KINGFISHER
CHILDREN'S
A TO Z
ENCYCLOPEDIA

Copyright © Macmillan Publishers International Ltd 1998, 2012, 2018
Published in the United States by Kingfisher,
120 Broadway, New York, NY 10271
Kingfisher is an imprint of Macmillan Children's Books, London.
All rights reserved.

First published as *The Kingfisher Children's Encyclopedia* in 1998
This revised and updated edition published in 2018
Cover design by Matthew Kelly

Distributed in the U.S. and Canada by Macmillan,
1720 Broadway, New York, NY 10271

Library of Congress Cataloging-in-Publication data has been applied for.

ISBN: 978-0-7534-7465-5

Kingfisher books are available for special promotions and premiums.
For details contact: Special Markets Department, Macmillan,
120 Broadway, New York, NY 10271.

For more information, please visit www.kingfisherbooks.com

Printed in Hong Kong
9 8 7 6 5 4 3 2

2TR/0919/UTD/HH/128MA

KINGFISHER
CHILDREN'S
A TO Z
ENCYCLOPEDIA

KINGFISHER

LONDON & NEW YORK

Maps
Hardlines

Contributors & Consultants
Sue Aldridge, Sarah Angliss, Max Benato, Martyn Bramwell, Enid Broderick, Tim Brown, David Burnie, Catherine Halcrow, Jack Challoner, Michael Chinery, Maria Constantino, Chris Cooper, Sophie Cooper, Alan Cowsill, Jeff Daniel, David Darling, Dougal Dixon, John Farndon, Sue Gordon, John Graham, Ian Graham, Catherine Headlam, Lesley Hill, Caroline Juler, Anne Kay, Robin Kerrod, J.C. Levy, Keith Lye, Tim Madge, David Marshall, Bob McCabe, Iain Nicolson, Steve Parker, Jane Parker, John Paton, Malcolm Porter, Sue Reid, Meg Sanders, Philip Steele, Richard Tames, John Tipler, Ian Westwell, Brian Williams
2018 Edition Consultant Philip Steele

Illustrators
David Ashby, Julian Baker Illustration, Julian Baum, Michelle Brand, Andy Burton, Tom Connell, Maggie Downer, Richard Draper, Andrew Farmer, Chris Forsey, Mick Gillah, Trevor Hill, Karen Hiscock, Christian Hook, Kevin Jones Associates, Ruth Lindsay, Ceri Llewellyn, Kevin Maddison, Nicki Palin, Peter Ross, Peter Sarson, Mike Saunders, Ron Tiner, Martin Woodward, Black Hat: Kevin Lyles, Blue Chip: Keith Harmer, David Lewis Agency: Mark Stacey, J.M. & A: Steinar Lund, Linda Rogers Associates: Peter Dennis, Linden Artists: Lindsay Graham, Richard Hook, Sebastian Quigley, Clive Spong, Specs Art: Richard Berridge, Virgil Pomfret: Luigi Galanti, W.L.A: Cy Baker, Derick Bown, Robin Budden, Robin Carter, Barry Croucher, Sandra Doyle, Brin Edwards, David Hardy, Dan Harvey, Philip Hood, Ian Jackson, Bridgette Jones, Rachel Lockwood, Pond/Giles, Jonathan Potter, Steve Roberts, Andrew Robinson, Mike Rowe, Chris Shields, Paul Staveley, Mark Stewart, Mike Taylor, Richard Tibbitts, Chris Turnbull, Simon Turvey, David Woods

INTRODUCTION

The word *encyclopedia* comes from the Greek for "all-round education," and the *Kingfisher Children's A to Z Encyclopedia* provides just that, in a way that is both accessible and stimulating.

This comprehensive encyclopedia covers everything from ancient history to up-to-the-minute developments in technology; from animal and plant life on Earth to the latest plans for exploring outer space. Geography, natural history, religion, the human body—all the topics that children explore at home and at school—are included here.

Detailed in-depth coverage of an impressive range of topics makes this encyclopedia perfect for project work and homework assignments. At the same time, the text is broken up into manageable paragraphs, suitable for both confident readers and younger browsers. Colorful photographs and superb illustrations and maps not only enhance the text, but also encourage readers to find out more for themselves.

Easy access is the key to this encyclopedia. Major subject areas, such as ELECTRICITY, have been arranged alphabetically, but the encyclopedia also has a comprehensive index so readers can refer quickly to related topics such as CIRCUITS and SWITCHES.

The encyclopedia has been written and checked by a team of specialist authors and consultants and produced by a team of editors and designers with years of experience in children's reference. This 2018 edition has been comprehensively updated under the expert guidance of consultant editor Philip Steele. We are confident that it is a book in which children, and parents, can put their trust.

Kingfisher

HOW TO USE THIS ENCYCLOPEDIA

This book is fun and easy to use. All the entries are arranged alphabetically and provide information on two levels—quick reference and in-depth knowledge. The features explained in the guide below will help you to get the most from your encyclopedia.

Eye-catching color photographs bring subjects to life

Main headings always appear in the top left corner of the page for quick reference

All entries begin with a concise definition of the subject

Headings divide the text into self-contained sections

Authoritative text is approachable and packed with facts

Typeface is clear and easy to read

Colorful identification panels amplify the main topic by highlighting specific subjects

ARCHITECTURE

Architecture is the art of designing buildings and other structures so that they are soundly built, pleasing to look at, and suitable for their purpose.

The classical style uses flat beams, columns, and sculpture.

The style of architecture used for a building depends on the materials available, the architect's ideas, and what the building is going to be used for.

The Romans built aqueducts with curved arches and thick walls.

ARCHITECTS AT WORK
As well as needing to know a building's purpose, an architect must know the space allocated and how much money can be spent. Detailed models and drawings are produced for the builders, showing every part of the building and how it is to be constructed. These plans include practical features, such as heating and lighting systems, and pipe work for plumbing.

Japanese castles have upturned roof edges and contrasting colors.

WESTERN STYLES
Western architecture began in Greece around 500 B.C. with the classical style. Pillars were built to precise mathematical patterns, such as those in the Parthenon, in Athens, built 447–438 B.C. From about 200 B.C., the Romans built domes, and curved arches for bridges and aqueducts.

MEDIEVAL IDEAS
During the Middle Ages, the pointed arches and colorful stained glass of the Gothic style began to appear, especially

India's Taj Mahal features domes and minarets typical of Islamic architecture.

▲ The Shard is London's tallest skyscraper, at 1016 feet (310 metres). It opened in 2012. City skylines change all the time. Some cities limit the spread of high-rise architecture, so that historical buildings are not overshadowed.

in churches. Like the classical styles of the Romans and Greeks, the Gothic style has been used by many architects since then.

MODERN MATERIALS
Since the mid-1800s, inventions such as heating and lighting, and new building materials such as steel, plastic, and reinforced concrete, have revolutionized architecture. Steel-framed skyscrapers were first developed in the United States after the invention of the elevator in 1854. Modern architecture is often characterized by a combination of borrowed ideas with the newest materials and techniques.

HIGH-TECH BUILDINGS
The Sydney Opera House in Australia uses high-tech materials such as glass, concrete, and ceramics in its structure. Complex calculations were used to work out whether the materials would take the weight of its unusual component parts. Modern architects begin with a series of drawings, and use computers to calculate weights and forces. Then building begins.

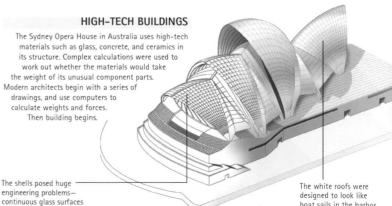

Glass walls and tall office buildings dominate modern architecture.

The shells posed huge engineering problems—continuous glass surfaces enclose a steel structure

The white roofs were designed to look like boat sails in the harbor

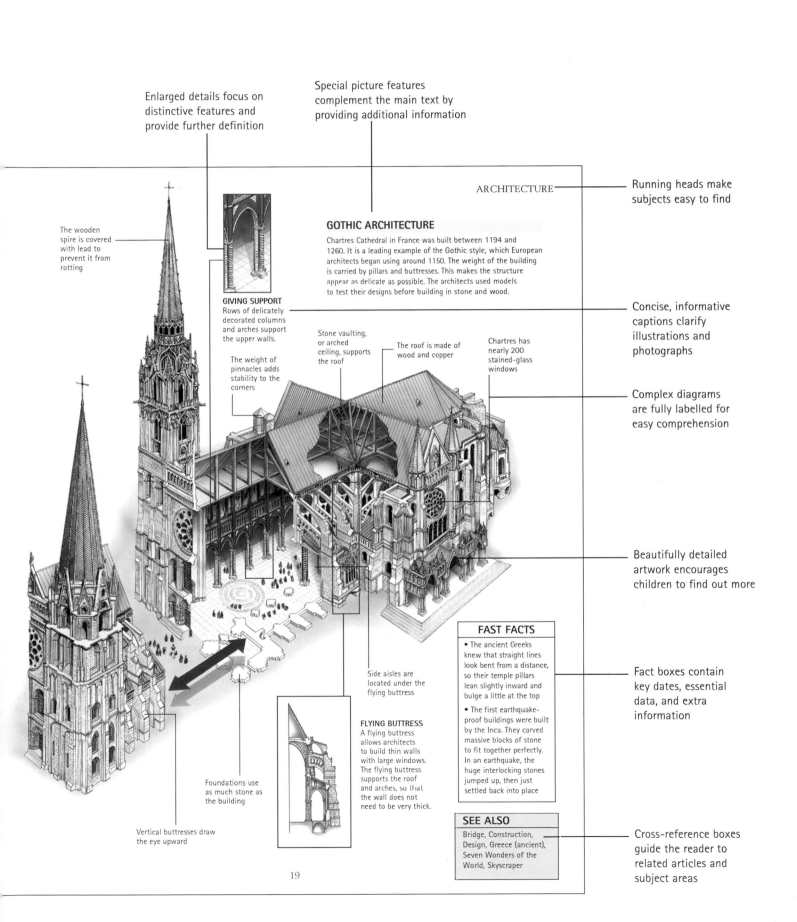

Enlarged details focus on distinctive features and provide further definition

Special picture features complement the main text by providing additional information

Running heads make subjects easy to find

GOTHIC ARCHITECTURE

Chartres Cathedral in France was built between 1194 and 1260. It is a leading example of the Gothic style, which European architects began using around 1150. The weight of the building is carried by pillars and buttresses. This makes the structure appear as delicate as possible. The architects used models to test their designs before building in stone and wood.

The wooden spire is covered with lead to prevent it from rotting

GIVING SUPPORT
Rows of delicately decorated columns and arches support the upper walls.

The weight of pinnacles adds stability to the corners

Stone vaulting, or arched ceiling, supports the roof

The roof is made of wood and copper

Chartres has nearly 200 stained-glass windows

Concise, informative captions clarify illustrations and photographs

Complex diagrams are fully labelled for easy comprehension

Beautifully detailed artwork encourages children to find out more

Side aisles are located under the flying buttress

FLYING BUTTRESS
A flying buttress allows architects to build thin walls with large windows. The flying buttress supports the roof and arches, so that the wall does not need to be very thick.

Foundations use as much stone as the building

Vertical buttresses draw the eye upward

FAST FACTS

• The ancient Greeks knew that straight lines look bent from a distance, so their temple pillars lean slightly inward and bulge a little at the top

• The first earthquake-proof buildings were built by the Inca. They carved massive blocks of stone to fit together perfectly. In an earthquake, the huge interlocking stones jumped up, then just settled back into place

Fact boxes contain key dates, essential data, and extra information

SEE ALSO

Bridge, Construction, Design, Greece (ancient), Seven Wonders of the World, Skyscraper

Cross-reference boxes guide the reader to related articles and subject areas

ABORIGINAL PEOPLE

The term "aboriginal" is used to describe the native inhabitants of any country. The Aboriginal people are the first inhabitants of Australia.

The Aboriginal people arrived in Australia from Southeast Asia over 50,000 years ago. They lived in nomadic groups, traveling around their territories, hunting with spears and boomerangs, fishing from canoes, and gathering fruit, but passed on valuable knowledge by word of mouth and in song.

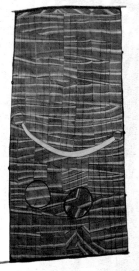

▲ These pieces of bark are painted with clan signs of the Napaljarri people of the Northern Territory. Originally, there were about 500 Aboriginal clans, each with its own territory and complex language.

◄ Example of Aboriginal bark painting by the artist Milpurrur, Arnhemland, Northern Territory, Australia.

EUROPEAN SETTLERS

When the British settled in Australia in the late 18th century, there may have been about 750,000 Aboriginal people living there. Many were killed by settlers or driven off their land. The population may have dropped to 150,000 by the early 20th century, but is now estimated at about 750,000 again. In 2008 the government formally apologized to the Aboriginal people for past mistreatment.

THE ABORIGINAL WAY OF LIFE

The Aboriginal people traditionally lived out in the open or in shelters made from branches and bark, and sometimes stone. They wore little, apart from body paint, ornaments, and waistbands or fur coats made from kangaroo skin. Today, a small number live in the Outback (interior) in the same way as their ancestors, but most have moved to towns and cities.

▶ A songman, accompanied by a didgeridoo player, tells stories through songs and poetry.

ART AND MUSIC

Aboriginal art mainly portrays religious beliefs in paintings on cave walls and on bark, or in poetry and songs. Today, some Aboriginal artists live by selling paintings made with earth pigments and charcoal. Aboriginal music is played on a didgeridoo (a long wooden pipe) and two clapping sticks, which are traditionally boomerangs.

▶ Witchetty grubs are the large, white larvae of various wood moths. The grubs are high in protein and are traditionally regarded as a great delicacy by Aboriginal people.

DREAMTIME

Rituals play an important role in Aboriginal beliefs, and body painting is a part of many rituals. Their beliefs are centered on the land and include an idea of eternity called Dreamtime—a world with no beginning and no end. Through Dreamtime, the ancestors—spirits that shaped mountains, rivers, plants, animals, and people—can be contacted.

SEE ALSO

Australia

AFRICA

Africa is the second-largest continent and covers about one fifth of Earth's land area. It includes 55 countries, six of which are islands.

▲ The Tuareg are a nomadic people who inhabit a large area of the Sahara Desert. Some still travel the desert with camel trains laden with goods such as dates and salt.

KEY FACTS

- **Area:** 11,701,210 sq. mi. (30,306,000km²)
- **Population:** 1,250,407,000
- **Number of countries:** 55
- **Largest country:** Algeria (919,595 sq. mi./ 2,381,741km²)
- **Smallest country:** Seychelles (176 sq. mi./455km²)
- **Highest point:** Mount Kilimanjaro (19,340 ft./ 5,895m)
- **Largest lake:** Lake Victoria (26,564 sq. mi./ 68,800km²)
- **Longest river:** Nile (4,160 mi./6,695km)

The world's hottest continent, Africa has rain forests and tree-scattered grasslands (known as savanna), which are inhabited by a huge variety of wild animals. A third of Africa is covered by the Sahara, the largest desert on Earth.

HIGHS AND LOWS

Much of Africa is made up of plateaus (flat areas of land high above sea level). The plateau in East Africa is broken up by two extinct volcanoes—Mount Kenya and Tanzania's Mount Kilimanjaro—and the East African Rift. The Rift is a long crack in the Earth's crust that runs from Mozambique through East Africa, the Red Sea, and into southwestern Asia. Elongated lakes have formed in the valley. Africa's special features include the Nile, the continent's longest river, which stretches for 4,160 mi. (6,695km) and Lake Tanganyika, the world's longest lake, which stretches for 385 mi. (620km).

HOT AND DRY

Because Africa lies across the equator, most of the continent gets extremely hot. The hottest yearly average temperature on Earth is 93°F (33.9°C), as recorded at Dallol in Ethiopia. The land around the tropics, on each side of the equator, is starved of rain and more than half of Africa's land has less than 20 in. (500mm) of rain per year.

RAIN FORESTS AND SAVANNA

In some regions, particularly around the equator in western and central Africa, rainfall is high and large rain forests grow. Debundscha in Cameroon has a mean annual rainfall of over 393.7 in. (10,000mm). Between the rain forests and the deserts are vast areas of tropical savanna. They are prone to drought, with a mixture of rainy and dry seasons.

▼ Chobe National Park in Botswana is home to herds of elephants and impala. Many African countries have set aside large stretches of land as wildlife reserves.

2

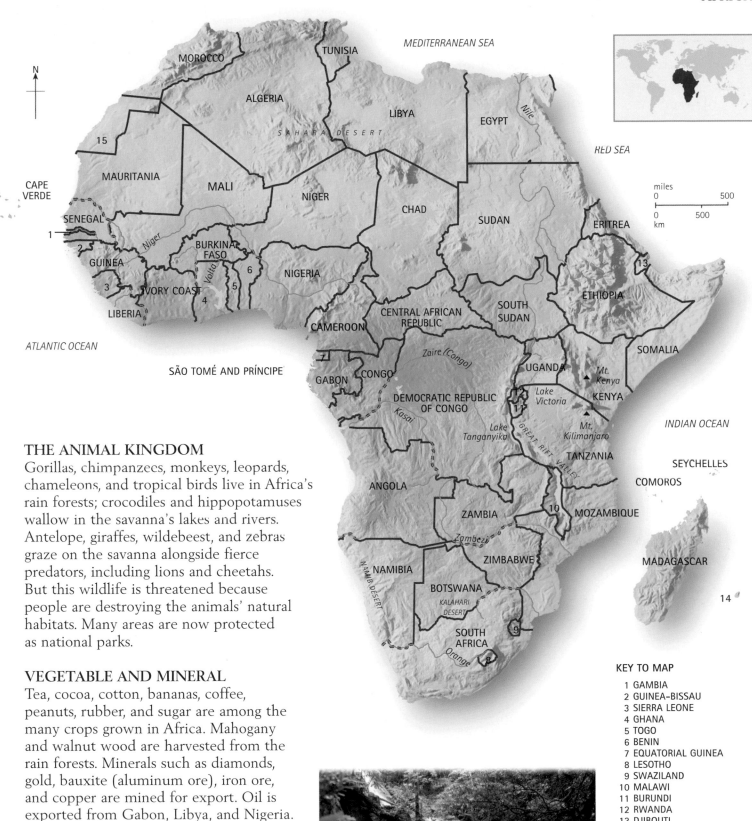

N

MEDITERRANEAN SEA

MOROCCO
TUNISIA
ALGERIA
LIBYA
EGYPT
SAHARA DESERT
Nile
RED SEA

CAPE VERDE

MAURITANIA
MALI
NIGER
CHAD
SUDAN
ERITREA

SENEGAL
1
2
GUINEA
BURKINA FASO
6
NIGERIA
3
IVORY COAST
Volta
5
4
LIBERIA
Niger
ETHIOPIA
13

CENTRAL AFRICAN REPUBLIC
SOUTH SUDAN

ATLANTIC OCEAN

CAMEROON
SOMALIA

SÃO TOMÉ AND PRÍNCIPE
7
GABON
CONGO
Zaire (Congo)
UGANDA
Mt. Kenya
KENYA

DEMOCRATIC REPUBLIC OF CONGO
Kasai
12
11
Lake Victoria
Lake Tanganyika
Mt. Kilimanjaro
GREAT RIFT VALLEY

INDIAN OCEAN

TANZANIA
SEYCHELLES
COMOROS

ANGOLA
ZAMBIA
10
MOZAMBIQUE
Zambezi
MADAGASCAR
14

NAMIB DESERT
ZIMBABWE
NAMIBIA
BOTSWANA
KALAHARI DESERT
9
SOUTH AFRICA
8
Orange

miles
0   500
0   500
km

THE ANIMAL KINGDOM

Gorillas, chimpanzees, monkeys, leopards, chameleons, and tropical birds live in Africa's rain forests; crocodiles and hippopotamuses wallow in the savanna's lakes and rivers. Antelope, giraffes, wildebeest, and zebras graze on the savanna alongside fierce predators, including lions and cheetahs. But this wildlife is threatened because people are destroying the animals' natural habitats. Many areas are now protected as national parks.

VEGETABLE AND MINERAL

Tea, cocoa, cotton, bananas, coffee, peanuts, rubber, and sugar are among the many crops grown in Africa. Mahogany and walnut wood are harvested from the rain forests. Minerals such as diamonds, gold, bauxite (aluminum ore), iron ore, and copper are mined for export. Oil is exported from Gabon, Libya, and Nigeria.

PEOPLE AND LANGUAGES

Many Africans live in tribal villages with their own cultures. Over 1,000 languages are spoken south of the Sahara alone. Country borders take little account of tribal differences, and in one country there may be many tribal groupings. ▶

KEY TO MAP

1 GAMBIA
2 GUINEA-BISSAU
3 SIERRA LEONE
4 GHANA
5 TOGO
6 BENIN
7 EQUATORIAL GUINEA
8 LESOTHO
9 SWAZILAND
10 MALAWI
11 BURUNDI
12 RWANDA
13 DJIBOUTI
14 MAURITIUS
15 WESTERN SAHARA
(occupied by Morocco)

◀ The Korup National Park in Cameroon is one of Africa's densest rain-forest areas.

▲ The people of Tahoua in Niger build reed huts from locally available materials. Huts like these are typical of the Sahel region, an area of dry grassland on the edge of the Sahara.

RELIGIOUS BELIEFS
The people who live in northern Africa are mostly Arabs and Berbers who speak Arabic and Berber languages and follow Islam. The countries in southern Africa are largely populated by black Africans. Although most are Muslims or Christians, ancient local traditions still flourish, and more than a quarter of Africa's people follow local beliefs.

THE EARLY DAYS
Many scientists believe Africa is the continent where human beings first evolved, about seven million years ago, but little is known about this very early history. Around 10,000 years ago, the Sahara had a moist climate, and many people lived there hunting animals, gathering plants for food, and later raising crops and herding cattle.

ANCIENT EGYPT AND ISLAM
In about 3100 B.C., ancient Egypt—one of the world's greatest early civilizations—was formed out of Upper and Lower Egypt in northern Africa. It thrived on the fertile banks of the Nile until, in 30 B.C., it became part of the Roman Empire. In the A.D. 600s, the Arabs conquered northern Africa and converted the people of Egypt and its neighbors to Islam.

GREAT KINGDOMS
For centuries, people outside Africa knew little about the continent south of the Sahara. Between 1100 and 1500, Arabs trading for gold, ivory, and slaves brought back news of great empires in West Africa such as Ghana, Mali, Benin, Songhai, and Kanem. Kingdoms such as Benin, which was founded around A.D. 900, produced beautiful

◄ The Masai people of East Africa are one of many tribal groups that live in Africa. A semi-nomadic people, they raise cattle and hunt wild animals.

▲ This fine brass head was made in the West African kingdom of Benin, which is now part of Nigeria. It dates from the 18th century and represents an Oba or ruler wearing a ceremonial headdress.

bronze sculptures that are highly prized today. Many of the sculptures symbolize the magical aspects of the obas (kings) of Benin. Kingdoms also arose in the south, such as the huge stone city of Great Zimbabwe. News of Africa's wealth attracted great curiosity among Europeans.

CONQUERING A CONTINENT
Portuguese explorers were the first Europeans to map the coasts of Africa. In 1498, the explorer Vasco da Gama rounded the Cape of Good Hope, in southern Africa, on a journey that led him to discover a new route to India. Others later sailed on to East Africa. The Portuguese were also the first Europeans to export slaves from West Africa, a trade that continued until the 1800s.

EUROPEAN INFLUENCE
The Dutch took over many Portuguese trading posts during the 1600s. In 1652, they founded a settlement at Cape Town, which became part of South Africa. By the late 1800s, almost all of Africa was ruled by European powers.

◄ About three fifths of Africa's people live in villages. In some areas, the markets are full of fresh produce, but in others, drought, poverty, and civil war have led to food shortages and widespread famine.

INDEPENDENCE
Colonial rule continued in Africa until the 1950s, when the colonies began to gain their independence. By the early 1970s, most countries were independent, but economic problems have led to instability in many areas. The African Union, which took over from the Organization of African Unity in 2001, aims to promote economic, political, and cultural cooperation in Africa.

A HARD WAY OF LIFE
Two thirds of the world's poorest nations are in Africa. Most Africans live in villages and farm the land. Poverty, disease, and war in many areas mean that people often do not reach old age. In many African countries, life expectancy at birth is between 50 and 60 years.

BUSY CITIES
Although most Africans live in villages, the continent has some large, bustling cities. Cairo, the capital of Egypt, is the largest, with a population of 19,500,000. It is followed by Lagos in Nigeria, which has 17,500,000 inhabitants, and Kinshasa in the Democratic Republic of Congo, with a population of 11,860,000.

TIME OF EQUALITY
One of the most important events in Africa's history took place in 1994, when South Africa became a democracy under the leadership of Nelson Mandela. This finally ended apartheid, the official policy that separated people of different races. Since 1948, this policy had given whites power, while denying people of other colors basic rights in education, at work, and in everyday life.

▲ Africa has produced many world-class soccer players. They include Pierre-Emerick Aubameyang (Gabon, see above) and Yaya Touré (Ivory Coast).

▲ Harare, named after the African chief Neharawe, is the capital of Zimbabwe in southern Africa. It is a modern city, with tall skyscrapers and tree-lined streets.

SEE ALSO
Civil war, Continent, Egypt, Egypt (ancient), Empire, Explorer, Grassland, Kenya, Nigeria, Roman Empire, Slavery, South Africa, Sudan and South Sudan

AIRCRAFT

An aircraft is a machine that can fly through the air. Airplanes, helicopters, gliders, airships, and balloons are all different types of aircraft.

The Wright brothers' *Flyer 1* made the first controlled, powered flight in 1903. It covered 118 ft. (36m).

A gas burner heats the air inside a hot-air balloon to make it rise. It can only go where the wind takes it.

Like all gliders, the Delphin SF-34 uses air currents to stay airborne. Long, thin wings give maximum lift.

Helicopters, such as the Robinson R-22, can hover in midair and fly in any direction.

The first aircraft were balloons and airships, which relied on lighter-than-air gases to keep them up. Sir George Cayley in Britain and Otto Lilienthal in Germany flew the first gliders in the 1800s. But it was the invention of the gasoline engine in the 1880s that led to powered flights in heavier-than-air craft, such as helicopters and airplanes.

EARLY AIRPLANES
Airplanes are aircraft with fixed wings that provide the upward force known as lift, engines to provide thrust, and hinged control surfaces for steering. Airplanes were developed at the start of the 1900s and were originally built with wood and canvas to make them light.

WHAT KEEPS A PLANE UP?
An airplane's wings hold it up as it flies. They have a curved upper surface and a flat lower surface. Air travels more slowly across the bottom of the wing than the top, creating an upward push.

KEY DATES

1903 Orville and Wilbur Wright make first powered, controlled flight in the USA in their aircraft *Flyer 1*

1937 Frank Whittle designs jet engine. In 1939, the Heinkel He 178 is first jet plane

1939 Igor Sikorsky designs the first modern helicopter, USA

1947 In the United States, the rocket-powered Bell X-1 is first aircraft to fly at supersonic speed

1950s The first jet airliners, the DeHavilland Comet and Boeing 707, enter service

1970 The Boeing 747 "jumbo jet" enters service

1976 Anglo-French Concorde, supersonic jet airliner runs its supersonic service

2016 Sun-powered Solar Impulse 2 completes flight around the world

PROPELLER VERSUS JET
All early airplanes had small piston engines that drove propellers. As the propeller turned, it pulled the aircraft forward. Most modern, large airplanes are powered by jet engines. These burn fuel and air to produce a stream of exhaust gases that thrusts the airplane forward. Jets provide more power, but are costly to maintain.

THE FUSELAGE
The main body of a plane is called the fuselage. It contains the crew, passengers, cargo, and equipment. The front of the fuselage houses the cockpit where the pilot sits, and at the rear is the tailplane, made up of a vertical fin and two small wings.

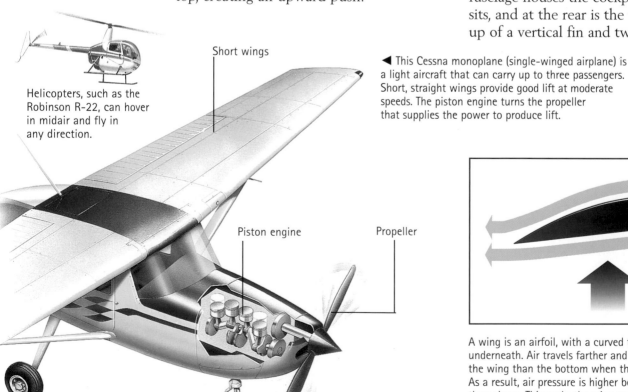

Short wings

Piston engine

Propeller

◀ This Cessna monoplane (single-winged airplane) is a light aircraft that can carry up to three passengers. Short, straight wings provide good lift at moderate speeds. The piston engine turns the propeller that supplies the power to produce lift.

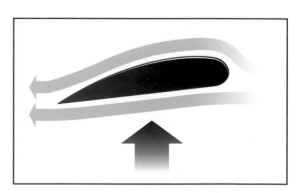

A wing is an airfoil, with a curved top and a flat underneath. Air travels farther and faster over the top of the wing than the bottom when the plane is in the air. As a result, air pressure is higher beneath the airfoil than above. This sucks the wing up, creating lift.

THE JET AIRLINER

Long-distance travel has been made cheap and reliable by jet airliners. The first wide-bodied jet was the Boeing 747, or jumbo jet, in 1970. It needed long runways and high take-off and landing speeds. The 747-8 Intercontinental, which entered service in 2012, can carry up to 467 passengers as far as 9,200 miles (14,800 km). Another major producer of wide-bodied airliners has been the European company Airbus. Aerodynamic design and electronics are improved all the time, but increasingly the emphasis is on environmental and safety rules, and low cost.

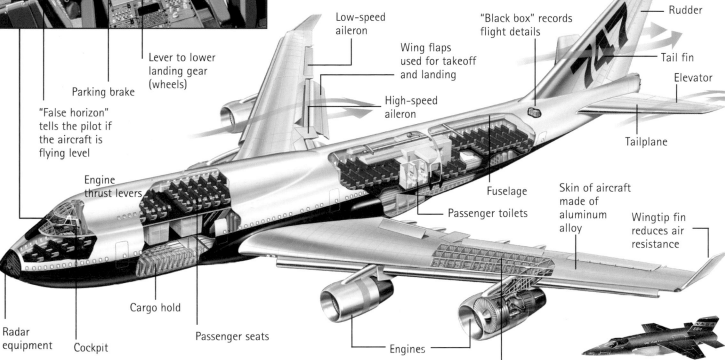

Low-speed aileron

Wing flaps used for takeoff and landing

"Black box" records flight details

Rudder

Tail fin

Elevator

High-speed aileron

Tailplane

Lever to lower landing gear (wheels)

Parking brake

"False horizon" tells the pilot if the aircraft is flying level

Engine thrust levers

Fuselage

Passenger toilets

Skin of aircraft made of aluminum alloy

Wingtip fin reduces air resistance

Cargo hold

Passenger seats

Radar equipment

Cockpit

Engines

Fuel tanks located inside wings

Propelled by rocket engines, the supersonic X-15 holds the world air speed record at 4,510 mph (4,274kph), set in 1967.

Concorde ran the world's only supersonic passenger airplane service, from 1976–2003, with a cruising speed of about 1,350 mph (2,170kph).

FLY-BY-WIRE

Large flaps on the back edge of the wings increase lift and reduce speed for landing, while ailerons, elevators, and the rudder change direction. These are usually controlled by the pilot, but the Airbus A3420 introduced the "fly-by-wire system," whereby the flaps and ailerons are adjusted with the help of computers.

FLYING AND FLOATING

Airplanes come in many forms. Jet airliners fly all around the world, while small airplanes, called light aircraft, ferry people, mail, and supplies over short distances. Some planes have floats instead of wheels to land on water. Military planes hold radar, cameras, and bombs. Biplanes (airplanes with double wings) are used by display teams and as crop dusters because they can fly slowly and make sharp turns.

The Harrier jump jet uses the downward thrust of its engines to rise straight up without needing a runway.

▶ The B-2 Stealth Bomber has flat, slablike panels made of special materials. These scatter beams from enemy radar, making the craft almost undetectable. Special paint also absorbs radar waves.

SEE ALSO

Airport, Engine, Helicopter, Transportation, Warfare

AIRPORT

Airports are places that airline passengers pass through and where freight is handled. They are also where aircraft are refueled, repaired, and maintained.

▲ Air traffic controllers are positioned high above the airport in the control tower. They use radar to track each plane on their screens and computers to plan flight paths. They radio their instructions to the pilots.

The biggest airports are like small cities with tens of thousands of people working in them 24 hours a day. Domestic airports handle passengers flying within the same country. People flying to or from another country go through international airports. Specialist services here include passport control, immigration, and customs.

ON ARRIVAL

All passengers arriving on international flights go through customs to make sure that they are not bringing anything illegal, such as drugs, into the country. Customs officers can stop and search anyone they think might be carrying illegal goods. They also check for goods on which travelers should pay tax.

KEEPING SAFE

Security at airports has become a high priority in recent years, as the number of terrorist attacks on planes has increased.

All passengers boarding a flight must go through a metal detector while their hand baggage is put through an X-ray machine. This is to make sure that they are not carrying any weapons or explosives onto the aircraft. International travelers also use passports to prove their identity.

CONTROLLING AIR TRAFFIC

Aircraft landing and taking off have to comply with air traffic control to make sure they do not collide, either on the ground or in the air. At very large airports, the area under air traffic control extends for hundreds of miles horizontally and thousands of feet vertically in all directions. Aircraft circle above the airport waiting for permission to land.

ON LANDING

Airplanes land on runways and then taxi (move slowly) to a gate. Here, the doors of the aircraft can be opened safely. Passengers leave the aircraft with their hand baggage and either walk or are driven by bus to the main terminal buildings.

Aircraft taking off use a different runway from aircraft landing

Control tower staff direct air traffic in the air and on the ground

Passenger terminal

Air bridges connect aircraft to the terminal gate

Aircraft are refueled between flights

Baggage and cargo are taken from the hold to the terminal

Service vehicles are used for carrying freight

SEE ALSO

Aircraft

ALLIGATOR AND CROCODILE

Alligators and crocodiles are large, scaly reptiles with powerful jaws. They live on the banks of rivers and in swamps, feeding on fish, mammals, turtles, and birds.

An alligator's lower teeth are not visible when its jaws are shut.

The fourth tooth on the lower jaw of a crocodile sticks out.

Closely related to alligators, caimans feed on fish and other prey.

The gavial has a long, thin, tooth-lined snout and feeds mainly on fish.

Alligators and crocodiles are some of the largest living reptiles on the planet—the biggest crocodiles can grow to around 23 ft. (7m) and weigh over 2,400 lb. (1,120kg). Alligators are usually smaller, and can be distinguished from crocodiles because they have a broader, flatter snout and their teeth are hidden when their jaws are closed. Caimans and gavials, alligators, and crocodiles belong to a group called crocodilians.

STRONG JAWS

Like crocodiles, alligators float with only the tip of their snout and their eyes protruding, waiting to pounce on prey. Although crocodiles have been known to attack humans, alligators rarely do so, even though their jaws are strong enough to crack the bones of an animal such as a pig. Alligators eat a wide variety of animals. Young ones feed on insects, crayfish, frogs, and minnows, while the diet of an adult may include waterbirds, turtles, and small mammals, including the occasional dog.

◄ A crocodile pounces on a wildebeest, seizing it in its strong jaws and spinning it around in the water.

ALLIGATOR HOLES

During the winter, alligators stay in the water to keep warm, burying themselves in mud or in holes they have made with their bodies. In times of drought, these holes are often the only places where water can still be found, and they are used as a refuge by alligators and other aquatic animals until the rain returns.

ENDANGERED CREATURES

There are 23 species of crocodilian, of which only two are true alligators: the American alligator of the southeastern United States and the Chinese alligator of the Chang (Yangtze) River. All crocodilians are hunted for their skin and meat. Their habitats are also threatened; the American alligator was protected by law from 1969 to 1987.

DEVOTED PARENTS

Alligators lay between 30 and 80 eggs in a concealed nest. After incubating for 60 days in the heat of the sun, the young make high-pitched yelps from inside the eggs. The mother then scrapes away the sand and waits until the young hatch out to carry them to the water in her mouth. She watches over them in their first year.

Bones and scales act like armor

The fourth tooth of the lower jaw fits into a pocket in the upper jaw

SEE ALSO

Africa, Animal, Reptile, Swamp and marsh, United States of America

AMPHIBIAN

Amphibians are cold-blooded animals that are able to live both in water and on land. Most start life breathing through gills, but later develop lungs.

▲ The extraordinary Mexican axolotl salamander usually spends its life as a tadpole, breathing through gills.

Like many frogs, the European common frog has smooth, moist skin and long legs for jumping.

Like many toads, the European common toad has dry, lumpy skin and walks rather than leaps.

The long-tailed salamander's bright color helps it warn off predators.

Newts, such as this smooth newt, are salamanders that spend long periods in water.

Caecilians have no legs and live underground. They are found only in tropical areas, and many are blind.

Frogs, toads, salamanders, newts, and caecilians are all types of amphibian. They are cold-blooded creatures that rely on their surroundings for warmth, and are found in most parts of the world. Adult amphibians usually have soft, thin, moist skin that absorbs oxygen from the air, helping them breathe. But some frogs and toads have thick, warty skin to help them survive in drier conditions. There are around 6,260 amphibian species, but one third of them are endangered.

JELLIED EGGS

The way amphibians breed and develop is unique in the animal kingdom. Females lay their jelly-covered eggs, called spawn, in water. These hatch into tadpoles, which develop limbs and lungs so that they can live on dry land. Some amphibians need only a small amount of water in which to lay their eggs. The tree frog lays its eggs on moist leaves and the male midwife toad carries the female's eggs on its back legs, dipping them into pools of water. The Australian gastric (stomach)-brooding frog swallows her eggs. Once they develop into froglets, they hop out of her mouth.

BIG EATERS

All amphibians are hunters. Many use their bulging eyes to track fast-moving prey, swallowing it whole. Small frogs and salamanders eat insects and tiny fish. Large toads gulp down mice and birds. They usually sit and wait, or crawl toward their prey, before lunging with mouth open. Some frogs and salamanders have a long, sticky-tipped tongue attached to the front of their mouth, which they can flick out to grab insects.

LEAPING FROGS AND TOADS

Over 80 percent of all amphibians are frogs and toads, known as anurans. They have long, five-toed back legs for leaping and shorter, four-toed front legs used to cushion the landing. There is no scientific difference between frogs and toads, but anurans with smooth, moist skin that usually jump are called frogs, and those that waddle and have drier, lumpy skin are called toads.

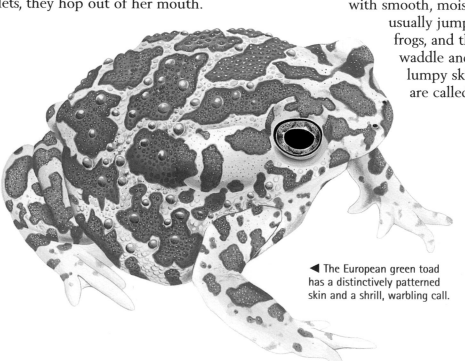

◄ The European green toad has a distinctively patterned skin and a shrill, warbling call.

THE GLANDS
Pores that hold the salamander's poison can be found across its back and on the sides of its head.

THE POISON
When the fire salamander is attacked by a predator, poison oozes out of the pores in its skin.

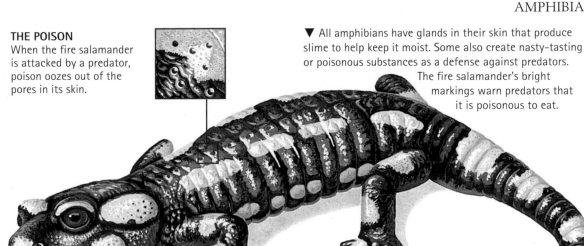

▼ All amphibians have glands in their skin that produce slime to help keep it moist. Some also create nasty-tasting or poisonous substances as a defense against predators. The fire salamander's bright markings warn predators that it is poisonous to eat.

SALAMANDERS AND CAECILIANS

Newts and salamanders (urodelans) have short limbs and long tails. Salamanders in Europe and North America that spend long periods in water are called newts. Most salamanders breathe with lungs and through their skin, although some have no lungs. Caecilians (apodans) are the third and smallest group of amphibians. They are wormlike, with blunt snouts for tunneling, tiny eyes, and wide mouths. They hunt mainly at night.

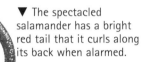

▼ The spectacled salamander has a bright red tail that it curls along its back when alarmed.

THE AMPHIBIAN LIFE CYCLE

When frogs mate, the male usually sits on the female's back for up to three days. As soon as the female lays her eggs in the water, the male releases sperm to fertilize them. The eggs hatch into tadpoles, which eventually metamorphose (change) into froglets (young frogs) and leave the water for life on land.

1 The female frog lays her eggs, or spawn, in large masses in a pond or stream. The eggs are protected by a special jelly.

2 The larvae, or tadpoles, develop inside the eggs. About a week later, the tadpoles hatch out and attach themselves to plants.

3 The tadpoles breathe through feathery gills and start to swim at about three days of age. They feed on waterweeds and algae in the water.

4 The tadpoles slowly turn into frogs, developing limbs and lungs so that they can live on land. Their tails are absorbed into their bodies.

5 Fully grown, the young frogs leave the water. They feed on small insects and will not reproduce themselves until they are a year old.

SEE ALSO
Animal, Frog and toad, Hibernation

ANIMAL

Animals are multicellular living creatures that can move, eat food, sense their surroundings, and reproduce, usually by mating with a partner.

The rotifer is one of the smallest animals—seen only through a microscope.

The octopus is a type of mollusk, a group that also includes snails and squid.

The angelfish is just one of 32,000 different species of fish.

The shield bug is part of the largest group—insects, with a million known species.

The peacock is one of 10,000 species of bird, most of which can fly.

The rabbit is a mammal. Its young are fed on milk produced by the mother.

Over one million known animal species live on the Earth, but six million or more may still be undiscovered. Every animal is unique, but there are common features that set creatures in the animal kingdom apart from other living beings such as plants, fungi, and single-celled organisms.

THE MATING GAME

Like all living creatures, animals must reproduce. Most do this by mating with a partner. It is usually the female that chooses a mate, so many males are brightly colored or use elaborate courtship rituals to attract a suitable partner.

BILLIONS OF TINY CELLS

All adult animals are multicellular, which means they are made up of more than one cell. Some animals, such as rotifers and hydras (aquatic animals), have just a few dozen cells, but large animals, such as humans, are much more complex and can have up to 50 billion cells.

▲ The galago, or bush baby, is a nocturnal animal, so it comes out at night to feed. Huge, round eyes, a good sense of smell, and an excellent sense of hearing are essential for hunting prey at night.

FOOD FOR LIVING

Unlike plants, animals cannot make their own food—they must eat ready-made plant or animal food. Most have some sort of mouth, but the way in which the food is broken down inside their body varies. Birds have no teeth, so the food is ground by stones in their stomach. Snakes swallow prey alive and whole, digesting it slowly with strong juices. The tapeworm has no mouth, but lives in another animal's intestines, soaking up digested food through its skin.

MOTHERLY LOVE

Many animals go to great lengths to keep their young alive. For example, the female scorpion, best known for her sting, is a very caring mother. She carries her newborn young on her back for up to 12 days, until they can fend for themselves.

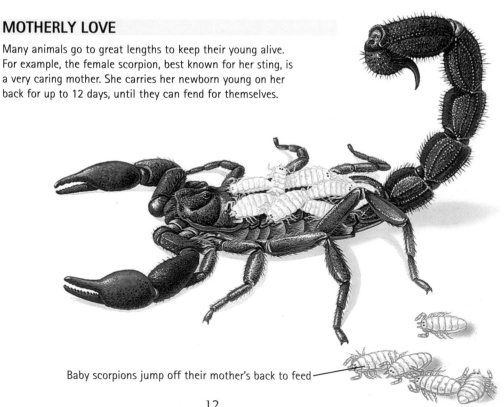

Baby scorpions jump off their mother's back to feed

NERVES AND SENSES

All animals sense their surroundings with a set of nerves and sense organs that are adapted to suit the way they live. For example, many night hunters have whiskers to find their way in the dark, and some snakes have infrared sensors to "see" the body heat of their prey. Sharks can smell blood in the water many miles away and home in on it accurately, while migrating animals, such as gray whales, have an extra sense that allows them to travel great distances without getting lost.

ON THE MOVE

All animals, from the slowest snail to the fastest gazelle, move, usually by using an efficient set of muscles. The way they move varies: some crawl or walk, some slither, while others hop or run—in the case of crabs, sideways. Even a drifting jellyfish pulsates to move itself up or down in the water. This ability to move has allowed some species to spread all over the world. Some animals, such as sponges and corals, can only move when young, and remain in one place as adults. ▶

The golden lion tamarin is a rare monkey, another type of mammal.

THE FASTEST ANIMAL

Predatory animals use many methods to catch their food. Some use stealth, others use camouflage, but the cheetah's strategy is speed. It is the fastest animal on four legs, reaching speeds of 70 mph (110kph) in mid-chase. Its favorite food is the young antelope that graze on the African savanna. But a cheetah's stamina is poor—if it does not catch the antelope in the first few hundred yards, the prey usually gets away.

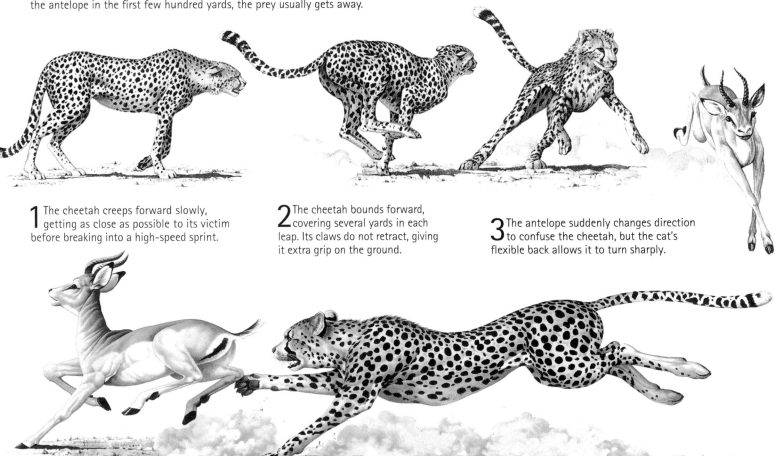

1 The cheetah creeps forward slowly, getting as close as possible to its victim before breaking into a high-speed sprint.

2 The cheetah bounds forward, covering several yards in each leap. Its claws do not retract, giving it extra grip on the ground.

3 The antelope suddenly changes direction to confuse the cheetah, but the cat's flexible back allows it to turn sharply.

4 The gap closes. The cheetah swipes with strong paws at the antelope's legs to knock it off balance and bring it down, before killing it with a bite.

A QUESTION OF CLASS

Zoologists divide the animal kingdom into about 30 major groups, or phyla (the largest of which are shown in this chart). Each group, or phylum, can be further divided into subphyla, classes (shown), then orders, families, genera, and species (not shown). Animals from different species cannot breed together, except in rare circumstances.

INVERTEBRATES
(animals without backbones)

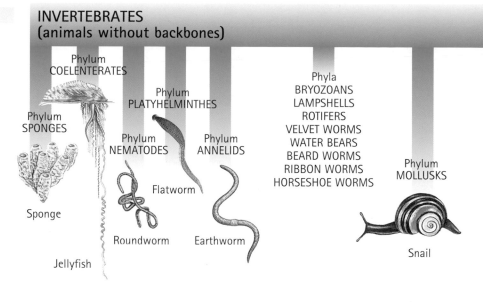

Phylum
COELENTERATES

Phylum
PLATYHELMINTHES

Phylum
SPONGES

Phylum
NEMATODES

Phylum
ANNELIDS

Phyla
BRYOZOANS
LAMPSHELLS
ROTIFERS
VELVET WORMS
WATER BEARS
BEARD WORMS
RIBBON WORMS
HORSESHOE WORMS

Phylum
MOLLUSKS

Sponge

Flatworm

Roundworm

Earthworm

Snail

Jellyfish

▲ The marbled polecat belongs to a family of carnivores (meat-eating mammals) that includes weasels, badgers, otters, and skunks. All of these animals have short legs and long, flexible bodies.

FAMILY GATHERINGS

Zoologists classify, or group, animals by their common features. For example, all insects have six legs, all birds have feathers, and all mammal mothers feed their young on milk from their own bodies. The grouping of animals in this way is known as taxonomy. It helps zoologists to work out when animals first appeared on Earth, how they have changed through time, and which creatures are closely related.

WITH BACKBONES

All animals can be divided into two main groups: those with backbones, called vertebrates, and those without backbones, called invertebrates.

▶ The anteater is an edentate. This is an order of mammal with few or no teeth. Other members of the group include sloths, which are herbivores (plant-eaters) and armadillos. The anteater is an insectivore (insect-eater), living solely on ants and termites, which it sniffs out with its snout and licks up with its long, sticky tongue. Its powerful front claws are used for digging.

Vertebrates include fish, amphibians, reptiles, birds, and mammals. All other animals are invertebrates.

THE MYSTERIOUS BARNACLE

It can be difficult for zoologists to tell if some creatures are animals at all. For example, an acorn barnacle attached to a rock on the seashore does not even look alive, let alone animal-like. By studying its life cycle, zoologists discovered that before the barnacle attaches itself to a rock, it looks like a young shrimp. This proved that barnacles are crustaceans, along with crabs and lobsters.

▲ Acorn barnacles

WHO IS RELATED TO WHOM?

Scientists study the genetic makeup of animals compared to other animals to reveal who is related to whom. For many years zoologists argued over whether red pandas were related to bears, raccoons, or

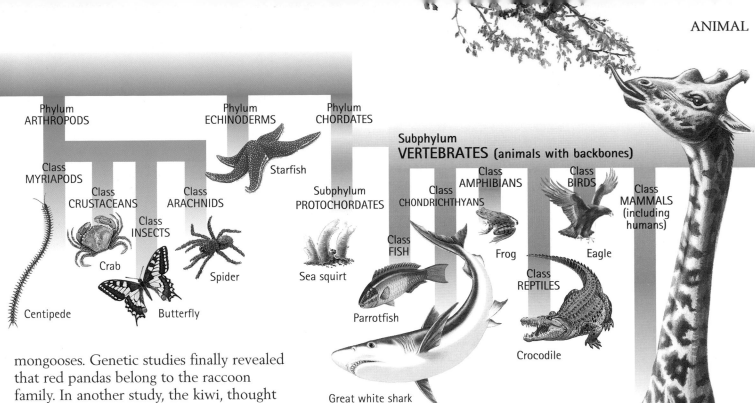

Phylum
ARTHROPODS

Phylum
ECHINODERMS

Phylum
CHORDATES

Subphylum
VERTEBRATES (animals with backbones)

Class
MYRIAPODS

Class
CRUSTACEANS

Class
ARACHNIDS

Class
INSECTS

Starfish

Subphylum
PROTOCHORDATES

Class
CHONDRICHTHYANS

Class
AMPHIBIANS

Class
BIRDS

Class
MAMMALS
(including
humans)

Class
FISH

Crab

Spider

Sea squirt

Frog

Eagle

Centipede

Butterfly

Parrotfish

Class
REPTILES

Crocodile

Great white shark

mongooses. Genetic studies finally revealed that red pandas belong to the raccoon family. In another study, the kiwi, thought to be one species of bird, was shown to have two species—they look very similar, but cannot breed together.

DEEP-SEA TREASURES

In the 1970s, when scientists sent deep-sea equipment down to new depths, over 200 new animal types were discovered living around deep-sea hydrothermal vents (jets of hot, mineral-rich water spurting out from the sea floor). Transparent fish, two-yard-long tube worms, plate-sized clams, and blind white crabs were among the amazing finds.

SPECIES UNDER THREAT

Many animals in the world are now rare or nearly extinct. Once an animal species has

died out, it is lost forever, which is why zoos have breeding programs for threatened species. Estimates vary, but scientists agree that there are millions of animal species still waiting to be discovered. These too are under threat as many natural areas, especially the tropical rain forests and coral reefs, are destroyed or polluted.

▶ The giraffe is the tallest animal. It is a mammal and grows up to 18 ft. (5.5m) tall. It lives in Africa and eats thorny acacia leaves, which it strips from the branches with its 20 in. (50cm)-long tongue.

▲ Some animals, called detritivores, help to recycle other animals' waste products. The dung beetle eats animal dung. Some species eat the dung where they find it, while others dig a hole and bury it to eat later.

AMAZING ANIMAL FACTS

• Insects are the most numerous animals on Earth. It is estimated that for every human there are 200 million insects

• The largest animal to have lived on Earth is the blue whale. Belonging to the order of mammals called cetaceans, blue whales can grow to over 100 ft. (30m) in length

• The fastest animal is the peregrine falcon. It can swoop at up to 220 mph (350kph)

• Unlike most animals, the sponge can regrow its entire body from a tiny fragment of itself

• The giant squid has the largest eye of any animal that has ever lived: 15 in. (40cm) in diameter, ten times the size of a human eye

SEE ALSO

Amphibian, Bird, Conservation, Crab, Evolution, Fish, Insect, Mammal, Microorganism, Reptile, Worm, Zoology

ANTARCTICA

Antarctica is the fifth-largest continent. It surrounds the South Pole, and 98 percent of it lies buried beneath a thick sheet of ice.

▲ Norwegian explorer Roald Amundsen was first to reach the South Pole, on December 14, 1911.

KEY FACTS

• **Area:** 5,405,430 sq. mi. (14,000,000km²)

• **Population:** no permanent population

• **Number of countries:** none, although some countries claim sections of the continent

• **Highest point:** Vinson Massif (16,066 ft./4,897m)

• **Largest ice shelf:** Ross (approx 182,240 sq. mi./472,000km²)

• **Position of South Pole:** 767 mi. (1,235km) from the nearest coastline

Only a few mountains and barren, rocky areas show above the ice that hides Antarctica. The thickness of the polar ice sheet makes Antarctica the highest continent—and also the windiest. It is largely a frozen desert, with snowfall near the Pole equivalent to less than 6 in. (150mm) of water per year. The world's coldest air temperature, –128.6°F (–89.2°C), was recorded there.

FIRE AND ICE

A string of mountains cuts across the icy mass. On their eastern side, near the coast, the ice sheet reaches depths of 15,750 ft. (4,800m). Ross Island, to the west, holds the active volcano Mount Erebus. Ice flows down to the coast as glaciers and spreads out as huge ice shelves over the sea. When the ice becomes too heavy, parts break away to form enormous, flat-topped icebergs up to 200 ft. (60m) high and many miles long.

FUR AND FEATHERS

Antarctica has few land animals because, even in the summer, most of the continent is covered with ice. The animals live mainly in the air or sea and have thick fur, feathers, or blubber (fat) to keep

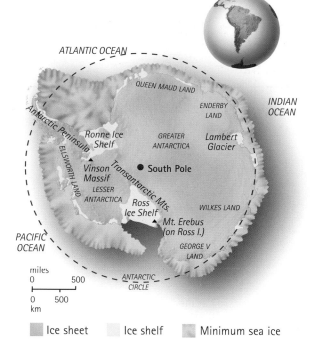

miles 0 — 500
km 0 — 500

■ Ice sheet ■ Ice shelf ■ Minimum sea ice

◄ Two emperor penguins with their chick. To withstand the winter cold, emperors have very dense feathers and large fat reserves. They also huddle together in groups of up to 5,000 birds to keep warm.

them warm. The ocean is home to many species of krill (tiny shrimplike creatures), squid, fish, seals, whales, and eight types of penguin. Antarctic birds include the predatory skua and large-winged albatross.

STUDIES ON ICE

Antarctica has a temporary population of up to 4,000 scientists from 18 countries. Their interests vary from space research to microbiology, and all must abide by the Antarctic Treaty. This agreement bans the mining of valuable mineral resources buried beneath the ice and prevents any military or industrial activities on the continent. More than 38,000 tourists also visit Antarctica each year during the summer.

◄ Icebergs break away from the ice shelves that surround Antarctica. The ice builds up in layers over thousands of years.

SEE ALSO

Animal, Bird, Climate, Conservation, Desert, Explorer, Glacier

ARCHAEOLOGY

Archaeology is the study of the remains of the past that people have left behind them such as objects and buildings. Often remains are buried or sunken.

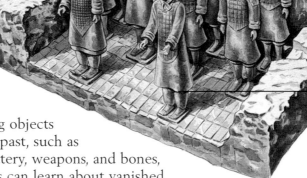

2 The site is divided into a grid with string. Squares are excavated one by one. Topsoil is removed with diggers and trowels.

1 Archaeologists use computerized equipment to find buried objects.

FAST FACTS

• Analysis of ancient seeds or pollen reveals what people ate or what plants or crops grew

• The skeleton of a person buried alive was found at the corners of four huge steps making up the Pyramid of the Sun at Teotihuacan, near Mexico City

• The most famous discovery in archaeology was King Tutankhamen's tomb in Egypt, found by Howard Carter in 1922

CHINA'S BURIED ARMY

In 1974, thousands of life-size clay soldiers were found near the tomb of Shi Huangdi, the first emperor of the Qin Dynasty in China who died in 210 B.C. They were part of a massive burial complex built to protect the emperor in the afterlife.

3 Finds are cleaned by carefully brushing away soil. Each find is recorded and numbered before it is removed.

4 The position of an object can reveal important information.

5 Objects are carefully examined before being restored and preserved. They can then be put on display.

▲ An Egyptian mummy, or preserved body, from about 600 B.C. Remains like this reveal a lot about the lives of ancient people.

By studying objects from the past, such as buildings, pottery, weapons, and bones, archaeologists can learn about vanished civilizations. Archaeology can take us back to a time before people began writing, more than 5,000 years ago.

CLUES TO THE PAST

To know where to dig, archaeologists often start from a small clue such as a coin or a fragment of pottery. Many archaeologists now work on rescue digs—recording a site before it is destroyed, usually by being built on. Aerial photography and scanners reveal what is under the ground.

SORTING THE FINDS

Finds are sorted by type and age. For objects up to 60,000 years old, a technique called radiocarbon dating is used. This measures the remaining carbon content. X rays can show up faded details on pottery, and tests on bones can reveal the illnesses people suffered from. Wood objects can be dated by dendrochronology—a technique that compares the tree rings.

LOST CITIES

Sites may be as small as a grave or as large as an entire city. The ancient city of Troy, for example, was uncovered in Turkey by German archaeologist Heinrich Schliemann in 1870, after years of searching. Many sites, however, are discovered by accident. The Indus Valley civilization in Asia, which was destroyed in about 1700 B.C., was found by chance in the 1920s by railroad workers.

◄ A Minoan vase from about 1500 B.C., found on the island of Crete. Distinctive styles in art and pottery allow archaeologists to identify different groups of people.

SEE ALSO

Aztec, Babylon, China, Egypt (ancient), Greece (ancient), Roman Empire

ARCHITECTURE

Architecture is the art of designing buildings and other structures so that they are soundly built, pleasing to look at, and suitable for their purpose.

The classical style uses flat beams, columns, and sculpture.

The Romans built aqueducts with curved arches and thick walls.

Japanese castles have upturned roof edges and contrasting colors.

India's Taj Mahal features domes and minarets typical of Islamic architecture.

Glass walls and tall office buildings dominate modern architecture.

The style of architecture used for a building depends on the materials available, the architect's ideas, and what the building is going to be used for.

ARCHITECTS AT WORK
As well as needing to know a building's purpose, an architect must know the space allocated and how much money can be spent. Detailed models and drawings are produced for the builders, showing every part of the building and how it is to be constructed. These plans include practical features, such as heating and lighting systems, and pipe work for plumbing.

WESTERN STYLES
Western architecture began in Greece around 500 B.C. with the classical style. Pillars were built to precise mathematical patterns, such as those in the Parthenon, in Athens, built 447–438 B.C. From about 200 B.C., the Romans built domes, and curved arches for bridges and aqueducts.

MEDIEVAL IDEAS
During the Middle Ages, the pointed arches and colorful stained glass of the Gothic style began to appear, especially

▲ The Shard is London's tallest skyscraper, at 1016 feet (310 meters). It opened in 2012. City skylines change all the time. Some cities limit the spread of high-rise architecture, so that historical buildings are not overshadowed.

in churches. Like the classical styles of the Romans and Greeks, the Gothic style has been used by many architects since then.

MODERN MATERIALS
Since the mid-1800s, inventions such as heating and lighting, and new building materials such as steel, plastic, and reinforced concrete, have revolutionized architecture. Steel-framed skyscrapers were first developed in the United States after the invention of the elevator in 1854. Modern architecture is often characterized by a combination of borrowed ideas with the newest materials and techniques.

HIGH-TECH BUILDINGS

The Sydney Opera House in Australia uses high-tech materials such as glass, concrete, and ceramics in its structure. Complex calculations were used to work out whether the materials would take the weight of its unusual component parts. Modern architects begin with a series of drawings, and use computers to calculate weights and forces. Then building begins.

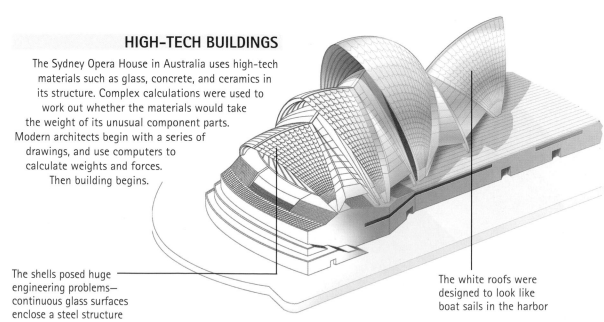

The shells posed huge engineering problems—continuous glass surfaces enclose a steel structure

The white roofs were designed to look like boat sails in the harbor

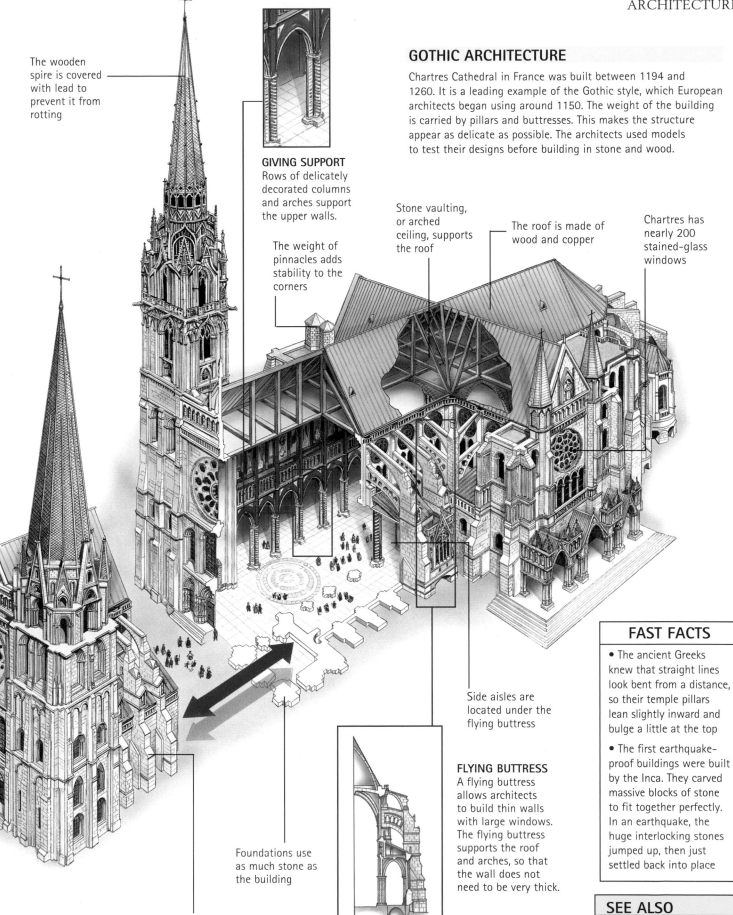

The wooden spire is covered with lead to prevent it from rotting

GIVING SUPPORT
Rows of delicately decorated columns and arches support the upper walls.

The weight of pinnacles adds stability to the corners

GOTHIC ARCHITECTURE

Chartres Cathedral in France was built between 1194 and 1260. It is a leading example of the Gothic style, which European architects began using around 1150. The weight of the building is carried by pillars and buttresses. This makes the structure appear as delicate as possible. The architects used models to test their designs before building in stone and wood.

Stone vaulting, or arched ceiling, supports the roof

The roof is made of wood and copper

Chartres has nearly 200 stained-glass windows

Side aisles are located under the flying buttress

FLYING BUTTRESS
A flying buttress allows architects to build thin walls with large windows. The flying buttress supports the roof and arches, so that the wall does not need to be very thick.

Foundations use as much stone as the building

Vertical buttresses draw the eye upward

FAST FACTS
• The ancient Greeks knew that straight lines look bent from a distance, so their temple pillars lean slightly inward and bulge a little at the top

• The first earthquake-proof buildings were built by the Inca. They carved massive blocks of stone to fit together perfectly. In an earthquake, the huge interlocking stones jumped up, then just settled back into place

SEE ALSO
Bridge, Construction, Design, Greece (ancient), Seven Wonders of the World, Skyscraper

ARCTIC

The Arctic is the area within the Arctic Circle—an imaginary line around the northern part of the globe with the North Pole at its center.

The Arctic is made up of the frozen Arctic Ocean, the surrounding seas and small islands, and the northern parts of Canada, Alaska, Russia, Finland, Sweden, Norway, and Greenland.

LAND OF THE MIDNIGHT SUN

Temperatures creep above freezing point for only about four months of the year. There are some days during the summer when areas near the North Pole are in constant daylight because the sun never sets. This is why the Arctic is sometimes known as the Land of the Midnight Sun.

TUNDRA LIFE

Treeless plains, or tundra, cover the land. In the summer, these plains are home to animals such as reindeer, lemmings, musk oxen, and Arctic hares, which graze on scrubby plants and shrubs. Migratory birds, such as the Arctic tern, return from winter homes to breed in the short warm season.

▲ Arctic hares live on the tundra. In summer, their fur is brown. They grow white coats in the winter.

THE DARK OF WINTER

Wintertime in the Arctic is cold, dark, and long. For a short time the sun does not come above the horizon at all. The ocean is frozen and the tundra snow-covered, with only a few mosses and lichens growing. Most animals and birds migrate south until summer returns. Polar bears thrive in these harsh conditions, hunting seals and catching fish in the icy water.

▼ An airplane arrives with supplies for the store at Savissivik, Greenland. Aircraft are a vital link for scattered settlements around the Arctic.

PEOPLE IN THE ARCTIC

A number of different people live in the Arctic, including the Inuit of Greenland, Canada, and northeast Asia and the Sami (Lapps) of Scandinavia. Those on the coast live by hunting and fishing. Those living inland hunt wild caribou or, like the Nenet tribe from Siberia in northern Russia (below), herd reindeer for a living.

SEE ALSO

Animal, Asia, Canada, Climate, Magnetism, Migration, North America, Ocean and sea, Russia and the Baltic States, United States of America

ARGENTINA

Bordered by the Andes Mountains to the west, Argentina is the second-largest country in South America and the eighth largest in the world.

Area: 1,073,500 sq. mi. (2,780,400km²)
Population: 44,293,200
Capital: Buenos Aires
Language: Spanish
Currency: Argentinian peso

▲ Cacti flourish in the warm, dry air of the plateaus (flat areas of land high above sea level) in the Andes Mountains. Many species of cactus grow across Argentina.

Argentina has two warm and rainy regions in the north: the Gran Chaco and Mesopotamia. The central areas are made up of a fertile, grassy plain called the Pampas, while Patagonia in the south is largely desert. In the far south is the cold and windswept land of Tierra del Fuego.

UNIQUE WILDLIFE
Jaguars, monkeys, and tapirs are found in rain forests in the north. Patagonia is home to unique animals such as the pudu, a tiny deer, and rhea, a flightless, ostrichlike bird.

TOWN DWELLERS
Ninety-seven percent of Argentineans are of European descent, with *mestizos* (people of mixed European and American Indian descent) making up just 3 percent. Skilled cowboys, known as *gauchos*, herd cattle across the plains. Around 92 percent of the population lives in cities and towns. Many people work in meat-packing industries and in factories using farm products, including wool and hides.

SPANISH TREASURE SEEKERS
Spanish explorers reached Argentina in 1516. They were looking for treasure, and they named the country after *argentum*, the Latin word for "silver." European

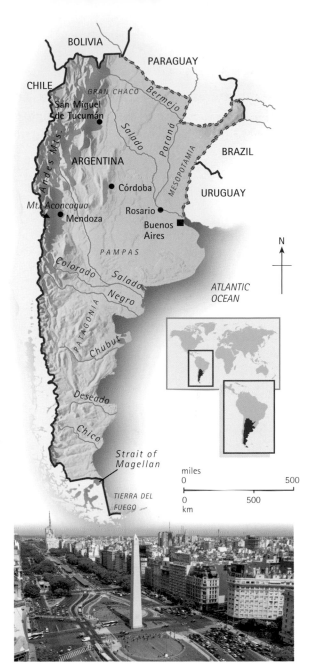

▲ Argentina's capital, Buenos Aires, whose name means "favorable winds," is one of the world's great ports.

settlers arrived soon afterward and became rich by farming the fertile land.

MODERN TIMES
In 1816, Argentina declared independence after almost 300 years of Spanish rule. Since the 1930s, the country has faced many problems, including harsh military rule and high unemployment. In 1982, Argentina invaded the Falkland Islands, a British dependency, but was defeated. Elections in 1983 ended military rule.

◄ *Gauchos* work on the huge cattle ranches of the pampas. They are regarded as folklore heroes.

SEE ALSO
Grassland, South America

21

ART

Art can be any creative work used to portray images and to express feelings—from drawing, painting, and sculpture to architecture and computer graphics.

▶ Jeweler Carl Fabergé (1846–1920) was famous for the jewel-encrusted eggs he made for the czars of Russia.

The first examples of art were cave paintings and images carved out of stone, the oldest of which were made about 40,000 years ago. Most early art was dedicated to gods, because religion and worship were important influences, but over the centuries new styles of art have evolved.

Japanese silk-screen prints, like this one from the 1800s, greatly influenced Western art in the 1900s.

Native American art, such as this mask, combines geometric styles with strong colors.

This pot by Clarice Cliff is typical of the 1930s' art deco style, with its bold lines, colors, and shape.

CLASSICAL STYLE
It was during the Renaissance, about 1300–1600, that the word "artist" was first used. Before that, painters were thought of merely as skilled craftworkers. Renaissance means rebirth, and artists such as Michelangelo and Leonardo da Vinci took their ideas from the classical lines of the ancient Greeks and Romans.

PAINTING FROM LIFE
The Renaissance artists were the first to use live models. By using light and shade, these artists gave their images depth, resulting in a three-dimensional appearance on the canvas. They also began to use perspective to indicate whether objects were near or far.

STRONG FEELINGS
In the late 1500s, art started to become more personal. Scientific advances made people question their religious beliefs, and this was reflected in the art of the baroque movement. Caravaggio's *The Death of a Virgin* was rejected by the priest who commissioned it, because it showed the Virgin Mary as an old woman. Artists like Rubens created paintings—many large-scale—full of passion and drama.

EVERYDAY LIFE
During the 1600s, artists began to paint everyday life and ordinary people. Before then, only important people and grand themes were thought to be worth painting. Rembrandt van Rijn seemed to reveal the sitter's character, and William Hogarth's work commented on social conditions.

▲ This scene, *The Creation of Adam*, is on the ceiling of the Sistine Chapel, Rome. It is one of nine scenes from the Old Testament painted by Michelangelo between 1508 and 1512.

▲ The vibrant, rapid strokes of Edgar Degas's *Danseuses* (1880s) capture a sense of movement.

22

◄ Pop art used mass-produced imagery to create a powerful impact. Artists Andy Warhol and Roy Lichtenstein were famous artists in this movement.

▲ *Marriage à la Mode* (1743) by William Hogarth was a series of scenes criticizing manners.

CAPTURING SUNLIGHT

By the 1700s and 1800s, many artists were trying out new methods and ideas. In the late 1800s, the French impressionists, such as Claude Monet and Edgar Degas, became more spontaneous, daubing their canvases with bold strokes of color to try and capture the fleeting effects of light.

THE SHOCK OF THE NEW

During the early 1900s, artists experimented in radical new ways. Cubists, such as Pablo Picasso and Georges Braque, began to show images as though they were seen from several sides at once, and opened the door for other forms of abstract art. Surrealists, such as René Magritte and Salvador Dali, used dreams to explore hidden feelings, painting unlikely objects together in surprising situations. Photography gained a new status as an art form, with haunting images of landscapes or witty and innovative surrealist images. Artists today continue to discover new styles and materials, including video and multimedia techniques, as well as taking inspiration from traditional folk art.

EASTERN ART

In some cultures, artistic styles have changed little over thousands of years. Chinese art has been very influential, with its accurately observed landscapes executed with simple brush strokes on silk and paper.

DECORATIVE ARTS

Distinctive styles can also be seen in the decorative arts—in ceramics, textiles, and metalwork. Art deco of the 1930s, for example, took art into every aspect of life.

◄ Pablo Picasso tried to see subjects from many different angles as in his *Tête de femme (Jacqueline)* (1963).

▲ *Still Water* (2011) by Nic Fiddian-Green is a modern, 33-feet (10-meter)-tall bronze sculpture in Marble Arch, London, England.

SEE ALSO

Architecture, Color, Design, Music, Paint and dye, Photography, Renaissance, Sculpture

ASIA

Asia is the largest continent. It covers 30 percent of Earth's land area and has a bigger population than all the other continents put together.

▲ A dragon boat festival in Taiwan. At the end of the race, the winning team raises its oars. Boats are an important means of transportation along Asia's wide rivers.

KEY FACTS

- **Area:** 16,837,143 sq. mi. (43,608,000km²)
- **Population:** 4,484,544,000
- **Number of countries:** 50
- **Largest country:** Russia, 75 percent of which is in Asia
- **Smallest country:** Maldives (115 sq. mi./298km²)
- **Highest point:** Mount Everest (29,029 ft./8,848m)
- **Largest lake:** Caspian Sea (143,550 sq. mi./371,800km²)
- **Longest river:** Chang (Yangtze) (3,915 mi./6,300km)

The immense size of Asia means it has a huge variety of environments and weather conditions. Its natural habitats include dense tropical forests, fertile plains, arctic regions, and deserts—both hot and cold. The world's ten highest mountains are found in Asia, as well as the lowest point on land: the shores of the Dead Sea, at 1,289 ft. (393m) below sea level.

NATURAL BORDERS
Asia is separated from Europe by the Ural Mountains in the northwest and from North America by the Bering Strait, a strip of water only 55 mi. (88km) wide, in the northeast. The Red Sea and the Suez Canal divide Asia from Africa in the southwest.

EXTREMES OF TEMPERATURE
Northern Asia is cold and often desolate, with few plants to support people or animals. Noril'sk in northern Russia is the coldest city in the world, with average temperatures of 12.4°F (–10.9°C). In contrast, Tirunelveli in India has average temperatures of 82.4°F (29°C).

WET AND DRY
Devastating floods occur in Asia, notably in China, Bangladesh, and India. The monsoon winds from the Indian Ocean bring heavy rain to much of southern and eastern Asia. Vast areas of central Asia, on the other hand, have very little rain, and deserts such as the Gobi dominate the landscape.

DANGER ZONE
Because Asia lies on faults in the Earth's crust, many Asian countries, especially Japan, have experienced devastating earthquakes. The coasts of eastern and Southeast Asia are also prone to typhoons—violent storms that come from the China Sea.

▲ The snow leopard is found in some of the most remote areas of central Asia. Its pale, spotted coat allows it to blend in with its surroundings.

▶ The yak is used in the mountainous regions of Tibet as a source of food, milk, and clothing, and for carrying goods.

KEY TO MAP
1 SYRIA
2 LEBANON
3 ISRAEL AND PALESTINE
4 JORDAN
5 UNITED ARAB EMIRATES
6 QATAR
7 BAHRAIN
8 KUWAIT
9 GEORGIA
10 ARMENIA
11 AZERBAIJAN
12 TURKMENISTAN
13 UZBEKISTAN
14 TAJIKISTAN
15 KYRGYZSTAN
16 AFGHANISTAN
17 NEPAL
18 BHUTAN
19 BANGLADESH
20 BURMA (MYANMAR)
21 THAILAND
22 LAOS
23 CAMBODIA
24 VIETNAM
25 SINGAPORE
26 BRUNEI

▲ Terraces are cut in the hillsides in the Philippines to provide land for growing rice and other crops.

ENDANGERED ANIMALS

Thousands of animal species live in Asia, especially in the tropical south and southeast. But the effect of people clearing the land for farming and hunting animals for their skins has been to put several species in danger of extinction, including the giant panda, the orangutan, the tiger, and the snow leopard.

THE LAND PROVIDES

Rice is the main crop of warm, wet southern Asia, while wheat, barley, and millet grow in the colder, drier north. Spices such as pepper and cloves have been a source of wealth for India, Sri Lanka, and Indonesia for centuries. Other major crops include tea, tobacco, cotton, sugar, coffee, cocoa, jute, and fruit. Forests cover nearly a third of Russia and nearly 20 percent of the rest of the continent.

NATURAL RESOURCES

Raw materials are among Asia's most important exports. Asia provides more than half of the world's tin. Coal, gas, aluminum, and other metals needed for manufacturing are exported worldwide. Seven of the ten countries with the largest oil reserves are in Asia: Saudi Arabia, Iran, Iraq, Kuwait, the United Arab Emirates, Russia, and Kazakhstan.

WAY OF LIFE

In the desert areas of Saudi Arabia and Iran, and the steppes (dry, grassy, treeless plains) of Mongolia and neighboring ▶

▲ Mongolians have traditionally survived off the infertile land of central Asia by herding cattle. Bactrian (two-humped) camels are used as beasts of burden.

▼ San'a, the capital of Yemen, is one of the most beautiful Islamic cities. Handmade goods, such as cloth, leatherware, glassware, and pottery, are sold in its bazaars.

countries, there are many nomadic (wandering) tribes. These nomads live by herding camels, goats, sheep, and horses. Farming is the most common occupation for the people of many Asian countries, including China, India, and Indonesia.

CROWDED CITIES
In Asia, 49 percent of people live in a city, compared to 74 percent in Europe and 82 percent in the United States. Nine of the ten megacities with the largest populations are in Asia: Guangzhou-Foshan, Beijing, Karachi, Shanghai, Seoul-Incheon, Manila, Delhi, Jakarta, and Tokyo-Yokohama.

BIG BUSINESS
Industry is a major employer in countries such as Japan, South Korea, and Taiwan, and it is becoming increasingly important in Thailand and Malaysia. Other areas such as Singapore and Hong Kong have become important financial centers. Fishing and forestry, as well as manufacturing, are important industries

▲ China is the world's largest rice producer. Rice is grown in wet regions south of the Chang River.

in many Asian countries. China is the world's largest manufacturer of cars, while South Korea makes more televisions than any other country. China has one of the world's fastest-growing economies.

CRADLE OF CIVILIZATION
Asia was the birthplace of some of the world's most ancient civilizations, including Mesopotamia (in modern-day Iraq), China, and the Indus Valley (in modern-day Pakistan). These areas had large cities and were ruled by a small governing class of priests, officials, and warriors. Their rich cultures attracted both trade and conquering armies.

▲ Followers of Buddhism worship outside a temple in Yangon (Rangoon), the former capital of Burma (Myanmar). Almost 90 percent of Burma's population is Buddhist.

GAINING INDEPENDENCE

Colonial rule continued until the 1900s, when many of the colonies won their freedom, and created independent nations such as India and Jordan. In other countries, such as the former Soviet Union and China, communism took a firm hold. Since the break-up of the Soviet Union in 1991, republics such as Kazakhstan and Tajikistan have become independent nations. In 2002, after years of violent clashes, East Timor, formerly part of Indonesia, became Asia's newest country. The 21st century has seen foreign invasions, civil wars, uprisings, tensions and terrorism across much of the Middle East.

MULTI-RELIGIOUS SOCIETY

Asia was where the world's major religions had their roots. Islam was carried from Asia to Europe and Africa by conquering armies such as the Mongols in the 12th century. Buddhism and Hinduism were spread from India by merchants and missionaries. Judaism and Christianity were exported from Asia as well as silk and spices during the Roman period. Today, these five religions still thrive in Asia, although Islam has the most followers.

GLITTERING EMPIRES

By the 1500s, the Ottoman Empire in the Middle East, the Safavid Empire in Iran, the Mogul Empire in India, and the Ming Dynasty in China were the richest and most powerful states in the world. They had grown rich on exports such as silk, spices, ceramics, and jewels. But these riches attracted European explorers.

▲ Trade routes, known as the Silk Road, were used to carry goods between Asia and Europe from 1000 B.C. until the 1400s. Luxury items, such as the Ming vase shown here, as well as silks and spices, were carried through Pakistan, Tajikistan, Uzbekistan, and Kazakhstan to the Middle East, from where they were taken by boat to Europe.

COLONIAL RULE

From the beginning of the 1800s, much of Asia was colonized by European powers, whose steamships and modern weapons gave them superior mobility and firepower. The colonists transformed large areas of Asia into plantations for growing tea, coffee, cotton, and rubber for export to Europe.

▲ A holiday in Uzbekistan brings out dancers in brightly colored costumes. This Asian republic exports silk and ranks third among world cotton producers.

SEE ALSO

China, Communism, Crop, Earthquake, Empire, Indian subcontinent, Indonesia, Japan, Mesopotamia, Middle East, Religion, Russia, Southeast Asia

ASTRONAUT

Astronauts are people who are specially trained to work in space. They often spend weeks or months carrying out research on a space station or spacecraft.

On April 12, 1961, Yuri Gagarin of the U.S.S.R. became the first man in space on board *Vostok 1*.

Valentina Tereshkova from the U.S.S.R. became the first woman in space on June 16, 1963 on board *Vostok 6*.

Apollo 11 astronaut Neil Armstrong of the U.S.A. was the first to walk on the Moon, on July 21, 1969.

Experiments carried out by astronauts help discover what exists in space and how conditions in space affect life on Earth. Since the first human space journey was made in 1961, astronauts have walked on the Moon and lived in orbit.

JOBS IN SPACE
Work aboard a spacecraft includes maintaining the equipment, conducting scientific experiments, and launching and repairing satellites. To fly a spacecraft, an astronaut must be trained as a military pilot; mission specialists are highly qualified engineers or scientists.

CRUSHING FORCES
Astronauts must be prepared for the unusual conditions found in space. First, they are trained to survive the g-forces (crushing forces of take off) which make the body seem up to six times heavier than usual. To get used to the lack of gravity in space, astronauts train in giant water tanks

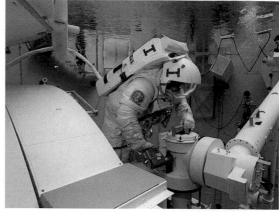

▲ Astronauts train for long periods in a giant water tank, known as the Neutral Buoyancy Simulator, in order to prepare for the work they will do on space walks. These astronauts are training for repair work on a satellite.

and high-altitude aircraft, which provide a sense of weightlessness.

SPACE SICKNESS
Over 40 percent of astronauts suffer from space sickness for the first few days, because weightlessness affects their sense of balance. Gradually, a lack of gravity also reduces the number of red cells carrying oxygen in the astronauts' blood, causing tiredness.

ASTRO-GYMS
Astronauts can grow about 2 in. (5cm) in space due to the lack of gravity, and their heart, muscles, and bones weaken. These

▲ Scientific experiments are carried out in space to observe the effects of the lack of gravity on such things as fungi and plants.

◄ Everything in the spacecraft, including the astronauts, floats around the cabin unless it is secured.

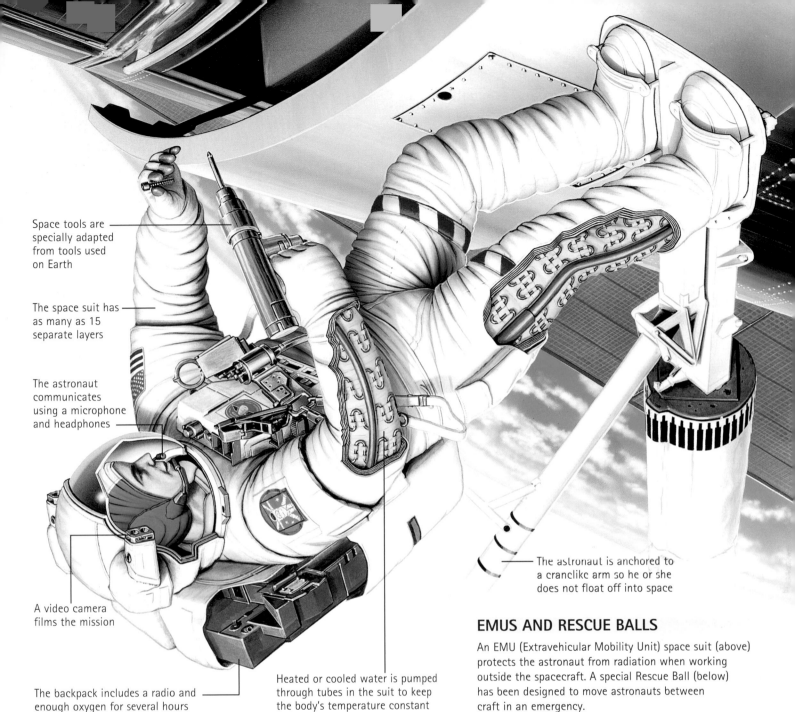

Space tools are specially adapted from tools used on Earth

The space suit has as many as 15 separate layers

The astronaut communicates using a microphone and headphones

A video camera films the mission

The backpack includes a radio and enough oxygen for several hours

Heated or cooled water is pumped through tubes in the suit to keep the body's temperature constant

The astronaut is anchored to a cranelike arm so he or she does not float off into space

EMUS AND RESCUE BALLS

An EMU (Extravehicular Mobility Unit) space suit (above) protects the astronaut from radiation when working outside the spacecraft. A special Rescue Ball (below) has been designed to move astronauts between craft in an emergency.

changes can be controlled with a special diet and by carrying out a regular exercise routine in a gym aboard the spacecraft.

THE OUTER LIMITS

Spacecraft are constantly bombarded with radiation particles that would normally be blocked by the Earth's atmosphere. Each astronaut carries an instrument to measure his or her exposure to radiation. The recommended limit in a lifetime is 100 rads (units of radiation). This restricts the amount of time an astronaut can spend in space and could jeopardize plans for long-distance missions to Mars or more remote

planets, which would take two or more years to reach.

NO DAYS AND NIGHTS

Temperature in space can change from extremes of –328°F (–200°C) to more than 212°F (100°C) when the craft is in the full glare of the Sun. It is important to maintain a steady temperature in the spacecraft, and this is done in the same way as in an air-conditioned office on Earth. There is no day or night in space, but astronauts keep to a routine that imitates the cycle on Earth so that they know when to sleep and when to work.

SEE ALSO

Gravity, Planet, Rocket, Satellite, Spacecraft, Space exploration

ASTRONOMY

Astronomy is the scientific study of objects in space, such as planets, stars, comets, and black holes, using equipment such as telescopes and space probes.

Nicolaus Copernicus discovered that the planets orbit the Sun.

Johannes Kepler claimed that the planets move in elliptical (oval) orbits.

Galileo Galilei was the first astronomer to use a telescope.

Isaac Newton described how gravity affects cosmic objects.

Early civilizations watched the stars and planets to predict the coming of the seasons. But it was the ancient Greeks who first studied them as a science. The word astronomy comes from two Greek words meaning "star laws."

▲ Our galaxy seen through a telescope.

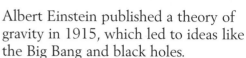

► An X-ray picture of our galaxy.

COPERNICUS TO EINSTEIN
Modern astronomy began with Nicolaus Copernicus, who realized that the Sun, not Earth, was at the center of our solar system. His ideas were published in 1543, the year he died. Galileo Galilei used his newly invented telescope in 1610 to help prove those ideas. In 1667, Isaac Newton put forward his laws of gravity, which explained how objects move in space.

Albert Einstein published a theory of gravity in 1915, which led to ideas like the Big Bang and black holes.

SIGNALS TO THE PLANETS
Modern astronomers can calculate Earth's distance from other planets in our solar system by bouncing radar signals off the planets' surfaces and timing how long they take to return to Earth. The distance to faraway stars can be figured out from their brightness and by using a method called parallax (see diagram far right).

THE KECK OBSERVATORY
Observatories are special buildings used to study the skies. The Keck at Mauna Kea, Hawaii, is one of the highest in the world. At the top of an extinct volcano, it is 13,780 ft. (4,200m) above sea level and has two telescopes in twinned domes that track the stars like binoculars.

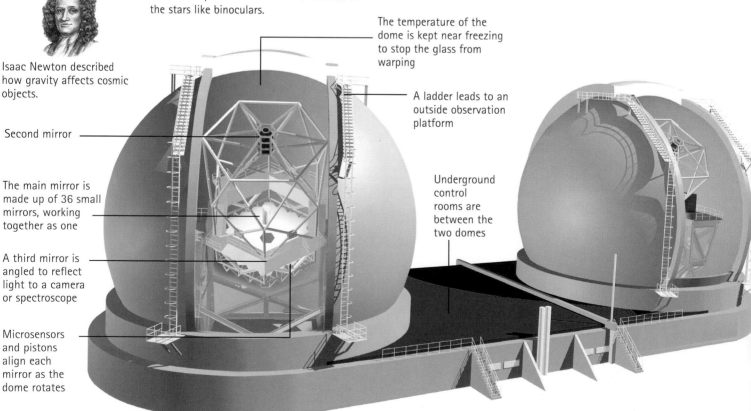

The temperature of the dome is kept near freezing to stop the glass from warping

A ladder leads to an outside observation platform

Second mirror

The main mirror is made up of 36 small mirrors, working together as one

A third mirror is angled to reflect light to a camera or spectroscope

Microsensors and pistons align each mirror as the dome rotates

Underground control rooms are between the two domes

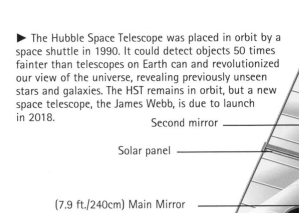

Radio antenna

▶ The Hubble Space Telescope was placed in orbit by a space shuttle in 1990. It could detect objects 50 times fainter than telescopes on Earth can and revolutionized our view of the universe, revealing previously unseen stars and galaxies. The HST remains in orbit, but a new space telescope, the James Webb, is due to launch in 2018.

Second mirror

Solar panel

(7.9 ft./240cm) Main Mirror

Cameras and other scientific recording equipment

Edmond Halley predicted that the comet of 1682 would return in 1758.

Albert Einstein created important theories about space and time.

LIGHT YEARS AWAY

The nearest star to our Sun is Proxima Centauri, more than 26 trillion miles (42 trillion kilometers) away. Star distances are measured in light years (light travels almost 6 trillion miles in one year). Proxima Centauri is 4.26 light years away, which means its light takes four years and three months to reach Earth.

SECRETS OF STARLIGHT

The temperature and chemical makeup of objects in space are revealed by the radiation that they give off. This radiation includes light, radio waves, microwaves, infrared, ultraviolet, X rays, and gamma rays. Astronomers use optical and radio telescopes as well as spectroscopes (radiation detectors), set up in observatories, to study cosmic radiation.

PLANETARY PROBES

Sending unmanned spacecraft to the planets is now the most technically challenging area of astronomy. The spacecraft are launched aboard rockets and either land on the planet or send down a probe that transmits information back to Earth.

◀ In 1997, a probe from the *Galileo* spacecraft plunged into Jupiter's gas clouds. It sent back photographs and chemical data to Earth for over an hour before being destroyed.

In 1997, a probe entered Jupiter's clouds, and the first remote-controlled, robotic probe roamed around on Mars. In 2004, two more rovers carried out research on Mars. In the same year, a spacecraft visited Saturn and its moons and released a probe that landed on the surface of Titan, Saturn's largest moon. In 2006, *New Horizons* was launched. It flew by Jupiter, Saturn, and Uranus on its way to the dwarf planet Pluto and the Kuiper Belt.

KEY DATES

3000 B.C. First known records of astronomy made by the Babylonians

125 B.C. Hipparchus groups the stars according to their brightness

1543 Nicolaus Copernicus proposes that Earth orbits the Sun

1600 Johannes Kepler discovers that the planets orbit the Sun in ellipses

1781 William Herschel discovers Uranus

1846 Neptune discovered

1908 Giant and dwarf stars first noted

1930 Clyde Tombaugh discovers Pluto

1997 Probe enters Jupiter's atmosphere to collect data; the *Sojourner* probe lands on Mars

2006 *Venus Express* orbits Venus

2011 *Messenger* enters orbit around Mercury

2016 European Space Agency's *Rosetta* mission places a lander on a comet

PARALLAX

The distances of nearby stars can be calculated by plotting their positions at different times of the year, and then applying a simple geometric equation. The bigger the parallax angle, the closer the star.

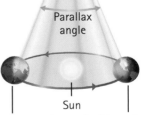

Where the star seems to be on January 1

Where the star seems to be on July 1

Real position of star

Parallax angle

Sun

Position of Earth on July 1

Position of Earth on January 1

SEE ALSO

Black hole, Constellation, Galaxy, Gravity, Solar system, Space exploration, Star, Telescope

ATMOSPHERE

The atmosphere is an envelope of gases surrounding Earth. It shields us from the Sun and contains the air we breathe. Without it, life would not exist.

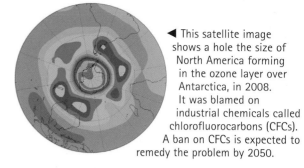

This satellite image shows a hole the size of North America forming in the ozone layer over Antarctica, in 2008. It was blamed on industrial chemicals called chlorofluorocarbons (CFCs). A ban on CFCs is expected to remedy the problem by 2050.

The gases that form the atmosphere are held in place around Earth by gravity. They can be divided into four layers: the troposphere, stratosphere, ionosphere, and exosphere. Each contains a mixture of gases, which gets thinner the farther away the layer is from Earth.

THE WEATHER ZONE
The lowest and densest layer is the troposphere, which extends about 8 mi. (13km) above Earth's surface. It contains 78 percent nitrogen, 20 percent oxygen, and small amounts of other gases and is where life exists, clouds form, and where most of Earth's weather occurs.

OZONE LAYER
Above the troposphere, up to about 30 mi. (50km), is the stratosphere. This is where jet planes usually fly, and near its top is the ozone layer, which absorbs most of the Sun's harmful ultraviolet radiation.

HIGH-ENERGY RAYS
Above the stratosphere is the ionosphere. In this layer, the Sun's rays break up some gas atoms into charged particles, or ions. Temperatures in the upper ionosphere (which is called the thermosphere) can reach 3,600°F (2,000°C).

MERGING INTO SPACE
Above 310 mi. (500km), the ionosphere merges into the exosphere, which stretches up to a height of several thousand miles. Any gas molecules found here are on their way out toward space.

GREENHOUSE GASES
Emissions from transport and factories are overloading the atmosphere with 'greenhouse' gases, such as carbon dioxide and methane. These are trapping radiation around the planet, causing it to overheat.

▲ In the atmosphere above the Arctic and Antarctic, colliding particles from the Sun create flickering bands of light known as auroras.

EVOLVING ATMOSPHERE
The atmosphere is constantly evolving. At first it was made up of high levels of carbon dioxide. Oxygen appeared about 1,800 million years ago, but advanced life was possible only after the ozone layer formed.

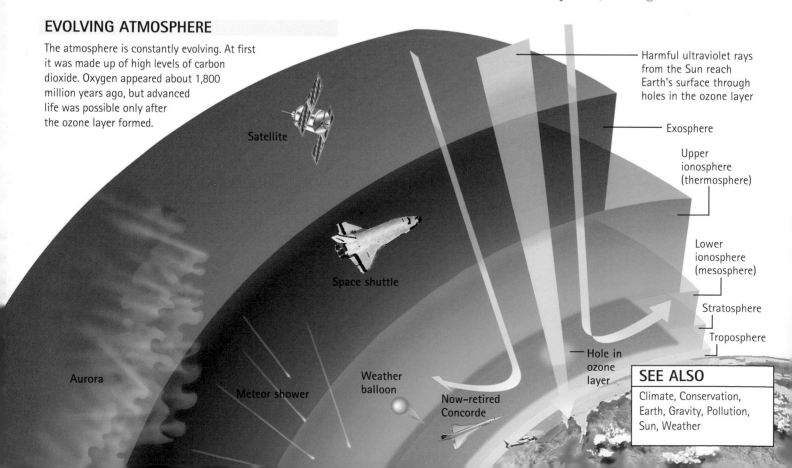

Satellite

Space shuttle

Aurora

Meteor shower

Weather balloon

Now-retired Concorde

Hole in ozone layer

Harmful ultraviolet rays from the Sun reach Earth's surface through holes in the ozone layer

Exosphere

Upper ionosphere (thermosphere)

Lower ionosphere (mesosphere)

Stratosphere

Troposphere

SEE ALSO
Climate, Conservation, Earth, Gravity, Pollution, Sun, Weather

ATOM AND MOLECULE

Atoms are the basic building blocks of everything around us, from plants and animals to planets and stars. A molecule is two or more atoms joined together.

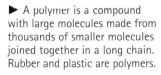

Crystals form regular shapes as their atoms are arranged in set patterns.

Pencil lead is soft because its atoms slide easily over each other.

Diamonds are very hard because their atoms are in a rigid framework.

DNA, the basis of life, consists of two strands of molecules in coils.

Every substance in the universe is made of atoms. An atom is the smallest part of any substance that can exist on its own—it is less than ten billionths of a yard in diameter. The period at the end of this sentence contains billions of atoms.

EMPTY SPACE
Most of an atom is made up of empty space, but at its center is a tiny nucleus. If an atom were scaled up to the size of a football field, the nucleus would be no bigger than a peppercorn.

THE NUCLEUS
The nucleus is the densest part of the atom and usually contains an equal amount of smaller, subatomic particles called protons and neutrons. Electrons are even lighter subatomic particles that whirl around the nucleus in all different directions at the speed of light.

INSIDE AN ATOM
The nucleus of every atom consists of particles called protons and neutrons (except for the hydrogen atom, which has no neutrons). Other particles, called electrons, flit around the nucleus in a random motion, making billions of trips in a millionth of a second.

▶ A polymer is a compound with large molecules made from thousands of smaller molecules joined together in a long chain. Rubber and plastic are polymers.

FORMING BONDS
Some substances consist of molecules that are formed from only one type of atom, and these are called elements. But when different types of atoms join to make molecules, they form compounds. A water molecule is a compound of one oxygen atom and two hydrogen atoms.

SOLID, LIQUID, OR GAS?
Water is a liquid, which means its molecules can move around (flow), whereas the molecules in a solid such as wood are fixed together in a definite pattern. Gas molecules buzz around randomly, filling all the available space.

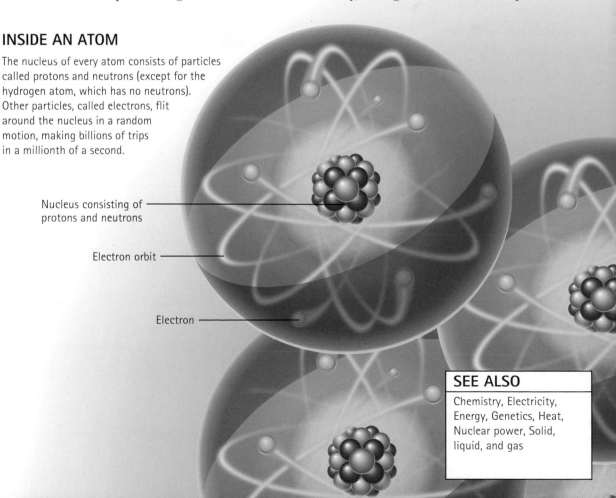

Nucleus consisting of protons and neutrons

Electron orbit

Electron

FAST FACTS

- The word "atom" comes from the Greek word *atomos*, meaning "uncut"

- A tiny speck of dust, just visible to the naked eye, contains a quadrillion atoms

- The lightest atom is hydrogen. The heaviest naturally occurring atom is uranium, which is 238 times the mass (weight) of hydrogen

SEE ALSO
Chemistry, Electricity, Energy, Genetics, Heat, Nuclear power, Solid, liquid, and gas

AUSTRALIA

Australia is the sixth-largest country in the world, covering about four percent of Earth's surface. It is also the smallest, flattest continent.

Area: 2,989,000 sq. mi. (7,741,200km²)
Population: 23,232,000
Capital: Canberra
Language: English
Currency: Australian dollar

KEY FACTS

• **Number of states:** 6 (Western Australia, South Australia, Queensland, New South Wales, Victoria, and Tasmania)

• **Number of territories:** 3 (Northern Territory, Australian Capital Territory, and Jervis Bay)

• **Highest point:** Mount Kosciuszko (7,316 ft./ 2,230m)

• **Longest permanent river:** Murray-Darling (2,330 mi./3,750km)

• **Largest lake:** Eyre (3,700 sq. mi./9,583km²)

Australia is often referred to as Down Under because it lies below the equator, in Earth's Southern Hemisphere. It is both a country and a continent.

THE GREAT DIVIDING RANGE

With the exception of a few mountain ranges, Australia is low and flat. The mountains of the Great Dividing Range run down the coast of Queensland and New South Wales. Fertile plateaus (flat areas of land high above sea level) lie along the top, where dense forests once grew. Today, many of the forests have been cleared for cities and farms.

SUNSHINE AND MONSOONS

The weather is cool and wet in the southernmost parts of the country, but most of Australia is hot or warm all year round. There are just two seasons in the far north: wet and dry. The wet season, from November to April, is hot and humid, with monsoon rains that turn huge areas of land into lakes.

▲ Rain forests on the northeast coast of Queensland, where the climate is wettest, are now national parks.

THE OUTBACK

The country's vast central region, which the Australians call the Outback, is hot and dry and mostly a desert—the second largest in the world. The temperature at Alice Springs, in central Australia, is often over 100°F (38°C). The rest of the interior is made up of land covered in coarse grass, low shrubs, and trees and provides grazing for cattle and sheep.

LIFE-BRINGING WATER

The many billabongs (waterholes) and rivers in the Outback are dry most of the year, and the parched plants sometimes catch fire. There are occasional heavy rains, however, when the buried seeds of flowering plants come to life and the riverbeds fill with water. The Australian

▼ Uluru (Ayers Rock) is a huge outcrop of sandstone sacred to the Aborigines.

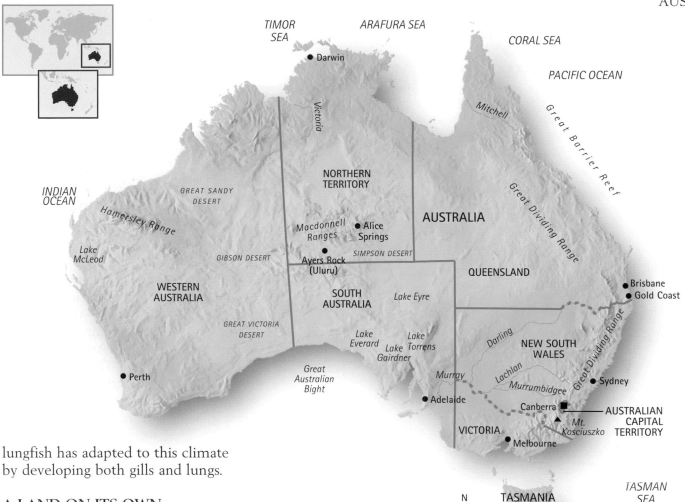

TIMOR SEA

ARAFURA SEA

CORAL SEA

PACIFIC OCEAN

INDIAN OCEAN

• Darwin

Victoria

Mitchell

Great Barrier Reef

GREAT SANDY DESERT

NORTHERN TERRITORY

Great Dividing Range

Hamersley Range

AUSTRALIA

Macdonnell Ranges

• Alice Springs

Lake McLeod

GIBSON DESERT

SIMPSON DESERT

• Ayers Rock (Uluru)

QUEENSLAND

WESTERN AUSTRALIA

SOUTH AUSTRALIA

Lake Eyre

GREAT VICTORIA DESERT

• Brisbane
• Gold Coast

Lake Everard

Lake Torrens

Lake Gairdner

Darling

NEW SOUTH WALES

Great Dividing Range

• Perth

Great Australian Bight

Murray

Lachlan

Murrumbidgee

• Sydney

• Adelaide

Canberra ■

AUSTRALIAN CAPITAL TERRITORY

VICTORIA

▲ Mt. Kosciuszko

• Melbourne

N

miles
0 — 500
0 — 500
km

TASMANIA

TASMAN SEA

• Hobart

lungfish has adapted to this climate by developing both gills and lungs.

A LAND ON ITS OWN

Australia has been isolated from any other landmass since about 65 million years ago, when it split from Antarctica. About 130 million years ago, Australia and Antarctica were both part of a great southern continent. Many species of animal that are unique to Australia evolved during this time. These include marsupials (pouched mammals), such as kangaroos, koalas, and wombats, as well as two unusual egg-laying mammals, the duck-billed platypus and the echidna (also known as the spiny anteater).

AUSTRALIA'S EXPORTS

Australia's farms produce wheat, beef, mutton, and wool, as well as wine made from grapes grown in the south. Australia is rich in minerals, such as coal, gold, iron ore, bauxite (aluminum ore), uranium, diamonds, and opals. Minerals and farm products are the country's main exports, with manufactured goods representing about 15 percent. Australia's factories ▶ produce goods such as cars and trucks, textiles, chemicals, and household goods.

▲ The kookaburra is often seen in parks and gardens. Its strange call, like a chuckling laugh, led to the name "laughing jackass."

◀ The Great Barrier Reef is a chain of more than 2,500 small reefs and coral islands. It stretches for 1,250 mi. (2,010km) along the northeast coast. The reef has suffered widespread environmental damage in recent years.

▲ New South Wales and Western Australia produce more than half of Australia's wool.

▼ Sydney is Australia's oldest and largest city, with a population of more than 5 million. The city is built around a huge natural bay, jutting out into which is the world-famous Sydney Opera House.

Australia also has a successful film and television industry.

SHEEP STATIONS

Most of the Outback is too dry to grow crops, but vast sheep farms, called sheep stations, cover thousands of acres. Huge cattle ranches are known as cattle runs, a few of which are the size of New York State. The cattle live and breed until it is time for market, when the rancher rounds them up, often using a helicopter.

SCHOOL ON THE AIRWAVES

People living on sheep stations and cattle runs are often hundreds of miles from the nearest town, although electronic technology and communications have made them less isolated. They may have to rely on flying doctors, who arrive by light aircraft, for medical help. Children in the Outback send and receive schoolwork by email and watch lessons on the internet. They can communicate with their teachers via phone or internet.

IN THE BIG CITIES

Nearly 90 percent of people in Australia live in cities, where most of the jobs are to be found. The largest cities—Sydney, Melbourne, and Brisbane—lie on the south and east coasts. In Sydney, the population of more than 5 million enjoys the attractions of city life, including the world-famous Sydney Opera House, as well as the beach. Bondi Beach lies about 5 mi. (8km) south of the center and attracts many swimmers and surfers.

▲ A favorite pastime in coastal cities is surfboat racing. Lifeguards give demonstrations of their skills at festivals.

FIRST INHABITANTS
Australia's first, or aboriginal, inhabitants arrived about 50,000 years ago from Southeast Asia. They lived off the land, hunting animals, gathering plants, and fishing, for thousands of years, until European settlers destroyed their way of life in the 1700s.

CAPTAIN COOK LANDS
The Dutch were the first Europeans to explore the coast in the 1600s, but they never established any settlements. The first Europeans to settle in Australia were the British. In 1770, Captain James Cook reached the east coast of Australia and immediately claimed it for Britain, calling it New South Wales.

CONVICTS ARRIVE
The first British fleet landed at Botany Bay in January 1788, with soldiers, convicts, and the colony's first governor, Arthur Phillip. The first settlement, named Sydney, was set up nearby, and as more free settlers arrived, other farming settlements grew up around the coast.

THE AUSTRALIAN GOLD RUSH
In 1851, many more people dashed to Australia seeking their fortune after news that gold had been found in New South Wales and Victoria. Melbourne, the capital of Victoria, soon became a wealthy city and Australia's population more than doubled. In 1854, gold miners at the Eureka Stockade rebelled against their colonial rulers, hastening reform and self-government.

AUSTRALIA—THE NATION
In 1901, Australia became a nation. The colonies became states and united as the Commonwealth of Australia. During World War I, Australian troops helped the British; in World War II they defended their country against Japanese invasion. People from many countries migrated to Australia after both wars, and the population rose from five million in 1918 to more than 23 million today. English is not the first language for 15 percent of Australians. Increasingly, Australia looks to Asia and Pacific countries for trade links, especially to Japan.

▲ Cattle ranches, or runs, can be thousands of square miles in size. Farmers use motorcycles and helicopters to round up huge herds of livestock.

◄ Tasmania has a cooler, wetter climate than the Australian mainland. Much of the island is unpopulated and covered in thick forest.

◄ Britain sent many thousands of convicts to Australia between 1788 and 1853 under a system called transportation. The early years in prison settlements were harsh.

SEE ALSO
Aboriginal people, Architecture, Continent, Explorer, Gold, Kangaroo, Platypus

AZTEC

The Aztecs were members of one of the last great native civilizations of the Americas. They created a large empire in Mexico during the 1400s.

▶ The Aztecs used two calendars: this solar one, divided into 18 months, and a sacred one.

Quetzalcóatl (meaning plumed serpent) was one of the main Aztec gods.

This ceremonial mask was made from precious stones on a human skull.

The Aztecs' rise to power began in the 1300s, when they built the city of Tenochtitlán on an island where Mexico City now stands. They began to create their great empire by conquering nearby cities, largely to the south and east.

THE PEOPLE

The Aztec ruler was an emperor who relied on a warrior class to defend and expand the empire. Next in importance were the priests. Ordinary people were farmers, traders, craftsworkers, and slaves. Food was farmed on floating gardens (called *chinampas*) on Lake Texcoco, which surrounded Tenochtitlán. Indian corn, vegetables, and cotton were grown; turkeys and dogs were kept for meat. The Aztecs were among the first to use cocoa beans to make a chocolate drink, and the words "tomato" and "avocado" come from the Aztec language.

TEMPLES OF DOOM

The main religious building was the Great Temple at Tenochtitlán, a stone pyramid with sacrificial altars at the top. Each ruler built a larger, more impressive temple on the same site. It was rebuilt six times.

CONQUERED BY A LEGEND

The Aztec Empire was at its height when Montezuma II became emperor in 1502 and built a vast palace. Under his rule, the empire stretched across Mexico from the east to the west. In 1519, a small force of Spanish soldiers and bounty hunters, led by Hernán Cortés, arrived in Mexico. Many Aztecs, including Montezuma, believed Cortés was the legendary god Quetzalcóatl, and at first welcomed the Spaniards. By 1521, Cortés's army had completely destroyed Tenochtitlán, and Cortés was made governor of Mexico.

Stone knives were used to cut out the heart

Feathers from the quetzal bird were used for headdresses

HUMAN SACRIFICE

Religion was very important to the Aztecs. They worshiped many gods—of war, rain, sun, and wind—and carried out human sacrifices to win the favor of their gods. Captives taken in battle were killed by the priests. They cut out the still-living hearts using ceremonial knives made of very sharp stone. The blood was used to bathe statues of the gods.

SEE ALSO

Mexico

BABYLON

Babylon was a large and wealthy city beside the Euphrates River in modern Iraq. It was founded around 2300 B.C. and flourished for 2,000 years.

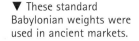

The city of Babylon was famous for its power, beauty, and magnificent buildings. The name Babylon means "gate of god," and it was a great religious center.

▲ Hammurabi's army conquered neighboring cities to form a large, strong empire.

PYRAMID TOWERS

The city was dominated by its pyramid-shaped temple towers called *ziggurats*, made from sun-dried bricks. Around the city was a great wall, and canals fed water from the river to fields outside the city for growing grain, vegetables, and fruit.

WEALTH OF KNOWLEDGE

The Babylonians were skilled in science, mathematics, and astronomy. They divided the circle into 360 degrees and the hour into 60 minutes, and grouped numbers into tens. They studied the Sun and stars in order to predict the future, and they used a form of writing, called cuneiform, scratched with pointed reeds in soft clay.

RIGHTS FOR CHILDREN

Babylon's rulers had military, religious, and legal powers. One of their greatest leaders was Hammurabi, who ruled from 1792 B.C. to 1750 B.C. He drew up a set of laws, the oldest surviving in the world, that protected women, children, and slaves. The Code of Hammurabi was carved on a black pillar, which is now in the Louvre Museum in Paris, France.

RISE AND FALL OF BABYLON

After Hammurabi, the Babylonians were ruled by Assyrians until a new empire arose under Nebuchadrezzar II in 605 B.C. He fortified Babylon and built fine buildings. After he died, in 562 B.C., Babylon collapsed into civil war. It fell to the Persians in 539 B.C., and was conquered in 331 B.C. by the Greeks, led by Alexander the Great.

GRAND ENTRANCE

Babylon's narrow streets were crowded with traders who entered through one of eight gates in the double city walls. The grand Ishtar Gate, named after a fertility goddess, was the main entrance. It was covered with blue tiles and decorated with figures of bulls and dragons.

The Ishtar Gate stood 39 ft. (12m) high

The city wall was so wide that a chariot could be driven along it

According to legend, hanging (terraced) gardens were built by Nebuchadnezzar to please his wife

SEE ALSO

Law, Mesopotamia, Seven Wonders of the World, Weights and measures

BALTIC STATES

Estonia, Latvia, and Lithuania are independent republics bordering the eastern shores of the Baltic Sea, in northern Europe. They are known as the Baltic states.

▲ Like Latvia and Lithuania, Estonia became independent in 1991. It had been taken into the Soviet Union in 1940.

ESTONIA
Area: 17,462 sq. mi. (45,228km2)
Population: 1,252,000
Capital: Tallinn
Language: Estonian
Currency: Euro

LATVIA
Area: 24,938 sq. mi. (64,589km2)
Population: 1,945,000
Capital: Riga
Language: Latvian
Currency: Euro

LITHUANIA
Area: 25,212 sq. mi. (65,300km2)
Population: 2,824,000
Capital: Vilnius
Language: Lithuanian
Currency: Euro

The landscape of the Baltic region was shaped by movements of ice in prehistoric times. It includes plains, peat bogs, marshes, lakes, and hills. There are large areas of forest and farmland. The two chief rivers are the Nemunas (Neman) and the Daugava (Western Dvina). The climate is moderate and moist.

PEOPLES AND WORK
Estonia is the smallest of the three nations. Its people are related to the neighboring Finns, and their language is linked to Finnish. The Estonian economy depends on trade, especially in electronic and telecommunications equipment. Latvian and Lithuanian are both Baltic languages. Latvia exports timber, processed wood, pork, and dairy products. Lithuania, the largest Baltic state, has gas and oil refineries.

INVADERS AND EMPIRES
For centuries the Baltic states were invaded and settled by their more powerful neighbors. German Crusaders and merchants arrived in the Middle Ages, leaving a lasting influence on culture, religion, and architecture. The Lithuanians united with the Kingdom of Poland. Denmark and Sweden extended their power eastward in the 1600s, and the Russian empire moved westward during the 1700s.

THE ROAD TO INDEPENDENCE
Struggles for independence between the two World Wars were short-lived. The Soviet Union invaded the Baltic states in 1940 and many Russians settled in the region. Estonia, Latvia, and Lithuania declared their independence in 1991, during the fall of the Soviet Union. Today they are all members of the European Union (EU).

▶ Riga, on the Western Dvina River, is Latvia's capital city and its main industrial center.

SEE ALSO
Civil War, Europe

BAT

Bats are the only mammals that are capable of true flight. Most are nocturnal (active at night). They live all over the world, except at sea and in polar regions.

The big brown bat of North America gives birth to twins. Other bats have only one baby.

Kitti's hog-nosed bat from Thailand is the world's smallest mammal. It was first recorded in 1974.

Free-tailed bats have a tail that extends beyond the wing membrane. These bats can fly high and fast.

Horseshoe bats have circular flaps of skin around the nose to direct sound while hunting.

The Rodrigues fruit bat lives on an island in the Indian Ocean. Its forest home has now almost gone.

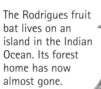

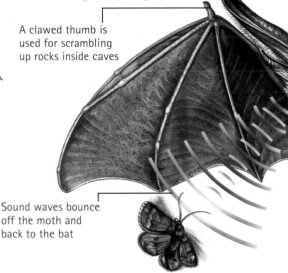

A clawed thumb is used for scrambling up rocks inside caves

Large ears help the bat hear the returning echoes

Bats use their tails to brake or change direction in flight

Sound waves bounce off the moth and back to the bat

ECHOLOCATION

Most bats can see in the dark, but the microbat also uses echolocation to find its way around. It makes very high-pitched (ultrasonic) squeaks—as many as 500 per second. The sound waves from these squeaks "hit" objects or prey in front of the bat, making an echo return. The bat can tell from these echoes exactly where the prey is.

With their large wings of leathery, lightweight skin held stretched out by very long finger bones, bats are the only mammals that can truly fly. There are so many different species of bat that, added together, they make up almost a quarter of the whole mammal group.

A MAMMAL WITH WINGS

Apart from its wings, the bat has the typical features of a mammal. It has a furry body, warm blood, and its young are fed on their mother's milk. When resting, the bat wraps its wings around its body and hangs upside down by its claws in a roost, such as a cave, a hollow tree, high up in a roof, or down in a cellar.

GROUPS OF BATS

Bats are divided into two main groups according to their size. Fruit bats are large bats, often called flying foxes because they have a face that looks like a fox. Most live in tropical forests and eat leaves and fruit. Other bats, called microbats, are much smaller and eat insects, which they hunt in flight. Microbats look like winged mice. Some bats are specialist feeders. The fishing bat of South America grabs fish in its long claws. Vampire bats, from South and Central America, feed on the blood of cattle and horses, but rarely of humans.

KEEPING WARM

Bats in colder climates hibernate in the winter by clustering in cool, dry places. Others, such as the Mexican free-tailed bat, migrate. Most bats give birth to one offspring a year, early in the warm season. The young cluster together in nursery roosts while the parents go off to feed.

PROTECTED BY LAW

Many bat species are threatened because their habitats have been destroyed by people building roads and houses. Bats are also often treated as pests. Fruit bats especially are accused of destroying crops and damaging trees. In many countries, bats are now protected by wildlife laws.

SEE ALSO

Conservation, Hibernation, Mammal, Migration, Radar and sonar, Seed and pollination

BEAR

Bears are large, strong mammals with stocky bodies, thick fur, and big claws. There are eight species, living mainly in Europe, Asia, and North America.

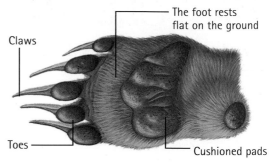

▲ Bears use their front feet for digging, hunting, and climbing. Their claws may grow up to 5 in. (12cm) long.

Sloth bears love honey so much they are also known as honey bears.

The spectacled bear is the only bear that lives in South America.

The American black bear lives in remote areas and feeds on almost anything.

There are several types of brown bear. The Kodiak is the world's largest bear.

Meat is the main source of food for most bears. They are classified as carnivores (meat-eaters), but bears will eat just about anything and are particularly fond of fruit, nuts, fish, and honey. They use their strong sense of smell to track down food, because their small eyes have only poor vision.

LIVING IN A DEN

Bears spend most of the year alone, but come together to mate or to scavenge on the bodies of dead animals. In regions with cold winters, most bears spend long periods asleep in dens, which can be caves, tree stumps, or holes under rocks. This is not true hibernation since they often wake up. It is during this time that the cubs are born—usually two every second year. The female polar bear gives birth to her cubs in a snow den.

COLOR AND MARKINGS

The eight species of bear include the polar bear, white-coated for camouflage in the snow, and two black bears, the American and the Asian. The sloth bear hangs from forest trees in India and Sri Lanka. South America's spectacled bear gets its name from white markings around its eyes; the Malayan or sun bear has a sun-shaped patch on its chest. Brown bears include the grizzly and Kodiak.

IN DANGER

Bears have almost no predators—except for humans, who hunt and kill them for their fur, teeth, or claws. Largely peaceful, bears will defend themselves and their cubs fiercely only if under attack. Wildlife conservation groups are fighting to protect the remaining bear population from human cruelty and destruction.

AS WHITE AS SNOW

The polar bear lives among the treeless tundra and cold seas of northern polar regions. It is white-coated for snow camouflage and can grow to over 2,200 lb. (1,000kg). Thick, water-repellent fur allows the bear to swim in icy seas, where it hunts seals, fish, walruses, and small whales. Polar bears are known to ambush seals by lying in wait at breathing holes in the pack ice.

SEE ALSO

Animal, Arctic, Forest, Hibernation, Mammal

BICYCLE AND MOTORCYCLE

Bicycles, which rely on pedal power, are the most energy-efficient form of transportation. Motorcycles are based on the bicycle design, but are powered by an engine.

▶ Off-road motorcycles are strong for rough terrain and jumping obstacles.

The dandyhorse, built in 1817 by Karl von Drais, had no pedals and was pushed along by foot.

The penny farthing, produced in 1870, had solid tires and a step to help the rider climb on.

Bicycle design has changed little since the 1880s, when the chain-driven rear wheel and air-filled tires arrived.

Early motorcycles, such as this one built by Gottlieb Daimler in 1885, were slow and uncomfortable to ride.

The first bicycle with pedals appeared in the 1860s, when Frenchman Pierre Lallement introduced the velocipede. Twenty years later, the German Gottlieb Daimler fitted a gasoline engine to a bicycle and made the first motorcycle.

MODERN BICYCLES

All modern bicycles have the same basic design. The front wheel, connected to the handlebars, steers the bike, while the back wheel drives it. Types include BMXs and touring, road, mountain, and racing bikes. Modern bikes are built for speed and strength from tough, yet lightweight materials, including aluminum and carbon fiber. The number of gears on a bicycle ranges from 3 to 21, and tires can be very thin to reduce friction or extra wide to absorb shocks from rough, uneven ground as on cross-country bikes.

ENGINE POWER

Motorcycles have either a four-stroke engine like a car or a simpler two-stroke engine. The smallest are just 50cc (cubic centimeters) in size; the most powerful can be over 1,100cc. Scooters and mopeds are the smallest motorcycles. Most have electronic ignition and up to five gear speeds.

RACING MOTORCYCLES

Motorcycle racing is an international sport and includes motocross (dirt-track racing), enduros (endurance racing), and speed racing. The fastest models can have 18 gear ratios and reach speeds of 174 mph (280kph).

BICYCLE GEARS

Gears make it easier to cycle. If the cyclist selects a low gear, a device called a derailleur moves the chain onto the largest sprocket on the rear wheel. This allows the back wheel to turn with less pedaling, making it easier (but slower) to go uphill. Selecting a high gear to go downhill has the opposite effect.

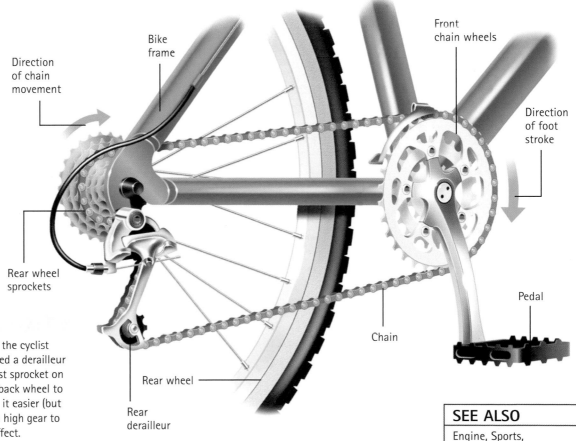

Direction of chain movement

Bike frame

Front chain wheels

Direction of foot stroke

Rear wheel sprockets

Rear derailleur

Rear wheel

Chain

Pedal

SEE ALSO

Engine, Sports, Transportation

BIG BANG THEORY

The Big Bang is the term used to describe a huge explosion that scientists believe happened about 13.7 billion years ago, creating our universe.

Matter, energy, space, and time are all thought to have been created in a fraction of a second 13.7 billion years ago, when there was a colossal explosion called the Big Bang that created tremendous heat.

PEA-SIZED UNIVERSE
Nobody knows what caused the Big Bang, since we cannot look back to a time before it. But just after the event, the universe is believed to have been a knot of tightly packed particles only about the size of a pea. Its temperature was 18 thousand trillion, trillion degrees Fahrenheit.

COSMIC COOLING
From that moment on, the universe began to expand and cool. First, hydrogen and helium (the two most common atoms in the universe) were created. Over the next billion years, the first stars and galaxies formed, gathered together by the force of gravity. Finally planets began to form.

MICROWAVES IN SPACE
A discovery made in 1965 seems to support the Big Bang theory. A steady glow of microwave radiation comes from every direction in space. Scientists believe that this is the cooled remains of the fireball in which the universe was formed.

SPEEDING GALAXIES
Scientists have also found that, apart from a few nearby galaxies, everything in space is racing away from us. This suggests that all matter and energy in the universe were once concentrated at a single point, just before the Big Bang. The universe may expand forever, or it may eventually stop expanding and collapse inwards.

▲ A microwave map of our galaxy, showing radiation ripples thought to be left over like an afterglow of the Big Bang.

THE UNIVERSE IS BORN

In the first split second after the Big Bang, matter was created in the heat of the newborn universe. As it cooled down, a dense fog of atoms, made up of protons, neutrons, and electrons, appeared.

5 One billion years later: gravity pulls matter together to form galaxies.

6 13.7 billion years later: the ever-expanding universe that we see today.

4 300,000 years later: electrons begin to orbit the nuclei to form atoms. The universe fills with light.

3 Three minutes later: protons and neutrons combine to form hydrogen and helium nuclei.

2 A fraction of a second later: the temperature begins to drop. Protons and neutrons form.

1 The Big Bang takes place.

SEE ALSO
Atom and molecule, Energy, Galaxy, Planet, Solar system, Star, Universe, Wavelength

BIRD

Birds are warm-blooded, egg-laying vertebrates (animals with backbones). They have wings, and are the only animals with feathers.

The large beak of the toucan is useful for plucking fruit from trees.

An avocet's long, slender bill probes for shellfish in soft mud.

The eagle uses its hooked beak to tear meat into chunks.

A swift gathers insects in its wide beak while flying.

There are about 10,000 different species of bird. They are found all over the world, even on polar ice caps. Only a few birds cannot fly at all. These include the long-legged, fast-running ostrich of Africa, the rhea of South America, the emu of Australia, and penguins in the Southern Hemisphere, which use their flipperlike wings to "fly" through water.

HOLLOW BONES

A bird is designed for lightness. Its bones are thin and hollow, and its beak is toothless. In the front limb, the upper-arm and forearm bones are long. The wrist, hand, and three finger bones are joined together to support the feathers.

BIRD SENSE

Birds have excellent eyesight and good hearing, but their sense of smell is less developed. A bird's feeding habits vary with habitat and species. Some, such as

▶ A hummingbird can flap its wings 100 times per second, creating a humming sound as it hovers to drink nectar.

the parrot, are nut-eaters; others, such as the snipe, feast on worms. Some birds like to scavenge dead bodies. The raven has a reputation as an evil bird because in medieval times it pecked at the dead bodies of executed criminals.

CHEWING STONE

Since they have no teeth to chew with, seed-eating birds grind food in the gizzard, a muscular stomach part. Digestion is aided by pieces of stone and grit that they have swallowed for this purpose. ▶

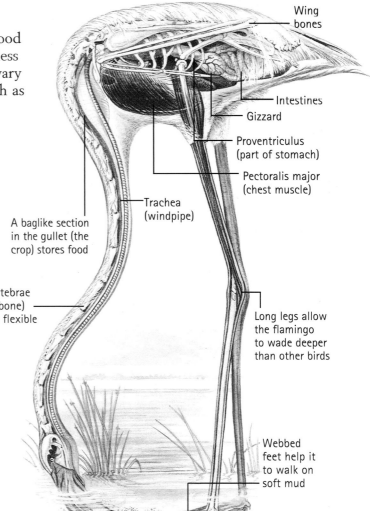

Wing bones

Intestines

Gizzard

Proventriculus (part of stomach)

Pectoralis major (chest muscle)

Trachea (windpipe)

A baglike section in the gullet (the crop) stores food

Sections of short vertebrae (as in a human backbone) allow the neck to be flexible

Long legs allow the flamingo to wade deeper than other birds

Webbed feet help it to walk on soft mud

THE FLAMINGO'S BEAK AND DIET

The shape of a bird's beak depends on what it eats. The flamingo strains its food from mud and water, so its long beak contains a filter of little hooks to trap tiny plants and crustaceans (shellfish). It is the algae that the shellfish eat that give the flamingo its bright pink color. If the flamingo doesn't eat them, its feathers turn grayish white.

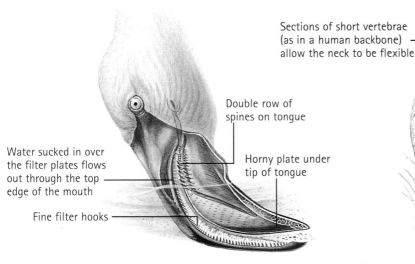

Double row of spines on tongue

Horny plate under tip of tongue

Water sucked in over the filter plates flows out through the top edge of the mouth

Fine filter hooks

NESTS

Birds' nests vary widely, from the bare cliff ledge of the guillemot to the stick-and-twig pile of an eagle's aerie.

Swallows build nests of mud high up on cliffs or on the sides of buildings.

The Indian tailorbird builds its nest by sewing leaves together with spider silk.

A plover lays its eggs on shingle—their only protection is camouflage.

Some ducks, grebes, and other waterbirds build floating nests.

The ovenbird builds an oven-shaped nest of mud on a branch or fence post.

Down feather

Contour feather

FEATHERS
Birds have three types of feathers. Fluffy down feathers near the body keep the bird warm. Contour feathers give the body a streamlined shape. Flight feathers, on the wings, have barbs that form smooth, flat surfaces.

Flight feather

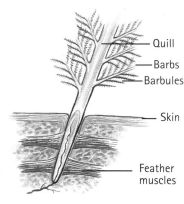

Quill
Barbs
Barbules
Skin
Feather muscles

MICROSCOPIC HOOKS
Each feather is made of keratin (found in the hair and nails of humans) and has a long, stiff shaft, or quill, with side parts called barbs, linked by tiny hooklike barbules.

COLORS AND BREEDING

The colors of a bird's feathers usually help to conceal, or camouflage, it in its natural habitat. Most birds molt (shed) their old feathers and grow new ones each year. This molting may be linked to breeding, as some male birds, such as the bird-of-paradise and peacock, grow colorful feathers to attract mates. The females, however, tend to be drab in color so that they are hidden from predators while sitting on the nest.

COURTING COUPLES

As the spring or mating season arrives, a male and female pair up to mate. Most birds court with a variety of calls and displays. Some males give gifts of food such as insects to the females. Usually the males show off their colors and skills in flight and on perches, or try to outsing and outdance rivals. Grebes perform a very elaborate dance that involves crouching, head wagging, and swaying.

LAYING EGGS

Most bird pairs breed alone, but some, such as rooks or puffins, breed in large groups called colonies. The female lays hard-shelled eggs and sits on them to keep them warm until they are ready to hatch. This process is called incubation. The number of eggs laid in one clutch varies— a kiwi lays a single egg, while a North American bobwhite can lay up to 25. Eggs can take at least ten days to hatch; albatross eggs take the longest, up to 70 days.

MATCH-MAKING

Larger, long-lived birds, such as gannets, storks, cranes, and albatrosses, often return to the same nest site and the same partner each year. The male ostrich, however, courts several females, which all lay eggs in one nest. He then guards all the eggs (there may be up to 30) and—when they hatch—the chicks.

▲ Male birds-of-paradise have beautiful feathers. They show off their plumes in a dance to attract a mate.

HOW A BIRD FLIES

The goose, like other birds in flight, lowers its wings using its strong pectoral (chest) muscles. The wings push the air down and back, thrusting the bird up and forward in the air. The wing and tail feathers can be twisted and fanned to help the goose maneuver as it flies.

1 The powerful downstroke lifts the bird upward.

2 Legs and tail are in line with body to keep the bird streamlined as it flies.

3 The upstroke is less powerful. Feathers are twisted, letting air through.

4 The tail is used for steering and for braking.

MOVING HOUSE

Birds are warm-blooded. Their average body temperature is 105.9°F (41°C)—slightly hotter than humans'. This means they can stay active in cold weather but they need food, so many species leave colder climates and migrate to warmer places somewhere else in the world.

BETWEEN CONTINENTS

Birds such as geese and waders fly from the Arctic to Europe, Asia, and North America. Birds from Europe, like swifts and bee-eaters, fly south to Africa and India. The Arctic tern is the greatest migrator of all birds, flying an amazing 9,320 mi. (15,000km) to the Antarctic.

FAST FACTS

• A large bird such as a swan has about 25,000 feathers, whereas a tiny hummingbird has 1,000

• The world's largest bird, the ostrich, is too heavy to fly. The largest flying bird is the Kori bustard, weighing 40 lb. (18kg)

• The pitohui of New Guinea is the only bird that is poisonous

FEEDING THE CHICKS

The crow belongs to the group known as perching birds, which is the largest of the 26 bird groups. Its toes are designed for gripping, as crows build their nests in trees or on the sides of cliffs. The chicks are often born blind and helpless, and the parents feed them until they are ready to leave the nest.

The bones are thin and hollow, so that birds are very light

The inside of the chick's mouth is bright red to attract its parent's attention

Like all birds, the crow has thousands of feathers

These two-week-old chicks have soft, downy feathers, and their eyes are now open

SEE ALSO

Animal, Eagle, Migration, Prehistoric animal, Zoology

BLACK DEATH

The Black Death was a disease that struck Asia, Europe, and North Africa during the 1300s. It killed over one third of the people living there.

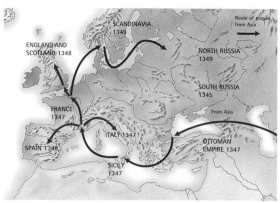

▲ The Black Death swept through Europe from Asia in 1347, reaching its peak in 1349. Only a few areas, such as Belgium and eastern Germany, were unaffected.

Fleas passed on the bubonic plague when they bit people.

The fleas lived on black rats, which thrived in the tightly packed houses.

Medieval artists often portrayed the Black Death as a murderous skeleton.

More people were killed by the Black Death in the late 1340s than by any other disease in history. Milder outbreaks of the disease, also called the bubonic plague, continued for about 300 years.

DEADLY SYMPTOMS

The name Black Death came from the blood spots that turned black under the skin. Some victims died within hours. Only about five percent of people who caught the disease survived. Fleas from diseased rats spread the plague by biting humans. It was also possible to catch the plague from an infected person.

THE PLAGUE SPREADS

The Black Death began in central Asia in about 1339, and in 1347 Italian soldiers brought it back from the Crimea, on the Black Sea. It spread rapidly through North Africa and Europe, where rats and fleas thrived in conditions of poor hygiene. As people fled the disease-infested cities, the Black Death spread with them.

A TERRIBLE PUNISHMENT

The appearance of the Black Death was a horrible mystery. Many saw it as God's punishment; some whipped themselves in public and prayed to be saved. Doctors did not know what caused the disease and so had no idea how to treat it. Many believed cats and dogs spread the plague, so they killed them. The true carriers, black rats, only increased. Today, cases of plague would be cured by antibiotics.

DEVASTATED POPULATIONS

Many doctors and priests died looking after the sick, leaving few educated people alive. Because so few workers survived after the worst of the plague was over, those remaining demanded higher wages instead of simply working to pay rent for land. The economy became based on money, as it is today.

"BRING OUT YOUR DEAD!"

During an outbreak of the plague, people tried to control the disease. Infected houses were marked with a cross to warn visitors. Prisoners or volunteers patrolled the streets with wheelbarrows, calling for people to bring out the bodies of the dead. The bodies were then taken to large plague pits outside the town and quickly buried.

SEE ALSO

Asia, Disease, Medicine, Middle Ages

BLACK HOLE

A black hole is a region of space where the pull of gravity is so strong that nothing can escape from it, not even light.

INVISIBLE FORCE

When a black hole lies close to another star, its immense gravity sucks particles or gas away from the star. These are pulled into a gassy spiral, called an accretion disk. The gas inside the disk is heated to millions of degrees Fahrenheit and gives off X rays. It is these powerful, flickering X rays that reveal the presence of a black hole.

Nearby star

Black hole

Particles, gas, and matter spiral downward

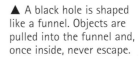

▲ A black hole is shaped like a funnel. Objects are pulled into the funnel and, once inside, never escape.

Scientists believe that a black hole forms after a massive, heavy star has exploded at the end of its life. The outer parts are hurled into space, but the core of the dead star, with no light and heat left to support it, shrinks very quickly.

DEAD STARS

The gravity of a dead star is thought to pull all the material left behind inward, squeezing it tighter to make it smaller and extremely compact. A tiny black hole, the size of a period, could hold enough matter to make a mountain. Vast black holes, thought to exist at the center of galaxies, may contain as much matter as tens of millions of stars.

COSMIC VACUUM

Black holes are invisible—they can only be tracked down by their effect on a nearby object. They tug matter away from

the surface of a star, like a vacuum cleaner. This debris enters a whirlpool, which spins around the black hole before disappearing inside, like water going down a giant drain.

THROUGH A WORMHOLE

Some black holes may be the entrances to strange tunnels through space and time known as wormholes. It has been suggested that a spacecraft could travel along a wormhole and reappear in a different part of the universe.

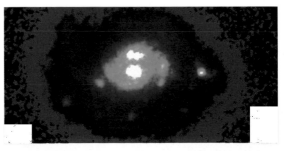

◄ This ultraviolet image shows galaxy M77. Its center is thought to be a black hole with the mass of several million suns.

SEE ALSO

Astronomy, Big Bang theory, Constellation, Galaxy, Gravity, Star

BLOOD

Blood is a vital liquid that is pumped through arteries and veins around the body by the heart. Blood carries oxygen, nutrients, hormones, and waste products.

KARL LANDSTEINER
This Austrian-born pathologist (1868–1943) discovered blood groups, making blood transfusions safe for the first time.

Most animals have a bloodlike fluid. It is red in most vertebrates (animals with backbones), but can be different colors in other animals. Lobsters have blue blood, snails have gray blood, some insects have green blood, and a worm's blood is colorless.

BLOOD PLASMA
Just over half (55 percent) of human blood is a pale yellow liquid called plasma. This contains hundreds of substances, including nutrients, sugars, salts, minerals, hormones, and chemicals.

OXYGEN CARRIERS
About 45 percent of blood is made up of blood cells and platelets. The vast majority of blood cells are small, red, and doughnut-shaped. They are made inside the bones and released into the blood, where they carry oxygen around the body. When red cells have plenty of oxygen, as in most arteries, they are bright red. When low in oxygen, as in most veins, they are dark red.

FAST FACTS
• An average human has 11 pt. (5l) of blood

• A blood spot the size of a pinhead contains about 5 million red cells, 10,000 white cells, and 250,000 platelets

• Anemia is a lack of oxygen in the blood

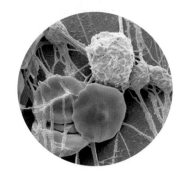

◄ Chemicals in the blood form a net over a wound. The net traps red blood cells, platelets, and white blood cells to form a clot.

DEFENDING THE BODY
Less than one percent of blood is made up of white blood cells and platelets. There are several types of white blood cell, all of which defend the body. Some fight invading bacteria and viruses by bombarding them with chemicals. Others surround invaders and eat them.

CLOTTING AND HEALING
Platelets are cell fragments that help wounds to heal. They gather around a cut and release chemicals to slow blood loss and form a clot. This stops the blood flow and seals the wound, stopping germs from getting in while new skin grows.

BLOOD GROUPS
There are several different types of human blood, including A, B, AB, and O. The blood group depends on the chemicals that the white blood cells produce. If a person needs a blood transfusion, the right group must be given because some chemicals do not mix. The wrong chemicals may clot with the existing blood and make the illness worse or even cause death.

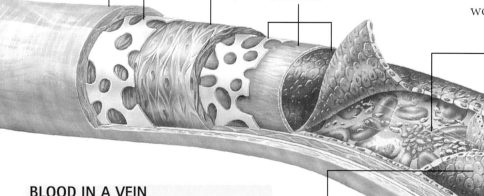

Outer layers of vein wall

Muscle

Inner layers of vein wall

White blood cell that makes chemicals to fight disease

White blood cell that eats dying and dead germs

Red blood cell

Valve to stop blood flowing the wrong way

Platelets help blood to clot

White blood cell that attacks invaders

BLOOD IN A VEIN

Blood is carried toward the heart by veins and away from the heart by arteries. Red blood cells returning to the lungs from the heart are dark red in color because they are no longer carrying oxygen. All blood contains plasma, platelets, red blood cells, and several types of white blood cells.

SEE ALSO
Cell, Disease, Heart and circulatory system, Immune system, Medicine

BOAT

Boats are small watercraft powered by oars, sails, or an engine. They are smaller than ships—usually no more than about 65 ft. (20m) long.

Boats in ancient Egypt were made by tying reed bundles together.

A coracle is a round boat made of animal skin stretched over a frame.

A junk is a traditional Chinese boat and is still in use today.

A catamaran is a sailboat with two hulls arranged side by side.

A paddle wheeler's engine turns a huge paddle wheel to drive the boat forward.

Small, powerful tugboats are used to tow much larger vessels into port.

► A sailboat can travel in almost any direction, but at different rates. Sailing with the wind behind the boat (running) is not the fastest. Sailing across the wind (reaching) is faster. To sail into the wind a boat must tack, or zigzag, at an angle of 45° to the wind direction with the sails drawn in as close as possible.

Close-hauled · Reach · Broad reach · Run · With the wind · Across the wind · Into the wind

Wind direction

POWERED BY THE WIND

The skill in sailing lies in positioning the sail so that it catches the wind most efficiently. Sails are adjusted by a sheet (rope). Sideways movement is reduced by the centerboard (keel) reaching far down into the water. The boat is steered using the tiller to adjust the position of the rudder (a board attached to the back of the boat).

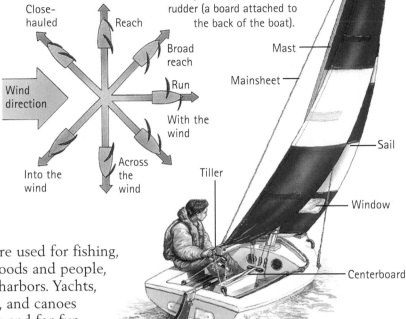

Mast · Mainsheet · Sail · Window · Centerboard · Tiller · Rudder

Working boats are used for fishing, transporting goods and people, and moving ships in harbors. Yachts, motorboats, sailboats, and canoes are all used for racing and for fun.

HOLLOWED-OUT TRUNKS
The first boats were built in prehistoric times, when people hollowed out tree trunks to make dugouts. Boats such as Inuit kayaks were made from animal skins. Ancient Egyptians made boats from bundles of reed.

DESIGNED FOR THE JOB
A boat's design depends on its use. A lifeboat must be built to travel long distances quickly and to cope with rough seas. A small motorboat must be tough enough to withstand the pounding of the waves as well as its own engine vibrations.

PARTS OF A BOAT
The keel runs along the base of a boat. It keeps it stable and provides a framework from which to build up the boat. The hull, or outer shell, can be made of wood, but plastic and fiberglass are tougher and cheaper. The bow, or front of the boat, cuts through the water and pushes it to the sides so that the hull can glide smoothly.

ON THE MOVE
Rowboats are moved by muscle power, using oars which have a wide blade at one end. The paddles of some canoes have blades at each end and this makes it much easier to steer in fast-moving rapids. Sailboats, or yachts, use sails to catch the wind and drive them through the water. Most working boats and some sports boats are powered by an engine. This makes a propeller spin in the water, moving the boat forward.

▲ Small, light motorboats rise out of the water when they travel at speed.

SEE ALSO
Egypt, Engine, Fishing industry, Ship, Transportation, Wind power

BRAIN AND NERVOUS SYSTEM

The brain is the body's control center, responsible for action, thought, memory, behavior, and emotion. It is linked to the body by the nervous system.

Fish have simple brains, with areas that process smell extending forward to the tip of the nose.

Snakes have brains with large sight areas, showing the importance of sight for hunting.

Birds have brains with large movement centers which control the complex movements used in flight.

Cats, like other mammals, have brains with large cerebrums for complex and adaptable behavior.

The average adult human brain weighs about 3.1 lb. (1.4kg). It is a large grayish-colored organ. The brain is made up of tiny cells that send electrical messages to the body along a network of nerves known as the nervous system.

IN THREE PARTS

All vertebrates (animals with backbones) have a brain that can be divided into three main areas: brain stem, cerebellum, and cerebrum. The brain stem and cerebellum keep the body functioning. The cerebrum deals with thought, memory, and sensation.

THE BRAIN STEM

The brain stem is at the bottom of the brain, where it joins the spinal cord (the bundle of nerves linking the brain to the body). The stem controls the body's automatic processes, such as heartbeat, breathing, body temperature, blood pressure, digestion, and getting rid of waste.

THE CEREBELLUM

The cerebellum lies at the back of the brain. When movement instructions come from the cerebrum, the cerebellum analyzes the instructions. It then sends signals to the muscles to make smooth and coordinated movements. The cerebellum also controls posture and balance.

THE CEREBRUM

About 90 percent of the human brain is taken up by the cerebrum—the center of all thought. It is split into two halves, called cerebral hemispheres, which contain gray matter and white matter. Gray matter lies on the surface and is made up of nerve cell bodies, which create messages. The inner white matter is packed with nerve fibers carrying the messages to the body.

CEREBRAL CENTERS

The human cerebrum looks the same all over, but different areas carry out special functions. One area receives and processes nerve signals from the eyes. Another is for touch, processing nerve signals from the skin. Just in front of this is the motor

HOW NERVE CELLS PASS ON MESSAGES

The brain and nervous system are made of microscopic nerve cells called neurons. Each nerve cell has two parts: a spiderlike cell body and a long nerve fiber. The cell body receives signals from other nerve cells and passes these along its fiber, like a tiny telephone wire, to yet more nerve cells, until the message reaches its final destination.

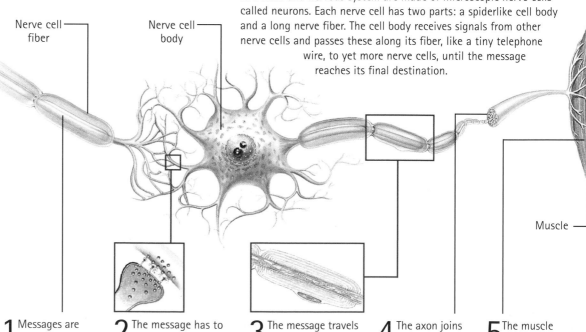

Nerve cell fiber

Nerve cell body

Muscle

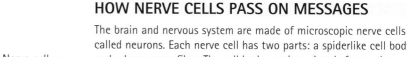

1 Messages are sent along a nerve fiber (axon) to another nerve cell.

2 The message has to jump the small gap (synapse) between the two nerve cells.

3 The message travels fast along the axon because it is insulated with a sheath of myelin.

4 The axon joins with other nerve fibers in a bundle, creating a pathway.

5 The muscle receives the message from the brain to move.

THE BRAIN AND SKULL

The brain is protected by a bony skull, three thin layers of membrane, called meninges, and a pool of fluid. The two sides of the cerebrum (the cerebral hemispheres) are joined by the corpus callosum. The left side of the brain usually controls logic, and the right side is more active in creative pursuits.

The hypothalamus is the site of emotion and instinct

The pituitary gland controls the hormones

Bony skull

Fluid

Meninges

Cerebrum

Corpus callosum

Cerebellum

Planning

Spatial awareness

Skilled movement

Touch

Thought and consciousness

Speech

Hearing

Sight

Memory

Brain stem

Cerebellum

Spinal cord

center, which sends nerve signals to the muscles. There are also areas for hearing, taste, speech, and other body processes. Consciousness and thought are believed to originate at the front of the cerebrum.

CROSSING THE DIVIDE

Nerve signals arriving or leaving one side of the brain cross over to affect the opposite side of the body, so signals from the body's right side go to the brain's left hemisphere and vice versa. The two sides are joined by a strip of nerve fibers, the corpus callosum.

INSTINCTS AND EMOTIONS

Basic instincts, such as hunger, thirst, and sleep, as well as strong emotions, such

as fear, anger, and joy, come from the hypothalamus, which lies at the top of the brain stem. Dangling beneath it is the pituitary, a pea-size gland that controls the body's hormones (chemical messages).

THOUGHTS AND MEMORIES

The human brain contains 100 billion nerve cells and is far more complex than the most advanced supercomputer. One thought or memory involves millions of nerve signals, flashing around billions of brain cells, along trillions of pathways. An electroencephalogram (EEG) records these electrical nerve signals.

A NETWORK OF NERVES

The brain is linked to a branching network of nerves by the spinal cord. Sensory nerves bring information from the senses to the brain. Motor nerves carry signals from the brain to the muscles. The brain and spinal column make up the central nervous system. The nerves in the rest of the body make up the peripheral nervous system.

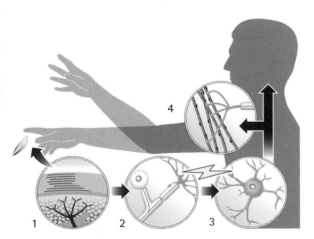

▲ A reflex is an automatic response. The flame's heat stimulates pain sensors in the finger (1) that send a signal to the spinal cord (2). The signal passes to a motor nerve (3), which makes muscles contract (4), pulling away the hand. Signals also pass to the brain, which registers pain.

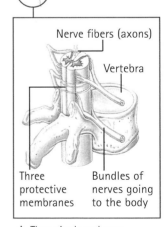

Nerve fibers (axons)

Vertebra

Three protective membranes

Bundles of nerves going to the body

▲ The spinal cord runs through a tunnel formed by vertebrae in the spine. Its nerves are surrounded by protective membranes.

SEE ALSO

Cell, Gland, Hearing, Human body, Sight, Taste and smell, Touch

BRAZIL

Brazil is the largest country in South America, covering almost half the continent. It is also South America's richest and most heavily populated country.

Area: 3,287,960 sq. mi. (8,515,770km²)
Population: 208,846,000
Capital: Brasília
Language: Portuguese
Currency: Real

Two thirds of Brazil is covered by the Amazon River basin, which contains the world's largest rain forest. Some 4,000 mi. (6,437km) long, the Amazon flows across the northwest of the country and carries about a fifth of the world's river water.

ON THE EQUATOR
Brazil is warm all year round, with temperatures rarely dropping below 68°F (20°C), because the equator lies across the north of the country. Rainfall is highest inland, with more than 11 in. (280mm) of rain falling in January, the wettest month.

LIFE IN THE RAIN FOREST
The Amazon rain forest is a dense and steamy region, with at least 40,000 kinds of plants and thousands of different insects, exotic birds, and wild animals, including macaws, monkeys, jaguars, sloths, armadillos, piranha fish, and anacondas. But the wildlife and the way of life of the small groups of Indians who inhabit the rain forest are under threat because of the number of trees being cut down. Efforts to protect the rain forest—an area of global environmental importance—are now being made. Farming, logging, and mining all threaten the region.

◀ Many families living in the heart of the Amazon rain forest still build their houses out of bamboo.

▲ São Paulo, Brazil's largest city, is ringed by shanty towns called *favelas*. Poverty is a serious problem for Brazil's rapidly growing population.

FARMING THE LAND
Most of Brazil's wealth comes from crops grown in mountainous areas. Coffee is the country's largest export—Brazil produces about a third of the world's supply. Other exports include orange juice, soybeans, rice, sugarcane, and cotton. Valuable timber, such as mahogany, as well as nuts, rubber, and medicines are harvested in the forests.

INDUSTRY AND MINING
Factories around the major cities make cars, aircraft, cement, and chemicals. Brazil's vast mineral wealth includes iron, lead, copper, magnesium, uranium, gold, and diamonds. Most of Brazil's power is hydroelectric, from projects such as the Itaipu Dam on the Paraná River at the Paraguay border.

▶ Sugarloaf Mountain overlooks the beautiful natural harbor of Rio de Janeiro, once the capital of Brazil. The mountain gets its name from the days when sugar was sold in pyramidlike, solid blocks.

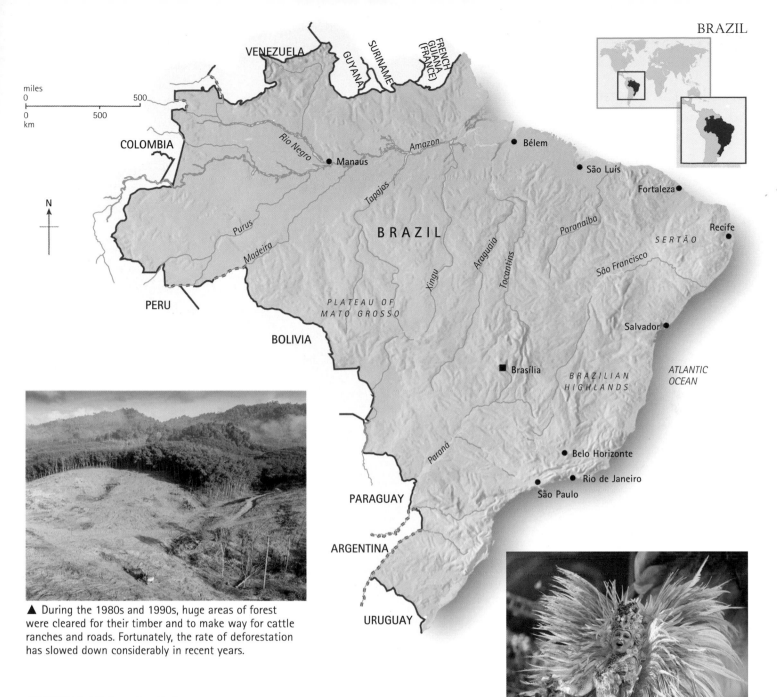

miles
0   500
km
0   500

VENEZUELA
GUYANA
SURINAME
FRENCH GUIANA (FRANCE)

COLOMBIA

Rio Negro
Amazon
● Manaus
● Bélem
● São Luís
Fortaleza ●

N

Tapajos

BRAZIL

Purus

Madeira

Paranaíba

SERTÃO

Recife ●

Xingu

Araguaia

Tocantins

São Francisco

PERU

PLATEAU OF
MATO GROSSO

Salvador ●

BOLIVIA

■ Brasília

BRAZILIAN
HIGHLANDS

ATLANTIC
OCEAN

Paraná

● Belo Horizonte
● Rio de Janeiro
● São Paulo

PARAGUAY

ARGENTINA

URUGUAY

▲ During the 1980s and 1990s, huge areas of forest were cleared for their timber and to make way for cattle ranches and roads. Fortunately, the rate of deforestation has slowed down considerably in recent years.

WHERE PEOPLE LIVE
As many as 87 percent of Brazilians live in cities on the Atlantic coast and in the south. The best farming and mining areas, as well as the two biggest cities—Rio de Janeiro and São Paulo—are found there.

CULTURAL MIX
About 75 percent of Brazilians are of European origin, many with Portuguese ancestry. The rest are of mixed Indian, European, and African descent. Ancient settlers reached Brazil thousands of years ago; the Portuguese arrived in the 1500s, bringing African slaves with them. Brazil declared its independence from Portugal in 1822.

BRAZIL TODAY
Brazil is now a country of 27 states, each with its own local government. The country's capital, Brasília, was built in the 1950s on the Central Plains to encourage development in inland areas of the country. Since the 1950s, Brazil's economic status in the world has grown, but at the expense of many of its natural resources. Almost one quarter of Brazilians are under 15 years of age. The population is set to reach 238 million by 2050. It is important that the country continues its economic growth if its population is to be housed, educated, and employed.

▲ The Brazilian carnival lasts for five days just before Lent. It is especially spectacular in Rio de Janeiro.

SEE ALSO
Conservation, Rain forest, South America, Sports

BRIDGE

Bridges are structures that are built to allow people, animals, or vehicles to cross rivers, canals, canyons, railroads, or roads.

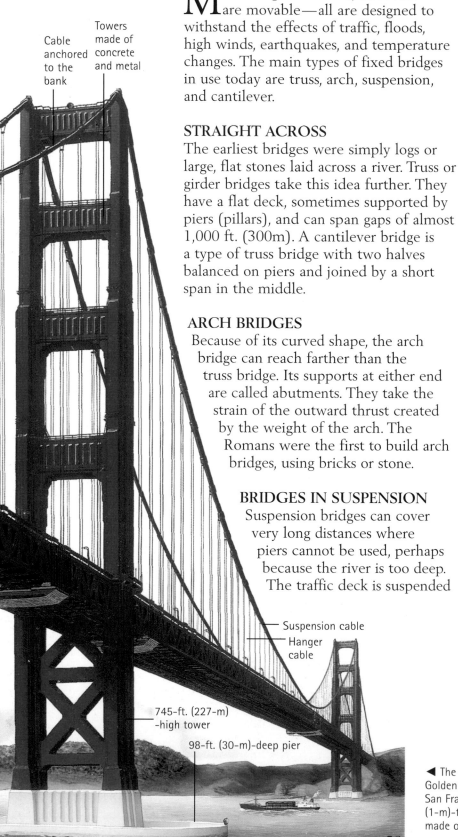

Cable anchored to the bank

Towers made of concrete and metal

Most bridges are fixed, but some are movable—all are designed to withstand the effects of traffic, floods, high winds, earthquakes, and temperature changes. The main types of fixed bridges in use today are truss, arch, suspension, and cantilever.

STRAIGHT ACROSS
The earliest bridges were simply logs or large, flat stones laid across a river. Truss or girder bridges take this idea further. They have a flat deck, sometimes supported by piers (pillars), and can span gaps of almost 1,000 ft. (300m). A cantilever bridge is a type of truss bridge with two halves balanced on piers and joined by a short span in the middle.

ARCH BRIDGES
Because of its curved shape, the arch bridge can reach farther than the truss bridge. Its supports at either end are called abutments. They take the strain of the outward thrust created by the weight of the arch. The Romans were the first to build arch bridges, using bricks or stone.

BRIDGES IN SUSPENSION
Suspension bridges can cover very long distances where piers cannot be used, perhaps because the river is too deep. The traffic deck is suspended

Suspension cable
Hanger cable

745-ft. (227-m)-high tower

98-ft. (30-m)-deep pier

HOW BRIDGES WORK
Bridges are designed to withstand huge forces (shown by the arrows in the diagrams below). They must be strong enough to carry their own weight, as well as that of the people and vehicles that use them. Bridges must also withstand the strong vibrations set up by high winds.

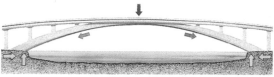

In an arch bridge, the downward pressure (load) is pushed out toward the foundations on each bank.

In a cantilever bridge, the load on the central span is balanced equally over each supporting pier.

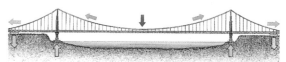

In a suspension bridge, curving cables transfer the bulk of the load to anchored points on each bank.

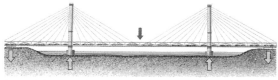

In a cable-stayed bridge, the load is balanced equally over one or more central supports.

→ Load   → Support   → Tension   → Compression

from towers by steel cables. A modern version of this is the cable-stayed bridge, which does not need the heavy anchorages required to stabilize a suspension bridge.

MOVABLE BRIDGES
Some bridges are built to move so large ships can pass through them. Drawbridges lift up by splitting in the middle or at one end, swing bridges turn sideways, and lift bridges have a central section that can be raised. Deck sections can also be floated on pontoons to create temporary bridges.

◄ The 4,200-ft. (1,280-m)-long Golden Gate suspension bridge in San Francisco hangs from two 3-ft. (1-m)-thick suspension cables, each made of 27,450 wires.

SEE ALSO
Architecture, Construction, Industrial Revolution, Iron and steel

BUDDHISM

Buddhism is a religion that was first practiced in Asia about 2,500 years ago. Today, it is estimated that there are around 350 million Buddhists across the globe.

▲ A young Thai Buddhist, in traditional orange robes, studies his blackboard in a temple. Buddhists believe that meditation plays a vital role in the path to enlightenment.

▲ The Wheel of Life symbolizes the process of change and rebirth. When we reach Nirvana, the process stops and we come off the wheel.

Buddhism was founded in northeast India by a prince called Siddhartha Gautama. Born around 563 B.C., he left his home at the age of 29 to lead a life of meditation and preaching. He became a great religious teacher before his death in about 483 B.C.

THE ENLIGHTENED ONE
While sitting under a fig tree, Gautama entered a peaceful state of mind called enlightenment—Nirvana ("absence of sorrow"). He taught others how to reach this state, and gained the title Buddha— "Enlightened One." The Buddhist religion spread from India to China, Japan, and other parts of Asia.

REBIRTH
Buddhists believe in reincarnation—being reborn until Nirvana is reached. The form of each new life, or reincarnation, depends on how the being behaved during previous lives. A human might have been an animal in the last life; a male might have been a female. This is known as their karma.

FOUR NOBLE TRUTHS
Buddha's teachings are based on the Four Noble Truths. These state that all suffering is caused by attachment to the material world. Buddhists believe that they will be free of these attachments, and therefore of suffering, if they follow the Eightfold Path. This consists of eight steps involving wisdom, understanding, morality, and meditation.

TYPES OF BUDDHISM
There are two main types of Buddhism: Theravada is common in Southeast Asia and teaches that Buddha was an ordinary human being who achieved enlightenment; Mahayana is popular in northern Asia and claims that Buddha was the divine spirit in human form. A branch of Mahayana, called Zen Buddhism, was established in Japan in the 1100s.

▲ A Buddhist monastery in Tibet. Buddhism was introduced into Tibet in A.D. 749. Tibetan monks are called lamas. The chief lamas are the Dalai Lama and the Panchen Lama.

◀ Many images of Buddha show him sitting serenely, legs crossed in the lotus position. The image reminds followers of Buddha's goodness and helps them to meditate and pray.

EIGHTFOLD PATH TO ENLIGHTENMENT
- Right views
- Right thought and intention
- Right speech, plain and truthful
- Right action, including never taking a life
- Right occupation, harming no one
- Right effort, always persevering
- Right awareness of the past, present, and future
- Right contemplation or meditation

SEE ALSO
Asia, Japan, Religion

BUTTERFLY AND MOTH

Butterflies and moths are flying insects with two pairs of wings, which are often brightly colored. They hatch as caterpillars and change into butterflies or moths as adults.

The turquoise blue has been hunted almost to extinction by collectors for its beautiful wings.

A peacock butterfly's eye spots may help it scare off small birds when it suddenly opens its wings.

The white admiral is a woodland butterfly. Its caterpillar is covered with protective spines.

Swallowtails are large and colorful butterflies, found in North Africa, Europe, and across Asia.

The large white is a very common butterfly. Its caterpillars feed in groups, often on cabbage plants.

There are more than 170,000 species of butterflies and moths in the world. They form the group of insects known as Lepidoptera, which means "scale-wing." Their wings are covered with thousands of tiny scales that give the wings their colorful appearance.

COLORFUL BUTTERFLIES
Most butterflies fly by day and have brightly colored wings that close together over their backs when they are resting. They have a slim body and thin antennae (feelers) with clubbed tips, which are used to detect smells. The monarch, cabbage white, tortoiseshell, and peacock are all types of butterfly.

DULL MOTHS
Most moths are dull in color, fly at night, and have feathery or hairy antennae and a stout and hairy body. At rest, a moth holds its wings open. A moth's forewing is often linked to its hindwing on each side by tiny hairs that act like hooks. The hawk moth, ermine, eggar, and tussock are all

◀ The back part of the hawkmoth caterpillar looks like a viper in order to deceive any predators into leaving it alone.

▲ Tropical birdwing butterflies, such as the Rajah Brooke, can have a wingspan of 11 in. (28cm).

types of moth. The scarlet tiger and burnet are examples of moths that are brightly colored and fly by day.

SENSING THE WORLD
An adult butterfly or moth sees well with its large eyes. Its sensitive antennae pick up the scents of flowers and fruit and can detect the smell of a mate. Most species of butterfly or moth feed on flower nectar, which is sucked up by a long, strawlike mouth called a proboscis.

EGG TO CATERPILLAR
After mating, female butterflies and moths lay their eggs on or near the plant that their caterpillars like to eat. The brimstone butterfly likes buckthorn, while the green oak tortrix moth chooses oak leaves. Some species will feed only on one type of plant.

LIVING TO EAT
Butterfly and moth eggs hatch into soft-skinned, wingless larvae called caterpillars. Their job is to eat—a large group of caterpillars can destroy crops within a few weeks. A caterpillar sheds its skin (molts) four or five times as it feeds and grows. Despite having a variety of devices to protect themselves from predators, such as sharp spines that secrete a stinging fluid, few caterpillars manage to escape their attackers and reach adulthood. Others are brightly colored as a warning.

◀ This peppered moth is a pale, speckled gray in color to camouflage it against lichen on tree bark.

LIFE SPAN

Most butterflies and nearly all moths live for just one breeding season or year. A few, such as peacock and monarch butterflies, survive the winter as adults. Their main predators are birds by day and bats at night. The breeding season is usually in the spring or summer, although tropical species can breed at any time of the year.

ALL CHANGE

When they are ready to become adults, caterpillars enter a pupal stage (chrysalis). Many moth caterpillars spin cocoons of silk. Butterfly caterpillars grow a hard skin. Inside these cases, they gradually change. After a few weeks, or the following spring, the chrysalis splits and the adult winged insect (imago) emerges.

Like all hawkmoths, the privet hawkmoth is a fast flyer. Its caterpillars have a curved horn at the end.

CATERPILLAR TO BUTTERFLY

The monarch butterfly lays its eggs on a milkweed plant. A week later, a single caterpillar emerges from each egg. First it eats its egg case, then it feeds on the plant. Once fully grown, the caterpillar becomes a chrysalis (pupa). Inside, it metamorphoses (changes form) before emerging as a butterfly. The whole cycle from egg to adult takes about five weeks.

1 The female monarch lays a cluster of eggs on the leaves of a milk-weed plant.

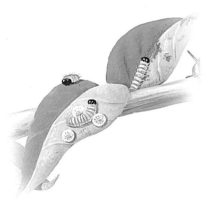

2 Each tiny caterpillar (larva) hatches and starts to eat. It grows very quickly.

3 When fully grown, the caterpillar spins a silken thread and firmly attaches itself to a twig.

4 The caterpillar sheds its striped skin, revealing a chrysalis (pupa). It now looks still and lifeless.

5 Inside the chrysalis a new body slowly begins to form. Finally, the skin splits and an adult butterfly emerges.

6 The butterfly clings to the twig of the milkweed plant, letting its new wings hang down to help force blood into them.

7 When the wings have dried and hardened, metamorphosis is complete and the adult monarch butterfly can fly away.

SEE ALSO

Animal, Flower, Insect

CANADA

Canada is the second-largest country in the world. It lies at the north of the continent of North America, and a large percentage of its area lies within the Arctic Circle.

▲ Moose are just one of the animals living in Canada's forests, which are also home to bears, beavers, bobcats, caribou, foxes, wolves, mountain lions, and goats.

Area: 3,855,100 sq. mi. (9,984,670km²)
Population: 35,624,000
Capital: Ottawa
Languages: English, French
Currency: Canadian dollar

▲ Forestry is one of Canada's most important industries. Trees are cut down to make paper as well as to build homes.

The Rocky Mountains run down the west of Canada, and four of the five Great Lakes lie on its border with the United States. These, together with other Canadian lakes, contain more than 17 percent of the world's freshwater.

CANADIAN FORESTS
Forests cover 53 percent of the country. British Columbia is the leading province in timber production, with 250-ft. (75-m)-high trees, such as Douglas fir, growing in its moist, coniferous forests. Maple syrup is collected from maple trees in Ontario and Quebec, and in the southwest there are orchards and vineyards.

THE GREAT PLAINS
Canada has vast grassland areas, or prairies, stretching across its center. Only about seven percent of these Great Plains is used for growing crops, but this land produces enough to make Canada the world's second-largest exporter of wheat. Cattle ranches on the drier grasslands supply beef and dairy produce.

INDUSTRY AND MINING
Manufacturing industries lie mostly in Ontario and Quebec.

Products include cars, trucks, aircraft, machinery, steel, paper, and chemicals, as well as processed food and minerals. Among Canada's resources are gold, iron ore, copper, petroleum, and natural gas. Fishing is important, but overfishing has greatly reduced stocks.

SPORTS AND LEISURE
Most Canadians share a love of the outdoors, enjoying baseball, football, soccer, skiing, and ice skating. Competitive ice hockey is usually played indoors. Rodeo enthusiasts flock to the annual Calgary Stampede. There are 36 national parks.

CANADIAN PEOPLE
The ancestors of Canada's Native Americans arrived from Asia at least 13,500

▶ The 1,814-ft. (553-m)-high Canadian National (CN) Tower dominates Toronto's skyline. The city is Canada's financial, manufacturing, and communication center.

◀ In the wintertime, temperatures can fall as low as –22°F (–30°C). Lakes and rivers freeze over, and people play games on the ice.

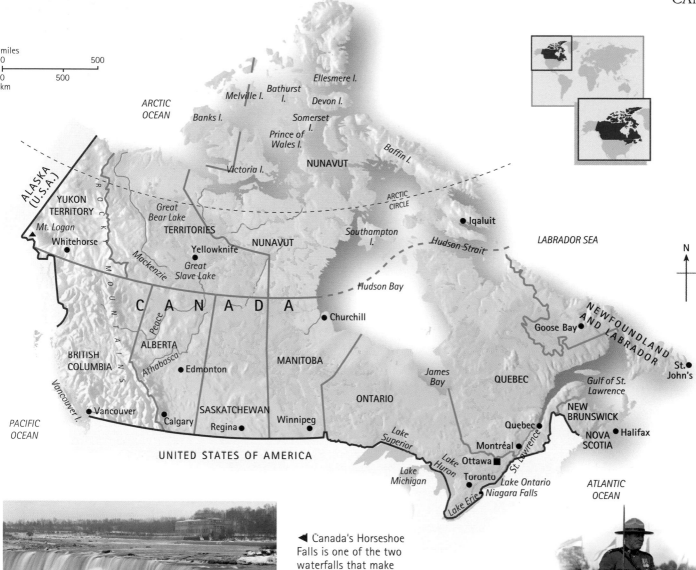

miles
0   500
0   500
km

◀ Canada's Horseshoe Falls is one of the two waterfalls that make up Niagara Falls.

years ago—possibly much longer. Those of the Inuit arrived much later and are not related to the earlier settlers. Europeans arrived during the 1500s. From 1754 to 1763, in the French and Indian War, Britain fought France for control of its Canadian territory (New France) and won. Since 1867, the country has been self-governing. Newfoundland became part of Canada in 1947.

THE GOVERNMENT

Canada is divided into ten provinces and two territories. The provinces make their own laws, but the territories are mainly under government control. National laws are made by an elected parliament that is located in Ottawa. There is also an unelected body of senators; they act as consultants and advise parliament.

TRANSPORTATION

Canada has a good system of roads, including the Trans-Canada Highway, which is more than 4,350 mi. (7,000km) long. The St. Lawrence Seaway, a waterway linking stretches of rivers and canals, allows ships to carry cargoes inland from the Atlantic Ocean as far as the Great Lakes.

▲ The Royal Canadian Mounted Police, nicknamed the Mounties, are Canada's national police force.

SEE ALSO

Arctic, Grassland, Native American, North America

61

CAR

Cars are motorized vehicles with an engine, wheels, and steering mechanism. They are designed to carry passengers or to race in competitions.

There will be an estimated 2 billion cars on the world's roads by 2050. Cars have had a huge impact on society and are one of the world's most important inventions.

THE FIRST CARS

The first successful gasoline (gas)-powered vehicles were developed by the German engineers Karl Benz and Gottfried Daimler in the 1880s. Benz designed a complete vehicle. Daimler simply added his engine to a horseless carriage.

HOW A CAR MOVES

Most cars today are powered by gas or diesel engines, or by electric motors. The engine turns a driveshaft, which is linked to the wheels by gears.

STREAMLINING

A car's shape is now designed using computers. It must look good, be safe and comfortable, and work well. The sleeker or more streamlined the car, the faster and more economical it will be to drive. Objects that stick out, such as windshield wipers, can be hidden under panels to reduce wind resistance and wind noise. In some modern designs, front and rear panels on the car can be adjusted electronically to change the airflow around the car's body.

Cugnot's steam gun carriage of 1769 was the first motorized vehicle.

Daimler's first car, built in 1886, was a coach fitted with an engine.

The Rolls Royce Silver Ghost of 1906 used automatic engine controls.

The 1914 Model T Ford was the first car made on a moving assembly line.

Volkswagen produced more than 20 million Beetles between 1938 and 2003.

The 1984 Ferrari Testarossa can reach a speed of 180 mph (290kph).

The GM Sunraycer of 1987 used solar energy from sunlight to power it.

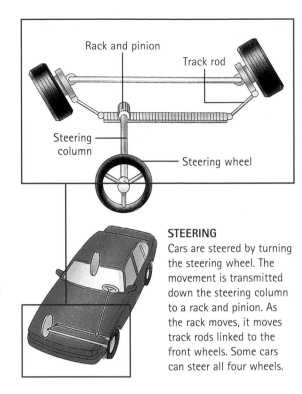

Rack and pinion
Track rod
Steering column
Steering wheel

STEERING
Cars are steered by turning the steering wheel. The movement is transmitted down the steering column to a rack and pinion. As the rack moves, it moves track rods linked to the front wheels. Some cars can steer all four wheels.

▼ Racing cars are designed to have minimum air resistance. They have a sleek shape and pointed nose.

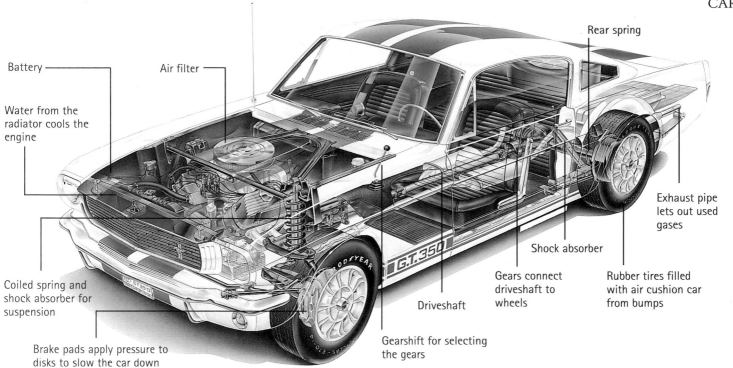

Battery

Air filter

Water from the radiator cools the engine

Rear spring

Coiled spring and shock absorber for suspension

Brake pads apply pressure to disks to slow the car down

Gearshift for selecting the gears

Driveshaft

Gears connect driveshaft to wheels

Shock absorber

Exhaust pipe lets out used gases

Rubber tires filled with air cushion car from bumps

CONTROL SYSTEMS

Gearboxes have up to five forward gears to vary the speed and power of the car and one gear for reversing. Gears are selected by a shift lever, although many gearboxes are automatic. An electrical system controls the engine, lights, and other instruments. The electric circuits are powered by a battery, which is charged from the engine. Computerized engine management systems in modern cars mean that problems can be diagnosed more easily.

ROAD SAFETY

Road safety is very important in the design of modern cars. Experiments using life-size dummies are carried out by safety experts to establish how a car collapses on impact and how this affects the passengers inside. These experiments have led manufacturers to introduce improvements in the design of the steering wheel, seats, and seat belts and to the invention and use of new safety devices such as inflatable air bags.

IMPROVING COMFORT

Passenger comfort is improved by smooth braking and suspension. Brakes are linked to all four wheels to slow down the car. Modern cars use antilocking brakes to prevent skidding when roads are wet or slippery. The suspension system cushions the car from bumps in the road and usually consists of a coiled spring and shock absorber (to reduce the spring's vibrations) attached to each of the four wheels.

▲ Crash test dummies are used to test cars for road safety. Here, an air bag is shown exploding after a crash. The dummy mimics how a person would be affected in the accident.

THE ENVIRONMENT

Cars have completely changed the way we live, but this has come at a cost to the environment, with vehicle emissions affecting air pollution and contributing to climate change. Some countries plan to switch to all-electric cars by 2040, and there will be rapid improvements in battery storage and recharging. An even bigger revolution is also on the way, as driverless cars are already being tested on the roads.

KEY DATES

1885 First petrol-driven motor car: Karl Benz

1887 First four-wheeled motor car: Gottfried Daimler

1891 First modern car layout: René Panhard and Emile Levasor

1895 World's first motor race: France

1908 First cheap mass produced car: Henry Ford's Model T

1940 General Motors brings in automatic transmission

1997 Toyota Prius, mass-produced hybrid (petrol-electric) car

2019 All Volvo cars fitted with electric motors

SEE ALSO

Invention, Transportation, Truck and bus

CARIBBEAN

The Caribbean islands lie between North and South America, forming a chain about 2,000 mi. (3,200km) long. They include Cuba, Jamaica, and Haiti.

ANTIGUA & BARBUDA
Area: 171 sq. mi. (442km²)
Population: 94,000
Capital: St. John's
Language: English
Currency: East Caribbean dollar

BAHAMAS
Area: 5,359 sq. mi. (13,880km²)
Population: 330,000
Capital: Nassau
Language: English
Currency: Bahamian dollar

BARBADOS
Area: 166 sq. mi. (430km²)
Population: 292,000
Capital: Bridgetown
Language: English
Currency: East Caribbean dollar

CUBA
Area: 42,804 sq. mi. (110,861km²)
Population: 11,147,000
Capital: Havana
Language: Spanish
Currency: Peso

DOMINICA
Area: 290 sq. mi. (751km²)
Population: 74,000
Capital: Roseau
Language: English
Currency: East Caribbean dollar

The region known as the Caribbean includes three island groups: the Greater Antilles and the Lesser Antilles, which lie in the Caribbean Sea, and the Bahamas, in the Atlantic Ocean. These islands are also known as the West Indies because, when the explorer Christopher Columbus first saw them in 1492, he believed he was near India.

TROPICAL ISLANDS
The Caribbean's tropical climate and steady ocean winds mean that temperatures rarely drop below 77°F (25°C), although the hot days are often relieved by cooling sea breezes. Violent hurricanes sometimes strike the islands, causing great damage to property and crops.

FOREST ANIMALS
Vegetation on the islands includes palm trees and exotic flowers such as orchids. Some islands also have very dense rain forests—home to parrots and macaws, as well as bats, snakes, and insects. In many places, these forests have been cleared to make way for crop plantations.

▲ Bananas are one of the chief crops. They are picked while still green and exported in refrigerated cargo ships.

HOMEGROWN PRODUCE
Sugarcane is the main crop grown on the islands. Stalks are crushed for raw juice or refined to make crystallized sugar. Bananas and other fruit are important crops, as are coffee, cocoa, and cotton.

ISLAND INDUSTRY
As well as farming, there is some mining. Jamaica has bauxite (aluminum ore), Trinidad has offshore oil and gas, and there is some manufacturing. Tourism is by far the largest employer—on some islands, more than one fifth of the working population is employed, directly or indirectly, by the tourism industry.

THE ORIGINAL ISLANDERS
The first settlers in the Caribbean were the Caribs and Arawaks from South America. Most were killed by Europeans who arrived

▼ Large markets, where people sell homegrown goods, are a familiar aspect of island life.

DOMINICAN REPUBLIC
Area: 18,792 sq. mi.
(48,670km2)
Population: 10,734,000
Capital: Santo Domingo
Language: Spanish
Currency: Peso

GRENADA
Area: 133 sq. mi. (344km2)
Population: 112,000
Capital: St. George's
Language: English
Currency: East
Caribbean dollar

HAITI
Area: 10,714 sq. mi.
(27,750km2)
Population: 10,647,000
Capital: Port-au-Prince
Language: French, Creole
Currency: Gourde

JAMAICA
Area: 4,244 sq. mi.
(10,991km2)
Population: 2,991,000
Capital: Kingston
Language: English
Currency: Jamaican dollar

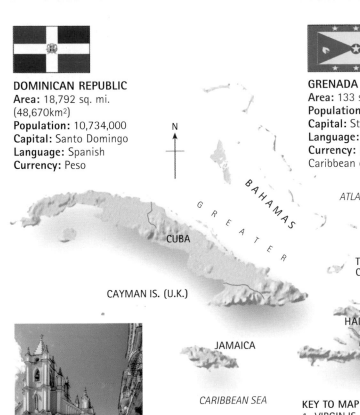

ATLANTIC OCEAN

BAHAMAS

GREATER

CUBA

CAYMAN IS. (U.K.)

JAMAICA

CARIBBEAN SEA

TURKS AND
CAICOS IS. (U.K.)

ANTILLES

HAITI DOMINICAN
REPUBLIC
HISPANIOLA

PUERTO
RICO (U.S.)

ST. KITTS & NEVIS

MONTSERRAT (U.K.)

GUADELOUPE (FRANCE)

DOMINICA

MARTINIQUE (FRANCE)

ST. LUCIA
BARBADOS

ST. VINCENT &
THE GRENADINES

GRENADA

TRINIDAD
& TOBAGO

ANTIGUA &
BARBUDA

LESSER

ANTILLES

1 2 3 4

◄ This square in Cuba
has architecture typical
of that built by the
European colonials.

KEY TO MAP
1 VIRGIN IS. (U.S.)
2 VIRGIN IS. (U.K.)
3 ANGUILLA (U.K.)
4 ST MARTIN (FRANCE/NETHERLANDS)
*Countries in parentheses are countries of which that island or group
is a dependency. Aruba and Curaçao (both Netherlands) is not shown.*

miles
0   100
0   100
km

soon after Columbus sighted the islands.
The Europeans brought slaves from Africa
to work on sugar and cotton plantations.
After the abolition of slavery in the 1800s,
people from India and China came to work
in the Caribbean.

A CULTURAL MIX
The people of the Caribbean reflect its mix
of cultures. They speak Spanish, French, or
English, often with a local dialect. Religion
is an important part of life. As well as
Christians, Hindus, and Muslims, there are
Rastafarians, who worship Haile Selassie
(emperor of Ethiopia until 1974) as a god.
On Haiti, many people practice voodoo,
a blend of African and Christian beliefs.

SELF-GOVERNING
Most larger islands are independent. Others
are dependent on the U.S.A., France, U.K.,
or the Netherlands. They include Puerto
Rico (U.S.A.), Guadeloupe and Martinique
(France), and Curaçao (Netherlands). The
governments are working to develop the
islands, many of which are poor. Many
islanders have migrated to the U.K.,
Canada, or the U.S. to find work.

ST. KITTS & NEVIS
Area: 101 sq. mi. (261km2)
Population: 52,000
Capital: Basseterre
Language: English
Currency: East
Caribbean dollar

ST. LUCIA
Area: 238 sq. mi. (617km2)
Population: 165,000
Capital: Castries
Language: English
Currency: East
Caribbean dollar

**ST. VINCENT & THE
GRENADINES**
Area: 150 sq. mi. (389km2)
Population: 102,000
Capital: Kingstown
Language: English
Currency: East
Caribbean dollar

TRINIDAD & TOBAGO
Area: 1,980 sq. mi. (5,128km2)
Population: 1,218,000
Capital: Port of Spain
Language: English
Currency: Trinidad dollar

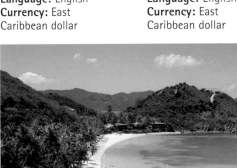

▲ The beautiful sandy beaches and warm waters of the
Caribbean islands lure tourists from all over the world.

SEE ALSO

Empire, Explorer, North
America, Slavery

65

CARTOON AND ANIMATION

A cartoon can be an animated film, a comic strip, or a single picture. The first printed cartoons, in the 1840s, ridiculed prominent people or political events.

The word "cartoon" was originally used by artists to describe the picture they produced as part of the preparation for a painting or tapestry. Today, cartoons are seen on screen and in print.

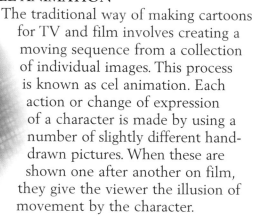

▼ Spiderman, created in 1962, has crossed over from comic book to animated film.

CEL ANIMATION

The traditional way of making cartoons for TV and film involves creating a moving sequence from a collection of individual images. This process is known as cel animation. Each action or change of expression of a character is made by using a number of slightly different hand-drawn pictures. When these are shown one after another on film, they give the viewer the illusion of movement by the character.

A CAST OF THOUSANDS

Between 15,000 and 20,000 images are used for a 20-minute animated film, so a whole studio of artists is often needed for longer films. Painters create a background picture for each scene, and illustrators draw the characters. Then other artists touch up the images. Disney's *Beauty and the Beast* (1991)

had 90 artists whose only job was to touch up the lines. Once the image has been colored in, it is placed on a clear plastic sheet of celluloid, called an acetate, by a paint and trace artist. Then, finally, the animation is shot onto film.

COMPUTER ANIMATION

Many artists still draw by hand and use computers to add color. Computers also speed up the rendering (the planning of the movements and the creation of the frames). Disney's *Toy Story*, made in 1995, was the first full-length film to be made entirely by computer animation.

COMIC STRIPS

Comic strips use a smaller creative team than animated films. A strip tells a story in a series of pictures. Speech balloons are used to put words into the mouths of characters.

COMPUTER EFFECTS

Computer-generated imagery (CGI) is the creation of any image using electronic technology. Computer animation refers to moving images, often in 3D. Three-dimensional structures are modeled onscreen, and changes in appearance can be made to key frames. The computer automatically adjusts or "morphs" these frames into a realistic motion sequence.

▶ *Up* was a 2009 computer-animated film produced by Pixar for Walt Disney Pictures. Computer magic could show the house being lifted by 20,622 balloons! The average amount of time required to render a single frame of film for *Up* was between five and six hours. For every second of film, 24 frames are required.

SEE ALSO
Computer, Design, Film, Newspaper and magazine

CASTLE

Castles are fortified homes that were owned by rich and powerful families during the Middle Ages. Some are still in use, but many are now in ruins.

Early castles, known as motte and baileys, were made of wood and soil.

Massive stone keeps began to be erected around 1070.

In the Middle Ages, castles were used to protect towns, river crossings, and frontiers. They were also used to guard against invasion and prevent rebellion.

MOTTE AND BAILEY
Castles were first built around A.D. 950 by knights or lords. The castles included a hill or mound surrounded by a ditch and topped by a wooden tower called a motte. A bailey, or courtyard, contained living quarters, stables, granaries, and barns. These early castles were protected by a high wooden fence, called a palisade.

STONE CASTLES
From about 1070, larger castles had a stone tower called a keep. The Tower of London, the first keep in England, was begun in 1078. Food and weapons were stored inside the tower, and the knight and his staff lived there. Prisoners were kept in dungeons.

TOWERS AND WALLS
From the 1100s onward, stone curtain walls were built to surround the keeps. Towers were added to the outside of the walls so that attackers could be shot at from different directions. After about 1270, a second outer wall was added to some castles to make them harder to attack. These castles, often built by Crusaders in the Middle East, were called concentric because of their double walls.

UNDER ATTACK
A castle was attacked with catapults, rams, and siege towers. Boulders and flaming missiles were hurled at it, and its walls undermined. If a castle was not captured quickly it was besieged. Most castles fell because of bribery, disease, or famine.

CANNON FIRE
By the 1450s, cannons and gunpowder became powerful enough to destroy walls. Castles were no longer safe from attack. Most fell into ruin, but some continued to be used as palaces or luxurious homes.

Concentric castles had two or more walls and strongly guarded gatehouses.

UNDER SIEGE
Armies attacked castles by smashing walls with catapults or rams and by digging out foundations so that the walls collapsed. The moat was drained and filled in so that siege machines could be wheeled right up to the walls. Attackers were shielded by frames covered with wet hides.

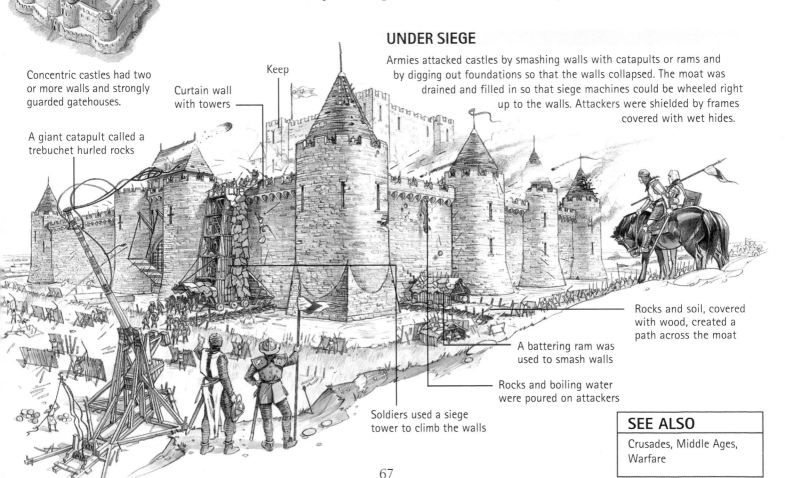

A giant catapult called a trebuchet hurled rocks

Curtain wall with towers

Keep

Rocks and soil, covered with wood, created a path across the moat

A battering ram was used to smash walls

Rocks and boiling water were poured on attackers

Soldiers used a siege tower to climb the walls

SEE ALSO
Crusades, Middle Ages, Warfare

CAT

Cats are agile, hunting mammals with keen senses and sharp teeth and claws. Domestic cats make some of the most popular pets.

The longhaired Persian needs regular grooming to keep its coat sleek.

The hairless sphinx was bred in the 1960s from a kitten born without fur.

The Manx cat from the Isle of Man, in the U.K., is famous for its lack of a tail.

The blue shorthair has copper eyes and a quiet, affectionate nature.

The Cornish rex has a curly coat of short, thin hair and large, open ears.

The Siamese has long been one of the most popular pedigreed (purebred) cats.

Large, sensitive ears pick up sounds too faint for human ears to hear

Pupils open wide to let in a maximum amount of light. A mirrorlike layer at the back of the eye intensifies the light

HUNTER IN THE HOME

Even a domestic cat, like this tabby, has the hunting instincts of its wild relations. Cats often toy with their prey, rather than killing it immediately. They hunt mostly at night, catching mice, small birds, and insects.

Whiskers are modified hairs with nerves at their base and are ultra-sensitive to touch

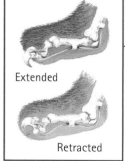
Extended

Retracted

THE CLAWS
Cats retract (pull back) their claws to keep them sharp when not in use. Each claw is attached to a toe bone. It is retracted by ligaments, which are worked by muscles.

The cat family is divided into two main groups, based largely on size. The first group is made up of big cats such as tigers, lions, and leopards. The second includes cougars, bobcats, and lynxes, as well as the many small wild cats and the domestic cat. In all there are 37 species of cat.

PET CATS
It is thought that the domestic cat was originally a small wild cat living in Africa. By 2000 B.C. it had been tamed by the ancient Egyptians, who used it to protect their stored food from mice and rats. Today, there are many breeds of domestic cat, including longhaired Persians and Angoras and the shorthaired Manx and Siamese.

CAT CHARACTERISTICS
Domestic cats resemble their wild relatives in many ways. They are excellent hunters, strong and agile, with a keen sense of hearing and very good eyesight. They have curved claws, strong jaws, sharp teeth, and whiskers that are sensitive to touch. Cats are naturally inquisitive and are expert climbers and jumpers. Their flexible backbones allow them to swivel their bodies into a wide range of positions.

CAT BEHAVIOR
Cats spend at least an hour a day grooming their fur by licking it with their rough tongues. This helps keep their fur in good condition and keeps them cool in hot weather. Cats sleep, on the average, twice as long as other mammals, spending up to three fourths of the day asleep, usually in short intervals—hence "catnaps."

HUNTING TACTICS
Although most domestic cats do not have to catch their own food, their instinct (inborn behavior) is to hunt. A cat's sensitive nose quickly picks up the scent of its prey. With its soft, padded paws, a cat can stalk its prey without being noticed until it is close enough to pounce. Then it grabs the prey with its claws and kills it with a powerful bite—usually at the back of the head, breaking the victim's neck.

SEE ALSO
Animal, Mammal, Sight, Tiger

CAVE

Caves are hollows that are formed in rock and ice by erosion (wearing away), usually by water. The largest, most impressive caves are found in limestone rock.

Some caves consist of just one hole barely large enough for a person to enter; others are intricate mazes of passageways and chambers. The Mammoth Cave network in Kentucky is the world's longest. Its labyrinth of caves stretches for 405 mi. (652km).

ROCK, ICE, AND LAVA

Caves sometimes form in sea cliffs, where waves attack weak spots in the rock. The pressure of the water and the salty spray gradually erode the cliff structures. Long, tunnel-like caves can also develop in glaciers where streams of melted water run beneath the ice. Similar caves can be found in volcanoes, where a crust forms over a liquid stream of molten lava.

LIMESTONE CAVES

The largest and most impressive caves are found in limestone rock, where rainwater (which is slightly acidic) trickles through cracks in the rock. The rock slowly dissolves and the thin cracks get wider and wider. The trickle of rainwater swells into a stream, which carves hollows in the stone to form caves and potholes.

THE INSIDE STORY

Where streams meet, they carve out very large caves, or caverns. The floor of the cavern may be filled by underground lakes, so that it can only be explored by diving. Water dripping from the ceilings of limestone caves is rich in minerals, such as calcium carbonate, from the dissolved rock. As the water drips, these minerals are often deposited in dramatic columns— long, slender stalactites hang down from the ceiling; shorter, stumpier stalagmites grow up from the floor. Where they join together, a pillar is formed.

MAKING CAVES

It takes thousands of years for a limestone cave to form. The process begins when rainwater starts to wear away the stone and seep through cracks. Horizontal caverns are made where the water forms underground lakes. These are left dry when the level of groundwater falls.

1 Rain falls on the ground and seeps through cracks in the rock.

2 The cracks get wider and form a pothole.

3 Passages appear as the water continues to dissolve the rock.

4 The water becomes an underground stream, gradually eroding more rock to form a cave.

5 Stalactites and stalagmites are formed from minerals deposited by the dripping water.

Stalactite

Stalagmite

Underground stream

SEE ALSO

Glacier, Rock, Seashore, Volcano, Water

CELL

Cells are the smallest units capable of all the functions of life. Some living things are single cells; others (such as ourselves) are made up of billions of cells.

Every living thing is made up of tiny chambers, called cells—the basic building blocks of all organisms. Every cell has its job, but works with the others to keep the plant or animal alive. Some things, such as bacteria, are just one cell; this contains all they need to survive.

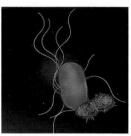

Bacteria have only one cell and can multiply fast.

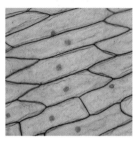

Onions, like most plants, have box-shaped cells.

Sperm cells are used in reproduction.

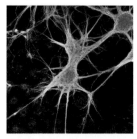

Nerve cells take messages to and from the brain.

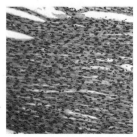

Muscle cells are long and thin and lie in bundles.

THROUGH THE WALLS

Each animal cell is surrounded by a thin membrane. This gives it shape and lets chemicals and waste pass in and out. Inside the membrane, tiny structures float in cytoplasm, a jellylike fluid.

INSIDE THE CHAMBER

Each tiny structure, or organelle, in a cell has a job. The nucleus, for example, contains genes (instructions that decide the cell's shape and function). Sausage-shaped structures called mitochondria release the energy in food. Other organelles store energy, make proteins, keep the cell clear of debris, or defend it against bacteria.

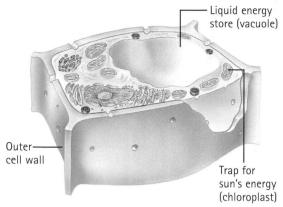

▲ Plant cells have a thick wall of cellulose, which gives them a rigid shape. Up to 90 percent of their space is taken up by the vacuole—a sack full of sugary water.

Liquid energy store (vacuole)
Outer cell wall
Trap for sun's energy (chloroplast)

PLANT CELLS

Unlike animal cells, plant cells have a thick cell wall and extra structures called chloroplasts. These structures are filled with a green pigment called chlorophyll. This traps the sun's energy and uses it to make food in a process called photosynthesis.

SPLITTING IN TWO

Cells multiply by splitting in two. Under a microscope, you can see some bacteria split as fast as once every 15 minutes. Most animal and plant cells multiply much more slowly than this for growth, to repair damage, and for reproduction.

ANIMAL CELLS

Every part of an animal—from its bones to its blood—is made of cells. Many of the cells are spherical, but unevenly shaped, because they do not have a thick outer wall like plant cells. They all have the same basic structures inside them, known as organelles.

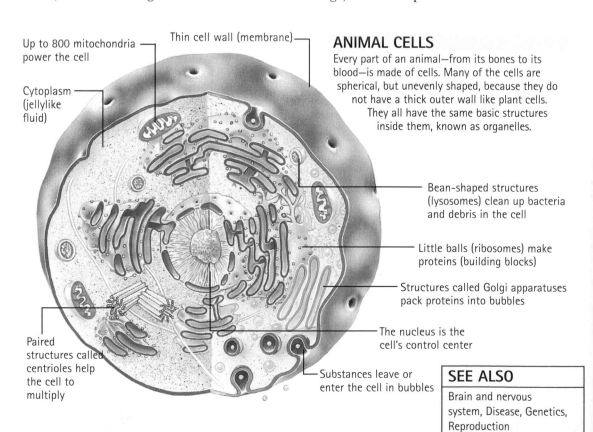

Up to 800 mitochondria power the cell

Thin cell wall (membrane)

Cytoplasm (jellylike fluid)

Bean-shaped structures (lysosomes) clean up bacteria and debris in the cell

Little balls (ribosomes) make proteins (building blocks)

Structures called Golgi apparatuses pack proteins into bubbles

The nucleus is the cell's control center

Paired structures called centrioles help the cell to multiply

Substances leave or enter the cell in bubbles

SEE ALSO

Brain and nervous system, Disease, Genetics, Reproduction

CELT

The Celts are a group of people who lived in Europe from about 2,500 years ago. They were fierce warriors who fought frequently.

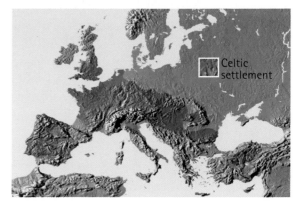

▲ This map shows Europe in about 200 B.C. It is home to many different peoples, but shares a culture that today we call 'Celtic'.

This silver and gold chalice was made in Ireland in the 8th century.

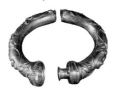

A noble might have worn this gold torc around his neck about 2,100 years ago.

A brooch, from the 500s, used to fasten a woolen cloak around the shoulders.

The first Celts lived in central Europe from about 500 B.C. and came to live in countries such as Germany, France, Britain, and Spain. Most of what we know about Celtic life and culture has been passed down in accounts written by the Romans.

GODS AND DRUIDS
Some tribes shared similar beliefs, worshipping gods and goddesses. Rituals were carried out by Druids, priests who were also law-makers and envoys.

FARMING AND TRADE
Most people lived in small farming villages. Chieftains were famous for feasting and drinking. Hill forts were strongholds in times of war, and perhaps also served as centers of administration or trading. There was rich trade with the Mediterranean region.

STYLE AND BEAUTY
Celts were expert workers in iron, bronze, and gold. A style of decoration, featuring swirling patterns, spread far and wide. It is named La Tène, after an archaeological site in Switzerland. Fine craft work was later a feature of Christian Ireland, in the early Middle Ages.

MODERN CONNECTIONS
Today's Celtic languages include Welsh, Cornish, Breton, Manx, Irish, and Scottish Gaelic. Celtic identity still plays a part in modern politics, especially in Scotland, Ireland, Wales and Brittany.

WARRIOR QUEEN
Many of the ancient myths and legends of the Gaels and Britons were written down in the Middle Ages. 'The Cattle Raid of Cooley' is set in about A.D.100 and tells of Queen Medb (Maeve) of Connacht, in Ireland. Her warriors are defeated by the heroic Cú Chulainn, champion of Ulster.

SEE ALSO
France, Ireland (Republic of), Roman Empire

CENTRAL AMERICA

Central America is a strip of land between North and South America. It consists of Belize, Guatemala, Costa Rica, El Salvador, Honduras, Nicaragua, and Panama.

▲ The Mayan temple of Altun Ha lies deep in the rain forest of Belize. Hundreds of palaces and pyramids were built by the Maya in Central America between A.D. 300 and A.D. 900.

BELIZE
Area: 8,867 sq. mi. (22,966km²)
Population: 360,000
Capital: Belmopan
Languages: English, Spanish
Currency: Belize dollar

COSTA RICA
Area: 19,730 sq. mi. (51,100km²)
Population: 4,930,000
Capital: San José
Language: Spanish
Currency: Costa Rican colón

EL SALVADOR
Area: 8,124 sq. mi. (21,041km²)
Population: 6,172,000
Capital: San Salvador
Language: Spanish
Currency: Colón

GUATEMALA
Area: 42,042 sq. mi. (108,889km²)
Population: 15,461,000
Capital: Guatemala City
Languages: Spanish, Mayan languages
Currency: Quetzal

Poverty, political instability, and civil war have troubled Central America for the last 100 years. All seven countries in this region are rich in natural resources, but wealth is spread unevenly. A growing number of people earn money from tourism. About 25 percent work on the land—far fewer than previously.

LAND AND CLIMATE
Lowland forests, plains, and swamps lie along the Central American coasts, and rivers and mountains crisscross the region. Its many volcanoes include Guatemala's Tajumulco, at 13,786 ft (4,202m), the highest peak in Central America. The region's climate is hot and moist, with temperatures seldom dropping below 75°F (24°C). Land along the coast has the highest temperatures, with cooler areas inland on the mountains and plateaus (flat areas of land high above sea level). More than 12 in. (300mm) of rain per month falls in some areas from July to September.

▼ Most Central Americans are Roman Catholic, but their religious festivals often have a local flavor. For example, All Saints' Day (November 1) is celebrated in Guatemala with riotous horse races.

FORESTS IN DANGER
Central America has some of the richest forests in the world, containing valuable hardwood trees, such as mahogany. But in some places, including Costa Rica, the trees are being cut down so fast for timber, or to make space for farming, that national parks have been set up to protect the remaining trees. Jaguars, monkeys, snakes, caimans (like small alligators), iguanas, many species of bird, as well as colorful butterflies and other insects are all at risk from deforestation.

AGRICULTURAL LIFE
A quarter of people in Central America are farmers. Cattle and sheep are raised in upland areas; export crops, such as bananas, sugarcane, cotton, and about one tenth of the world's coffee supply, are grown on plantations. Chicle (for chewing gum) is collected from sapodilla trees, and cacao beans are farmed for chocolate. Indian corn, beans, and rice are grown for food.

▲ The Panama Canal, opened in 1914, is an important shipping link between Atlantic and Pacific ports.

INDUSTRIAL GROWTH
Low labor costs have attracted industry to Central America, particularly clothing and textile manufacture, with Far Eastern companies setting up factories. Panama has a higher living standard than its neighbors, with insurance, banking, and other service industries.

PEOPLE AND LANGUAGE
Most Central Americans are of mixed European and Indian descent. In the 1500s, Spanish soldiers and gold seekers conquered the region. Before then, it was home to various Indian tribes, including the Maya, who ruled between A.D. 300 and A.D. 900. Many of the first European settlers brought African slaves, whose descendants still live in Belize, Nicaragua, and Panama. Spanish is spoken all over the region, although English is the official language in Belize. Many people also speak local Indian languages.

◀ There are many Indian communities in Guatemala, each with its own distinct style of dress.

INDEPENDENT NATIONS
Honduras, Guatemala, El Salvador, Costa Rica, and Nicaragua gained independence from Spain in the 1800s. Panama separated from Colombia in 1903, and Belize was a British colony until 1981. In the 1990s, the Central American Common Market, which had been set up in the 1960s, was replaced by the Central American Integration System. From the 1990s, Central American governments turned toward democratic rule, although there was a military coup in Honduras in 2009.

HONDURAS
Area: 43,277 sq. mi. (112,088km²)
Population: 9,039,000
Capital: Tegucigalpa
Language: Spanish
Currency: Lempira

NICARAGUA
Area: 50,540 sq. mi. (130,380km²)
Population: 6,026,000
Capital: Managua
Languages: Spanish
Currency: Córdoba

PANAMA
Area: 29,120 sq. mi. (75,420km²)
Population: 3,753,000
Capital: Panama City
Languages: Spanish, English
Currency: Balboa

◀ Many Guatemalan village women weave traditional textiles to sell to tourists.

SEE ALSO
Aztec, Civil war, Conservation, Maya

CHEMISTRY

Chemistry is the study of chemicals. These are substances that are used in, or created by, a reaction involving changes to atoms or molecules.

ANTOINE LAVOISIER
(1743–94). Lavoisier was a French chemist. He explained how chemical reactions worked. He was the first to understand the role of oxygen in combustion (burning).

Oxygen is an element. The two atoms that make up its molecules are of the same kind. The chemical formula for oxygen is O_2.

Carbon dioxide gas is a compound of two oxygen atoms with one carbon atom. Its chemical formula is written CO_2.

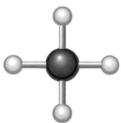

A molecule of methane gas has a carbon atom in the middle bonded to four hydrogen atoms. Its formula is written CH_4.

Water has one oxygen atom and two hydrogen atoms, giving it probably the best-known chemical formula, H_2O.

CHEMICAL ANALYSIS

Chemists use flame tests as a way of identifying chemical elements—by seeing which color they give off when held in the flame of a Bunsen burner. A compound of an element is burned on the end of a piece of platinum wire or asbestos. The flame burns a distinctive color and so the element can be identified. This type of chemical analysis is called qualitative, and shows what elements a substance contains. To show how much of an element is present, chemists use quantitative analysis.

Flame colors of elements

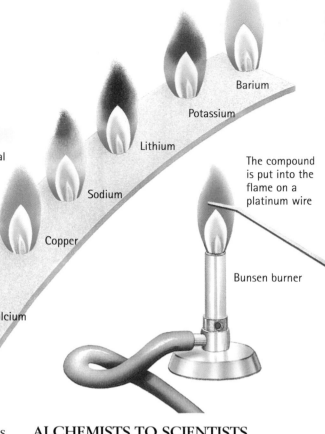

Barium

Potassium

Lithium

Sodium

Copper

Calcium

The compound is put into the flame on a platinum wire

Bunsen burner

Chemistry explains the way substances behave and how they combine with each other. Chemists use chemical reactions to create many substances used in everyday life, including plastics, dyes, glues, detergents, and medicines.

ELEMENTS AND COMPOUNDS

An element is a substance in which all the atoms are of the same kind. A compound is a combination of two or more elements. The compound sodium chloride (common salt), for example, is a combination of the elements sodium and chlorine. Many compounds, including salt and water, occur naturally. Others, such as nylon and plastic, were first made artificially in laboratories.

CHEMICAL REACTIONS

When different substances combine to form new materials, a chemical reaction has taken place. A substance's atoms are bonded together into molecules. During a reaction, the bonds between atoms break, allowing new molecules to form. A rusting car is an example of a chemical reaction, as iron in the car and oxygen in the air form iron oxide, or rust. Chemists use symbols (such as Fe for iron and O for oxygen) to record what happens in a reaction.

ALCHEMISTS TO SCIENTISTS

Medieval alchemists studied reactions, but it was not until the 1770s that Antoine Lavoisier showed how reactions work. In 1869, Russian chemist Dmitri Mendeleyev worked out the periodic table, grouping elements by how they react with each other.

WEAPONS AND DRUGS

Today, chemical substances of all kinds are mined or manufactured. Chemists search for new reactions to create fertilizers or drugs, which may contain long chains of molecules. Industry mass-produces useful chemicals through large-scale reactions. Poison gas and other chemicals have been used as weapons, but they are now banned.

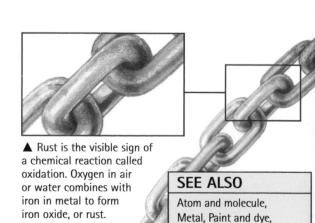

▲ Rust is the visible sign of a chemical reaction called oxidation. Oxygen in air or water combines with iron in metal to form iron oxide, or rust.

SEE ALSO

Atom and molecule, Metal, Paint and dye, Plastic, Warfare

CHINA

China is the third-largest country in the world and the nation with the largest population. Almost one fifth of Earth's people live in China.

Area: 3,705,407 sq. mi. (9,596,960km²)
Population: 1,379,303,000 (inc Hong Kong and Macau)
Capital: Beijing
Language: Guoyo (Mandarin Chinese)
Currency: Yuan

China is one of the world's oldest civilizations. Its name in English may be related to the ancient state of Qin (pronounced *Ch'in*). The Chinese call their country Zhongguo, which means "middle land." China's more than 1.3 billion citizens are ruled by one of the world's few remaining communist governments.

▲ The giant panda lives in the bamboo forests of western China. It is an international symbol of conservation. In 2016 this much-loved animal was taken off the endangered list, but it remains vulnerable.

NATURAL BARRIERS

China lies in eastern Asia; deserts and mountains form natural barriers with its neighbors. The Gobi Desert — 502,000 sq. mi. (1,300,000km²) — straddles the border with Mongolia. The Himalayas — the highest mountains on Earth, rising to almost 5 mi. (8km) — stretch along the border with India, Bhutan, and Nepal. The Chang (Yangtze) River is the longest in Asia and flows from the Tibetan uplands to the East China Sea, dividing the warm, moist southern regions from the drier and cooler north.

CHINA'S WILDLIFE

Plant life ranges from bamboos and other subtropical plants in the south to coniferous forests in the north. Garden plants now common around the world, such as wisteria, first came from China. With much of the country covered by mountains and desert, forests have been cleared to make way for villages and farms. This has reduced the habitats of animals such as the tiger (which is also prey to hunters) and the giant panda, making them rare in the wild. ▶

▲ Thirty years ago, bicycles were the most common transport in Chinese cities. Today, China is the world's biggest car manufacturer.

THE GREAT WALL OF CHINA

One of China's greatest early empires was ruled by the Qin dynasty. The first Qin emperor, Shi Huangdi, came to the throne in 221 B.C. He ordered the construction of the Great Wall to keep out invaders from the north. Stretching for 4,000 mi. (6,400km), the wall was built by joining together shorter walls that had been built earlier. The wall has been rebuilt many times. Most of the present wall was constructed during the Ming Dynasty (1368–1644).

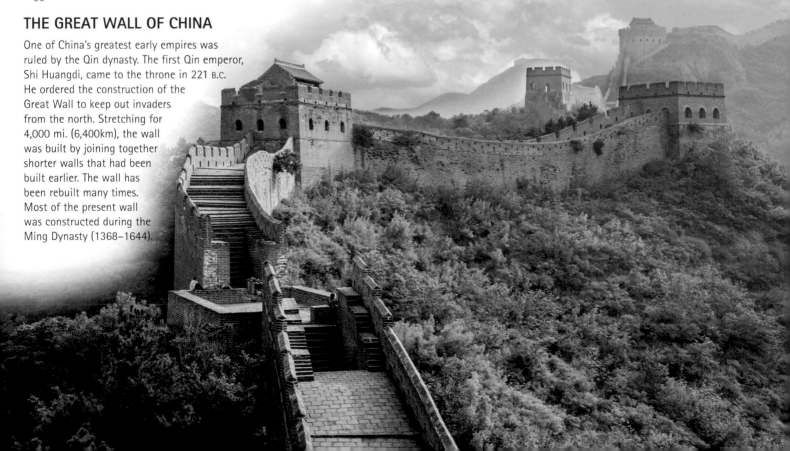

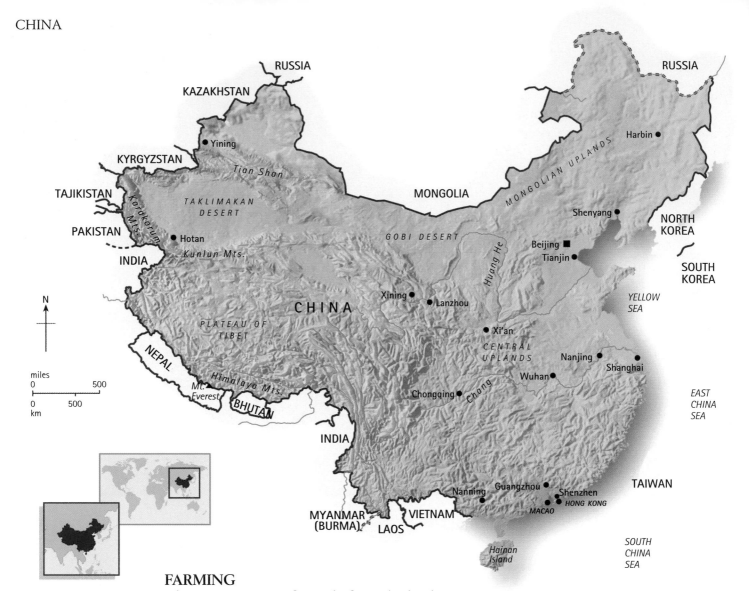

▼ Traditional ways of life are still strong in many parts of China. Here, fishermen use birds called cormorants to bring up fish from the water. They tie a thong around the bird's throat to stop it swallowing the catch.

FARMING

About 30 percent of people farm the land. Many farms are run as collectives, with people working together and dividing crops between the government and themselves. Important crops include rice, which is the main food of the south, and wheat, which is used to make bread and noodles in the north. Millet, tea, vegetables, soybeans, and cotton are also grown; and many farmers breed pigs, ducks, and chickens.

INDUSTRIAL GROWTH

Chinese industry has grown rapidly in the last 40 years. Factories produce machinery, transportation equipment, clothing, and electrical goods. Shanghai is the leading industrial city. In 1997, Hong Kong—then a British colony and wealthy financial and industrial center—was returned to China.

WRITING IN CHARACTERS

Over 90 percent of the people are Han Chinese, originally from the north of China. Mandarin is the main dialect, but many others are also spoken. Chinese writing does not use an alphabet. Instead, it uses symbols called characters that stand for words or ideas, not letters.

THE THREE TRADITIONS

China's traditional beliefs are known as the Three Teachings. The first of these is Confucianism, based on the teachings of Kongfuzi in the 6th century B.C. He called for people to respect their ancestors, family and state. The second is Daoism, which calls for respect for nature, harmony and simplicity. The third is Buddhism, which arrived in China in the 3rd century B.C. Communism brought atheism to China, but the Three Teachings are still at the root of many Chinese customs and social attitudes.

RULED BY DYNASTIES

For thousands of years, China was an empire ruled by emperors from successive royal families called dynasties. Many great inventions were made by the Chinese, including paper, ink, silk, printing, and gunpowder. In the 19th century, foreign powers forced China to open its borders to trade.

COMMUNIST RULE

In 1949, China adopted a communist government and was renamed the People's Republic of China, under the leadership of Mao Tse-tung. His strict policies meant that there were many changes as all aspects of life came under state control, and people found their freedom restricted.

▲ Preparing food on a street stall. Rice, noodles, and vegetables are the main ingredients used in Chinese cooking.

◄ Shanghai is China's largest city, with a population of 23,741,000. It is also China's leading industrial center.

CHINA TODAY

Since Mao's death in 1976, China's government has encouraged economic reform and foreign trade. By 2008, its economy was the world's second largest. However, China's rapid growth has led to problems such as air pollution, huge energy consumption, and water shortages. Political change is limited, and the state maintains tight controls on its people.

▼ This man is performing a traditional form of exercise that develops both mind and body. Called wushu, it is an ancient Chinese martial art.

◄ Farmers bring their produce to sell at a market in southern China. Here, farmers harvest three crops a year—two of rice and one of vegetables.

SEE ALSO

Asia, Buddhism, Communism, Mongol Empire, Paper, Zoology

CHRISTIANITY

Christianity is a religion based on the teachings of Jesus Christ, who lived in Palestine about 2,000 years ago. Today, it is practiced throughout the world.

The most well-known symbol of Christianity is the cross. It represents the cross on which Jesus was crucified.

Greek Christians used the fish as a code. The Greek word for fish spelled out the first letters of "Jesus Christ, God's Son, Savior."

The Christian Bible consists of the Hebrew Bible (Old Testament) and Christ's life and teachings (New Testament).

More people follow the Christian religion than any other. About 2.2 billion people believe that there is only one God and that he sent his son to Earth to save people from sin.

THE LIFE OF CHRIST

The life and teachings of Jesus Christ are contained in the New Testament of the Bible, the Christians' holy book. (The Old Testament of the Bible contains the sacred writings of the Jews.) Jesus is said to have performed miracles and healed the sick. The Roman rulers of Jerusalem crucified him by nailing him to a cross. Christians believe that three days later Jesus was raised from the dead and that some 40 days later he rose into Heaven.

CHRISTIANITY SPREADS

Jesus' teachings were spread by his disciples, or followers, who formed the early church. Despite persecution, Christianity became the religion of the Roman Empire in A.D. 324 and later spread across the world. Today, there are three main divisions in the Christian Church: Roman Catholic, Protestant, and

▲ Upon entering the Christian faith, followers are baptized, or dipped in water. This symbolizes cleansing and reflects the way Jesus was baptized by John the Baptist.

Eastern Orthodox. More than half of Christians are Catholics.

THREE-IN-ONE GOD

Christians believe that God is a Trinity: the Father (God), the Son (Jesus), and the Holy Spirit (God's influence on Earth).

THE HOLY MEAL

Before his Crucifixion, Jesus ate the Last Supper with his disciples. Christians reenact this meal with bread and wine in a special church ceremony called Holy Communion, or Mass, when Christ "becomes present" again. They celebrate Christ's birth at Christmas, his Resurrection at Easter, and the coming of the Holy Spirit at Pentecost.

▶ On Palm Sunday (the Sunday before Easter), many Christians carry palms in church. This commemorates Jesus' entry into Jerusalem, when he was greeted with branches of palm.

▼ Pope Francis became leader of the Roman Catholic Church in 2013. He is from Argentina.

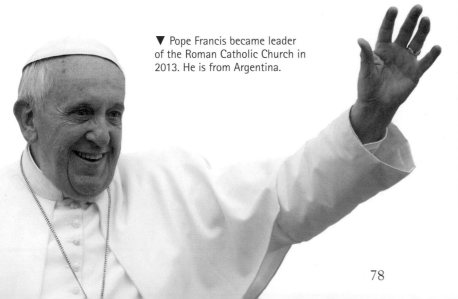

SEE ALSO

Crusades, Religion, Renaissance, Roman Empire

CITY

A city is a large community where thousands of people live and work. Nearly half of the world's population lives in cities.

Most cities are commercial or administrative centers. They are usually larger and more important than other towns in their region. Not all cities are huge. In Europe, a city is a town with a cathedral. In the United States, "city" is applied to an urban area with definite boundaries. The world's largest city is Tokyo in Japan, with over 34 million people, including those living in suburbs.

CITY LOCATIONS

The earliest cities grew in areas where the climate was suitable for growing crops. Access was also important so that trade could develop. Venice in Italy, London in England, and Kolkata (Calcutta) in India all grew because of their closeness to water, which provided transportation routes.

HOW CITIES WORK

With city centers becoming busier and more densely packed, high-rise buildings make the most of limited space. People working in the city often move farther out, where land is cheaper. This means that good road and train systems are necessary to bring them into the center.

PLANNING AHEAD

Most of today's cities were not planned, but spread out as they grew. In 1692, William Penn, the founder of the state of Pennsylvania, drew a plan for Philadelphia that resembled a grid. This became the pattern for most U.S. cities. In the mid-1800s, a French administrator named Georges-Eugène Haussmann redesigned Paris with wide boulevards and open squares rather than the chaotic maze of small streets that the city had been before.

CAPITAL CITIES

Most countries have a capital city where the national government is located. During the 1900s, a few capital cities were designed and built from new, including Canberra in Australia, Brasília in Brazil, and Islamabad in Pakistan. But more often, capitals have grown over time and have a mixture of old and new buildings alongside each other. The oldest parts of a city often form the center. Many people live outside the city center in areas known as suburbs.

▲ Large, elegant department stores attract tourists and shoppers to cities.

▲ The opera and other forms of entertainment bring people to the city center. They are often performed in grand and ornate buildings.

▲ Placing mass transit systems underground creates more space in cities.

▲ A good road network and public transportation are important to link the city with the suburbs.

SEE ALSO

Housing, Road, Skyscraper, Train, Transportation

CIVIL RIGHTS

Civil rights are the laws and customs that entitle everyone to fair and equal treatment. They give people the freedom to speak and act within the law.

▲ A demonstration held in 1997 against the military government in Myanmar (Burma). The government had refused to recognize the results of recent elections.

▲ Amnesty International works for the freeing of political prisoners and prisoners of conscience. It campaigns against torture and the death penalty.

▲ The flag of the United Nations, which was set up in 1946, after the end of World War II. The aim of the UN is to maintain international peace and cooperation.

The idea of civil rights in the West dates back to the writings of ancient Greek and Roman philosophers, and to the ideas of Judaism and Christianity. In some countries, civil rights are protected by a written constitution, as in the United States; in others, such as the United Kingdom, they consist of laws and customs built up over hundreds of years.

FAIR AND EQUAL
Civil rights mean people must be treated fairly and equally, no matter what their sex, religion, or ethnic origin. They are allowed freedom to express what they believe in speech or in the media. They also have the right to organize a political party, to have a fair trial if accused of a crime, and to vote in elections.

THE FIGHT FOR THE RIGHT
Many rights have been won only after a long and painful struggle. During the 1950s and 1960s, Dr. Martin Luther King, Jr., led the civil rights campaign to win equality for black Americans. In South Africa, Nelson Mandela was imprisoned in 1962 for opposing apartheid (the separation of whites and nonwhites). He was finally released

in 1991, when apartheid was abolished. In 1994, Mandela was elected South Africa's first black president. He led the country until he retired in 1999.

CIVIL RIGHTS ABUSES
International bodies, such as the United Nations and the European Court of Human Rights, protect civil rights; other organizations, like Amnesty International, campaign on behalf of people who are persecuted. However, some governments continue to ban civil rights. Dictators and single-party states deny rights to their people because they do not want their power threatened. Communist countries, such as China, traditionally stress the importance of social rights—for example, the right to work—often at the expense of human rights like freedom of speech.

"I HAVE A DREAM"
In 1963, Martin Luther King, Jr., led 200,000 people on a civil rights march in Washington, D.C. In his speech he declared, "I have a dream," demanding equal rights for black Americans. The Civil Rights Act of 1964 followed, and King was awarded the Nobel Peace Prize. In 1968 he was shot.

SEE ALSO
Communism, Democracy, Fascism, South Africa

CIVIL WAR

Civil war is an armed struggle between people who live in the same country or state. Civil war is usually triggered by political, religious, or ethnic differences.

▲ An Angolan UNITA rebel soldier pictured in 1986. Angola suffered years of civil war, backed, until 1990, by countries such as Cuba, the Soviet Union, South Africa, and the United States.

Families, communities, and whole countries have been divided by civil war. Because fighting takes place wholly within a country, no one escapes its effects. Prisoners are often murdered, homes destroyed, and civilians terrorized.

FIGHTING FOR RIGHTS

Civil wars erupt because of a difference in people's beliefs. They are often begun by minorities fighting for greater political or religious rights, for union with a similar group in a nearby state, or for the right to keep their way of life. These minorities are often led by strong figures.

OUTSIDE INFLUENCE

In some civil wars, outside countries give their support to one side, often for political gain or to protect human rights. During the 1980s, for example, a desperate civil war raged in Nicaragua between the socialist government and the right-wing Contras. The U.S.A. supported the Contras in order to combat the spread of left-wing socialist and communist regimes in Central America. Such foreign interference was typical of the Cold War, a period of rivalry and deep distrust between the Soviet Union, the U.S.A., and their supporters.

KEY DATES
1918–21 Russian Civil War. Fought between Bolsheviks and anti-Communists. Bolsheviks win
1967–70 Nigerian Civil War. Fought between Biafra and the Federal government. Biafra is defeated
1968–1994 Civil war, Northern Ireland. Prolonged conflict between Protestants and Catholics. A cease-fire is called and peace talks begin in 1994
1991–1995 and **1998–1999** In Yugoslavia, Kosovo, Slovenia, Croatia, and Bosnia fought for independence
2011 Many rebel groups, some backed by foreign countries, battle with the Syrian government of President Bashar al-Assad

ETHNIC CLASHES

Civil wars started by ethnic (racial) hatred have produced some of the worst cruelties of recent times. In the early 1990s, fighting broke out in Yugoslavia, as three provinces—Bosnia, Croatia, and Slovenia—fought for independence from the Serbian-dominated state. During the long-running war, thousands of civilians became the innocent victims of ethnic cleansing—the murder or forced eviction of one racial group by another through the use of violence and terror.

AFRICAN UNREST

When colonial rule ended in many African nations in the 1960s and 1970s, civil war followed. Within countries like Nigeria and Angola, different peoples had been forced together by colonial boundaries and these differences caused conflict. Some of the bloodiest civil wars caused by political and ethnic differences have broken out in Somalia, Congo, and Chad. ▶

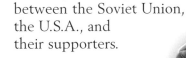

A Kurdish fighter goes to war in Syria in 2016. The homeland of the Kurds is divided between Turkey, Syria, Iraq, and Iran. They have often fought for an independent state of their own. ▶

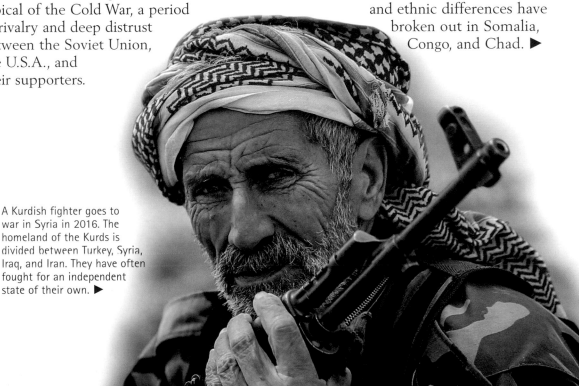

▲ A United Nations soldier helps an old woman cross the main street in Sarajevo, in the former Yugoslavia. An armored vehicle shields them from sniper fire.

▼ Spanish army soldiers forcing Republicans to surrender at Sanosierra on August 6, 1936.

▲ Posters are often used to rally support. This poster declares, "Peasants, the land is yours." It was designed by Republicans in the Spanish Civil War.

CHARLES I
English ruler (1600–49), came to the throne in 1625. He was executed during the English Civil War.

OLIVER CROMWELL
(1599–1658) ruled England, Scotland, and Ireland as Lord Protector after the king's execution.

▶ The Roundheads' crushing defeat of Royalist forces at Naseby in 1645 was the decisive victory of the English Civil War.

ROMAN CIVIL WAR

Civil wars are not a new phenomenon. Many of the earliest civil wars were fought between influential individuals and their backers in the search for power. In 49 B.C., civil war was started in Rome when Julius Caesar ordered his armies to cross the Rubicon River and march on Rome. He drove out his opponents and succeeded in making himself dictator.

ENGLISH CIVIL WAR

The English Civil War, which lasted from 1642 to 1649, was a struggle between the English king, Charles I, and parliament over who should govern the country. Charles believed that kings were appointed by God and should rule alone. Parliament believed it should have greater power. Parliament refused to cooperate with the king and this caused civil war.

ROYALISTS AND ROUNDHEADS

England divided into two factions: the Royalists, or Cavaliers, supported the king; the Roundheads supported Parliament. Two great generals, Lord Fairfax and Oliver Cromwell, led the Roundheads, and eventually the king's forces were defeated. In 1649, Charles was executed and England was declared a republic.

THE SPANISH CIVIL WAR

In 1936, a left-wing Republican government was elected in Spain. Most of the right-wing army rebelled and tried to overthrow the government. The right, led by General Franco, received support from Germany and Italy. Thousands of Spaniards died in the war. In 1939, the Republican army collapsed and Franco became dictator of Spain.

Royalist

Roundheads

SEE ALSO
Africa, Civil War (American), Greece and the Balkans, Refugee, Spain and Portugal, Warfare

CIVIL WAR, AMERICAN

More Americans died in the Civil War than in any other conflict. It was caused by the deep divisions between northern and southern states.

The Union flag (above) and the Confederate flag (left)

The American Civil War (1861–65) was caused by deep political differences. The southern states believed in the right of states, not Congress, to make their own laws, including the right to hold slaves. The South felt that this right was threatened by the election of Abraham Lincoln in 1860.

NORTH AND SOUTH

The North was a land of industry and manufacturing—and home to a strong movement against slavery. The South was a land of farms and plantations and depended on slaves for labor.

DECLARATION OF WAR

After Lincoln's election, 11 southern states seceded (separated) from the Union to create the Confederate States of America. Southern forces attacked Fort Sumter on April 12, 1861. Lincoln, determined to keep the nation intact, formed the Union army against the slaveholding states.

A Union soldier

A Confederate soldier

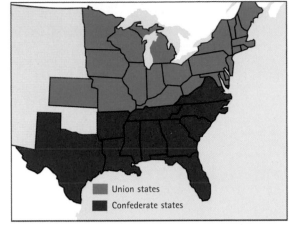

Union states
Confederate states

▲ The American Civil War was fought mainly in the East and Southeast between the southern, or Confederate states, and the northern, or Union states, including Oregon and California on the West Coast.

FOUR YEARS OF FIGHTING

The American Civil War was a fight the South could not win. More people lived in the North, it had a stronger industrial base, better communications, and a navy capable of stopping food and supplies reaching the South. In 1865, the South surrendered. More than 600,000 had died in the struggle, and most southern cities had been destroyed by the war. That same year, the 13th Amendment was added to the Constitution, abolishing slavery. Five days after the South's surrender, Lincoln was assassinated.

THE BATTLE OF GETTYSBURG

The Battle of Gettysburg in July 1863 was a major turning point in the American Civil War. About 85,000 Union troops, led by General George Meade, defeated some 75,000 Confederate soldiers led by General Robert E. Lee. The Confederates never truly recovered from the crushing defeat.

SEE ALSO

Slavery, United States of America, Warfare

CLIMATE

The climate of a region is its weather pattern over a long period of time. The weather may change from day to day, but the climate stays the same.

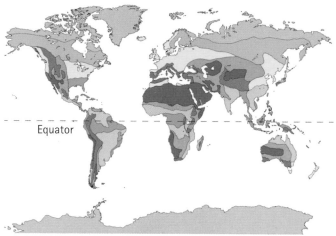

▼ The world can be divided into different climate zones. These vary from tropical regions, characterized by hot and humid weather, to freezing polar areas.

Equator

Key:
- Polar
- Subarctic
- Temperate
- Grassland
- Mediterranean
- Mountain
- Subtropical/monsoon
- Tropical
- Hot desert

▲ At the equator, the sun's rays are direct and strong. Away from the equator, the sun's rays are weaker because they strike Earth at an angle and must travel farther through the cool air of the atmosphere.

The climate of a region depends on how close the region is to the sea, how high up it is (its altitude), and, most importantly, how far it is from the equator (its latitude). Climate is usually measured as a combination of the average rainfall in an area and the temperature.

THE POWER OF THE SUN
The two extremes of climate on Earth are found at the equator and at the Poles. The climate is hottest in the zones on either side of the equator—the tropics—because the sun is almost directly overhead. The Poles are the coldest areas: temperatures drop below –58°F (–50°C).

THE TROPICS
The tropics are not only the hottest areas but also the wettest. The intense heat evaporates water from the rivers and oceans, forming rain clouds that drench the tropics. However, either side of the tropics lie some of the world's largest deserts.

COLDER HIGHER UP
Air is cooler the higher you go in the atmosphere. So mountainous regions have a colder climate than low areas. On a mountain, air cools by 42.8°F (6°C) for each 3,300 ft. (1,000m) climbed.

CLIMATE CHANGE
Climates can change over the ages, and natural causes such as volcanic eruptions can have a global effect. Most scientists agree that rapid warming of the planet in recent decades is the result of human activity. The increased release of gases, such as carbon dioxide and methane, into the atmosphere is trapping warmth around the planet. This may cause ice melt, severe storms, floods, and droughts.

WIND CIRCULATION
At the Poles, cold air sinks and disperses and is replaced by warmer air flowing in from above. The cold air moving away from the Poles meets warm winds from the subtropics and pushes the warm air back to the equator.

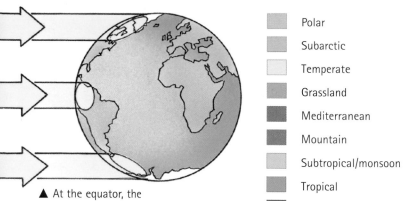

Polar front

Subtropical jet stream

Wind direction

AFRICA

Warm air from the equator

SEE ALSO

Desert, Forest, Habitat, Mountain and valley, Pollution, Water, Weather

CLOCK

Clocks are instruments used to measure time in hours, minutes, and seconds down to the smallest fraction. They include mechanical, quartz, and atomic clocks.

Chinese candle clocks "chime" when the candle burns the string to release a weight onto the cymbal.

Sundials show the time by plotting the changing position of the sun's shadow during the day.

Chronometers, invented in the 1700s for use on ships, have a slowly unwinding spring, not a pendulum.

A quartz watch tells the time by recording the vibrations of a quartz crystal inside.

Atomic clocks count the vibrations of light given off by atoms, and are used in satellites and aircraft.

People first learned to tell the time using sundials, sandglasses, marked candles, and water clocks. But during the 1200s, the first mechanical clocks were made.

MECHANICAL CLOCKS
Mechanical clocks are set in motion in one of two ways—by winding up a spring or by raising a weight. Gearwheels with teeth move the hour, minute, and second hands—this is called the clock's movement. Some clocks need to be wound every day, but others can run for about a week.

THE PENDULUM
In 1582, the Italian scientist Galileo Galilei discovered that every swing of a pendulum, or hanging weight, takes the same length of time. The time the swing takes depends on the length of the pendulum arm. A Dutch astronomer called Christiaan Huygens used this knowledge to make the first pendulum clock 74 years later. In a pendulum clock, the swinging weight moves from side to side to regulate the movements of the clock's hands around the clock face.

QUARTZ CRYSTAL
Most of today's clocks and watches are battery-operated and have a tiny quartz crystal inside. The crystal vibrates when it receives a charge of electricity from the battery. It gives out regular, fast pulses of current, which are slowed down by a microchip to one per second.

ATOMIC CLOCKS
The most accurate clocks are cesium-beam atomic clocks, which were first made in 1955. These measure the frequency of an atom's vibrations. They lose only a fraction of a second every million years.

TURNING TIME
When a grandfather clock is wound up, a weight is pulled up to the top of its case. As the weight falls, tiny toothed gearwheels turn and move the hands around the clock face. The swing of the pendulum makes the weight fall evenly as the gears catch against the pallet at every swing, turning one notch of the escape wheel. This makes the "tick-tock" sound.

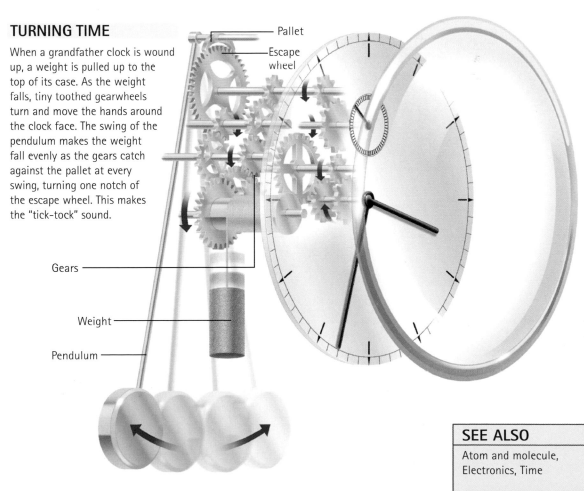

Pallet

Escape wheel

Gears

Weight

Pendulum

SEE ALSO
Atom and molecule, Electronics, Time

CLOTHING

Clothing is worn to protect the body and to make it look attractive. The kind of clothes people wear reflects where they live, their lifestyle, and their personality.

People started wearing clothes more than 100,000 years ago in colder parts of the world. Ice Age hunters 25,000 years ago stayed warm by sewing animal furs together. About 10,000 years ago, early farming communities learned how to spin plant and animal fibers to make thread that could be woven into cloth. Wool, cotton, silk, and flax for linen were used. Woolen cloth was used in cold northern areas; linen was preferred in hot countries such as Egypt.

▲ Firefighters' protective suits were developed from space suit technology. The suits have many layers, which were originally intended to protect astronauts from the sun's lethal radiation while they worked in space.

THE FIRST PANTS
Among the first people to cut clothes into the kinds of shapes used today were the ancient tribes of Persia (Iran). Men wore coats with sleeves and an early form of pants designed for life on horseback.

READY TO WEAR
In 1785, the steam-powered loom marked the birth of the modern clothing industry; and in the 1850s, sewing machines arrived. Clothing factories soon started making large amounts of inexpensive, ready-to-wear clothes so that people could afford to buy garments instead of making their own or having expensive designs made up by dressmakers and tailors.

CHANGING SHAPES
Advances in technology have continued to shape fashion in the 20th and 21st centuries. Synthetic nylon was first used to make stockings in the 1940s, polyester appeared in the 1960s, Lycra in the 1980s, and smart fabrics in the 2000s.

▲ In the 1960s, designers responded to a new teenage market, and the miniskirt arrived. Twiggy, shown here, was a British fashion model who became the symbol of the new look.

▲ Simple clothes, in natural fibers, worn in loose flowing styles, kept both women and men cool in ancient Egypt.

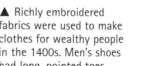

▲ Richly embroidered fabrics were used to make clothes for wealthy people in the 1400s. Men's shoes had long, pointed toes.

▲ Knee breeches in pale colors were worn by gentlemen in the 1700s. Long pants became fashionable during the 1800s.

▲ In the mid-1800s, women wore tight corsets and hoops made of wicker or steel, called crinolines, to make their skirts stick out.

FASHION VICTIMS

Wearing the latest styles to be fashionable began as a way for rich people to show their wealth. But sometimes, staying in fashion was painful. During the 1800s, women in search of the "hourglass" figure wore laced corsets with whalebone inside. This compressed the waist, making it as tiny as possible. People still follow design trends, but since World War II, when many women started working in factories, clothes have become more practical.

WORKWEAR TO CLASSICS

Trends do not always come from designers. Tough denim jeans, originally made as workwear for Californian gold miners in the 1850s, have become fashion classics. Many people today choose clothes to express their personality.

NATIONAL DRESS

In many parts of the world, traditional dress is worn every day. The *sari*, worn by Hindu women, is a long wrap of light fabric worn over a tight-fitting top called a *choli*. In some countries, national dress is kept for festivals and family celebrations.

MIX AND MATCH

National dress has had a strong influence on Western fashion. American cowboys learned to make leather leggings (chaps) by watching Native Americans stretch and soak buffalo hides. Today, designers continue to borrow from different eras and cultures in a constant search for new ideas.

▲ This wet suit is made of neoprene (a synthetic rubber). It gives the diver protection and warmth under water. Clothes like these allow people to explore previously inaccessible places.

▲ Designers' creations are shown on the catwalk, then toned down and reproduced for the ready-to-wear market.

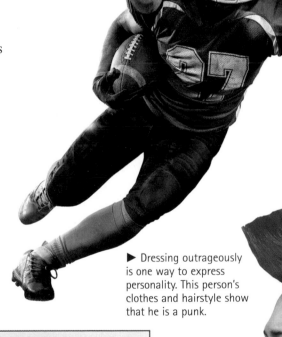

▶ Clothes for sports must be light, protective, and easy to move in. Uniforms often promote a sense of team spirit.

▶ Dressing outrageously is one way to express personality. This person's clothes and hairstyle show that he is a punk.

▲ In the 1800s, young boys and girls from wealthy families dressed alike. Both wore dresses over ankle-length pantaloons.

KEY DATES

1500s Whalebone is first used to stiffen corsets

1850s Tightly laced corsets and crinolines are used to create the "hourglass" figure

1870s The introduction of the bustle in women's dresses

1899 The "Gibson Girl" is created in the U.S.A.

1920s Coco Chanel revolutionizes women's fashion by creating short, simple shift dresses

1947 Christian Dior's "New Look" with very full skirts ends the austerity of the war years

1957 The sack dress dominates U.S. fashion

1960s André Courrèges (France) introduces the miniskirt, which is popularized in the U.K. by Mary Quant

SEE ALSO

Design, France, Material, Paint and dye, Textile

COAL

Coal is a rock formed under the ground from the remains of decayed prehistoric plants. It burns easily and is widely used as a fuel.

Anthracite is the highest quality coal. It gives the most heat but little smoke.

Most coal mined today is used in power plants to produce light and heat.

Some perfumes are made from coal tar—a black liquid produced from coal.

Coal, like petroleum and gas, is a fossil fuel. It was formed under the ground from the remains of plants over millions of years. It is used to make fires and to make electricity, chemicals, and steel.

CARBON CONTENT

Coal is made up of carbon, tar, oils, and minerals. There are three different types of coal, depending on the amount of carbon each contains. Lignite, or brown coal, contains less than 50 percent carbon; bituminous coal around 70 percent; and anthracite, the most valuable, has about 95 percent carbon. Over 7.5 billion tons of coal are mined each year, and 1.1 trillion tons remain underground.

INDUSTRIAL COAL

In about 1750, the Industrial Revolution led to a huge demand for coal as a fuel for steam engines. Today, many power plants burn coal to produce electricity. The iron industry uses coke—coal which has been heated to make the tar and oils evaporate—to produce iron and steel. The tar and oils are then used to produce dyes, fertilizers, and fibers such as nylon.

POLLUTION

When coal is burned, it releases smoke containing soot and poisonous gases, such as carbon monoxide. These can harm the environment, so most power plants have filters to clean the smoke.

▲ Different equipment is needed to mine coal. Cutting machines dig out coal within the mine, while a conveyor belt transports it back up the shaft.

HOW COAL IS FORMED

About 300 million years ago, in an age known as the Carboniferous period, the climate was warm and wet, ideal for swampy forests. Dead plants rotted and formed peat, which was buried under layers of sand and mud as sea levels rose, flooding the swamps. These layers slowly turned to rock. Their weight squeezed the peat, turning it into coal.

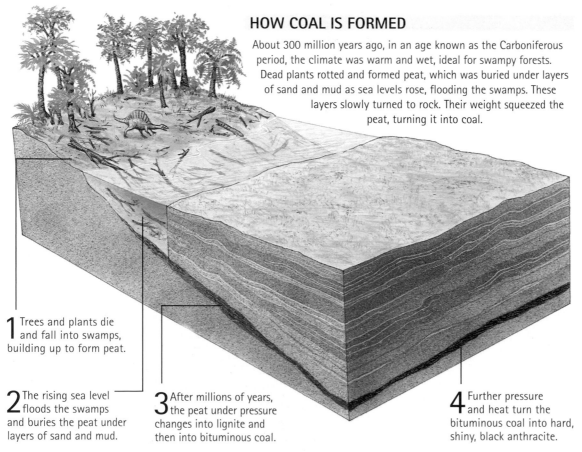

1 Trees and plants die and fall into swamps, building up to form peat.

2 The rising sea level floods the swamps and buries the peat under layers of sand and mud.

3 After millions of years, the peat under pressure changes into lignite and then into bituminous coal.

4 Further pressure and heat turn the bituminous coal into hard, shiny, black anthracite.

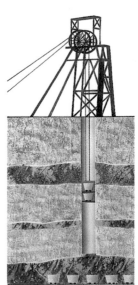

▲ A shaft is dug down to a seam many hundreds of feet below. A few mines are opencast—coal is mined at the surface.

SEE ALSO

Climate, Electricity, Fossil, Gas, Industrial Revolution, Iron and steel, Mining, Oil, Pollution

COLD WAR

The Cold War was a period of hostility between the capitalist and communist countries of the world. It began after the end of World War II.

▲ The U.S.S.R.'s Nikita Khrushchev (left) and U.S. President John F. Kennedy, fingers poised over their nuclear buttons, confront each other in this 1962 cartoon.

▼ U.S. soldiers in a burning village during the Vietnam War. The U.S. backed South Vietnam in its fight against Viet Cong guerrillas and Soviet-backed North Vietnam.

For more than 45 years, between 1945 and 1991, two superpowers, the United States and the Soviet Union (U.S.S.R.), fought each other using spies, alliances, trading bans, and local wars as their weapons.

IRON CURTAIN

After World War II, the U.S.S.R. and the U.S.A. distrusted each other. As communist governments took control of Eastern Europe, the Western nations reacted by forming a military alliance called the North Atlantic Treaty Organization (NATO). The frontier between West and East became known as the Iron Curtain.

CONFRONTATION

The Cold War was marked by a series of crises. The first was the Berlin Airlift in 1948, when the West flew in supplies to a Soviet-blockaded Berlin, the former capital of Germany. The superpowers began stockpiling nuclear weapons. They took opposing sides in other conflicts, such as the Korean War (1950–53) and Vietnam War (1954–75). In 1962, people feared that nuclear war would break out when the U.S. demanded that the U.S.S.R. withdraw nuclear weapons from Cuba. Eventually, the Soviets backed down and the crisis ended.

THE COLD WAR THAWS

After 1970, tension between the superpowers began to ease. The Cold War finally ended in 1991 with the fall of communism in many European countries, and the breakup of the Soviet Union, as states such as Lithuania, Kazakhstan, Belarus, and Georgia gained independence.

THE BERLIN AIRLIFT

After World War II, Germany was divided up. The U.S., France, and the U.K. controlled the West, and the U.S.S.R. controlled the East. The capital, Berlin, was also divided. In 1948, the West, including West Berlin, was united into one country, West Germany, with one currency, the German mark. In protest, the U.S.S.R. cut off West Berlin's road, rail, and water links with the West. For 11 months, U.S. and British planes flew food, fuel, and other vital supplies into the city until the Soviets lifted their blockade.

SEE ALSO

Communism, Democracy, Russia, United States of America, World War II

COLOR

Color is what we see when light from an object reaches our eyes. White light seems colorless, but it is actually made up of a mixture of colors.

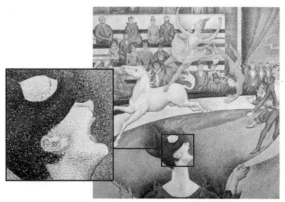

The primary colors of light are red, blue, and green. Mixed together they make up white light.

The primary colors of paint are yellow, blue, and red. Mixed together they produce black.

When you see a rainbow, you are seeing sunlight split apart by raindrops. The rainbow has seven colors: red, orange, yellow, green, blue, indigo, and violet. This range of colors is called the spectrum.

REFLECTING LIGHT
An object only appears to be a particular color because of the light it reflects. For example, a leaf looks green because it reflects green light and absorbs all the other colors in the spectrum.

PRIMARY COLORS
During the 1800s, scientists were amazed to discover that almost any color of light can be created by combining different amounts of a basic set of three colors—red, blue, and green. These are known as the primary colors of light.

MIXING IT UP
If equal amounts of red, blue, and green light are mixed together, they make white light. Mixing just red and green light together makes yellow; blue and green

▲ Georges Seurat's *The Circus* (1891) is painted using a technique called pointillism. Pure color is applied as dots. These merge at a distance to create the subtler shades.

makes cyan (a green-blue); and blue and red makes magenta. In photography, printing, movies, and television, light is mixed to produce millions of different colors.

PAINTING A DIFFERENT PICTURE
Pigments (used in paints) have a different set of primary colors. The primary colors are yellow, blue, and red, and when they are mixed together they make black.

SEEING IN COLOR
We see color when light falls on the retina at the back of the eye. The retina is full of cells, called rods and cones, that are sensitive to light. Cones are sensitive to particular colors, and rods, which are not color sensitive, help us to see in dim light.

REFLECTION AND ABSORPTION

When light hits an object, the object absorbs (soaks up) some of the colors of the spectrum and reflects (throws off) others. A tomato, for example, looks red because it reflects red light back into our eyes, but absorbs the other colors of the rainbow: orange, yellow, green, blue, indigo, and violet light.

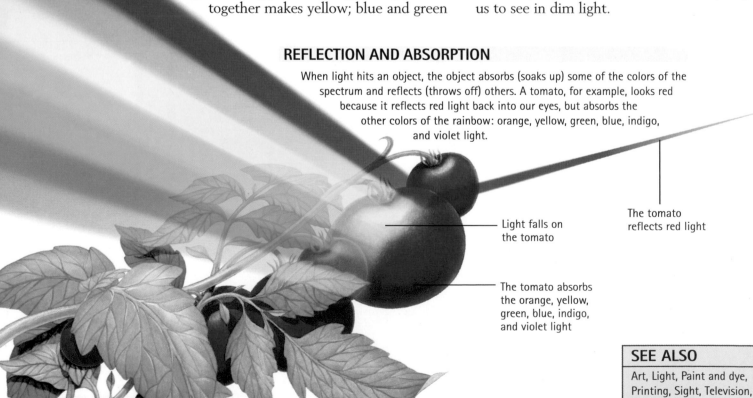

The tomato reflects red light

Light falls on the tomato

The tomato absorbs the orange, yellow, green, blue, indigo, and violet light

SEE ALSO
Art, Light, Paint and dye, Printing, Sight, Television, Wavelength

COMET, METEOR, AND ASTEROID

Comets, meteors, and asteroids are chunks of ice, rock, or metal that circle the Sun. As they travel closer to Earth, some can be seen lighting up the night sky.

Shooting stars are meteors burning up as they enter Earth's atmosphere.

The 12-mi. (20-km)-long asteroid Gaspra was photographed by the *Galileo* space probe.

Arizona's Barringer Crater was made by a meteorite over 20,000 years ago.

The space between the planets is littered with debris left over from when the solar system formed. Balls of ice and rock with tails are called comets, small particles that blaze through Earth's atmosphere are meteors, and larger chunks of rock and metal are asteroids.

ICE-COLD COMETS
A comet has a fuzzy head and one or more tails. Its head is a lump of ice, dust, and rock, 6–18 mi. (10–30km) across. Surrounding it is a cloud of gas and dust called a coma. The Sun's heat and the solar wind (a stream of particles given off by the Sun) drive dust and gas out from the coma to form the comet's tails. In 2014, the European Space Agency's Rosetta mission managed to land a spacecraft on a comet.

SHOOTING STARS AND SHOWERS
Many meteors have been around since our solar system formed, but others are chips off comets and asteroids, or even the Moon and Mars. These can be as small as grains of sand and most burn up as they hurtle into Earth's atmosphere at speeds of up to 25 mi./sec. (40km/sec). These are called shooting stars. Some travel in swarms and create a meteor shower in the night sky. Such showers can appear at the same time each year, when Earth crosses the swarm's path. Every year, a few meteors hit Earth's surface and are called meteorites.

THE ASTEROID BELT
Asteroids (sometimes called minor planets) are chunks of rock and metal smaller than planets that circle the Sun. There are billions of asteroids in the solar system, and more than 90 percent of them are in the asteroid belt between Mars and Jupiter.

A COMET IN FLIGHT
Comets are surrounded by clouds of dust, called comas, which can be up to 620,000 mi. (1,000,000km) across. Comets travel in long loops around the Sun. Each time they approach the Sun, more gas and dust evaporate from their centers, making the comas grow larger and the comets form tails. Comets' tails always point away from the Sun.

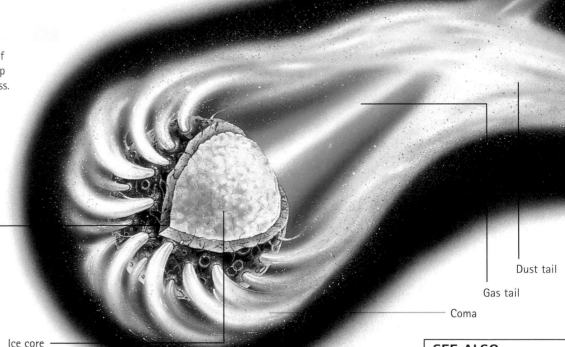
Rocky crust

Ice core

Dust tail

Gas tail

Coma

▲ Halley's Comet is visible from Earth every 76 years. It was studied closely on its last return in 1986.

SEE ALSO
Astronomy, Moon, Planet, Solar system, Spacecraft, Space exploration, Sun, Universe

COMMUNICATION

Communication is the process of sending and receiving messages. This can be done by using spoken and written language or recognized signs and signals.

◀ Sign language for the deaf uses hand signals and is based on ideas, not words.

The Sumerians developed the first known writing system in about 3500 B.C.

From the 1400s, printing became a means of mass communication in Europe.

The telephone, invented in 1876, allowed long-distance communication.

A satellite dish receives images and sounds sent from around the world.

People usually communicate with each other individually or in small groups. However, they sometimes need to relay messages to a much larger audience. This is known as mass communication.

SIGNS AND SIGNALS

Humans have developed ingenious ways of conveying messages to one another, using signs and signals when language cannot be used. Some Native Americans sent smoke signals, and African tribes used drumbeats. Signals are still in use today—navies send messages using flags, and road users rely on roadside signs and traffic lights.

POSTAL COMMUNICATIONS

One of the earliest, cheapest, and most reliable forms of communication was mail. Stamps were first used in Britain in 1840. Letters today are sorted by machine, and then carried by truck, train, or airplane to their destination.

TELEGRAPH MESSAGES

For a long time, the fastest way to communicate over long distances was to deliver messages on foot, on horseback, or by boat. Then in 1840, the American inventor Samuel Morse introduced the first simple telegraph, which used electricity to send messages down wire cables. The messages were coded using a system of dots and dashes. This became known as Morse code.

FASTER THAN EVER

Since the 1800s, many inventions, such as the telephone, radio, and television, have made communication across the world faster and easier. Today, a message can be sent to the other side of the world in seconds using satellite and computer links. The Internet enables all types of computers to communicate and share services using fiber optics. Video conference centers allow people thousands of miles apart to see and talk to each other directly.

THE PONY EXPRESS

In 1860, the Pony Express was the fastest delivery system in the United States, delivering letters along a 1,966-mi. (3,164-km) route in less than ten days—it had previously taken over three weeks by boat or stagecoach. The riders rode in all weather, changing to fresh horses at every pony express station—spaced 10–12 mi. (16–20km) apart. The service was closed in October 1861, once the telegraph and Morse code came into use.

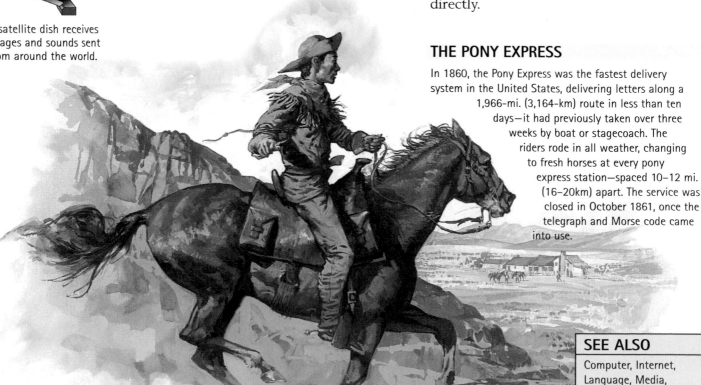

SEE ALSO

Computer, Internet, Language, Media, Printing, Radio, Satellite, Telecommunication, Telephone, Television

COMMUNISM

Communism is a political theory based on the idea that everybody should share all wealth, property, and industry equally.

The German journalist Karl Marx developed the idea of communism in the 1800s.

Mao Tse-tung led the Communists to victory in China in the 1940s.

Guerilla warfare brought Fidel Castro to power. He led Cuba from 1959 to 2008.

Ho Chi Min led North Vietnam for most of the Vietnam War.

◄ Since North Korea became communist in 1948, many statues to heroic workers have been erected.

In 1848, Karl Marx and Friedrich Engels published the *Communist Manifesto*, which stated that private ownership should be replaced by common ownership. Marx wanted to see an end to the way of life in which most people worked for a low wage, while a few wealthy people owned the factories and land. He believed that the only way to achieve this was by revolution.

THE FIRST REVOLUTION

The first successful communist revolution took place in Russia in 1917, after which the Union of Soviet Socialist Republics (U.S.S.R.) was set up under the leadership of Vladimir Lenin. The state took control of farms, factories, mines, and railroads in the name of the people. Lenin and his successor, Joseph Stalin, ruled as dictators. Most people were better fed and housed, but personal freedoms were severely restricted.

SPREAD OF COMMUNISM

After World War II, communism spread to Eastern Europe, China, and some countries in Africa, Asia, and Central America. During the Cold War, there was hostile rivalry between communist countries and the United States-led Western democracies.

THE COLLAPSE

From 1989 to 1992, communism in countries such as Poland, Hungary, and East Germany collapsed. With the break-up of the Soviet Union in the 1990s, China remains the only major nation with a communist government.

KEY DATES

1848 Journalist Karl Marx and philosopher Friedrich Engels publish the *Communist Manifesto*

1917 Lenin leads Russia's Bolshevik Revolution

1949 China becomes a communist state under Mao Tse-tung

1989 Communism collapses in Eastern Europe

1991 The breakup of the U.S.S.R. leaves only China, Cuba, Vietnam, and North Korea as communist states

---

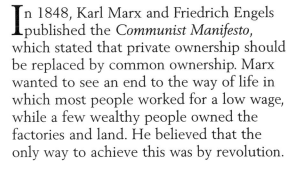

► Vladimir Lenin, leader of the Bolshevik Party, led a revolution that overthrew czarist rule in Russia. He set up the world's first communist regime in 1917.

SEE ALSO

China, Cold War, Democracy, Eastern Europe, Europe, Fascism, Revolution, Russia

93

COMPUTER

Computers are machines that handle information according to sets of instructions. They then give the results in a form that people can understand.

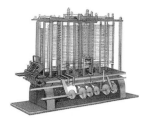

In 1834, Charles Babbage (1792–1871) designed the first mechanical computer, but he never saw it built.

In the 1960s, computers used transistors and stored data on tape. They could fill a whole room.

The British Sinclair ZX81 was one of the first home computers to be launched on the world market.

Portable laptop computers, small enough to fit inside a briefcase, have been available since the 1980s.

Smartphones have powerful operating systems. They run small programs called apps.

The computer is an electronic device that can do calculations millions of times faster than the human brain. First, the computer receives data, or information, put in by the user; then it processes the data as simple electrical signals according to its program and produces a result.

BINARY NUMBERS

All computers use a language called the binary system. Binary numbers are entirely made up of the digits 0 and 1. When a letter is typed on the keyboard or the mouse or joystick is moved, tiny electric currents are sent to the computer. These currents are stored by the computer as binary numbers.

MINIATURIZATION

The first computers took up a whole room, but by the 1960s, electronic components had become much smaller and computers began to shrink in size. The home computer became possible through the invention of the microchip, which contains tens of thousands of electronic components within a space no larger than a fingernail.

HIGHLY VERSATILE

A PC (personal computer) can tackle jobs from word processing to 3-D design and animation. Music can be recorded, edited, and played back on the PC. Desktop publishing means books and magazines can be designed on the PC.

HOW IT WORKS

Data in a PC is usually stored in random-access memory (RAM). The central processing unit (CPU) calls it up when it is needed, according to a list of instructions (the program), which is also stored in memory. Data flows to and from the CPU along an electronic pathway called the bus. After processing, data is stored in RAM again.

SCIENCE FRONTIERS

Computers have revolutionized science and technology. Space probes, satellite TV, and weapons detection systems all rely on computers. Computers make it possible to test chemical and nuclear reactions without real-life experiments.

AUTOMATION

In the automotive industry, computers are used to design a car and then build it with the aid of robots. Inside the car itself, a computer can check the engine, the brakes, and the steering. Computers can even be used in the home to control temperature, lighting, and security.

GLOBAL LINKS

Computers are increasingly changing the way we live by connecting people and places. The Internet links up computers all over the world, allowing messages and information to be sent across the globe in a matter of seconds.

BILL GATES (born 1955) In 1975, American Bill Gates founded Microsoft, now the largest software company in the world.

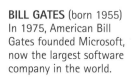

HOW A COMPUTER WORKS

A computer system has four basic parts. An input device such as the keyboard, mouse, or joystick enters information into the computer. Then the central processing unit (CPU), acting as the computer's brain, performs the tasks. The information is sent to an output device, such as the screen or printer, to display the results. And finally a memory unit stores programs and data.

A plasma screen is a light and quiet computer screen that provides sharp, vivid, high-quality images

The CPU is the brains of the computer

The hard disk is made up of magnetic layers that store information when the computer is turned off

Speakers are used to output sound from the computer

A mouse is used to point to different areas of the screen

The keys on the keyboard act as switches, sending tiny electric currents to the computer when pressed

COMPUTER ADD-ONS

Game Pad
A game pad is a powerful, dual-control input device used to play computer games.

Digital Camera
Photographs can be viewed on the screen of the camera and then imported to a computer for storage.

MP3 Player
This is a digital music player which can store and play songs downloaded from the computer.

SEE ALSO

Electronics, Internet, Robot, Satellite, Space exploration, Technology, Telecommunication

CONSERVATION

Conservation is the protection and careful use of natural resources, including animals, plants, and fossil fuels. It also includes care of historical treasures.

◄ The care and preservation of paintings is a painstaking process. An art conservator must understand a painting's history and content in the same way that an animal conservationist must know the habits of an endangered animal.

Conservationists try to find a balance between the needs of human beings and care of the environment. There are around 7.5 billion people alive today, and they all need land to live on, food to eat, and fuel for power. Without care, habitats can be destroyed, resources used up, and Earth damaged.

▲ Recycling plastic, paper, tin, and glass conserves Earth's resources. In many states, there are laws that specify that households can be fined for failing to separate trash for recycling.

GLOBAL AWARENESS
Some conservation issues are local, as when acres of forest are threatened with felling to make way for a new road. Others, such as recycling, saving energy, and stopping animals from becoming extinct, are shared worldwide. In 1992, world leaders got together at the Earth Summit in Brazil to draw up the very first global action plan to save the planet. One scheme that was introduced to encourage people to stop destroying their habitats—by logging trees or draining marshes—is the "debt-for-nature" idea. This means that a poor country has some of its international debt canceled in exchange for setting aside areas for conservation.

FACING EXTINCTION
Around 150 rare plant and animal species become extinct each day—far more than when the dinosaurs died out, 65 million years ago. The tiger, rhinoceros, Asian snow leopard, and even some species of insects are all in danger of disappearing forever. The last 700 or 800 mountain gorillas live on the borders of Rwanda, Uganda, and Zaire in Africa. Their rain forest home has been destroyed by farmers and timber firms, and they are also killed for food.

NATURE RESERVES
One of the best ways of protecting wildlife is to preserve an entire habitat in a national park. Zoos also help by breeding rare animals, such as the giant panda.

SAVING THE HELPLESS GIANT

Many species of large whale, such as the humpback whale (below), are threatened with extinction because they have been overhunted for their blubber, meat, oil, and bones. A global conservation body known as the International Whaling Commission (IWC) outlawed the killing of such rare whales in 1985, but not all countries have agreed to stop hunting.

SEE ALSO
Animal, Asia, Dinosaur, Ecology, Energy, Habitat, Pollution, Rain forest, Whale and dolphin, Zoology

CONSTELLATION

Constellations are groups of stars that form recognizable patterns in the night sky. Astronomers have named a total of 88 constellations.

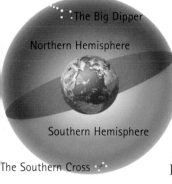

▲ The Northern and Southern hemispheres are domes of sky seen above and below the equator.

Thousands of years ago, people in Asia, Europe, and the Middle East realized that the stars formed patterns in the sky and named them after characters and creatures in their lives and legends. By A.D. 300, the Greek astronomer Ptolemy had named 48 constellations. Many of the names he gave them are still in use, including Taurus (the Bull), Ursa Major (the Great Bear), and Andromeda (a mythical Greek heroine). Today, astronomers use the position of the constellations to map the stars.

THE ZODIAC

If we could see the stars during the day, the Sun would pass in front of 13 constellations over the course of the year. The ancient astronomers counted only 12 constellations and called them the signs of the zodiac—claiming that babies born under each sign would have certain traits.

NEAR AND FAR

Stars in a constellation seem close to each other, but are usually far apart. Orion contains the stars Betelgeuse (300 light years from Earth), Rigel (900 light years away), and Mintaka (2,300 light years away). One light year equals 5.88 trillion miles (9.46 trillion kilometers).

MAPS OF THE STARS

Two maps of the constellations are needed because people who live north of the equator (in the Northern Hemisphere) see different stars from those who live south of the equator (in the Southern Hemisphere). The constellations in the center of each map can usually be seen all year round, while those near the edge can be seen only during particular seasons or at certain times of the night.

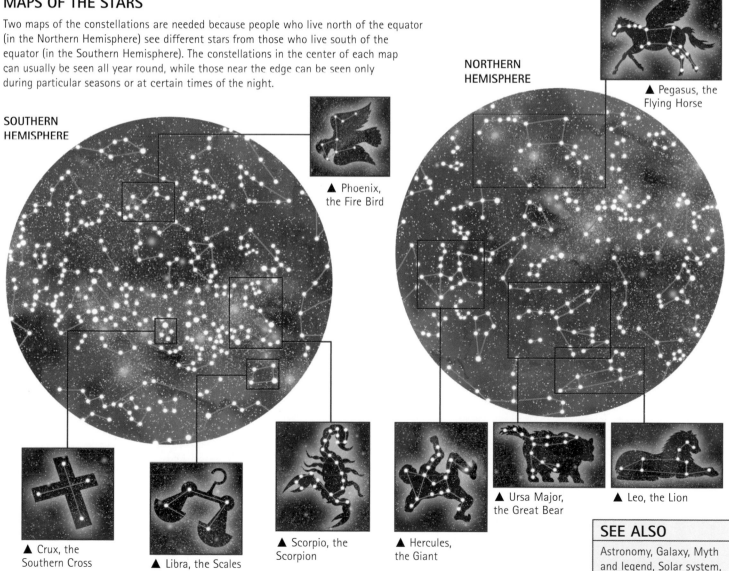

SOUTHERN HEMISPHERE

NORTHERN HEMISPHERE

▲ Pegasus, the Flying Horse

▲ Phoenix, the Fire Bird

▲ Crux, the Southern Cross

▲ Libra, the Scales

▲ Scorpio, the Scorpion

▲ Hercules, the Giant

▲ Ursa Major, the Great Bear

▲ Leo, the Lion

SEE ALSO

Astronomy, Galaxy, Myth and legend, Solar system, Star

97

CONSTRUCTION

Construction is the process of putting something together. This can include houses, skyscrapers, bridges, dams, roads, and even ships.

▲ Construction of the Queensferry Crossing over the Firth of Forth, Scotland. The bridge opened to the public in 2017.

Bricks are still the most popular construction material in house building.

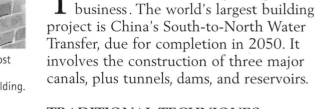

Carpentry is used to make the main frame, doors, and windows in many houses.

The frames of tall buildings and ships used to be fixed with hot nails, or rivets.

The construction industry is big business. The world's largest building project is China's South-to-North Water Transfer, due for completion in 2050. It involves the construction of three major canals, plus tunnels, dams, and reservoirs.

TRADITIONAL TECHNIQUES
In the past, most construction was domestic. Each family built a house, pens for animals, and dams to irrigate their crops. The materials were usually natural and found locally and included wood, clay, stone, bone, skin, or grass. Work was done by hand.

THE DAWN OF CIVILIZATION
As more complex civilizations developed, so did building skills. The first bricks were made in Palestine in 6000 B.C., and the construction of the pyramids in Egypt required thousands of workers, as well as skilled mathematicians. Ancient cranes were used on Roman building sites.

MODERN CONSTRUCTION
The size and height of constructions used to be limited by the skill of the stonemason or carpenter. But from the late 1800s, new techniques using steel frames and molded concrete allowed skyscrapers to be built.

A BUILDING GOES UP
There are two main stages in constructing a building. First, the foundations must be laid below ground to support the structure. Tough materials, concrete (poured in trenches) or steel columns (driven into the ground), are used. The second stage is the construction of the building above ground. Either the walls or a steel frame are constructed first to support floors and other features. Finally, the roof is added.

STEEL-FRAMED CONSTRUCTION

Modern high-rise buildings usually have a steel frame onto which floors and wall panels are bolted. The frame supports the weight of the building so walls can be thin with large windows.

▲ H-shaped, reinforced steel girders are bolted together to form the building's frame.

▲ Metal floor panels are bolted to the frame, then a wire mesh is laid and concrete is poured over it.

A crane, or derrick, is used for lifting building materials into place

Molded concrete wall panels are fixed to the outside of the frame

SEE ALSO
Architecture, Bridge, Dam, Housing, Road, Ship, Skyscraper, Tunnel

CONTINENT

Continents are large stretches of land unbroken by sea. There are seven continents on Earth.

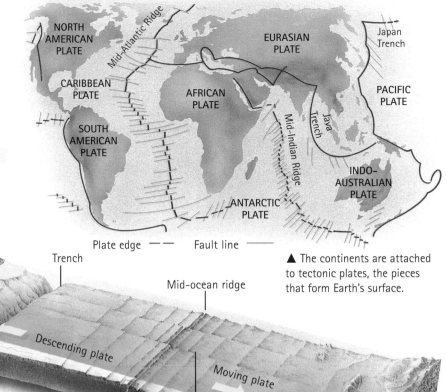

▲ The continents are attached to tectonic plates, the pieces that form Earth's surface.

HOW CONTINENTS DRIFT

All the land on Earth is fixed to giant plates which float on a sea of magma (melted rock). As the magma moves slowly, so do the continents, but some toward each other and others apart. Where two giant plates rub together, a crack sometimes appears in Earth's surface, allowing magma to escape. Two such cracks, known as mid-ocean ridges, run through the Atlantic and Indian oceans.

Continental crust

Volcano

Trench

Descending plate

Mid-ocean ridge

Moving plate

Seabed spreading

Rising magma

Oceanic crust

As it moves, the plate cracks to form fault lines

Earth's crust is like a giant jigsaw puzzle made up of eight large pieces and several small pieces, called tectonic plates. On top of these plates sit seven land masses, or continents: Africa, Antarctica, Asia, Australia, Europe, North America, and South America. They make up 95 percent of Earth's land area; islands form the rest. The largest continent is Asia, with an area of just over 17 million sq. mi. (44 million km²), and the smallest is Australia, covering about 3 million sq. mi. (7.7 million km²).

CONTINENTAL CRUST

The continents are the thickest parts of Earth's outer layer, or crust—in some places reaching down 38–45 mi. (60–70km). At the center, the continents contain the oldest rocks on the planet, with some dating back three billion years. As newer rocks were added around the fringes of these ancient cores, the continents grew.

FLOATING WORLD

The tectonic plates on which the continents sit are floating on a hot, molten layer called magma. Heat from deep inside Earth keeps the magma moving slowly, and as it moves, so do the plates and continents. The slow movement of the continents is called continental drift.

VANISHED LANDS

More than 300 million years ago, all the land on Earth formed just one continent, called Pangaea. Then, about 180 million years ago, it split into two continents, called Gondwanaland and Laurasia. Slowly, North and South America broke away, India joined Asia, and Australia split from Antarctica and moved northward, until today's seven continents were created.

TOMORROW'S CONTINENTS

The movement is still continuing, and the continents we know today will look very different in 50 million years' time. Africa and the Americas, for example, will be even farther away from each other. North and South America will no longer be joined, and Australia will have moved farther northward.

▼ At first there was just one large continent, then two, and finally the seven continents that we know were formed.

180 million years ago

65 million years ago

SEE ALSO

Africa, Antarctica, Asia, Australia, Earth, Europe, North America, Ocean and sea, South America

CRAB AND OTHER CRUSTACEANS

Crabs belong to a group of animals called crustaceans. These creatures have no bones and are covered with a hard shell called an exoskeleton.

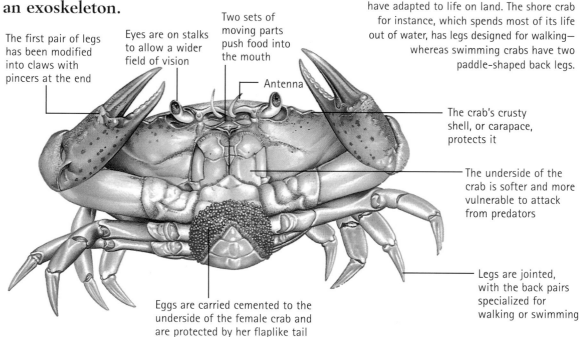

The first pair of legs has been modified into claws with pincers at the end

Eyes are on stalks to allow a wider field of vision

Two sets of moving parts push food into the mouth

Antenna

The crab's crusty shell, or carapace, protects it

The underside of the crab is softer and more vulnerable to attack from predators

Legs are jointed, with the back pairs specialized for walking or swimming

Eggs are carried cemented to the underside of the female crab and are protected by her flaplike tail

The male fiddler crab has a very large claw, which it waves as part of a display to attract the female.

The hermit crab lives in an empty seashell, which it drags around with its two pairs of walking legs.

The lobster has one narrow claw for slicing dead fish and a heavier claw for crushing clams.

The crayfish grows up to 16 in. (40cm) long. It lives in fresh water and has ten legs.

The water flea is one of the smallest crustaceans, growing to 0.008–0.7 in. (0.2–18mm) long.

The woodlouse is the only crustacean that lives entirely on land. It can roll itself up for defense.

LIVING ON THE SHORELINE

Most crabs live in or near the sea, but many have adapted to life on land. The shore crab for instance, which spends most of its life out of water, has legs designed for walking—whereas swimming crabs have two paddle-shaped back legs.

Crustaceans include shrimps, lobsters, woodlice, water fleas, and barnacles. Altogether, there are about 70,000 species of crustaceans. Beneath its hard body shell, a crustacean's body is divided into sections, with jointed legs attached. Crabs, lobsters, and barnacles have especially thick shells, which contain a lot of chalklike material. This makes their shells feel like crusts.

EYES ON STALKS

There are about 7,000 species of crab. The smallest are the tiny pea crabs, which are less than 0.4 in. (1cm) across. The biggest are spider crabs, which live on the seabed and measure up to 13 ft. (4m) across from the tip of one leg to another. Crabs have ten legs, two of which are claws, and their eyes can move up and down on the end of stalks.

CRAB HABITS

Crabs usually live in water or close to the shore. Large crabs feed mainly on dead animals, which they tear up with their claws; small crabs pick up tiny scraps of food from the seabed. Many crabs move sideways on land. The robber crab climbs palm trees to pick young coconuts, which it bores into with its powerful claws.

WITHOUT A SHELL

A crab's body is armored by a shell which molts as the crab grows. The hermit crab, however, does not have a shell and must inhabit empty mollusk shells to protect its soft abdomen. As it grows, it searches for a larger shell to make its home.

HATCHED FROM EGGS

Crabs and other crustaceans reproduce by laying eggs. On hatching, the tiny larvae drift about in water, passing through several body changes before they become adults. In a few species, including the woodlouse, the young hatch out looking like mini-adults.

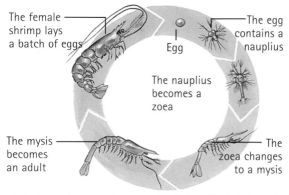

The female shrimp lays a batch of eggs

Egg

The egg contains a nauplius

The nauplius becomes a zoea

The zoea changes to a mysis

The mysis becomes an adult

▲ A shrimp larva must pass through several stages before becoming an adult.

SEE ALSO

Animal, Seashore

CROP

Crops are plants that are grown to provide food for people and animals. They are also grown for useful materials like cotton and linen.

◄ Cotton is a cash crop. It is grown for its fibers, which are spun to make thread or fabric. Its seeds are also crushed to produce oil and fodder.

Wheat grows worldwide, in areas with moist, mild winters and dry summers.

Rice grows best in warm, wet areas such as China, where it is a staple food.

Potatoes came from Peru, but have long been an important crop in Europe.

Sugar beet is grown for its sugar-rich root. Its leaves are used as animal fodder.

Coffee is the major cash crop in tropical regions. It is grown on plantations.

Grapes are grown in vineyards and harvested for wine, raisins, and fresh fruit.

The type of crop grown by farmers depends on the climate of the country, the quality of the soil, and its demand in the market. In developing countries, especially in tropical parts of the world, people grow just enough of a crop for their own needs. These are called subsistence crops. Other people, usually farmers, grow large amounts of crops so that they can be sold. These are called cash crops.

ESSENTIAL CEREALS

The most important food crops are cereals—large grasses grown for their seeds or grains. Cereals include wheat, rice, corn, oats, sorghum, and millet, which cover about three fourths of the world's farmland. Wheat is the most popular cereal, with about 740 million tons grown every year, mainly for people to eat, but also as animal feed. Rice is the main ingredient in the diet of over half the world's people, particularly in Asia.

ROOTS TO FRUIT

Another vital food source is root crops—plants with edible fleshy roots. The potato is an important root crop in Europe and the Americas, and yams and cassavas are staples in many parts of Africa. Cotton and flax are grown for their fibrous flowers, which are used to make cotton and linen. Other major crops include tea and tobacco, which are grown for their leaves, and fruit such as bananas and apples.

WILD ANCESTORS

All crops have come from wild plants, but they have been bred over time to provide bigger and better yields in soils or climates that are not their natural homes. Some crops have changed so much that it is hard to say which wild plants were their ancestors. As field and crop sizes have grown, the use of fertilizers, insecticides, and fungicides has also risen.

HARVESTING THE CROP

Combine harvesters automatically cut, thresh, and clean cereals such as wheat ready for transportation to market. Special attachments can be added to harvest different crops such as soybeans and corn.

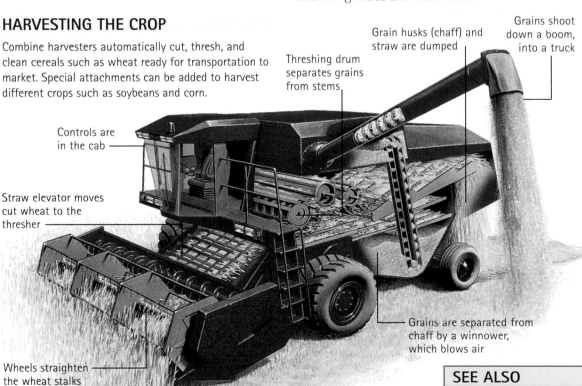

Controls are in the cab

Straw elevator moves cut wheat to the thresher

Wheels straighten the wheat stalks before they reach the cutting wheel

Threshing drum separates grains from stems

Grain husks (chaff) and straw are dumped

Grains shoot down a boom, into a truck

Grains are separated from chaff by a winnower, which blows air

SEE ALSO

Farming, Food, Fruit, Fungi, Genetics, Nutrition, Plant, Vegetable

CRUSADES

The Crusades were a series of religious wars that mostly took place in the Holy Land in the Middle Ages. These were fought between Christians and Muslims.

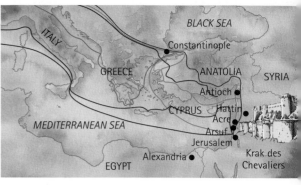

For nearly 200 years, starting in 1096, Christians from Europe marched to Palestine to fight the Muslims for control of the Holy Land, especially of Jerusalem. They carried the Pope's blessing, but many fought for power and wealth.

Nuredin was the Muslim leader who united the Islamic forces that Saladin took into battle at Hattin.

THE BEGINNING
From the 600s, Muslim Arabs ruled the Holy Land, but Christian pilgrims were allowed to visit Jerusalem. Then, in 1071, the Muslim Turks captured Jerusalem and threatened the Christian Byzantine Empire. Pope Urban II called for Christian soldiers to unite and march to the Holy Land to recapture Jerusalem and protect pilgrims.

PILGRIM PEASANTS
The response to the Pope's call was vast. With cries of *Deus Vult!* (meaning "God wills it" in Latin), thousands of people began the long march eastward. The first to set out for the Byzantine capital of Constantinople were bands of poorly armed pilgrim peasants under the leadership of Peter the Hermit and Walter

Sultan Saladin led the united Muslim armies and took Christian strongholds after the Second Crusade.

▲ The Crusaders traveled to the Holy Land by land and sea from all the Christian kingdoms of Europe. They built more than 100 castles and fortresses in the area. One of the best preserved is Krak des Chevaliers in Syria, which withstood 12 sieges before falling to the Muslims in 1271.

— First Crusade (1096–99)
— Second Crusade (1147–49)
— Third Crusade (1188–92)
— Fourth Crusade (1202–4)

the Penniless. Many died on the way, and the rest were killed by the Muslims as soon as they reached Anatolia.

AN ARMY OF KNIGHTS
The First Crusade began in November 1096, when a large army, mostly of French and Norman knights under the leadership of noblemen such as Godfrey de Bouillon, gathered at Constantinople. It defeated the Muslims, capturing the cities of Antioch and Jerusalem, and set up a Christian kingdom along the Palestinian and Syrian coast.

THE BATTLE OF ARSUF
In 1191, King Richard I secured victory over the Muslim leader Saladin at Arsuf, with a charge of armored knights. The charge was led by the Knights Templars and Knights Hospitallers—two military orders of skilled knights who were fanatical enemies of Islam and, like monks, took religious vows.

JERUSALEM IS LOST

Muslim counterattacks started the Second Crusade (1147–49), in which King Louis VII of France and King Conrad II of Germany led separate attacks on Anatolia. These ended in failure for the Christians and weakened their hold on the Holy Land. In 1187, a new Muslim leader, Saladin, led Islamic opposition and wiped out the Crusaders at the Battle of the Horns of Hattin. He then captured Jerusalem and most of the Holy Land.

RICHARD THE LIONHEARTED

The Third Crusade (1189–92) was led by Richard I (Richard the Lionhearted of England), Frederick I of Germany, and Philip II of France. Unfortunately, Frederick drowned on the way, but the Crusaders defeated Saladin and retook much of the Holy Land, except Jerusalem.

LATER CRUSADES

The Fourth Crusade (1202–4) ended in chaos. Its leaders wanted power and riches, and concentrated on Constantinople instead of fighting for the Holy Land. The Christians had little success in the Fifth Crusade (1217–21), but gained Jerusalem by treaty during the Sixth (1222–29). The Seventh Crusade (1248–54) ended with the capture of Louis IX of France, who was freed only after a ransom was paid.

FINAL BATTLE

During the Eighth Crusade (1270–72), the Muslims continued to advance. In 1291, they secured the last of the vital ports of Acre. No more Crusades took place and many of the knights retired to the island of Cyprus.

In 1212, thousands of children went on a children's crusade to the Holy Land. They did not reach their destination and many of them died or were sold as slaves.

King Richard I of England led the Third Crusade and was given the nickname "Richard the Lionhearted."

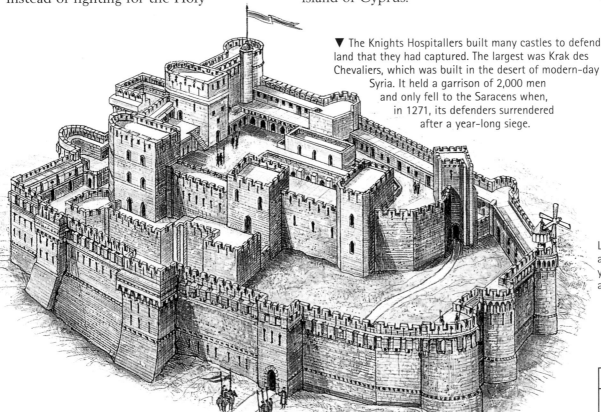

▼ The Knights Hospitallers built many castles to defend land that they had captured. The largest was Krak des Chevaliers, which was built in the desert of modern-day Syria. It held a garrison of 2,000 men and only fell to the Saracens when, in 1271, its defenders surrendered after a year-long siege.

Louis IX ruled the coast around Acre, Syria, for four years between the Seventh and Eighth Crusades.

SEE ALSO

Castle, Christianity, Empire, Islam, Middle Ages, Middle East, Warfare

CUSTOM

Customs are the traditions, rituals, and ways of behaving in a society that are passed on from generation to generation and are sometimes turned into laws.

Some Portuguese fishermen paint eyes on their boats to watch over them at sea and bring them back safely.

The *haka*, performed by New Zealand rugby teams before a match, is based on a Maori war dance.

The custom of carving pumpkin faces comes from the Celtic Day of the Dead, celebrated on October 31.

The *chanoyu*, a Japanese tea ceremony which can last for four hours, came originally from China.

The painting of eggs is a symbol of new life which has been adopted by Christians at Easter.

DANCING DRAGON

During the Chinese New Year festival, dancers inside a dragon costume move through the streets while firecrackers are set off. The dragon is believed to bring rain for a successful crop, and so has become a symbol of good fortune for the coming year. The firecrackers are to frighten away evil spirits.

Every society has its own customs, waiting politely in line, for example, or wearing a particular costume during a celebration. Learning about different customs helps us to understand people from other countries or cultures.

RITES OF PASSAGE

Across the world, customs are different, but there are times of life, known as rites of passage, when a person's status changes. Such times include birth, coming of age, marriage, and death—occasions that are marked by elaborate customs in every society. The custom of keeping mother and baby secluded from society for a month after birth is a common custom in many countries, probably based on fear of infection. There are also many customs marking a young person's move from childhood to adulthood, ranging from throwing a party to a religious ritual.

LINKS WITH THE PAST

Customs may be adapted over time, often as a result of industrialization or contact with other cultures. A custom's original meaning may be forgotten, or it may continue as a way of keeping a link with the past. The special Thanksgiving meal, for example, is usually celebrated with the whole family and commemorates the survival of Pilgrim families long ago.

CUSTOMARY GREETINGS

Everyday customs help people to bond with other members of their society. For instance, every culture has a customary way of greeting—Europeans kiss or shake hands, the Inuit rub noses, and the Chinese bow. By taking part in customs, people demonstrate their membership of a group or society.

GOING AGAINST THE GRAIN

Refusing to follow a custom can offend; it may even lead to the exclusion of an individual from a group of society. Customs are not laws, but because they are designed to help us understand what is acceptable behavior in a society, customs are often included in laws or religious codes.

▲ In Hindu weddings, everything is brightly colored, and the bride usually wears a red sari with lots of gold jewelry.

SEE ALSO
Clothing, Dance, Food, Judaism

DAM

A dam is a barrier built across a river or stream to hold back water. The stored water may be used for irrigation, as drinking water, or to provide power.

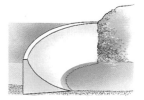

Arch dams, used in tall, narrow canyons or gorges, are often surprisingly thin.

Concrete gravity dams are built to hold back water in broad, shallow valleys.

Embankment dams have a reinforced inner wall to hold back shallow lakes.

The earliest dams were built in the Middle East about 5,000 years ago. These dams were used to direct water to fields of crops, through canals called irrigation channels. A dam built on the Orontes River in Syria about 1300 B.C. still irrigates fields near the city of Homs.

CONTROLLING THE FLOW

Today, dams are still built for irrigation, as well as to stop flooding and to provide water power for electricity. In low-lying areas of China, Bangladesh, and the United States, dams have been built to stop flood disasters. Other dams are built so that water can be stored in artificial lakes, or reservoirs. The water is then supplied to homes and industry.

HYDROELECTRIC DAM

Hydroelectric dams use water power to produce electricity. They require large quantities of water and a very long drop from the top to the bottom of the dam. About 6.6 percent of the world's electricity is generated by hydroelectric dams.

EMBANKMENT DAMS

The simplest dams are embankment dams. They are made from earth and rock and have a waterproof core to stop water from seeping through. The Aswan High Dam in Egypt controls the annual flooding of the Nile River and provides hydroelectric power for the whole country.

GRAVITY AND ARCH

Gravity dams are made of stone or concrete. They rely on their weight and strength to hold back the water. Arch dams are curved so that the weight of the water is pushed out from the dam to the canyon or gorge. They can be very thin—for example, the Vaiont Dam in the Italian Alps is 870 ft. (265m) high but only 75.5 ft. (23m) thick at its base.

ENVIRONMENTAL IMPACT

Dam building affects the surrounding environment, and wildlife can be destroyed. Some dams have fish ladders, which enable fish such as salmon to make their journey upstream to breed.

FAST FACTS

• The Itaipu Dam on the border of Paraguay and Brazil produces more electricity each year than any other dam

• At 548 ft. (167m), the Grand Coulee Dam, in the state of Washington, is 65 ft. (20m) taller than the Great Pyramid in Egypt

• Dams were so important in ancient Mesopotamia that King Hammurabi's laws said that anyone who broke a dam should be sold into slavery to pay the farmer

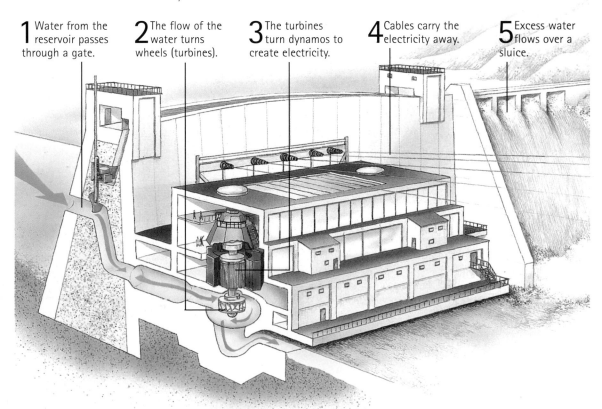

1 Water from the reservoir passes through a gate.

2 The flow of the water turns wheels (turbines).

3 The turbines turn dynamos to create electricity.

4 Cables carry the electricity away.

5 Excess water flows over a sluice.

SEE ALSO

Construction, Egypt, Waterpower

DANCE

Dance is one of the oldest art forms. It is the rhythmic movement of all or part of the body and includes ballet, the waltz, flamenco, tap, rumba, and disco.

Dancing can express emotion, tell a story, create a specific atmosphere, or show off physical strength. There are three main types of dance: social dancing for enjoyment; dance created to entertain an audience; and religious or ritual dance.

DANCING THROUGH HISTORY

People have been dancing for thousands of years—dancing figures appear in cave paintings in Europe and Africa dating back to prehistoric times. Many of the earliest dances that are still popular today were connected with religious ceremonies or superstitious beliefs. English morris dancing is based on ancient war rituals, and voodoo dancers in Haiti go into a trance in which they attempt to summon the spirits. The expressive dance drama of the ancient Greeks has had a long-lasting influence in the West.

GETTING TOGETHER

Formal social dances, where set steps are followed, go back many centuries. Bugaku dancing in Japan originated in the A.D. 600s. In medieval Europe, grand social dances were popular at court. Most were adapted from the simple country dances of ordinary people. As early as the 1400s, there were dance teachers who taught the steps to the latest dances.

CLASSIC BEAUTY

Ballet originated in the royal courts of Italy during the 1400s, but was developed in France. King Louis XIV was an enthusiastic dancer and opened the first European dance academy in Paris in 1661. Until then, most dancers had been amateur, but professional dancers soon began to appear. The academy's director, Charles-Louis Beauchamp, helped standardize the classic movements. He is thought to have set out the five basic ballet positions of the feet and arms. By the mid-1800s, romantic ballets such as *La Sylphide* were popular in Europe.

▲ Contemporary dance is less structured than ballet and does not always tell a story. It often uses choreography (arrangement) of the dancers' bodies to form striking poses.

▼ Ballet tells a story, whether it is a classical tale such as *Swan Lake* or a favorite children's story like *Alice in Wonderland*. Here, Alice (far left) meets the March Hare, Mad Hatter and Dormouse during her journey through Wonderland.

◄ Ice-skating competitions feature ice dancing in their freestyle section. Couples are not allowed to lift one another, but often imitate traditional ballroom dance routines using daring athletic poses.

▶ Music and dance are important in the cultures of many tribal countries, such as Zimbabwe, Africa. Here, a Shangaan dancer, in an elaborate costume with wings, mask, and grass skirt, performs a tribal dance.

▲ Dancing to repetitive music with a powerful underlying beat, often in strobe lighting, swept clubs in the 1990s.

BREAKING AWAY

The second half of the 1800s was the era of classical Russian ballet, with great masterpieces such as Tchaikovsky's *Swan Lake*. But by the early 1900s, some dancers were beginning to create a freer style, breaking away from the rigid patterns and training of classical ballet. The American dancer Isadora Duncan was a big influence on contemporary dance. She performed barefoot, basing her moves on ideas inspired by ancient Greece.

TAKE YOUR PARTNERS

As time went by, trends in social dances changed along with styles of music. In the 1800s, the waltz caused a scandal because the man and woman dancing held each other so close. Exciting new dances in the 1900s were based partly on African-American and Irish traditions, like jazz and tap. In the 1920s, while dramatic Russian ballets toured Europe, ordinary people in the United States were dancing the high-kicking Charleston.

DANCE FADS

Jitterbugging to the music of the big bands became popular in the 1930s and 1940s, developing into the sensational rock'n'roll jive of the 1940s and 1950s. The twist was popular in the 1960s, and the latter part of the last century was marked by disco, break dancing, and free expression.

▶ In the popular Japanese theater of Kabuki, an all-male cast performs comic dance, drama, and singing shows, often in female dress. To give a visual climax, each scene ends with a pose called the *mie*.

SEE ALSO

Africa, Custom, Music, Theater

DEMOCRACY

Democracy is a form of government in which the people take part in ruling the state. The people may rule directly or through elected officials.

◀ Two metal voting disks were given to each man in ancient Athens. They were used in criminal trials to vote guilty or not guilty.

People who live in a democracy either vote for officials who make laws for them, or they vote directly on laws in a meeting known as an assembly. Democracy allows people freedom of speech and the right to choose between competing political parties in regularly held elections.

◀ In some elections, a person votes by making a mark next to the candidate's name on a ballot paper. The papers (votes) are posted in a sealed ballot box, to be counted later.

POWER TO THE PEOPLE
The first democracy appeared in ancient Greece in the 500s B.C., when men in cities could vote in assemblies. The word democracy is Greek for "rule by the people."

ELECTION VICTORY

India is the world's largest democracy, and election time plays an important part in the lives of the people. Candidates make speeches, distribute leaflets, advertise, and design posters to persuade people to vote for them. Most candidates belong to a political party whose members share the same ideas about how the country should be run.

ELECTED ASSEMBLIES
The reign of Alexander the Great and a succession of Roman emperors gradually put an end to democracy, and the Middle Ages saw the rise of feudalism and monarchy. Democracy reappeared in the 1600s, when elected assemblies began to take power in some countries. At first only wealthy men could vote, but today nearly every adult in a democracy is allowed to vote.

MAJORITY RULE
Voters choose people to represent them in legislatures (law-making bodies), such as the U.S. Senate or the House of Representatives. For a law to be passed, a majority in the legislature must vote for it. On important issues, there may be a vote of all the people, called a referendum.

CHOOSING REPRESENTATIVES
Some elections are decided by a system in which the candidate with the most votes wins. Others are decided by proportional representation—each party gets candidates in parliament in relation to the number of votes it receives.

GOVERNMENTS AND THE LAW
There are many kinds of democracy. In Britain, there is a monarchy, but an elected parliament makes laws. France is a republic with a president and prime minister, as well as a legislature. In recent years, democracy has come under threat from authoritarian leaders in certain countries.

SEE ALSO

Civil rights, Government, Greece (ancient), Law, Politics

DESERT

Deserts are dry areas of land which receive very little rainfall and support few plants or animals. They may be sandy or rocky, and be very hot or very cold.

▲ Deserts are not always hot. Some places in Antarctica and Greenland are known as polar deserts because the ground there is so dry. For example, on the western side of Antarctica, there are areas that receive less than 5 in. (13cm) of snow each year.

More than a fifth of the world's land is so dry that it is known as desert. Most deserts receive less than 10 in. (250mm) of rain each year. Others receive more rain, but it quickly evaporates in the strong heat and winds or sinks into the parched ground. The driest place in the world is Chile's Atacama Desert, parts of which have less than 0.004 in. (0.1mm) of rain each year.

WHERE DESERTS FORM

Most deserts, such as the Kalahari and Sahara in Africa, lie between the Tropic of Cancer and the Tropic of Capricorn (25° to the north and south of the equator). These are the tropics, where the air is often too hot and dry for rain clouds to form. The cold Gobi Desert in central Asia exists, however, because it is far from the sea's moist winds. Other deserts occur because the winds that sweep across them lost all their moisture passing over neighboring mountainous regions.

SURVIVAL TACTICS

Desert plants and animals have developed ways of coping with the lack of water. Plants usually have long, spreading roots to reach any available moisture. Most have spines or small leaves that are rolled or waxy to cut down on water loss through evaporation. Other plants spend most of their lives as seeds—only growing when rain falls. Desert animals often hide during the heat of the day and come out at night. Camels can go for many days without water.

POCKETS OF WATER

Oases are pockets of fertile land in a desert. These occur where an aquifer, or underground stream, comes to the surface. Plants such as palm trees thrive, and animals and people gather there.

CREEPING DESERTS

Deserts can spread. This may happen because the climate becomes drier or nearby land is overgrazed by farm animals.

IN THE SHADOW OF THE SIERRA NEVADA

The deserts of North America are shielded from rain by the towering mountain wall of the Sierra Nevada. In some areas, less than 4 in. (100mm) of rain falls, making the gravelly ground inhospitable except to a few plants and animals. Temperatures during the day can reach 212°F (100°C), but at night it is often near freezing because there is no cloud cover.

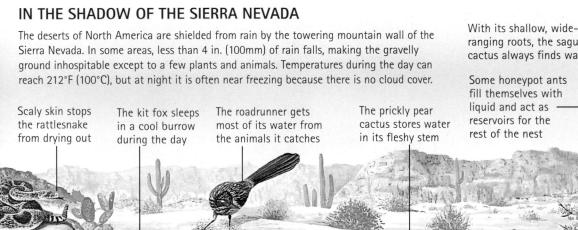

Scaly skin stops the rattlesnake from drying out

The kit fox sleeps in a cool burrow during the day

The roadrunner gets most of its water from the animals it catches

The prickly pear cactus stores water in its fleshy stem

With its shallow, wide-ranging roots, the saguaro cactus always finds water

Some honeypot ants fill themselves with liquid and act as reservoirs for the rest of the nest

SEE ALSO

Africa, Antarctica, Climate, Habitat, Plant, South America

DESIGN

Everything we use today, from a toothbrush to a car, has been designed according to its function, trends in fashion and art, and the latest available materials.

◄ Fashion designers sketch their ideas first. They show the outfits from different angles and in a variety of colors, adding swatches of fabric.

Professional designers must create an object that does the job it is supposed to do as efficiently as possible. But they must also think carefully about the aesthetic value, or appearance, of the object, how and where it will be used, who will be using it, and changing trends in technology and materials.

Even household appliances, such as the kettle, are always being redesigned.

AGE OF DESIGN
The word 'design' comes from the Italian word *designare*. From the 1300s to the mid-1500s, during the great Italian artistic era called the Renaissance, the word was used to describe the basic idea behind a work of art, as well as rough sketches of it. Today, the term covers a huge area, from detailed drawings and engineering plans for buildings to the graphic design of books, magazines, and product containers.

Scottish designer and architect Charles Rennie Mackintosh designed all his chairs with unusually high backs.

SKETCHING IT OUT
The first step for many designers, whether painters, architects, film set designers, or fashion designers, is to sketch out their ideas, or create storyboards on paper. If it is a building or product, they may then make up a small model to scale. Fashion designers often make up a sample garment, using inexpensive cloth.

DESIGNING ON COMPUTERS
Computers are now used extensively in design, especially for industry. They allow people to experiment with three-dimensional, often animated, models on the screen. Using CAD (computer-aided design), a designer can quickly change a detail and the computer will calculate and apply the changes to the rest of the design. Specialist programs help experts create cars, shoes, and electrical goods.

THE CREATIVE PROCESS
Computers can be used to highlight stress points, illustrate aerodynamics, and show other crucial design features of a prototype car. Newspapers and magazines are designed on computers and sent digitally to the printer, as was this book.

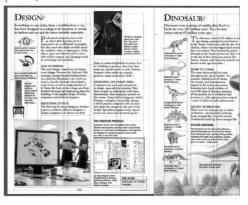

▲ Desktop-publishing software has revolutionized page design—changes can now be made in seconds.

SEE ALSO
Architecture, Art, Clothing, Computer

DINOSAUR

Dinosaurs were a type of reptile that lived on Earth for over 160 million years. They became extinct about 65 million years ago.

Tyrannosaurus rex was a theropod, or "beast-footed" dinosaur.

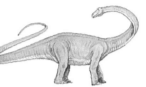

Diplodocus was a sauropod, or "lizard-footed" dinosaur.

Camptosaurus was an ornithopod, or "bird-footed" dinosaur.

Stegosaurus was a stegosaur, or "roofed" dinosaur.

Sauropelta was an ankylosaur, or "jointed" dinosaur.

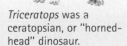

Triceratops was a ceratopsian, or "horned-head" dinosaur.

The dinosaurs evolved 225 million years ago during a geological period known as the Triassic. Some were only the size of a chicken, others were the largest land animals that ever existed. They roamed the planet throughout the Jurassic period and died out at the end of the Cretaceous period. The Triassic, Jurassic, and Cretaceous periods are known as the "age of reptiles."

MORE TO COME

The same dinosaurs did not exist throughout the age of reptiles. For example, *Diplodocus* lived during the Jurassic and *Tyrannosaurus* reigned in the Cretaceous period. Scientists have found evidence of over 900 species of dinosaur, spanning all the periods, but it is believed that many more existed and are still to be discovered.

LIZARD OR BIRDLIKE

There were two main groups, or orders, of dinosaur—the Saurischia (with hipbones arranged like a lizard's) and the Ornithischia (with hipbones arranged like

KILLING MACHINE

The theropods were the meat-eating dinosaurs, which all had large jaws full of teeth for tearing flesh. *Deinonychus* was a terrifying killing machine equipped with deadly tools, including a slashing claw on the second toe of its back foot which gave it its name—"terrible claw."

a bird's). The Saurischia can be divided into two smaller groups known as the theropods and the sauropods. The Ornithischia include four groups: the ornithopods, the stegosaurs, the ankylosaurs, and the ceratopsians.

MEAT-EATERS

The theropods were meat-eaters. They had long mouths full of teeth for tearing flesh, they walked on their hind legs, and had small bodies which they balanced with long, heavy tails. Some, such as *Compsognathus*, were chicken-size, while the biggest were 39.4 ft. (12m)-long killers, such as *Tyrannosaurus*. ▶

Sharp teeth were used to tear flesh

Each toe and finger had a razor-sharp claw

The second toe of its back foot had a "terrible claw"

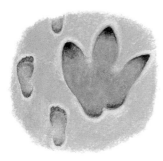

DINOSAUR GIANTS

Sauropods were plant-eaters. They had large, heavy bodies and moved around on all fours, using their long necks to reach leaves on trees. They were the largest land animals that ever lived and included *Diplodocus* and *Brachiosaurus*.

PLANT-EATERS

The Ornithischia dinosaurs were also all plant-eaters. The only ones that could walk on their hind legs were the ornithopods. They had a more sophisticated chewing system than the long-necked sauropods, with cheeks for holding the food while they chewed it. *Iguanodon* is probably the most famous of the ornithopods.

▲ A comparison between the size of mighty *Tyrannosaurus*'s feet and those of an average man.

▼ This fossil skeleton of *Tuojiangosaurus* was discovered in China in the 1970s. *Tuojiangosaurus* was a stegosaur that lived in the late Jurassic period, about 150 million years ago.

▲ In 1978, a fossilized nest of 15 young *Maiasaura* was found in Montana. Evidence showed that the young were very small and would have had to be cared for by the mother to survive. *Maiasaura* means "good mother lizard."

BONY ARMOR

Three ornithischian groups evolved from the ornithopods (bird-footed dinosaurs). They all had armor of some kind that made them heavy, so they walked on four legs. The first was the stegosaurs—the "roofed" dinosaurs. They had large bodies and either a double row of bony plates down the back like *Stegosaurus*, or an arrangement of spines like *Kentrosaurus*.

Archaeopteryx—one of the first birds

A SCENE FROM THE LATE JURASSIC

The late Jurassic is the period from 157 to 145 million years ago. It is known for its many plant-eating dinosaur species, such as spiny *Stegosaurus* and long-necked sauropods, including *Apatosaurus*. The main dinosaur predator was the meat-eating *Allosaurus*, but the reptile *Diplosaurus*, an ancestor of the crocodile, was also frightening.

A SCENE FROM THE LATE CRETACEOUS

The Late Cretaceous was a period from 95 to 65 million years ago. It was dominated by herds of duckbilled *Edmontosauruses*, which had replaced the sauropods as the main plant-eaters. Meat-eating *Tyrannosaurus* probably hunted these animals, because other plant-eaters like *Triceratops* and *Ankylosaurus* had developed spectacular defensive armor. Large flying reptiles may have scavenged like vultures on the bodies of dead dinosaurs.

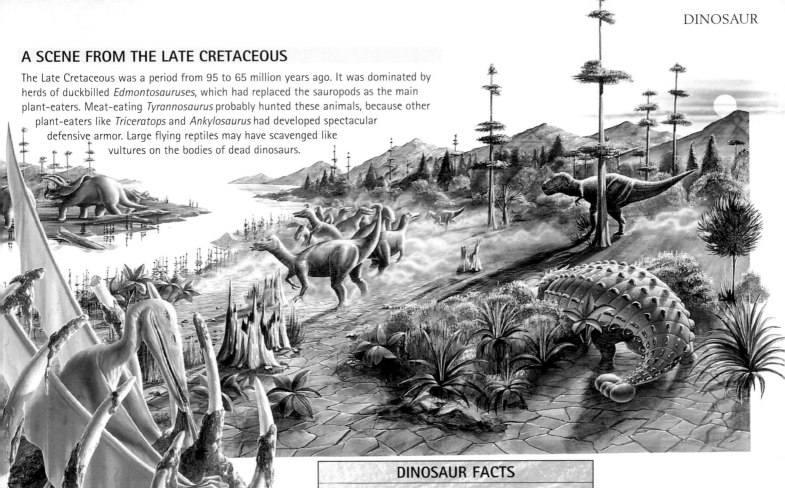

JOINTED DINOSAURS

The second ornithischian group was the ankylosaurs, or "jointed" dinosaurs. They had bony armor that lay flat over their broad backs, and were also armed with spikes along the sides, as in *Edmontonia*, or a tail with a club, as in *Euoplocephalus*.

HORNED HEADS

The last ornithiscian group was the ceratopsians. They had armor on their faces and heads, where it formed big bony frills around the neck. These "horned-head" dinosaurs included *Triceratops*, which had a small horn on the nose and two long horns over the eyes, and *Styracosaurus*, which had an enormous horn on the nose and a series of smaller horns around the frill.

REPTILE NEIGHBORS

Dinosaurs were not the only reptiles that lived at the time. Many groups of swimming reptiles, such as the fish-shaped ichthyosaurs and the long-necked plesiosaurs, lived in the sea; pterosaurs flew in the air.

DINOSAUR FACTS

- The smaller meat-eating dinosaurs hunted in packs like wolves, preying on young or weak plant-eaters

- Large plant-eating dinosaurs like *Diplodocus* must have had to eat continuously to avoid starvation

- Dinosaurs may have been warm-blooded like mammals and birds

- Many different types of insect and mammal also lived during the time of the dinosaurs

- The dinosaurs' legs were not at the side like reptiles', but under their bodies like mammals'

DEATH OF THE REPTILES

All of these unusual reptiles became extinct along with the dinosaurs at the end of the Cretaceous period. No one knows for sure how this happened, or why other reptiles, such as crocodiles and turtles, survived. It may have been a gradual process, due to a slow climatic change, or there may have been a sudden catastrophc, such as the Earth's being hit by a gigantic meteorite. The dinosaurs did leave some relatives, however. During the Jurassic period, birds evolved from the small meat-eating theropods, which means today's birds are the direct descendants of the dinosaurs.

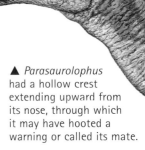

Male

Female

▲ *Parasaurolophus* had a hollow crest extending upward from its nose, through which it may have hooted a warning or called its mate.

SEE ALSO

Evolution, Fossil, Mammal, Prehistoric animal, Reptile

DISEASE

A disease is an illness that disturbs the normal healthy functioning of a plant, animal, or person. Each disease produces symptoms (physical changes).

▲ Many diseases have almost been wiped out by the widespread use of inoculation (also called immunization and vaccination). This is when a milder form of the disease is introduced into the body, by injection or via the mouth, so that the person develops long-term resistance to the disease.

The human body may be attacked by thousands of diseases. These range from relatively harmless ones, such as the common cold and athlete's foot, to life-threatening diseases, such as typhoid and some cancers. Plants and animals also suffer from diseases—potatoes suffer from blight, and cats can get the flu (influenza).

BACTERIA AND VIRUSES
Flu, AIDS, and tetanus are all infectious diseases. They are caused by harmful microscopic organisms we call germs that invade the body and multiply. Tetanus is caused by bacteria (living creatures); flu and AIDS are caused by viruses (bundles of DNA wrapped in protein). Infectious diseases are spread from person to person by, for example, breathing in germs. A sudden outbreak of an infectious disease which affects many people is called an epidemic. Some infectious diseases can

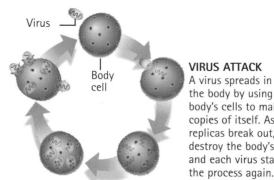

VIRUS ATTACK
A virus spreads in the body by using the body's cells to make copies of itself. As the replicas break out, they destroy the body's cell, and each virus starts the process again.

be prevented with vaccinations, and others can be treated with medicines such as antibiotics.

NONINFECTIOUS DISEASES
Many diseases are not caused by germs, but are the result of a poor diet. An example of this is scurvy, which is the result of not eating enough vitamin C. Others may be caused by an unhealthy lifestyle. For example, smoking and stress can lead to heart disease. Some diseases, such as hemophilia, run in families as a result of faulty genes.

LOOKING FOR CLUES
Symptoms such as pain or fever tell the person suffering from a disease that something is wrong, and give clues to doctors as to the cause. A doctor can also detect signs of disease by taking X rays or blood tests.

AFRICAN SLEEPING SICKNESS

In some areas of Africa, the tsetse fly spreads a disease called sleeping sickness. When it feeds on human blood, this tiny fly injects some of its saliva into the person's bloodstream. If its saliva contains microorganisms called *Trypanosoma brucei*, these enter the bloodstream also, and multiply inside the body, causing fever, headaches, and sleepiness. The person may die if not treated quickly.

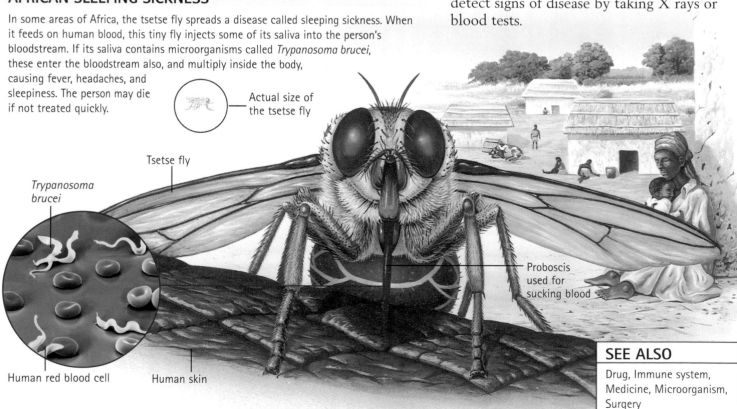

Actual size of the tsetse fly

Tsetse fly

Trypanosoma brucei

Proboscis used for sucking blood

Human red blood cell

Human skin

SEE ALSO

Drug, Immune system, Medicine, Microorganism, Surgery

DOG

The domestic dog (*Canis familiaris*) belongs to the dog family, known as Canidae, and is believed to be descended from the gray wolf.

The chihuahua is the world's smallest dog: 10 in. (15cm) to the shoulder.

The poodle is an intelligent dog. There are three types: toy, miniature, and standard.

The greyhound, bred for speed, can reach 35 mph (57kph).

The bulldog was originally bred for the "sport" of bull-baiting in the Middle Ages.

The husky is a powerful sledge dog, able to pull twice its own weight.

The Airedale is the largest breed of terrier, probably bred for hunting otters.

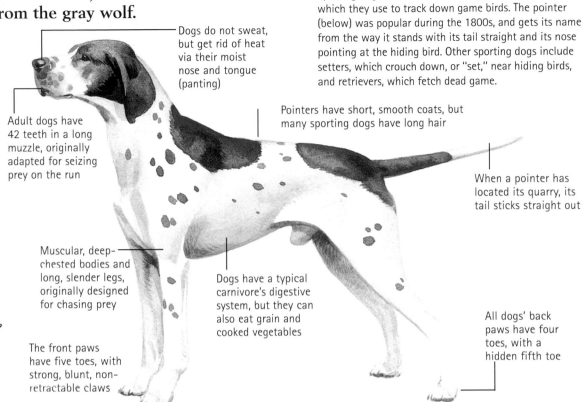

Dogs do not sweat, but get rid of heat via their moist nose and tongue (panting)

Adult dogs have 42 teeth in a long muzzle, originally adapted for seizing prey on the run

Muscular, deep-chested bodies and long, slender legs, originally designed for chasing prey

The front paws have five toes, with strong, blunt, non-retractable claws

Dogs have a typical carnivore's digestive system, but they can also eat grain and cooked vegetables

SPORTING DOGS

Sporting dogs are bred for their acute sense of smell, which they use to track down game birds. The pointer (below) was popular during the 1800s, and gets its name from the way it stands with its tail straight and its nose pointing at the hiding bird. Other sporting dogs include setters, which crouch down, or "set," near hiding birds, and retrievers, which fetch dead game.

Pointers have short, smooth coats, but many sporting dogs have long hair

When a pointer has located its quarry, its tail sticks straight out

All dogs' back paws have four toes, with a hidden fifth toe

Dogs were the first animals to be tamed. Fossil remains of a domestic dog dating back 10,500 years have been found in Idaho. The relationship between human and dog probably began because dogs are natural scavengers, and hung around camps looking for food scraps.

BREEDS AND GROUPS

Since then, humans have selectively bred dogs—the American Kennel Club (AKC) recognizes 190 breeds of dog, and Great Britain's Kennel Club includes 220. These breeds are divided into seven groups by appearance, use, and size: hounds, working dogs, gundogs, terriers, utility dogs, pastoral dogs, and toy dogs. The dog's most acute senses—smell and hearing—were selectively bred early on for guarding and hunting. Other physical features were bred for specific uses. For example, the dachshund's short legs were selected for going down badger sets, and the bulldog's set-back nose was selected to help it breathe while biting. Nowadays, a gentle, nonaggressive nature is selected for pets.

A DOG'S LIFE

Most domestic dogs are fully grown by the age of 2, are old by the age of 12, and rarely live past 20. Female dogs can become pregnant from about seven months, and give birth to an average of three to six puppies, although some breeds may have up to ten puppies. The puppies open their eyes on the tenth day and are ready to leave their mother at six weeks. Dogs are pack animals and follow a leader. This loyalty can be transferred to a human, especially if the dog is trained while young.

▲ The border collie uses the hunting instincts of its wild ancestors to round up sheep.

SEE ALSO
Hearing, Wolf

DRUG

Drugs are substances that affect the way in which the body or mind works. Most drugs are used medicinally, to cure or prevent an illness.

Medicinal liquids called syrups make swallowing drugs easy for children.

Pills or capsules are the most common form of a drug.

A drug is injected into the blood when a quick response is needed.

Eyedrops and inhalers act fast by sending the drug to the exact spot.

Creams and gels often contain drugs which disinfect a cut or graze.

Skin patches release drugs slowly through the skin into the blood.

Cigarettes are made from tobacco leaves, which contain the drug nicotine.

Over 4,000 years ago, a mythical ruler of ancient China, called Shennong, is said to have put together a book of more than 300 medicinal plants, many of which are still used in medicine today. But it was not until the 1700s, when the English doctor William Withering studied the heart drug digitalis (extracted from foxgloves), that drugs were looked at scientifically. The modern drug industry began in 1899, when the German company Bayer manufactured the painkiller aspirin.

WHICH TYPE OF DRUG?

Doctors use many types of drugs to treat patients. For example, antibiotics such as penicillin kill the bacteria that cause infections. Analgesics (painkillers), such as aspirin and codeine, stop pain messages from reaching the brain. Sedatives have a calming effect and can help a person sleep. Anesthetics deaden the body's nerves and are used in operations. Vaccines help the immune system fight diseases, and insulin is given to people when their body fails to make enough of it naturally.

▶ The foxglove is listed in the oldest surviving book on drugs and their uses, written between A.D. 20 and A.D. 70 by the ancient Greek doctor Dioscorides.

DANGERS AND ADDICTION

Some drugs, such as heroin or cocaine, are addictive, which means people cannot stop taking them. They are illegal because they are so dangerous. Even medicinal drugs or everyday drugs, such as alcohol, caffeine in tea and coffee, or nicotine in cigarettes, can be harmful if taken in large amounts.

TIMED-RELEASE CAPSULES

Drugs sometimes need to be released into the bloodstream slowly over a few hours, especially if they are painkillers. Timed-release capsules contain hundreds of tiny pellets with coatings of different thicknesses. Some of the pellets release the drug in the stomach; others release it later in the intestines.

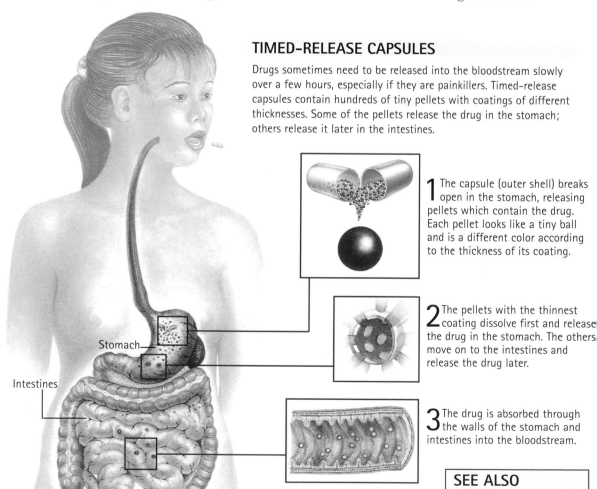

Stomach

Intestines

1 The capsule (outer shell) breaks open in the stomach, releasing pellets which contain the drug. Each pellet looks like a tiny ball and is a different color according to the thickness of its coating.

2 The pellets with the thinnest coating dissolve first and release the drug in the stomach. The others move on to the intestines and release the drug later.

3 The drug is absorbed through the walls of the stomach and intestines into the bloodstream.

SEE ALSO

Medicine, Plant

EAGLE AND OTHER BIRDS OF PREY

Eagles and other birds of prey survive by hunting animals. They swoop down on their prey from the air, grabbing them with their sharp talons.

► Unlike hawks and eagles, owls, like this little owl, hunt their prey at night.

The Andean condor is the largest bird of prey. It can weigh 26.5 lb. (12kg).

A diving peregrine falcon can reach speeds of over 155 mph (250kph).

Northern goshawks can strike in midair, often attacking from below.

Vultures, such as this black vulture, feed on the bodies of dead animals.

Golden eagles carry prey equal to their own weight in their powerful talons.

Birds of prey are born hunters. They have sharp eyesight to spot far-off prey, sharp, curved talons to catch their food, and strong, hooked beaks to tear at flesh. Most have large, broad wings with flight feathers that spread out when they soar in updrafts. As well as eagles, birds of prey include buzzards, falcons, hawks, kites, ospreys, and vultures. Owls are also often included, but belong to a different bird group.

HUNTING SKILLS
Most birds of prey soar high into the air and then swoop down on their prey on the ground at high speed. Some, such as the peregrine falcon, can also attack birds in midair. The kestrel is unusual because it hovers just a few yards above the ground before swooping. Vultures usually scavenge dead meat.

DIFFERENT TASTES
There are more than 60 species of eagle scattered throughout the world, although many are endangered. Most live in wild, remote places where humans cannot disturb them. Eagles eat a wide range of animals. The golden eagle attacks hares, small rodents, and other birds; the serpent eagle gorges on snakes. Some are experts at snaring fish, and the harpy eagle catches monkeys.

FISH FOR DINNER
The bald eagle, the national bird of the United States, is one of the most endangered birds of prey. It feeds on birds and small animals, but particularly likes fish. It scoops them from the surface of the water and flies off, gripping them in its powerful, sharp talons.

NEST RECYCLING
Many eagles use the same nest, or aerie, again and again, adding more material each time they breed. Their nests can become enormous—a bald eagle's can measure 10 ft. (3m) across and weigh over a ton. Most eagles lay just two eggs. Once the young have hatched, they do not leave the nest for up to two months.

SEE ALSO

Bird

EARTH

Our planet, Earth, is one of the eight planets that move around the Sun. It is made up of rocks and metals, and is the only planet known to support life.

Planet Earth is an almost perfectly round ball of rock, with a metal core, which travels around the Sun. It is surrounded by a blanket of gases called the atmosphere, has one moon, and, as far as we know, is the only planet that supports life.

NIGHT AND DAY

Approximately every 24 hours, Earth does a full circle on its axis—an imaginary line joining the North and South poles. As it spins, one side turns to face the Sun and is in daylight, while the other side turns away, experiencing night. Earth spins eastward, which is why the Sun seems to rise in the east and set in the west.

Magnetic fields
North magnetic pole
South magnetic pole

▲ As Earth spins, electrical currents beneath the surface turn the planet into a huge magnet, with a north and south pole just like any ordinary magnet.

AROUND THE SUN

As well as spinning on its own axis, Earth is constantly moving around the Sun. One complete path around the Sun is an orbit. The length of a year is determined by the time it takes a planet to make one orbit. This means that Earth travels 595 million miles (958 million km), at an average speed of 19 mi./sec. (30km/sec).

CHANGING SEASONS

Earth is tilted toward the Sun at an angle of 23.5°. As Earth orbits, those places that are tilted toward the Sun receive more warmth and light for the part of the year that is known as summer. As these places move farther around, they tilt away from the Sun, experiencing winter.

CORE TO CRUST

Beneath its thin shell, or crust, the interior of Earth is very hot. Below about 45 mi. (70km), there is a mantle of rock that is semimolten (partly melted). The outer layer of Earth's core is molten, too, but enormous pressure keeps the inner core (the center) solid, even though temperatures here reach over 10,800°F (6,000°C). The upper layer of the mantle is made of plates, like pieces of a jigsaw, with the continents on top. Sometimes, the plates rub together, causing pressure. Earthquakes occur when the plates move.

FROM CORE TO CRUST

If we could cut a large section out of Earth, we would see a planet made in four layers. At its center is a solid inner core of almost pure iron, surrounded by an outer core of liquid iron and nickel. Enveloping this is a mantle of silicon compounds, crystals, and lighter metals topped with a hard rock crust.

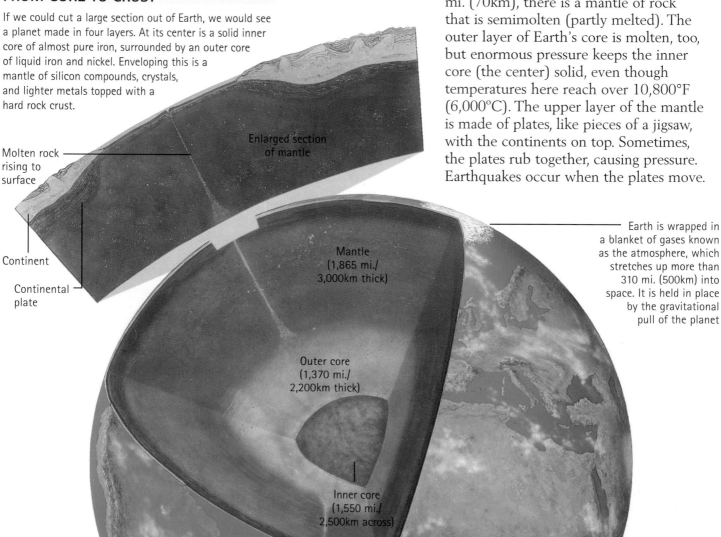

Enlarged section of mantle

Molten rock rising to surface

Continent

Continental plate

Mantle (1,865 mi./ 3,000km thick)

Outer core (1,370 mi./ 2,200km thick)

Inner core (1,550 mi./ 2,500km across)

Earth is wrapped in a blanket of gases known as the atmosphere, which stretches up more than 310 mi. (500km) into space. It is held in place by the gravitational pull of the planet

EVOLVING EARTH

Astronomers believe that Earth began to form about 4.6 billion years ago, when the solar nebula (a vast cloud of hot debris circling the newly formed Sun) began to cluster together into lumps that eventually became the planets of our solar system. The process took millions of years to complete, and Earth, like the other planets, developed a unique chemistry and atmosphere.

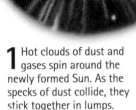

1 Hot clouds of dust and gases spin around the newly formed Sun. As the specks of dust collide, they stick together in lumps.

2 The forces of gravity pull more passing lumps into the spinning ball. Heavy elements such as iron sink to the center.

3 Lighter metals and rocks come to the surface and red-hot Earth cools enough for a hard shell to form.

4 Gases escaping from Earth form clouds and rain falls, creating oceans containing small oxygen-producing plants.

5 Originally one large mass, Earth's land surface is now split into seven large bodies, known as continents.

LIFE ON EARTH

Why exactly there is life on Earth is still a mystery to scientists. The theories are numerous, but the answer is probably a combination of reasons. First, Earth's distance from the Sun is ideal—not too hot like Venus, nor too cold like Mars. Second, Earth has water, which covers more than 70 percent of its surface. Scientists believe that electrical storms on the newly formed planet caused chemical reactions between gases in the atmosphere. These created the first building blocks of life, which fell into the oceans, where they combined to become simple plant-like forms. All plants make oxygen, and so an ideal atmosphere was soon created for the evolution of oxygen-breathing life-forms.

EARTH FACTS AND FIGURES

- Earth's diameter (the distance from Pole to Pole through the center) is 7,900 mi. (12,714km)

- Earth's circumference (the distance around its middle at the equator) is 24,901 mi. (40,075km)

- As Earth spins, places near the equator move much faster than places at the Poles, causing the planet to bulge slightly in the middle and be flattened at the top and bottom

- The temperature of Earth's inner core may be as hot as 11,200°F (6,200°C)

- Of the eight planets in our solar system, Earth is the third closest to the Sun

- The Sun and Earth are about 93 million miles (150 million km) apart

- Earth's path around the Sun is not a circle but an ellipse (an oval), which means it is closer to the Sun on January 1 than on June 1

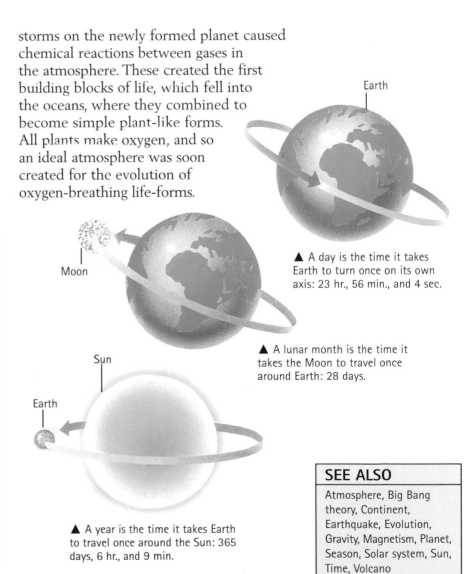

Earth

▲ A day is the time it takes Earth to turn once on its own axis: 23 hr., 56 min., and 4 sec.

Moon

▲ A lunar month is the time it takes the Moon to travel once around Earth: 28 days.

Sun

Earth

▲ A year is the time it takes Earth to travel once around the Sun: 365 days, 6 hr., and 9 min.

SEE ALSO

Atmosphere, Big Bang theory, Continent, Earthquake, Evolution, Gravity, Magnetism, Planet, Season, Solar system, Sun, Time, Volcano

EARTHQUAKE

An earthquake is a shaking of the Earth's surface. It is caused by the sudden release of pressure through weak parts of the Earth's crust.

The vast majority of earthquakes do not cause any serious damage. Small tremors can happen with an erupting volcano, an avalanche, or a landslide. However, the largest earthquakes occur as a result of pressure or tension deep under the ground being released through weak areas (fault lines) in the Earth's crust.

TECTONIC PLATES

The Earth's crust is broken into giant slabs called tectonic plates. Sometimes, pressure builds up underground as a result of the plates moving against each other. The pressure is suddenly released, sending out shock waves in all directions and causing the Earth's crust to shake and even crack.

EARTHQUAKE ZONES

There are two great earthquake zones. Both are where two tectonic plates meet. One stretches across southern Asia, through the Mediterranean, and into eastern Africa. The other is the "ring of fire" around the Pacific Ocean, which includes the United States. In 1906, a large part of San Francisco was destroyed by an earthquake in this zone.

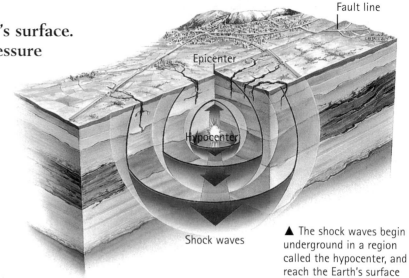

▲ The shock waves begin underground in a region called the hypocenter, and reach the Earth's surface directly above, at the epicenter. From here, they radiate in all directions.

SHOCK WAVES

Earthquake shock waves are known as seismic waves. They are measured using an instrument called a seismometer. A severe earthquake can be felt as much as 250 mi. (400km) away. The intensity of it is plotted on the Richter scale. Geologists measure the size of an earthquake using the Moment Magnitude Scale (MMS), which indicates how much energy it has released.

DISASTER IN JAPAN

In 2011, Japan was devastated by the effects of a Magnitude 9.0 offshore earthquake. It triggered powerful tsumanis up to 130 ft. (40m) high. The worst-hit region was Tohoku, in the northeast. More than 15,000 people died, 125,000 buildings were destroyed or damaged, and reactors at the Fukushima nuclear plant blew up, leaking radiation into the countryside.

SEE ALSO

Continent, Earth, Mountain and valley, Ocean and sea

EASTERN EUROPE

Eastern Europe includes several countries that were either part of the former Soviet Union, or once part of the communist bloc controlled by the Soviet Union.

▲ Expanses of steppe once covered Ukraine, but this land, covered with rich soil, is now heavily farmed.

Eastern Europe lies between the Baltic Sea, the Balkan Peninsula, the Black Sea, and Russia. It makes up more than one sixth of Europe's land area and is a region of plains, low hills, and mountains.

PEAKS AND PLAINS
To the south lie the rugged Carpathian Mountains and Transylvanian Alps. The highest point is Gerlachovsky Stit, a peak of 8,714 ft. (2,656m) in the Carpathians. To the west is the Hungarian Plain, and to the east are the vast rolling steppes (treeless plains) of Ukraine.

A REGION OF RIVERS
The area is watered by some of Europe's major rivers. The Danube, Europe's second-longest river at 1,725 mi. (2,776km), forms much of Romania's southwestern border; the Dnieper and the Dniester both flow through Ukraine. Europe's largest swamp, the Pripet Marshes, straddles the border between Belarus and Ukraine.

CONTINENTAL CLIMATE
Away from the mountains, Eastern Europe has warm summers; temperatures average 68°F (20°C) or more in July. Winters get colder as you travel from west to east. Most of the region has moderate rainfall, with 20–40 in. (500–1,000mm) per year, but the southeast is drier, with less than 20 in. (500mm) of rain per year.

BREADBASKET OF EUROPE
In the lowlands, many of the region's forests have been cleared for farming. The fertile steppes, once an area of natural grassland, are also farmed. Ukraine is sometimes called "the breadbasket of Europe" because of its high production of grain and other crops. ▶

▼ The medieval city of Prague, capital of the Czech Republic, has some of Europe's most beautiful and well-preserved architecture.

BELARUS
Area: 80,155 sq. mi. (207,600km²)
Population: 9,550,000
Capital: Minsk
Languages: Belarussian, Russian
Currency: Belarusian rouble

CZECH REPUBLIC
Area: 30,450 sq. mi. (78,860km²)
Population: 10,675,000
Capital: Prague
Language: Czech
Currency: Czech koruna

HUNGARY
Area: 35,920 sq. mi. (93,030km²)
Population: 9,851,000
Capital: Budapest
Language: Hungarian
Currency: Forint

MOLDOVA
Area: 13,070 sq. mi. (33,850km²)
Population: 3,474,000
Capital: Chisinau
Language: Moldovan
Currency: Moldovan leu

POLAND
Area: 120,730 sq. mi. (312,685km²)
Population: 38,476,000
Capital: Warsaw
Language: Polish
Currency: Zloty

N

miles
0   100
0   100
km

BALTIC SEA

LATVIA

LITHUANIA

RUSSIA

■ Minsk

BELARUS

RUSSIA

GERMANY

Vistula

Warsaw ■

POLAND

Pripet
Marshes

■ Prague

CZECH REPUBLIC

Kiev ■

UKRAINE

Dnieper

▲ Gerlachovsky
Stit

Dniester

SLOVAKIA

AUSTRIA

Carpathian Mountains

■ Bratislava

MOLDOVA

HUNGARY

Budapest ■

Chisinau ■

SLOVENIA

Danube

Hungarian Plain

SEA OF
AZOV

ROMANIA

CROATIA

Transylvanian Alps

BLACK
SEA

Bucharest ■

SERBIA

Danube

BULGARIA

BALKAN PENINSULA

ROMANIA
Area: 92,043 sq. mi.
(238,400km²)
Population: 21,530,000
Capital: Bucharest
Language: Romanian
Currency: Leu

SLOVAKIA
Area: 18,932 sq. mi.
(49,036km²)
Population: 5,445,000
Capital: Bratislava
Language: Slovak
Currency: Koruna

UKRAINE
Area: 233,032 sq. mi.
(603,550km²)
Population: 45,039,000
Capital: Kiev
Language: Ukrainian
Currency: Hryvna

▶ Old-fashioned factories,
such as this one in Romania,
cause air, water, and soil
pollution in many parts
of Eastern Europe.

DISAPPEARING WILDLIFE

As in the rest of Europe, the wildlife in
Eastern Europe has been reduced by the
destruction of forests and grasslands. A
number of large mammals that once grazed
on the steppes, such as the saiga antelope,
have now disappeared. The rare wisent
(European bison) is found in western
Belarus and central Poland; the Danube
Delta on the Black Sea is a major wetland
and home to many birds.

HEAVY AND LIGHT INDUSTRY

Coal, oil and natural gas, iron ore, and
other minerals are found in this region.
Heavy industry produces machinery,

▲ The practice of Eastern Orthodox Christianity is widespread in Belarus, Moldova, Romania, and Ukraine. Here, priests celebrate the Eucharist in Kiev in Ukraine.

transportation equipment, and steel and the manufacture of electronic goods, clothes, and processed food is increasing.

CITY DWELLERS

Many people live in rural areas, and a few people still follow nomadic lifestyles. But more than two thirds of the people live and work in towns and cities. In Ukraine, 3.4 million people live in Kiev and its suburbs.

RELIGIOUS WORSHIP

Religion is an important part of life for many people in Eastern Europe. The two dominant faiths in the region are Roman Catholic and Eastern Orthodox Christianity. There is a Muslim minority in Romania, which was once part of the Muslim Ottoman Empire.

FOREIGN POWERS

All of the countries of Eastern Europe have at times in their

history been under the influence of a foreign power. In 1793, Poland disappeared after being divided up among Prussia, Austria, and Russia. Hungary and Czechoslovakia formed part of the Hapsburg Empire until 1918. Romania gained its independence from Turkey in 1878. More recently, Ukraine, Belarus, and Moldova were part of the Russian-dominated Soviet Union.

COMMUNIST RULE

In World War II, the region was invaded by Nazi Germany, and millions of Jews, Roma, and Slavs were murdered. After 1945, Eastern Europe came under communist rule, either as part of the Soviet Union or as members of the Soviet bloc. Romania remained outside Soviet control, but under the communist dictator Nicolae Ceauşescu.

THE NEW MAP

Belarus, Moldova, and Ukraine gained their independence in 1991, following the breakup of the Soviet Union. In 1993, Czechoslovakia split peacefully into two countries: the Czech Republic and Slovakia. All but Belarus, Ukraine, and Moldova are now part of the European Union. All these countries have experienced a considerable migration of people to western Europe in search of work since 1990.

▲ Vacationers in Budapest play chess in one of Hungary's many natural hot springs.

AN AGE OF CHANGE

In 1990, Hungarians celebrated their first democratic election in 42 years. Since then, political changes have swept across the region. However, there are still tensions rooted in the past. In Ukraine, there has been fighting between supporters of a nationalist, pro-Western government in Kiev and pro-Russian rebels in the east of the country. In 2014, Russia annexed the Crimea region.

SEE ALSO

Cold War, Communism, Democracy, Europe, Russia

ECOLOGY

Ecology is the study of how plants, animals, and humans live together in their natural surroundings, and the ways in which they affect one another.

THE FOOD CHAIN

Each organism in a food chain feeds on and gets energy from the previous level. Ecologists divide plants and animals in a chain into groups, depending on how they get their energy. Plants are energy producers, using the sun's energy to produce new growth. Animals are consumers, obtaining energy by eating plants or other animals.

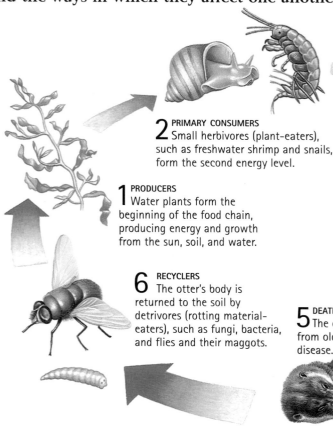

2 PRIMARY CONSUMERS
Small herbivores (plant-eaters), such as freshwater shrimp and snails, form the second energy level.

1 PRODUCERS
Water plants form the beginning of the food chain, producing energy and growth from the sun, soil, and water.

3 SECONDARY CONSUMERS
The third level of energy usage is by larger carnivores (meat-eaters) such as trout, which feed on the shrimp and snails.

4 TOP PREDATOR
In the fourth level of energy transfer, a bigger carnivore such as an otter preys on the trout.

6 RECYCLERS
The otter's body is returned to the soil by detrivores (rotting material-eaters), such as fungi, bacteria, and flies and their maggots.

5 DEATH
The otter dies from old age or disease.

Every plant and animal depends on a cycle of food, energy, and waste disposal that links it to other plants and animals. Ecologists study how plants and animals are linked to each other in food chains and webs.

CHAINED TOGETHER

All living things need energy. Plants use light energy from the sun to turn substances in the soil, air, and water into food. Insects eat the plants and fish, birds, and other animals eat the insects. In this way, energy is passed along a food chain. When living things die, their bodies break down and release nutrients back into the ground to start the process again.

ECOSYSTEMS

An ecosystem consists of the plants and animals in a certain area, together with the air, soil, climate, and other nonliving things. A forest is one type of ecosystem, but there are many others. An ecosystem can be as small as a pond or as large as an ocean.

HUMANS INTERVENE

Humans are part of the biggest ecosystem of all—the Earth itself. Some human actions can affect the entire planet. Logging a rain forest, for example, affects the forest by destroying its plants and animals. Since trees produce the oxygen needed by humans and other life-forms, the world's oxygen supply is also affected.

GRAY SQUIRREL INVASION

The introduction of plants or animals from foreign lands can have harmful effects on ecology. When gray squirrels from North America were introduced to Britain, the native red squirrels were pushed out of the food chain in most areas.

▲ Many timber companies manage their forests ecologically, using a process known as artificial reforestation. This means that a constant supply of seed is sown in a nursery and transplanted to the forest to replace felled trees.

SEE ALSO

Animal, Brazil, Conservation, Forest, Habitat, Plant, Pollution

EDUCATION

Education is the development of skills and knowledge. It can be formal, as provided by schools, or informal— through playing, watching, and learning in everyday life.

Learning to play a musical instrument is free as part of the curriculum in some countries. In other places, pupils must pay for lessons.

Many people feel that the main reason for educating children is to benefit society, by teaching skills needed to keep the community going. Others feel that it is more important to develop an individual's talents and interests. The ancient Greek philosopher Socrates believed that education could make people happier.

SCHOOL FOR ALL

The ancient Greeks were the first to set up a formal education system, but only for boys of rich families. Lessons included the art of public speaking for budding politicians. In many countries, the church or charities governed schooling. It wasn't until the 1800s that governments began to take control and the 1900s before education became free for most girls and boys. However, millions of people worldwide still do not possess the basic skills of reading and writing.

BEST YEARS OF YOUR LIFE

In most countries, it is compulsory for children to go to primary school at the age of 5 or 6, then on to a secondary (high) school at about 13 years of age. Some start earlier. Friedrich Froebel opened the first kindergarten (nursery) in Germany in 1837. In many parts of the world, attendance drops after the age of 11, but education can continue into adulthood at colleges or universities. Courses offer vocational (career) training or specialist qualifications.

THE CURRICULUM

The curriculum (subjects taught) varies in each country. It may emphasize religion, local crafts, or history. Many schools in the 1800s concentrated on reading, writing, and arithmetic. Subjects and teaching methods have changed over the years, as have educational theories. The Czech educationalist Comenius (1592–1670) thought pictures were a vital teaching tool. Italian reformer Maria Montessori (1870–1952) created wooden devices to help children learn through exploration.

School trips are a fun and exciting way of relating subjects learned in the classroom to real-life objects and situations.

SCHOOLS OF THOUGHT

Styles of teaching, subjects taught, and classroom settings have changed over the years. Once children had to sit in rows in silence while the teacher lectured them. Now, there is more emphasis on interaction and small-group tuition. Educators argue about which is best—formal instruction (presenting facts to learn) or learning through activity and experience.

▲ A government health advisor known as the Food Fairy visits a classroom in the United States in 1925 to instruct children on healthy eating.

SEE ALSO
Greece (ancient)

EGYPT

Egypt lies in the northeast of Africa. More people live there than in any other African nation, except Nigeria and Ethiopia, yet just four percent of its land is inhabited.

Area: 386,662 sq. mi. (1,001,450km²)
Population: 99,413,000
Capital: Cairo
Language: Arabic
Currency: Egyptian pound

Most of Egypt's people live around the Nile Delta and Valley and along the Suez Canal, a vital shipping link for world trade. The Nile River, controlled by the Aswan High Dam, provides fertile land stretching from Egypt's border with Sudan right up to the Mediterranean Sea. Egypt's main cities are its capital, Cairo, and the port of Alexandria—two of the largest cities in Africa.

DESERT AREAS

On either side of the Nile lie two deserts that together cover more than 90 percent of the country—the vast, low-lying Western Desert and the hilly Eastern Desert, which borders the Red Sea.

AGRICULTURAL LIFE

Agriculture is the country's most important industry, employing about a third of all Egyptians. These farmers, known as *fellahin*, grow cotton and food crops such as corn and rice in the fertile Nile Delta. The manufacturing industry is growing, and tourists attracted by the ancient ruins also generate income for many Egyptians. Oil, cotton, and cloth are major exports.

Traders, such as this man selling herbs and tea, set up their stalls in open street markets, or bazaars.

PEOPLE AND FAITH

Most Egyptians are descended from the people of ancient Egypt or from Arabs who invaded the country in the A.D. 600s. Ninety percent of the people are Muslim. The rest are mostly Christians of the ancient Coptic Church.

EGYPT TODAY

Egypt was part of the Ottoman Empire from 1517 until 1922. Britain controlled the Suez Canal and had administrative power in the country from the 1880s until the 1950s. President Hosni Mubarak ruled as dictator from 1981 until 2011, when massive protests forced him to step down.

Egypt's main port of Alexandria was the world's greatest trading city 2,000 years ago.

▶ Triangular-sailed wooden boats called *feluccas* carry goods and passengers along the Nile.

SEE ALSO
Africa, Egypt (ancient), Islam, Middle East

EGYPT, ANCIENT

Ancient Egypt developed along the Nile River around 5,000 years ago. Over the next 2,500 years, it grew into one of the greatest civilizations of all time.

▲ Pyramids were burial monuments for kings. The Sphinx (half man, half lion) stands beside the pyramids at Giza.

The funeral mask of Tutankhamen, boy king of Egypt (1361-52 B.C.), was discovered in 1922.

The ancient Egyptians chose to settle by the Nile in Africa because each year the river flooded, spreading mud over the banks. This provided them with fertile land to farm.

PYRAMID BUILDERS
The ancient Egyptians were the first real engineers and built impressive temples, cities, and pyramids. The largest of the pyramids needed over two million blocks, each weighing almost 3 tons. Some of the stones were from distant quarries and carried down the Nile on rafts.

The tombs of some important officials contained models of items that they might need in the next world.

A CREATIVE PEOPLE
The ancient Egyptians used papyrus reeds to make shoes, boats, ropes, and writing paper. Papyrus scrolls preserve ancient Egyptian hieroglyphic writing. The Egyptians also invented a 365-day calendar.

LIFE AFTER DEATH
Many gods were worshiped, including the sun god Ra and Osiris, god of the dead. The Egyptian kings, or pharaohs, were also believed to be gods. When they died, the kings and queens were buried in tombs full of things needed in the next world—food, jewelry, even small statues of servants (*shabtis*). Most royal tombs were robbed, but in 1922, the tomb of the boy pharaoh Tutankhamen was found, with most of its treasures untouched.

END OF A CIVILIZATION
Ancient Egypt included three great ages: the Old Kingdom, the Middle Kingdom, and the New Kingdom. In 31 B.C. Cleopatra died, and Egypt fell to the Roman Empire.

MUMMIFIED BODIES

The ancient Egyptians believed in life after death. Their bodies were mummified (preserved) before burial to prevent decay. It took 70 days to mummify a body.

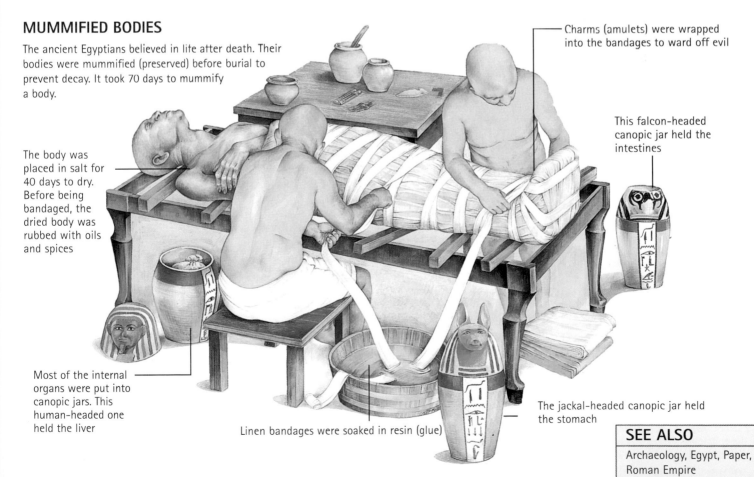

Charms (amulets) were wrapped into the bandages to ward off evil

This falcon-headed canopic jar held the intestines

The body was placed in salt for 40 days to dry. Before being bandaged, the dried body was rubbed with oils and spices

Most of the internal organs were put into canopic jars. This human-headed one held the liver

Linen bandages were soaked in resin (glue)

The jackal-headed canopic jar held the stomach

SEE ALSO
Archaeology, Egypt, Paper, Roman Empire

ELECTRONICS

Electronics is a branch of engineering which studies the components and circuits that make up modern electrical devices, like radios and toasters.

Modern electrical devices contain tiny electronic parts called components, which are joined together by lines of metallic paint on circuit boards. Electronic engineers know how to put the right components together to make circuits that can perform specific jobs.

Until the 1950s, radios used glass tubes. They were bulky and fragile.

WORKING PARTS
Components affect the way electrons (tiny charged particles) flow through a circuit. The simplest component, the switch, breaks the flow of electrons, or current. Resistors make it harder for the current to flow, while capacitors store current as electrical charge. Diodes let current flow in only one direction.

In the 1950s, the small, durable transistor began to replace the valve.

TRANSISTOR TECHNOLOGY
The first circuits used bulky glass vacuum tubes, which could magnify a current or switch it on or off. This ability to turn a current on or off electronically is the principle behind all computers. In the 1950s, the valve was replaced by a device called the transistor, which was much smaller, cheaper, and more durable, paving the way for the huge electronic advances that were to follow.

BIRTH OF THE MICROCHIP
In the 1970s, the invention of the microchip, which contained thousands of tiny transistors on a piece of material smaller than a stamp, allowed complex circuits to be squeezed into a tiny space. This made the home computer possible. More recently, very large-scale integration (VLSI) has enabled hundreds of millions of transistors to be put on a single chip, meaning that even smaller computers can be made.

ELECTRONICS TODAY
Electronics is now part of virtually all electrical devices. The microprocessor, a complex circuit on a single chip, is used in devices from robots and space rockets to DVD players, laptops, and smartphones.

In the 1970s, microchips made hand-size radio-cassette players possible.

Today's radios are often tiny, and digital radios are replacing analogue radios in many cases.

HOW A DIGITAL WATCH WORKS

A digital watch is powered by a battery. Its timing is controlled by a quartz crystal, which vibrates thousands of times a second. The microchip uses these vibrations to keep time, which it displays in numbers.

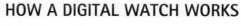

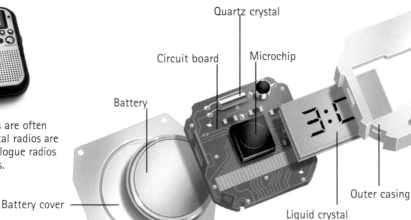

Quartz crystal

Circuit board

Microchip

Battery

Battery cover

Liquid crystal display (LCD)

Outer casing

Plastic window

SEE ALSO

Atom and molecule, Clock, Computer, Electricity, Robot, Rocket, Telephone

ELEPHANT

Elephants are the largest animals on land. They have very thick skin, a trunk, and ivory tusks. There are three species: two live in Africa and one in Asia.

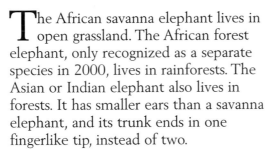

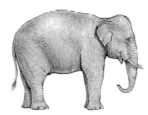

The Asian or Indian elephant grows to around 10 ft. (3m) at the shoulder and weighs up to 5 tons.

The African savanna elephant is the largest land animal. It can reach 13 ft. (4m) and weighs up to 6 tons.

The African savanna elephant lives in open grassland. The African forest elephant, only recognized as a separate species in 2000, lives in rainforests. The Asian or Indian elephant also lives in forests. It has smaller ears than a savanna elephant, and its trunk ends in one fingerlike tip, instead of two.

EATING MACHINES

Elephants live on leaves and bark, eating up to 440 lb. (200kg) of food a day. They use their trunks, which are giant, flexible nostrils, to pull up plants and to bring food and water to their mouths. They have 12 back teeth (molars), but only 4 are fully developed and in use at any one time. Most elephants have tusks, or extra long, curved teeth, which they use to strip bark off trees and to dig for water.

PROTECTIVE INSTINCTS

Female elephants start to breed when they are about ten years of age. They are pregnant for 20 months, before giving birth to a single calf. When a calf is about to be born, other females gather around the mother and the herd stays in one place until the young calf, which stands nearly 3 ft. (1m) tall, is on its feet and ready to move on.

▶ An elephant's tusks are long, curved teeth called incisors. About one third of the tusk is hidden in the skull.

- Skull
- Upper jaw
- Lower jaw
- Tusk (incisor tooth)

COOLING DOWN

Because elephants have no sweat glands, they lose very little body heat. They cool down by hiding in the shade and flapping their ears, or by bathing in water and using their trunks to shower themselves.

OLD AGE

All elephants, except the old bull males, are sociable animals and live in herds led by the oldest females. They can live for over 60 years, but many are killed for their ivory tusks. In many places the bull elephants, which have the biggest tusks, have become rare. The spread of human settlements has also led to both Asian and African elephants becoming endangered.

SEE ALSO

Africa, Animal, Indian subcontinent, Mammal

EMPIRE

An empire is a group of nations or states under the control of a single power. Most empires are built up when one country conquers others.

Octavian, later called Augustus, became the first emperor of Rome in 27 B.C.

From A.D. 527 to 565, Justinian ruled the Byzantine Empire with his wife.

In 1525, Babar founded the Mughal Empire by conquering northern India.

Süleyman enlarged the Ottoman Empire in the 1500s.

Maria Theresa and Francis I unified the Hapsburg Empire in the 1740s.

Haile Selassie, emperor of Ethiopia, was overthrown by the army in 1974.

BRITISH INDIA
Over 600 small states, ruled by leaders including rajahs and maharajahs, came under the British Empire. They had their own laws, armies, and finances, but there were British troops in some states to guarantee loyalty.

Some of the greatest empires in history were the Roman, British, Byzantine, Japanese, Ottoman, and Russian empires. Each was ruled by an emperor or empress, but there have been other types of rule.

POWER GROWTH
Empires are usually built up when a country becomes richer or has larger armed forces than its neighbors, allowing it to spread its power and influence. The Macedonian king Alexander the Great trained his army with new weapons and tactics before conquering a vast empire from 334 to 323 B.C. The European Hapsburg dynasty used royal marriages and treaties to expand its Holy Roman Empire for more than 300 years from the 1400s. In the 1800s, the British Empire was won by economic strength, backed up by military superiority when needed.

IMPERIAL RULE
Many empires are ruled by a single state or nation, often with great brutality. The Assyrians in the ancient Middle East used their army to enforce the king's rule and to collect taxes. Those who disobeyed were cruelly punished. The Mongol Empire was run as a dictatorship in which the khan's wishes were enforced by the army. Other empires allowed some freedoms to their subjects. The states in the Athenian Empire of the 400s B.C. met each year to discuss events. Many of the cities and states in the Holy Roman Empire were free to run their own affairs, make their own laws, and even go to war.

KEY DATES

1500–1100 B.C. Egyptian New Kingdom rules an empire in southwest Asia

850–609 B.C. Assyria rules the Middle East

559–326 B.C. Persian Empire flourishes

264 B.C.–A.D. 410 Rome expands to rule vast areas before falling to barbarian invasion

228 B.C. China united under the Qin Dynasty

A.D. 800 Holy Roman Empire begins with the coronation of Charlemagne

1206 Genghis Khan founds the Mongol Empire

1492–1828 Spain conquers an empire in the Americas before colonies win independence

1880–1950s European powers build empires in Africa and Asia, then grant colonies independence

A SCRAMBLE FOR POWER
The Industrial Revolution made European states richer and better armed than other peoples. By 1850, several European nations owned colonies in Africa and Asia, which produced wealth and trade. In 1882, the British took over Egypt, while other European nations had already conquered vast areas of Africa, Asia and the Pacific and turned them into colonies. Within 40 years it became clear that these colonies produced little wealth and were costly to maintain.

COLLAPSE OF EMPIRES
Empires may collapse as the result of foreign attack, member states breaking away, or internal dispute. The ancient Persian Empire was defeated in war by the Greeks under Alexander the Great. The Roman Empire was weakened by internal power struggles, and then fell to barbarian attacks during the 400s. In 1917, the German and Austro-Hungarian Empires were divided up into smaller states by the victorious Allies at the end of World War I, and the new states were racked by revolution, bringing an end to their empires.

A POSTIMPERIAL WORLD
Since 1945, very few empires have continued to exist. The colonial empires

▲ The great palace of Persepolis was the center of the Persian Empire, founded by Darius the Great in 559 B.C. Nations subject to the Persian "King of Kings" brought tributes to Persepolis each spring as part of a great festival.

of the British, French, and other European nations broke up when, weakened by World War II, they could not afford to keep the colonies in the face of nationalist independence movements. In 1990, the Soviet Union broke up, as the states of the old Russian Empire declared themselves independent. There are few multinational empires in the world today, because most nations are able to survive economically, and do not need to be part of an empire to be protected from invaders.

▲ The Forbidden City, inside the city of Beijing, includes palaces of the Chinese emperors from 1421 to 1911. They are now preserved as museums and galleries.

◀ The Assyrian Empire, with its capital at Nineveh, was a military state based on cruel and constant warfare. It collapsed in 609 B.C. when its enemies united to capture Nineveh.

SEE ALSO
Aztec, Babylon, Inca, Mongol Empire, Napoleonic Wars, Roman Empire

ENERGY

Energy is the ability to do work. An object or substance has energy if it can move or if it can generate such things as heat, sound, or electricity.

The Sun provides most of the heat and light energy that we use on Earth.

When things move, they are using kinetic energy—like this car.

Dynamite's explosive power comes from stored chemical energy.

A radio produces sound energy by making the atoms in the air vibrate.

A hammer coming down to strike a nail uses the potential energy of gravity.

Nuclear energy takes its most dramatic form in a nuclear explosion.

Energy is everywhere—in sunlight as heat and light energy, in a smartphone as sound energy, even in a lump of coal as stored chemical energy. Energy can be converted from one form into another, but it can never be destroyed.

MOVING OBJECTS

One of the most basic forms of energy is the energy of movement, or kinetic energy. Heavy, fast-moving objects have more kinetic energy than light, slow-moving ones. The kinetic energy of a car is less than that of a truck traveling at the same speed. A parked car has no kinetic energy at all.

HEAT ENERGY

Kinetic energy is also closely related to heat energy. An object is hot because its atoms (the tiny particles that it is made of) are constantly in motion. So an object's heat energy can be thought of as the kinetic energy of its atoms. The faster its atoms move, the hotter the object becomes.

▲ A runner waiting on the blocks to start a race is like a coiled spring ready to expand. When the starter's gun goes off, the potential (stored) energy in her muscles is converted into the kinetic (motion) energy of running.

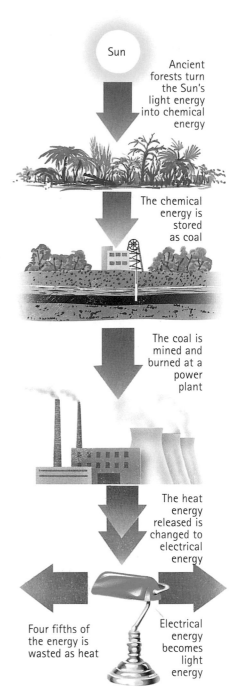

Sun

Ancient forests turn the Sun's light energy into chemical energy

The chemical energy is stored as coal

The coal is mined and burned at a power plant

The heat energy released is changed to electrical energy

Four fifths of the energy is wasted as heat

Electrical energy becomes light energy

ENERGY CYCLE

Carbon-based fossil fuels such as coal, oil and gas are examples of stored energy. Today we can use the Sun's energy directly, to generate power without using up finite resources.

SAVING IT FOR LATER

Energy can be stored to be used later. This energy in storage is called potential energy. A spring stores energy as it is squeezed. When it is released and expands back to its original shape, the potential energy becomes motion (kinetic energy).

CHANGING FORM

The law of conservation of energy says that energy can never be destroyed or lost, but will change its form. For example, if a boy gliding on a pair of roller skates slowly comes to a halt, his kinetic energy will gradually decrease to zero. But the energy does not vanish, it is transformed into two other energy forms: heat and sound. The heat, created by the friction of the roller-skate wheels rubbing on the ground, warms up both the wheels and the ground. The sound energy can be heard as a swish or squeak of the wheels.

ENERGY AND POWER

Scientists measure energy using units called joules (J). Power—the rate at which energy is used—is measured in watts (W). The idea of power involves time. If two hotpots heat a pint of water from 50°F (10°C) to 212°F (100°C), they both give the water the same amount of heat energy. But if one hotpot does the job in half the time, it has twice the amount of power as the other. Nuclear power works by releasing the energy locked inside the nucleus of an atom and using it to do work.

MAKING IT WORK

Energy is never lost, but it can be wasted if not put to work. Heat is the main cause of energy wastage. For example, an ordinary lightbulb converts only one fifth of its electrical energy into light; the rest is wasted as heat. Inefficiency of car engines also means that the Earth's natural energy resources, such as oil, are constantly being wasted.

AN ENERGETIC GAME OF PINBALL

Energy is constantly changing its state. In a game of pinball, potential energy is converted into kinetic energy. The moving ball will tend to slow down through friction as it comes into contact with parts of the machine. Energy is used up in overcoming friction, but it is not lost—it is changed into heat. When the player adds energy to the ball, by pushing it with a flipper, the ball speeds up.

1 Pulling back the plunger coils a spring just behind the ball. In energy terms, the potential energy in the player's hand is transferred to the spring.

2 Letting go of the plunger shoots the ball into play. The spring's potential energy is changed into the kinetic energy of the moving ball.

3 As the ball moves inside the machine, it starts to slow down—its kinetic energy is being changed, mainly into heat. Flippers and obstacles have springs to speed up the ball.

SEE ALSO

Ecology, Electricity, Force and motion, Heat, Light, Magnetism, Nuclear power, Solar power, Sound

ENGINE

Engines are machines that convert energy into mechanical work to power vehicles, to drive other machines, or to generate electricity.

FRANK WHITTLE
(1907–87) An officer in the British Royal Air Force, designed a successful turbojet engine in 1941.

WERNHER VON BRAUN
(1912–77) Head of the team of German scientists during World War II that created the V2: the first rocket-powered guided missile, and the inspiration for later moon rockets.

The main types of engine are steam, gasoline (gas), diesel, jet, and rocket. Each one is supplied with energy by burning, or combusting, fuels such as coal, gas, and diesel oil. Nearly all engines are internal combustion engines, which means the fuel is burned inside the engine. The exception to this is the steam engine, which uses external combustion.

EARLY STEAM ENGINES
In the 1700s, much of the power for the Industrial Revolution was provided by the steam engine. In 1712, Englishman Thomas Newcomen developed the first practical steam engine for pumping water from mines. In 1765, a Scottish engineer, James Watt, began to improve the Newcomen steam engine and developed a much more efficient machine. Soon steam engines were powering factory machinery, as well as railroad cars, such as the *Rocket* locomotive, built by English engineer George Stephenson in 1829.

▲ An ultralight is a hang glider with an engine. It uses a two-stroke engine, which is lighter, cheaper, and more powerful for its size than a four-stroke engine.

THE POWER OF STEAM
In a steam engine, a fire is used to boil water to produce high-pressure steam. As the steam expands, it pushes a piston back and forth in a cylinder, or turns the blades of a fanlike wheel called a turbine. These then drive the machine. Most steam engines have been replaced by internal combustion engines. However, many power plant generators today are still worked by steam turbines.

GASOLINE ENGINES
Nowadays, cars, trucks, buses, and many trains and aircraft use internal combustion

STEAM LOCOMOTIVE
Steam locomotives powered the world's railroads for over 130 years. Hot gases from the burning coal surround the water tubes, turning the water to steam. The steam passes to the cylinder, driving the piston backward and forward. The piston in turn pushes the connecting rod backward and forward, which rotates a crank and drives the wheels. Water and coal are carried in the tender.

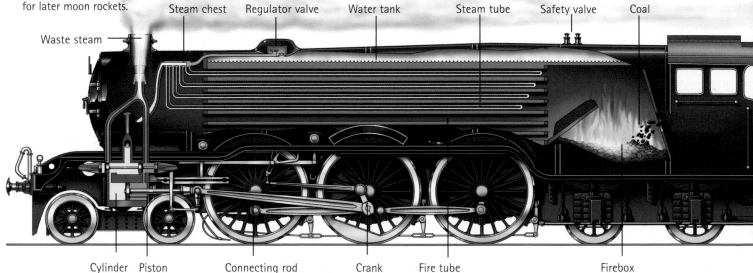

Steam chest   Regulator valve   Water tank   Steam tube   Safety valve   Coal

Waste steam

Cylinder   Piston   Connecting rod   Crank   Fire tube   Firebox

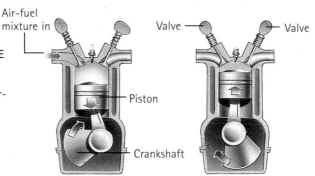

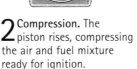

A FOUR-STROKE ENGINE
Cars have internal combustion engines with pistons that work in a four-stroke cycle (the piston makes two movements up and two down). Air and fuel are let into the piston cylinder by valves at the top. The explosion of ignited fuel moves the piston, which turns a crankshaft. This spins the driveshaft.

Air-fuel mixture in — Piston — Crankshaft

Valve — Valve

Spark plug

Exhaust gas out

1 Induction. As the piston goes down, it draws a mixture of air and fuel into the cylinder.

2 Compression. The piston rises, compressing the air and fuel mixture ready for ignition.

3 Power. A spark lights the fuel, forcing the piston down and turning the crankshaft.

4 Exhaust. On the final stroke of the engine, the piston rises to expel exhaust (waste) gases.

engines fueled by diesel oil, gas, or biofuels. In a gas engine, the fuel mixes with air inside a cylinder, and a spark sets the mixture on fire, pushing the piston up and down (see above).

DIESEL ENGINES

Like gas engines, diesel engines have cylinders, pistons, valves, and a fuel supply, but there are no spark plugs or ignition system. The fuel explodes because of the heat created when the piston compresses the fuel and air inside a cylinder. The explosion pushes the piston up and down, which powers the vehicle.

THE GAS TURBINE

A jet, or gas turbine, engine does not have pistons. Instead, air is sucked in at the front of the engine and compressed, or squashed, by the rotating blades of the compressor. The air is blown into the combustion chamber and ignited with aviation fuel. The hot gases are expelled from the back of the engine, pushing the plane forward.

TO THE STARS

Like jet engines, rocket engines also use their exhaust gases to push the vehicle forward. Unlike jets, however, rockets cannot burn fuel by taking in oxygen from the air, since there is no air in space. Instead, they carry their oxygen supply with them, usually as liquid oxygen. The fuel either ignites spontaneously when mixed with the oxygen, or is lit by a spark.

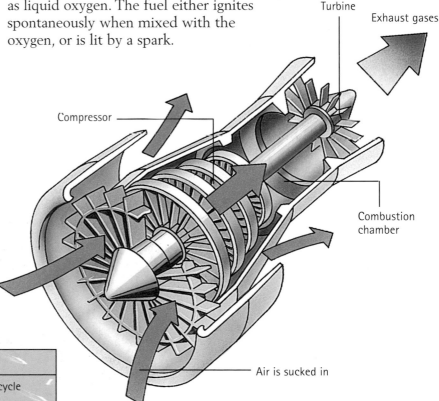

Turbine

Exhaust gases

Compressor

Combustion chamber

Air is sucked in

A JET ENGINE
In a jet engine, air is sucked in at the front of the engine by giant rotating blades. The air is then compressed and passed into a combustion (burning) chamber, where it is ignited. The plane is thrust forward by the exhaust gases. These gases also turn a turbine, which drives the compressor.

KEY DATES

1862	Alphonse Beau de Rochas invents the four-stroke cycle
1876	Nikolaus Otto develops the prototype automobile engine
1878	Sir Dougald Clerk invents the two-stroke cycle
1892	Rudolph Diesel patents the diesel engine
1897	C.P. Steinmetz's *Future of Electricity* predicts air pollution from use of coal as fuel
1939	The first jet-engined aircraft, the Heinkel, flies in Germany
1944	The first V2 missile is fired on enemy targets

SEE ALSO
Aircraft, Car, Electricity, Energy, Rocket, Train, Transportation

EUROPE

Europe is the second smallest of the world's seven continents. It has 44 countries recognized as nation states, including parts of Russia, Turkey, and Kazakhstan.

▲ Iceland in the North Atlantic Ocean is known as the "Land of Ice and Fire" because of its volcanoes and hot springs set against a landscape of ice fields and glaciers.

KEY FACTS

- **Area:** 10,180,000 sq. mi. (26,366,000km²)
- **Population:** 741,400,000
- **Number of countries:** 44
- **Largest country:** Russia, 25 percent of which is in Europe
- **Smallest country:** Vatican City (0.17 sq. mi./0.44km²)
- **Highest point:** Mount Elbrus (18,510 ft./5,642m)
- **Largest lake:** Lake Ladoga (6,835 sq. mi./17,700km²)
- **Longest river:** Volga (2,292 sq. mi./3,688km²)

Only the continent of Australia is smaller than Europe, but Europe's moderate climate, rich resources, and fertile land support a large population. Between them, the people speak about 50 major languages and many more dialects. With its 44 countries, Europe is a continent of diverse cultures.

NEVER FAR FROM WATER
The northwest and west of Europe are bordered by the Arctic and Atlantic oceans, and the Mediterranean Sea surrounds the south. The coastline is broken up by thousands of fjords and other inlets. However, 17 European countries have no access to the sea.

NORTH EUROPEAN PLAIN
Many of Europe's most populated areas lie on the North European Plain, which stretches from the southern part of the United Kingdom through northern France, Germany, and Poland to the Ural Mountains in Russia. To the north are forests of coniferous trees such as fir, larch, and pine. Deciduous forests of ash, elm, and oak grow in central and southern Europe. In the southeast are large areas of dry grassland called steppes.

SCANDINAVIA
In the far north of Europe lies the cold and mountainous region of Scandinavia, which includes the countries of Norway, Sweden, and Denmark. The climate around the Arctic Ocean is cold and snowy, with temperatures in January averaging below 3°F (–16°C). Few trees grow in the extreme north, but the forests farther south contain large animals such as brown bears, reindeer, and wolves.

▼ Wine is produced throughout Europe, particularly in France (shown here), Germany, Spain, Italy, and Bulgaria.

ARCTIC OCEAN

NORWEGIAN SEA

ICELAND

NORTH SEA

UNITED KINGDOM

IRELAND

ATLANTIC OCEAN

PORTUGAL

SPAIN

FRANCE

Pyrenees

1
2
GERMANY

NORTH

EUROPEAN

Alps

4
5

AUSTRIA

SWITZERLAND

6
7
8
9
10
11
12
13
14
15
16
17

ITALY

MEDITERRANEAN SEA

MALTA

NORWAY

SWEDEN

DENMARK

FINLAND

Lake Ladoga

BALTIC SEA

ESTONIA

LATVIA

RUSSIA

LITHUANIA

BELARUS

POLAND

CZECH REPUBLIC

SLOVAKIA

HUNGARY

PLAIN

Carpathian Mts.

18

ROMANIA

BULGARIA

Bosporus

TURKEY (European part)

GREECE

RUSSIA (European part)

Ural Mountains

KAZAKHSTAN (European part)

Volga

Caspian Sea

Mt. Elbrus

BLACK SEA

N

miles
0
500
0
500
km

KEY TO MAP
1 THE NETHERLANDS
2 BELGIUM
3 LUXEMBOURG
4 SWITZERLAND
5 LIECHTENSTEIN
6 MONACO
7 ANDORRA
8 VATICAN CITY
9 SAN MARINO
10 SLOVENIA
11 CROATIA
12 BOSNIA–HERZEGOVINA
13 SERBIA
14 MONTENEGRO
15 KOSOVO
16 NORTH MACEDONIA
17 ALBANIA
18 MOLDOVA

THE MEDITERRANEAN

The southern part of Europe is divided from the north by three mountain ranges: the Pyrenees, the Alps, and the Carpathian Mountains. The Mediterranean countries of southern Europe, including Italy, Spain, and Greece, have mild, rainy winters and hot, dry summers.

A FERTILE CONTINENT

Europe is a fertile continent; farms cover more than half the land. Crops include barley, oats, potatoes, and wheat, and citrus fruit and olives in the south. Vast areas of steppe in Ukraine and southern Russia are heavily farmed for grain.

EUROPE AND ENERGY

Europe has reserves of oil, natural gas and coal, but most new power in Europe is now coming from renewable sources, especially wind. Europe was the world's first industrial continent, but much of its economy now depends on finance and services.

A MIXED POPULATION

Most Europeans are the descendants of people who lived on the continent in prehistoric times, but there is a long history of immigration from Africa, Asia, and the Caribbean. About 77 percent of the population lives in cities and towns, working in factories or service industries, such as finance and tourism. ▶

▲ The number of red squirrels decreased in Europe in the 1900s, following the introduction of the gray squirrel from North America and loss of large areas of woodland.

BRANCHES OF CHRISTIANITY

Christianity is Europe's leading religion. Many follow the Roman Catholic Church, which has its headquarters in Vatican City, in Rome, Italy. Protestantism is a branch of Christianity with its highest European representation in the north of the continent. The Orthodox Church flourishes in the east and southeast.

HISTORICAL CITIES

Many of Europe's large cities are steeped in history, but are also characterized by modern architecture and a modern way of life. Paris in France contains magnificent buildings dating from the Middle Ages, and is at the same time a leading fashion center. Moscow in Russia and London in England are important international cities, as well as historic sites. Athens and Rome, the capitals of Greece and Italy, have impressive ruins surviving from the days of Ancient Greece and the Roman Empire.

DEMOCRACY AND LAW

Throughout history, Europe has had an important influence on world politics. The system of democracy—where the government is chosen by the people—was first tried in Ancient Greece about 2,500 years ago. Similarly, many of the laws developed during the Roman

▲ Istanbul in Turkey lies on the shores of the Bosporus, the strait that divides Europe from Asia. Its buildings reflect a mixture of Eastern and Western styles.

▲ The ruins of Delphi, a sacred site from as early as 1100 B.C., stand on Mount Parnassus in the southern part of mainland Greece.

civilization (from 590 B.C. to A.D. 476) still influence legal systems today.

THE RENAISSANCE

From the 1300s, Europe became an increasingly important center of art and learning, with people interested in new ideas about art, science, and literature. This period is known as the Renaissance. At the same time, a desire for trade led European seafarers to set out to explore unknown lands and later to start colonies abroad. In the late 1700s, the continent was the birthplace of the Industrial Revolution, which brought great power and prosperity to the West.

END OF EMPIRES

The map of Europe has often changed throughout history, largely because of wars between rival countries. In the 1900s, two great world wars were fought between European powers. In the years following World War II (1939–45), the empires created in Africa and Asia by European countries

◀ Many European countries, including Germany, the Netherlands, Romania, and Italy, have strong national soccer teams and attract enthusiastic fans, like these from Switzerland.

such as Belgium, Britain, France, the Netherlands, and Portugal came to an end. Former colonies became independent countries, but many people living there continued to follow European customs and speak European languages. A large number of them have since made their homes in Europe.

EAST AND WEST

By the 1950s, Europe was divided between the noncommunist countries of the West and the Soviet-backed communist countries of the East. Until the 1980s, the two sides remained armed and hostile throughout the period known as the Cold War. But from the late 1980s, the Eastern European countries threw off their communist governments. A new map of Europe was shaped, with new countries and partnerships. Yugoslavia split into five separate countries at this time; a sixth nation was added in 2006, when Montenegro broke away from Serbia and became Europe's newest nation state.

THE EUROPEAN UNION

From the 1950s onwards a group of European nations set up treaties to promote economic cooperation, as well as human rights and democracy, with an eventual goal of political unity. The European Economic Community (EEC or Common Market, 1957) became the European Union (EU) in 1993. As of 2017 the EU has 28 members, although the United Kingdom is negotiating withdrawal ('Brexit') following a referendum in 2016. The Euro currency is shared by 19 EU nations.

▲ After World War II, about a seventh of Berlin was in ruins. The city was divided between East and West until 1990, when Germany was reunited.

▶ German car-making factories are among the most highly automated in the world, and the cars they produce are exported worldwide.

SEE ALSO

Eastern Europe, France, Germany, Greece and the Balkans, Italy, Netherlands, Belgium, and Luxembourg, Scandinavia, Spain and Portugal, Switzerland and Austria, United Kingdom

EVOLUTION

Evolution is the way in which an organism changes over many generations, resulting in a species that is very different from its early ancestors.

JEAN BAPTISTE LAMARCK
(1744–1829) was a French biologist who believed, mistakenly, that animals evolved during their own lifetimes. For example, each giraffe, by stretching, elongated its neck.

CHARLES DARWIN
(1809–1882) shook the world, and especially the Church, with his theory of natural selection, which he published in *On the Origin of Species* in 1859.

Most scientists believe that the first simple organisms appeared on Earth over 3.5 billion years ago, and that all today's plants and animals have arisen from these by a process of gradual change. This process, which is constantly happening from one generation to the next, is known as evolution.

DARWIN'S THEORY
The idea of evolution has been around since the time of the ancient Greeks. However, the first convincing theory of how evolution works was provided in the mid-1800s by the English naturalist Charles Darwin. He recognized that plants and animals produce lots of offspring, but that only a small number of these offspring survive. Darwin concluded that only the individual with the most useful characteristics is able to survive in a process that he called the struggle for existence.

SURVIVAL OF THE FITTEST
Darwin noticed that individuals that are not well suited to their surroundings die out. This leaves only the fittest individuals to breed and pass the useful characteristics

that have allowed them to survive on to their offspring. In popular terms, this process is known as "the survival of the fittest." It explains the enormous variety of plant and animal life that is found throughout the world—because the conditions vary from place to place, animals and plants adapt to fit their environment.

LITTLE BY LITTLE
With each new generation of plant and animal life, the struggle for existence continues. The result is that, over a long period of time, plants and animals gradually change and become better adapted to the place where they live

---

EVOLUTION FACTS AND FIGURES

- Scientists estimate that 99.9 percent of all the species that have ever lived are now extinct

- The idea of evolution was first suggested by the ancient Greeks more than 2,500 years ago

- A naturalist called Alfred Russel Wallace came up with the same theory of evolution as Darwin (and at the same time), but Darwin published his ideas first

- By looking at fossilized animals in different layers of rock, scientists can see how the animals evolved

- When Darwin visited the Galapagos Islands, he saw that all the finches had different beaks to suit their food, such as a long, hooked beak for catching insects or a nutcracker-shaped beak for eating seeds

---

THE EVOLUTION OF MAN

Hominims (early humans) evolved from apelike ancestors around seven million years ago. Australopithecines, such as *Australopithecus afarensis* (3.9–2.9 m.y.a.), walked upright on their back legs. *Homo habilis* (2.4–1.5 m.y.a.) made basic tools from stone and bone, while *Homo erectus* (1.8 m.y.a.–40,000 y.a.) was probably the first human to use fire. The Neanderthals (*Homo neanderthalensis*, 230,000–28,000 y.a.) lived alongside and even interbred with modern humans (*Homo sapiens*), who first appeared 195,000 y.a.

AUSTRALOPITHECUS   HOMO HABILIS   HOMO ERECTUS   NEANDERTHALL MAN   HOMO SAPIENS

Hyracotherium (55–40 million years ago [mya]) was 10 in. (25cm) tall, and had four toes.

THE EVOLUTION OF THE HORSE

All life-forms probably developed from single-celled sea organisms. From there, evolution branched out in different directions. One group of fish, for example, evolved into amphibians, and one group of amphibians then gave rise to the reptiles. Birds and mammals evolved from different groups of reptiles. Today's hoofed horse evolved over millions of years from an animal the size of a dog.

Mesohippus (40–25 mya) was much larger and had three toes.

Merychippus (25–5 mya) was better suited to firm, grassy plains.

▲ Hungry Dutch explorers on the island of Mauritius in the 1500s were new predators for the trusting, flightless dodo, extinct by 1680.

and the dangers that surround them. To an observer, each change may be almost invisible, but over millions of years they all make a big difference.

NATURAL SELECTION

Conditions of habitat and climate are not the same everywhere, so a variation in the evolution of a plant or animal that is useful in one area of the world might be less useful in another. A species that spreads out may therefore evolve, or change, over a long period of time into several different species. Because this process of weeding out the inefficient individuals and favoring the fittest ones is an entirely natural one, Darwin gave it the name natural selection.

EVIDENCE FROM THE ROCKS

Some of the strongest support for the idea of evolution comes from the fossilized remains of plants and animals that are found in rocks formed from layers of sand and mud on ancient seabeds. In each layer of rock, the organisms look slightly different from the ones below. This provides the evidence for a process of change over hundreds, thousands, or even millions of years.

A COMMON ANCESTOR

The bone structure of living animals also gives clues to evolution. A human's arm, a bird's wing, and a whale's flipper all

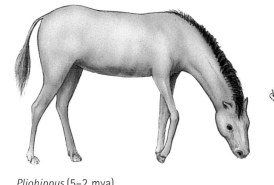

Pliohippus (5–2 mya) had stronger legs and single hooves.

Equus caballus (1.5 mya) was similar to today's horses.

look very different and have different uses in everyday life. However, their bones are actually very similar. This suggests that these animals have all evolved from a common ancestor, which spread out over a wide geographical area. The arms then adapted for different jobs according to the demands of the different environments.

SEE ALSO

Dinosaur, Fossil, Genetics, Horse, Prehistoric animal, Prehistoric people

EXPLORER

People explore to discover the unknown. Through exploration we have learned much about the Earth. We are still exploring the oceans and outer space.

Christopher Columbus opened up America to European trade in 1492.

Captain Robert Scott died on the way back from the South Pole in 1912.

Jacques Cousteau helped invent the aqualung so he could explore under water.

The Phoenicians were among the first explorers, sailing the Mediterranean around 3,000 years ago. Pytheas, a Greek sailor, ventured into the Atlantic Ocean in 300 B.C. and, in A.D. 1000, Norway's Leif Ericsson reached North America.

THE SILK ROAD
Chinese and Arab travelers made long overland journeys. In 138 B.C., Zhang Qian became the first Chinese man to explore central Asia. Later, European merchants took the Silk Road to China, visited by the Italian Marco Polo in 1275 and described in his book *Description of the World*.

AGE OF DISCOVERY
In the 1400s, stronger ships and the invention of navigational aids such as the backstaff (used to plot the ship's position by the Sun and stars) prompted European explorers to head to sea. They went in search of lands to conquer and for trade, riches, and slaves. Seeking a sea route to India, Portuguese sailors headed south along the African coast. In 1488, Bartholomeu Días reached the southern tip of Africa, and in 1498, Vasco da Gama crossed the Indian Ocean. Columbus arrived in America from Spain in 1492.

MAPMAKERS
In 1522, Ferdinand Magellan's ship from Spain completed the first voyage around the world. He died on the way, but the trip proved that the Earth was round. In the 1770s, James Cook of the British navy sailed the Pacific, mapping the coast of New Zealand and landing in Australia.

LAST FRONTIERS
Later explorers moved inland. The Scottish missionary David Livingstone traveled into Africa. Robert Peary of the United States conquered the North Pole in 1909, and Norway's Roald Amundsen reached the South Pole in 1911. In 1960, the *Trieste* dived 35,800 ft. (10,910m) under the sea, and in 1969 a human being walked on the Moon.

INTO THE UNKNOWN
Early sea voyages advanced navigational knowledge and helped mapmakers to produce more accurate maps. In the 1400s, Prince Henry the Navigator, of Portugal, skilled in mathematics and astronomy, helped organize 50 expeditions to West Africa. These trips pushed back the frontiers of navigation and paved the way for future trade and navigation.

SEE ALSO

Antarctica, Asia, Australia, Map, Ocean and sea, Space exploration, Submarine, Viking

EXPLOSIVE

An explosive is a substance such as gunpowder or dynamite that creates a huge burst of energy and a shock wave when it is triggered.

Demolition gangs use explosives to bring down old buildings. Mining companies use them to blast apart rocks, tunnelers to blow holes in mountains, and scientists to send rockets into space. Fireworks are pyrotechnic explosions that create a display of sound, light, and smoke.

Sticks of dynamite are removed from their waxed wrappers and a detonating cap is inserted.

CREATING SHOCK WAVES

When explosives release energy, they heat up the surrounding air. Fuels such as gas and coal release heat slowly, but an explosive heats the air rapidly. As the air around an explosive heats, it expands, creating a fast-moving shock wave that breaks apart any objects in its path. We hear the shock wave as a bang.

GUNPOWDER AND DYNAMITE

Gunpowder is the oldest explosive— it was discovered by the Chinese over 1,400 years ago. Its main ingredients are charcoal (charred wood), sulfur, and saltpeter, which are ground up and set on fire in air. Gunpowder is still used in fireworks today.

DETONATING SAFELY

The destructive power of an explosive is great, and it must therefore be controllable. When nitroglycerin (a combination of carbon, hydrogen, nitrogen, and oxygen) was invented in 1846, it was too dangerous to use, as it could detonate (ignite) by being shaken. The Swedish scientist Alfred Nobel solved the problem in 1867 by adding porous matter called kieselguhr, which created a new, safe explosive— dynamite. Dynamite does not need air to work and today is widely used for demolition.

UP AND DOWN AGAIN

Demolishing a tall structure using explosives is an act of patience and precision. Preparation can take days, using tons of dynamite and yards of fuse wire. The skill lies in making sure that the construction falls safely, in the right direction, away from obstacles.

Holes are bored in the bricks and the dynamite is inserted. Fuse wire links each detonator cap. The structure is weakened by carefully knocking out rows of bricks near the ground, leaving a zigzag of concrete struts. The demolition team has now finished its job, so everyone stands back and the electronic switch is flicked. The dynamite has been placed so that the structure falls without damaging any other buildings in the surrounding area.

SEE ALSO

Chemistry, Energy, Mining

FARMING

Farming is the growing of crops and raising livestock on the land to produce food, drink, textiles, and other products.

Items such as food, leather, cotton, and rubber come from farms. Farming is the world's biggest employer, taking up 35 percent of the working population.

ORIGINS OF FARMING

Archaeological evidence shows that farming began around 11,000 B.C., when Stone Age people began to herd wild animals. By around 8000 B.C., people had learned that scattered seeds would grow and multiply, providing food for themselves and their animals. The first crops were probably wheat and barley.

AGRICULTURAL REVOLUTIONS

Dramatic developments in farming have occurred since then. Irrigation of crops in Mesopotamia in 4000 B.C. and the ox-drawn plow, invented in about 3000 B.C., made it possible to work difficult soils. From the A.D. 1400s, the potato,

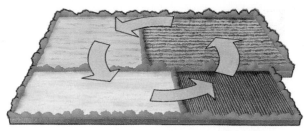

▲ In the early 1700s, English politician Charles Townshend created a four-field crop rotation system, which meant that a field did not have to be left fallow (empty) each year.

tomato, turkey, chili, and corn were brought from America to Europe and Asia. New machinery, such as Jethro Tull's seed drill (1700), Eli Whitney's cotton gin (1793), and steam-powered tractors (mid-1800s) made farming less labor-intensive.

NEW METHODS AND OUTLOOKS

Since the 1970s, a "green revolution" based on artificially improved crops and fertilizers has increased food production in poorer nations. In developed countries, new machines and the rearing of livestock on mechanized farms have increased production.

▲ Rows of green crops growing in the middle of a barren, sandy desert are evidence of the enormous achievements in farming and irrigation techniques.

DAIRY FARMING

Milk is produced on dairy farms from cattle, although goats, buffalo (bison), and sheep may also be kept for milk. On modern dairy farms, cattle are milked by machine. The milk is cooled and stored in a large tank before being sent to a plant to be put into containers or processed into butter, cheese, and other products.

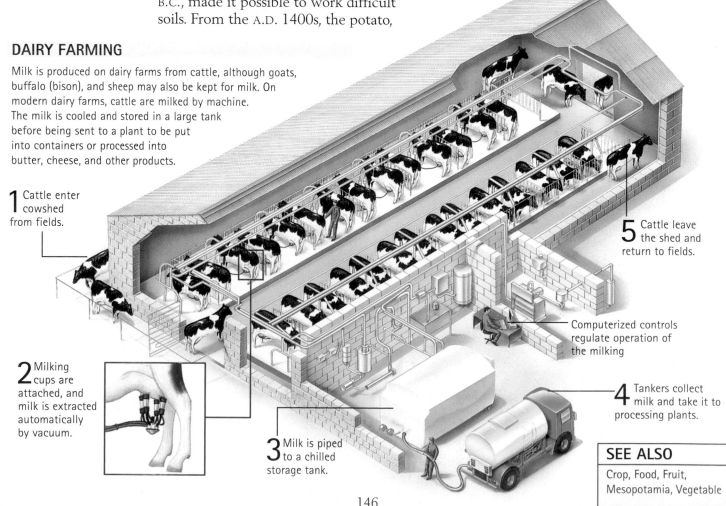

1 Cattle enter cowshed from fields.

2 Milking cups are attached, and milk is extracted automatically by vacuum.

3 Milk is piped to a chilled storage tank.

4 Tankers collect milk and take it to processing plants.

5 Cattle leave the shed and return to fields.

Computerized controls regulate operation of the milking

SEE ALSO
Crop, Food, Fruit, Mesopotamia, Vegetable

146

FASCISM

Fascism is a political belief that states that the government of a country is all-powerful and that the citizens must obey it for the good of the nation.

Juan Perón, with his wife Eva ("Evita"), ruled Argentina in the 1940s and 1950s.

General Francisco Franco won a civil war before ruling Spain (1939–75).

Antonio Salazar was dictator of Portugal from 1932 until 1968.

Oswald Mosley was the leader of the British Union of Fascists in the 1930s.

Fascist ideas gained support after World War I (1914–18), with the first fascist government appearing in Italy in the 1920s. The term fascism comes from *fasces*, bundles of rods with an ax that were symbols of state power in ancient Rome.

SUCCESS THROUGH STRENGTH

Fascism is based on the idea that a nation will only succeed through disciplined, ruthless action and a determined will. Fascists believe that achieving a worthwhile aim makes all actions acceptable. Schools, religion, newspapers, the arts, and sciences are expected to serve the nation. Military power and a secret police back up a fascist government. Fascists often believe that their race or nation is superior to all others.

SEIZING POWER

In 1922, the Italian fascist leader Benito Mussolini took advantage of chaos caused by a general strike to seize power. He called himself *Il Duce* (The Leader) and, with backing from big business, brought prosperity to Italy. But he led Italy to defeat in World War II and in 1945 was murdered by his own people. Fascist-style governments held power in Japan and Hungary in the 1930s and 1940s.

NAZI GERMANY

In Germany, the Nazi leader Adolf Hitler was voted into power in 1933, promising to end unemployment and poverty. As *Führer* (Leader), he crushed opposition, and ordered the murder of millions of Jews, gypsies, and others. In 1939, he started World War II, but killed himself in 1945 when Germany faced defeat.

MODERN EXTREMISTS

Some governments still follow fascist ideas, but none admits to fascism because of its association with the regimes of Hitler and Mussolini. Small, extremist political parties in many countries openly support racism and fascism, but win few votes in elections.

PACT OF STEEL

In May 1939, the two fascist dictators, Adolf Hitler in Germany and Benito Mussolini in Italy, agreed to a military treaty called The Pact of Steel. In 1940, Mussolini entered World War II on Hitler's side. They were later joined by other fascist states in Eastern Europe when Hitler invaded the Soviet Union in 1941. All shared in Hitler's downfall four years later at the end of World War II.

SEE ALSO
Government, Politics, World War I, World War II

FILM

A film is made up of a number of photos, or frames, projected in rapid sequence onto a screen to create moving images. It is a popular form of entertainment.

KEY DATES

1877 Photographer Eadweard Muybridge makes the first moving pictures on film

1895 The Lumières make the first motion picture

1903 Edwin Porter releases *The Great Train Robbery*

1905 Thousands of nickelodeon movie theaters (it cost a nickel to get in) open across America

1927 First talking film, *The Jazz Singer*, appears

1995 First full-length CGI animation, *Toy Story*

2009 Revival of 3-D filmmaking, with *Avatar*

In 1877, British-American photographer Eadweard Muybridge took a series of photographs of a horse running, using 24 cameras. By putting the photos together in sequence, Muybridge created the concept of moving pictures on film. This became the movies—the most popular art and entertainment form of the 1900s.

THROUGH THE PEEPHOLE
Thomas Edison picked up Muybridge's idea and made a machine called a kinetoscope, which showed up to 90 seconds of moving pictures, viewed through a peephole. The French brothers Louis and Auguste Lumière took things one step further by inventing a machine that took these images, stored them on rolls of celluloid, and projected them onto a wall for an audience to see.

ADVENT OF AN INDUSTRY
Film screenings became popular all around the world, but especially in the United States. The film that broke new ground in movie history was Edwin Porter's dramatic 11-minute epic *The Great Train Robbery* (1903) in which a group of gunmen robs a train, and is then tracked down and brought to justice.

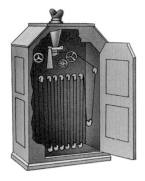

The kinetoscope, invented by Thomas Edison, was the first machine to produce moving pictures. Over 160 ft. (50m) of film revolved on spools, and the viewer looked through an eyehole to see the pictures move.

MAKING MOVIES

Making films can involve literally hundreds of technicians, actors, and camerapeople, but it is the director of the film who controls what is seen on screen. He or she decides how a film should be shot, where the cameras should be set, and what kind of lighting to use. Today, many directors use computer-generated special effects in their films, and some of the footage shot in the conventional way with the camera is changed completely by computer enhancement.

Second camera takes shot from different angle

Cameraman

Director

Microphone

Console controls sound

SCREENPLAY

The principles of Porter's film still define filmmaking today. A written script details the scenes to be shot; these scenes are filmed, in any order, and then edited together in the order of the original script. This is known as postproduction. It is at this stage that computer effects and the soundtrack are added.

SUN AND STARS

The sunny weather and open landscape of a small suburb of Los Angeles, California, called Hollywood, made it the center of filmmaking in America, and later the world, from 1907. Once sound was added to films in 1927, other countries formed film industries, too.

SMALL SCREEN COMPETITION

The popularity of television in the 1950s left cinema in a slump. Filmmakers tried gimmicks such as 3-D (viewers wore green and red tinted glasses) or "smell-o-vision" to attract audiences. This slump continued until the 1970s when the modern blockbuster was born. *Jaws*, Steven Spielberg's tale of a deadly killer shark, started the trend in 1975, but was eclipsed two years later by George Lucas's *Star Wars*. The 2000s saw 3-D movies return to popularity (viewers now wore dark-tinted, polarized glasses): the beginning of this new wave came with the release of *Avatar*.

SLAPSTICK MOVIES
Early movies were in black and white. Props and scenery provided the special effects, as in *Modern Times* (1936), one of Charlie Chaplin's first films with sound.

MUSICALS
Color was introduced in the 1930s, making films such as *The Wizard of Oz* (1939), shot in Technicolor, possible. However, until the 1950s, many films were still made in black and white.

MOVIE FRANCHISES
Franchises are movie series, where the same characters star in multiple movies. Successful series have included *The Pirates of the Caribbean* (above), *X-Men*, *Star Wars*, and *James Bond*.

ANIMATED MOVIES
In the past, cartoons were hand-drawn. Today, most animations are produced on computer, using CGI (Computer Generated Imagery). Many, like *Finding Dory* (2016), are released in 2-D and 3-D simultaneously.

SEE ALSO

Cartoon and animation

149

FISH

Fish are vertebrates (backboned animals) which breathe oxygen dissolved in water through their gills. They are found in salty and fresh water around the world.

▲ Mudskippers survive low tides in the swamps of Africa and Southeast Asia by breathing air. They use their strong pectoral fins as "arms" to climb trees in search of food.

FOUR TYPES OF FISH

Fish can be divided into groups by body structure. Examples are jawless fish, sharks and rays, and bony fish—primitive and modern.

Lampreys (above) and hagfish are ancient fish. They have no jaws, and, like sharks, their skeletons are made of soft cartilage.

Sharks usually have a torpedo-shaped body with a skeleton of cartilage. All have strong jaws, many with several rows of teeth.

Primitive bony fish, such as the coelacanth (above) and lungfish, are related to fish that lived over 400 million years ago.

Perch (above) are modern bony fish. Unlike primitive bony fish, they do not have a fleshy lobe at the base of each fin.

Most fish are streamlined for easy movement through water. The tail pushes the fish forward, and the fins are used for steering and balance. Most fish have two pairs of fins on their sides. There is one dorsal fin, running down the middle of the back, and another fin at the base of the tail. The tail is usually forked.

COLD-BLOODED CREATURES

As cold-blooded creatures, fish stay at the same temperature as the water they live in. If the water is very cold, fish slow down and may stop moving altogether. Apart from using sight and smell, fish also have a row of sensors on their sides, known as the lateral line, that picks up vibrations in the water even if the fish cannot see clearly.

BONE OR GRISTLE

There are over 32,000 known species of fish—more than all other vertebrates put together. Fish can be divided into cartilaginous fish and bony fish. Cartilaginous fish, whose skeletons are made of soft cartilage, or gristle, include sharks, skates, and rays. There are only about 900 species, all of which live in the

sea. Bony fish include some of the most colorful animals on earth, and the fastest—sailfish—can reach speeds of 60 mph (100kph).

BROWN AND GRISTLY

Most cartilaginous fish are brown or gray and have five or more gill slits on each side. Their fins are solid and their bodies are covered with rough, toothlike scales. Sailors once used shark skins to scrub the decks of wooden ships. The whale shark is the largest fish, measuring 40 ft. (12m) long and weighing up to 20 tons.

FISH BONES

Bony fish have smooth, overlapping scales. Their fins are delicate membranes stretched over slender spines. The gills are covered by a flap called an operculum, so there is only one gill opening on each side of the body. Most bony fish have an

TEMPERATE SEAS

Fish are adapted to suit their environment. Sea fish constantly lose water and must drink a lot, whereas freshwater fish take in water through their skin. Temperate waters, which get colder in winter, are home to dull-colored fish, commonly caught for food. These fish often swim deeper or migrate in cold weather.

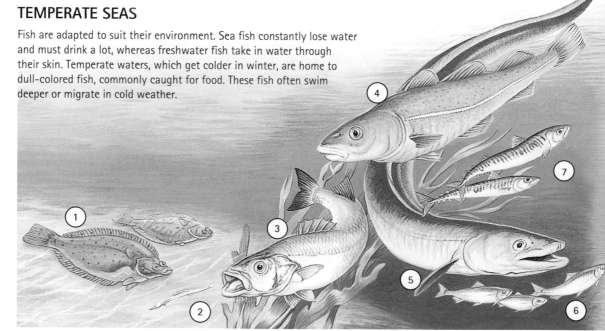

KEY TO TEMPERATE SEA

1 PLAICE
2 SAND EEL
3 BASS
4 COD
5 CONGER EEL
6 HERRINGS
7 MACKEREL

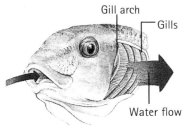

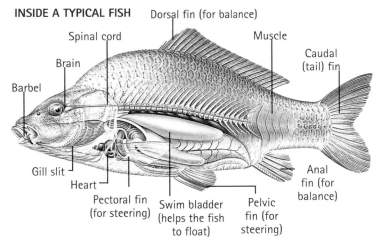

INSIDE A TYPICAL FISH

Gill arch
Gills
Water flow

Dorsal fin (for balance)
Muscle
Caudal (tail) fin
Spinal cord
Brain
Barbel
Anal fin (for balance)
Gill slit
Heart
Pectoral fin (for steering)
Swim bladder (helps the fish to float)
Pelvic fin (for steering)

▲ Oxygen from the water passes through the thin walls of the gills (tiny blood-filled threads arranged in pockets on each side of the throat) and into the blood. The water then passes out through the gill slits.

air-filled swim bladder, allowing them to float motionless in the water. Sharks have no swim bladder and would sink if they stopped swimming.

JAWLESS FISH

There are 70 species of lamprey and 43 species of hagfish. These eel-shaped creatures make up the jawless fish. Lampreys have a round, suckerlike mouth and toothed tongue, used to rasp flesh from other fish. Hagfish have a slit-shaped mouth and sharp teeth. They eat dead fish.

MILLIONS OF EGGS

Some fish give birth to live young, but most species lay eggs. These are usually released into the water by the female, where they are fertilized by the male. Fish lay many eggs, as most get eaten. The ocean sunfish may lay 300 million eggs in its lifetime. Fish that protect their eggs do not lay many, and it is often the male that looks after them. The female sea horse lays eggs in a pouch on the male's abdomen, where they can be protected.

TROPICAL SEAS

The most brightly colored fish live in the tropics, blending in with the vivid coral reefs—their camouflaged colors hide them from predators.

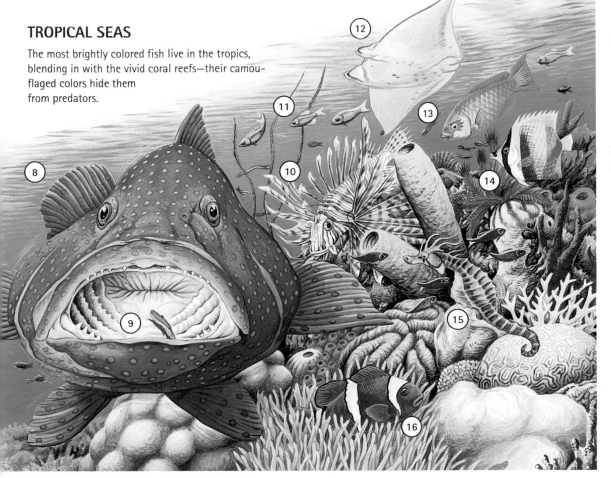

FRESHWATER FISH

About two fifths of all fish live in freshwater streams, lakes, rivers, ponds, marshes, and swamps.

Guppies, native to the Caribbean islands, are attractive and popular aquarium fish.

Piranha live in South American rivers, feeding on fish or other animals with their razorlike teeth.

This African catfish is typical of its group, which has long barbels (whiskers) and fins that lock upright.

Rainbow trout are native to North America, but because of trout farming, now live in European rivers.

The climbing perch can be seen taking short "walks" across land—it has a gill chamber for breathing air.

KEY TO TROPICAL SEA
8 GROUPER
9 CLEANER WRASSE
10 LION FISH
11 FAIRY BASSLET
12 MANTA RAY
13 PARROT FISH
14 BUTTERFLY FISH
15 SEA HORSE
16 TOMATO CLOWNFISH

SEE ALSO

Animal, Fishing industry, Fossil, Jellyfish, Ocean and sea, Prehistoric animal, Shark

FISHING INDUSTRY

The fishing industry is the organized business of catching or breeding fish and shellfish for food, from seas, rivers, or lakes.

Gill nets hang like curtains beneath the surface with weights to hold them down.

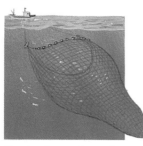

Trawl nets are dragged along the bottom to catch demersal (seabed) fish.

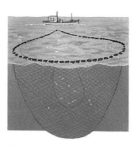

Purse seines are nets pulled in a circle around pelagic (surface) fish.

Fishing is one of the world's most important industries. About 109 million tons of fish are caught each year. China, Peru, the U.S., Indonesia, Chile, Japan, India, and Russia catch the most. People have caught fish since prehistoric times, but large-scale commercial fishing did not begin until the 1600s.

FISHING GROUNDS

The oceans are vast, but most fish are caught in well-known fishing grounds within 60 mi. (100km) of land, in the shallower waters of the continental shelf. There are rich fishing grounds off Canada's east coast, near Iceland, and around Japan. Fish are attracted to these places by plentiful supplies of plankton to eat.

FISH TYPES

Two types of fish are caught at sea: pelagic and demersal. Pelagic fish, including herring, salmon, tuna, and anchovies,

HARVESTING THE SEA

Many large fishing boats are equipped as floating fish factories. The net is winched in, and the haul is sorted into types of fish. Often they are cleaned and gutted before being placed in boxes of ice and stored in freezer compartments below deck to keep them fresh on the way to market. Long-range fishing boats may be at sea for several months at a time.

live near the sea's surface. Demersal fish, including cod, sole, and haddock, live near the seabed. Fishermen use different fishing methods and nets to catch the two types of fish. Nowadays, the size of fishing catches is limited by international agreements. This is because some species of fish have been overfished and are in danger of extinction.

FISH-FARMING

Keeping fish for food in tanks, ponds, or underwater cages is called fish-farming. Fish and shellfish, including salmon, trout, oysters, mussels, and scallops, are farmed. Fish farms produce nearly half of the fish people eat. In China, fish farms yield more than 35 million tons of fish a year. By comparison, Chinese fishing boats bring in 19 tons of fish a year.

▲ Onboard trawlers, sonar equipment detects large groups of fish.

SEE ALSO

Fish, Ocean and sea

FLAG

The United Nations recognizes 195 sovereign states. These are UN member and observer countries, each of which has a national flag flown at home and outside their embassies abroad.

Afghanistan

Albania

Algeria

Originally flags led the troops in warfare and identified friend or foe. The color and design of national flags reflect the nations' history or religion. In the U.S. flag the stars represent the states; the color red stands for courage, white for purity, and blue for justice and perseverance. In European heraldry white and yellow (representing metal) were never placed next to each other. Only the Vatican City flag breaks this rule. ▶

Andorra

Angola

Antigua and Barbuda

Argentina

Armenia

Australia

Austria

Azerbaijan

The Bahamas

Bahrain

Bangladesh

Barbados

Belarus

Belgium

Belize

Benin

Bhutan

Bolivia

Bosnia-Herzegovina

Botswana

Brazil

Brunei

Bulgaria

Burkina Faso

Burma (Myanmar)

Burundi

Cambodia

Cameroon

Canada

Cape Verde

Central African Republic

Chad

Chile

China

Colombia

Comoros

Congo, Republic of the

Costa Rica

Côte d'Ivoire

Croatia

Cuba

Cyprus

Czech Republic

Democratic Rep. of Congo

Denmark

Djibouti

Dominica

Dominican Republic

East Timor

Ecuador

Egypt

El Salvador

Equatorial Guinea

Eritrea

Estonia

Eswatini

Ethiopia

Fiji

153

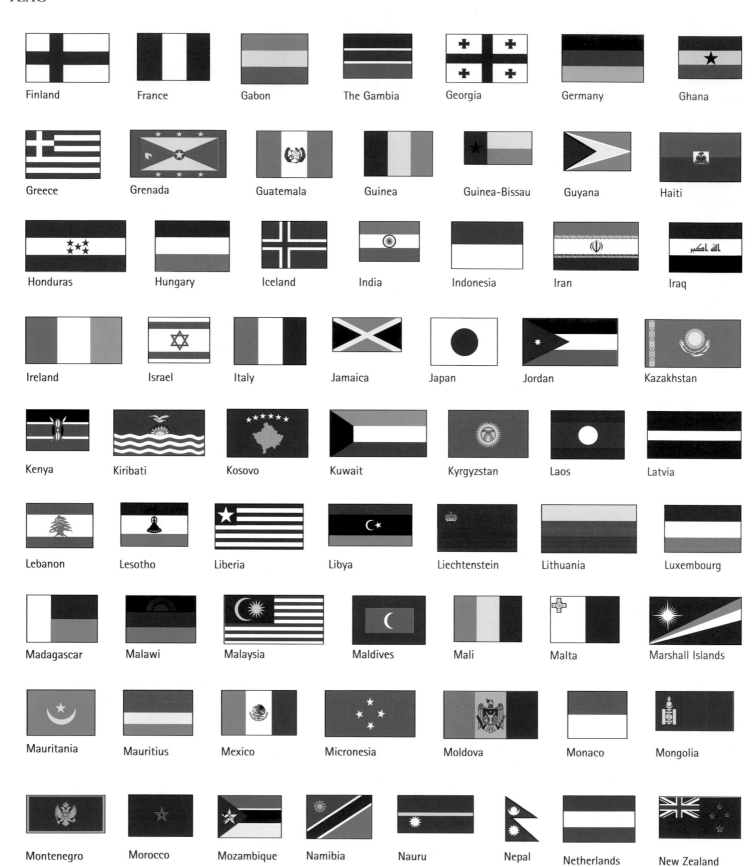

Finland · France · Gabon · The Gambia · Georgia · Germany · Ghana

Greece · Grenada · Guatemala · Guinea · Guinea-Bissau · Guyana · Haiti

Honduras · Hungary · Iceland · India · Indonesia · Iran · Iraq

Ireland · Israel · Italy · Jamaica · Japan · Jordan · Kazakhstan

Kenya · Kiribati · Kosovo · Kuwait · Kyrgyzstan · Laos · Latvia

Lebanon · Lesotho · Liberia · Libya · Liechtenstein · Lithuania · Luxembourg

Madagascar · Malawi · Malaysia · Maldives · Mali · Malta · Marshall Islands

Mauritania · Mauritius · Mexico · Micronesia · Moldova · Monaco · Mongolia

Montenegro · Morocco · Mozambique · Namibia · Nauru · Nepal · Netherlands · New Zealand

Nicaragua · Niger · Nigeria · North Korea · North Macedonia · Norway · Oman

Pakistan
 Palau
 Palestine
 Panama
 Papua New Guinea
 Paraguay
 Peru

 Philippines
 Poland
 Portugal
 Qatar
 Romania
 Russia
 Rwanda

 St Kitts-Nevis
 St Lucia
 St Vincent and the Grenadines
 Samoa
 San Marino
 São Tomé and Príncipe
 Saudi Arabia
 Senegal

 Serbia
 Seychelles
 Sierra Leone
 Singapore
 Slovakia
 Slovenia
 Solomon Islands

 Somalia
 South Africa
 South Korea
 South Sudan
 Spain
 Sri Lanka
 Sudan

 Surinam
 Sweden
 Switzerland
 Syria
 Taiwan
 Tajikistan
 Tanzania

 Thailand
 Togo
 Tonga
 Trinidad and Tobago
 Tunisia
 Turkey
 Turkmenistan

 Tuvalu
 Uganda
 Ukraine
 United Arab Emirates
 United Kingdom
 United States of America
 Uruguay

 Uzbekistan
 Vanuatu
 Vatican City
 Venezuela
 Vietnam
 Yemen
 Zambia
 Zimbabwe

FLOWER

Flowers are the reproductive parts of some kinds of plants. They make seeds that will form a new generation of the same type of plant.

Bats are attracted to the nighttime scent and infrared colors of some tropical flowers.

Flowers are really specialized leaves that have evolved over millions of years to help plants reproduce efficiently. There are more than 350,000 species of flowering plants, called angiosperms, which range from huge, long-lived trees to tiny annuals. Flowers may vary greatly in appearance, but they are all made up of the same basic parts.

MALE AND FEMALE PARTS

The main reproductive parts of a flower are the female carpel and the male stamens. Each stamen is made up of the anther, which produces tiny powdery grains of pollen, and the filament, or stalk. The carpel has a stigma, which is often sticky and colored. The stigma is found at the end of a style—a kind of stalk that leads down to the ovary. Inside the ovary are egg cells that develop into the seeds that will later become new plants.

POLLINATION

For seeds to form, pollen grains from the anther must come into contact with the

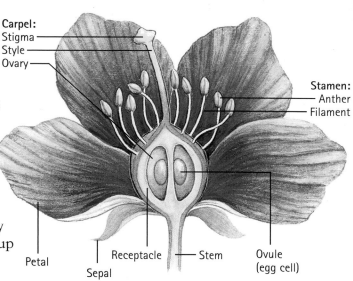

Carpel:
Stigma
Style
Ovary

Stamen:
Anther
Filament

Petal
Sepal
Receptacle
Stem
Ovule (egg cell)

▲ Flowers have four main parts: sepals and petals (the outer parts), and carpels and stamens (the reproductive parts). The stamens are male and the carpels are female.

stigma. This process is called pollination. Most flowering plants are pollinated by insects. For example, as a bee pushes inside the flower looking for nectar, its body gets dusted with pollen from the anthers of the flower. The bee will then transfer this pollen dust to the stigma of the next flower it visits.

FLOWER APPEAL

The varying colors, scents, and shapes of individual flowers have developed to appeal to pollinators—usually insects, but also birds and small mammals, such as bats. Many flowers have glands called nectaries, which produce nectar—a sugary liquid on which the pollinators feed. The pollinators must push past the male and female parts of the flower to reach the nectar.

Many alpine flowers are tough and lie low on the ground, to help them withstand the cold.

Desert plants, such as cacti, have bright flowers to attract insects for the few weeks they are in bloom.

▲ One of the petals of the bee orchid looks like a real bee. This signals to other pollinators that the flower is a good source of nectar, and they land on it. Other flowers attract bees with ultraviolet markings on their petals that only bees can see.

Water flowers, such as white water lilies, float above the surface to attract insect pollinators.

FLOWER FACTS

- The first flowering plant—thought to have been a magnolia—appeared about 160 million years ago

- The world's largest flower, *Rafflesia arnoldii*, grows in Indonesia and can measure up to 3 ft. (1m) in diameter. Its smell of rotting meat is irresistible to the flies that pollinate it

- Opium, which comes from the opium poppy, is used to make pain killing drugs like codeine

- The Madagascan periwinkle, once thought of as a weed, is now farmed to produce anticancer drugs

1 The poppy flower buds remain tightly closed until the pollen grains are ripe.

2 The buds begin to open, revealing the brightly colored petals and other flower parts.

Bee pollinator

3 The red flowers attract bees and flies, which climb into the flowers looking for nectar. Pollen from the carpels sticks to them and is carried to the stigma of the next flower that they visit. This is called pollination.

THE REPRODUCTIVE CYCLE

All flowering plants grow from seeds, which germinate into tiny plants, each with a root, shoot, and leaves. New buds on the shoot expand into leaves, branches, and more buds. When the plant is mature, some buds open to reveal flowers. The flower's male parts (anther and filament) release pollen grains. When these land on the stigma, a tiny tube grows down the style toward the egg cells in the ovary. When the tube meets an egg cell, the contents of both fuse together. This is fertilization, which results in a new seed.

BLOWN BY THE WIND

Some flowers are pollinated by the wind, which blows the pollen grains through the air. These flowers are rarely showy or scented. They often have feathery stigmas to catch the clouds of pollen as they fly through the air.

A GARDEN IN BLOOM

Particular flowering plants are selected for a garden because of when, and how often, they produce their flowers. This can depend on how long the flowering plants live. Annuals are plants that sprout, mature, flower, produce seeds, and die all in the same year. Biennials live for two years, and perennials live for three years or longer. Most garden plants are perennials, because once they have flowered, they flower every year for as long as they live.

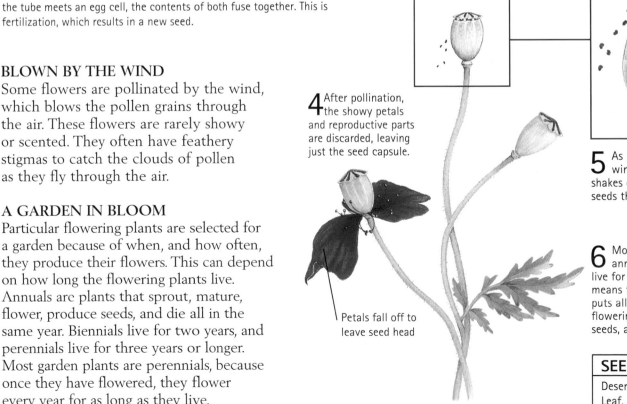

4 After pollination, the showy petals and reproductive parts are discarded, leaving just the seed capsule.

Petals fall off to leave seed head

5 As it sways in the wind, the seed capsule shakes out the ripened seeds through holes.

6 Most poppies are annuals (plants that live for one year). This means that the plant puts all its energy into flowering and producing seeds, and then dies.

SEE ALSO

Desert, Fruit, Grassland, Leaf, Plant, Rain forest, Seed and pollination

FOOD

Food is any substance that is a source of nutrition to a living organism. Without it, nothing can live. The food we eat is supplied by plants and animals.

Modern diets contain a wide range of foods. Some, such as fruits and vegetables, are still in the original state in which they were grown. Others, such as bread and hamburgers, are processed foods, which means they arrive at our tables looking very different from the ingredients that were used to make them.

THE FIRST FARMERS
Until about 15,000 to 10,000 years ago, humans were hunter-gatherers, spending much of their time hunting animals and gathering fruits and vegetables for food. By about 8000 B.C., people in fertile parts of the world were managing the land for agriculture. They started to grow food crops and to domesticate animals such as cattle, sheep, and poultry for milk, meat, and eggs.

DIFFERENT DIETS
Meat and dairy products are a major part of the diet in the West, but in many places people do not eat dairy at all—fewer than 30 percent of people in the world can digest lactose (the sugar in milk). In tropical countries, people eat mainly rice, cassava, and potatoes, with very few vegetables, while in Mediterranean countries, it is usual to have a high intake of all kinds of different fruit and vegetables.

FOOD INTAKE WORLDWIDE
Although there is more than enough food to support the world's population, it does not always reach those in need. One in seven people goes hungry—and 65 percent of the world's hungry live in only seven countries. Around 20 million people die of hunger each year. In the U.S., people eat 60 percent more food than they need, which can cause its own set of health problems.

STAPLE FOODS
Our food comes from many different sources, either plant or animal. The main foods obtained from plants are grains, fruits, and vegetables. Products made from grains, or cereals, such as rice or bread, have been the basis of the human diet for thousands of years. Food from animals includes meat, eggs, and dairy products. They cost more to produce than plant foods.

▶ Cereals such as wheat (right), rice, and corn together make up more than 60 percent of the world's food intake.

Breakfast cereal

Bread

Flat bread

Noodles

Cookies

Pasta

FOOD PROCESSING

Humans have been processing food—by cooking it—ever since the discovery of fire. Today, there are many other ways of processing food, such as milling, freezing, canning, and ultraheat treatment. Processing makes some foods, such as potatoes and wheat, easier to digest. It also stops food from rotting, which encourages germs to grow. Heat treatment kills germs, and chilling and freezing slow down their growth to a safe level.

ADDITIVES

Substances known as additives are usually added to foods during processing. Some, such as the vitamins and minerals added to bread and cereals, improve the nutritional value of food. Other additives include preservatives, which are added to foods to stop them going rotten, and colorings, such as the natural pigment of beets.

FOOD SAFETY

A small percentage of the population suffers from food poisoning each year, usually caused by food contaminated with harmful bacteria such as *E. coli* or *Salmonella*. Preparing food hygienically lowers the risk of food poisoning. Foods such as meat, fish, milk, and eggs should be heated and cooked thoroughly before eating to kill any dangerous bacteria.

RELIGION AND CULTURE

The food people eat often depends on their culture or religion. For example, some Jews eat a kosher diet governed by religious laws, such as cooking and eating meat and dairy produce separately. In the Hindu religion, every living creature is believed to have a soul, so eating animals is often avoided. Many vegetarians believe animals should not be killed for humans to eat.

▲ Paella is a Spanish dish made with rice, shellfish, vegetables, and chicken, named after the shallow frying pan in which it is cooked. Each country has unique local ways of preparing food that have often been passed down through the generations, and are usually made from local produce.

FRUIT AND VEGETABLES

We eat fruits, such as oranges, and vegetables, such as cauliflowers, in their natural state. However, oranges can also be processed to make juice or preserved by canning. Vegetables such as peas can be frozen or dried to last longer.

DAIRY PRODUCTS

Dairy cattle produce milk, from which other products such as butter, cheese, and yogurt are made. Beef comes from cattle that have been specially reared for their meat. Beef is cut up into joints or steaks, or ground for foods such as burgers.

Picking in an orange grove

Cauliflower

Fresh oranges

Orange juice

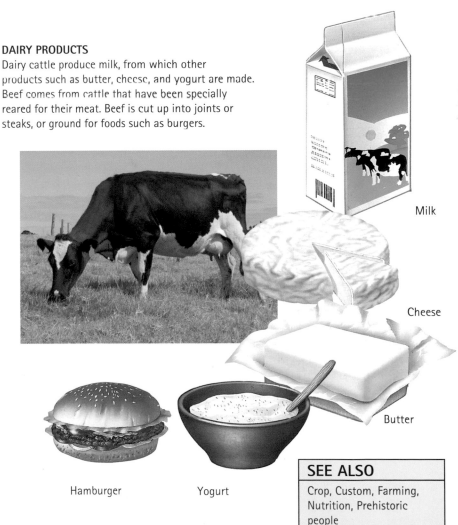

Milk

Cheese

Butter

Hamburger

Yogurt

SEE ALSO

Crop, Custom, Farming, Nutrition, Prehistoric people

FORCE AND MOTION

A force changes the way an object moves. If the object is stationary, a force will set it in motion. If it is moving, a force will change its speed or direction.

Force is a word we use in everyday speech. For example, we may talk about forcing a door open or forcing a suitcase shut. In both, a force—either a push or pull—is being applied by a person to move the door or suitcase lid.

▲ This amusement park ride is kept spinning in a circle by two competing forces: centrifugal force, which pulls outward, and centripetal force, which pulls inward.

▲ An object's weight affects how fast it moves and how long it takes to stop. This is called its momentum, and it can be transferred from one object to another, as between two pool balls.

CHANGING VELOCITY
A force is anything that changes an object's velocity (speed in a given direction). A ball rolling along the ground has a certain velocity, but if it is kicked, the ball increases velocity. An increase in velocity is known as acceleration, and a decrease in speed is called deceleration.

STATE OF INERTIA
An object that stays at the same velocity—neither speeding up, nor slowing down or changing direction—is said to be in a state of inertia. This rarely happens, however, because moving objects usually slow down because they bump into something, come into contact with the ground, or are blown by the wind. The force created by wind, or when two items rub together, is known as friction. It works against motion, slowing things down.

FAST FACTS
• A bus is harder to push than a car because an object with greater mass (more material) has more inertia, which means it needs a greater force to accelerate

• Two forces that balance each other exactly, producing no movement, are known as static forces. A bridge stays up in this way

---

MIGHTY FORCES
Pulling a door open or pushing it shut requires direct force and human strength. But sometimes we are not strong enough (do not have enough force) to move an object. People have invented machines such as levers and pulleys to increase the effect of human force. Powerful natural forces such as electricity and magnetism have also been harnessed to work for us. Another natural force, gravity, literally keeps our feet on the ground.

NEWTON'S LAWS
Most of the principles of force and motion were first discovered in the 1660s by the English scientist Isaac Newton. Today, in honor of his work, we measure force in newtons (N). One newton is roughly the force that you feel when you hold a large orange in the palm of your hand.

ACTION AND REACTION
Whenever force is applied to an object, it always creates another force, called a reactionary force, that works in the opposite direction. A kayaker paddling through water moves forward by such action and reaction. The kayaker's paddle pushing the water backward is the action, while the reaction is the force exerted by the water on the paddle, which pushes the kayak forward through the water.

Action: the paddle pushes against the water

Reaction: the kayak moves forward in the water

SEE ALSO
Bridge, Electricity, Gravity, Heat, Invention, Machine, Magnetism

FORENSIC SCIENCE

Forensic science is the scientific investigation of a crime, such as theft or murder, by scientifically trained specialists—doctors, dentists, chemists, and biologists.

▲ Surfaces are dusted for fingerprints. Victims have their fingerprints taken, so that only unknown prints are included in a search.

▲ Dried blood is scraped off the murder weapon, diluted, and analyzed for blood type and DNA code.

No matter how careful a criminal may be, he or she will leave clues behind. It is the job of the forensic team to examine the scene of the crime for fingerprints and footprints, bloodstains, and other evidence.

AT THE SCENE OF THE CRIME

Equipment such as cameras, lasers, and materials for casts make a record of the position of everything at the scene. Samples of hair, paint, glass, and other substances are also taken away for analysis. These samples have to be handled very carefully. The investigating team wears paper bodysuits, overshoes, and gloves so that they do not contaminate the samples. They will also wrap and seal the samples in plastic before sending them for analysis.

ANALYZING CLUES

Fingerprints can reveal the identity of a criminal, if they can be matched to samples kept on a computer network. Analysis of DNA (genetic code) from blood and other samples taken from the scene of the crime has been used since 1986 for more serious crimes. Each person has a unique DNA fingerprint or profile, which can be checked against samples taken at the scene. Laboratory analysis of a single fleck of paint is enough to identify a car used in a crime, for example. Similarly, bite marks in food found at the scene can lead to an arrest, if they can be matched with dental records.

CAUSE OF DEATH

Suspicious deaths involving murder, suicide, or an accident are usually investigated by a coroner (an official who specializes in forensics). The coroner will order an autopsy (an examination of the body to determine the cause of death). The forensic pathologist (a doctor who specializes in autopsies) examines the appearance of the body and then dissects it, looking at each organ in turn. He or she also analyzes blood and flesh samples.

WHO DUNNIT?

Every item at the scene of the crime tells a story. Criminals often wear gloves, so fingerprints are rare, but clothing fibers caught on the corner of a photocopier in a scuffle may lead police to the murderer.

FIBERS
Fibers from clothing worn by the criminal and the victim are taken away and studied under a microscope.

FINGERPRINTS
Finding just one print can solve the crime—even identical twins have different fingerprints.

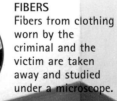

BLOOD
Originally, only the blood group could be established, but now a unique DNA code can be found.

FOOTPRINTS
Footprints can reveal the criminal's shoe size and the store where the shoes were bought.

SEE ALSO
Chemistry, Genetics

FOREST

Forests are large areas of land covered mainly by trees and other plants. Today, they occupy almost 30 percent of the world's land area.

There are three basic types of forest: coniferous (boreal), broad-leaved deciduous, and dense, tropical rain forests. Many forests include a combination of coniferous and deciduous trees.

CONIFEROUS FORESTS

Coniferous forests are found in the cold northern areas of Canada, Europe, and Asia and include spruce, fir, or pine. These trees are evergreens (do not shed their leaves in winter) and carry their seeds in cones.

DECIDUOUS FORESTS

The temperate regions of the United States and Europe have warm summers, mild winters, and rain all year round. Here, the native forest trees, such as oak, ash, and beech, are all deciduous, which means they drop their leaves in the fall.

THE LIFE OF THE FOREST

A forest's highest layer is formed by the treetops and is called the canopy. Below this are shorter trees, then a layer of bushes and shrubs. Lower still, there are ferns, grasses, and wildflowers, and then the mosses and fungi that grow on the forest floor. In addition to the larger animals, such as deer and squirrels, there are thousands of smaller creatures living under the leaves, and in the bark and forest soil.

THE TROPICS

In the hot, permanently wet regions of the tropics, there are dense rain forests full of teak, ebony, rosewood, mahogany, and other evergreen trees. Often the trees grow so closely together that sunlight cannot reach the ground. Other regions in the tropics with both wet and dry seasons have deciduous woodlands and savanna—grasslands with scattered clumps of trees.

WHY WE NEED FORESTS

Forests provide food and shelter for animals and refresh the atmosphere by turning carbon dioxide into oxygen. More than three billion people use firewood for cooking and heating. There is also a large trade in forest products: softwoods (conifers) for building and making paper, and hardwoods (deciduous) for furniture. Other products include fruits, nuts, and spices, gums and resins, rubber, and many vital medicines.

▲ In deciduous forests, the fallen leaves form a carpet on the floor which nourishes new growth.

FAST FACTS

- Before forests were cleared to make way for farms and cities, forests covered about 60% of the world's land area

- 29% of the forests are boreal, 21% temperate, and 50% tropical

- Some rain forests have up to 300 different trees in 1,076 sq. ft. (100 sq m)

- In the United States, under 10% of the original forests remain

---

1 At first, there is a grassy meadow, into which pine seeds fall and grow to become seedlings.

2 Pine trees need full sun to grow, so they form the top layer of forest, with deciduous trees beneath.

3 The type of forest changes as old pines die and deciduous trees fill in gaps in the canopy.

4 In the final stage, a totally deciduous forest develops. It is the climax of this ecological succession.

SEE ALSO

Brazil, Habitat, Plant, Rain forest, Tree

FOSSIL

Fossils are the remains of once-living things found in rocks. They are preserved in different ways and show us what conditions were like in the past.

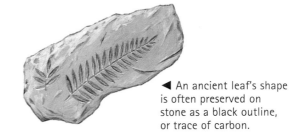

◄ An ancient leaf's shape is often preserved on stone as a black outline, or trace of carbon.

Dead insects can be preserved whole in tree resin (sap) that has turned into amber over time.

Ammonites (fossilized shells of extinct mollusks) are often found as molds or casts in rock.

A dinosaur footprint, made over 65 million years ago, may be preserved in rock as a trace fossil.

Fossils can include shells, bones, teeth, leaves, skeletons, or even whole animals. Most fossils are found in areas that were once in, or near, water, such as the sea or a river. Layers of mud in the water settle over the animal, creating the perfect conditions for its remains to be preserved.

TYPES OF FOSSIL

A living substance can be preserved whole, but more often it is changed in some way over time. It can be replaced by another material, such as stone, or may rot away leaving an empty mold of the organism.

PRESERVED WHOLE

An insect stuck in resin (sap) oozing from a tree will be preserved whole when that resin turns to the semiprecious stone amber. When larger animals die, usually only the hard parts like bones and teeth are preserved. Sometimes, pools of natural tar can preserve mammoth bones unaltered since the Ice Age (over 10,000 years ago).

PETRIFIED WOOD

Fossilized wood is petrified. This means that the wood has been replaced, molecule by molecule, by a stony material. The carbon

in a leaf can survive as a black outline on a stone surface. Millions of leaves preserved in this way produce coal.

A STONE REPLICA

Stone copies of plants or animals are created when water seeps through the rock in which they lie, removing all of the remains. This leaves an empty mold in the shape of the living creature, which is filled by minerals seeping into the rock—creating an exact copy of the creature, known as a cast. Seashells are often fossilized as casts in limestone. Trace fossils are marks in the rock that show where an animal once existed, as in the case of wormholes.

USEFUL FOSSILS

We can tell how old a rock is from its fossils. Many animals existed for only a short time in history and, when we find their fossils in rock, we can tell the age of that rock. Other fossils tell us about the climate or habitat of an area in the past. For example, finding a fossil palm leaf in a cool region indicates it once had a tropical climate, and fossil seashells found far inland reveal that the area was once under the sea.

HOW FOSSILS ARE FORMED

When a dinosaur dies, its flesh rots away, leaving only the bones behind. Scavengers may also remove parts of the body, so complete fossilized remains are rare. Over time, the bones are covered by layers of soil, which harden into rock. Millions of years later, the fossil is exposed by wind and rain or movements in the Earth's crust.

1 The dinosaur's body falls into a sea, river, lake, or swamp. Under water the remains are more likely to be buried fast by soil and sand deposited by the water.

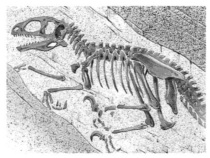

2 The dinosaur's flesh rots away or is eaten by water animals. Its bones and teeth are covered by many layers of sand and soil, which change to rock over time.

3 Thousands of years later, the strata of rock shift, bringing the bones to the surface.

SEE ALSO

Coal, Dinosaur, Evolution, Oil, Prehistoric animal, Rock

FRANCE

France is Europe's third-largest country. Only Russia and Ukraine are larger. France has a rich cultural tradition and a turbulent history.

Area: 212,900 sq. mi. (551,500km²)
Population: 67,364,000
Capital: Paris
Language: French
Currency: Euro

Most French landscape is plains or low hills. Three of its borders are high mountain ranges: the Vosges in the northeast; the Pyrenees in the southwest; and the Alps, including France's highest point, Mont Blanc (15,771 ft./4,807m), in the southeast. The Massif Central rises in central France. Paris, the capital, lies in flat country on the Seine River. Other major rivers include the Loire, Rhône, and Gironde.

A NATION OF FARMERS

France is the European Union's leading farming nation. Its soil and climate are good for crops. The north is cool and moist, averaging about 1.5 in. (35mm) of rainfall per month. The south is drier and hotter, with summer temperatures above 77°F (25°C). Farmers grow wheat, barley, oats, flax, sugar beet, fruit, and vegetables and raise cattle and sheep. France is famous for its wines and cheeses, and French cooking is admired and copied all over the world.

PARIS THE CAPITAL

Paris is the center of government, arts, and fashion. It is France's largest city—home to about a sixth of the nation's people. Its 2,000-year-long history means the buildings are a mixture of old and new. Visitors come to see the Louvre Museum, the tomb of Napoleon, Notre Dame Cathedral, the Eiffel Tower, and other famous sights.

▲ Peaceful rural communities are farm-based. Typical crops include wheat, apples, and grapes.

FRENCH LIFE

Although France is a land of forests and green countryside, 81 percent of the people live in towns and cities. They meet in sidewalk cafés and restaurants, or enjoy a game of *boules* (a kind of outdoor bowling). Favorite sports include bicycle racing, soccer, rugby, and tennis. There are parades and speeches on Bastille Day (July 14), France's national holiday commemorating the beginning of the French Revolution in 1789.

AN INDUSTRIAL GIANT

After Paris, the largest French cities are Marseilles (the main seaport), Lyon, Lille, Nice, and Toulouse. France has a highly developed industrial economy. French factories produce many goods, including cars, aircraft, chemicals, machinery, and textiles. Fishing and mining are important. France also has a world reputation for luxury goods, such as perfume and elegant clothes. Europe's fastest trains speed between French cities, and there is also a fine road system.

▲ Many French people, and other Europeans, ski in the Alps on the border between France and Italy.

▶ This spectacular glass pyramid, finished in 1989, is the entrance to the Louvre Museum in Paris. The Louvre, originally built as a residence for the kings of France, now houses one of the world's largest art collections.

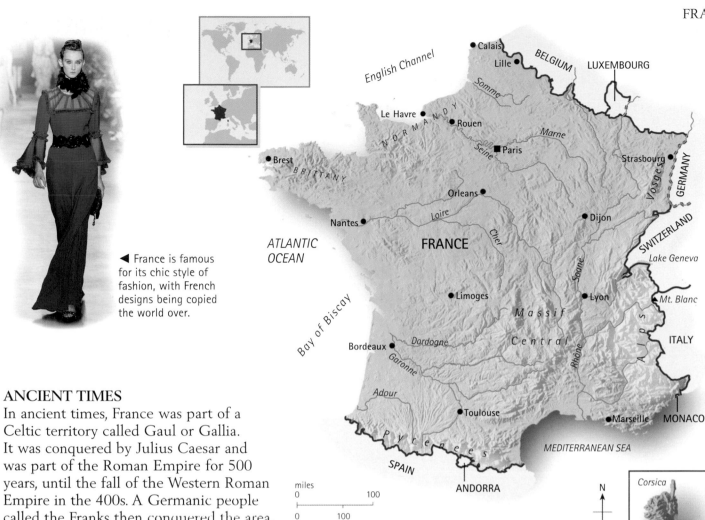

◀ France is famous for its chic style of fashion, with French designs being copied the world over.

ANCIENT TIMES

In ancient times, France was part of a Celtic territory called Gaul or Gallia. It was conquered by Julius Caesar and was part of the Roman Empire for 500 years, until the fall of the Western Roman Empire in the 400s. A Germanic people called the Franks then conquered the area, bringing it within their empire. France gets its name from the Latin *Francia*, meaning "country of the Franks."

A TURBULENT HISTORY

France became an independent country in the 800s, but there was no common language until the founding of the French Academy in the 1630s. France has had a turbulent history, including wars with England and Spain and rule by greedy or inept kings. The Revolution of 1789 removed the king and many of the old ways, and during the rule of Napoleon Bonaparte (1799–1815), France dominated Europe. France suffered great damage and loss of life in two world wars, but recovered to become a founding member of the European Union (EU) and a strong voice in world affairs.

ACROSS THE WORLD

France also ruled colonies overseas, which is why today the French language and culture are found in places as far apart as Quebec and North Africa. There are still many French dependencies, mainly in the Caribbean and the Pacific. The island of Corsica, which lies off the southeast coast, is also a region of France.

▲ Each summer, the world's top riders take part in the Tour de France, a bicycle race across France. The final stage is in Paris, from Disneyland to the Champs-Élysées.

▲ The 984 ft. (300m)-high Eiffel Tower in Paris won a design competition for the World's Fair in 1889.

SEE ALSO

Celt, Europe, Napoleonic Wars, Revolution, World War I, World War II

165

FROG AND TOAD

Frogs and toads belong to the group of animals known as amphibians. Most spend their early life as tadpoles in water, but the adults live mainly on land.

◄ The male edible frog has large vocal sacs to call females in the mating season.

Gliding frogs have rounded sucker pads to help them climb.

Bullfrogs can grow up to 8 in. (20cm) and may even eat newly hatched alligators.

South American arrow-poison frogs are extremely dangerous.

Frogs are related to toads, but frogs generally have a slimmer body with smooth skin, and toads have drier, warty skin. All amphibians have thin skin; their lungs are inefficient, and they breathe mainly through their skin. Oxygen from the air passes through the skin and into tiny blood vessels just under the surface. This can happen only if the skin is moist, so they are usually found in damp places.

STICKY TONGUE

Most frogs feed on slugs, insects, and worms, which they catch with a long, sticky tongue. Larger frogs, such as the American bullfrog, also feed on prey such as mice, and even small ducklings.

MUSCULAR LEGS

Frogs are great jumpers. Their long, muscle-packed hind legs can send them shooting over 12 times their own length through the air. Webbed feet help frogs swim; tree frogs make huge leaps from branch to branch, aided by sticky pads on their toes. Toads have less powerful back legs than most frogs and waddle.

BRIGHT COLORS

Green or brown is the typical color of most frogs, but some tropical frogs are brilliantly colored. Some species change their skin color with changes in light or temperature, and all frogs shed the outer layer of their skin several times a year, pulling it over their head with their legs.

NOISY COURTSHIP

Frogs and toads can be very noisy at breeding time, when males croak to attract females. The European marsh frog is one of the noisiest—a colony sounds like a crowd of people laughing.

INSIDE A FROG

A frog's internal organs are similar to those of higher animals such as dogs. Externally, their bulging eyes help them look around in many directions, while the disk above the eyes is the eardrum (called a tympanum). Some frogs have a sticky-tipped tongue fixed to the front of their mouth that they flick out to capture prey.

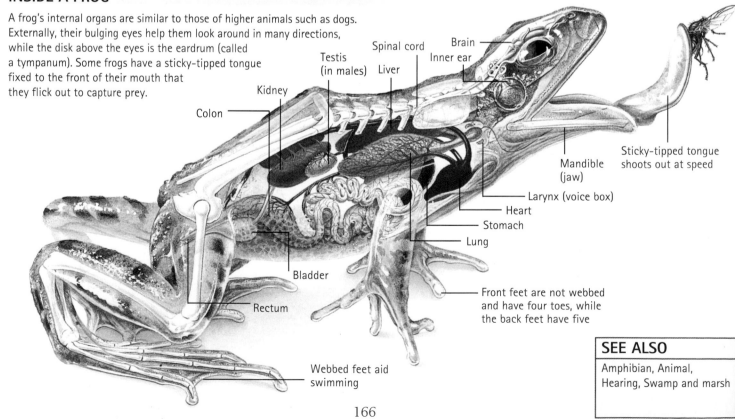

Testis (in males)
Spinal cord
Liver
Brain
Inner ear
Kidney
Colon
Mandible (jaw)
Sticky-tipped tongue shoots out at speed
Larynx (voice box)
Heart
Stomach
Lung
Bladder
Front feet are not webbed and have four toes, while the back feet have five
Rectum
Webbed feet aid swimming

SEE ALSO

Amphibian, Animal, Hearing, Swamp and marsh

FRUIT

Fruits contain the seeds of flowering plants. They protect the developing seeds and help them to reach a suitable place to grow into new plants.

Pomes are fleshy fruits like pears which have their seeds in a core formed from the flower stem.

Berries, such as tomatoes, cucumbers, and oranges, hold many seeds inside a single fruit with soft pulp.

Drupes have a single stone which contains the seed. Blackberries are a cluster of many small drupes.

Dry fruits range from chestnuts to corncobs, but all are seed-bearing.

For a new generation of plants to grow successfully, the seed must be spread away from the parent plant so that the new plants are not all grouped together. Fruits are the means by which flowering plants ensure that their ripe seeds get to new, fertile locations.

FLESHY FRUITS

Fruits can be divided into two basic groups: fleshy and dry. Fleshy fruits are juicy and taste good to mammals and birds, which eat the seeds along with the fruit. The seeds pass through the animals' bodies undigested and drop to the ground, where they grow into new plants. Strawberries are false fruits. They develop from a swollen stem. The seeds on the surface are the real fruits.

DRY FRUITS

Fruits such as poppy seedheads or walnuts become dry as the seed ripens. Some, such as pea pods, split open so that the seed is scattered in all directions. Others, such as the maple key, are light and can be blown by the wind. Nuts are also fruits. They have a hard outer casing that rots when the seed inside is ripe and ready to germinate (start growing).

SEED CONTAINERS

Fruits develop from the ovary of the flower after it has been pollinated. The seeds inside the fruit develop from the fertilized egg cells within the ovary. Some fruits, including peaches, cherries, and plums, contain a single seed. However, most fruits, such as apples, raspberries, tomatoes, and squashes, contain more than one seed. Occasionally, the sepals (leaves outside the flower petals) remain after the petals of the flower have fallen, and enclose the fruits, as in acorns.

FRUIT TO EAT

Some fruits are poisonous to humans, but there are many that are delicious and nutritious. Fleshy fruits often contain fruit sugars, which are a useful source of energy, and the fiber provided by the skin, flesh, and sometimes the seeds, aids healthy digestion. Fruits contain vitamins, minerals, and other nutrients that help the body fight off illness. Nuts are also an excellent source of protein.

EATING THE FRUIT

The bright color and pleasant smell of fruits such as blackberries attract birds and animals to eat them. After digesting the soft outer part, they pass the seeds out of their body with the rest of their waste. By this time, they will often be at some distance from the original plant.

1 The dispersed seed falls on fertile soil and the first shoots appear.

2 Flowers on the mature plant are pollinated and produce seeds.

3 The petals drop off and the fruit forms. It is hard and unappealing to birds.

4 The fruit becomes succulent and sweet when it is ready to be eaten.

SEE ALSO
Flower, Food, Leaf, Nutrition, Plant, Seed and pollination

FUNGI

Fungi are neither plants nor animals, but have their own kingdom, which has over 120,000 species and includes mushrooms, toadstools, molds, and yeasts.

◄ The mold on this peach comes from airborne spores that have started to breed.

The earth star lifts its fruit body clear off the ground on starlike rays.

The giant puffball is as big as a man's head and makes billions of spores.

Truffles, which grow close to tree roots, are considered the tastiest of fungi.

Unlike plants, fungi need a supply of organic food in order to grow and reproduce. Plants have a green pigment, called chlorophyll, which allows them to make their own food using the Sun's energy. Fungi have no chlorophyll, so they take food from plants and animals.

WHERE THEY LIVE

There are more than 80,000 different types of fungus. Some, like yeast, are only a single cell. Most form masses of threads, called mycelium, which spread inside whatever they feed on. Many live inside plants or in the soil, where they help to break down dead plant and animal matter.

HOW THEY BREED

To reproduce, fungi must release minute spores into the air. Some fungi, such as mushrooms and toadstools, grow large fruit bodies to help the spores travel farther. Others grow tall, threadlike stalks with spore capsules at the end. If they land in a suitable place, the spores will grow to form new fungi of the same type. There are fungus spores around us all the time.

USEFUL FUNGI

Some fungi are useful because they help to break down the remains of dead plants and animals or make medicines. An example is the antibiotic penicillin. Certain yeast fungi are used to make bread and alcohol. Some mushrooms are good to eat, but others contain deadly poison, and it is difficult to tell them apart.

NO-FUN FUNGI

Fungi can grow on and spoil food, paper, wood in buildings, and damp clothes. Fungal diseases can damage and even kill plants, including crops such as potatoes and strawberries. Some affect animals and people: athlete's foot is a common fungal disease that causes itchy, flaky skin between the toes.

HOW FUNGI BREED

Like most fungi, the poisonous fly agaric has a web of threadlike mycelium through which it feeds on decaying matter. To reproduce, it releases spores from the surface of its gills into the air. When the spores land, they develop their own mycelium. But they can only grow fruit bodies by joining up with mycelium from the same species of fungus.

Cap

Developing gills

Developing cap

Mycelium

Upturned cap allows spores to disperse farther

Gills, where spores are produced

Spores

Stipe (stem)

SEE ALSO

Medicine, Microorganism, Plant

GALAXY

A galaxy is a huge collection of stars held together by gravity. The Sun is just one of as many as 400 billion stars contained within our home galaxy, the Milky Way.

There are probably over a billion galaxies in the universe. They come in three basic shapes: spiral, elliptical, and irregular.

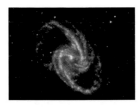

Barred-spiral galaxies have a well-defined bar with arms attached to it.

Elliptical galaxies can be round or oval and have very little gas or dust.

THE NUCLEUS

The central part of a galaxy is called the nucleus. Here, stars are crowded much closer together than on the galactic outskirts. Astronomers now know that massive black holes may lie deep within the nucleus of many large galaxies. There is probably a black hole at the center of our own galaxy.

LIGHT YEARS AWAY

Enormous distances separate galaxies. The closest large galaxy to the Milky Way is the Andromeda Galaxy, located about two million light years away. It is the farthest object visible to the naked eye.

CLUSTERS AND SUPERCLUSTERS

Galaxies are arranged in clusters, which are themselves part of superclusters. The Milky Way and the Andromeda Galaxy are the two largest members of a small cluster of about 30 galaxies known as the Local Group. This, in turn, forms a tiny part of the Local Supercluster.

ACTIVE GALAXIES

Galaxies vary greatly in the amount of energy they give off. Some galaxies, known as active galaxies, are so-called because they give out more energy than is available from all the stars they contain. The extra energy is believed to be supplied by matter falling into a black hole at their center.

ELLIPTICAL

Elliptical galaxies are round or oval in appearance and usually have very little gas or dust. They vary greatly in size, from giants to dwarfs. Giant ellipticals may contain up to ten trillion stars and are the largest type of galaxy.

Irregular galaxies are small and shapeless and contain a great quantity of gas.

Nucleus

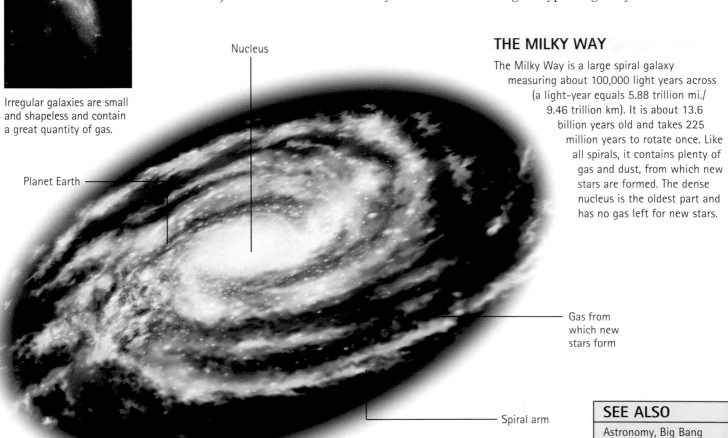

Planet Earth

THE MILKY WAY

The Milky Way is a large spiral galaxy measuring about 100,000 light years across (a light-year equals 5.88 trillion mi./ 9.46 trillion km). It is about 13.6 billion years old and takes 225 million years to rotate once. Like all spirals, it contains plenty of gas and dust, from which new stars are formed. The dense nucleus is the oldest part and has no gas left for new stars.

Gas from which new stars form

Spiral arm

SEE ALSO

Astronomy, Big Bang theory, Black hole, Constellation, Solar system, Star, Universe

GAS

Gas that is burned for cooking and heating is a fossil fuel consisting mainly of methane. It is usually brought into homes and industries via pipelines.

Gas is useful because it releases heat when it burns. It is used for heating and cooking in homes, and many industries burn gas for welding or smelting.

FOSSIL FUEL

Most domestic gas is natural gas, found underground, often with oil or coal but sometimes on its own. Like oil, gas was formed over millions of years from the remains of plants and animals. These organisms are made up largely of hydrogen and carbon, which change to a hydrocarbon called methane when they decay. The natural gas is then mined. Bottled gas, used by campers, is not natural gas. It is propane or butane, two by-products of oil refining.

PROCESSING GAS

Most natural gas is found under the sea. It flows under pressure through

92 percent Methane

3.5 percent Ethane

2.5 percent Nitrogen

1 percent Propane

1 percent Other

◄ The composition of natural gas varies, although its main ingredient is always methane. These are the percentages for gas from the North Sea.

a pipe connected to a gas terminal on land, although some is made into a liquid and shipped across the sea. There are a few unwanted substances in natural gas, which are removed at the terminal. The resulting gas does not smell, and a leak could go unnoticed. So a chemical with a distinct smell called a thiol is added.

GAS—THE BURNING ISSUE

The Chinese used natural gas thousands of years ago to evaporate seawater to obtain salt. In the early 1800s, oil prospectors set alight wells which produced only gas because it was worthless to them. Then, in the 1870s, experiments were carried out in which natural gas was piped into U.S. homes. Methane is one of the gases believed to be affecting climate change.

1 Exploration teams search for gas by drilling from rigs in areas with the right rock formation. Gas is often found with oil.

2 The gas reaches terminals in seamless steel pipes.

3 Smaller pipes then supply homes and industries.

4 The gas is used in stoves and heating systems.

DRILLING FOR GAS

Gas is usually found many thousands of feet below the Earth's surface in a rock such as sandstone. A layer of hard, impermeable rock above it prevents the gas from reaching the surface unless it is drilled by a gas or oil company.

SEE ALSO

Climate Change, Mining, Oil, Rock

GENETICS

Genetics is the science that studies how animals and plants pass their features to their offspring, generation after generation.

Gregor Mendel (1822–84) bred pea plants and studied how they passed features on to offspring.

Nobel Prize-winning scientists James Watson of the U.S.A. and Francis Crick of the U.K. discovered the structure of DNA in 1953.

Babies look like their parents. This tendency for offspring to resemble their parents was known in ancient times. People bred particular plants or animals with features they wanted, such as cows that gave the most milk. Over many generations, this selective breeding led to cows that gave even more milk.

PATTERNS OF INHERITANCE
In the 1850s, an Austrian monk called Gregor Mendel discovered the basics of inheritance by breeding pea plants. He found that some features of pea plants, such as height and color, were not passed on to the next generation as a blend of both parents' features. Instead, a feature from one parent was dominant.

IT IS IN THE GENES
We now know that the features inherited by the peas were decided by their genes.

▶ Dolly, the first artificially cloned sheep, was created from a cell taken from another adult sheep. This meant that both sheep had exactly the same genes.

Genes are the instructions which decide the appearance and function of each living cell or organism. They are arranged on corkscrew-shaped chemicals called DNA (deoxyribonucleic acid), visible only under an electron microscope.

PASSING ON GENES
When a human or other living thing reproduces, it passes on a copy of half of its genes to its offspring. Each reproductive cell (sperm or egg) contains a different combination of genes, guaranteeing that each offspring will be unique.

GENETIC ENGINEERING
Scientists can now change animals and plants by genetic engineering. The required gene is extracted from the DNA using chemicals called enzymes and inserted into a host organism to obtain the desired characteristic.

PASSING ON THE MESSAGE

DNA is made of thousands of chemical subunits (known as bases), strung in a line like beads on a necklace. There are four different bases, called A, T, G, and C, which are arranged along the DNA. Their sequence determines the cell's genetic code, in the same way that letters of the alphabet arranged in a certain order become a sentence.

The DNA strands are separated while the code is copied during reproduction

C = Cytosine, which always links to Guanine

T = Thymine

G = Guanine

A = Adenine, which always links to Thymine

A gene is made up of three pairs of subunits

Genes are contained inside the nucleus of each microscopic living cell

Nucleus

The DNA strands are coiled up into chromosomes —human cells contain 23 pairs

The DNA strand looks like a twisted ladder—a shape known as a double helix

The DNA is wrapped around a core of proteins

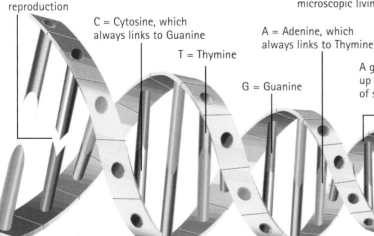

SEE ALSO

Atom and molecule, Cell, Crop, Farming, Forensic science

GERMANY

Germany is a large country that lies in the middle of Europe and borders nine other countries. East and West Germany were reunited in 1990.

Area: 137,847 sq. mi. (357,021km²)
Population: 80,594,000
Capital: Berlin
Language: German
Currency: Euro

Germany has a varied landscape, with a broad, flat plain in the north and uplands in the central region. The south is mountainous and includes the Black Forest, and Bavarian Alps. The country is crossed by several major rivers, including the Danube, Rhine, Oder, Weser, Ems, and Elbe. The climate is rarely severe, with warm summers and mild winters, and most places receive from 20–40 in. (500–1,000mm) of rain a year.

FARMING AND INDUSTRY
Fewer than 1.5 percent of Germans are farmers, growing crops such as wheat, barley, rye, and potatoes, as well as grapes to make wine. Many more people work in manufacturing or service industries. There are factories almost everywhere, especially in the Ruhr region—the heart of the iron, steel, and chemical industries. German goods include cars, cameras, computers, and textiles. Factories in the east are being modernized to match those in the west, the most prosperous part of the country.

GETTING AROUND
Germany has a high standard of living, and many people own cars. Expressways, called *Autobahnen*, were built from the 1930s, and the country also has an

▲ Many locals wear Bavarian national costume during the famous Munich Beer Festival, held every October. It attracts thousands of people from all over the world.

▶ Germany is the world's fourth-largest producer of cars after Japan and the United States. Car manufacturers from all over the world exhibit their latest models at the Frankfurt Motor Show each year.

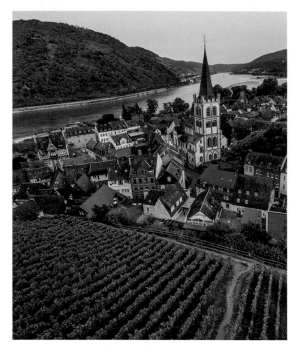

▲ The Rhine is one of Europe's most important rivers. Its banks are lined with vineyards and picturesque towns.

efficient modern railroad system. Barges carry heavy goods along the Rhine and other waterways.

A LAND OF VARIETY
Germany is divided into states called Länder. There are great regional differences, affecting the spoken dialect, building traditions, religion (Catholic or Protestant), festivals and customs. Food has many regional specialities, especially for sausages, meats, cheeses, pickles, and breads, and also for its famous local beers and wines. From the 1950s to the present day, immigration has added to the mix of languages, faiths, cultures and foods.

ARTS AND ARCHITECTURE
Germany has produced philosophers such as Kant and Hegel, and writers such as Goethe and Schiller. Bach, Beethoven, Brahms, and Wagner were all German. The automobile was invented by the German engineers Daimler and Benz, and German scientists pioneered the jet engine and space rocket. The country is also famous for Meissen china, as well as for its architecture, which includes many magnificent churches and palaces.

WARS AND RECOVERY
For hundreds of years, Germany was a patchwork of independent states, each with its own rulers. By the 1700s, Prussia

emerged as the strongest, uniting most of the other states to form a German Empire, in 1871. Germany suffered defeat in World War I (1914–18) and was then ruled by the Nazi dictator Adolf Hitler, who led the country into World War II (1939–45). Defeat in this war left Germany divided. East Germany was under communist rule, and West Germany became the richest capitalist democracy in Europe. In 1990, the two parts—an economically prosperous west and an impoverished east—were reunited, bringing many economic and social problems. However, Germany is still a powerful economic and political force within the European Union (EU).

▲ Since reunification, Berlin has become a cosmopolitan city, known for its alternative arts and music scene, its clubs and cafes, its new architecture, galleries and museums.

DENMARK
BALTIC SEA
NORTH SEA
Rostock
Hamburg
Bremen
POLAND
Elbe
Oder
NETHERLANDS
Weser
Berlin
Hannover
Ems
Harz Mts.
Rhine
Dortmund
Essen
GERMANY
Leipzig
Düsseldorf
Dresden
RUHR
Cologne
Bonn
BELGIUM
OBE MTS.
Mosel
Frankfurt
CZECH REPUBLIC
LUXEMBOURG
Main
Mannheim
Nürnberg
N
FRANCE
Stuttgart
Danube
BLACK FOREST
Munich
AUSTRIA
SWITZERLAND
Bavarian Alps

miles
0   100
0   100
km

▼ Sigmaringen Castle, built on top of a mountain in the Black Forest region, is typical of many castles that dot the German landscape.

SEE ALSO

Europe, Fascism, Industrial Revolution, Industry, World War I, World War II

GLACIER

A glacier is a mass of ice that flows slowly, under the influence of gravity, either from high in the mountains or in polar regions where it is very cold.

Take a handful of snow and squeeze it hard. It turns to ice in your hand. This is what happens when snow falls, year after year, in the valleys of high mountains. The snow at the bottom of the valley is compressed by the weight of the snow above, until it turns to ice.

ICE RIVERS

As the ice comes under greater pressure from the snow above, it begins to soften and flow like putty. At this point, a glacier has formed. The glacier moves slowly—perhaps 10 ft. (3m) per year.

DESTRUCTIVE POWER

A heavy glacier is a powerful force of erosion. As it moves downward, it grinds the valley into a distinct U-shape. A valley that once held a glacier is obvious from its flat bottom and vertical sides.

GATHERING RUBBLE

The debris that is worn away by the glacier is carried along, either embedded in the ice or lying on the top. This rubble is called moraine. When it is dropped at the glacier's snout (front edge) as the ice melts, moraine forms a landscape of irregular heaps of sand, clay, and rocks.

POLAR ICE CAPS

Glaciers that form near the North and South poles can cover whole countries or continents, and are usually known as ice caps or ice sheets. Snow falls at the center of the continent and spreads out toward the sea. Antarctica and Greenland are both covered by ice sheets.

FREEZING—AND MELTING

Between 1,600,000 and 10,000 years ago, the Earth went through periods of intense cold, known as ice ages. For thousands of years in each ice age, vast glaciers covered much of North America, Asia, and Europe as far south as London, England. Many of the lakes, valleys, and hills that we see today were carved by these ice sheets. The 21st century has seen a widespread and accelerating melting of glaciers, which is believed to be associated with global warming.

1 The top of the valley is eroded by the glacier into a sheer-sided basin called a cirque.

2 As the glacier travels, its surface cracks to form crevasses.

3 The glacier picks up soil and rocks (moraine), which pile into ridges.

Snout

4 Melting ice forms a lake at the bottom of the glacier.

This is also moraine

SEE ALSO

Antarctica, Arctic, Lake, Mountain and valley, Prehistoric animals, Prehistoric people

GLAND

Glands are organs that make and release chemicals that the body needs. One group of glands makes hormones, which control growth, life, and development.

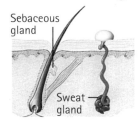

▲ The skin has two exocrine glands beneath its surface: sebaceous glands, which make oil to keep skin and hair soft, and sweat glands, which keep the body cool.

Sebaceous gland

Sweat gland

FAST FACTS

• Tear glands are exocrine glands that release tears to clean the front of the eye

• Human endocrine glands produce over 50 hormones

• Women's breasts are mammary glands, which produce milk

Some glands in the body have little tubes known as ducts, through which they release chemicals directly to an area where they are needed. These are the exocrine glands. They include sweat glands in the skin and salivary glands in the mouth. Other glands have no ducts and release chemicals called hormones into the blood. These are the endocrine glands.

THE MASTER GLAND
The pituitary gland is the smallest but most important gland in the body. It is attached to part of the lower brain called the hypothalamus. Together, these two areas of the brain control all of the body's nerves and endocrine glands.

SUGAR IN THE BLOOD
The body stores and uses energy as glucose (blood sugar). A gland in the neck, called the thyroid gland, makes a hormone called thyroxine which controls metabolic rate (how fast the cells use up glucose). The amount of glucose in the blood is regulated by two more hormones, called insulin and glucagon, which are made in the pancreas.

HEALTHY TEETH AND BONES
On the thyroid gland are four tiny, pea-size glands called parathyroids. Together, the thyroid and parathyroids make hormones which affect levels of calcium for healthy teeth and bones.

PUMPING UP THE ADRENALINE
There is an adrenal gland on top of each kidney. The outside of each gland makes steroid hormones that control the body's water balance and bodily reactions to stress and illness. The inside makes adrenaline (epinephrine), the hormone that gets the body ready for emergency action. A fast heartbeat, more sweat, and the need to urinate frequently are all effects of adrenaline. Today, we may feel these effects in a stressful situation, such as an exam, but their original purpose was to prepare the body to run from danger, such as a wild animal.

ENDOCRINE GLANDS

Hormones circulate around the body in the bloodstream. Their levels are often regulated by a system known as feedback. This means that sensor cells check how much of each hormone is present in the blood, and tell the glands to release more or less, as is needed.

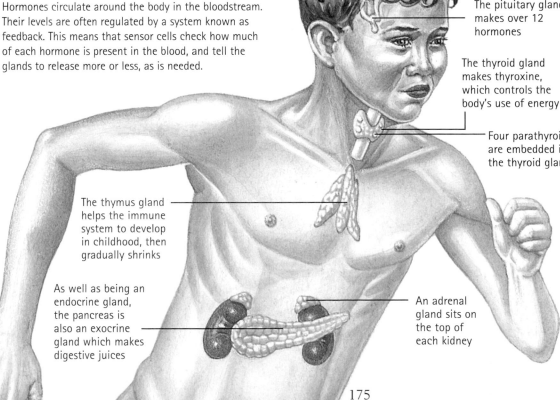

The pituitary gland makes over 12 hormones

The thyroid gland makes thyroxine, which controls the body's use of energy

Four parathyroids are embedded in the thyroid gland

The thymus gland helps the immune system to develop in childhood, then gradually shrinks

As well as being an endocrine gland, the pancreas is also an exocrine gland which makes digestive juices

An adrenal gland sits on the top of each kidney

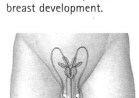

Ovaries

▲ Ovaries make female hormones which control the menstrual cycle and breast development.

Testes

▲ Testes make male hormones which control sperm production and growth of facial hair.

SEE ALSO
Brain and nervous system, Hearing, Human body, Mammal, Reproduction, Sight, Skin and hair

GLASS

Glass is a transparent material made by melting together sand, salt, and other substances at high temperatures, then leaving them to cool gradually.

People first made glass over 6,000 years ago, to use as a colored glaze on stone or clay beads. The earliest surviving glass containers, dating from about 1500 B.C., came from Egypt and Mesopotamia. They were molded around stones as they cooled, or carved once they had set. There are many more ways to make glass today. It can be molded, blown into shape, or rolled into flat sheets like pastry.

USES FOR GLASS

Glass is used to make countless objects around us—from windowpanes and lenses in eyeglasses to cookware and ornaments. It can also be pulled into long strands, like spaghetti, to make fiberglass. Fiberglass can be spun into thicker strands, called fiber-optic cables, that carry information as pulses of light over vast distances. It can also be matted to make glass wool, a material that traps heat like a blanket. Glass wool is often used to insulate attics.

SODA-LIME GLASS

Modern, manufactured glass is about 72 percent silica (the main ingredient of sand), but also contains other substances to make it easier to produce. Ninety percent of all glass is a type called soda-lime glass. This contains soda (sodium carbonate) to reduce its melting temperature from 2,372 to 1,292°F (1,300 to 700°C), and lime to stop it dissolving in water.

TOUGHENING IT UP

Tiny amounts of other chemicals can change glass properties. Boron, for example, can make it ovenproof, copper can make it a red color, and lead can make it more transparent. Because glass shatters, it can be laminated (toughened by sandwiching acrylic plastic or wire meshwork between layers of glass). Such glass can be made to withstand bullets.

1 A powder containing about 72 percent silica (the quartzlike part of sand), 15 percent soda, 6 percent lime, 4 percent magnesia, 2 percent alumina, and 1 percent boric oxide is poured into the furnace.

2 The glass is heated until soft and workable. The s͏c gives a melting point of abo͏ 1,292°F (700°C).

3 The glass passes between rollers and onto a bath of hot metal, usually tin, where it floats until its surface is smooth and hard.

FLOAT GLASS FOR WINDOWS

Traditionally, window glass was made by hand, either by spinning or blowing a lump of melted glass flat and cutting it. Then, at the beginning of the 1900s, sheet glass began to be made by drawing melted glass straight from the furnace through rollers. The surface was rough, though, and needed costly polishing, so in the 1950s, English glass manufacturer Alistair Pilkington invented the float process shown here.

4 The glass passes over cooling rollers until its surface is hard enough not to be scratched by handling.

5 The glass is cut for use in windows and mirrors.

▲ Stained-glass windows are made from small pieces of colored glass, joined together with lead strips. The colors come from metal oxides which are added to the glass during smelting. For example, red is from copper, and yellow is from manganese and ferrous oxide. Features are painted on later.

SEE ALSO

Materials,
Telecommunication

GOLD

Gold is a shiny, yellow precious metal. It is a stable chemical element that is not affected by air or water, which means that it never rusts or tarnishes.

Unlike most metals, gold occurs in its pure state. Some of it is found as grains in sand or gravel, but most of it occurs as veins in rock. It has been valued by people for thousands of years because of its qualities as an attractive metal that never tarnishes and is easy to shape.

▲ Most gold is found in lodes, or veins, in rock. This must be crushed before the gold can be collected.

GOLD MINING

Most gold—about 2,500 tons a year—is extracted by mining. After crushing the rock in which it is found, gold is collected using one of several chemical methods, the most common of which is the cyanide process. Sodium cyanide is added to a pulp of powdered rock and water. This dissolves the gold, which is filtered before zinc is added. The gold settles as a fine mud, and the zinc is dissolved.

ORNAMENTAL AND PRACTICAL

Gold has been used for making jewelry and ornaments for thousands of years. Today, it is used for many other things, including wiring electronic circuits, making dental fillings, and forming part of satellite reflector shields.

▲ This mask belonged to King Kofi Karikari of Ashanti, in what is now Ghana, West Africa. It is made of pure gold weighing nearly 3.3 lbs. (1.5kg). It was part of royal treasures seized by British invaders at Kumasi in 1874.

STRENGTHENING GOLD

Pure gold is very soft and needs to be hardened by mixing it with other elements, such as copper, nickel, or silver. The amount of gold in an object is measured in carats. Eighteen-carat gold contains 18 parts of gold and 6 parts of silver and copper. The purest gold is 24-carat gold.

THE GOLD RUSHES

Nearly half of the world's gold is held by governments as ingots (gold bars). Gold has always been prized. From 1840 to 1900, thousands sought their fortune in California, Colorado, the Yukon in Canada, South Africa, and Australia in what came to be called gold rushes.

PANNING FOR GOLD

Rocks containing tiny nuggets, veins, or flakes of gold may become eroded (worn away) by rain or ice. When this happens, the gold can be carried into streams. During a gold rush, prospectors would be seen standing in streams panning for gold. After dipping the pan into the stream they would swirl and tip it gently to throw off water, leaving gravel—and, with luck, gold.

▶ If the prospector was lucky, he would find small grains of gold mixed in with the gravel at the bottom of the pan.

SEE ALSO
Australia, Chemistry, Metal, Mineral and gem

GOVERNMENT

The government of a country is the system by which laws are made, social services provided, and the country organized.

The structure of governments varies, but most governments are responsible for the same tasks and have a constitution (a set of rules that they must obey).

BRANCHES OF GOVERNMENT

Most governments today have three branches: the executive (a president or prime minister), the legislative (a congress, assembly, or parliament), and the judiciary (the highest courts of law). A democratic legislature is composed of elected representatives, and it makes the laws by which the country is governed. New laws are debated by the legislature, then a vote is taken. Once a law is passed it is enforced by the judiciary.

THE JOB OF GOVERNMENT

National matters, such as defense or foreign policy, come under the national government. Services such as education, police, fire, parks, trash collection, road-building, transportation, and urban planning come under local (municipal) administration. Governments may also provide social services to help the aged, the unemployed, or those on low incomes. Costs for such services may be shared between national and local governments.

DICTATORS AND OLIGARCHS

In ancient Rome, an oligarchy (men from a small number of noble families) met in the Senate to run the government. In 82 B.C., Lucius Sulla was made dictator with supreme power to solve disputes. Against strong opposition, he reformed the constitution and the legal system and cut government power. In 79 B.C., Sulla retired to his country estate.

RAISING TAXES

Running a country is expensive. Governments raise money by placing taxes on how much people earn or inherit and on how much they spend. Income taxes vary wildly—in some countries, people pay nothing on their earnings, while in others top rates can be as high as 67 percent. To pay for local services, local governments may collect additional taxes.

▲ The House of Commons, inside the Houses of Parliament at Westminster, London, is where elected members of the British parliament sit and vote on new laws.

TYPES OF GOVERNMENT

Communism A system based on the political theories of Karl Marx and Friedrich Engels in the 1800s. They advocated class war and a society in which all property is owned by the people. Communist states are usually dictatorial.

Dictatorship Rule by one person, a group, or a committee whose word is law. Often accompanied by censorship and restricted rights. The idea of dictatorship comes from ancient Rome, when the Roman Senate could appoint individuals as dictators in times of national emergency.

Federalism A union of two or more states that can pass individual state laws, but that accept the national government's rule in matters such as the country's defense. The United States, Australia, Canada, and Switzerland all have federal governments.

Monarchy Rule by a king, queen, emperor, or empress. Traditionally, a monarch would have supreme power, but nowadays most monarchs have only constitutional power. This means that their power is limited by the country's constitution or government to ceremonial duties. The U.K. has this system.

Oligarchy Government by a small ruling group. A republic would be an oligarchy if only a few people were entitled to vote for the leader. Most ancient Greek city-states were oligarchies because only the free men (not slaves or women) could vote. Ancient Rome was an oligarchy ruled by a few nobles.

Republic A state or country where power is held by elected representatives acting on behalf of the people who elected them. An elected president is head of state and sometimes of the government. This is the most common form of government in the world today.

SEE ALSO

Civil rights, Democracy, Empire, Revolution, Women's rights

GRASSLAND

Grasslands are large areas of flat or gently rolling land covered by grasses, often with trees and bushes scattered across them or clustered along streams.

▲ Damp, long-grass prairies are rich in bluestem, switch grass, and needlegrass.

Between dry, rainless deserts and dense, wet forests there are usually areas known as grasslands. These regions have definite wet and dry seasons. The grasses grow quickly, flower, and produce seeds in the wet season, then die back or do not grow in the dry season. Most of a grass plant is below ground. This means that it can survive droughts and fires better than other plants.

GRASSLAND TYPES

Different types of grass grow all over the world, and grasslands are given different names wherever they exist. In North America, they are called prairies or plains; in Africa, savanna. The cooler grasslands of Argentina are called pampas, and in Russia they are steppes.

AFRICAN SAVANNA

Temperatures on the savanna are hot all year, and rain falls only during the summer. The long red oat, bluestems, and dropseed grasses plus scattered trees produce up to 18.2 tons of vegetation per acre (45 tons per hectare) each year, providing food for animals that include zebras, antelope, and ostriches. Frequent fires encourage fresh growth of grasses and trees.

ANIMALS AND PLANTS

Antelope in Africa, kangaroos in Australia, and bison in the United States graze the grasslands. Marmots, rabbits, and ground squirrels burrow for roots and shelter. These plant-eaters are hunted by lions, wolves, hyenas, and birds of prey such as hawks and eagles. Invertebrates (animals without backbones), such as insects, are the largest group of grassland animal. These provide food for rodents and small birds.

HARVESTING THE LAND

Wild grasslands once covered almost a third of the world's land, but most have been changed by humans. Sheep farmers in Australia, cattle ranchers in the U.S., dairy farmers in Europe, and nomadic goat herders in North Africa all depend on natural or cultivated grasslands to feed their animals. Grasslands have also been plowed to produce cereal crops such as wheat, corn, and oats.

Scattered trees grow where roots can reach deep, permanent water

Waterholes fill during the wet season, storing water for the dry season

Grazing animals wander across the grasslands in herds, usually settling near a source of water

SEE ALSO

Africa, Animal, Argentina, Canada, Crop, Farming, Food, Habitat

GRAVITY

Gravity is a force that exists between any two objects, pulling them together. On Earth, the force of gravity pulls you toward the ground and gives you weight.

◄ The speed at which a rocket is launched determines whether it escapes Earth's gravity and flies into space or plummets back to Earth.

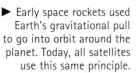

► Early space rockets used Earth's gravitational pull to go into orbit around the planet. Today, all satellites use this same principle.

When you jump up in the air, you come back down again. This is because Earth's gravity pulls you down toward the planet. If there were no gravity, we would drift off Earth and into space. Gravity explains why the stars and planets move in the way that they do, and how the Moon affects the tides each day. It is also the force that gives us our weight.

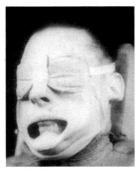

▲ Astronauts and fighter pilots feel the effects of g-forces (gravity) during takeoff. Not only does gravity distort their faces, but it can also send all the blood to their legs, sometimes making them feel faint.

FAST FACTS

• Isaac Newton (1643–1727) discovered the law of gravity, supposedly when he saw an apple fall from a tree

• Gravity keeps the rings of Saturn in orbit around the planet

• To escape Earth's gravity, a spacecraft must reach 6.9 mi./sec. (11.2km/sec). This is called escape velocity

MASS AND WEIGHT

The less gravity there is, the less you weigh. If you were in outer space, far away from any other objects, you would not feel any gravity. This means you would be completely weightless, even though your mass (quantity of matter) would not have changed. On Earth, the weight of something depends on its mass. A walrus has more mass than a mouse, for example, so it feels a greater force of gravity. That is why a walrus weighs more than a mouse.

FREE FALL

Sky divers experience a feeling of weightlessness in a free fall from a high airplane. In fact, they are still being pulled by Earth's gravity, but the air resistance is pushing against them. Only outside Earth's atmosphere, in space, are we truly weightless.

PULLING TOGETHER

We normally think about gravity only as it applies to Earth, but gravity exists between any two objects. The greater their mass and the closer they are together, the larger the force of gravity between them. Two ships at sea, for example, will attract each other, but their gravitational pull is so small compared to other forces on Earth that it is not noticeable. However, two nearby spaceships, far away from other objects in space, will create a noticeable gravitational attraction, called microgravity.

DROPPED FROM ON HIGH

Like all forces, gravity alters the velocity (speed) of objects. Near Earth's surface, gravity makes all objects accelerate at the same rate—32.19 ft./sec.^{2} (9.81m/sec^2)—no matter how heavy. If a full and an empty box fall from the top of a tall building, they reach the ground together.

SEE ALSO

Earth, Force and motion, Moon, Solar system, Spacecraft

GREAT DEPRESSION

The Great Depression was a worldwide slump in trade and economies. It began with the Wall Street stock market crash in 1929 and lasted well into the 1930s.

President Franklin D. Roosevelt launched the New Deal: a national program to aid the poor through community projects. Preparations for World War II aided recovery in Europe.

In the 1930s, trade between nations collapsed, businesses closed, and millions of people lost their savings and their jobs. This worldwide slump was known as the Great Depression.

THE CAUSES

Trouble began after World War I (1914–18). The loser, Germany, was ruined by having to make huge payments to the victorious Allies. Many Germans lost all of their savings as the value of their money collapsed. There were fears of a revolution like the one in communist Russia (1917).

HOME FROM WAR

In Britain, France, and the United States, factories struggled to adjust to peacetime trade. Millions of soldiers came home and looked for jobs. Trade unions called workers to strike against employers who demanded wage cuts. In 1926, a general strike (all workers) happened in Britain. Food prices fell so low that many farmers were ruined and were forced to give up their land.

THE CRASH

In 1929, the United States's financial market crashed after a period of frantic buying. Share prices fell sharply, ruining many investors. Banks and businesses shut down. The Wall Street Crash (named after New York's financial district) affected money markets around the world. World trade plunged. The Great Depression had begun.

EFFECTS OF THE SLUMP

The Great Depression cast a shadow across the 1930s. Jobless people lined up for food and clothing handouts. Some lost their homes and wandered the streets, begging or looking for work. Droughts and dust storms brought more misery to farming communities in the United States.

▲ Few were immune to the effects of the Great Depression. Many well-qualified people were out of work.

FLEEING THE DUST BOWL

In 1930, a drought hit large areas around Oklahoma, where grassland had been plowed to produce wheat. By 1933, the soil had turned to dust, leaving farms useless. Thousands of poverty-stricken families fled the Dust Bowl looking for work in California and elsewhere. By the 1940s, the grassland had regrown.

SEE ALSO

Communism, Money, Revolution, World War I, World War II

GREECE AND THE BALKANS

More than ten countries make up the Balkans, a region that includes the Balkan Peninsula, named for a mountain range that runs through it.

ALBANIA
Area: 11,100 sq. mi. (28,748km²)
Population: 3,048,000
Capital: Tirané
Languages: Albanian, Greek
Currency: Drachma

BOSNIA-HERZEGOVINA
Area: 19,767 sq. mi. (51,200km²)
Population: 3,856,000
Capital: Sarajevo
Language: Serbo-Croatian
Currency: Convertible Mark

BULGARIA
Area: 42,811 sq. mi. (110,880km²)
Population: 7,100,000
Capital: Sofia
Languages: Bulgarian, Turkish
Currency: Lev

CROATIA
Area: 21,851 sq. mi. (56,590km²)
Population: 4,292,000
Capital: Zagreb
Language: Croatian
Currency: Kuna

GREECE
Area: 50,949 sq. mi. (131,957km²)
Population: 10,769,000
Capital: Athens
Language: Greek
Currency: Euro

▶ Remains of the Parthenon, a temple built in the 400s B.C. for the goddess Athena, stand on the Acropolis in the center of Athens.

The Balkan peninsula has seas on three sides: the Adriatic and Ionian to the west, the Mediterranean to the south, and the Aegean and Black seas to the east.

MOUNTAIN COUNTRY
Apart from the Balkan Mountains, there are several other mountain ranges. One famous peak is Mount Olympus in Greece, which is 9,550 ft. (2,911m) high. The Danube River is the most important waterway, forming the border between Romania and Bulgaria. The Balkan region has a mild climate. Summer temperatures reach 86°F (30°C); winters can be cold and snowy in the mountains.

NATIONS AND PEOPLES
There is a rich cultural and religious diversity as a result of many invaders to the region. Ancient Greece ruled an empire until the Roman invasion in 146 B.C. Then, in the A.D. 300s, the Roman Empire became split into east and west, and the Balkans fell into the eastern part, known as the Byzantine Empire. During the 500s, Slavs came down from the north, scattering into distinct tribes, which are reflected in the languages present today: Bulgarian, Serbian, Croatian, Slovenian, and Macedonian. The Ottoman Turks ruled the region from the 1400s, but most Balkan people stayed Christian under Islamic rule.

▲ A fisherman rows across the harbor on the Greek island of Symi. Balkan coastlines break up into chains of rocky islands. The warm seas and sunshine attract many tourists.

THE BALKANS TODAY
Yugoslavia, Bulgaria and Albania became communist countries. The Federal Republic of Yugoslavia broke up amid savage civil wars in 1991, and is now made up of seven independent nations. The entire Balkan region has faced economic challenges in recent years. Greece, Bulgaria, Slovenia and Croatia are members of the European Union. Greece has struggled to cope with the arrival of many refugees escaping from war or poverty in the Middle East, and other parts of Asia and Africa.

KOSOVO
Area: 4,203 sq. mi. (10,887km²)
Population: 1,895,000
Capital: Pristina
Languages: Albanian, Serbian
Currency: Euro

NORTH MACEDONIA
Area: 9,928 sq. mi. (25,713km²)
Population: 2,104,000
Capital: Skopje
Languages: Macedonian, Albanian
Currency: Denar

MONTENEGRO
Area: 5,333 sq. mi. (13,812km²)
Population: 643,000
Capital: Podgorica
Languages: Montenegrin, Serbian
Currency: Euro

SERBIA
Area: 29,913 sq. mi. (77,470km²)
Population: 7,111,000
Capital: Belgrade
Languages Serbian
Currency: Dinar

SLOVENIA
Area: 7,827 sq. mi. (20,273km²)
Population: 2,102,000
Capital: Ljubljana
Language: Slovenian
Currency: Euro

TURKEY
Area: 302,535 sq. mi. (783,560km²)
Population: 81,257,000
Capital: Ankara
Languages: Turkish, Kurdish
Currency: Turkish lira

▲ The Festival of Roses is held each year in Kazanluk, Bulgaria, one day before rose picking begins. The petals are crushed for their oil (attar), used in perfume.

HOW PEOPLE LIVE
Many of the Balkan people are farmers, living in small towns and villages as their ancestors did 100 years ago. They grow corn, barley, fruit, and vegetables and raise sheep, goats, cattle, and pigs. Donkeys and horse-drawn wagons can still be seen carrying produce to market. There are few big cities, apart from national capitals such as Athens (Greece) and Belgrade (former Yugoslavia), where skyscrapers tower over older buildings. Factories make vehicles, textiles, chemicals, and electronic goods, and mines produce coal, iron, and lead.

WHERE EAST MEETS WEST
Along the sunny Balkan coasts, with their beaches and medieval towns, tourism is an important industry. New hotels and roads cater for the growing tide of visitors. Eastern and Western building styles can be seen side by side: here a Christian church in Byzantine style, there an Islamic mosque. Bulgaria is famous for growing roses to make perfume. Visitors from all over the world visit Greece to see the wonders of its ancient civilization.

◄ Albanian children stand in front of a military defense pillbox.

SEE ALSO

Civil war, Empire, Europe, Greece (ancient), Refugee

GREECE, ANCIENT

The ancient Greeks created one of the world's greatest civilizations. They gave us enduring styles of architecture, art, literature, and government.

Not many paintings are left from ancient Greece, but there are many decorated pots—usually showing myths or festivals.

This silver, four-drachma coin, made in Athens, was used all over ancient Greece. The owl symbolized Athena, goddess of wisdom.

Corrupt politicians were ostracized (sent into exile) if enough voters scratched their name onto *ostraca* (pieces of broken pottery).

The Greeks moved south into what is now Greece some 4,000 years ago. The Minoans developed a great civilization around 2000 B.C., on the island of Crete, but most achievements in the arts, sciences, and government were made during the Golden Age. This was a period between 477 and 431 B.C., when Athens was the ruling city-state.

A RUGGED COUNTRY

The nature of the Greek countryside helped shape the country's history. Its mountain ranges made travel by land difficult. Fiercely independent and patriotic communities grew up in the fertile pockets between the mountains, and ancient Greece became a country divided into many city-states.

THE OLYMPIANS

The people were deeply religious. They believed in many gods—all of whom had human form, but possessed superhuman powers and were, of course, immortal. The chief gods were known as the Olympians because they were believed to live at the top of Mount Olympus in northern Greece. Zeus ruled the gods with his wife Hera. Other gods and goddesses included Aphrodite, goddess of love; Apollo, god of the sun, music, and poetry; Ares, god of war; and Athena, goddess of wisdom. The ancient Greeks built temples to their gods, in which they made offerings of food, wine, and sometimes live animals. Rich families had shrines in their homes to less important household gods.

▲ Women were usually married at the age of 13, often to men over twice their age. They were in charge of the house and wove all the material for the loose-fitting garments, known as *chitons*, worn by men and women.

DECORATIVE ARTS AND FESTIVALS

The Greeks decorated their temples and palaces in a new, natural style of marble statues and reliefs. Music, drama, dance, and sports were celebrated at festivals, such as the Olympic Games, held every four years, from 776 B.C., in honor of the gods.

LITERATURE AND LEARNING

The poet Homer, who created the epic poems the *Odyssey* and *Iliad*, was just one of many great writers. Dramatists such as Aeschylus, Euripedes, and Sophocles wrote plays for open-air theaters. Socrates, Plato, and Aristotle discussed philosophy in *agoras* (marketplaces) and academies, while scientific discoveries were made by Pythagoras, Archimedes, and others.

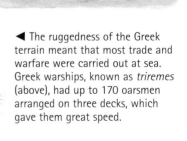

◄ The ruggedness of the Greek terrain meant that most trade and warfare were carried out at sea. Greek warships, known as *triremes* (above), had up to 170 oarsmen arranged on three decks, which gave them great speed.

ATHENS VERSUS SPARTA

The two most powerful city-states were Athens and Sparta, which were constantly at war with each other. They had different approaches to education, the arts, and warfare. Athens and other city-states had democratic governments where all male citizens could vote, and their children were educated in the arts and sciences. Sparta was a military state with a tough, warlike people. Boys were sent away to military camps at the age of seven, and girls were also trained in gymnastics and warfare— a fact which shocked the Athenians.

EMPIRE AND LEGACY

Early in the 400s B.C., Athens and Sparta united against a new common enemy, Persia. The ancient Greeks won, but fighting resumed and the city-states began to crumble. Then, in 335 B.C., Alexander the Great united ancient Greece once more and went on to conquer almost the entire Middle East, from Egypt to northern India. In 146 B.C., the Romans conquered Greece, but adopted much of its culture.

▲ The actors in the amphitheaters wore clay masks so that even people in the top rows could tell the characters apart.

▲ Lyres were stringed instruments made from turtle shells. Athenian boys learned to sing and play the lyre and *aulos* (flute) at music schools.

▲ Amphitheaters, like this one at Delphi, were carved into the sides of hills. Their clever design meant that a whisper on stage could be heard by the whole audience.

KEY DATES

2000 B.C. Minoan civilization in Crete flourishes

1600–1200 B.C. Mycenaean civilization on the mainland rules Greece

900–800 B.C. Homer writes *Iliad* and *Odyssey*

490 B.C. Persian army invades Greece—the Greeks win at the battle of Marathon

480 B.C. Battles of Thermopylae and Salamis

431–404 B.C. Peloponnesian War between Athens and Sparta. Plague kills a third of Athenians. Sparta wins

356–323 B.C. Reign of Alexander the Great

146 B.C. Roman Empire conquers Greece

BATTLE OF THERMOPYLAE

The Greek cities fought frequent wars with each other, but in 480 B.C. they united against an invasion by the Persian emperor Xerxes. A force of 300 *hoplites* (armored infantry) from Sparta held thousands of Persians at the mountain pass of Thermopylae for three days before being wiped out. This gave the Greek fleet of ships time to gather at the Straits of Salamis and defeat the invasion.

SEE ALSO

Architecture, Astronomy, Democracy, Europe, Greece and the Balkans, Medicine, Mesopotamia, Myth and legend, Olympic Games, Sculpture, Seven Wonders of the World, Theater

HABITAT

A habitat is the home of particular species of animal or plant. It provides them with the food, shelter, and conditions that allow them to survive.

◀ Oystercatchers living on the coast of the Netherlands depend on clean seas for the survival of the shellfish they feed on.

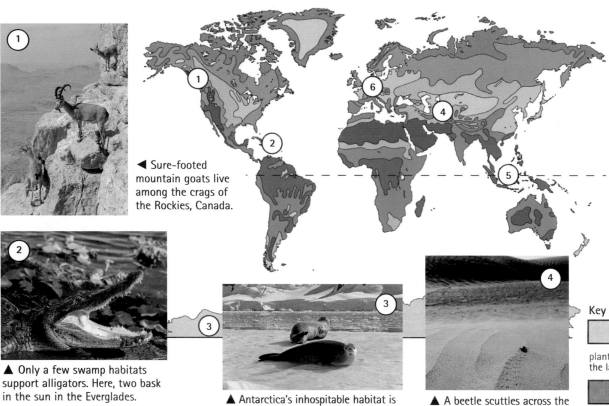

◀ Sure-footed mountain goats live among the crags of the Rockies, Canada.

▲ Only a few swamp habitats support alligators. Here, two bask in the sun in the Everglades.

▲ Antarctica's inhospitable habitat is home to animals with a thick layer of fat, such as this Weddell seal and pup.

▲ A beetle scuttles across the cold desert of Turkmenistan. Its small size helps it keep warm.

▲ An orangutan sits in a rain-forest canopy in Borneo—a threatened habitat.

Key

Cold desert: cold region with little rain. Animals and plants must be able to survive the lack of water and cold.

Tundra: treeless plains near Arctic. Snow-covered in winter. Migratory animals, moss, and lichens in summer.

Temperate woodland: tree-covered areas in climate that changes between winter and summer. Trees usually shed their leaves.

Coniferous forest: areas (usually northern) with trees bearing pine cones. Wildlife includes deer, bears, wolves.

Savanna grassland: grassland areas with scattered trees, lying between desert and rain forest. Large predators and herbivores.

Tropical rain forest: dense forest around equator in Asia, Africa, and South America. Habitat with the most wildlife.

Steppe and dry grassland: hot summers and cold winters. Short grasses, with many snakes and rodents.

Hot desert: hot with little rain. Can be sandy or rocky. Many animals hide during the day.

Climate, soil, plants, and animals—from the tiniest insect to the tallest tree—all create a habitat. Scientists classify them into types, such as grassland, forest, desert, mountaintop, river, swamp, or sea. These groups show great variation.

HABITATS AND BIOMES
When scientists talk about a habitat in general, they use the word biome. For example, a grassland is a biome, but a specific grassland such as the Argentinian Pampas is known as a habitat. Within each habitat there are also thousands of small, specialized living spaces, such as the dark, damp world under a rock on a riverbank, or a pool of water in the fork of a forest tree. These are known as microhabitats.

OCEAN WORLDS
The biggest biome of all is the oceans, which cover 71 percent of the Earth's surface. This biome is divided into layers

according to how warm or salty the water is and how far down the sunlight reaches. It also varies from place to place—from the warm, blue seas of the Caribbean to the cold, windswept Antarctic Ocean. Around the edges of the seas are other special habitats, such as coral reefs, rocky and sandy shores, and river mouths.

UPSETTING THE BALANCE
Each habitat is a complex system, with all the plants and animals perfectly suited to, and yet dependent on, their environment, as well as on one another. When something upsets the balance, a habitat can be badly damaged. Parts of Africa's savannas have been turned into desert because too many people, goats, and cattle have stripped off the vegetation. Lakes and rivers in many countries have been poisoned by industrial chemicals. Forests may be damaged by acid rain, and some seashores are being scarred by oil spillages.

SEE ALSO

Desert, Forest, Grassland, Ocean and sea, Pollution, Rain forest, Seashore

HEARING

Hearing is one of the five senses. It depends on the detection of sound waves in the air which are changed into nerve signals and sent to the brain for processing.

Bats use their high-pitched (100,000Hz) squeaks to locate flying insects to eat.

Frogs can hear only low frequency sounds of 5,000Hz and below.

Dogs hear both high and low-pitched sounds. Dog whistles are 35,000Hz.

Human ears hear frequencies from about 30 to 18,000Hz.

For most people, hearing is the second most important sense, after sight. It allows communication, warns us of danger, and gives pleasure, from music to birdsong.

THE OUTER EAR
We hear with our ears. The outer ear is just a skin-covered flap of gristle, or cartilage, that catches sound waves in the air. Most of the delicate working parts are behind it, protected inside the skull.

INSIDE THE EAR
Sound waves funnel into the ear canal. At its end, they hit a small patch of flexible skin, the eardrum. The sound waves bounce off it and make the eardrum vibrate (shake back and forth). Vibrations pass from the eardrum, along a chain of three tiny bones, called the hammer (malleus), anvil (incus), and stirrup (stapes). These bones pass the vibration to the oval window.

THE COCHLEA
The oval window is a membrane in the wall of a fluid-filled chamber, the cochlea, which is coiled like a snail, small enough to sit on your fingernail. Vibrations of the oval window push ripples into the fluid inside the cochlea. As the ripples go around the coil, they shake almost two million tiny hairs protruding from 25,000 hair cells.

SOUND TO ELECTRICITY
The hair cells send signals to the brain. Here they are analyzed for volume and frequency, and compared with soundprints in the memory. Sound waves travel at about 1,115 ft./sec. (340m/sec). If sound comes from the side, waves reach the closer ear a fraction of a second before the farther ear. From this tiny difference, the brain works out the direction of the sound source. This is only possible with two (or more) ears and is called stereophonic hearing. Frequency of sound is measured in vibrations per second, hertz (Hz), and our ears can hear only certain frequencies.

CAPTURING SOUNDS ON THE AIRWAVES

The outer ear collects sound waves in the air and sends them toward the eardrum. They travel through the middle ear, via the hammer, anvil, and stirrup to the cochlea, where they become electrical messages that are sent to the brain along the cochlear nerve.

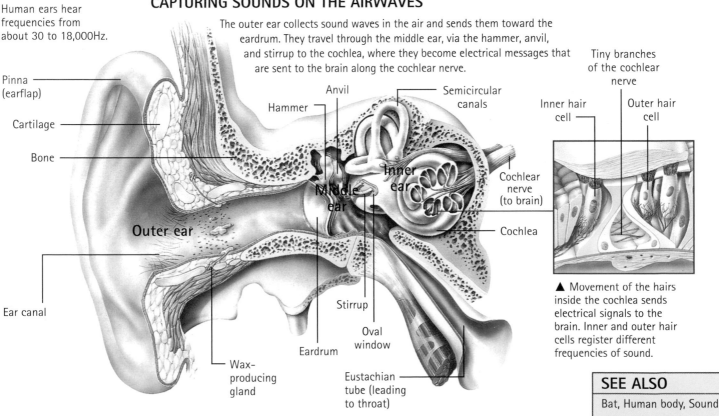

Pinna (earflap)

Cartilage

Bone

Outer ear

Ear canal

Hammer

Anvil

Middle ear

Inner ear

Semicircular canals

Cochlear nerve (to brain)

Cochlea

Tiny branches of the cochlear nerve

Inner hair cell

Outer hair cell

Wax-producing gland

Eardrum

Stirrup

Oval window

Eustachian tube (leading to throat)

▲ Movement of the hairs inside the cochlea sends electrical signals to the brain. Inner and outer hair cells register different frequencies of sound.

SEE ALSO
Bat, Human body, Sound

HEART AND CIRCULATORY SYSTEM

The heart is a hollow, muscle-walled pump in the chest. It squeezes at least once every second to pump blood around the body. If it stops, so will life.

WILLIAM HARVEY
(1578–1657) The English doctor who showed that blood circulates (moves around the body) in only one direction, along arteries and veins.

The heart is a muscular pump with four chambers (pockets) which drives the blood around the body by means of a network of arteries, veins, and capillaries known as the circulatory system.

IN AND OUT
As the muscles in the heart contract, blood is squeezed from the heart into arteries, which carry the blood around the body. As the heart muscles relax, blood flows into the heart from the body, via veins. Each squeeze–relax cycle is a heartbeat.

A TIRELESS MUSCLE
The cardiac (heart) muscle never tires. In an average lifetime, the heart beats more than 2.5 billion times. On average,

the heart beats 70 times per minute, although heartbeat rate varies with age or health. Each beat pumps about 2.5 fl. oz. (70ml) of blood. As the body has only about 5.3 qt. (5 l) of blood, all the blood passes through the heart in one minute. An active body uses more energy and oxygen, so the heart beats faster and pumps more blood with each beat.

CHECKING THE HEART
Each heartbeat starts in a small area of the wall in the right atrium. This is the heart's natural pacemaker. It sends tiny electrical signals through the heart's walls, telling them to contract. The action is controlled by nerve signals from the brain and chemicals in the blood called hormones. Electronic sensors placed on the skin can detect the electrical signals of the heart. The signals are displayed as a graph on an ECG (electrocardiograph) machine.

TWO PUMPS IN ONE
The heart is not one pump but two, separated by a muscular dividing wall. The right pump receives low-oxygen blood from the body, along the main veins. It sends this blood out through the pulmonary arteries to the lungs, where it receives oxygen, and returns to the heart's left pump. This sends it out around the body again.

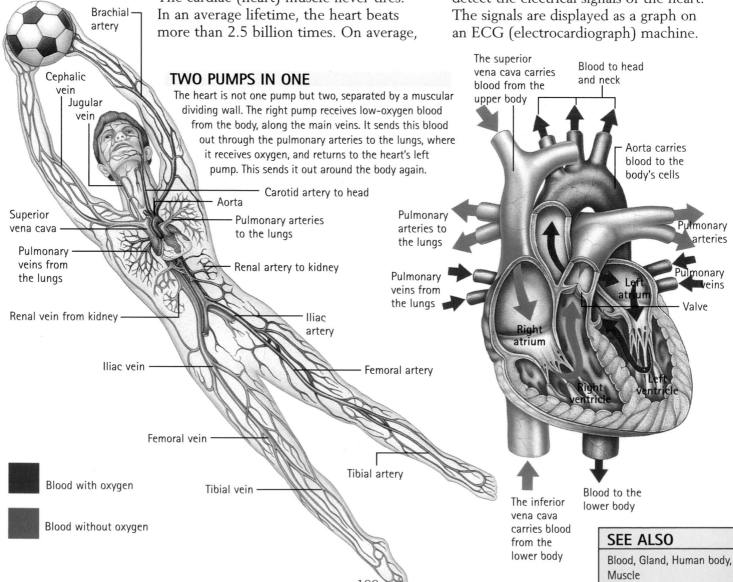

Brachial artery

Cephalic vein

Jugular vein

Superior vena cava

Pulmonary veins from the lungs

Renal vein from kidney

Iliac vein

Femoral vein

Tibial vein

Carotid artery to head

Aorta

Pulmonary arteries to the lungs

Renal artery to kidney

Iliac artery

Femoral artery

Tibial artery

Blood with oxygen

Blood without oxygen

The superior vena cava carries blood from the upper body

Blood to head and neck

Aorta carries blood to the body's cells

Pulmonary arteries to the lungs

Pulmonary veins from the lungs

Pulmonary arteries

Pulmonary veins

Left atrium

Valve

Right atrium

Right ventricle

Left ventricle

The inferior vena cava carries blood from the lower body

Blood to the lower body

SEE ALSO
Blood, Gland, Human body, Muscle

HEAT

Heat is a form of energy that is created by the vibration of atoms within a substance. Heat always moves from warm places to cooler ones.

Only a fraction of the Sun's rays reaches us, yet it is our most important heat source.

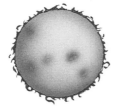

By striking a match, we start a chemical reaction which produces heat.

Pressure deep inside the Earth produces heat that escapes via volcanoes.

The flow of electricity through wires creates heat that we use to toast bread.

Friction (two objects rubbing together) creates heat used to start a fire.

Everything is made up of atoms and molecules that are always moving, even when an object is perfectly still. Their motion gives the object internal energy, or heat. The faster the atoms and molecules move, the hotter an object is. We usually measure heat with a thermometer.

CONDUCTION

If two objects of different temperatures touch each other, the hotter object will always transfer some of its heat to the cooler object. For example, when you stir hot coffee with a cold teaspoon, the heat from the coffee flows into the teaspoon. This happens because atoms in the coffee touch atoms in the spoon, making them vibrate more. This is called conduction. Metal is a good conductor of heat but some materials, such as polystyrene, transfer heat poorly. They are called insulators.

▲ The Earth's inner heat escapes through cracks in the crust, creating hot springs in Iceland. People bathe in them, and geothermal plants use the heat to make electricity.

RADIATION AND CONVECTION

Heat also travels by radiation and convection. The Earth is warmed by heat which radiates (spreads out) through space from the Sun to the Earth. Heat radiates very fast—it takes just over eight minutes for heat to radiate from the Sun to the Earth. Convection occurs only in liquids or gases that are unevenly heated. Warm parts of a liquid or gas flow into cooler ones, spreading heat with them.

HEAT IN OUR LIVES

When we eat food, our bodies break it down, releasing energy that heats us inside. We burn fuels, such as wood and coal, to help us stay warm, or to make heat to drive machines. Power plants make electricity, which we convert into heat in our homes.

FEELING THE HEAT

Boiling water in a kettle over an open fire requires heat to travel in each of its three ways: radiation, conduction, and convection. Air molecules are set in motion by heat, radiating from the fire. The hot air molecules hit the kettle bottom, making its molecules vibrate. The heat travels through the metal via conduction and through the water by convection.

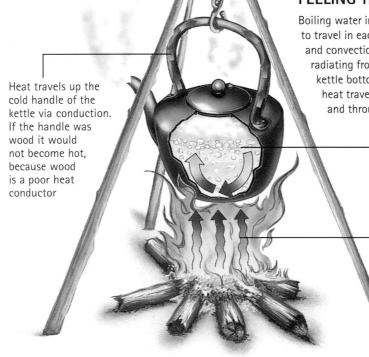

Heat travels up the cold handle of the kettle via conduction. If the handle was wood it would not become hot, because wood is a poor heat conductor

Heat circulates through the water via convection until all of the water is the same temperature

Heat from the fire radiates through the air until it hits the bottom of the kettle

SEE ALSO

Atom and molecule, Electricity, Energy, Solid, liquid, and gas

HELICOPTER

Helicopters are aircraft with spinning rotor blades instead of wings. These make them able to fly in ways that are impossible for most other aircraft.

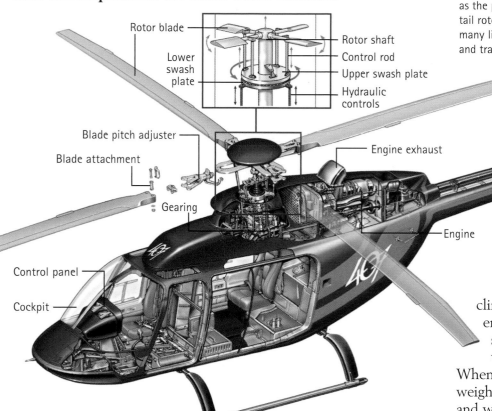

Rotor blade
Lower swash plate
Rotor shaft
Control rod
Upper swash plate
Hydraulic controls
Blade pitch adjuster
Blade attachment
Gearing
Control panel
Cockpit

BELL 407

The Bell 407 helicopter is a popular commercial helicopter, capable of carrying six passengers as well as the pilot. It has one main rotor and a small vertical tail rotor. It is used as an air taxi and for many light tasks such as police searches and traffic surveillance.

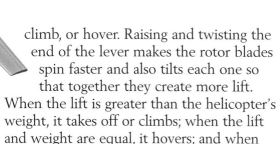

Tailplane
Engine exhaust
Tail rotor
Tail rotor shaft
Engine

The Ka-26 Kamov Hoodlum has two sets of main rotors, rotating in opposite directions.

The Russian Mil-24 gunship has one main rotor on top and a small vertical rotor at the back.

The Boeing CH-47 Chinook military helicopter has two rotors—one at each end.

H elicopters are very maneuverable aircraft—they can take off and land vertically in a small space, hover in one place, and fly in any direction: forward, sideways, even backward!

ONE ROTOR OR TWO
Most helicopters have one set of long, thin rotor blades (the main rotor) on top and a smaller tail rotor. The main rotor provides lift to keep the helicopter in the air. The tail rotor is used for changing direction. It also stops the helicopter from being spun around by the main rotor. Some helicopters have two main rotors which rotate in opposite directions to prevent the vehicle from spinning around.

TAKING OFF
The angle of the rotor blades is called the pitch. By changing the pitch of the blades, with a control lever in the cockpit, the pilot can make the helicopter take off, land,

climb, or hover. Raising and twisting the end of the lever makes the rotor blades spin faster and also tilts each one so that together they create more lift. When the lift is greater than the helicopter's weight, it takes off or climbs; when the lift and weight are equal, it hovers; and when the lift is less than the weight, it descends.

MOVING AND STEERING
A helicopter moves forward when the whole of the main rotor is tipped forward. To slow down, the rotor is tipped back. Tipping the blades to the side makes the helicopter fly sideways. To turn, the tail-rotor angle is altered with foot controls.

SPINNING INTO ACTION
The first helicopters flew in the early 1900s, but they were clumsy and could barely take off. The first successful modern helicopter was the Vought-Sikorsky VS-300, built by Igor Sikorsky in 1940.

HELICOPTERS AT WORK
The helicopter's versatility in flight means it can be used for search and rescue at sea, police observation, or as an air ambulance. Military helicopters can fly lower than planes, and take off from small clearings or the decks of ships.

SEE ALSO
Aircraft

HIBERNATION

In the cooler parts of the world, many mammals pass the winter months in a very deep sleep. This is called hibernation.

Many types of bat are active during the night and go into a type of hibernation each daytime.

Some butterflies, such as the monarch, hibernate in groups in hollow trees or attics over the winter.

The deep winter sleep of some bears is hibernation, but their body temperature only drops slightly.

Snakes, such as adders, hibernate under rocks or in holes under the ground when the weather is cold.

Some animals, such as the lungfish, estivate (become inactive in summer to survive drought).

Many animals hibernate during the winter when it is cold and there is little food. While hibernating, their body temperature falls greatly until it is little more than that of the surroundings.

GETTING READY
During the autumn, an animal will eat a lot to increase its body fat; this will give it energy while hibernating. It then looks for a safe spot in which to settle down. Most rodents take food supplies into their sleeping quarters to hibernate.

ONLY JUST ALIVE
While hibernating, an animal's heart and breathing rates drop until it is only just alive. It may stir and stretch itself from time to time, but does not really wake up until the outside temperature rises in the spring. By this time, most animals have used up all their food reserves and are very thin. They have to look for food right away and will die if they do not find any.

WHO HIBERNATES?
Insect-eating bats in cool climates have to hibernate because there are not enough insects for them to eat in the winter. Ground squirrels, such as the prairie dog, also hibernate. Among birds, only the whippoorwill and some other nightjars are known to hibernate. Small hummingbirds also huddle together at night in a type of nightly hibernation.

COLD-BLOODED ANIMALS
Reptiles, amphibians, and many fish living in cold climates become inactive in the winter. As the air or water temperature falls, the animals get slower and slower and then come to a complete stop. But there is not such a dramatic change as in the hibernating mammals, because they are cold-blooded animals, and their temperature is always similar to that of the surroundings.

WARM WINTER SLEEP

Before hibernating, the chipmunk tunnels underground and builds a nesting place. It also collects seeds and nuts, which it stores in the tunnel. After it has pushed the earth out, it often loosely plugs up the entrance with earth. The chipmunk sleeps through most of the winter but may wake up on warm winter days, when it will eat some of its food.

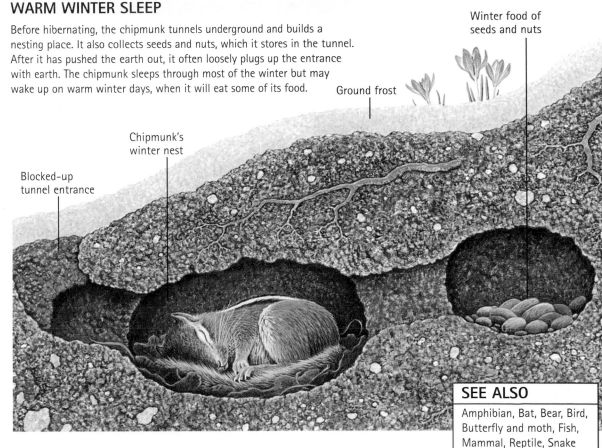

Winter food of seeds and nuts

Ground frost

Chipmunk's winter nest

Blocked-up tunnel entrance

SEE ALSO
Amphibian, Bat, Bear, Bird, Butterfly and moth, Fish, Mammal, Reptile, Snake

HINDUISM

Hinduism is one of the oldest existing religions. It began in northern India about 4,000 years ago and is now the most popular religion in southern Asia.

▲ Many small shrines exist by the sides of roads as well as in most Hindu homes. Here, food and flowers are offered and incense and candles burned.

▲ Shiva is one of the most important Hindu gods and represents destruction and rebirth.

Today, about 80 percent of Indians are Hindu and there are over 900 million Hindus worldwide. Hinduism developed from various religious beliefs and social customs which came together in northern India from the 1500s B.C.

EARLIEST WRITINGS
The earliest Hindu writings, called the *Vedas*, date from about 1000 B.C. Later, there were the famous epic stories, the *Ramayana* and *Mahabharata*. Other important writings led to the creation of the Indian caste system. This is a social and religious system where people are divided into different groups by birth.

MANY GODS
Hindus believe in one overall god, called Brahman. They worship other gods and goddesses who represent various

expressions of Brahman. The chief of these are Brahma (the creator), Shiva (the destroyer), and Vishnu (the preserver). Respect for all forms of life is a key belief, and this is reflected in reverence for the cow, which may not be killed.

CYCLE OF LIFE
Like Buddhists, all Hindus believe in reincarnation, or being born again after death. They also believe in the importance of living a good life and in karma, which means that one is punished or rewarded for one's past actions in the next life.

HINDU TEMPLES
Like most Hindu temples, this one in India's capital city, Delhi, is highly ornate. The goddess of good fortune, Lakshmi, is worshiped here in religious rituals, which are usually led by Hindu priests and teachers, who are members of the Brahman caste.

SEE ALSO
Buddhism, Religion

HIPPOPOTAMUS

Hippopotamuses are large, thick-skinned animals with short legs and a massive head and muzzle. They live in the lakes and rivers of tropical Africa.

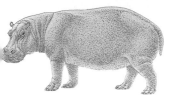

The large, or river, hippo has thick, gray skin and spends much of its time wallowing in shallow water.

The small pygmy hippo has oily, blackish skin and spends less time in the water than the river hippo.

Hippopotamus means "riverine horse" and comes from the Greek words *hippos* (horse) and *potamos* (river). In reality, however, the animal is more like a giant pig.

BARREL ON SHORT LEGS

After the elephant and rhinoceros, the hippopotamus is the world's largest land animal. It is like a barrel with short legs—about 11.5 ft. (3.5m) long, weighing up to 4 tons, and only about 5 ft. (1.5m) high. Hippos generally live in groups of around 5 to 30 strong. They spend most of the daytime wallowing in pools of mud or shallow water, usually with their heads appearing just above the surface. Their eyes, ears, and nostrils are all at the top of the head, so they can see, hear, and breathe without being seen. They have a good sense of smell, although their eyesight is relatively poor.

▲ Hippos normally stay under water for up to six minutes without breathing, and they can actually run under water.

FEEDING HABITS

In the evening, hippos leave the water to feed. Grass is their favorite food, but they also eat crops and often damage them by trampling through fields. Adult hippos have no enemies apart from people. Calves (young hippos) are sometimes eaten by lions on land and by crocodiles in the water, but they are usually well protected by the adults. An adult hippo can easily bite a crocodile in half with its huge jaws.

A SMALL COUSIN

The pygmy hippopotamus is no more than about 5.75 ft. (1.75m) long, has oily, blackish skin and a rounded head. It lives in the swamps and damp forests of West Africa, but spends less time in the water than its larger, gray-skinned cousin.

FEROCIOUS FIGHTERS

The hippopotamus has a huge head and can open its mouth very wide to reveal curved, daggerlike teeth up to 20 in. (50cm) long. With its mouth wide open, the hippo looks as if it is yawning, but this is really a challenge made by one male to another. The males often fight and can cause terrible wounds with their teeth.

▲ Huge tusklike teeth are used for fighting.

▲ The ears remain closed when under water.

▲ Each hoofed foot has four webbed toes.

▲ The hippo's nostrils close up under water.

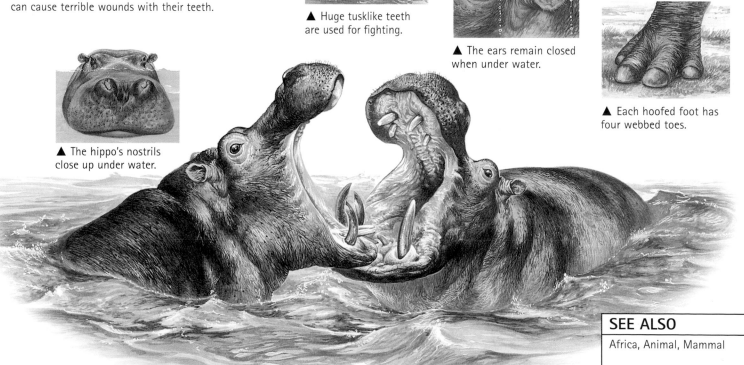

SEE ALSO

Africa, Animal, Mammal

HORSE

Horses are four-legged, plant-eating mammals with a single hoof on each foot. Long ago they were wild but today almost all horses are domesticated.

THE HORSE FAMILY
All animals that have a single-toed hoof on the end of each leg belong to the horse family—the group called *Equidae*.

The common zebra has black-and-white stripes and lives wild in Africa.

The ass is smaller than the horse, has long ears, and is usually colored gray.

The Shetland pony is a hardy breed of horse with thick coat and long mane.

Przewalski's horse, found in Mongolia in 1870, is the only truly wild horse left.

Most grazing mammals are cloven-hoofed, which means that their feet end in a pair of hoofed toes. Horses' feet, however, end in a large single hoof. This feature, combined with long and powerful legs, makes horses fast and tireless runners. They are therefore perfectly suited to life in open places, where there is nowhere to hide from danger.

WILD HORSES
Horses are sociable animals, and in the wild live in herds of about 10 to 20. Mares (female horses) usually breed at the age of about two or three years, and normally have one foal a year. At one time, herds of wild horses roamed across the grassy plains of eastern Europe and central Asia. They were preyed upon by wolves and other predators, and hunted by people for food. But about 6,000 years ago, humans began to tame horses. From that moment, the history of the horse abruptly changed.

PRZEWALSKI'S HORSE
Domesticated horses soon outnumbered wild ones, which became increasingly rare. There were originally two kinds of wild horse: the tarpan and Przewalski's horse. The last tarpan died in a zoo in 1909. The rare Przewalski's horse died out in the wild but has been successfully reintroduced to the grasslands of Mongolia.

PULLING POWER
Horses have been bred for a wide variety of uses. Some of them were originally bred for their pulling power, and were used by farmers to pull plows and farm carts in the days before tractors were invented. Today, there are hundreds of different breeds of horse. They include huge draft horses, which can measure nearly 6.5 ft. (2m) high at the shoulder, Shetland ponies, and the Falabella horse from Argentina, which is smaller than many dogs.

▲ Many North American rodeo events such as steer wrestling have evolved from working with cattle.

HORSES TODAY
Today, horses are used in every continent except Antarctica. In many countries, they still carry on traditional roles of providing transportation and a livelihood for their owners. In North America, they have played a vital role in cattle herding for over 350 years; Australians still use hardy horses called walers that were bred by early settlers. Other uses today include policing, ceremonial and sports events, hunting, and riding for fun. But one of the most popular events is horse racing. For this, thoroughbreds descended from Arabian stallions of the 1700s are mostly used.

▲ Horses used for showjumping need to have a combination of power, stamina, boldness, and agility in order to handle the tough demands of the sport.

PARTS OF THE HORSE

The overall shape and appearance of a horse is called its conformation, while the parts of the horse's body are called the points. A horse's skeleton gives clues about its breed. For example, a draft horse has large, thick bones to support its weight whereas a racehorse has long, fine bones that help it to run swiftly.

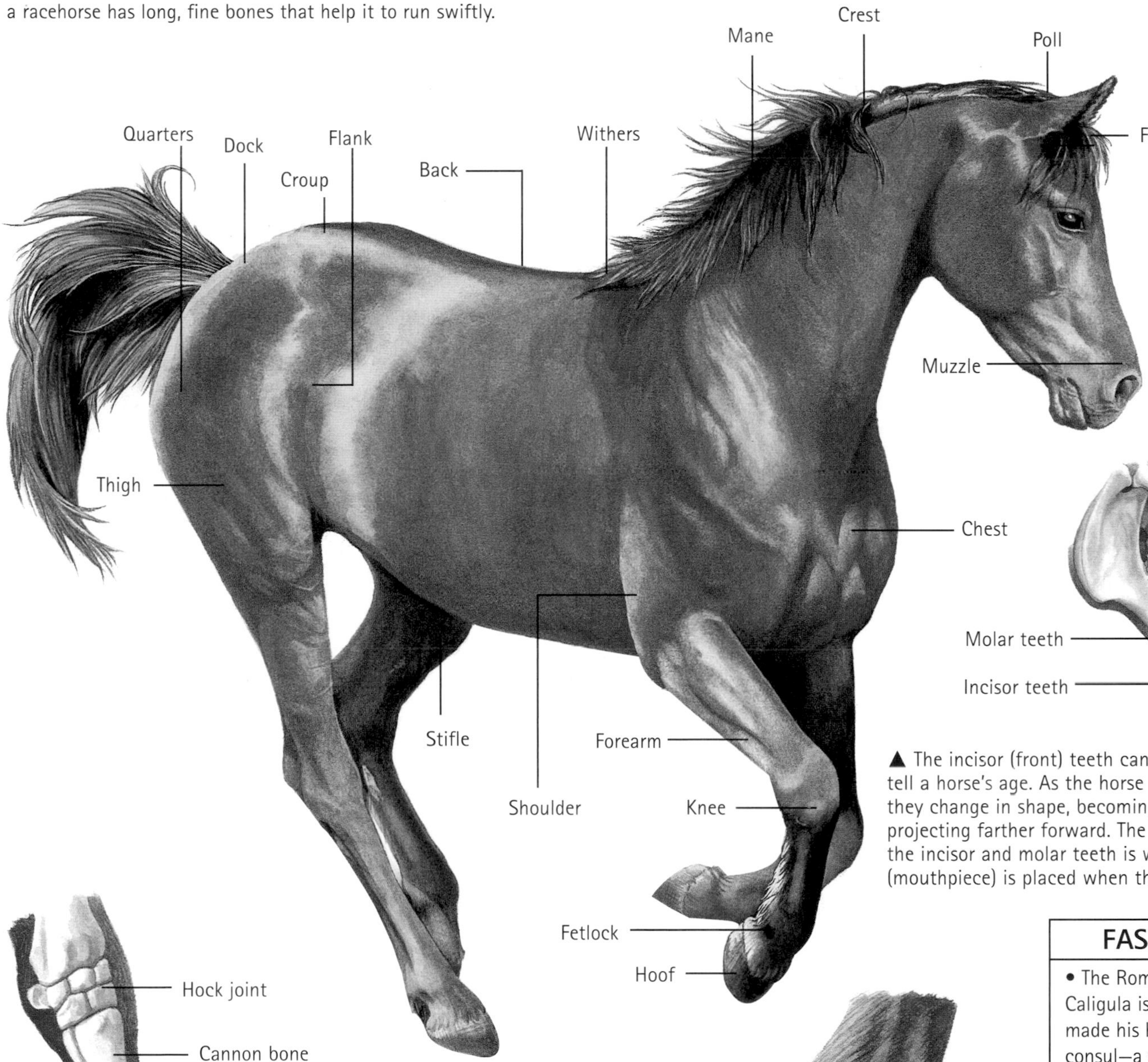

Mane
Crest
Poll
Forelock
Quarters
Dock
Flank
Croup
Back
Withers
Muzzle
Thigh
Chest
Molar teeth
Incisor teeth
Stifle
Forearm
Shoulder
Knee
Fetlock
Hoof

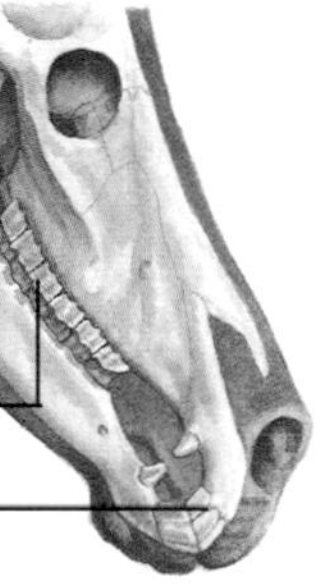

▲ The incisor (front) teeth can be used to tell a horse's age. As the horse grows older, they change in shape, becoming longer and projecting farther forward. The gap between the incisor and molar teeth is where the bit (mouthpiece) is placed when the horse is bridled.

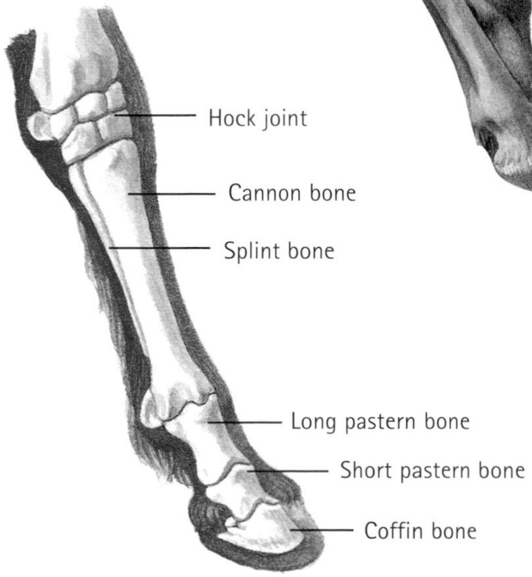

Hock joint
Cannon bone
Splint bone
Long pastern bone
Short pastern bone
Coffin bone

Heel
Frog
Hoof wall
Sole
Shoe

FAST FACTS

• The Roman Emperor Caligula is said to have made his horse, Incitatus, consul—a very high rank in Roman government

• The earliest ancestor of the horse had four toes and was the size of a fox

• Horses are measured in hands from the ground to the top of the withers. A hand is 4 in. (10cm)

• A horse goes through four gaits, from slow to fast: walk, trot, canter, and gallop

▲ The modern horse stands on only one toe (its hoof), but the two splint bones on either side of the cannon bone are remnants of the early horse's other toes.

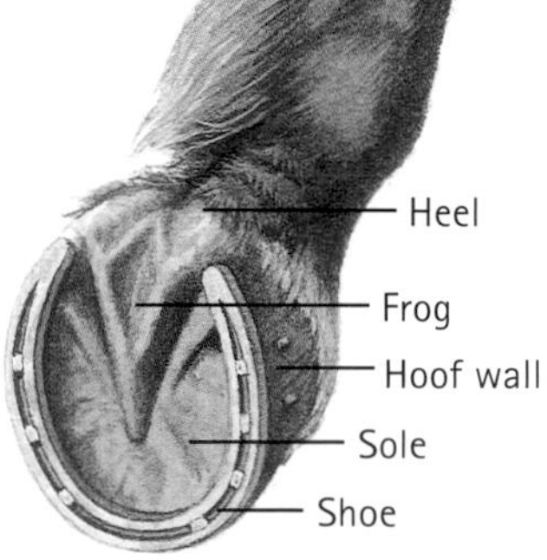

▲ Horses have metal shoes nailed to their hooves to protect the hoof wall from wearing down on rough or hard ground. Shoes must be replaced every few weeks. Before they can be fitted, the new growth of hoof has to be trimmed and the hoof reshaped.

SEE ALSO

Animal, Evolution, Mammal, Mongol Empire, Sports, Transportation, World War I

HOUSEHOLD APPLIANCE

Household appliances are devices that make day-to-day jobs around the house easier. They have changed our lifestyles and improved public hygiene and diet.

► Percy Spenser (U.S.A.) invented the microwave oven in 1945 using technology developed for military defense during World War II.

Most toasters pop up when sensors inside detect that a set temperature has been reached.

This wipe-clean ceramic stove uses electricity.

The first washing machine (invented by Hamilton Smith, U.S.A., 1858) relied on muscle power.

Early refrigerators (invented by Ferdinand Carre, France, 1858) were cooled by blocks of ice.

Irons have been used for centuries, first heated on a stove, then by gas, then, in 1891, by electricity.

Houses in developed countries contain a wide range of appliances. Many, including stoves, refrigerators, freezers, food processors, and microwave ovens, are used in the kitchen to preserve and prepare food. Others, such as washing machines, tumble dryers, dishwashers, and vacuum cleaners, help with cleaning. Since the invention of electricity— a form of energy that can be converted into movement or heat—more sophisticated appliances have been produced.

WASH DAY
Before labor-saving appliances, routine housekeeping was a full-time job. A day was set aside to wash clothes using a washboard and a mangle. Perishable food could not be stored easily, so people shopped almost every day, and preparing meals took longer. Rugs had to be hung up outside and beaten to get the dust out.

MAKING A MEAL OF IT
Most stoves use gas or electricity, and these are easy to control. Methane, butane, or propane gas goes through a valve and burns in the air, releasing heat. Electric stoves have elements containing wire which resists the flow of electricity. As the current is forced along this wire, electrical energy is turned into heat energy. Coffeemakers and toasters work in the same way.

MICROWAVE OVENS
Microwave ovens contain a magnetron, which turns electricity into microwaves, or high-frequency radio waves. Microwaves make molecules of water and fat in the surface of the food vibrate very fast, producing heat. This heat spreads from the outside to the middle of the food.

WASHING MACHINES
These have microprocessor control systems. A powerful electric motor turns the drum full of wet clothing back and forth through a series of cycles, which duplicate the stages of washing by hand. The clothes are agitated in hot detergent, then rinsed and spun at high speed, which forces out most of the water.

VACUUM CLEANERS

While the suction pulls dirty air in, a spinning brush helps dislodge dirt. Bags are finely perforated and act as a filter, while bagless designs (right) use a whirling vortex of air to spin dirt out—air is pushed out, but dirt is trapped inside.

Air spins at up to 923 mph (1486kph)

Air minus dirt and dust

Brush

Dirty air

Dust particles

The electric motor turns a fan which creates a partial vacuum and causes air to rush in, pulling dust with it

SEE ALSO

Design, Electricity, Invention, Machine, Technology, Wavelength

HOUSING

Housing includes any form of building or structure in which people live. It can provide shelter for a single person, a family, or several family groups.

Romas of Europe live in horse-drawn wagons.

Indonesians build houses on stilts in damp areas.

The Mongolian *yurt* can be folded and moved.

Native American *pueblos* are made of mud bricks.

Sudanese huts have small windows to keep out heat.

Suburban houses have garages and yards.

Since at least 50,000 years ago, people have built tents or shelters from sticks, animals hides, or turf. When people settled down to farming, they began to build more permanent houses.

BUILDING MATERIALS
For thousands of years, people used natural materials, such as wood or stone, that they found nearby. Clay and chopped straw were mixed, then shaped into bricks, and dried in the sun. Later, people learned to bake the bricks in ovens to make them tougher and more waterproof. Modern houses may still be made of bricks, or of modern materials such as concrete, steel, and glass.

INTO THE CITY
In the 1700s and 1800s, during the Industrial Revolution, people crowded into cities to find work. Whole streets of new houses were built, often by mill or factory owners, to meet demand. Today, cities continue to expand, but homes in outlying surburbs take advantage of space by having front or back yards.

CLIMATE AND DESIGN
In forested areas of North America and Scandinavia, wood is an important building material. Elsewhere, houses are more likely to be built of bricks or stone. In hot countries,

▲ The shanty homes of the poor contrast sharply with apartments for the wealthy in Mumbai (Bombay), India.

houses have thick walls to keep the inside cool. Houses in areas with a lot of snow or rain usually have sloping roofs so the water can run off.

COMPUTER CONTROL
Modern houses are equipped with gas, electricity, water, and drainage systems. Soon houses may be computer-controlled, with lighting, heating, security, TV, and other features run automatically.

◄ Millions of people around the world live in tall apartment buildings, many of which were built during the 1950s and 1960s, especially in heavily populated areas.

▼ Energy-saving ideas, such as these solar panels, make modern houses more efficient.

SEE ALSO

Architecture, Castle, City, Construction, Materials

HOVERCRAFT

Hovercraft travel on a cushion of air, which greatly reduces water resistance. They can travel over both water and land, something no other craft can do.

The British *SRN6* hovercraft, built in 1965, is still in service over 30 years later.

The *ABS* hovercraft circumnavigated the Baltic Sea in 1994.

The Russian giant assault hovercraft delivers troops and equipment onto land.

The American *Hovermarine* was designed to seat up to 150 passengers.

When a boat moves, the surrounding water pushes against it and slows it down. It could go much faster if it could travel above the water instead of through it. The hovercraft and its cousin, the hydrofoil, both provide a solution to this problem.

CUSHIONS AND SKIRTS

The air cushion that holds a hovercraft up is created by one or more powerful lift fans. Air pumped by these fans is prevented from escaping too quickly by a flexible rubber skirt all around the edge. Hydrofoils, on the other hand, use winglike foils to lift them from the water.

THE FIRST HOVERCRAFT

People experimented with vehicles supported by air cushions as long ago as 1877, but the technology to build a hovercraft was not available until the

▲ Hydrofoils have aerofoil-shaped underwater wings, or foils, which lift the craft's hull out of the water as it speeds up. They are powered by propellers or water jets.

1900s. The first successful hovercraft was built by the British engineer Christopher Cockerell in 1959.

SKIMMING WAVES

Hovercraft have a number of uses. The largest hovercraft carry passengers and their cars across short stretches of water. Small, one-person hovercraft often race against each other in sports events. Military hovercraft transport troops and equipment onto beaches.

HOW THE HOVERCRAFT WORKS

Because a hovercraft is raised up on a cushion of air, it can travel over water or land and reach speeds of up to 80 mph (130kph), much faster than an ordinary ship. Two large fans on each side of the hovercraft suck in air and push it underneath the craft to lift it up. Another two large fans at the rear, with rudders for steering, propel the craft forward.

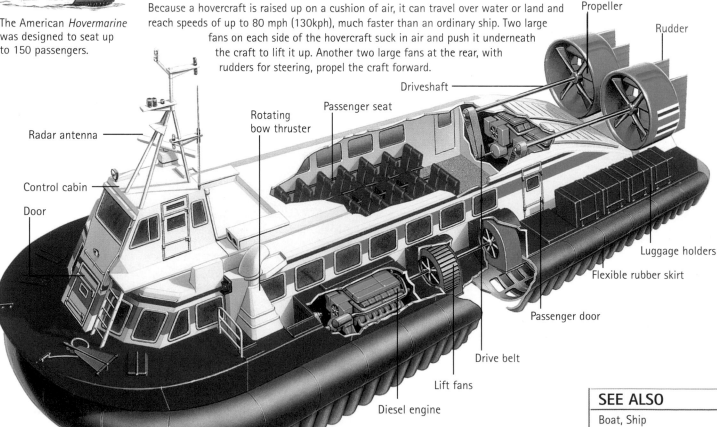

Propeller
Rudder
Driveshaft
Radar antenna
Rotating bow thruster
Passenger seat
Control cabin
Door
Luggage holders
Flexible rubber skirt
Passenger door
Drive belt
Lift fans
Diesel engine

SEE ALSO

Boat, Ship

HUMAN BODY

The human body is made up of a skeleton, organs, outer skin, and specialized systems, all of which work together to make it one of the most complex of all life-forms.

▼ The human face reveals a person's identity—his or her age, gender, and genetic inheritance.

▶ Athletes train hard in order to build up their muscles and reach peak body fitness.

The human body is similar to the bodies of other large mammals, especially apes. But it is also unique in many ways. It can walk upright on its two back legs. Its fingers are capable of precise, delicate movements, and its large brain is far more complex than that of any other creature. These features make humans a separate species in the animal kingdom, called *Homo sapiens*.

BUILDING BLOCKS

The human body is made up of more than 50 trillion tiny building blocks, called cells. These are all microscopic in size and vary in shape and structure according to their functions. Every second, the body makes more than five million cells of various kinds, to replace those that wear out and die.

BODY TISSUES

Cells of the same kind are grouped together to form tissues. For example, bone tissue is strong and stiff, to provide the body with an inner supporting framework— the skeleton. Cartilage tissue is also strong, but softer and smoother. It covers bones where they join and is found inside flexible parts like the nose and ears.

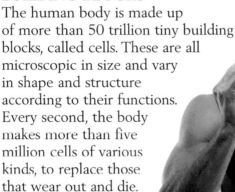

▲ Through regular stretching exercises, the human body can become very supple and capable of bending and twisting in extreme ways.

BODY ORGANS

Groups of tissue make up the main parts of the body, called organs. Examples are the intestines, which absorb digested food into blood; the kidneys, which filter waste products from blood; and the heart, which pumps blood. Several organs work together as a major body system.

BODY SYSTEMS

Each system has a very important job to keep the body alive and healthy. For example, the respiratory system consists of the nose, trachea, and lungs. It breathes in air and absorbs oxygen from the air into the blood. Oxygen is needed to release the energy from digested food substances, in order to power life processes. ▶

DIGESTIVE SYSTEM

The body needs to maintain its cells and tissues, and repair worn-out parts. The raw materials for growth and repair come from food, which is processed by the digestive system: the mouth, teeth, esophagus, stomach, and intestines. Food is broken down into nutrients and energy-rich chemicals, which pass into the blood. Waste matter passes out of the body as feces.

URINARY SYSTEM

The life processes inside cells produce waste products, some of which are removed by the urinary system. This consists of the kidneys, which filter the wastes from the blood to form urine, and the bladder, which stores the urine before it is removed from the body.

COORDINATION AND CONTROL

The body parts and organs do not work on their own. Two main control systems keep them functioning together in a coordinated fashion. The hormonal system consists of body parts called endocrine glands that make substances called hormones. These pass into the blood and around the body. Each hormone affects the chemical activity of certain cells and tissues, making them speed up or slow down.

NERVOUS SYSTEM

The second control system, the nervous system, is a network of wirelike nerves throughout the body, with the brain as the control center. The brain receives information as tiny nerve signals from the sensory system—mainly the eyes, ears,

SKIN AND MUSCLES

The skin protects the inside of the body from dirt, too much dryness or wetness, injury, harmful rays, and germs. It also helps to keep the body warm in cold weather and cool in hot conditions. The muscular system consists of more than 640 muscles. In most cases, each end of a muscle is joined to a bone. When the muscle shortens or contracts, it pulls on the bones and moves that part of the body.

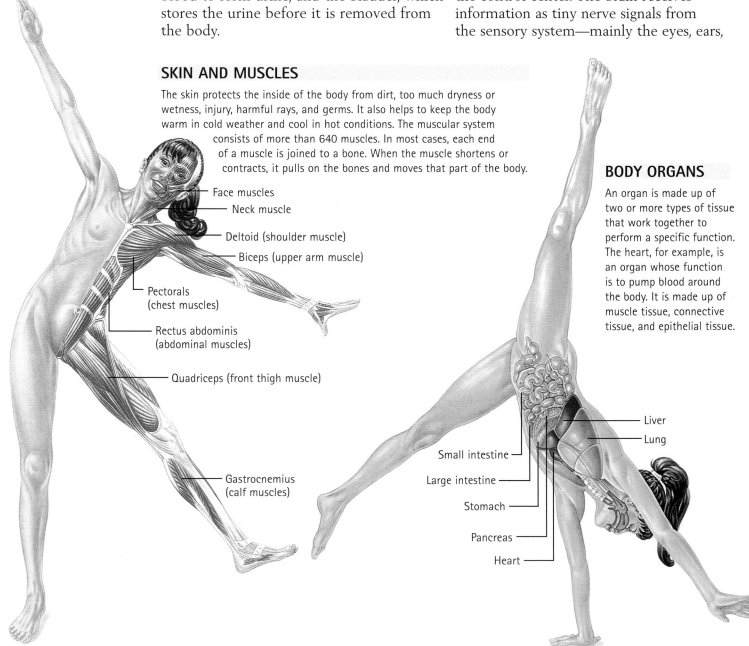

Face muscles

Neck muscle

Deltoid (shoulder muscle)

Biceps (upper arm muscle)

Pectorals (chest muscles)

Rectus abdominis (abdominal muscles)

Quadriceps (front thigh muscle)

Gastrocnemius (calf muscles)

BODY ORGANS

An organ is made up of two or more types of tissue that work together to perform a specific function. The heart, for example, is an organ whose function is to pump blood around the body. It is made up of muscle tissue, connective tissue, and epithelial tissue.

Small intestine

Large intestine

Stomach

Pancreas

Heart

Liver

Lung

nose, tongue, and skin. These sense organs detect what is happening around the body. The brain also sends signals to muscles, telling them when and how to contract and produce movements. It is also the site of mental processes such as thoughts, feelings, emotions, and memories.

REPRODUCTION

The human body reproduces like any other mammal's. The reproductive system consists of either female or male sex organs. The male ones make sperm cells; the female ones contain egg cells. When a sperm cell fertilizes an egg cell, the egg begins to multiply rapidly. Over a period of nine months, it grows and develops within the mother's body into an embryo, then a fetus, and is born as a baby.

◄ The average body reaches its peak physical power and maximum size around the age of 18 to 25 years. After this it begins to age. Signs of aging include wrinkled skin, gray hair, balding in men, shrinking, weaker muscles, slower reactions, and less sharp senses.

GROWING UP

Some animals are active and independent within minutes of birth. But a human baby needs food, warmth and care for many months. As it grows into a child, it learns to sit, stand, walk, talk, read, write and acquire many other skills. This takes years because human society is very complex, with many customs, traditions, rules and laws.

CIRCULATORY AND LYMPHATIC SYSTEMS

The circulatory system consists of the heart, blood vessels, and blood. It transports oxygen from the lungs, and nutrients and energy-rich substances to all parts of the body. The lymphatic and immune systems produce antibodies which are released into the bloodstream to fight off disease.

■ Oxygenated blood

■ Deoxygenated blood

■ Lymphatic system

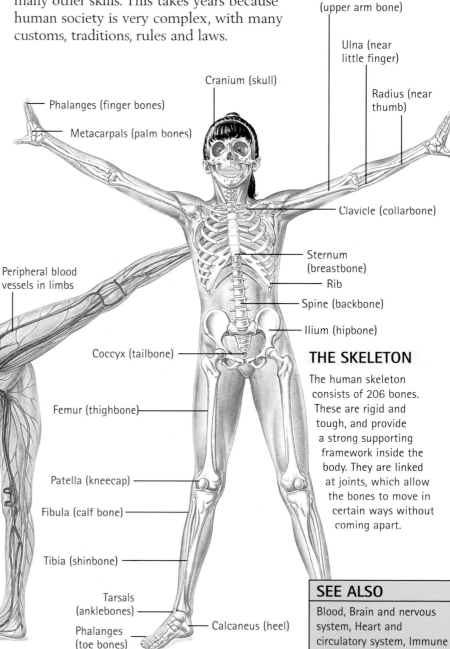

Peripheral blood vessels in limbs

Lymph vessels

Lymph nodes

Heart

Aorta (main artery from heart)

Phalanges (finger bones)

Metacarpals (palm bones)

Cranium (skull)

Humerus (upper arm bone)

Ulna (near little finger)

Radius (near thumb)

Clavicle (collarbone)

Sternum (breastbone)

Rib

Spine (backbone)

Ilium (hipbone)

Coccyx (tailbone)

Femur (thighbone)

Patella (kneecap)

Fibula (calf bone)

Tibia (shinbone)

Tarsals (anklebones)

Phalanges (toe bones)

Calcaneus (heel)

THE SKELETON

The human skeleton consists of 206 bones. These are rigid and tough, and provide a strong supporting framework inside the body. They are linked at joints, which allow the bones to move in certain ways without coming apart.

SEE ALSO

Blood, Brain and nervous system, Heart and circulatory system, Immune system, Reproduction

IMMUNE SYSTEM

The body protects itself from illness and disease using its immune system, which constantly cleans the blood and body tissues and attacks invading germs.

EDWARD JENNER
Jenner was a British doctor (1749-1823) who developed the technique of vaccination—a way to provide artificial immunity against disease. In 1796 he vaccinated patients with harmless cowpox to protect them against deadly smallpox.

The immune system is one of the body's most complicated systems. It includes a series of glands—known as lymph glands, or lymph nodes—that are found throughout the body, but especially in the neck, armpits, and groin. These glands are connected by a network of tubes called lymph vessels, and both glands and vessels contain a pale, milky fluid called lymph.

MILLIONS OF CELLS

Lymph and lymph glands are home to the main kind of cell in the immune system, called the lymphocyte. These cells are also found in large quantities in the blood, where they form one kind of white blood cell, and in the fluids that bathe all the body parts. There are about two trillion lymphocytes in the human body.

RECOGNIZING INVADERS

Germs such as bacteria and viruses are continually entering the body by being breathed in, or swallowed, or through a cut. As soon as germs enter, lymphocytes called T- and B-cells identify them as "non-self," or foreign particles. They do this by detecting unfamiliar substances, or antigens, on the germs' outer surface.

ON THE ATTACK

Some of the B-cells then start to multiply and form plasma cells. These cells produce Y-shaped substances known as antibodies that attach themselves to the antigens and cause the germs to burst, or clump together so they cannot multiply. T-cells produce chemicals that kill infected cells. They also help another type of white blood cell, called a macrophage, to destroy germs by engulfing, or eating, them.

LONG MEMORIES

Different germs carry different antigens. When a germ infects the body, causing an illness, B-cells known as memory cells remember its antigens so that, if the germ enters again, the memory cells can quickly activate the immune system to fight off the illness. This protection against disease is called immunity.

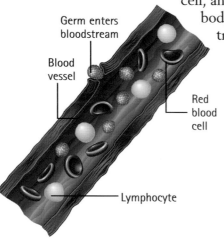

Germ enters bloodstream

Blood vessel

Red blood cell

Lymphocyte

1 When a germ enters the bloodstream—for example, through a cut—white blood cells, known as lymphocytes, are drawn to the site.

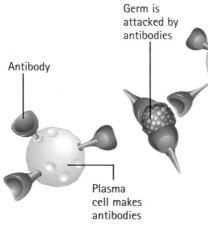

Antibody

Germ is attacked by antibodies

Plasma cell makes antibodies

2 Some lymphocytes multiply and form plasma cells which make antibodies that attack the germ.

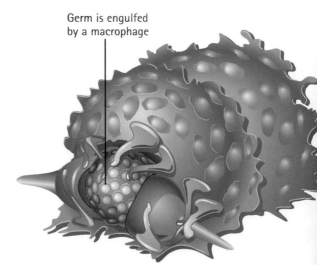

Germ is engulfed by a macrophage

3 Other lymphocytes—certain types of T-cell—help to attract macrophages to the site. These swallow the germ and dissolve it.

IMMUNITY AGAINST DISEASE

Lymphocytes and macrophages work together to destroy germs that cause disease. Often, they do not succeed in killing a new germ before it has multiplied and caused an illness. However, once the memory cells have been primed, the immune system is ready for action. Next time it meets the germ it can quickly make the right antibodies to fight off the infection. Immunity can also be artificially induced. A specially weakened form of the germ is swallowed or injected into the body. It is not strong enough to cause illness, but it activates the immune system to remember the real germ in the future.

SEE ALSO
Disease, Gland, Human body, Medicine

INCA

The Inca were people who lived in the Andes Mountains of South America. From about 1200 to the mid-1500s, they ruled a rich and sophisticated empire.

The Inca Empire was centered around Cuzco—an upland valley in the Andes Mountains of Peru. The empire stretched into present-day Ecuador, Colombia, Bolivia, Argentina, and Chile. Although made up of many tribes, its ruling emperor and nobles were members of the Inca tribe. The empire collapsed after the Spanish invaded in 1532.

The Inca had no writing system. They used knotted, colored strings, called *quipus*, to keep records.

GOD ON EARTH

The first great Inca emperor was Pachacuti Yupanqui, a warrior who came to power in 1438. His son, Tupac, and grandson, Huayna Capac, extended the empire. The emperor was known as "Inca." He was considered a god, a descendant of the sun.

RUNNING AN EMPIRE

The empire was strictly governed. The ordinary people worked many days each year for the emperor, planting crops, fighting battles, or building bridges and roads. The roads ran throughout the empire, crossing mountain ravines by rope bridges. In places,

Gold, silver, and precious stones were used to craft beautiful objects used by noble families and in religious rituals.

roads were carved from rock, elsewhere they were paved. The roads were mostly used by *chasquis*, the royal messengers, and merchants, who used llamas to carry goods. There were no wheeled vehicles.

EVERYDAY LIFE

Most of the 12 million people were farmers. They kept llamas and alpacas for wool and meat, and grew Indian corn, potatoes, and other vegetables in terraced fields. Wool and cotton cloth was woven by hand, and pots made from clay. Stone fortresses guarded cities and roads, but most families lived in houses made from mud bricks.

GREAT FESTIVAL OF THE SUN

The Capac Raymi, the Great Festival of the Sun, was held in Cuzco on the longest and shortest days of the year. At dawn, the emperor offered a golden cup of sacred beer and sacrificed a white llama to Inti, the sun god, to gain his help and protection. Other important gods included the supreme deity Viracocha and the goddesses of the earth and the sea.

SEE ALSO

Aztecs, Empire, South America

INDIAN SUBCONTINENT

The Indian subcontinent is a huge land mass that includes the countries of India, Pakistan, Bangladesh, Nepal, and Bhutan. It makes up one tenth of Asia.

BANGLADESH
Area: 57,452 sq. mi. (148,800km²)
Population: 157,827,000
Capital: Dhaka
Language: Bengali
Currency: Taka

BHUTAN
Area: 14,824 sq. mi. (38,400km²)
Population: 758,000
Capital: Thimphu
Language: Dzongkha
Currency: Ngultrum, Indian rupee

INDIA
Area: 1,477,613 sq. mi. (3,827,000km²)
Population: 1,296,834,000
Capital: New Delhi (part of Delhi)
Languages: Hindi, English, Bengali, and 20 other official languages
Currency: Rupee

MALDIVES
Area: 115 sq. mi. (298km²)
Population: 330,000
Capital: Malé (Malé Island)
Language: Divehi
Currency: Rufiyaa

NEPAL
Area: 56,827 sq. mi. (147,181km²)
Population: 29,384,000
Capital: Kathmandu
Language: Nepali
Currency: Nepalese rupee

Three quarters of the Indian subcontinent is covered by India itself. As well as Pakistan, Bangladesh, Nepal, and Bhutan on the mainland, there are two island nations in the south—Sri Lanka and the Maldives.

FROM HIGH TO LOW
High mountain ranges lie in the north of the region, including the Himalayas, which contain the world's highest peak, Mount Everest (29,029 ft./8,848m), on the border between Nepal and China. Southern India consists largely of a plateau called the Deccan. Bordering the Deccan are two low mountain ranges, the Eastern and Western Ghats, edged by narrow coastal plains.

WATER AND WINDS
The longest river in the region, the Indus (1,975 mi./3,180km), flows from the Himalayas through Pakistan. The Brahmaputra (1,800 mi./2,900km) and Ganges rivers (1,550 mi./2,494km) join in Bangladesh and flow across the world's largest delta, into the Bay of Bengal. Mawsynram, near Shillong, just north

▲ Religion and festivals play an important part in Indian life. Many people go on pilgrimages to holy places like the city of Varanasi on the banks of the Ganges river. The waters of the river are considered sacred.

of Bangladesh, is the rainiest place on Earth—a record of about 1,024 in. (26,000mm) a year. Most rain falls from June to October, when monsoon winds blow from the sea. These have little effect on the dry northwest—the Thar Desert along the Pakistan–India border has less than 10 in. (250mm) of rain a year.

TROPICAL TREES
Few plants grow in the northwest, except on the wetter mountain slopes, but most of the Indian subcontinent has plenty of farming and grazing land. Valuable trees in tropical forests include ironwood, rosewood, and teak. Bamboo also grows in many areas.

▼ Spices provide a major industry for India and are sold at markets like this one in Udaipur.

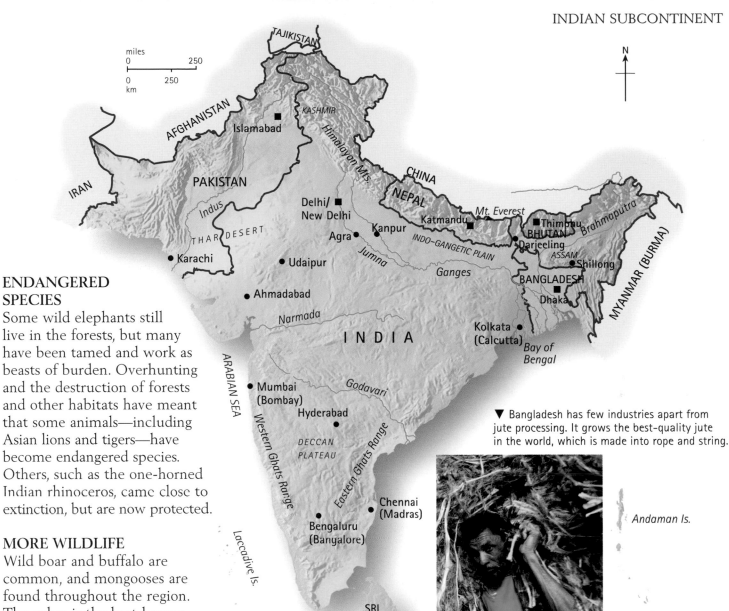

miles
0 — 250
0 — 250
km

N

TAJIKISTAN

AFGHANISTAN

IRAN

PAKISTAN

KASHMIR

Himalayan Mts.

CHINA

NEPAL

Islamabad

Indus

THAR DESERT

Delhi/
New Delhi

Agra

Kanpur

Katmandu

Mt. Everest

Thimphu
BHUTAN

Brahmaputra

Darjeeling

ASSAM

Shillong

MYANMAR (BURMA)

Karachi

Udaipur

Jumna

INDO-GANGETIC PLAIN

BANGLADESH

Ahmadabad

Ganges

Dhaka

ARABIAN SEA

Narmada

I N D I A

Kolkata
(Calcutta)

Bay of
Bengal

Mumbai
(Bombay)

Godavari

Hyderabad

Western Ghats Range

DECCAN
PLATEAU

Eastern Ghats Range

Chennai
(Madras)

Bengaluru
(Bangalore)

Laccadive Is.

MALDIVES

Malé I.

INDIAN
OCEAN

SRI
LANKA

Colombo

Andaman Is.

Nicobar Is.

ENDANGERED SPECIES

Some wild elephants still live in the forests, but many have been tamed and work as beasts of burden. Overhunting and the destruction of forests and other habitats have meant that some animals—including Asian lions and tigers—have become endangered species. Others, such as the one-horned Indian rhinoceros, came close to extinction, but are now protected.

MORE WILDLIFE

Wild boar and buffalo are common, and mongooses are found throughout the region. The cobra is the best-known reptile, and the region's many birds include the myna bird, which can imitate human speech. Mountain animals include brown and black bears, deer, the rare snow leopard, the markhor (a kind of wild goat), various kinds of wild sheep, and wild yaks.

▼ Bangladesh has few industries apart from jute processing. It grows the best-quality jute in the world, which is made into rope and string.

▲ Ihuru Island is one of 1,200 coral islands that make up the Maldives. Most are just 6.5 ft. (2m) above sea level.

GROWING POPULATIONS

With a population of over one billion, India has more people than any other country apart from China. Pakistan, with a population of 158 million, ranks sixth in the world, and Bangladesh, with 133 million people, is the world's seventh-largest country.

INDIA'S LANGUAGES

India has 23 major languages and more than 448 dialects and minor languages. The two main language groups are the Indo-European, which includes Hindi—the most widely spoken language—and the Dravidian languages, including Tamil, which are spoken mainly in the south. English is also spoken by many Indians. ▶

PAKISTAN
Area: 307,374 sq. mi. (796,095km2)
Population: 204,925,000
Capital: Islamabad
Languages: Urdu, English, and Punjabi
Currency: Pakistan rupee

SRI LANKA
Area: 25,332 sq. mi. (65,610km2)
Population: 22,409,000
Capital: Kotte (Colombo)
Languages: Sinhala, Tamil
Currency: Sri Lankan rupee

▲ Agriculture is Sri Lanka's main economic activity. Important crops, including tea, are grown on large plantations.

▼ Nepal's Sherpa people live on the southern slopes of the Himalaya Mountains, where the spectacular landscape, which includes Mount Everest, attracts many tourists. Timber is used for cooking and heating by locals and tourists, and less than a third of the country's forests remain.

URDU AND BENGALI

Pakistan's official language is Urdu, but only eight percent of the people speak it as their first language. Instead, they speak the language of their community. The largest communities are the Punjabi, Pashtun, Sindhi, and Sariaki. In Bangladesh, more than 95 percent of the people speak the official language, Bengali.

RELIGIONS OF INDIA

Beautiful temples, mosques, and other religious buildings are everywhere. In places such as Udaipur, India, there are spectacular palaces built hundreds of years ago for princes. Today, Hindus make up 81 percent of India's population, with Muslims forming another 13 percent. India also has large numbers of Christians, Sikhs, Buddhists, and Jains. Islam, the Muslim religion, is the chief religion in Pakistan, Bangladesh, and the Maldives.

INFLUENCE OF BUDDHA

Hinduism is the official religion of Nepal, but the country was the birthplace of Buddha, so many Nepalese have combined the beliefs and practices of the two religions. Buddhism is the chief religion in Bhutan and of the Sinhalese in Sri Lanka, although

▲ The Taj Mahal at Agra was built between 1632 and 1653 at the request of the Mogul emperor Shah Jahan, who wanted it as a tomb for his wife.

a minority group in Sri Lanka, the Tamils, mainly follows Hinduism. Differences between these groups have led to civil war between government troops and Tamil guerrillas, which ended in 2009.

FARM LIFE

Around three fifths of the people of the Indian subcontinent are farmers who live in villages and farm the land around them. Farming is the leading activity, and rice is the main crop in India, Bangladesh, and Sri Lanka. In Pakistan, wheat is the leading food crop. Tea is grown in northeast India, around Darjeeling and in Assam, as well as in Sri Lanka. Most farmers have a low standard of living and live in houses made of mud and straw. India has more cattle and buffalo than any other country, but Hindus consider them sacred and they cannot be killed for food. Fishing is also a major activity.

▲ In Bhutan, local women make cheese from yaks' milk.

DEVELOPING INDUSTRY

The Indian subcontinent has plenty of coal, iron ore, and other minerals. There is some oil, and petroleum refining is an important industry. India has a fast-growing high-tech sector and is now the seventh-largest economy in the world.

CITY LIFE AND EDUCATION

The region has six cities with more than ten million people. These are the Indian cities of Mumbai (formerly Bombay), Kolkata (formerly Calcutta), and Delhi. (Delhi is made up of the walled city of Old Delhi and the capital New Delhi.) Karachi and Lahore in Pakistan and the Bangladeshi capital Dhaka make up the six. Sri Lanka has a good education system, but in the rest of the Indian subcontinent there are millions of people who cannot read or write. The education system in India is, however, gradually improving.

EARLY TIMES

From 1857, India (which included modern India, Pakistan and Bangladesh) came under direct or indirect British rule. In 1947, British India split into two independent parts—modern India and Pakistan, which was created for Muslims. In 1971, East Pakistan broke away and became the separate country of Bangladesh. Sri Lanka became independent from Britain in 1948, as did the Maldives in 1968.

DIFFICULT DIVISION

At the time of the partition of British India, the status of Kashmir in the north was not satisfactorily settled. Part of this territory now falls within northeast Pakistan, but the bulk lies within the Indian states of Jammu and Kashmir. Guerrillas and governments are in dispute over whether Kashmir should remain part of India, become part of Pakistan, or become independent.

GANDHI
Mohandas K. Gandhi was born in India in 1869. From the 1920s, he used peaceful protests to lead India to independence. He became known as Mahatma, meaning "great soul." He was assassinated in 1948.

FAST FACTS

• Indians call their country Bharat after a legendary monarch

• The name India comes from an ancient word *Sindhu* meaning "river"

• India is the world's seventh largest country by area

• India's railroad system is the largest in Asia

◄ Pakistan's national cricket team is world famous. Children play the game from an early age.

SEE ALSO

Asia, Buddhism, Hinduism, Islam, Mountain and valley

INDONESIA AND EAST TIMOR

Indonesia, in Southeast Asia, has 13,466 islands, of which 922 are inhabited. They are part of the Malay Archipelago, the world's biggest island group by area.

INDONESIA
Area: 735,298 sq. mi.
(1,904,569km²)
Population: 260,581,000
Capital: Jakarta
Language: Bahasa Indonesia
Currency: Rupiah

EAST TIMOR (TIMOR-LESTE)
Area: 5, 743 sq. mi.
(14,874km²)
Population: 1,067,000
Capital: Dili
Languages: Tetum, Portuguese
Currency: US dollar

The majority of Indonesia's islands lie close to or just south of the equator. They are mountainous with many volcanoes, 77 of which have erupted in recent times. The climate is hot and humid, and tropical rain forests cover large parts of the country. The main areas are the islands of Java, Sumatra, and Sulawesi and the regions of Kalimantan (part of Borneo) and West Papua (part of the island of New Guinea). In 2002, East Timor split from Indonesia and became independent.

VARIED WILDLIFE
The westerns islands of Indonesia were once part of the Asian mainland, and are home to Asian animals such as elephants and orang-utans. The eastern islands, once linked to Australia, contain animals such as cockatoos and birds of paradise.

WEALTH OF LANGUAGES
Indonesia is home to many ethnic groups, the largest being Javanese. Apart from the national language, about 700 other languages and dialects are spoken. More than 86 percent of the people are Muslims, making Indonesia the world's largest Islamic country.

◄ Bali is famous for its music and dance. Dyed batik cloth is used to make traditional clothing.

▲ Rice, Indonesia's main food, is grown on terraced fields. Volcanic ash makes the soil rich and fertile.

LIFE AND WORK
Many Indonesians live in rural villages, some in houses raised on stilts. Industry is growing rapidly, however, leading to the development of large modern cities such as Jakarta and Surabaya on Java. The forests are rich in timber, and the seas provide good fishing. Minerals include tin, nickel, copper, and oil. Factories make clothing and electrical goods for export.

PREHISTORIC PEOPLES
People have lived in Indonesia since prehistoric times. There were Hindu and Buddhist kingdoms from the 700s, before the arrival of Islam. Portuguese traders came in the 1500s, and Dutch ones from the 1600s. In 1800, the area became the Dutch colony of the East Indies. Eventually, in 1949, Indonesia became a republic.

SEE ALSO
Asia, Islam, Malaysia, Rain forest, Southeast Asia, Volcano

INDUSTRIAL REVOLUTION

The Industrial Revolution is the name given to the great changes that took place when people began to use steam power to make goods in factories.

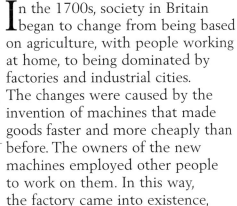

Thomas Newcomen built the first steam engine in 1712 to pump water.

In the 1700s, society in Britain began to change from being based on agriculture, with people working at home, to being dominated by factories and industrial cities. The changes were caused by the invention of machines that made goods faster and more cheaply than before. The owners of the new machines employed other people to work on them. In this way, the factory came into existence, surrounded by houses for the workers. Often several factories were built together, from which a new town developed.

The spinning jenny of 1764 could spin several threads at one time.

WOMEN'S WORK

Factory jobs often required skill rather than strength. Women were as good as men for such work, and many single women gained independence by earning a wage for themselves. Most women gave up work when they married, to run the household and family.

KING COTTON

The Industrial Revolution began around 1760, when new machines that could spin cotton thread very quickly were invented in Britain. These made thread so fast that hand weavers could not keep up. So weaving machines were invented. At first, waterwheels powered the machines, but by 1780 these could not cope. In 1785, British clergyman Edmund Cartwright (1743–1823) invented a power loom that used steam power to drive it.

THE POWER OF STEAM

Simple steam engines were already being used to pump water out of mines. Between 1764 and 1790, Scottish engineer James Watt (1736–1819) improved the steam engine so that it used heat more efficiently and could drive machines. By 1800, there were about 500 steam engines at work in Britain. For the first time, people had an artificial source of power that was cheap and efficient. ▶

In 1777, the world's first iron bridge was erected in Shropshire, England.

Eli Whitney's cotton gin of 1794 separated cotton seeds from fiber at speed.

Locomotives, such as the German *Der Adler* of 1835, powered the rail boom.

BRUNEL
The British engineer Isambard Kingdom Brunel (1806–59) built railroads, bridges, and the world's largest ship.

RAW MATERIALS

The Industrial Revolution required iron for machines, coal to burn in steam engines, and money to pay for them both. By 1750, Britain had all three and became the first country to industrialize. The iron industry grew quickly after 1709, when Abraham Darby first used coke to smelt iron (melt the iron ore). This was cheaper and more efficient than the old way using charcoal. New coal mines were dug to supply coal for steam engines and coke for ironworks.

CANALS AND RAILROADS

The new industrial products required a transportation system to move them to people. Between 1750 and 1830, canals were dug, linking major cities and rivers. Most roads remained poor, but in 1804, Richard Trevithick built the world's first steam locomotive. By the 1830s, Britain had embarked on a railroad craze, and railroads were soon being built across western Europe and North America. By

1870, many of their cities had been linked by rail. Belgium, France, Germany, and the United States began industrializing after 1815. By 1900, the U.S. and Germany had overtaken Britain in steel production.

BUSINESS BOOM

The new machines made goods faster and more cheaply. Factory and mine owners made huge profits, some of which they spent on more machines, so creating new jobs. Investors saved small amounts of money in banks, which then lent large amounts to industrialists. This developing "capitalist" system raised money to build factories, offices, and houses.

A HARD LIFE

For many workers, life in the factories and mines was hard and dangerous. Men, women, and children worked 13 or more hours a day, often for low wages. Many workers

DEVELOPING INDUSTRIAL AREAS

The new factories were built near canals and railroads so that raw materials could be brought in and finished goods taken to markets easily. Houses were built to accommodate the workers, but many industrial areas became slums and lacked running water, drains, and other basic services.

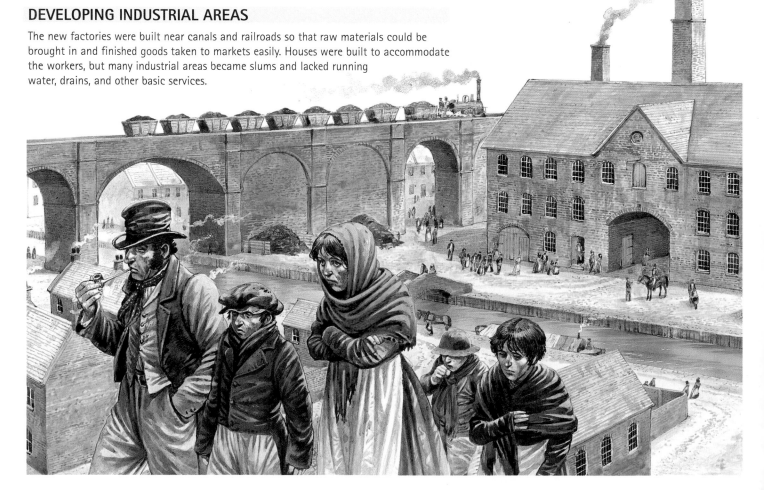

KEY DATES

1769 James Watt perfects the steam engine

1794 Eli Whitney invents the cotton gin

1807 Robert Fulton's first steamboat

1831 First U.S. steam-powered railroad (South Carolina)

1834 Cyrus McCormick demonstrates his reaper

1844 Samuel Morse sends first telegraph message

1849 Elias Howe patents the sewing machine

were killed or injured by unsafe machinery before new safety laws were enforced. Towns grew rapidly and without proper planning, leaving some areas without drains or clean water. Diseases that were caught from unclean water (like cholera) or in crowded conditions (tuberculosis) became common and killed thousands of people. These conditions caused social unrest and even riots.

CAMPAIGNERS AND REFORMERS

Gradually, laws to shorten working hours and stop child labor were introduced. Trade unions, at first banned, campaigned for better pay and conditions for workers.

In time, reformers won improved working conditions and schooling for all children. Slums were cleared and new laws controlled factory and housing development.

LONG-TERM EFFECTS

During the Industrial Revolution, cities grew rapidly as people began to leave the countryside to find work. Industrialization spread worldwide during the 1900s, and the world economy today is geared to the production of goods, though some countries in Africa and Southeast Asia remain dependent on agriculture or services. People now enjoy higher standards of living than ever before, but at a high cost to the environment. Industrialization has caused pollution and used up resources such as coal, oil, and minerals. However, new technology is being developed to solve some of the problems created by industrialization.

URBAN DEVELOPMENT

Streets of attached houses were built around factories to house the workers. Gradually, some factory owners or town councils improved conditions for the workers by building schools and churches.

CHILD LABOR
In the 1700s and 1800s, factory owners employed children, many of them under ten years of age, to work in factories and mines. They had to work long hours in dangerous and unhealthy conditions. However, by 1900, most industrialized countries had banned child labor.

SEE ALSO

Coal, Engine, Iron and steel, Machine, Pollution, Train, Transportation, Water power

INDUSTRY

Industry covers all the different kinds of work people do, from producing raw materials and manufacturing goods to providing services.

Borer

Grinder

Puncher

Turning machine

▲ Machine tools such as these are widely used to manufacture machinery and motor components.

Manufacturing industries, such as the aircraft and automotive industries, make goods for people to buy. The electronics industry, for example, produces tiny wafers of silicon that are the brains of our computers, and the chemical industry manufactures a wide range of chemicals, from fertilizers to lifesaving antibiotics. The steel industry is one of the most important of all industries because it produces the metal that many other industries rely on. The construction industry uses steel to build towering skyscrapers and massive dams and bridges.

PRIMARY INDUSTRIES

Mining produces the raw materials, such as ores and petroleum, on which manufacturing industries depend. It marks the beginning of the industrial production process and is therefore called a primary industry. Agriculture, forestry, and fishing are also primary industries. Manufacturing is next in the production chain, and is called a secondary industry.

GETTING SERVICE

When the manufacturing industries have produced the goods, they have to be sold to the consumer. This is the job of stores. They do not produce goods, but

▶ Researchers in the chemical industry develop new materials such as drugs and plastics.

they provide a service by buying goods from the manufacturers and selling them on to customers. Stores are an example of a service industry, often called a tertiary (third) industry. Other examples of service industries include transportation and tourism, insurance and banks, restaurants and hotels, hospitals, and local government.

MASS PRODUCTION

A key feature of today's global industry is mass production—the manufacture of goods in large quantities at a relatively low cost. In a typical mass-production operation, goods are built up piece by piece on an assembly line, with people often working side by side with industrial robots.

▲ Some industries, such as this textile factory in India, involve hundreds of people working together. Others have people working in smaller groups, or alone at home.

AUTOMATION TAKES OVER

Today, many assembly lines are fully automated, with machines now controlled by computers instead of humans. Robots are increasingly being used, particularly in the automotive industry. They are ideal for performing highly repetitive, hazardous, or awkward tasks, such as spot welding or paint spraying. Fitted with a gripper, they can also be used to move objects.

SEE ALSO

Construction, Farming, Fishing industry, Industrial Revolution, Mining, Robot

INSECT

Insects belong to the large group of animals called arthropods, which means "jointed legs." An insect's legs are made up of small segments and flexible joints.

Male stag beetles have large jaws that look like the antlers of a stag.

Crickets have long hind legs for hopping, and rub their wings together to "sing."

Earwigs are flat with pincers at their tail and wings that fold away.

Aphids have soft brown or green bodies up to 1 in. (3mm) long.

A human louse, like all sucking lice, feeds on the blood of mammals.

IDENTIFYING AN INSECT

All adult insects have a body that is divided into three parts: the head, the thorax (where legs and wings are joined), and the abdomen (where the insect digests its food and makes its eggs). They also have three pairs of legs and a tough body case, or exoskeleton.

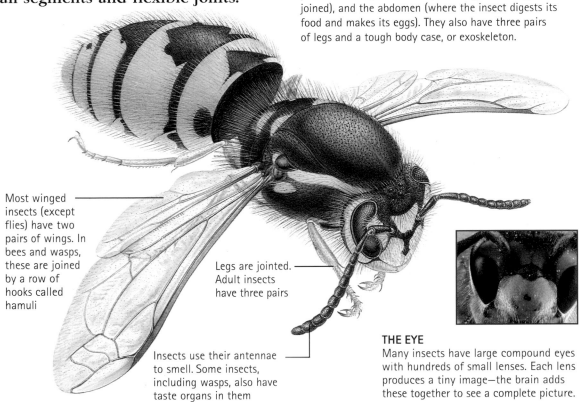

Most winged insects (except flies) have two pairs of wings. In bees and wasps, these are joined by a row of hooks called hamuli

Legs are jointed. Adult insects have three pairs

Insects use their antennae to smell. Some insects, including wasps, also have taste organs in them

THE EYE
Many insects have large compound eyes with hundreds of small lenses. Each lens produces a tiny image—the brain adds these together to see a complete picture.

More than a million species of insect have been found on Earth. That's more than all the other types of animal put together. They are split into over 30 groups and include grasshoppers, beetles, butterflies, flies, and bees. Insects have no backbone or skeleton inside the body, but the whole insect is covered with a tough, horny material called chitin. This forms an external skeleton rather like a suit of armor. It is made up of segments, some of which are loosely connected by soft membranes so that the insect can move.

WITH OR WITHOUT WINGS

Most insects have two pairs of wings, but some, including fleas and worker ants, never have wings. Flying ants only have wings for a short time, then lose them. Beetles and many bugs look as if they have no wings because their front wings form hard cases and completely cover the delicate hind wings.

BREATHING WITH TUBES

Insects do not have lungs. They breathe by way of a system of fine tubes, called tracheae. These branch through the body and carry air and oxygen. In most insects, air enters the tubes through small holes on the sides of the body—mainly on the abdomen. The openings are called spiracles and they are best seen in large caterpillars, which are the young stages of butterflies and moths.

WATER BUGS

Insects that live in water usually have to come to the surface to renew the air in their breathing tubes, but many young insects can absorb dissolved oxygen straight from the water into their tracheae. ▶

▶ Beetles form the largest insect order, with more than 370,000 species.

◀ The praying mantis has powerful jaws so it can munch through the hard outer case of insects.

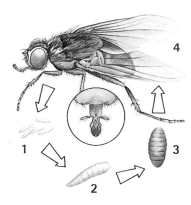

MOUTHPARTS
Insects have a variety of mouthparts adapted to suit their diets. Some have chewing jaws, others suck up their food, and some have piercing needles.

Tiger beetles are fierce carnivores (meat-eaters), with prominent biting mandibles (or jaws).

Weevils' mouthparts are extended into a snout. They can be serious pests, infesting flour and grain.

A fly's proboscis is like a straw with a sponge tip. It dribbles on food to dissolve it, then sucks it back up.

INSECTS ARE EVERYWHERE
Very few insects live in the sea, but they live everywhere else, and they feed on just about everything. Many are pests and cause a lot of damage by eating our food and crops. Termites and other insects, such as the woodworm and deathwatch beetle, can even destroy our houses. Fleas and mosquitoes suck our blood and carry dangerous diseases. But there are also some very useful insects. Honeybees pollinate many of our crops and give us honey, silkmoths give us silk, ladybug beetles eat huge numbers of greenflies (aphids) and other plant pests, and dung beetles and their grubs help to keep the countryside clean by eating the dung of cows and other animals.

AN INSECT GROWS UP
Most insects start life as eggs, but the insect that hatches from an egg does not usually look much like its parents. A caterpillar, for example, looks nothing like an adult butterfly or moth: it has no wings, and instead of sipping nectar from flowers it munches its way through leaves with its biting jaws. Before it becomes an adult, the caterpillar has to pass through a chrysalis, or pupa stage, during which its body is broken down and rebuilt in the adult form. Bees, flies, and beetles pass through similar stages as they grow up. Young insects of this kind are called larvae, and this way of growing up is called a complete metamorphosis, meaning "a complete change."

THE EMERGING INSECT
Insects molt several times as they grow up, because their tough outer coats, or exoskeletons, cannot grow. At each molt, the old skin splits open and the insect crawls out.

INSECT LIFE CYCLE
Advanced insects, such as flies, have a four-part life cycle. The eggs hatch into larvae which change their skins twice as they grow. Then comes the pupa stage where they change into the adult form.

SMALL ADULTS
Grasshoppers and dragonflies have a slightly different kind of life cycle. The young insects do not have wings, but they do look fairly like the adults apart from being smaller. They are called nymphs, and they gradually turn into adults without passing through a chrysalis stage. This way of growing up is called an incomplete metamorphosis—"an incomplete change."

INSECT HOMES

Ants are the most successful social insects. In the leaf-cutter ant's communal home, the queen lays the eggs, nursery workers look after them, and larger workers cut leaves and bring them back, leaving scent trails by touching the ground with the tips of their abdomen. Soldier ants have a big head with strong jaws and bite to protect the nest, while smaller workers build new tunnels and tend the fungus gardens to feed the others.

Nursery worker

Soldier ants use their sting and powerful jaws to defend the colony

A queen ant can lay one egg every ten seconds.

Ants chew the leaves to pulp and mix it with their droppings. A fungus grows on the mixture and the ants eat the fungus.

Smaller worker protects leaf

A large leaf-cutter can grow up to 3/4 in. (2cm) and carry a gigantic weight in its mouth.

A worker takes the eggs to the nursery chambers and tends the growing larvae.

The nest has its own air conditioning system—air tunnels keep it at a constant temperature and humidity.

Ants can carry leaves through the network of tunnels.

Waste chamber

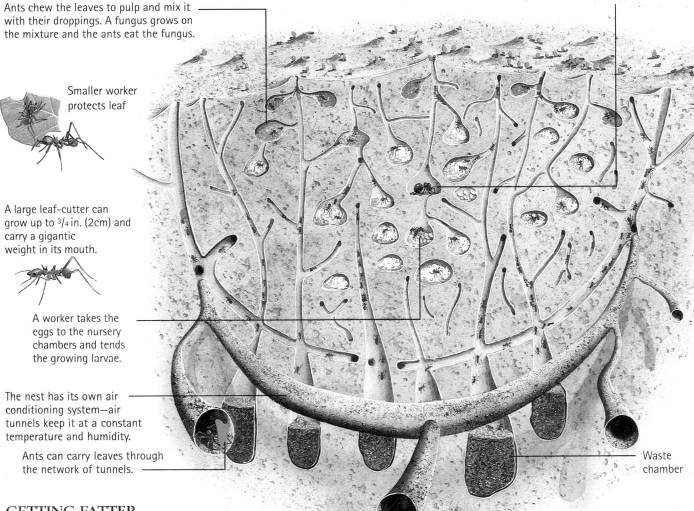

GETTING FATTER

As insects grow they shed their old body cases—but not before growing a soft new one. The insect pumps itself up with air or water for a few hours until the new skin has hardened, and then gets rid of the air or water to leave enough space for the next stage of growth. Most insects molt between 4 and 10 times as they grow up, but some may molt as many as 50 times before they are fully grown adults.

LARGE AND LITTLE

The heaviest species is the African Goliath beetle, which is about as big as a man's fist and weighs about 3.5 oz. (100g). Some stick insects are longer, but their bodies are extremely thin. The tiniest insects are smaller than a period on this page.

HOME ALONE

Most insects are solitary—living alone and finding a safe place to lay their eggs. This could be inside the body of another insect, in the case of the tarantula hawk wasp which lays an egg on a paralyzed but living spider. Social insects always live together in large family groups. Each insect has its own job, and only the queen lays eggs.

◀ Bumblebees are social insects that have pollen baskets (hairs) on their hind legs to collect pollen.

FAST FACTS

• Ants and bees recognize members of their own colony through smell

• The number of lenses in an insect's eye varies from about 6 in a worker ant to 30,000 in some dragonflies

• There are around 3,500 species of cockroach. Most live in tropical countries

SEE ALSO

Black Death, Butterfly and moth, Disease, Fossil, Prehistoric animal

INTERNET

The Internet is a global computer and telecommunications network. It offers instant access to information, knowledge, entertainment and opinions from around the world.

▲ Today's electronic media are acccessed via computer, tablet, smartphone, or television.

The Internet, or "Net," allows vast amounts of information to be streamed electronically, linking computers, tablets, smartphones, radios, televisions, household appliances and even satellites in space.

IN THE BEGINNING

Computer networking began with military communications. In the 1970s universities used the same idea to share research data. The 1980s and 90s saw the development of the Internet and the spread of personal computers. Soon e-mail (electronic mail) became one of the most common ways for people to communicate. The World Wide Web could be used by the public from 1993, allowing people to "surf" the Internet at the click of a mouse. At first it needed to be accessed by a slow telephone line ("dial-up").

THE WORLD WIDE WEB

The web is a system for placing pages of information and images on the Internet. The text is written in HTML (Hypertext Markup Language) and then uploaded to a server. A web browser such as Google Chrome is used to search out and display the pages when requested. The transfer is carried out using HTTP (HyperText Transfer Protocol). Pages contain hyperlinks, which take you straight to the next page when clicked.

SEARCH ENGINES
Search engines greatly speed up the process of finding Web pages and specific pieces of information on the Web.

HOW WE USE THE INTERNET

Since the 2000s, multiple ("broadband") frequencies have been used to allow fast and easy downloads. The applications of the Internet today affect almost every aspect of our lives, from education and healthcare to business, art, design, manufacture, shopping and advertising. We can live-stream entertainment, play games, message each other and use social media. We can see and chat to relatives on the other side of the world using Skype. The wonders of the Internet are matched by concerns. Do we spend too much time online? Is the Internet abused by criminals? Is our privacy safeguarded?

EMAIL
Using email, people can send letters and pictures to one another across the world within seconds.

SHOPPING
Many goods and services can be ordered and paid for over the Internet.

EVERYDAY INTERNET
We now use the Internet every day for all sorts of information and entertainment, from maps and weather to movies and games.

SEE ALSO
Communication, Computer, Technology, Telecommunication

INVENTION

An invention is the creation of something new. In the past 200 years, the number of inventions has boomed, changing the world dramatically.

▲ Wheels were used in Mesopotamia about 3200 B.C. The cart wheel was developed from the earlier potter's wheel.

Civilization has been driven forward by inventions. Each invention has been based on those that came before it and has made further progress possible.

GETTING THE BASICS RIGHT

Prehistoric people were the first inventors. They learned how to farm and to make fire, pottery, the wheel, and metal tools. One invention often leads to others. Without the wheel, for example, there could be no wagons, watermills, or machines driven by gears. Key inventions of the 1800s included photography, electric light, plastics, and automobiles. In 1946, the first electronic computer was built, changing the way we live.

THE INVENTORS

Some people stand out as lone inventors. In the late 1400s, the Italian Leonardo da Vinci designed a flying machine, but could not build it because there was no suitable engine. The American Thomas Alva Edison is credited with more than 1,000 inventions, including the lightbulb and

the phonograph. Other pioneers who worked alone were Alexander Graham Bell (the telephone), Guglielmo Marconi (the radio), and Karl Benz and Gottfried Daimler (the automobile). More recent inventions, such as the television and computers, were developed by large research teams with many specialists.

GOOD OR BAD?

Most people would agree that painkilling drugs are "good" inventions and that poison gas is "bad," but poison gas can be put to good use to kill pests that eat our food. It is how inventions are used that makes them useful or harmful.

The flushing toilet was developed in the 1840s.

Safety matches were invented in 1844.

An early experimental photocopier of 1940.

John Logie Baird invented the television in 1926.

Alexander Graham Bell invented the telephone in 1876.

PHONOGRAPH
Thomas Edison's phonograph of 1877 used a cylinder of tinfoil to record sound.

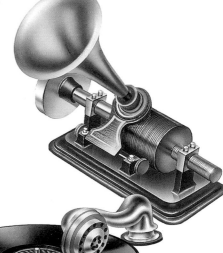

RECORDED SOUND

Sound recording has traditionally been by analog means. The sound waves in the air are reproduced as peaks and troughs in a groove on a solid object. These were read by passing a needle along the groove. CDs, mp3 players, i-Pods and phones treat sound as digital computer data instead.

COMPACT DISK
The compact disk, or CD, of the early 1980s contained digital music, read by a laser beam for accurate reproduction.

HI-FI VINYL
In 1958, stereo sound from long-playing records produced high-fidelity sound, or hi-fi, for the first time. Vinyl records have made a comeback in recent years.

78RPM GRAMOPHONE
In 1921, a flat plastic disk, or record, with sound fed through electric speakers gave better quality sound.

> ### SEE ALSO
> Aircraft, Car, Clock, Electronics, Industrial Revolution, Nuclear power, Printing, Warfare

IRELAND, REPUBLIC OF

The Republic of Ireland occupies 80 percent of the island of Ireland, which lies off the west coast of Britain. It is also called by its Gaelic name, Eire.

Area: 27,133 sq. mi. (70,273km²)
Population: 5,011,000
Capital: Dublin
Languages: English and Irish Gaelic
Currency: Euro

Ireland is a land of green fields, rolling hills, lakes, known as loughs, and winding rivers. The center of the country is flat, and low mountain ranges line the coasts. The Shannon, at 240 mi. (386km) the longest river in the British Isles, is used for hydroelectric power. Ireland has a mild, moist climate, and rich green grass grows on the limestone that forms much of the country, giving it the name Emerald Isle.

FARMING AND EUROPE
Ireland is a farming country famous for dairy foods such as butter. Wide bogs in the midlands are full of peat (decayed plants), which is cut and dried for fuel. Ireland voted to join the European Union (EU) in 1972, and from 2002, used the Euro as its currency. The country has gone through rapid social changes in recent years.

INDUSTRY AND CITIES
Irish factories make electronic equipment, textiles, plastics, and other goods. The country also brews alcoholic beverages. Industry is centered mainly around Dublin, Cork, and Limerick—three fifths of the people now live in towns or cities, where they are more likely to find work.

IRELAND AND BRITAIN
England gained control of Ireland in the 1500s, after which Protestants from England and Scotland settled there. When Ireland became self-governing in 1921, the six Protestant-dominated counties of Northern Ireland stayed part of the United Kingdom. In the republic, most people are Roman Catholics. The division of the island causes continuing tensions.

▲ Live music, traditional and modern, is a large part of Irish culture. The country has also produced many great writers.

▼ The city of Dublin is popular with tourists. Landmarks include the Ha'penny Bridge over the Liffey River.

▲ The Irish are famous for breeding horses. Their thoroughbred yearlings are often used as racehorses.

SEE ALSO
Christianity, Civil war, Europe, U.K.

IRON AND STEEL

Iron is one of the most common metals in Earth's crust. It is often used mixed with other ingredients in the form of steel—a cheap, strong building material.

▲ Glowing red-hot, molten iron is poured from a giant ladle into molds and left to cool as ingots.

In its natural state, iron is found combined with other elements, such as oxygen, as a rocky material called iron ore. Before it can be used, the iron has to be extracted (removed) from its ore by a process called smelting.

Steel can be shaped in various ways. It can be rolled into tubes . . .

. . . or drawn through a hole to make wire.

A series of rollers shapes solid steel into girders.

Steel is used for a wide range of everyday objects.

EXTRACTING THE IRON

The iron ore is mixed with coke (a form of carbon) and limestone (a chalky rock). Then it is blasted with hot air until it reaches a temperature of over 2,732°F (1,500°C). The iron melts, and most of the impurities (unwanted materials) float to its surface. The impurities, known as "slag," are then removed. The iron remaining is called pig iron. This still contains some impurities, especially carbon, but after further heat treatment, it can be poured into molds to make cast-iron parts such as engine blocks.

MAKING STEEL

Most pig iron goes for refining, or purifying, to make steel. This involves mixing it with scrap steel and blasting it with oxygen so that most of the carbon burns off. Steel is a tough, strong material that is used to make bridges, buildings, and many other objects that carry heavy loads. Manufacturers often add other elements to steel to give it special properties. Adding chromium and nickel makes stainless steel—a material that never rusts. This is used to make such things as engine parts and surgical tools.

PROCESSING THE IRON

Iron is extracted from its ore in a blast furnace. The resulting pig iron contains about four percent carbon, which comes from the coke in the furnace. This carbon makes the iron very brittle, so the iron is processed again before it is used. Steel is made by blasting the pig iron with oxygen inside a furnace called a converter. The oxygen combines with the carbon in the iron to form gases that are easily removed.

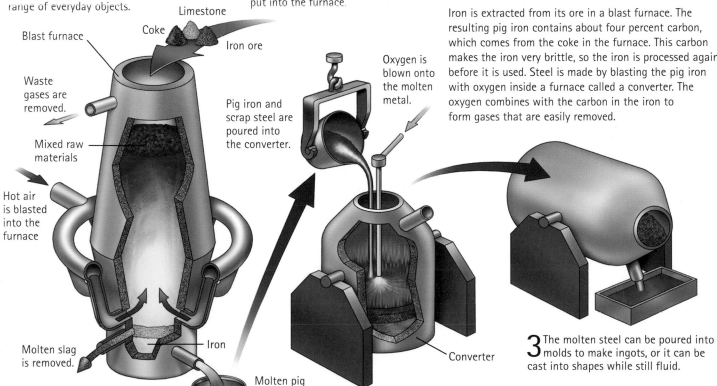

The raw materials are put into the furnace.

Limestone

Coke

Iron ore

Blast furnace

Waste gases are removed.

Mixed raw materials

Hot air is blasted into the furnace

Molten slag is removed.

Iron

1 As the coke burns inside the furnace, it removes the oxygen from the iron ore to leave pig iron.

Molten pig iron pours into ladle.

Pig iron and scrap steel are poured into the converter.

Oxygen is blown onto the molten metal.

Converter

2 Inside the converter, oxygen is used to burn off most of the carbon, leaving steel.

3 The molten steel can be poured into molds to make ingots, or it can be cast into shapes while still fluid.

SEE ALSO
Bridge, Construction, Earth, Metal, Skyscraper

ISLAM

Islam is the second most common religion in the world after Christianity. People who follow Islam are called Muslims.

▲ The crescent and star are the symbols of Islam.

There are 1.6 billion Muslims across the world, many in the Middle-East, East, southeast Asia and Africa. They believe in one all-powerful god, who created everything. Their name for this god is Allah. Islam means "submission" in Arabic, and devout Muslims try to live their lives according to Allah's word.

THE STORY OF MUHAMMAD
Islam began with the Prophet Muhammad, an Arab born in about A.D. 570 in the city of Mecca (in what is now Saudi Arabia). When he was 40, Muhammad was called by Allah to preach his words, and he spread Islam throughout much of the Arab world. He died in 632.

PILGRIMAGE TO MECCA
The pilgrimage to Mecca, called the hajj, takes place during the 12th month of the Muslim year. Nearly two million Muslims from across the world converge on Mecca to perform rituals, such as walking around the holy shrine, or Kaaba (the black structure seen below), which contains a black stone dating from ancient times.

▲ Islam has no priesthood. There are congregations and their leaders, as well as scholars and teachers.

LAWS OF ISLAM
Islamic Law, or the Shariah, is very important to Muslims. It was laid down by early Islamic teachers and tells Muslims how they should live their lives. The holy book of Islam is the Koran (or Qur'an), said to be Allah's exact words, as told to Muhammad. A Muslim's main religious duties are the "Five Pillars of Islam"—faith, prayer, almsgiving, fasting, and pilgrimage.

MUSLIMS AT PRAYER
The Muslim place of worship is called a Mosque. The call to prayer is heard from mosques five times a day. Muslims may pray in any clean and suitable place or visit the mosque on Fridays to pray together.

SEE ALSO
Crusades, Middle East, Pilgrim, Religion

ISRAEL AND PALESTINE

Israel and the Palestinian territories stand on a narrow strip of land in southwest Asia, on the eastern shore of the Mediterranean Sea. They make up most of the area once known as the Holy Land.

ISRAEL
Area: 7,876 sq. mi. (20,400km²)
Population: 8,300,000
Capital: Jerusalem (claimed)
Languages: Hebrew, Arabic
Currency: New Shekel

PALESTINE (Gaza and West Bank)
Area: 2,402 sq.mi. (6,220km²)
Population: 4,950,000; Israeli settlers 380,000
Capital: East Jerusalem (claimed)
Languages: Arabic, Hebrew
Currency: Israeli New Shekel, Egyptian Pound, Jordanian Dinar

The hills of Galilee lie in the north, while lowlands and fertile plains lie to the west. Most of southern Israel is taken up by the Negev Desert.

LAND AND CROPS
The Jordan River flows along eastern borders, into the Dead Sea. Summers in the region are dry and hot, while winters are cool. Farming depends on irrigation, and crops include oranges and other fruit, olives and vegetables.

TOWNS AND FACTORIES
Ninety-two percent of Israelis are city dwellers, working in factories or service industries. Exports include high-tech equipment, cut diamonds and pharmaceuticals.

A TROUBLED HISTORY
The Holy Land is sacred to Jews, Christians and Muslims. In the Middle Ages it was fought over during the Crusades. It later became part of the Ottoman Empire and after World War I was administered by the British. The state of Israel was founded in 1948, as Jews, many escaping from persecution in Europe, reclaimed their ancient homeland. This led to a series of wars with the displaced Arab population and in 1967 Israeli troops occupied Gaza and the West Bank. Today Palestinians have strictly limited control of these territories. The West Bank is being settled by Israelis.

▲ The Dead Sea is the saltiest body of water in the world. The salt crystallizes to form lumps in the water.

▲ The Dome of the Rock has been a Muslim shrine since 691A.D. It stands on a sacred hill known to Jews as the Temple Mount and to Muslims as the Noble Sanctuary.

▶ The education of future generations of schoolchildren will be an essential key to peace in Israel and Palestine.

SEE ALSO
Asia, Christianity, Islam, Judaism, Middle East, Pilgrim

ITALY

As the seat of the Roman Empire and cradle of the Renaissance, Italy has been at the center of European civilization for centuries.

Area: 116,348 sq. mi. (301,340km²)
Population: 62,128,000
Capital: Rome
Language: Italian
Currency: Euro

▲ ▼ Venice's annual carnival is a major event, and carnival-goers dress flamboyantly for the occasion. Boats known as gondolas are used for transportation in Venice, where the main "streets" are canals—the Grand Canal at the Rialto Bridge has been the scene of many regattas, or races.

▲ Italy has many old and beautiful churches. Even a tiny country church, like this one near Siena, may have a priceless medieval *fresco* (painting on plaster) or a carving.

Some of the highest mountains in Europe, the Alps, tower across northern Italy. Another mountain chain, the Apennines, stretches from north to south. The independent state of San Marino stands on the three peaks of Mount Titano in the Apennines—it is the oldest republic in Europe, founded in the A.D. 300s, and covers just 24 sq. mi. (61sq km).

POWER FROM WATER

Rushing mountain streams are used in hydroelectric schemes, and solar panels also provide power for a country with little coal or oil of its own. Italy's largest rivers, the Po, Arno, and Tiber, are all in northern Italy, as are lakes Garda, Como, and Maggiore. Southern Italy, which includes the islands of Sardinia and Sicily, is hotter and drier than the north.

FOOD AND DRINK

Italy is the world's largest wine producer. Italian dishes vary from north to south and range from veal in subtle, light sauces to seafood in rich, spicy tomato sauces. Italian recipes have inspired cooking around the world, and pizza and pasta have become international dishes.

AGRICULTURE

Many Italians are farmers. The major crop is wheat, used to make pasta and bread. Others are olives, grapes, corn, and sugar beets. Cattle are reared mainly in the north, and many sheep and goats are kept on rough pastures in Sardinia and Sicily.

INDUSTRIOUS NORTH

In northern Italy, industry is based around the cities of Turin, Milan, and Genoa. Factories make a wide range of goods including automobiles, clothing, machinery, and chemicals. Milan is particularly famous for its fashion houses, where clothes are designed. Many raw materials have to be imported, and Italy has a large fleet of merchant ships.

SPEAKING ITALIAN

Almost everyone in Italy speaks Italian, although a few communities speak another language—German is the first language of people living near the Austrian border. Most Italians are Roman Catholics, and the head of the Catholic Church, the pope, lives in Vatican City, in Rome.

▲ Italy is rich in artistic treasures, spectacular buildings, and historic remains such as those of the Colosseum, an ancient amphitheater in Rome.

VATICAN CITY
Vatican City, the smallest independent state in the world, is under one fifth of a square mile (0.44km²). St. Peter's Basilica, at its center, is almost 690 ft. (210m) long and is shaped like a cross.

VARIETY FOR VISITORS
Tourism is one of Italy's main industries. Every year, millions of people visit the country to enjoy its peaceful countryside, sunny beaches, snowcapped mountains, and historic cities such as Venice, Florence, Naples, and Rome.

ROME TO RENAISSANCE
Italy was where the Roman Empire was founded. Roman rule ended in the West in A.D. 476, but Rome remained the headquarters of the Roman Catholic Church. Italy broke up into smaller city-states, and from the 1300s to the early 1500s, it was the center of the Renaissance. The country has produced explorers such as Marco Polo, artists such as Leonardo da Vinci, and scientists such as Galileo.

UNITING THE STATES
From the 1500s, France and Austria tried to control Italy. During the 1800s, Giuseppe Garibaldi and other patriots led the fight to unite the Italian states. They drove out the Austrians and, in 1861, Italy became an independent and united kingdom.

MODERN ITALY
During the 1920s and 1930s, the Fascists, led by Benito Mussolini, held power. After World War II (1939–45), Italy held its first free election for 20 years and a republic replaced the monarchy. From the 1950s to the 2000s, Italy had many different governments. It was a founder member of the European Economic Community (EEC) in 1957. In recent years, large numbers of refugees have fled to southern Italy by boat, crossing from North Africa.

◀ Motorcycles and scooters are a popular form of transportation with young Italians, meeting here at the Piazza del Popolo in Rome.

▲ Modern opera began in Italy in the early 1600s, with the composer Claudio Monteverdi. The Italian tenor Luciano Pavarotti helped popularize opera worldwide.

SEE ALSO
Art, Christianity, Europe, Fascism, Renaissance, Roman Empire, Volcano

223

JAPAN

Japan is an island country in northeast Asia, off the east coast of China. The Japanese call their country Nippon or Nihon, which means "source of the sun."

Area: 145,913 sq. mi. (377,915km²)
Population: 126,451,000
Capital: Tokyo
Language: Japanese
Currency: Yen

▲ Today, Japan's leading industries include the manufacture of electrical goods such as televisions.

By area, Japan is Asia's 18th-largest country. Its largest island is Honshu, followed by Hokkaido, Kyushu, and Shikoku. There are also thousands of small islands, such as the chain of Ryukyu Islands.

ERUPTIONS AND EARTHQUAKES

Most of Japan is hilly or mountainous and the rivers are fast flowing, providing water power for electricity. Japan's highest peak, Mount Fuji at 12,389 ft. (3,776m), is a volcano which last erupted in 1708. In 2011 the worst earthquake in Japan's history occurred off the coast, creating tsunami waves over 130 ft. (40m) high and causing a disastrous meltdown at the Fukushima Daiichi nuclear power plant.

VARIED CLIMATE

The northernmost island of Hokkaido, just south of the Russian territory, is cool and snow is common in winter; Kyushu in the south is much warmer. Most of Japan has plenty of rainfall.

PINK-FACED MONKEYS

Forests cover more than two thirds of the land and many animals, including bears, wild boar, deer, and foxes, live in them. Pink-faced monkeys called Japanese macaques live as far north as the northern tip

of Honshu. They have long, thick fur and swim in hot springs in the snow to keep warm.

FIRST ARRIVALS

The first people in Japan were probably descendants of a group of people called the Ainu, a few thousand of whom live in Hokkaido today. The ancestors of most modern Japanese people probably reached the islands from mainland Asia around 2,200 years ago. The country ranks tenth in the world by population.

SHARED RELIGIONS

More than 93 per cent of the people live in crowded cities and towns. The largest city is Tokyo, and other large cities include Osaka and Nagoya, all situated on Honshu, where 80 percent of the people live. Japan follows two main religions:

▲ Japan is a leading fishing nation. It supplies not only its own people with fish, but also many other countries.

▼ Many beautiful temples, like the Kinkaka Ji with its spectacular gardens, can be found in Japan's former capital, Kyoto.

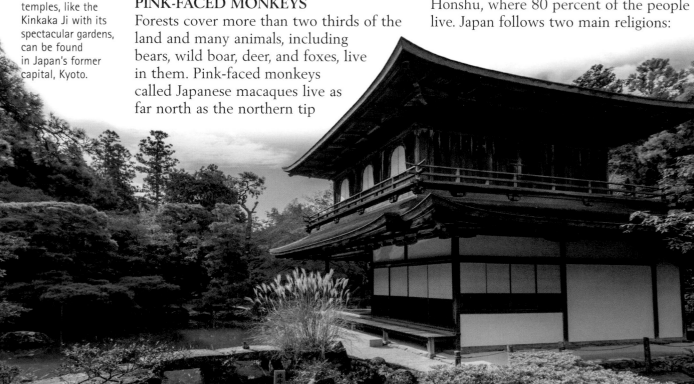

Shintoism (the oldest) and Buddhism. Many people follow both.

MEETING ITS NEEDS

Although it lacks natural resources, Japan is a wealthy country. Because it is so hilly, only about 11 percent of the land is farmed. Japan produces only 39 percent of the food it needs. Rice is the leading crop and food. Fruit, sugar beet, tea, and vegetables are also important.

MADE IN JAPAN

Manufacturing is the most valuable activity, and Japan ranks third among the world's top industrial countries, after the United States and China. Its products sell around the world and include chemicals, electrical and electronic equipment, iron and steel, machinery, ships, textiles, vehicles and transportation equipment.

POWERFUL NATION

Japan became a powerful nation during the late 1800s. It won some important battles against China in 1894 and defeated Russia in 1905. In 1937, it attacked China and, in 1941, it attacked the American naval base in Pearl Harbor, Hawaii. This act drew it and the United States into World War II.

MOVING TO DEMOCRACY

In 1945, after the United States had dropped atomic bombs on Hiroshima and Nagasaki, Japan surrendered. The United States occupied Japan until 1952. During this time, Japan became a democratic country, and the once all-powerful emperor became the head of state with only ceremonial duties. The country is now ruled by an elected prime minister and government, and is one of the world's great economic powers.

SEA OF OKHOTSK

Hokkaido

Sapporo

Hakodate

N

J A P A N

Sendai

Shinano

miles
0   125

0   125
km

SEA OF JAPAN

H o n s h u

Mt. Fuji ▲

Tokyo ■

Yokohama

Kyoto ●

Kobe ●   Nagoya ●

Hiroshima ●   Osaka ●

S h i k o k u

PACIFIC OCEAN

Nagasaki ●

Kyushu

EAST CHINA SEA

Osumi Is.

▶ Sumo, a Japanese style of wrestling in which opponents try to push each other out of a ring, is a popular national sport.

Ryukyu Is.

Okinawa

Sakishima Is.

▼ Japan's bullet train, here seen against a backdrop of Mt. Fuji, is one of the fastest in the world. High-speed rail connects Japan's big cities.

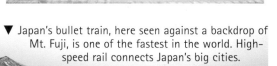

SEE ALSO

Asia, Buddhism, China, Industry, Southeast Asia, Volcano, World War II

225

JELLYFISH AND OTHER CNIDARIANS

Jellyfish, sea anemones, and corals belong to a group of animals called cnidarians. They all have soft bodies armed with stinging tentacles.

▶ Jellyfish move by pumping water backward with their bodies.

A Portuguese man-of-war is not a true jellyfish. Like corals, it is a colony of animals living together.

The hydra is a freshwater cnidarian. It forms new buds that break off and grow into new animals.

Sea anemones are tube-shaped animals that attach themselves, with a suckerlike base, to rocks in the sea.

Cnidarians are invertebrates—which means "no backbone." In fact they have no trace of a skeleton at all—except for corals, whose soft bodies are surrounded by a hard case made of limestone. Cnidarians have no brain, but have simple nerves and muscles. The largest individuals are found among the jellyfish, which are nearly all umbrella- or bell-shaped animals with a mouth on the underside. There are about 17,700 different kinds. Most of them are no bigger than a saucer, but there are a few real giants, with bodies up to 6.5 ft. (2m) across and tentacles as long as 230 ft. (70m).

STINGING STRINGS

Most cnidarians use tentacles to catch prey. Even corals are carnivores, or meat-eaters, using stinging cells on their tentacles to paralyze microscopic animals in the water. The stings of some jellyfish are very dangerous to swimmers. Those of the Australian sea wasp jellyfish can kill a person in minutes.

ENTANGLING PREY

The jellyfish's tentacles are covered with powerful stinging cells and are used to catch and kill fish, shrimp, and other small animals. The lion's mane jellyfish, here, can have a 6.5-ft. (2-m) body and tentacles reaching 130 ft. (40m). The tentacles pull the victim into the mouth, which is hidden under its bell-like body.

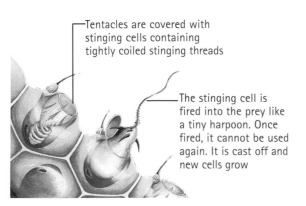

Tentacles are covered with stinging cells containing tightly coiled stinging threads

The stinging cell is fired into the prey like a tiny harpoon. Once fired, it cannot be used again. It is cast off and new cells grow

A STICKY END

Some jellyfish have bodies covered with sticky slime that traps any small animals they touch. Aurelia, the common jellyfish found washed up on beaches, uses stinging cells and then envelops its paralyzed prey in mucus.

BREAKING UP

Jellyfish scatter eggs or tiny babies into the water, but these do not grow directly into jellyfish. Instead, they settle on a rock or seaweed and grow into cone shapes. They gradually divide until they look like piles of miniature saucers. Each saucer floats away and grows into a new jellyfish.

SEE ALSO

Animal, Evolution, Ocean and sea

JUDAISM

Judaism is the religion of the Jewish people. It teaches that there is one true God, who revealed himself to the Jews and has given the human race rules to live by.

The six-pointed star became a symbol of Judaism during the Middle Ages. It signifies the protection of God given to David, king of Israel in about 970 B.C.

Jewish women pray at Jerusalem's Western Wall, at the site of the ancient Temple.

Jews light a candle a day during the eight days of Hanukkah, to celebrate the rededication of the Temple in 165 B.C.

Jews believe that there is one eternal, invisible God who created the universe. There are about 14 million Jews living in Israel and all over the world.

MOSES AND THE HEBREWS
The first followers of Judaism were the Hebrew people of the Middle East. According to the Bible (Old Testament), the Jewish holy book, God made an agreement with Abraham and his descendants in about the year 1900 B.C. In about 1200 B.C., God sent Moses to lead the Hebrews out of slavery in Egypt. God revealed his teachings about how to live and serve God to Moses. These teachings are the basis of Judaism and are contained in the Torah, laws based on the first five books of the Bible. Later works, the Talmud, tell people how to lead good lives and how to observe rituals.

THE HOLY SABBATH
The Hebrews worshiped at the Temple in Jerusalem, but this was destroyed in a war with the Roman Empire in A.D. 70. Modern Jews study their faith in buildings called synagogues. Here, they are guided by teachers known as rabbis. The most religious day of the week is the Sabbath, which lasts from sunset Friday to sunset Saturday. Jews cannot work on this day, because they believe this was the day when God rested after creating the world.

▲ A rabbi preparing to sound the *shofar* (ram's horn) at Yom Kippur wears a *tallith* (prayer shawl) and phylactery boxes.

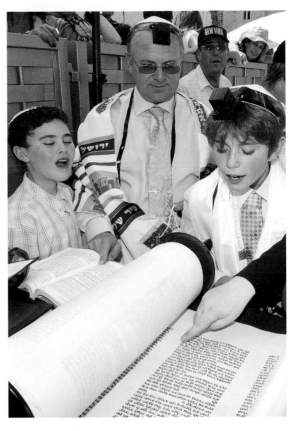

BAR MITZVAH
When a Jewish boy officially becomes a man, at the age of 13, the bar mitzvah ceremony is held. The boy reads from the books of the prophets during the Sabbath service. The service is often followed by prayers and a family celebration. A girl of 13 has a similar ceremony, the bat mitzvah. She is not yet officially a woman, but now has religious responsibilities.

KOSHER RITUALS
Jews observe various festivals, including Yom Kippur in September or October, when sins are confessed and forgiveness asked. At Passover, in March or April, the departure from Egypt is celebrated. Orthodox Jews have strict rules about what they eat, how their food is prepared, and the way ritual objects should be treated. These rules are called kosher.

PERSECUTION
For centuries, Jews have lived among other nations, which have sometimes persecuted them. During World War II, the Nazis murdered millions of Jews in what is called the Holocaust. After this, many Jews created a new homeland, Israel, in the area where the Hebrews lived.

SEE ALSO
Israel and Palestine, Religion, World War II

KANGAROO AND OTHER MARSUPIALS

Marsupials are mammals that normally carry their young in pouches. There are about 320 different kinds, most of which live in Australia and New Guinea.

Koalas live in and feed off eucalyptus trees.

Common opossums are found in North America.

Wombats are nocturnal burrowing animals.

The Tasmanian devil is stocky with sharp teeth.

Kangaroos are the biggest of the marsupials, some of them reaching nearly 6.5 ft. (2m) tall. They are Australia's equivalent of the herds of antelope that live on the African plains. Kangaroos are not hoofed animals and they move by leaping instead of running, but they graze and browse like antelope and they have a similar head and jaws. Farmers do not like kangaroos because they eat the grass intended for sheep.

ALL KINDS OF KANGAROO

There are about 50 kinds of kangaroo. The smallest are about the size of a rabbit and are called rat kangaroos. The middle-size ones are often called wallabies. The red kangaroo and the gray kangaroo are the biggest species. They usually live in small groups called mobs. Although they are about as tall as a man when they stand upright, their young, called joeys, are only about 1 in. (2.5cm) long when they are born.

A WIDE VARIETY

Not all marsupials are grazers. Just like the mammals in other parts of the world, Australia's marsupials have adopted all sorts of habits. Possums and gliders live in the trees like monkeys and squirrels; the koala is like a small bear. There is even a marsupial mole. There are also many carnivorous, or meat-eating, marsupials, including the doglike Tasmanian devil.

EXTINCT SPECIES

The Tasmanian wolf, or thylacine, is another doglike carnivore, but it has not been seen alive since 1936 and is probably extinct. Farmers hunted it because they thought it killed their sheep. Many other Australian marsupials have died out because they were killed by cats and dogs and other mammals introduced by man.

THE LONG JOURNEY

A kangaroo is born blind and helpless, and looks more like a grub than a kangaroo. As soon as it is born it has to climb up to its mother's pouch, where it starts to feed and grow. It develops long back legs and a long tail, and by six months it is ready to leave the pouch for the first time.

▲ Red kangaroos can bound along on their huge back legs at speeds of about 24 mph (40kph) and can cover 26 ft. (8m) in a single leap.

1 The newly born kangaroo crawls up its mother's body until it reaches the security of the pouch.

2 Inside the pouch, the baby suckles on its mother's milk and starts to grow rapidly.

3 By six months, the joey is old enough to leave its mother's pouch, but it soon jumps back inside if danger threatens.

SEE ALSO
Animal, Australia, Mammal

228

KENYA

Kenya is a country on the east coast of Africa with beautiful scenery and spectacular wild animals. The equator runs through its center.

Area: 224,081 sq. mi.
(580,367km²)
Population: 47,616,000
Capital: Nairobi
Languages: English, Swahili
Currency: Kenyan shilling

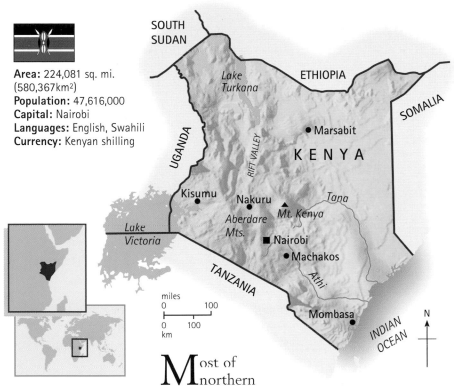

▲ The Kenyan capital of Nairobi has many modern buildings.

▲ Kenya's many national parks and their wildlife are major tourist attractions.

Most of northern Kenya is made up of dry plains. There are also forested uplands in the west and savannas (grasslands) to the south. Part of Africa's largest lake, Victoria, is in the west.

MOUNT KENYA
Volcanic mountains lie in the middle of the country, close to the equator. They include Mount Kenya, now extinct. At 17,058 ft. (5,199m), it is the country's highest peak, second only to Tanzania's Mount Kilimanjaro in the whole of Africa.

FARMS AND CITIES
The mountainous areas have fertile soil that is good for farming. On large plantations, Kenyan farmers grow coffee, tea, vegetables, and fruit for export. On small plots of land, people raise crops of corn, beans, cassava, and potatoes for food. Only 15 percent of the land is suitable for farming, and many Kenyans have left their villages to seek jobs in towns and cities such as Mombasa—the main port—and the capital city, Nairobi.

NATIONAL PARKS
Kenya's wildlife is threatened by poaching. There are 23 national parks, 16 nature reserves, and six marine parks. Tourism plays an important part in Kenya's economy.

KENYA'S PEOPLE
Most Kenyans are black Africans, although a small number are of European, Asian, and Arab descent. Three fifths of Kenyans are from four ethnic groups: the Kikuyu, the Luhya, the Luo, and the Kalenjin. Kenyans are enthusiastic about soccer and athletics. Kenyan runners have won many medals at the Olympic Games.

MODERN KENYA
Some of the earliest-known fossil remains of human beings have been found in parts of Kenya. Kenya was British from 1895 to 1920. It gained its independence in 1963 and became a republic in 1964. The country's most famous leader of modern times was Jomo Kenyatta, president from 1964 until his death in 1978.

► People such as the Samburu live in Kenya's semidesert areas.

SEE ALSO
Africa, Animal, Fossil, Mountain and valley

229

KIDNEY

The kidneys are vital organs that clean the blood by filtering out unwanted substances and excess water. These are then removed from the body as urine.

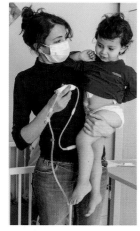

▲ A young girl whose kidneys are not working properly is given regular "dialysis" treatment. This involves linking her up to a special machine called a hemodialyzer that filters out the waste materials in her blood. Once a suitable donor has been found, she can be given a kidney transplant.

Body processes, such as digesting food or burning energy, produce various waste substances. These are collected from all parts of the body by the blood system and are carried to the kidneys, where they are filtered out. The kidneys are the most important part of the body's excretory system, which is responsible for getting rid of, or excreting, liquid wastes.

A MILLION MICROFILTERS

Inside each kidney are two layers. The outer layer—the renal cortex—contains about a million tiny filtering units, called nephrons. Each nephron has a tiny knot of microscopic blood vessels, or capillaries, called a glomerulus, which is surrounded by a double-layered cup—Bowman's capsule. As blood flows through the glomerulus, water, minerals, salts, and wastes seep out into Bowman's capsule. These substances ooze from the capsule through a long, thin U-shaped tube, called the nephron loop, or loop of Henle, which lies in the kidney's inner layer—the renal medulla.

KEEPING USEFUL SUBSTANCES

Each nephron loop is surrounded by more capillaries, so that useful substances such as minerals and salts can pass from the loop back into the blood. A certain amount of water is also taken back, or reabsorbed. The amount depends on the body's water supplies and is controlled by chemical messengers called hormones.

COLLECTING THE WASTES

The unwanted substances that are left form the urine. This trickles into larger tubes, or collecting ducts, and gathers in the renal pelvis—a space in the middle of the kidney. From here it dribbles into a tube called the ureter and is carried down to the bladder, a small muscular sac in the lower abdomen. The bladder empties by squeezing its muscular walls to force the urine along another tube, the urethra, to the outside.

THE KIDNEYS AT WORK

The kidneys, which are bean-shaped, are positioned centrally in the rear of the body, one on either side of the spine. They receive blood via the renal arteries and, after the blood has been filtered, it is carried away by the renal veins. All of the body's blood flows through the kidneys about 350 times a day—that's more than 1,800 qts. (1,700l)! This is constantly cleaned and filtered to produce about 3 pt. (1.5l) of urine each day.

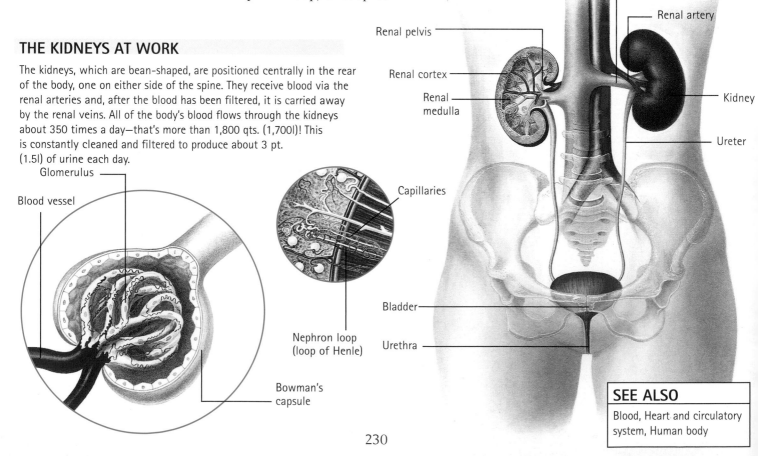

Glomerulus

Blood vessel

Capillaries

Nephron loop (loop of Henle)

Bowman's capsule

Renal pelvis

Renal cortex

Renal medulla

Renal vein

Renal artery

Kidney

Ureter

Bladder

Urethra

SEE ALSO

Blood, Heart and circulatory system, Human body

LAKE

A lake is a body of still water that fills a hollow in Earth's surface. These hollows form in a number of ways, and the water in them can be fresh or salty.

An oxbow lake is a curved section cut off from a meandering river.

Crater lakes form in the tops of old volcanoes or in meteorite craters.

The water that fills a lake comes from rain, inflowing streams, or, sometimes, from underground springs. As well as providing an important habitat for many kinds of plant and wildlife, lakes are used by people as a source of water, for fishing, for transportation, or for fun.

GREAT DEPTHS

The deepest lakes lie in rift valleys, where parts of Earth's crust have cracked and sunk. Lake Baikal in Siberia is over 5,250 ft. (1,600m) deep and was formed more than 30 million years ago. It is the world's oldest and deepest lake. Other such lakes include Lake Nyasa in Malawi and Lake Turkana in Kenya.

THE DEATH OF A LAKE

Lakes begin to die as soon as they form. Rivers entering the lake bring sand and gravel that form a delta and silt that fills up the bottom of the lake. At the same time, rivers leaving the lake cut a gorge, lowering the water level. Eventually, the falling water level and rising deposits combine to turn the lake into dry land.

The deepest lakes are fault valley lakes that form where rocks subside.

GLACIAL WATERS

Most lakes were formed in hollows left behind by the retreating glaciers of the last Ice Age, about 10,000 years ago. Others were formed in depressions between heaps of rocky debris dumped by the glaciers. The Great Lakes of North America and most of the Scottish lochs were formed in this way.

SALT LAKES

Sometimes a lake forms in a hollow with no outlet. Water can then escape only by evaporating, which leaves behind large deposits of salt. The lake between Israel and Jordan known as the Dead Sea is eight times saltier than seawater.

UNIQUE WILDLIFE

Larger lakes support their own wildlife. Lake Baikal is home to 745 animal species and 150 plant species found nowhere else. But pollution has become a major problem in many lakes, wiping out numerous species.

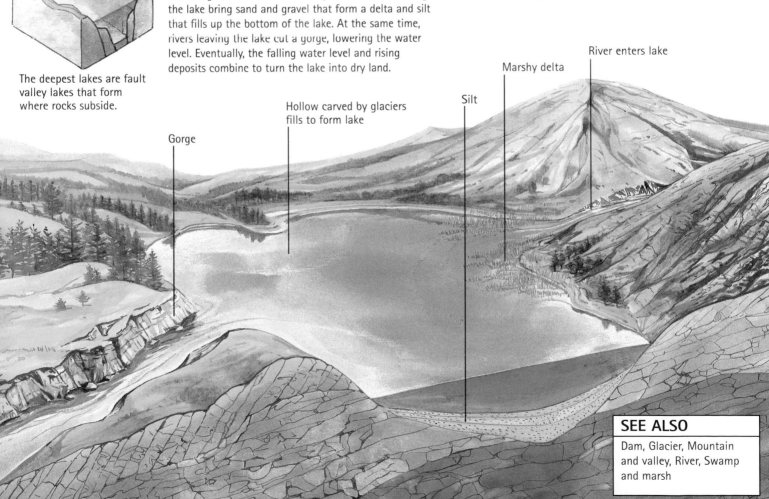

Gorge

Hollow carved by glaciers fills to form lake

Silt

Marshy delta

River enters lake

SEE ALSO

Dam, Glacier, Mountain and valley, River, Swamp and marsh

LANGUAGE

Language is how humans communicate with one another, either through speech, writing, or even sign language. It comes from the Latin word *lingua*, meaning tongue.

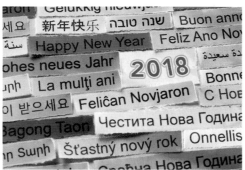

▲ "Happy New Year" written in a number of different languages.

Language starts as a collection of sounds, arranged so that they mean something. Over time, people developed different languages and then organized the sounds into alphabets. An alphabet is a collection of signs that represent the sounds we use.

ABCDE
Roman

ابتثج
Arabic (read right to left)

АБВГД
Cyrillic (Russian)

ΑΒΓΔΕ
Greek

חטיבב
Hebrew (read right to left)

▲ The first five written symbols of five different alphabets.

香氣治療
Chinese characters

▲ Chinese has no alphabet, but consists of 40,000 characters, each of which represents an object or idea.

WORLD LANGUAGES
Today, there are around 6,900 languages in the world. Mandarin Chinese is the language spoken by the largest number of people. Next comes English, which is spoken in more countries than any other language. About 820 languages are spoken in Papua New Guinea. People have tried to make up artificial "universal" languages. The best known and most widely used is Esperanto, invented in 1887.

HOW LANGUAGES CHANGE
Languages constantly change. New words, such as "cyberbully," come into use. Old words disappear, for example, "bombard," meaning a cannon. Latin, the language of the ancient Romans, is not spoken, but people can read it. Words can also move from one language to another. English contains many of these words, such as "video" (I see) from Latin and "planet" (wanderer) from Greek.

LANGUAGE FAMILIES
Languages belong to families—groups of related languages that developed from an original parent language. English belongs to the Germanic branch of the large Indo-European language family; French belongs to the Romance branch.

▲ The Rosetta Stone, found in Egypt in 1799, helped scholars to read ancient Egyptian hieroglyphs (left), as the same inscription was written in three languages, including ancient Greek.

SIGNS AND CODES
Language is not just confined to spoken or written words. Deaf people use sign language and blind people read Braille, a special alphabet using raised dots. Even codes, such as those used by computers, are called languages.

◄ "The Tower of Babel" story tells how people tried to build a huge tower to reach Heaven. God stopped it from being built by making everyone speak different languages, so that they could not understand each other.

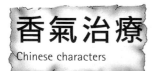

SEE ALSO

Communication, Internet, Literature, Media, Newspaper and magazine

LASER

A laser is a machine that produces a powerful beam of concentrated light. The word "laser" is short for Light Amplification by Stimulated Emission of Radiation.

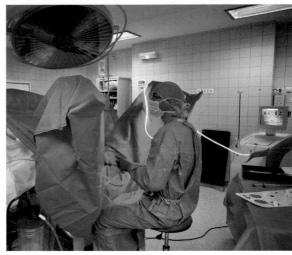

▲ A laser seals as it cuts, so there is less bleeding, making lasers useful for making precision cuts in surgery.

Lasers give out light in a narrow, concentrated beam which is all one wavelength—unlike light from a bulb which goes out in all directions. And while ordinary light spreads out and fades away over long distances, a beam of laser light does not. It can travel for thousands of miles as a strong, straight beam.

Light shows use beams and holograms (3-D images) created by lasers.

RUBY OR GAS LASERS

The most common type of laser produces a beam of red light. It is the "ruby laser," which has a rod-shaped red crystal inside of it. Ruby lasers produce flashes or pulses of powerful light. Gas lasers produce a continuous beam. These use colored liquids or gases instead of crystals. Lasers that use colored liquids are called "dye lasers."

Sensors in the nose of a bomb can home in on laser light aimed at a target.

DIRECTING THE BEAM

As laser beams are narrow and intense, they have hundreds of uses. Low-powered laser beams can be reflected (bounced) off objects to find out if they are dark or light, smooth or pitted, still or vibrating. They are used in this way in stores to read bar codes on products, to register the pits (tiny dents) on CDs, or to monitor the vibrations of machines. Since laser beams are completely straight, they can also be used as guides on construction sites to help build walls and floors.

In industry, the high temperature of the laser cuts holes in solid steel.

THE CUTTING EDGE

High-powered laser beams create enough energy to burn exact holes through solid metal. They are used to cut precise parts for machines and clothes. Laser beams may also replace the surgeon's knife in delicate operations, such as those on the eye.

3–D IMAGES

One of the most amazing uses of the laser is the hologram. This is a set of ridges that creates a three-dimensional picture (image with depth) when it is seen in the right light. A hologram is produced by scanning a laser beam across the surface of an object. The ridges of the hologram record the way the object reflects light, so they can create a 3–D image when light shines on them.

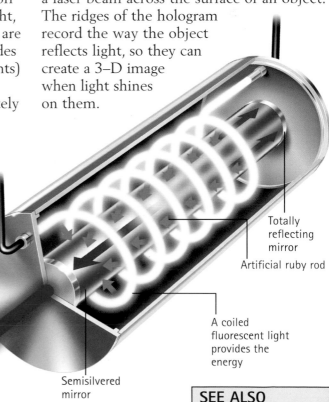

Totally reflecting mirror

Artificial ruby rod

A coiled fluorescent light provides the energy

Laser beam

Semisilvered mirror

INSIDE A RUBY LASER

A rod of artificial ruby is used as a "lasing medium." A powerful lamp directed at the ruby crystal energizes the atoms inside it, so it flashes light. This light is reflected back and forth between two mirrors so that the light waves become coherent (all the same wavelength). It escapes through a tiny hole in one of the mirrors as a narrow "laser beam" ready to be focused.

SEE ALSO

Astronomy, Light, Surgery, Technology, Telescope

LAW

Laws are the rules people live by. Governments make laws, and law officers and courts see that laws are obeyed and disputes settled.

▲ A traffic policeman in Samoa controls the flow of pedestrians across the road. Police act on behalf of the government to enforce the laws of a country and maintain order. They investigate crimes and arrest suspects, patrol the streets, direct traffic, find missing persons, and help in times of disaster.

About 4,000 years ago in Babylon, King Hammurabi issued a list of laws dealing with such things as stealing and bad workmanship. The ancient Jews based their laws on the Ten Commandments given to Moses by God, as told in the Bible. The early Greeks invented democracy—lawmaking by all the people—and the Romans gave us most of the kinds of law we still use today, such as family law, property law, and criminal law. Emperor Justinian I of the Byzantine Empire drew up his famous Code of Civil Law in A.D. 534.

TOWARD MODERN LAW
A big step toward modern law came in 1215, when King John of England signed the Magna Carta—an agreement to govern according to laws. Later, parliaments rather than kings began to make laws. In 1804, Emperor Napoleon I of France introduced the Napoleonic Code, still the basis for much French law today.

UPHOLDING THE LAW
In a democracy, laws are proposed by governments, passed by legislatures (a congress or parliament), and enforced by the police and courts. People accused of breaking a law may have to go to court, where lawyers argue the case, presenting evidence and questioning witnesses. A group of ordinary people, called the jury, decides whether the accused is guilty or not guilty. The judge decides the punishment—perhaps a number of years in prison, a fine, or community service.

WHAT HAPPENS IN A CRIMINAL LAW TRIAL?

A person accused of breaking the criminal law is innocent until proven guilty by a court of law. The lawyers put the case to the jury. The prosecution tries to prove that the defendant is guilty, and the defense tries to show that he or she is innocent. Then it is up to the jury to decide.

Jury A body of people (usually 12) who swear under oath to listen to the evidence and make an unbiased decision based on it alone.

Judge The person who oversees court proceedings, rules on law, and, where guilt is proven, decides on the form of punishment.

Prosecution lawyer He or she provides evidence of the defendant's guilt, questioning witnesses and scientific experts, and presenting physical evidence.

Defendant The person accused of breaking the law. In the witness box he or she can be questioned by lawyers.

Stenotypist The person who keeps a record of everything that is said during the course of a trial.

Defense lawyer The lawyer who acts on behalf of the defendant to show his or her innocence.

Physical evidence Items which are put before the jury, presented to prove the defendant's guilt or innocence.

SEE ALSO

Civil rights, Democracy, Mesopotamia, Roman Empire

LEAF

Leaves use energy from sunlight to make food for plants, and are themselves a source of food for animals. They also produce the oxygen we need to breathe.

The horse chestnut has a compound leaf made up of separate leaflets.

Maple leaves are hand-shaped, or palmate, with no separate leaflets.

The ash leaf is made up of several leaflets.

The cherry has a pinnate (feather-shaped) leaf.

Pine needles are long, thin evergreen leaves that grow in clusters.

Leaves are the food factories of green plants. They come in a variety of shapes and sizes, and help us to identify the different plant species. The branching pattern of veins on the surface of a leaf is part of a network of tubes that carry water and food to all parts of the plant. The large vein that runs across the center of the leaf is called the midrib.

MAKING FOOD

The main function of leaves is to make food for the plant. This process, known as photosynthesis, takes place in tiny bodies, called chloroplasts, in the leaf cells. These contain a green-colored substance called chlorophyll that absorbs light energy. The energy is used to turn water and the gas carbon dioxide from the air into food molecules, such as starch and sugar. The by-product of this process is oxygen gas, some of which is used by the plant for respiration. The rest passes into the air. Nearly all living things need oxygen to survive.

TRANSPIRATION

Leaves also help the plant to draw water up from the soil, by a process called transpiration. As the water evaporates (dries) from tiny pores, or stomata, in the leaf's surface, more water is sucked up from the roots to replace it. Each pore is bound by two special "guard" cells that can open or close the opening to control water loss. The water moves up the stem through fine tubes called xylem vessels. Another set of tubes, the phloem vessels, carries food around the plant.

LEAF DESIGN

Leaves are designed to catch as much sunlight and lose as little water as possible. Stiff veins hold the leaf out to the light, and cells are transparent so that light can reach the chloroplasts. The outer layer, or cuticle, is waterproof, and most of the stomata are on the underside of the leaf, shielded from drying breezes.

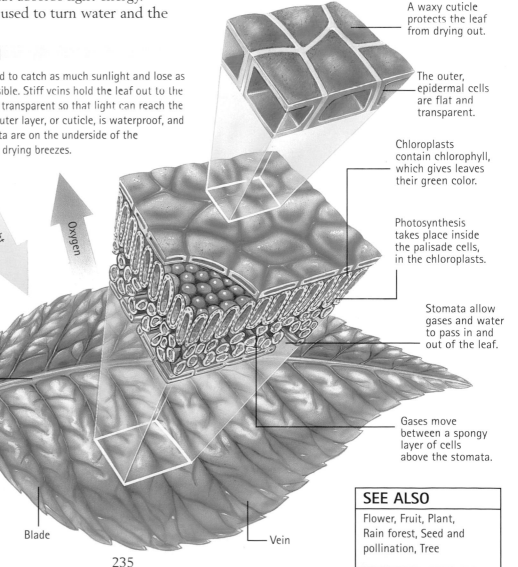

A waxy cuticle protects the leaf from drying out.

The outer, epidermal cells are flat and transparent.

Chloroplasts contain chlorophyll, which gives leaves their green color.

Photosynthesis takes place inside the palisade cells, in the chloroplasts.

Stomata allow gases and water to pass in and out of the leaf.

Gases move between a spongy layer of cells above the stomata.

Sunlight

Oxygen

Carbon dioxide

Midrib

Water

Blade

Vein

SEE ALSO

Flower, Fruit, Plant, Rain forest, Seed and pollination, Tree

LENS

A lens is a transparent object with at least one curved surface that helps us focus on an image by bending rays of light. It is normally made of glass or plastic.

Glasses help us see if our eye lenses don't work properly.

The lens in a camera focuses light onto the film inside.

Microscopes use lenses to magnify objects from 100 to 1,600 times.

Lenses in a pair of binoculars help you see things that are far away.

Some periscopes use lenses to enlarge the image reflected from the mirrors at either end.

When light travels through a lens, it slows down. This is because light travels faster through air than through other transparent substances like water, glass, and plastic. As it slows down it bends off course. This effect, called "refraction," is why a straw put in a glass of water at an angle looks bent. The bending distorts the image seen by the eye and can be used to make an object seem bigger or smaller.

DISTORTED IMAGES

If you put a magnifying glass close to the page of a book, you'll see a larger-than-life version of the page below it. This happens

BENDING LIGHT

There are two kinds of simple lens: convex (or converging) lenses which enlarge the image and concave (or diverging) lenses which are thicker at the edges than the middle and reduce the image.

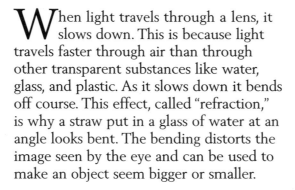

Focal length— distance from lens center to the focus

Virtual image

Actual image

Virtual image

Actual image

CONVEX LENS
Rays of light passing through the lens are bent inward. A magnified image is produced behind the object.

CONCAVE LENS
Light rays are bent outward, so they spread out (diverge), producing a reduced image between the object and the lens.

▶ A magnifying glass has a convex lens—a lens much thicker at the middle than the edges. The image seen depends on how close you hold the glass.

because light rays from the page have been bent away from each other by the lens. Light rays from distant objects are bent toward each other by a magnifying glass. If it's dark enough, you can catch these rays on a sheet of paper. If you put the paper the right distance from the lens, they will form a focused (sharp) image.

GETTING FOCUSED

The distance from the lens to the piece of paper is called the "focal length" of the lens. In general, a thick lens bends light more than a thin one, so it has a shorter focal length. A camera uses a convex lens to produce sharp images on photographic film. Specialist cameras also use concave lenses (that are thicker at the edges than the middle). These are used to compress large images, like landscapes, onto a photograph.

EYE LENSES

Our eyeballs act like giant convex lenses that focus (bend) light onto the backs of our eyes. The muscles of our eyes pull the lenses flatter when we want to focus on objects in the distance, or make the lenses thicker to focus on nearby objects.

SEE ALSO

Astronomy, Laser, Light, Microscope, Photography, Sight, Telescope

LIGHT

Light is a visible form of energy. It moves faster than anything else in the universe, traveling about 186,000 mi. (300,000km) in one second. Without light, we cannot see.

SIR ISAAC NEWTON
The English scientist and mathematician (1642–1726) demonstrated that light was broken into different colors by shining light through a prism.

The Sun, our nearest star, is our main source of light. Although it is nearly 93 million mi. (150 million km) away, the light it makes reaches Earth in eight minutes and is so strong that it damages our eyes if we look straight at it. At night, when our part of Earth faces away from the Sun, we have to use lightbulbs or candles for light. Compared to the Sun, the light energy made by these is tiny. They can only light up objects a few yards away.

CASTING SHADOWS

Light can travel through air, water, and other transparent (see-through) materials. Unlike sound, it can also travel through a vacuum, or empty space. Materials that only allow some light through, and are not transparent, are said to be translucent.

▲ The Moon has no light of its own—it shines only because it reflects the Sun's light. Stars, however, are luminous because they produce their own light.

Many materials, like wood and metal, are opaque—they block light. If you shine a light at an opaque object, you will see a dark area behind it—the shadow. This has exactly the same outline as the object, because light travels in straight lines.

INVISIBLE ENERGY

There are many other types of energy, including radio waves, microwaves, and X rays, that travel just like light. In fact, light is only one tiny part of a huge range of energy forms, called the electromagnetic spectrum. Over the last century or so, people have built a variety of machines, such as scanning equipment, microwave ovens, and radios, that can detect or make use of the invisible parts of this spectrum.

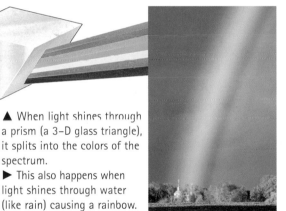

▲ When light shines through a prism (a 3–D glass triangle), it splits into the colors of the spectrum.
▶ This also happens when light shines through water (like rain) causing a rainbow.

▲ Glowworms, the glowing larvae of fireflies, have light organs under their abdomen that produce a heatless light known as bioluminescence.
▶ Many deep-sea fish have similar light organs on their sides to help them find food and mates in the dark.

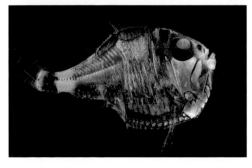

▲ There are two basic ways to produce artificial light: through heat (known as incandescence), as in an electric lightbulb or by making a gas glow, as in a fluorescent light.

> **SEE ALSO**
> Color, Electricity, Energy, Laser, Lens, Microscope, Moon, Sun, Wavelength

LITERATURE

Literature is the art of writing fine prose or poetry. This often involves storytelling, but may also include history, biography, and information books.

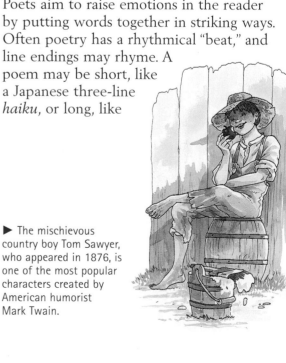

▶ Rapunzel used her hair as a climbing rope in a German tale recorded by the Grimm Brothers.

People told each other stories and poems long before they learned to write. This is "oral" (spoken) literature. Most modern literature is written in the form of books or is performed as drama.

▲ Good literature is written to be enjoyed, and it provides hours of entertainment for the cost of a single book.

GREAT STORYTELLERS
The ancient Greeks told stories in poetry and in drama about heroes and gods. The poem by Homer called the *Iliad* tells of the heroes who fought at the siege of Troy. In China and India, poets told tales of how the world began and of the mysteries of life and death.

▶ Long John Silver, the charming but deadly pirate, appeared in *Treasure Island*, a novel written by the Scottish author Robert Louis Stevenson in 1881.

WRITING IT DOWN
A few oral works were written down, such as the epic English poem *Beowulf* in about A.D. 750. Books were copied by hand throughout the Middle Ages, when Geoffrey Chaucer (c.1342–1400) wrote a collection of stories called the *Canterbury Tales*. After 1455, the printing press made it possible to copy books cheaply and easily. A "golden age" of literature began in many countries.

THE NOVEL
The novel is a long story in prose. During the 1800s, ordinary people learned to read, and the novel became popular. Some novels were published as serials in magazines. Leading novelists of the time included Britain's Charles Dickens, France's Victor Hugo, and Leo Tolstoy in Russia.

POETRY
Poets aim to raise emotions in the reader by putting words together in striking ways. Often poetry has a rhythmical "beat," and line endings may rhyme. A poem may be short, like a Japanese three-line *haiku*, or long, like

▶ The mischievous country boy Tom Sawyer, who appeared in 1876, is one of the most popular characters created by American humorist Mark Twain.

◄ Hamlet, the moody Danish prince, was created by the English playwright William Shakespeare, based on an old Danish tale.

▶ D'Artagnan, hero of the French novel *The Three Musketeers*, was created by Alexandre Dumas in 1844 and has featured in several movies.

Charles Dickens (1812–70) was a great English novelist.

John Milton's 12-book *Paradise Lost*. A poem can tell a story, make the reader laugh, or reveal the poet's innermost feelings.

work in every field, from aviation to zoology. Writers produce articles for newspapers, magazines, and the Internet, and scripts for radio, television, and movies.

Dante (1265–1321) began modern Italian literature with his *Divine Comedy*.

DRAMA

Plays were performed in ancient Greece, but modern drama dates from the 1500s. Although there may be stage directions, dramatic literature is largely dialogue and relies on acting for its power. Movie scripts use special effects, lighting, and camera angles to make the dialogue more effective.

CHILDREN'S WRITERS

There were few books written for children before the 1700s. Today, some of the best writers create stories for children. A few books, such as A. A. Milne's *Winnie the Pooh*, become classics, with their characters known around the world.

American writer Edgar Allan Poe (1809–49) mastered the horror story.

HOW WRITERS WORK

Writers watch and listen, invent plots and characters, and note down interesting things that happen. Many writers stick to one kind of book, such as humor, horror, crime, romance, religion, art, or philosophy. Some writers tell their own life story in an autobiography; others write about famous people in a biography or about the past as history. Writers

PUBLISHING A WORK

There are two main kinds of literature: fiction (stories) and nonfiction (factual books, from cookbooks to encyclopedias). Every book starts with a writer who either thinks up an idea or is asked to write a book by a publishing company. The publisher pays the writer for the book and sees to the editing, design, illustration, and printing or publishing as an e-book. By selling large quantities of books to readers, the publisher hopes to make a profit.

Murasaki Shikibu (c.978–c.1014) wrote the *Tale of Genji* in Japan, about 1005.

▲ Alice, from the book *Alice in Wonderland* by Lewis Carroll, which appeared in 1865.

▶ The 1605 story of Don Quixote and his servant Sancho Panza, by the Spanish author Miguel de Cervantes, has been translated into over 60 languages.

SEE ALSO

Film, Greece (ancient), Language, Myth and legend, Printing, Theater

LUNGS AND RESPIRATORY SYSTEM

The lungs are two pinkish-gray, spongy, cone-shaped organs inside the chest. The respiratory system consists of the nose, throat, trachea, lower airways, and lungs.

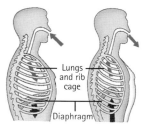

Breathing in   Breathing out

▲ When breathing in, the rib cage expands and the diaphragm is lowered. These actions happen in reverse when breathing out.

FAST FACTS

- The lungs cover an area as large as a tennis court

- At rest, an average person takes about 12-15 breaths every minute. Each breath consists of just over a pint of air

- After great activity, the breathing rate can rise to 60 breaths per minute, with over six pints of air per breath

Oxygen is essential for almost every living thing, including the human body. When we breathe in, our lungs take in fresh air, absorb oxygen from it, and pass it to the blood, which carries it to all the parts of the body. Fresh air is taken into the lungs by breathing, or respiration. This process is powered by two sets of muscles—the diaphragm below the lungs and the intercostal muscles between the ribs, in front of the lungs.

IN AND OUT

To breathe in, the diaphragm tenses, shortens, and flattens. The intercostals also shorten and pull the ribs upward and forward. These movements stretch the lungs, making them larger, and suck fresh air in through the nose and mouth, down the throat and trachea, into the lungs. To breathe out, the diaphragm relaxes, and the stretched lungs spring back to their normal size, pushing stale air out.

OXYGEN IN

Dark, bluish-red, low-oxygen blood flows to each lung along the pulmonary artery. This divides many times to form a network of microscopic blood vessels, or capillaries, which enclose tiny balloons called alveoli. Oxygen from the air inside each alveolus seeps easily through its thin lining and the thin capillary wall, into the blood. This makes the blood bright red. The capillaries join to form the pulmonary vein, which carries the high-oxygen blood away.

CARBON DIOXIDE OUT

In addition to taking in oxygen, the respiratory system also removes one of the body's waste products, carbon dioxide. This seeps the opposite way to oxygen— from the blood into the alveolus—and is breathed out as stale air.

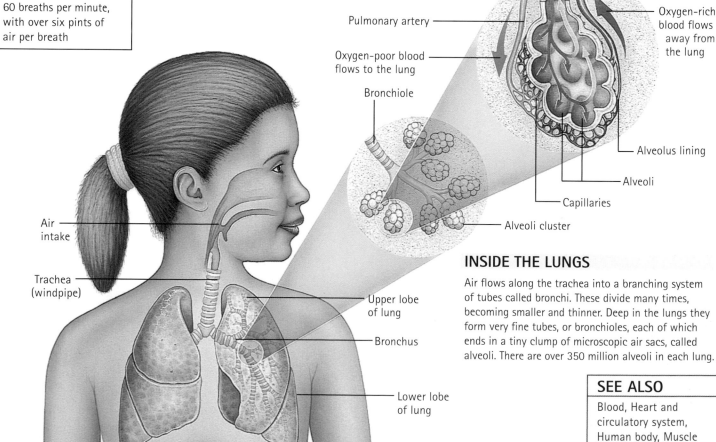

INSIDE THE LUNGS

Air flows along the trachea into a branching system of tubes called bronchi. These divide many times, becoming smaller and thinner. Deep in the lungs they form very fine tubes, or bronchioles, each of which ends in a tiny clump of microscopic air sacs, called alveoli. There are over 350 million alveoli in each lung.

SEE ALSO

Blood, Heart and circulatory system, Human body, Muscle

MACHINE

A machine is a device that makes work easier by allowing us to use force to complete a task. It can be simple, like a screwdriver, or complicated, like a car.

Simple machines make work easier and can be used as parts of more complex devices. There are six main types of machine: the lever, pulley, and wheel and axle (which are all forms of levers); and the screw, inclined or sloping plane, and wedge (all forms of inclined planes).

BASIC MACHINES

By using a lever, you can increase the effect of the force, or effort, you apply. The machine needs a fulcrum (a fixed point) to support it. By positioning the fulcrum carefully, you can apply a small effort at one end of the lever to raise a big load at the other end. Heavy weights can be moved using an inclined plane (pushing goods up a ramp is easier than lifting them); on rollers, like the logs used by pyramid builders to move slabs; or by a wheel turning on an axle.

MAGNIFIED FORCE

A screw can either pull things together or push them apart (like a jack). A pulley system uses wheels to change the direction of a force produced by pulling on a rope. The wedge (an ax, for example) can be used to split materials.

Corkscrews make use of screw and lever actions. The screw's spiral thread gives a tight grip.

A pair of scissors is a double lever. The screw is the fixed point or fulcrum; the blades pivot around it.

A can opener acts as a wedge, forcing its way into the lid while cogged wheels turn the cutter.

THE EARLIEST MACHINES

The potter's wheel, invented around 3500 B.C., was one of the earliest machines. Others include the spindle, for spinning fibres into yarn; the loom, for weaving yarn into cloth; the plow, for turning heavy soil; and bellows, for blowing air into fires.

WAR AND WORK

Early war inventions include the battering ram (a wedge), and the catapult (a lever). An important development of the wheel was the gear. A gearwheel combines the principles of wheel and lever. As it turns, its teeth, or cogs, mesh with other toothed wheels. In this way it can change the speed and direction of the force applied, depending on the number and spacing of the teeth.

INVENTIVE PAST

The ancient Greeks used screws, lathes (used for turning wood), construction cranes, and watermills—the first machines to use nonanimal power. They discovered that steam could be used to drive machines. But neither the Greeks nor the equally inventive Chinese were interested in labor-saving machines, because slaves were cheap and plentiful. ▶

Pulley wheels

Having four wheels allows four times the load to be lifted with the same effort.

Effort

RAISING THE LOAD

The simplest type of pulley is a wheel with a grooved rim. A rope or chain is passed around the groove. The pulley changes the direction of a force, so by pulling down on the rope, a person can raise a heavy weight. The more pulleys there are with one rope running through them, the greater the load that can be lifted with the same effort.

Load

TAKING THE STRAIN

Elevators can be hydraulic or operated by electric traction, like the one here. Hoisting ropes, made of steel cables, are raised or lowered by a pulley wheel, turned by an electric motor. In the 1850s, engineer Elisha G. Otis invented the first elevator featuring an automatic safety device—a safety clamp—which would prevent the elevator from falling if the rope broke.

MEDIEVAL MACHINES

Important mechanical inventions in Europe during the Middle Ages included the crossbow, windmill, clockwork, and the printing press. During the 1200s, the English monk Roger Bacon predicted the use of cars, airplanes, and submarines long before the technology and materials required for such inventions were even available.

MACHINES REPLACE WORKERS

As labor became more expensive, it made economic sense to make machines do more work. From the 1700s, a new kind of mechanized industry developed. The Federal Armory in Springfield, Massachusetts, pioneered the mechanized manufacture of muskets for the army. In Britain, the engineer Marc Brunel designed 43 machines that could make 10,000 pulley blocks a year, enabling the Royal Navy dockyard to reduce the workforce required for the task from 110 to just 10 men.

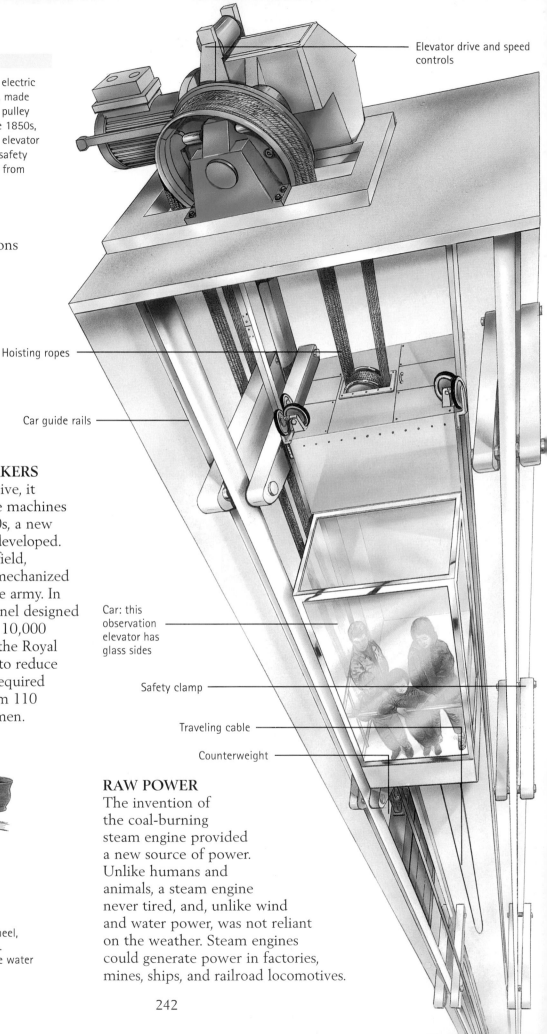

Elevator drive and speed controls

Hoisting ropes

Car guide rails

Car: this observation elevator has glass sides

Safety clamp

Traveling cable

Counterweight

▲ From the invention of the potter's wheel, someone got the idea for the cart wheel. Fitted with pots, a wheel could also raise water from one level to another, for irrigation.

RAW POWER

The invention of the coal-burning steam engine provided a new source of power. Unlike humans and animals, a steam engine never tired, and, unlike wind and water power, was not reliant on the weather. Steam engines could generate power in factories, mines, ships, and railroad locomotives.

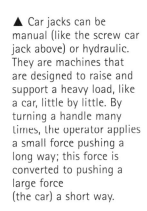

▲ Car jacks can be manual (like the screw car jack above) or hydraulic. They are machines that are designed to raise and support a heavy load, like a car, little by little. By turning a handle many times, the operator applies a small force pushing a long way; this force is converted to pushing a large force (the car) a short way.

THE FACTORY AGE

To make machines, machine tools were needed to stamp out metal plates, cut screws and gears, and shape metals by cutting, drilling, grinding, or polishing. Standardization of parts made it easier to keep machines working and repair them quickly. Important new inventions included the dynamo, the electric motor, and the hydraulic press and ram. The clothing and shoemaking industries were transformed by the sewing machine, invented in 1846.

THREAT TO JOBS

The use of machines in industry greatly increased output and made factory goods cheaper. But there was a human cost. Workers, including women and children, toiled for low pay in bad conditions. In the 1880s, social critics like the Englishman William Morris complained that machines were destroying craftsmanship, reducing people to a form of slavery. Some people smashed machines they thought were going to take away their work.

WORK REVOLUTION

The machine revolution affected farming, where machines took over harvesting, baling, and threshing. Transportation and trade were revolutionized in the mid-1800s by the locomotive, steamship, and conveyor belt. Machines invaded offices and stores, at first in the form of typewriters and cash registers.

THE MODERN WORLD

New machines, such as the car and the airplane, began to transform the world at the beginning of the 1900s. The invention of the jet engine and the rocket allowed people to travel at speeds that had been unimaginable before. In the home, old-fashioned devices were being discarded in favor of new time- and energy-saving appliances such as the washing machine, vacuum cleaner, and the food processor. In industry, robots and increasingly efficient computers took over many basic production processes. New materials, such as plastic, ceramics, and carbon fibers, have replaced metals to make machines that are smaller, yet more efficient.

▶ A forklift truck is a machine that raises weights using liquid pressure (hydraulics). Simple hydraulic machines have a cylinder with a large and a small piston inside. The cylinder is filled with fluid. A force applied to the small piston is transferred to the larger one, increasing the force.

◀ A snowblower has two engines: one drives the truck, the other turns the drum. As it turns, blades on the drum churn the snow, forcing it upward through the chutes. As the truck moves forward, it takes in more snow.

SEE ALSO

Car, Engine, Household appliance, Industrial Revolution, Industry, Invention, Robot

MAGNETISM

Magnetism is a force that can attract (pull towards) or repel (push away) objects that have a magnetic material such as iron, nickel or cobalt inside them.

The horseshoe magnet has a pole at each end.

So does the simple bar magnet.

A ring magnet has one pole on its outer surface and another pole on its inner one.

If you have ever moved a magnet toward a pin, you have experienced magnetism. Pins are made of steel—a material that consists mainly of iron—and they feel a strong force pulling them toward the magnet, which may even be strong enough to make them stick to it. Any material, like steel, that is attracted toward a magnet in this way is called a magnetic material.

MAGNETIC POLES

When an object is attracted to a magnet, it sticks to its ends—this is where the magnet exerts, or gives out, the greatest force. The two ends of the magnet are called its poles. One of them is north-seeking and the other is south-seeking. They should be marked in some way so you can tell them apart. If you bring the same poles of two magnets face to face, they will repel each other; and if you bring different poles of two magnets face to face, they will attract each other.

► Industrial-strength electromagnets can lift heavy pieces of scrap iron.

ELECTRO-MAGNETISM

In 1820, a Danish physicist, Hans Christian Ørsted, discovered that magnetism was produced by an electric current. This led to the development of the electromagnet—a temporary magnet formed when an electric current passes through a conductor such as wire, which is wrapped around an iron core. Electromagnets are useful because they can be turned on or off and altered in strength. They can produce magnetic fields strong enough to drive generators and electric motors. Smaller ones are used to make doorbells and buzzers work.

MAGNETIC EARTH

The Earth itself acts like a huge magnet with magnetic poles at its north and south ends—known as the magnetic north pole and the magnetic south pole. These poles act like the ends of a magnet and make compass needles point north. They are close to the geographic North and South Poles, which are at the top and bottom of the imaginary line, or axis, around which the Earth spins.

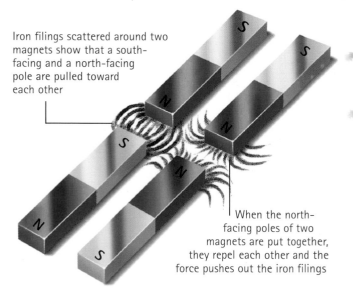

Iron filings scattered around two magnets show that a south-facing and a north-facing pole are pulled toward each other

When the north-facing poles of two magnets are put together, they repel each other and the force pushes out the iron filings

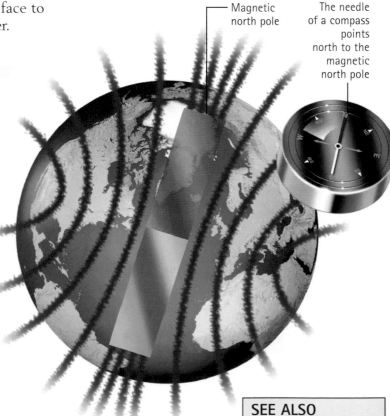

Magnetic north pole

The needle of a compass points north to the magnetic north pole

SEE ALSO

Antarctica, Arctic, Earth, Electricity, Iron and steel, Metal

MALAYSIA

Malaysia is a fast-growing nation in Southeast Asia, consisting of Peninsular Malaysia and the areas of Sabah and Sarawak on the island of Borneo.

Area: 127,355 sq. mi. (329,847km²)
Population: 31,382,000
Capitals: Kuala Lumpur and Putrajaya
Language: Malay
Currency: Ringgit (Malaysian dollar)

The two regions that make up Malaysia lie 400 mi. (650km) apart, across the South China Sea. The climate is hot, humid, and rainy, and there are swamps, rain forests, and golden beaches. The many mountains include Mount Kinabalu (13,435 ft./4,095m), the highest peak in Southeast Asia.

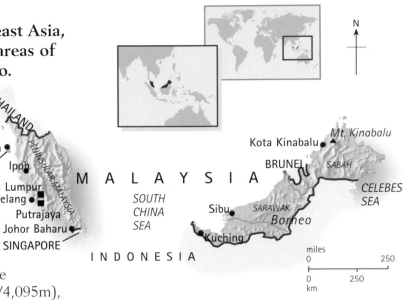

▲ Sarawak has a swampy coastal plain and many rivers. In some villages, people live in houses raised on stilts.

▲ Workers tap rubber trees for their latex. Rubber is a major export, as well as tin, gas, oil, palm oil, hardwood, tea, cocoa, and pineapples.

RURAL AND CITY LIFE
Wildlife includes giant turtles and over a thousand types of orchid. Traditionally, Malays lived in rural areas, in villages called *kampongs*, but 75 percent of the population now lives in towns and cities. Kuala Lumpur has many modern buildings, including the 1,483-ft. (452-m) Petronas Twin Towers, and is Malaysia's largest city.

GROWING INDUSTRIES
Malaysia has fertile soil, and the most important food crop is rice. There are also large deposits of minerals. The country is growing rapidly as an industrial power, and is a major producer of components for the electronics industry, textiles, cement, cars, and tires. Tourism is also growing.

MALAYSIA'S PEOPLE
Half the people are Malay, and nearly a quarter are Chinese. Other groups include native peoples Borneo and the Malay peninsula and Indians (mainly Tamils). Malay is the national language, but Chinese, Tamil, and English are also widely spoken. Islam is the official religion, but about 40 percent of the people practice other religions, including Buddhism, Christianity, and Hinduism.

OVER THE AGES
Waves of migrants from different regions have settled in Malaysia over thousands of years. The Arabs, Portuguese, and Dutch all occupied the area before the British seized control in the early 1800s, eventually granting independence in 1957. Today's Malaysia was eventually formed in 1963.

▲ Traditional crafts include working with textiles. In the north of Peninsular Malaysia, batik work is popular.

SEE ALSO
Indonesia, Rain forest, Southeast Asia

MAMMAL

Mammals are vertebrates (they have backbones). They have adapted to a wider range of habitats and show a greater variety of forms than any other animal group.

Orangutans are one of about 300 primates. This group includes humans.

The bat is the only mammal that can fly. Its forelimbs act as wings.

There are about 334 types of marsupial, mostly found in the Australian region.

Mammals like the hyena have strong teeth called canines for stabbing flesh.

Marine mammals like the seal have short fur and streamlined bodies.

The duck-billed platypus is one of only five species of egg-laying mammal.

◄ The armadillo is covered in bony plates that protect it from predators. When attacked, it curls up into a tight ball.

All mammals are warm-blooded, which means they can keep their bodies warm and stay active even in the coldest weather. The only other animals that can do this are birds. Most mammals are covered with hair or fur, which helps keep them warm. Unlike other animal babies, young mammals feed on their mother's milk. Mammals also have larger brains than other animals.

A SUCCESSFUL GROUP

The first mammals appeared on Earth about 200 million years ago as small, insect-eating creatures. When dinosaurs died out about 65 million years ago, mammals began to explore different habitats and try different foods. They became larger and took on many different shapes. Thousands of "experimental" mammals have come and gone during the last 50 million years, but only about 5,448 different species live in the world today.

VARIETY OF HABITATS

Mammals are not as numerous as birds or fish, but they can be found in almost every habitat: some live in seas and rivers; some spend their lives high up in the trees of the forest; antelopes and other grazing mammals form huge herds on grasslands. Some mammals manage to survive in the driest deserts and on the coldest mountaintops. Bats have taken to the air; seals, whales, and dolphins to the seas.

THE RIGHT TEETH

Mammals eat a wide range of foods and most have teeth designed to suit their diets. Most plant-eating mammals (herbivores), such as horses and elephants, have large grinding teeth at the back of the mouth. Rodents have sharp, chisel-like front teeth for gnawing nuts and other hard foodstuffs. Flesh-eating mammals (carnivores), such as lions and wolves, have large, sharp canines for stabbing and seizing prey, and sharp-edged cheek teeth for slicing through flesh.

CARE OF THE YOUNG

Young mammals learn many of their survival skills during the period that they are with their mother, feeding on her milk. At birth, lion cubs are blind and helpless, weighing only about 3.3 lb. (1.5kg). The mother carries them in her mouth from one hiding place to another, and the male protects his family from intruders. Only when the cubs are between 18 and 24 months old will the lioness have another litter.

MAMMAL OF THE DESERT

The two-humped Bactrian camel of central Asia is well adapted to life in the desert. It can travel for days or even weeks with no food or water because it carries a large store of fat in its humps, which it converts into food. At the end of a long period without food, the humps lose much of their firmness, and may even flop to one side. With its bushy eyebrows and long lashes, the camel can shield its eyes from the sand. It can even close its nostrils during a sandstorm. A close relative of the Bactrian camel is the Arabian camel, or dromedary, which has only one hump.

COVERED IN FUR
One of a mammal's main characteristics is its fur. A Bactrian camel's fur can grow to 10 in. (25cm) on its head, neck, and humps. Camels grow a new coat once a year.

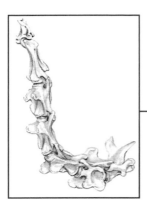

NECK BONES
All mammals, apart from the manatee and sloth, but including the giraffe, have seven cervical vertebrae (bones that make up the neck).

A MOTHER'S MILK
Mammals are the only animals to feed their young with milk, produced in special glands called mammae.

Omnivorous mammals, which include humans, eat plants and animals. Insect-eaters, such as shrews and hedgehogs, have lots of small, sharply pointed teeth, but anteaters have no teeth at all: they lap up ants with their sticky tongue. Some whales have no teeth: they feed on small animals which they sift from the water with plates of horny material in the roof of their mouth called baleen or whalebone.

EGGS AND POUCHES

A tiny number of mammals, such as the duck-billed platypus, are unusual because they lay eggs. Others, called marsupials, are also known as pouched mammals, because the female nurses her babies in a pouch or pocket on her body. About 50 million years ago, marsupials lived all over the world, but they are now found mainly in the Australian region, with a few in North and South America. All other mammals, known as placental mammals, give birth to live young.

THE LARGEST GROUP

Placental mammals are by far the biggest group of mammal. While the baby is inside its mother, it gets food and oxygen from her blood through a structure called the placenta. A placental mammal baby can stay inside its mother's body for much longer than a marsupial baby. A baby elephant, for example, grows inside its mother for about 22 months and is well developed when it is born. Some baby mammals can run around soon after they are born, but many others, including human babies, are quite helpless at birth.

FAST FACTS

- With their relatively large brains, mammals have a greater ability to learn than other animals

- Special mammal senses include the bat's sonar and the mole's ultrasensitive whiskers

- The largest mammal, the blue whale, can be 100 ft. (30m) long

SEE ALSO

Animal, Bat, Bear, Cat, Dog, Hippopotamus, Horse, Kangaroo, Monkey, Platypus, Prehistoric animal, Rat, Rhinoceros, Tiger, Whale and dolphin, Wolf

MAP

A map is a diagram or image of land or sea.
It can be used to show people the way, or to
provide statistics or other useful information.

A pedometer is used
to measure distance.

A theodolite gives the
direction of distant objects.

Stereo viewers give a 3-D
image from aerial photos.

Maps may show symbols, points of
the compass or grid lines to help
the reader locate places. They may
show lines of latitude and longitude.

MAPS TO SCALE
Maps are often drawn to an accurate scale.
Distances on the map represent distances
on the ground. For example, 1 inch on a
map might equal 1 mile on the ground (or
a scale of 1:1,00,000 means that 1 cm on
the map equals 1 km on the ground).

TYPES OF MAP
Physical maps show hills, valleys, rivers,
and mountains. Political maps show
nations, regions, and borders. Road maps
show routes for driving, or city streets.
Weather maps may show wind directions
or air pressure. Sea charts may show rocks,
reefs, currents, and depths.

THE FIRST MAPS
The first maps were drawn in
Mesopotamia, in about 2300 B.C. They

▲ Maps using Mercator projection, invented in 1569,
allow sailors and pilots to plot their course accurately,
but distort areas close to the North and South Poles.

▶ Maps using
Peters projection,
developed in
1973, give
accurate areas
but distort
shapes.

MAP PROJECTIONS
Unless the Earth's surface is being mapped onto a round globe, it cannot be shown
exactly as it is. The curve of the Earth's surface has to be flattened out onto a page of
paper or a screen, moving from three-dimensional (3D) to two-dimensional (2D). Imagine
peel being taken from an orange and squashed flat onto a plate. A map maker uses
geometry to transfer the dimensions, using a "projection."

were sketched on clay tablets and were
not accurate. One of the first great
geographers and mapmakers was a Greek
called Ptolemy, who lived in Alexandria,
Egypt, in about 140 C.E. The Romans
mastered the skills of surveying land while
building roads across their empire.

THE SEARCH FOR ACCURACY
As sailors began to explore the wider
world after the Middle Ages, accurate
maps became very important and precious.
Newly discovered lands were mapped
with great skill in the 1700s and 1800s.
Modern map making (cartography) is
assisted by aerial photography, by satellite
imagery and the use of computer software.

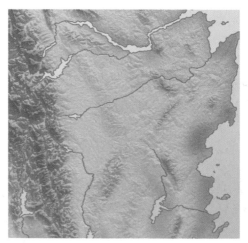

▲ Relief maps show physical features, such as
rivers, plains, hills, and mountains.

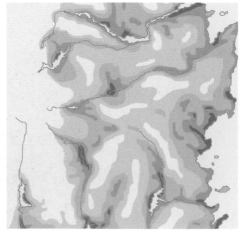

▲ Here, population density is shown by colors.
Dark colors are areas with the most people.

▲ Route maps may show roads, railroads, and
built-up areas to help travelers find their way.

SEE ALSO
Mesopotamia, Navigation,
Weather

MATERIALS

People use a huge range of different materials with which to make things. These include metal, plastic, rubber, ceramics, glass, and wood.

▲ A lathe spins an object quickly, so that it can easily be smoothed to a perfect round shape.

Leather is strong but soft, and easily cut to shape.

Rubber can be stretched, but bounces back to shape.

Plastic may be soft or hard and can take any shape.

Glass is hard but shatters easily when hit.

Wood is relatively light and strong.

Bricks of clay can bear heavy weights.

All the materials people use originally come from the Earth. Materials that are used in their natural state are called raw materials. These may be processed or mixed together to make manufactured or "synthetic" materials.

RAW AND SYNTHETIC

Wood, which comes from trees, is a raw material. It can be used in its original state or processed to make manufactured materials such as cardboard and paper. Glass is a synthetic material made by mixing together sand, salt, and other raw materials at a high temperature.

PROPERTIES

Materials must be chosen carefully. A ladder, for example, must be made of something strong and rigid, like steel. If it is made of something soft and stretchy, like rubber, it will bend when people walk up it, making it dangerous to use. Every material has properties, such as strength and hardness. Other properties characterize a material

▲ Metal is heated until it becomes liquid, then poured into a mold. When it cools and hardens, the metal takes the shape of the mold.

as ductile, elastic, or plastic. A ductile material is one that can be stretched easily. Metal is ductile when it is hot; it can be pulled into thin wires. Materials like rubber that go back to their original shape after stretching are elastic. Wet clay and other materials that can be pushed into any shape, and then stay like that, are plastic. Most plastics have this property when they are hot, which is how they got their name.

COMPOSITES

Sometimes people need to combine materials to benefit from two properties which a single material does not have. For example, car windshields need to be transparent like glass, but as strong as steel. Manufacturers often mix materials or sandwich them together to make new ones called composites. Laminated glass is a composite material. The strongest type has a thin steel mesh sandwiched between panes of glass. It is almost completely transparent, but is strong enough to stand or walk on.

◀ Clay is an example of a material that changes easily. As clay it is soft and weak. But when heated, or fired, it changes to pottery, which is very hard and strong. Adding different substances, such as bone ash or white clay, gives pottery different properties.

SEE ALSO

Bridge, Construction, Design, Housing, Solid, liquid, and gas, Textile

MAYA

The Maya people dominated Central America from about A.D. 250 to A.D. 850, building cities deep in the rain forest. Their descendants still live in the region.

The Maya were great astronomers and carved dates of religious ceremonies on stones.

The Maya wrote using glyphs (picture symbols) to show sounds of words or to convey ideas.

The Maya were among the most highly developed civilizations in Central America. Their achievements in art, architecture, astronomy, and mathematics were outstanding.

MIGHTY MAYA
The Maya had begun to live in cities as early as 750 B.C. By A.D. 250 these had become city states, probably led by priest-kings. They erected stone pillars to record their achievements. Within a few generations, the Maya were building vast cities, such as Tikal (now in Guatemala), with populations of up to 50,000 people. These spread across the Yucatan Peninsula to the Pacific Ocean. This was known as the Classic Period.

WEALTH FROM THE EARTH
The wealth of the Maya was based on trade and farming. As early as 1500 B.C., people in the area were growing Indian corn, the basic food of the Maya. The

▲ Modern Maya at a market on the steps of a church in Guatemala.

seeds were either boiled or ground into a powder to make a porridge. Mayan farmers grew tomatoes, string beans, avocados, and sweet potatoes. They had no farm animals, but hunted wild game and fish. Most people lived in forest huts, coming into the city only to attend markets or religious ceremonies.

SCIENCE OF THE STARS
Mayan priests learned how to calculate the solar year, lunar months, and even the movements of the planet Venus. For these calculations, the Maya developed complex mathematics and used writing more skillfully than any other American people.

DEATH OF A CULTURE
In about A.D. 800, some of the southern cities were abandoned. By 950, most of the great cities had collapsed. The reasons for this are unknown. People continued to live in their homeland, but in villages. There was a revival around 1200, and then, in the 1500s, the Maya were conquered by Spanish invaders.

MAYAN MONUMENTS
With only stone hand tools, the Maya managed to build great pyramids and palaces. The Castillo Pyramid in Chichén Itzá reached 100 ft. (30m) above the ground. Chichén Itzá survived longer than most Mayan cities—it was inhabited until about 1440.

The Castillo is 180 ft. sq. (55m sq.) at the base

Four staircases each had 91 steps. These, plus the step at the temple entrance, added up to 365—the number of days in the Mayan year.

SEE ALSO
Central America, Explorer, Mexico

MEDIA

The communications media are the channels through which news, information and views are made public. They include newspapers, magazines, radio, television and electronic media.

Printed media include newspapers, magazines, and books. Broadcast media include radio, television, cinema, and live-streaming. The electronic age has created entirely new media, which cross over traditional boundaries and are changing the way we live.

TRADITIONAL MEDIA

The content of traditional media has aimed to inform, entertain, influence public opinion, or advertise. Some public print or broadcasting is a public service, but most is produced to make a profit from sales or advertising. Media companies are increasingly large multimedia international corporations.

ELECTRONIC MEDIA

Electronic media include websites, blogs, and social media sites such as

▲ Paparazzi photographers spy on celebrities and take photographs for international papers and magazines.

Facebook, Twitter, Instagram, and Snapchat, Vk.com in Russia and Sina Weibo and Renren in China. Users control input, sharing links, messages, opinions, music or video clips by computer or smartphone. The new media have affected sales of newspapers, magazines, books, and music, which have had to find new electronic outlets.

MEDIA, POWER AND FREE SPEECH

People and governments have always wanted to control, influence, or censor the traditional media, whether for political, moral or economic reasons. In some ways social media have got around this problem, but there are concerns about privacy, data protection, political interference, online abuse, and "cybercrime." Freedom of expression remains one of the most important human rights.

Game, set, and match to Murray

Scotland the brave! Andy Murray wows the center court at Wimbledon with another classic victory.

ANDY MURRAY took the trophy for the second time with a storming performance against Canada's Milos Raonic, 6-4, 7-6, 7-6.

CHAMPION'S CELEBRATION Murray, 29, and his wife Kim Sears, 28, were smiling broadly as they arrived for the Champion's Dinner at the Guildhall in the City of London last night.

By JANE SMITH

NEWSPAPER
A reporter and photographer will go along to a match to record results and comments from players.

COVERING AN EVENT

A news event will be covered in different ways by the media: newspapers send a reporter and photographer; radio shows may have just one broadcaster with an outside broadcast unit; television needs visual images and sound.

TELEVISION
Television coverage of a news event demands camera operators, sound technicians, and a commentator on site.

RADIO
Results are given during a radio news bulletin, while sports programs are recorded live from events.

THE EVENT
Major sports attractions, such as the Wimbledon or U.S. Open tennis tournaments, give press passes to TV and radio stations and accredited journalists.

SEE ALSO

Internet, Newspaper and magazine, Photography, Radio, Television

MEDICINE

Medicine is the scientific study of human disease. It covers the causes, prevention, diagnosis, and treatment of all types of different sicknesses.

The name of the ancient Greek Hippocrates (c.460–377 B.C.) lives on in the Hippocratic oath, a code of principles for doctors.

French chemist Louis Pasteur (1822–95) invented pasteurization—a process of killing germs in liquids such as milk.

English surgeon Joseph Lister (1827–1912) introduced antiseptics into surgery, reducing the risk of bacterial infection.

Alexander Fleming (1881–1955) was a British bacteriologist who discovered the antibiotic drug penicillin.

The Greek physician Hippocrates is often called the "founding father of medicine." He examined patients and recorded their symptoms. He also prescribed many remedies, including willow bark tea—later shown to be the source of aspirin. But medicine could not progress in a scientific way until doctors understood how the body works.

UNDERSTANDING THE BODY
In the 1500s, the Belgian anatomist Andreas Vesalius was the first to show where bones, muscles, blood vessels, and organs were situated in the body. Then William Harvey (1578–1657), a British doctor, discovered that the blood was pumped around the body by the heart. During the 1800s, scientists showed that microbes (microscopic organisms such as bacteria) could cause disease, and medicine began to progress as a modern science.

MAKING A DIAGNOSIS
The identification, or diagnosis, of a disease begins with the doctor taking a history of the illness. This includes asking about symptoms, previous illnesses, and details of the patient's lifestyle. Then the doctor carries out a physical examination.

This may include listening to the sounds of the patient's chest and abdomen with a stethoscope, feeling organs such as the liver, and looking into the eyes, ears, and throat with special instruments. Most illnesses can be diagnosed from the history and physical examination alone. The doctor may also send blood, urine, and other samples to a hospital laboratory for testing. Sometimes the patient will need to have an X ray or a scan. These create pictures of the inside of the body, which can give a better idea of what is wrong.

MEDICAL TREATMENT
Most illnesses are treated by drugs or surgery. There are around 6,000 drugs available today, including painkillers,

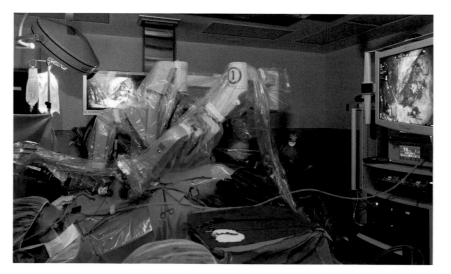

◀ Medicine is a scientific frontier which changes all the time. Advances in pharmaceuticals, electronics, scanning and surgical methods have saved countless lives. Here, surgeons in a hospital's operating theatre are making use of robotics.

antibiotics, anticancer drugs, and drugs for mental illness. Surgery is often used in the treatment of heart disease and cancer to remove or repair diseased tissue. It is possible to replace major organs such as the heart, lungs, kidneys, and liver by transplant surgery.

PREVENTATIVE MEDICINE
Prevention is always better than a cure. Doctors and nurses use what they know about the causes of disease to help stop patients getting sick in the first place. Smoking is known to cause both heart disease and lung cancer, so the medical profession tries to discourage patients from smoking. Smokers can attend antismoking clinics, for example, and there are health warnings on cigarette packs. People can also look after themselves by eating a healthy diet, exercising, getting enough rest, and having regular checkups.

Vaccination protects people from diseases such as polio.

ALTERNATIVE TREATMENT
There are also complementary or alternative medicines, which take a different approach to healing. Acupuncture comes from the Chinese medical tradition. It depends upon balancing the body's lifeforce, or *chi*, which flows along invisible channels in the body called meridians. During treatment, an acupuncturist uses needles to help the chi flow more freely. This and other forms of alternative medicine, such as reflexology, homeopathy, and aromatherapy, are popular with patients, although their effects may not be scientifically proven.

▲ Acupuncture involves thin metal needles being inserted into selected points in a patient's body. In China, where the technique originated, it is used as an anaesthetic during surgical operations.

VIEWING THE BODY IN CROSS SECTIONS
One of today's fastest and most accurate forms of imaging (to help diagnosis) is the computerized tomography (CT) scanner, which creates a "virtual reality" image of the patient's body. The patient is moved slowly through the scanner, inside of which an X-ray source rotates around the body. A ring of detectors relay the information to a powerful computer for processing. The information is then displayed on screens on the main console as a series of cross sections, or slices, through the patient's body.

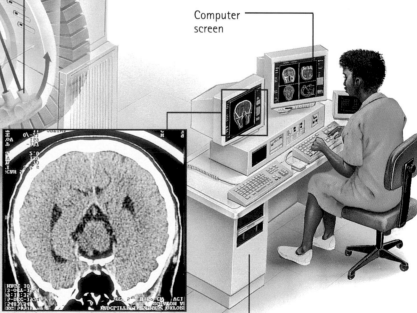

Revolving X-ray source

Continuous spiral (ring) of detectors

X-ray beam

Movable patient couch

Computer screen

Main console

▲ This image, produced by a CT scanner, provides details of a slice through the patient's brain.

SEE ALSO

Disease, Drug, Human body, Immune system, Nutrition, Surgery, X ray

MESOPOTAMIA

Mesopotamia lies along the valleys of the Tigris and Euphrates rivers in the Middle East. The world's earliest cities and organized civilizations grew up here.

Cast copper work, a bust of King Sargon of Akkad.

A wooden lyre shows the importance of music at Ur.

Elaborate gold jewelry was worn by the nobles.

Cylinder seals were used by merchants and priests.

After 2000 B.C., chariots dominated warfare.

Watered by the mighty Tigris and Euphrates rivers, Mesopotamia (a Greek word meaning "between the rivers") was a fertile and wealthy land. It was here that early farmers developed writing, founded cities, and built a series of empires which dominated surrounding lands.

FIRST FARMERS
Farming spread into Mesopotamia from the hills to the north and west. By about 6000 B.C., people living along the rivers had learned how to irrigate fields to grow barley, wheat, dates, and beans. Sheep and goats were kept for their meat and wool. In the fertile valley more food could be grown, and the population boomed. By about 3500 B.C., villages along the twin rivers had grown into cities of over 10,000 people.

CITY-STATES
The buildings in the cities were made of mud bricks, with only a few being built of kiln-baked bricks. The people learned how to weave wool and flax into clothing, make copper tools, and produce high-quality pottery for the first time. Each city was independent, but traded with other towns and people, even importing ivory and gemstones from India.

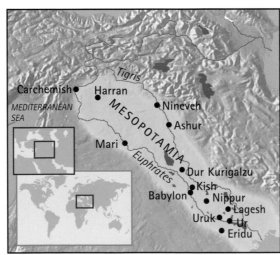

▲ A number of powerful cities ruled the area that surrounded them until the growth of empires.

▶ A ceremonial helmet made of an alloy of gold and silver, which belonged to King Meskalamdug of Kish in about 2200 B.C.

THE WORLD OF GILGAMESH
The need to organize irrigation schemes led to the growth of strong central governments by kings or priests. Gradually, a few powerful cities, such as Eridu, Kish, and Uruk, came to dominate the surrounding area, known as Sumer. Writing was invented to keep track of government and temple records, but was soon used to record events and the deeds of kings. In about 2700 B.C., Gilgamesh became king of Uruk and fought several wars. He was so famous that many stories were told and written about him.

SACRED CITIES
At the center of each city was a *ziggurat*, a massive artificial hill topped by a temple. Built of layers of mud brick and straw, the ziggurats were up to 330 ft. (100m) across and 330 ft. (100m) tall. Mud bricks were not strong enough to support these

THE LAW CODES

Rulers set out law codes, often carved on a stone pillar and set up for public display. The oldest-known was made by Ur-Nammu, who ruled Ur in about 2100 B.C. The code dealt with slaves, personal injury, and witchcraft. Ur was also famous for its ziggurat, an enormous stepped temple to the Moon god Nanna, also built by Ur-Nammu.

structures for long, and most ziggurats were repaired about every 100 years. The ziggurat was dedicated to the god or goddess of the city, whose prestige depended on the power of his or her city. Gods could win or lose worshipers if their city won or lost a battle. Many rulers were both kings and priests or the posts were held by the same family.

WARRIOR EMPIRES

Around 2334 B.C., King Sargon of Akkad, the area around Nippur, conquered Mesopotamia. He and his successors conquered lands as far as Syria. By about 2160 B.C. the empire had collapsed. By 1900 B.C. its lands had been conquered by the Amorites, nomads from the deserts to the west. The invaders settled in Mesopotamia and adopted local customs. By about 1792 B.C., King Hammurabi of Babylon claimed to rule all of Mesopotamia. Gradually the northern cities grew more wealthy and powerful. In 1250 B.C. the Assyrians, based at Nineveh, conquered a new empire covering Mesopotamia, Syria, Palestine, and Egypt.

END OF AN ERA

Mesopotamia enjoyed a final period of power from 626 B.C. to 539 B.C., under the Chaldean rulers. It was then conquered by Persia and became a part of larger empires. Mesopotamia is now divided among Iraq, Syria, and Turkey.

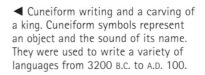

◄ Cuneiform writing and a carving of a king. Cuneiform symbols represent an object and the sound of its name. They were used to write a variety of languages from 3200 B.C. to A.D. 100.

▲ This gold bull's head which once decorated a harp was found in one of the royal tombs at Ur.

SEE ALSO

Babylon, Egypt (ancient), Empire, Middle East, Seven Wonders of the World

METAL

A metal is a shiny material such as iron, gold, or copper. Most are solid at room temperature, easy to shape when hot, and good at conducting heat and electricity.

▲ Metals can be joined by welding—the application of heat, pressure, or both. Here, an electrical current is being used to heat steel in a process called arc welding.

▼ Aluminum alloys are used in aircraft construction because they are light but strong.

The Earth has a huge supply of some metals, such as tin and iron —used to make tools, machines, and large structures. Other metals, such as gold and platinum, are rare. They are usually used in small quantities.

WORKING WITH METAL
People have known how to extract and use metals since about 8000 B.C. If a metal is heated until it becomes molten (liquid), it can be poured into a mold. As soon as it cools, it hardens and keeps its shape until melted again. Metals can also be hammered into any shape or pulled into long strands. Most solid metals are very strong and hard, which is why they are used to make things like building frames and engine parts that have to keep their shape when put under pressure.

METALS THAT RUST
If something made of iron is left outside, it will go rusty. This is because the surface of the iron reacts with oxygen in the air to form a new compound—iron oxide. Many other metals react with oxygen or other elements, and so are not found in their pure state in the ground. Instead, they are found as ores—compounds of metal and oxygen. A common way of extracting metal from oxide ores is to heat them with charcoal to remove the oxygen, leaving the pure metal.

ALLOYS
People have discovered many ways to mix metals both with each other, and with nonmetals, to make useful materials. These mixtures are called alloys. Steel is an alloy made from iron and small amounts of carbon and other metals. It is harder and stronger than pure iron. Bronze is a hard alloy made from copper and tin.

METAL FATIGUE
You need a large force to break a lump of metal apart all at once. But some metals break when bent many times by a small force. This way of breaking a metal, called metal fatigue, is a serious hazard. Machines like airplanes that must not fail are checked for signs of metal fatigue.

ALUMINUM	TUNGSTEN	MERCURY	STEEL
Soft and light, it forms a strong alloy when mixed with other metals.	Used in lightbulb filaments, which glow white hot when electricity passes through.	A poisonous liquid metal used in thermometers and barometers.	An extremely strong alloy made of iron, carbon, and other metals.
GOLD AND PLATINUM	IRON	CALCIUM	BRASS AND BRONZE
Precious metals used for jewelry and electrical circuits.	A strong metal used for outdoor railings and furniture.	Found in dairy products, it is essential for healthy bodies.	Copper alloys used for sculpture and decorative objects.
SILVER	ZINC AND NICKEL	SODIUM	PEWTER
A precious metal used for jewelry and decorative objects.	Commonly used as alloys, along with copper, for making coins.	A common metal found in salt as sodium chloride, it is used in lamps to create a glow.	An alloy of tin and lead, once widely used for tableware.
COPPER	TIN	MAGNESIUM, STRONTIUM, AND BARIUM	
A good conductor of electricity, commonly used for electrical wiring.	Commonly used to cover steel cans to stop them rusting.	Used to create the bright colors in fireworks.	

SEE ALSO
Construction, Gold, Iron and steel, Mineral and gem, Mining, Silver

MEXICO

Mexico, North America's third-largest country, lies between the United States to the north and Central America to the south.

Area: 758,449 sq. mi. (1,964,375km²)
Population: 124,575,000
Capital: Mexico City
Language: Spanish
Currency: Mexican peso

In north and central Mexico, mountain ranges called *sierras* enclose a high plateau. This plateau, Mexico's most thickly populated region, contains active volcanoes. Mexico's highest peak, Pico de Orizaba (18,491 ft./ 5,636m), is a dormant volcano.

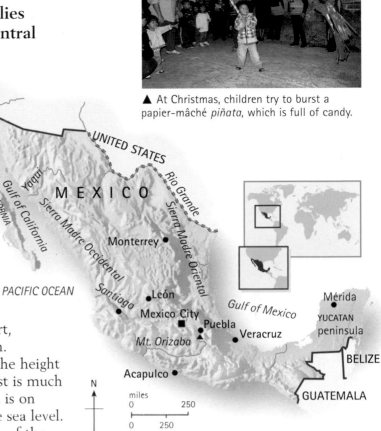

▲ Ruins such as El Castillo, the Pyramid of Kukulkan, may be seen at the ancient Mayan city of Chichen Itza.

▲ At Christmas, children try to burst a papier-mâché *piñata*, which is full of candy.

DESERTS AND FORESTS
Seven tenths of Mexico has little rainfall. The north is largely desert, but rain forests grow in the south. Temperatures vary according to the height of the land. Acapulco on the coast is much warmer than Mexico City, which is on average 7,380 ft. (2,250m) above sea level. Mexico City was built on the site of the ancient Aztec capital Tenochtitlán, founded around 1325.

MESTIZOS
Many Mexicans are *mestizos*, of mixed European and Native American origin. Most white people are descendants of Spaniards who arrived in Mexico in 1519. Spanish is the official language, but some Mexicans speak Native American languages. Most Mexicans are Roman Catholics, and more than three fourths of the people live in cities and towns.

TRADE AND FOOD
Mexico is rich in minerals, including silver. Oil, gas, and oil products are the main exports. Factories also produce chemicals, clothing, iron and steel, processed foods, and vehicles. Food crops include corn (used to make flour for pancakes called *tortillas*), beans, rice, and wheat. Coffee, cotton, vegetables, and fruit are also important.

MODERN TIMES
Mexico became independent from Spain in 1821. It lost land to the United States in the Mexican War (1846–48), and this war ruined Mexico's economy. There were revolutions between 1910 and 1921, but since then Mexico has been mainly at peace. Poverty has led many people to illegally enter Mexico's rich neighbor, the United States, in search of jobs.

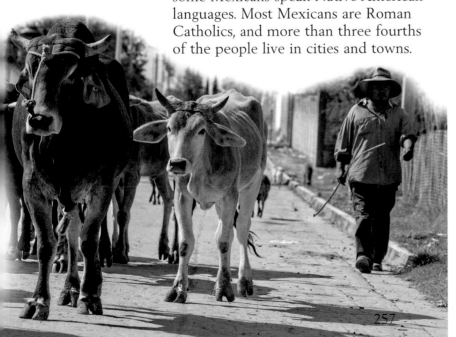

◄ Cattle are reared in the northern part of Mexico's plateau, where there is little rainfall.

SEE ALSO
Aztec, Central America, Maya, North America

MICROORGANISM

Microorganisms are tiny living creatures that cannot be seen without a microscope. They can be bacteria, viruses, protists (protozoans), or tiny algae or fungi.

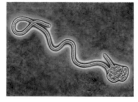

The Ebola virus is long and wormlike in shape. It is often deadly.

A colony of rodlike, food-poisoning bacteria growing on cooked roast beef.

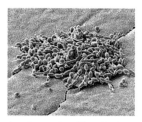

Yeast cells are fungi and can be used to ferment alcohol and make bread.

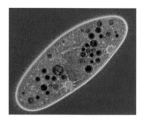

Paramecium protists are abundant in water and soil and feed on bacteria.

Many varieties of single-celled algae form colonies in or on top of water.

Bacteria are single-celled specks of living matter, mostly well under one hundredth of a millimeter long. There are three main shapes: rods, spheres, and spirals. Bacterial cells differ from other cells because their DNA, which controls all living things, floats free through the cells instead of being contained in a nucleus. They get food and energy by breaking down all kinds of living or dead substances and, unlike most other living things, many of them can survive without oxygen.

GOOD AND BAD

Bacteria reproduce by simply splitting into two. This can happen every 15 minutes in good conditions, so bacteria exist in huge numbers. Many bacteria cause illnesses, including tuberculosis, cholera, and food poisoning. These are often called germs or microbes. But not all bacteria are harmful. Some help to keep the soil in good condition, and others can be used to manufacture yogurt and other foods.

PROTISTS

Protists are single-celled organisms in which the DNA is wrapped up in a nucleus near the cell's center. They live everywhere, especially in watery surroundings. The best-known members of the group are amoeba, which continually change shape as they move. Some live harmlessly in water and swallow bacteria by simply flowing over them. Others live inside animals and cause illness. Many protists cause diseases such as malaria and sleeping sickness.

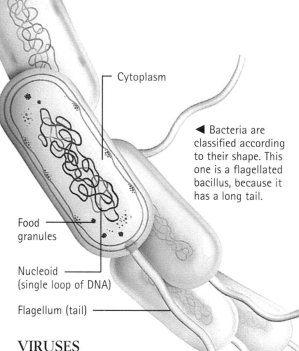

Cytoplasm

◀ Bacteria are classified according to their shape. This one is a flagellated bacillus, because it has a long tail.

Food granules

Nucleoid (single loop of DNA)

Flagellum (tail)

VIRUSES

Viruses are even smaller than bacteria. On the border between living and nonliving things, most consist of a piece of DNA inside an envelope of protein. Viruses can form crystals like salt and other chemicals, and can survive in this state for a long time. But they can reproduce only when they get inside other living things. In such cases, the DNA of a virus invades the cells, forcing them to make more viruses. All viruses therefore cause disease in other living things. Human illnesses caused by viruses include measles, AIDS, and the common cold. Prions are even smaller than viruses and have only recently been discovered. BSE, or mad-cow disease, is thought to be caused by prions.

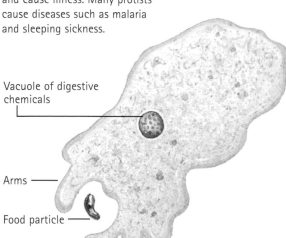

Vacuole of digestive chemicals

Arms

Food particle

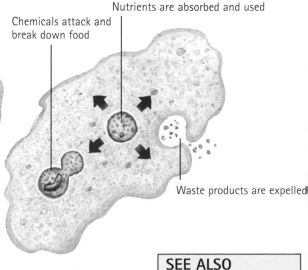

Nutrients are absorbed and used

Chemicals attack and break down food

Waste products are expelled

SEE ALSO
Cell, Disease, Fungi, Genetics, Microscope

MICROSCOPE

Microscopes are instruments that magnify tiny objects or reveal fine details on larger objects. They have opened up a whole world that was invisible to our eyes.

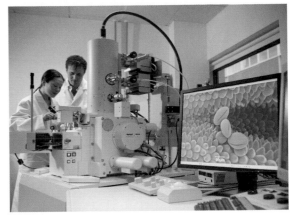

▲ In an electron microscope, the electrons are invisible, so a fluorescent screen is used instead of an eyepiece.

The first microscope was made by the Dutch eyeglass maker Zacharias Janssen in around 1590. The first scientist to see bacteria was the Dutchman Anton van Leeuwenhoek, who made his own microscopes in the 1670s. The first microscopes were optical, which means that the object, or specimen, being studied was viewed through an eyepiece. For this to work, the specimen needed to be thin enough to let light through.

ELECTRON MICROSCOPES

Electron microscopes first appeared in the 1930s. Instead of light, they use a beam of electrons controlled by magnetic fields. Electron microscopes are very powerful and can show details 1,000 times larger than optical microscopes can show. However, the specimen must be dried out

and sliced very thinly (about a thousandth of the thickness of this page). In addition, the air must be removed from inside an electron microscope and from around the specimen, as electrons are easily scattered.

OTHER MICROSCOPES

Scanning electron microscopes move a beam of electrons over the surface of the specimen. The electrons that bounce off are collected to make an image. Scanning probe microscopes and atomic force microscopes were invented in the late 1980s. They can magnify a million times, showing up individual atoms. An extremely sharp probe moves over the surface of the specimen, "feeling" its shape in tiny detail. A computer turns signals from the probe into a 3-D image, which is displayed on a monitor screen.

OPTICAL MICROSCOPES

In an optical microscope, light shining through an object is bent as it passes through a lens. This makes the object appear much bigger. Adding a second lens makes the magnification even greater. Optical microscopes with several lenses are called compound microscopes and can magnify things by up to about 2,000 times their real size.

An electron scan (x20) of Velcro, used as a clothes fastener, showing the nylon hooks and loops.

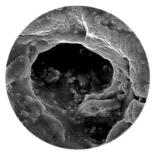

A false-color electron scan (x200) of a sweat pore from a blister on the palm of a man's hand.

An electron scan (x500) of individual cotton fibers, which make up a single thread of cotton.

An electron scan (x1,300) of human hairs protruding from the surface of the scalp (colored pink).

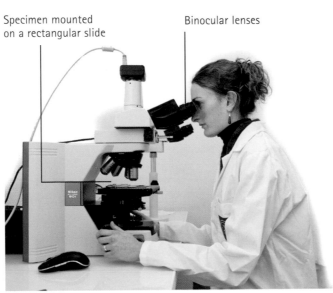

Specimen mounted on a rectangular slide

Binocular lenses

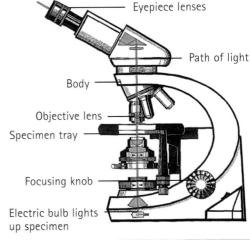

Eyepiece lenses

Path of light

Body

Objective lens

Specimen tray

Focusing knob

Electric bulb lights up specimen

SEE ALSO

Atom and molecule, Lens, Microorganism, Telescope

MIDDLE AGES

The Middle Ages make up a period of European history lasting from around the fall of the western Roman Empire in 476 A.D., to the fall of Constantinople in 1453.

▶ During the 1400s in France, Christine de Pisan wrote for a living. This was unusual in an age when few people, particularly women, knew how to read and write.

The Middle Ages saw invasions by Germanic peoples, Huns, Avars, Turks, and Moors. However most of Europe became Christian. As the Middle Ages ended, Europe was beginning a long period of global exploration, trade, and conquest.

Society was divided into three estates: the clergy and the nobility...

... and the third estate, made up of farm workers, traders, and craftspeople.

EMPEROR AND POPE

In 800, Charlemagne, king of the Franks, was crowned Emperor of the Romans by the pope. This was an attempt to reunite Europe under a Christian ruler. The rival powers of pope and emperor dominated the Middle Ages.

FEUDAL SOCIETY

In this period, Europe was divided into many kingdoms, dukedoms, bishoprics, and other states. The source of most wealth was farmland. The feudal system of controlling land and people was developed in France during the 900s. Kings gave land to lords and knights in return for military services. Each lord had to swear fealty (loyalty) to his overlord. The lord's land was farmed by peasants, who paid him in labor and surplus crops. The Church also held a lot of land, and many monasteries used their wealth to encourage learning and the arts.

A VIOLENT PERIOD

At the height of the Middle Ages, Muslims and Avars, the ruling families of Europe fought each other for power and wealth. The Hundred Years' War (1337–1453) was fought between the kings of England and France over who should rule France. The Hapsburg family of Austria and the Hohenzollerns of Germany fought long wars to conquer new lands.

TRADE AND INDUSTRY

After about 1100, Europe became increasingly wealthy. Merchants and craftspeople formed guilds— organizations that imposed regulations and controlled prices. They helped to spread skills and encourage trade between regions. By 1400, a growing number of people were working in manufacturing and trade.

MEDIEVAL BANQUETS

The wealthy lords and ladies of the Middle Ages held banquets for special occasions. These formal meals began early in the day—around 10 or 11 A.M.—and continued for several hours. Guests ate with their fingers or with knives and spoons (forks had yet to be invented). The food included a great many meat dishes and was often heavily spiced.

SEE ALSO
Castle, Crusades, Renaissance, Roman Empire

MIDDLE EAST

The Middle East is a group of countries in southwest Asia lying between Africa and Europe. It has great economic importance and is an area of unrest.

AFGHANISTAN
Area: 251,827 sq. mi. (652,230km²)
Population: 34,125,000
Capital: Kabul
Languages: Pashto, Dari
Currency: Afghani

BAHRAIN
Area: 293 sq. mi. (760km²)
Population: 1,441,000
Capital: Manama
Languages: Arabic and Indian languages
Currency: Bahraini dinar

IRAN
Area: 636,372 sq. mi. (1,648,195km²)
Population: 82,022,000
Capital: Tehran
Languages: Farsi and Azeri
Currency: Rial

IRAQ
Area: 169,235 sq. mi. (438,317km²)
Population: 39,192,000
Capital: Baghdad
Languages: Arabic, Kurdish
Currency: Iraqi dinar

ISRAEL
Area: 7,876 sq. mi. (20,400km²)
Population: 8,300,000
Capital: Jerusalem (claimed)
Languages: Hebrew, Arabic
Currency: New Shekel

Much of the Middle East is desert, with rugged mountain ranges in eastern Turkey, Iran, and northern Afghanistan. Afghanistan contains the region's highest peak, Nowshak (24,560 ft./7,485m), in a range called the Hindu Kush. Most people live along the coasts, in inland valleys, or around oases.

ANCIENT RIVERS

The main rivers, the Tigris and Euphrates, rise in Turkey and flow through Syria and Iraq. They join to form a river called the Shatt al Arab, which empties into the Persian Gulf. The world's first city-states were founded along these rivers in Mesopotamia, by a people called the Sumerians, in around 3500 B.C. The Middle East's most famous inland body of water is the Dead Sea, which lies in a deep valley between Israel and Jordan. Its shoreline is the world's lowest point on land, 1,417 ft. (432m) below sea level.

▲ The Elburz Mountains in Iran, close to the Caspian Sea, make up one of the Middle East's many mountain ranges.

RAIN, SNOW, AND DESERT

The areas with the highest rainfall are in the northeast: the Turkish city of Istanbul has an average rainfall of 31 in. (787mm) a year, while Saudi Arabia's capital Riyadh has only 4 in. (101mm). Snow falls on the mountains, and temperatures drop below freezing in the winter. The desert plains are hot. Few plants grow in the deserts, but date palms flourish around oases. ▶

▼ The Middle East has been transformed by the discovery of oil and gas. This has brought riches to the region, but has also created conflict in some areas.

261

JORDAN
Area: 34,495 sq. mi. (89,342km²)
Population: 10,248,000
Capital: Amman
Language: Arabic
Currency: Jordanian dinar

KUWAIT
Area: 6,880 sq. mi. (17,818km²)
Population: 4,200,000
Capital: Kuwait City
Language: Arabic
Currency: Kuwaiti dinar

LEBANON
Area: 4,015 sq. mi. (10,400km²)
Population: 6,230,000
Capital: Beirut
Language: Arabic
Currency: Lebanese pound

OMAN
Area: 119,500 sq. mi. (309,500km²)
Population: 3,424,000
Capital: Muscat
Language: Arabic
Currency: Omani rial

PALESTINE (GAZA AND WEST BANK)
Area: 2,402 sq. mi. (6,220km²)
Population: 4,950,00
Capital: East Jerusalem (claimed)
Language: Arabic, Hebrew
Currency: Israeli New Shekel, Egyptian Pound, Jordanian Dinar

QATAR
Area: 4,474 sq. mi. (11,588km²)
Population: 2,314,000
Capital: Doha
Languages: Arabic and Indian languages
Currency: Qatari riyal

SAUDI ARABIA
Area: 830,000 sq. mi. (2,149,690km²)
Population: 28,572,000
Capital: Riyadh
Language: Arabic
Currency: Riyal

SYRIA
Area: 71,500 sq. mi. (185,180km²)
Population: 18,029,000
Capital: Damascus
Language: Arabic
Currency: Syrian pound

▲ In Saudi Arabia, men often relax and drink tea together. Tradition dictates that women do not attend such gatherings.

DESERT ANIMALS

In some areas, nomadic tribes herding camels, goats, and sheep move around in search of pastures. The best-known animal of the Middle East is the camel, which can go for long periods without water. Another desert animal, the Arabian oryx, once lived throughout the Arabian Peninsula and in Lebanon, Iran, and Iraq. By 1972, it was extinct in the wild because people had overhunted it in their cars. Arabian oryxes bred in captivity have now been released in Oman and are increasing in number.

PEOPLE AND RELIGION

Many of the people of the Middle East are Arabs, and Arabic is their chief language. There are also Turks, Iranians, Kurds, Pashtuns, Azeris, Uzbeks, Armenians, and Jews. The Middle East was the birthplace of Judaism, Christianity, and Islam, and all three religions regard Jerusalem in Israel as a holy city. Muslims also make pilgrimages to Mecca and Medina in Saudi Arabia. Islam has two main branches, known as Sunni and Shia. Israel is the centre of Judaism, and there are smaller Christian communities across the region.

SADDAM HUSSEIN
Saddam Hussein (1937–2006) became Iraq's president in 1979. He led Iraq into war with Iran, which lasted from 1980 to 1988. In 1990, Iraq invaded Kuwait, but an international force drove the Iraqis out during the Gulf War in 1991. In 2003, a U.S.-led coalition invaded Iraq and overthrew Hussein and his government. He was executed in 2006 for crimes against humanity.

◄ In cities such as Damascus in Syria, handicrafts are sold at markets called *souks*.

HOW PEOPLE LIVE
Until about 50 years ago, most people lived on farms or in farming villages. Today, more than 70 percent of people live in towns and cities. The largest cities are Tehran, capital of Iran, Istanbul in Turkey, and Baghdad, capital of Iraq. Many cities have tall modern buildings as well as older areas.

OIL POWER
The region's chief resource is oil, and Saudi Arabia has about 16 percent of the world's known oil reserves. Other leading oil producers are Iran, Kuwait, the United Arab Emirates, Qatar, and Oman. Qatar's riches also derive from huge reserves of natural gas. Money from oil sales has been used to build new cities and roads and to develop new industries to make oil products such as chemicals and plastics.

INDUSTRY AND FARMING
Iran and Turkey have many other industries, and Israel, the most developed country in the Middle East, is known for its aircraft, electrical goods, electronics, precision instruments, and textiles. Agriculture employs over three quarters of people in Afghanistan and Yemen, but in desert nations such as Bahrain and Qatar only one percent of the population are farmers.

► Kuwait's water towers are part of a desalination plant, where fresh water is produced by removing salt from seawater.

MIDDLE-EASTERN WARS
The boundaries of many countries in the Middle East were set after World War I (1914–18). Israel was created in 1948, leading to several Arab-Israeli wars. The Palestinians are still fighting to have their own land. In 1991 and 2003, U.S.-led coalitions fought Saddam Hussein's regime in Iraq. The Kurds, who live in Armenia, Iran, Iraq, Syria, and Turkey, are fighting to have their own country, Kurdistan. In the Arab Spring of 2011, there were uprisings and protests across the Middle East. In Syria, the uprising became a civil war with many rebel groups fighting government forces as well as each other.

TURKEY
Area: 302,535 sq. mi. (783,562km²)
Population: 80,845,000
Capital: Ankara
Languages: Turkish and Kurdish
Currency: Turkish lira

UNITED ARAB EMIRATES
Area: 32,278 sq. mi. (83,600km²)
Population: 6,072,000
Capital: Abu Dhabi
Languages: Arabic and Indian languages
Currency: Dirham

YEMEN
Area: 203,850 sq. mi. (527,968km²)
Population: 28,037,000
Capital: Sana
Language: Arabic
Currencies: Rial

SEE ALSO
Asia, Christianity, Europe, Islam, Israel and Palestine, Judaism, Mesopotamia, Oil

MIGRATION

Migration is the regular, instinctive movement of animals between one place and another. Their journeys are usually made to tie in with the seasons.

▶ Caribou (also known as reindeer) migrate from the Arctic tundra in vast herds to winter in the great coniferous forests farther south.

▲ Humpback whales migrate thousands of miles to reach warm waters, but they do not cross the equator.

▶ Monarch butterflies fly more than 1,860 mi. (3,000km) to reach their winter home.

▼ When the insects on which swallows feed die out in the fall, the birds fly south to find a fresh supply.

FINDING THE WAY

The map shows the routes taken by various migratory animals. Migrants are believed to use a range of methods to find their way. Some follow geographical features such as mountains and coastlines; others use their sense of smell. Birds, in particular, may be guided by the sun or the stars or by sensing Earth's magnetic field.

◀ The Arctic tern is a long-distance flyer, making an annual round trip of up to 25,000 mi. (40,000km).

Swallow
Caribou/reindeer
Monarch butterfly
Arctic tern
Humpback whale

FAST FACTS

• Migrating wildebeest in search of water can sense rain 60 mi. (100km) away

• Green turtles may swim over 1,250 mi. (2,000km) to lay their eggs on Ascension Island in the mid-Atlantic

• The shorter days of fall trigger migrating behavior in many animals

▲ Salmon battle their way upstream to reach their breeding grounds.

Every year, many animals journey hundreds, sometimes thousands, of miles to avoid cold winters—when food is hard to find—or to reach their summer breeding grounds. The animals usually travel in one direction before the onset of winter, then make the return journey the following spring.

BIRD MIGRANTS

Birds are among the most common migrants. Cuckoos, swallows, and many other insect-eating birds live in Europe and North America during the summer, when insects are plentiful, then fly south to spend the winter in warmer lands. Certain geese and ducks breed during the summer in the far north, but when the lakes begin to freeze, they fly south in search of food. The Arctic tern makes the longest journey of all. Each year, it flies from the Arctic to the Antarctic and back again, so that it can enjoy the summer months in both places.

BREEDING TIME

Whales commonly feed in cold waters in the far north and south, but they migrate to warmer subtropical waters to breed. Seals travel long distances across the sea to rocky islands where they bear their young, and turtles head for warm sandy beaches in which to lay their eggs. Some fish also migrate, though not annually. Salmon live in the sea, but return to the same river in which they hatched in order to spawn (breed). European eels, on the other hand, live in fresh water but travel to the Sargasso Sea, east of Florida, to breed.

INSECT MIGRANTS

Some insects migrate. Millions of monarch butterflies, for example, fly south from Canada and the northern United States to winter in warmer areas. They breed in the spring and die soon afterward, but their young complete the journey north.

SEE ALSO

Bird, Butterfly and moth, Reptile, Whale and dolphin

MILLIPEDE AND CENTIPEDE

Millipedes and centipedes are long-bodied animals with many pairs of legs. Millipedes feed mainly on rotting vegetation, but centipedes are active hunters.

The word millipede means "thousand legs," whereas centipede means "hundred legs." Neither animal tends to have as many legs as its name suggests, but both have an impressive number, which makes them easy to identify.

SEGMENTED BODIES

Millipedes and centipedes belong to a group of animals called arthropods. Like other arthropods, they have a tough outer case, or exoskeleton, and their bodies are divided into segments. In most millipedes, the segments are circular in cross section, and each one carries two pairs of tiny legs. In centipedes, the segments are flatter and, instead of carrying four legs, each segment carries just two.

DANGERS OF DRYING OUT

Millipedes and centipedes do not have fully waterproof bodies, which means they have to be careful not to dry out. To avoid this they tend to live in damp places, such as scattered or piled leaves and soil, and are active mainly at night.

▶ When threatened, millipedes usually coil up tightly to protect their legs.

DIFFERENT LIFESTYLES

In other ways, these animals live quite differently. Millipedes have small jaws and they feed on the remains of decaying plants. They move quite slowly and, if they are threatened, rarely run away. Instead, they often protect themselves by coiling up into a spiral. Some millipedes have special glands that produce a poisonous fluid. If another animal tries to eat them, the fluid soon puts the attacker off its meal. Centipedes, on the other hand, are aggressive hunters with large claws surrounding their head. Many can move quite fast, either to scurry after their prey or to escape danger.

Two of the 10,000 identified species of millipede. Most have 120 to 160 legs, but the record is 750.

Two of nearly 3,000 types of centipede. Most have 30 to 50 legs, though one species has 177 pairs.

FEROCIOUS HUNTERS

A centipede's flattened body allows it to slip easily in and out of crevices while it is hunting. Centipedes are armed with special claws on either side of the head that inject poison into their prey. Most centipedes feed on small creatures such as worms, snails, and beetles, but large tropical species—which can reach over 10 in. (25cm) long—sometimes attack frogs, mice, and even birds. Their claws are strong enough to pierce human skin, with very painful results.

Leg muscles anchored to the rigid body wall allow the limbs to move freely

Overlapping membranes between the segments allow greater flexibility of movement

The poisonous claws around a centipede's head are actually modified front legs

A centipede has long antennae which it uses to search for food

SEE ALSO
Animal, Insect

MINERAL AND GEM

Minerals are the natural elements or compounds that make up rocks in the Earth's crust. Gems, metal ores, sand, salt, and even talc are all types of mineral.

Jade is a hard, usually green, semiprecious gemstone that can be carved to form fine ornaments.

Turquoise ranges in color from blue to gray-green. Sky blue specimens are popular as gems.

The gem opal shows a characteristic play of colors, known as opalescence.

There are well over 4,000 officially recognized mineral species, and as many as 100 new ones are described each year. Some minerals form glassy crystals, others are like brightly colored rocks. They vary in color, density, and hardness, and also in their ability to reflect light and conduct heat or electricity.

MINERAL COMPOUNDS

Some minerals, such as gold, consist of one pure element. Many others are made up of two or more elements, combined to form a compound. The most common mineral—quartz—is a combination of silicon and oxygen. Most grains of sand are quartz, which is used for making glass.

MINERAL ORES

Many mineral compounds contain metals. The mineral hematite, for example, is iron oxide and galena is lead sulphide. Minerals such as these, from which the metals can easily be removed, or extracted, are called ores and are widely mined.

FORMING CRYSTALS

Many minerals form distinct three-dimensional shapes called crystals. The shapes are the result of the arrangement of atoms and molecules inside the mineral. Minerals that produce fine, hardwearing crystals that can be cut and polished to a beautiful finish are called gemstones.

PRECIOUS GEMS

Gems are most commonly worn as jewelry. They include diamonds, rubies, sapphires, and emeralds. Diamonds, because they are incredibly hard, are also used in industry and mining for drilling, cutting, and grinding. Industrial-grade diamonds can now be made artificially.

SCALE OF HARDNESS

An Austrian scientist, Friedrich Mohs (1773–1839), devised a scale to grade the hardness of minerals. His scale ranges from grade 1 for talc, the softest, to grade 10 for diamond, the hardest.

On Mohs's scale, a fingernail rates as 2.5, a copper coin as 3.5, and a steel penknife as 5.5.

A SELECTION OF MINERALS

The iron ore hematite often forms kidney-shaped lumps, which earn it the name kidney ore.

Quartz forms fine crystals and comes in many colors. The colorless variety is called rock crystal.

Galena has a metallic gray color and forms cubic crystals. It is the main ore of lead, and is commonly found with quartz.

Talc (magnesium silicate) is the softest mineral on Mohs's scale. It is widely used as talcum powder.

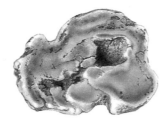

Gold is a soft, malleable (easily worked) metal which has been used since ancient times to make jewelry.

Malachite is a copper ore, well known for its bright green color. It is often granular, and rarely forms crystals.

SEE ALSO

Earth, Gold, Metal, Mining, Oil, Rock, Silver, Soil

Mining

Mining is the process of taking from the Earth useful or valuable substances such as coal, gas, salt, mineral ores, gemstones, or building stone.

▶ A vast bucket-wheel excavator is used to dig up rocks and minerals in an opencast mine.

▲ Gold is found as small grains, or nuggets, of pure metal. Here, gold nuggets are being washed out of the soil using water.

The earliest mines were built to find useful metals like lead, copper, iron, and tin and precious metals such as silver or gold. But, because there were no effective methods for removing excess water or supplying workers with air, the mines always had to be near the surface.

MINING AND MACHINES

Over the last two centuries, problems with drainage and ventilation have been solved by using machines, and mines can now be sunk deep into the ground. As well as pumping out water and circulating air, machines are used for drilling and cutting and carry materials, men, and equipment to and from the surface. Deep mining has always involved dangers from cave-ins, flooding, and poisonous gases. In the future, work in dangerous conditions is likely to be done by robots controlled from the surface.

REACHING THE DEPOSITS

There are many different methods of mining—the type and depth of deposit usually determine the method used. Materials such as stone, gravel, and sand are mined in quarries. Mineral deposits near the surface can be removed by opencast mining, using mechanical diggers or high-pressure water jets. Deep deposits are reached by sinking vertical shafts into the ground, or by driving a tunnel into the side of a hill or mountain—called drift mining. Explosives are often used to blast rocks apart so the minerals can be broken up.

MINING METHODS

A shaft mine is used to reach deep deposits. Where deposits are closer to the surface, minerals can be hauled up a slope in wagons. Drift mines are used where the seam reaches the surface, as on a hillside. Deposits close to the surface are removed in an opencast mine, and oil beneath the sea is tapped by an oil rig.

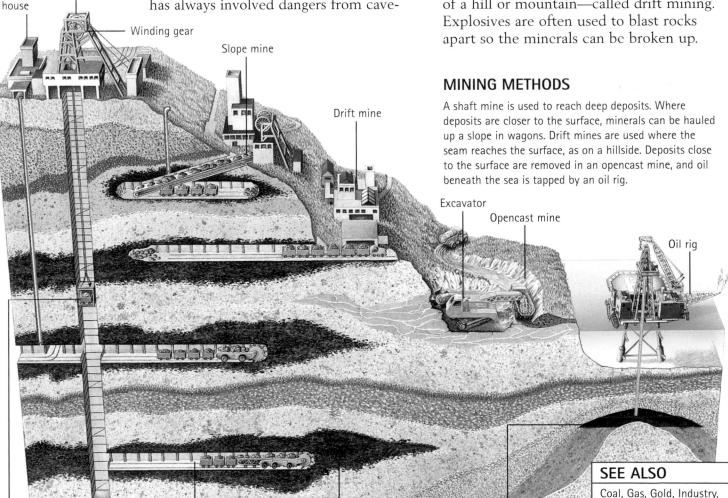

Shaft mine

Air ventilation house

Winding gear

Slope mine

Drift mine

Excavator

Opencast mine

Oil rig

age (elevator)   Main shaft   Tunnel   Ore vein (or coal seam)   Oil reservoir

SEE ALSO

Coal, Gas, Gold, Industry, Iron and steel, Metal, Mineral and gem, Oil, Rock, Silver

MONEY

Money is used to buy things or to save wealth for future needs. Money may take the form of bills, coins, or anything accepted as payment.

Native Americans used beads and shells made into decorative patterns.

The ancient Chinese used bronze cast into spade, knife, and other shapes.

Coins are popular because they are easy to produce and last a long time.

Before there was money, trade took place through barter, the exchange of one item or service for another. Barter only works if the person with one item wants what the other has to offer. Money allows people to sell things for money, then swap the money for what they want. It also makes borrowing possible, so that exchanges can be spread over time.

BEADS TO COINS

Many things have served as money. Useful products, such as salt or knives, have been used, as have decorative beads or even natural items such as shells or cattle. Coins made of precious metals and stamped with a design to show how much metal they contain were probably invented in Lydia (part of modern Turkey) around 700 B.C.

PAPER, PLASTIC, OR ONLINE?

Paper money is not valuable itself, but is a promise to pay real money. It was invented in China around 1000 A.D. Today many non-cash payments are made using paper checks, plastic debit and credit cards, or using online shopping or banking.

Paper money began as promises by banks to pay a certain amount of coins.

Credit cards and checks are useful because they can be used instead of cash.

► In 1923, German money lost value rapidly. Money became so worthless that bundles of bills were used as toys.

MAKING COINS

Coins are made from metals such as bronze or copper, which are stamped with a design showing how much they are worth and which country produced them. First, an artist draws the design on paper.

The design is engraved, in reverse, onto metal dies.

The metal for the coins is melted into thin sheets.

Round "blanks" are cut from the metal sheets.

The dies stamp the coin design onto the blanks.

THE MEASURE OF WEALTH

Money can be used to store and measure wealth, but the value of money is not stable. Wars may cause governments to collapse, so that their money becomes worthless. If a government prints too many bills, or allows excessive borrowing, the money loses value and inflation occurs.

HIGH FINANCE

Large sums are lent and borrowed by governments and large companies in the money markets. Brokers and banks arrange loans or sell shares, allowing businesses to trade and grow.

SEE ALSO
Gold, Great Depression, Silver, Trade

MONGOL EMPIRE

The Mongol Empire was created by the Mongols of eastern Asia. During the 1200s, they conquered vast areas of Asia and Europe to form a powerful empire.

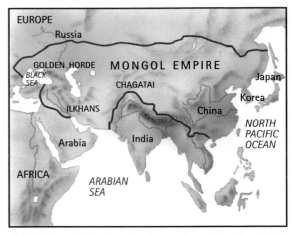

▲ The Mongol Empire at its largest in 1280 under Kublai Khan. The Golden Horde, Chagatai, and Ilkhans later became smaller independent empires.

Genghis Khan (c.1162-1227) united the Mongols and founded the empire.

Kublai Khan (c.1217-94) organized the conquests in China into a stable state.

Tamerlane (1336-1405) conquered an empire in central and western Asia.

The speed and brutality of the Mongol conquests stunned and terrified their enemies. But the Mongols failed to organize their new empire, and it collapsed as quickly as it had been created.

THE TIDE OF CONQUEST

In 1206, Temujin, leader of the Mongols, united the nomadic Asian tribes, taking the title Genghis Khan, or supreme ruler. By 1215, he had conquered northern China, killing about 35 million Chinese. Genghis Khan then turned west, taking western Asia, the Caucasus region, and southern Russia before his death in 1227. Genghis's son Ogedai then became khan, smashing Russia, Hungary, and Poland by 1241. That year Ogedai died, and the new khan, Mongke, turned on China and Persia.

MONGOL WARFARE

Mongols were mounted on hardy ponies, able to travel long distances in a short time. The light cavalry was armed with bows and trained to shoot while galloping. Heavier cavalry had lances and armor. This combination of speed and shock smashed every army they met.

THE NEW EMPIRE

By 1279, all of China had been conquered, and the Mongol Empire stretched from Korea in the east to the Black Sea in the west. Kublai Khan moved his capital to China, from where he was able to enjoy the wealth and luxuries of the conquests.

COLLAPSE OF THE KHANS

After 1300, the khan in China lost control of Mongol rulers elsewhere. The Mongols abandoned the tough life of warriors, and in 1368 were driven out by the Chinese. In the west, Mongol power was broken by the early 1400s. Today, Mongolia is a vast but poor country north of China.

SEE ALSO

Asia, China, Empire

MONKEY AND OTHER PRIMATES

Monkeys and apes belong to a group of mammals
known as primates, which also includes lorises, lemurs,
and galagos, as well as human beings.

The woolly monkey is a New World monkey.

The South American spider monkey uses its tail as an extra hand.

The Old World colobus monkey rarely comes down from the trees.

The mandrill is one of the largest Old World monkeys.

Monkeys differ from apes in having a
tail, although this is sometimes very
short. Both have their eyes at the front
of the head, giving them human-looking
faces. They are intelligent creatures with
good brains, and they learn quickly. They
live in family groups or larger colonies and
spend a lot of time grooming each other
and looking after their babies. Apes are the
nearest living relatives of human beings.

LIFE IN THE TREES
Monkeys and apes are very active and
nimble animals, with excellent eyesight.
Except for the South American night
monkey, or douroucouli, they feed in the
daytime and sleep at night. Most of them
live in the trees, where they can run along
branches and swing from branch to branch
with amazing ease. They grasp branches
with hands and feet, and some South
American monkeys can even hold on to
the branches with their tail. Baboons,
the largest of the monkeys, live mainly
on the ground, although they usually sleep
in the trees at night. With their pointed
muzzle and large teeth, they look more
like domestic dogs than monkeys.

TWO MONKEY GROUPS
There are about 260 species of monkey,
nearly all of which live in the tropical and
subtropical parts of the world. They fall
into two main groups—the New World
monkeys of South and Central America
and the Old World monkeys of Africa and
Asia. New World monkeys,
which include the little
tamarins and marmosets,
have a broad nose with
the nostrils facing to the

▲ Ring-tailed lemurs walk on the ground holding their
long tail up in the air. The word lemur means "ghost,"
a name derived from the weird cry of some species.

sides. Old World monkeys have a narrower
nose with the nostrils pointing downward.

THE BIGGEST APE
About 19 different kinds of ape live in
the forests of the Old World; no apes are
found in the Americas. The gorilla, the
chimpanzee, and the pygmy chimpanzee,
or bonobo live in Africa. Weighing up to
440 lb. (200kg), the gorilla is the largest
and strongest of all the primates. It usually
walks on all fours, with its knuckles on
the ground. Gorillas are not the fierce
creatures that people once thought them
to be. In fact, they live peacefully in the
forest in small family groups.

◄ Baboons live in close family
groups called troops. As with
other monkeys and apes, the
female carries her babies until
they are old enough to look
after themselves.

▲ An adult chimpanzee, closely observed by its young,
uses a stick as a tool to probe for termites. Chimpanzees
are among the most intelligent apes, able to imitate
humans and solve simple problems.

INTELLIGENT CREATURES

Chimpanzees look like small gorillas, but usually have a paler face. They live in large communities, often with over 100 individuals. They are probably the most intelligent of the apes, often using simple tools to help them find food.

ORIENTAL APES

The orangutan and a dozen species of gibbon live in Southeast Asia. Orangutans reach up to 4.3 ft. (1.3m) when upright, and their bodies are covered in sparse, reddish-brown hair. Gibbons are small apes, rarely weighing over 13–15 lb. (6–7kg), and they are wonderful acrobats. They use their long arms to swing and leap through the branches at high speed. Unlike chimps, gibbons and orangutans rarely come down to the ground.

FAMILY LIVING

Gorillas live in family groups, or troops. Each group is made up of one or more males and several females with their young. The group is ruled by a large mature male, known as a silverback because of the silver-gray hairs on his back. Gorillas are vegetarian, eating a diet consisting mainly of leaves and shoots, but also of bark, stems, roots, and fruit. They may live for up to 37 years.

VEGETARIAN DIETS

Monkeys and apes are basically vegetarian, although they often eat insects and other small animals. Chimpanzees even catch monkeys and small antelopes. Fruit is plentiful at all times of the year in the tropical areas, and is the main food of most monkeys and apes. The gorilla and a few monkeys feed mainly on leaves and shoots.

OTHER PRIMATES

Galagos, or bush babies, lorises, and lemurs have smaller brains than monkeys and apes, and are often called lower primates. Their snouts are more pointed than those of most other primates. They live mainly in the trees and feed mostly on fruit, leaves, or insects. Galagos live in tropical Africa and lorises in southern Asia. Both are active at night and have very large eyes. Lemurs are found only on the island of Madagascar, off the east coast of Africa.

▲ The loris is a slow-moving primate that lives in Southeast Asia. It has huge, forward-pointing eyes and broad, grasping hands and feet.

▲ The orangutan is an endangered species. Special rehabilitation centers in Sumatra and Borneo care for young animals and introduce them back into the wild.

SEE ALSO

Animal, Conservation, Mammal

MOON

The Moon is Earth's only natural satellite. Its diameter is 2,160 mi. (3,476km), and it lies at an average distance of 238,855 mi. (384,400km) from Earth.

Crescent Moon (waxing)

Half Moon (first quarter)

Full Moon (appears round)

Half Moon (last quarter)

Crescent Moon (waning)

The Moon shines because it reflects light from the Sun. The phase of the Moon (how much of its surface we can see) depends on the position of the Moon in its orbit.

SOLAR ECLIPSE

Sometimes the Moon passes exactly between Earth and the Sun. When this happens, there is a total solar eclipse, and, for a few minutes, the Sun's bright disk is blotted out. Since the Moon takes exactly the same time (27.3 days) to complete one orbit of Earth as it does to spin around once on its axis, it always keeps the same side facing toward us.

BLEAK AND LIFELESS

The Moon is a bleak place with no atmosphere, which means there is no weather either. There is no life, though ice has now been found on the dark side. The Moon consists mostly of solid rock with a small central core of molten rock or iron. A thin layer of dust covers its surface. During the day, the surface temperature may climb to 260°F (127°C), but at night it can plunge to as low as –279°F (–173°C).

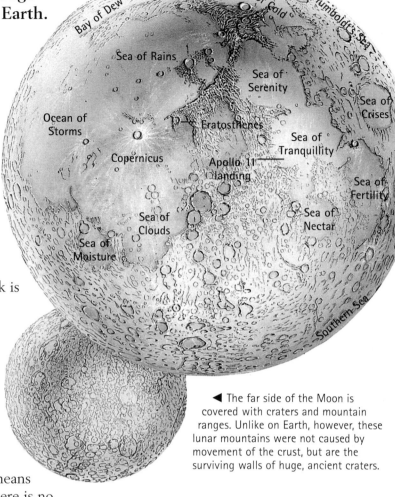
◄ The far side of the Moon is covered with craters and mountain ranges. Unlike on Earth, however, these lunar mountains were not caused by movement of the crust, but are the surviving walls of huge, ancient craters.

ORIGIN OF THE MOON

The Moon was formed just over four and a half billion years ago. It may have been gouged out of our own world when a large object struck Earth. Another possibility is that the Moon has always been a separate body and was captured by Earth when it strayed too close.

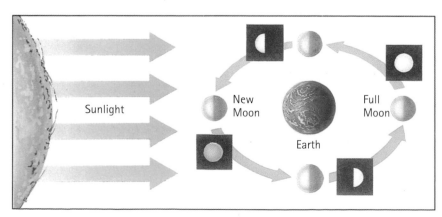

◄ At New Moon, the unlit side of the Moon, which is invisible to us, faces Earth. It grows (Crescent Moon) until half, then all, of the unlit side becomes visible (Full Moon). The phases then continue in reverse until the Moon is new again.

PLAINS AND CRATERS

The dark regions of the Moon's surface, known as maria (seas), are low-lying plains of solidified lava surrounded by brighter, mountainous areas. Craters, formed by the impact of meteorites and asteroids, occur everywhere on the Moon,

▼ The Collision Theory suggests that the Moon was formed when a large body struck Earth.

but are especially common in the uplands. They range in size from a few yards to 685 mi. (1,100km) across—Imbrium Basin in the Sea of Rains.

PULL OF THE MOON

Just as the Moon is held in orbit around Earth by gravity, so Earth itself is affected by the Moon's gravity. The oceans and seas are pulled up when the Moon is directly above them. As Earth rotates, these tidal bulges shift from east to west twice daily, causing high tides.

MYTHS AND LEGENDS

For centuries, the Moon has given rise to various myths and legends. Early people saw it as a god or goddess, and some philosophers thought it was linked with birth and death, because it waxed and waned. It was also feared that eclipses signaled war or famine. In astrology, the Moon is believed to have an important influence over our lives and destinies.

▼ Moon rocks brought back from the *Apollo* missions range in age from about 4.5 billion years, just after the Moon was formed, to 3.1 billion years, when the lava plains were created.

Anorthosite

Vasicular basalt

Typical basalt

► The Capture Theory suggests that the Moon was a passing body caught by Earth's gravity. This explains its different composition, although calculations show that a collision with another body was more likely.

Moon's new orbit

Original path of the Moon

Moon   Earth

1

2

◄ This body added its own material to the debris thrown off into space (1). The debris formed an orbiting cloud (2), which finally solidified into a solid mass—the Moon (3).

3

1   2   3

▲ Earth and the Moon may have formed together as a double planet from the cloud of debris left over after the formation of the Sun. However, this argument does not explain why their surface rocks are so different and why the Moon has such a small iron core compared with Earth's.

SEE ALSO

Astronaut, Earth, Gravity, Planet, Solar system, Space exploration

MOUNTAIN AND VALLEY

A mountain is a mass of land that is much higher than its surroundings, pushed upward by movement of the Earth's crust. Valleys are formed on mountain slopes.

As glaciers melt, they leave deep U-shaped valleys gouged out by the ice.

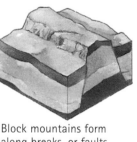

Erupting volcanoes build up mountains made of lava and ash.

Block mountains form along breaks, or faults, in Earth's crust.

A mountain is higher than a hill, but there is no strict distinction between the two. Mountains are natural barriers to communication, and valleys offer trade routes, places for settlement, and pastures for farming. Some mountains are found under the sea. One of them, Mauna Kea in the Pacific Ocean, is higher than Everest.

HIGHEST PEAKS

Mountains are formed over millions of years through plate tectonics—movement of Earth's crust. The crust is made up of rigid plates that are continuously moving. The highest mountains are the youngest. The longest mountain range on Earth, the Andes (4,475 mi./7,200km long), is being formed as the Pacific plate plunges beneath the South American plate. The highest range, the Himalayas, is being formed as the Indian plate crushes up against the Asian plate.

FOREVER WEARING AWAY

All the time a mountain is being pushed up, forces of erosion (such as wind and water) are wearing it down. Water flowing down the slopes gathers in streams and rivers, which carve out deep V-shaped valleys. Flat-bottomed, U-shaped valleys are formed by glaciers. Some straight valleys like the Great Rift Valley, East Africa, are formed along a crack or fault in Earth.

MOVING EARTH

The highest mountains are fold mountains. These are found in chains, or ranges, and are formed like folds in a blanket when the ends are pushed together. They are pushed up when rocky plates of Earth's crust collide. When one plate plunges beneath another, the rocks of the uppermost plate crumple up, making the mountain range.

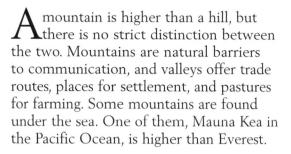

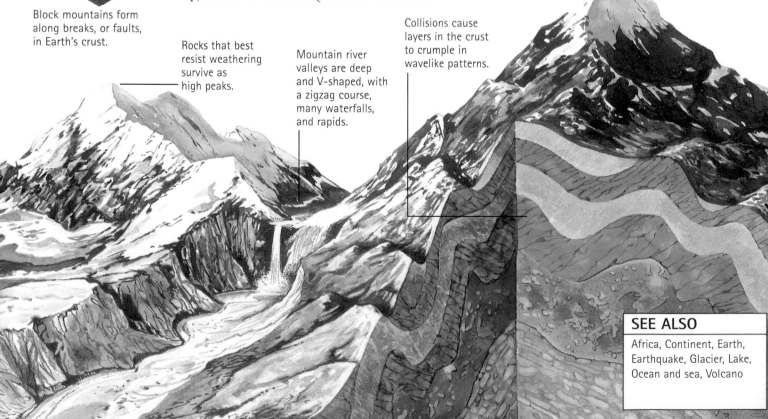

Rocks that best resist weathering survive as high peaks.

Mountain river valleys are deep and V-shaped, with a zigzag course, many waterfalls, and rapids.

Collisions cause layers in the crust to crumple in wavelike patterns.

SEE ALSO

Africa, Continent, Earth, Earthquake, Glacier, Lake, Ocean and sea, Volcano

MUSCLE

The body has 640 muscles, each specialized to contract (become shorter) to make the body move. All body actions, from blinking to sprinting, are muscle-powered.

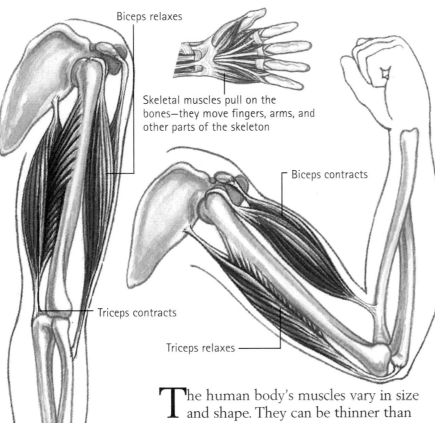

Biceps relaxes

Skeletal muscles pull on the bones—they move fingers, arms, and other parts of the skeleton

Biceps contracts

Triceps contracts

Triceps relaxes

▲ When you bend your arm, the biceps muscle in the upper arm pulls the forearm, and so bends the elbow. Its opposing partner, the triceps, pulls the forearm the other way and straightens the elbow.

The human body's muscles vary in size and shape. They can be thinner than cotton thread, long and bulging in the middle, or wide and slablike—the largest, the gluteus maximus, is in the buttocks. Most are firmly attached to the skeleton by their tapering ends, called tendons.

WORKING IN PAIRS
Muscles can only pull, not push. So they are arranged in opposing pairs. One of the pair pulls the body part one way. To move the part back again, its opposing partner pulls it the other way. Animal muscles have the same structure, and work in the same way as human muscles.

INSIDE A MUSCLE
Muscles are made up of bundles of long fibers called muscle fibers, or myofibers. Each contains bundles of even thinner microscopic parts—muscle filaments, or myofilaments. In turn, muscle filaments

▼ Inside a muscle are bundles of long muscle fibers (myofibers), thinner than human hair, joined by connective tissue.

Skeletal muscle

Smooth muscle

Cardiac muscle

are made of bundles of threadlike structures, called actins and myosins.

MUSCLE POWER
For a muscle to pull, each myosin "grabs" its neighboring actin and makes it slide past—like pulling in a rope with a hand-over-hand movement. Millions of myosins and actins doing this make the whole muscle shorten. The amount and strength of contraction are controlled by nerve signals to each muscle from the brain.

THREE MUSCLE TYPES
Skeletal muscles have a striped appearance under the microscope, so they are known as striped, or striated, muscles. As we can make them contract when we want to (by thinking), they are called voluntary muscles. Cardiac muscle (called the myocardium) forms the thick walls of the heart. It contracts regularly to pump blood. Visceral muscle forms layers and sheets in the walls of the body's inner parts—viscera—such as the stomach, intestines, and bladder. Both of these work automatically, so they are known as involuntary muscles.

The eye has six muscles which help rotate the eyeball in its socket

Ligaments

Tendons and ligaments are tough elastic tissues. Ligaments connect one bone to another; tendons connect a muscle to a bone

Achilles tendon

Tendons

SEE ALSO
Heart and circulatory system, Human body, Lens, Sight, Touch

MUSIC

The word "music" comes from the Greek muses (goddesses), who were said to inspire song and dance. In more scientific terms, music is the art of organized sounds.

As painters or sculptors use lines, colors, and shapes, so musicians use the properties of sound. They use notes of different pitch (highness or lowness) and combine them with the beat of a rhythm to make a melody, or tune. They can add harmony—the sounding together of two or more notes of different pitch. Tone, or timbre, the special quality of sound produced by different instruments or voices, is another aspect of music.

African traditional music is one of the oldest surviving musical forms and is always accompanied by the rhythm of drums.

John Lee Hooker (1917–2001) was a leading player of the blues, which have greatly influenced U.S. pop music.

Elvis Presley revolutionized pop music in the 1950s, becoming one of the first stars of rock'n'roll music.

▶ These marble steps are really an architectural sound art object. The Sea Organ in Zadar, Croatia, uses sea waves pushing air through tubes underneath the steps to make music. The sound comes out of many pipes on the top step.

MUSIC WITH A PURPOSE
The earliest music was probably functional. People danced and sang or chanted because the strange power of music gave them courage to hunt wild animals. They also sang and danced to honor their gods, or to accompany themselves as they worked. All of these ancient types of music are still with us.

MUSIC AS ART
With the growth of civilizations, people turned music into an art. The ancient *ragas* of India—rhythmic or melodic patterns—are a fine example of this. In the Western world, music as an art grew and changed rapidly. In medieval Europe, music still had a functional purpose, since it was sung in church and so served religion. But there was also the singing and the playing

▲ Jazz music originated in New Orleans during the early 1900s, and has remained a major form of music ever since. Unlike written music, it requires musicians to improvise, or make up music on the spur of the moment.

of minstrels, whose music was intended for pleasure and entertainment.

THE RENAISSANCE
From about 1400 to the present day, Western music has been divided into periods. The Renaissance, about 1400-1600, was a period when the rich had more time to enjoy themselves. There was a big increase in secular (nonreligious) music, and much more music for instruments, including the harpsichord and lute, by such composers as William Byrd and John Dowland.

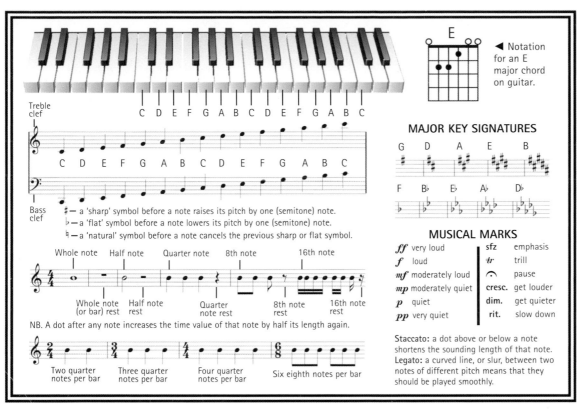

Treble clef — C D E F G A B C D E F G A B C

C D E F G A B C D E F G A B C

Bass clef

♯ — a 'sharp' symbol before a note raises its pitch by one (semitone) note.
♭ — a 'flat' symbol before a note lowers its pitch by one (semitone) note.
♮ — a 'natural' symbol before a note cancels the previous sharp or flat symbol.

Whole note Half note Quarter note 8th note 16th note

Whole note (or bar) rest Half note rest Quarter note rest 8th note rest 16th note rest

NB. A dot after any note increases the time value of that note by half its length again.

Two quarter notes per bar Three quarter notes per bar Four quarter notes per bar Six eighth notes per bar

E

◄ Notation for an E major chord on guitar.

MAJOR KEY SIGNATURES

G   D   A   E   B

F   B♭   E♭   A♭   D♭

MUSICAL MARKS

ff	very loud	sfz	emphasis
f	loud	tr	trill
mf	moderately loud	⌢	pause
mp	moderately quiet	cresc.	get louder
p	quiet	dim.	get quieter
pp	very quiet	rit.	slow down

Staccato: a dot above or below a note shortens the sounding length of that note.
Legato: a curved line, or slur, between two notes of different pitch means that they should be played smoothly.

THE BAROQUE PERIOD

During the baroque period, about 1600-1750, much music was composed on a grand and opulent scale. There were operas by Monteverdi and Handel, great choral works by Handel and J. S. Bach, and clear-sounding music for string orchestras by Vivaldi and others.

CLASSICAL ERA

The classical period, about 1750-1820, focused on new music forms for orchestras and instrumental groups: string quartets, sonatas, concertos, and symphonies. Haydn, Mozart, and Beethoven were masters of these new forms, with their emphasis on systematic development and "classical" order and proportion.

THE ROMANTICS

Beethoven's dramatic and expressive music also opened the way for the romantic period, about 1820-1900. Composers now wanted to express their own thoughts and feelings through poetic songs, descriptive pieces, or operas full of passion and drama. Schubert, Mendelssohn, Schumann, Chopin, Berlioz, Wagner, Verdi, Brahms, and Tchaikovsky all lived during this period.

GROWTH OF WORLD MUSIC

The 20th century saw an explosion of musical styles. Blues and jazz developed and later gave rise to rock and pop. Composers have been influenced by jazz and music from the Far East and elsewhere. Every type of music has been touched by electronics and computers. TV, radio, recorded music, and electronic media make music instantly available to people all around the world.

► Traditional instruments, as well as synthesizers, can be connected to a computer using MIDI (Musical Instrument Digital Interface). Once stored in the computer's memory, the notes can be made to trigger any sound or effect.

J. S. Bach (1685-1750) influenced almost every composer who followed.

Mozart (1756-91) was a child prodigy who began to compose at the age of five.

Beethoven (1770-1827) composed very powerful music, despite being deaf.

Liszt (1811-86) was a brilliant pianist who wrote very difficult piano music.

Wagner (1813-83) wrote dramatic operas of a highly romantic nature.

Gershwin (1898-1937) was famous for his popular songs and musicals.

SEE ALSO

Dance, Film, Musical instrument, Radio, Sound

MUSICAL INSTRUMENT

Musical instruments create vibrations that are turned into sound. Most have their own range of pitched (high or low) notes. All have their own tone, timbre, or "voice."

Musical instruments may be classified scientifically as: aerophones, in which the air itself vibrates; chordophones, in which one or more strings vibrate; membranophones, in which a stretched skin, or membrane, vibrates; and idiophones, in which the whole body of the instrument vibrates as one. The better-known way of classifying them is: strings, woodwind, brass, percussion, as well as keyboard instruments, electronic instruments, and the voice.

Irish harps were carried from town to town by wandering minstrels.

The 6 ft. (1.8m)-long serpent was very popular during the 1600s and 1700s.

From the 1100s, the hurdy-gurdy accompanied singers at feasts and dances.

The Jew's harp is placed inside the mouth, while a finger plucks its tongue.

STRINGED INSTRUMENTS

Stringed instruments produce their sounds from vibrating strings. With violins, violas, cellos, and double basses, the strings are usually scraped with a bow to make them vibrate. In other stringed instruments, notably the guitar, the strings are plucked. The player presses down on the strings with his or her fingers to change their "playing length," which is the section that vibrates. This is called "stopping." The wooden body vibrates in sympathy with the strings, giving them volume and tone.

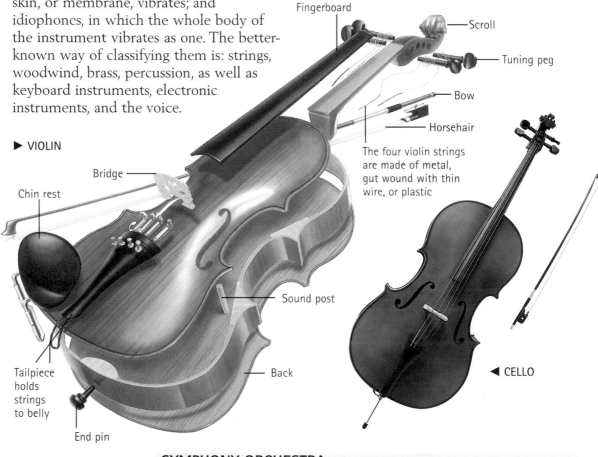

▶ VIOLIN

Fingerboard

Scroll

Tuning peg

Bow

Horsehair

The four violin strings are made of metal, gut wound with thin wire, or plastic

Bridge

Chin rest

Sound post

Tailpiece holds strings to belly

Back

End pin

◀ CELLO

SYMPHONY ORCHESTRA

A typical orchestra includes a string section of violins, violas, cellos, and double basses; a brass section of French horns, trumpets, trombones, and tuba; a wind section of clarinets, oboes, bassoons, flutes, and piccolos; and a percussion section of timpani, gong, glockenspiel, bass drum, and various other percussive instruments.

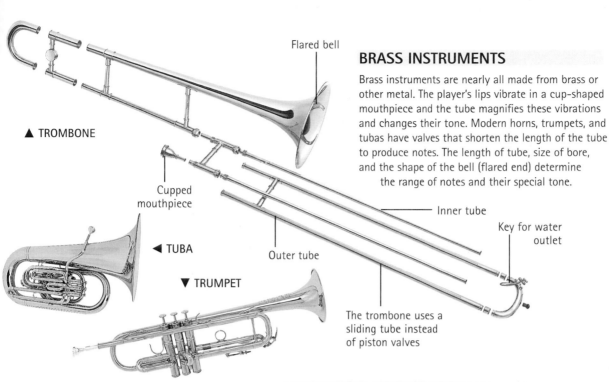

▲ TROMBONE

Flared bell

BRASS INSTRUMENTS

Brass instruments are nearly all made from brass or other metal. The player's lips vibrate in a cup-shaped mouthpiece and the tube magnifies these vibrations and changes their tone. Modern horns, trumpets, and tubas have valves that shorten the length of the tube to produce notes. The length of tube, size of bore, and the shape of the bell (flared end) determine the range of notes and their special tone.

Cupped mouthpiece

◀ TUBA

Outer tube

Inner tube

Key for water outlet

▼ TRUMPET

The trombone uses a sliding tube instead of piston valves

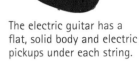

The electric guitar has a flat, solid body and electric pickups under each string.

The saxophone has a flared bell, single-reed mouthpiece, and is very popular in jazz.

WOODWIND INSTRUMENTS

Woodwind instruments make air vibrate in a tube. Many are made from wood, but this is not what classifies them as woodwind—it is the way they are played. Some, like the flute and recorder, have a mouthpiece that turns the player's breath directly into vibrations. The oboe, clarinet, and bassoon have small vibrating reeds. The player sounds different notes by opening or closing holes in the tube's side, and so changing the length of the tube in which the air vibrates.

▼ FLUTE

Finger key

Foot joint

Finger hole covered by key

Cork pads make airtight seal

Head joint

Lip plate

▼ CLARINET

Body joint

Mouth hole

▼ OBOE

Single (clarinet) reed
Double (oboe) reed

The rock drum kit includes a bass drum, floor toms, cymbals, and a snare drum.

▼ TIMPANI (KETTLEDRUM)

Drumhead

Tightening screws

Tuning gauge shows pitch

Tension rod

Supporting strut

Copper bowl

Foot pedal changes pitch of drum

The powerful church organ has one or more keyboards and several banks of pipes.

PERCUSSION INSTRUMENTS

Percussion instruments are struck. Drums have a tight membrane across a frame, which the player strikes with hands, fingers, or sticks. The air inside the frame, or the frame itself, makes the vibrating membrane sound louder. Bells, cymbals, and gongs are all made from a single piece of material and vibrate as a whole when struck. Some percussion instruments, such as drums and bells, sound notes of definite pitch. But with gongs and cymbals it is difficult to place the pitch.

SEE ALSO

Dance, Music, Sound

MYTH AND LEGEND

Myths and legends are the names given to the stories that early people told about their heroes and religious beliefs and to explain the world about them.

In earlier times, when people knew little about science or nature, they explained things like how the sun rose and set or how the world began through stories called myths. Before writing was developed, myths were passed down from generation to generation by word of mouth. By studying myths, we can learn much about a people's way of life, customs, and values.

▲ In Greek legend, the magical winged stallion Pegasus was ridden by the hero Bellerophon. Pegasus later became a carrier of thunderbolts for Zeus.

HEROIC EXPLOITS

Unlike myths, which early people regarded as sacred and true, legends are folktales about the imaginary exploits of a hero. The hero often existed, but over many tellings the story became exaggerated. The earliest recorded literature in the world is the Sumerian legend *The Epic of Gilgamesh*. It was based on a real person, King Gilgamesh, who lived around 2700 B.C. However, in the legend, the hero Gilgamesh is described as being half-god.

▲ Baba Yaga is a witch in Slavic mythology who guards the gate to the Other World. She has power over animals and birds and day and night.

THE UNKNOWN EXPLAINED

All early people had their own myths to explain how natural events happened. The ancient Greeks believed that the sun was their god Apollo driving a flaming chariot across the sky each day. The ancient Egyptians believed that the sun god Ra sailed across the sky in a boat.

▲ The Japanese often placed clay figures of ferocious, warriorlike gods in holy places to frighten off the demons.

▲ The Zuni Indians of the Southwest believe that the first people came from underground and were trained by the medicine man Yanauluha to farm the land and maintain order.

CREATION MYTHS

Most early people had their own myths to explain how the world began. Many myths start with nothingness, darkness, or water. Out of this comes a god, who then starts the process of creation. According to an Indian myth, the world began when a creature shaped like a man divided into man and woman. From their marriage came the human race and, later, animals.

FAVORITE GODS

At the center of most myths was a group of people's gods. The functions of particular gods depended on what was important to the people. For instance, farming was very important to the Aztecs of Mexico and so they worshiped, among others, a group of corn gods. The gods of the seafaring Vikings were mostly concerned with war.

HOMES OF THE GODS

People's gods usually belonged to one "family." Often they looked and behaved like people. They had mythical homes, usually in the sky or on a mountaintop, as gods needed to be all-seeing. Some gods inhabited sacred groves or the sea. However, the chief god in African mythologies lived on Earth.

EPIC TALES

The Greeks and Romans also told long stories to entertain. Among them are the Greek poet Homer's epic poems about Troy—the *Iliad* and *Odyssey*. He wrote these during the 700s B.C., and they are great works of literature. Such myths have inspired artists and writers ever since.

▶ The Norse (Scandinavians) believed that giants were a constant threat to both gods and human beings. Here, Surt leads the fire giants of Muspell against the gods at Ragnarok in what would be the last battle—and the end of the world.

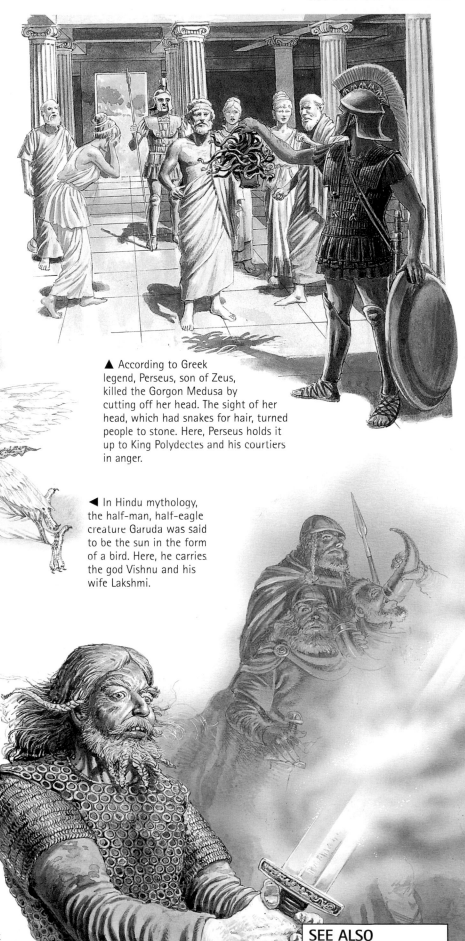

▲ According to Greek legend, Perseus, son of Zeus, killed the Gorgon Medusa by cutting off her head. The sight of her head, which had snakes for hair, turned people to stone. Here, Perseus holds it up to King Polydectes and his courtiers in anger.

◀ In Hindu mythology, the half-man, half-eagle creature Garuda was said to be the sun in the form of a bird. Here, he carries the god Vishnu and his wife Lakshmi.

SEE ALSO

Greece (ancient), Language, Literature, Mesopotamia

NAPOLEONIC WARS

The Napoleonic Wars were fought between Napoleon, ruler of France from 1799 to 1814, and his allies and other European states, such as Britain and Russia.

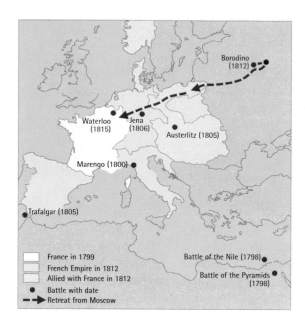

Napoleon was helped on campaigns by marshals like Michel Ney (1769–1815).

Cavalry Marshal Joachim Murat (1767–1815) became king of Naples.

Marshal Louis-Alexander Berthier (1753–1815) was chief of staff from 1805.

In 1799, General Napoleon Bonaparte (1769–1821) seized power in France. He introduced liberal freedoms and went to war with countries who opposed his rule. In 1804, he crowned himself emperor of France and crowned his wife empress.

THE CONQUEST OF EUROPE
In 1805, Napoleon defeated Austria at Ulm and Austerlitz. Prussia was defeated at Jena in 1806, and in 1807 the Russian army lost at Friedland. From 1808 to 1814, a British army fought in Portugal and Spain against a French invasion. In 1812, Napoleon invaded Russia, but was cut off by winter weather. Of his 500,000 men, only 75,000 returned. In 1814, Napoleon was forced to go into exile.

STRATEGY AND TACTICS
Napoleon tried to cut the enemy off from supplies and force them to fight where and when he chose. On the battlefield, he relied on artillery to pound the enemy before columns of infantry broke through the enemy lines, followed by cavalry to hunt fugitives. Bright uniforms helped soldiers recognize each other through the dense battlefield smoke.

DEFEAT AT WATERLOO
In 1815, Napoleon returned to France. His new army marched quickly, but was defeated by the British and Prussians at Waterloo. He was banished to the Atlantic island of St. Helena, where he died in 1821.

BATTLE OF MARENGO
Napoleon made his reputation at the Battle of Marengo in Italy on June 14, 1800. Attacked by 31,000 Austrians, Napoleon led a fierce defense by his 18,000 men until 10,000 reinforcements arrived under General Louis Desaix. Napoleon's brilliant counterattack crushed the Austrians.

SEE ALSO
France, Revolution, Warfare

NATIVE AMERICAN

Native Americans were the first people to settle the Americas, long before the discovery and settlement of those lands by Europeans.

The Tlingit lived along the northwest coast.

Navajo farmed the southwest of North America.

The Creek lived in the eastern woodland area.

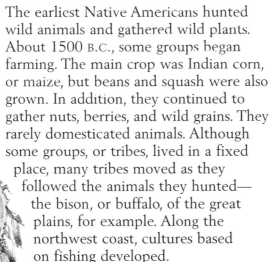

◄ The Cheyenne were one of the plains tribes. During war, the warriors were organized into seven societies, with the "dog soldiers" acting as scouts and forward troops.

Native Americans developed many different cultures and civilizations, but were overwhelmed by European invaders after the 1400s. Today they make up a minority of the American population.

EARLY ARRIVALS

Before 20,000 B.C., humans crossed into the Americas along a land bridge that stretched from eastern Asia across the Bering Strait. By about 10,000 B.C., they had spread south to the tip of South America. The Inuit of Canada and Alaska came from Asia only 3,000 to 5,000 years ago.

NATIVE CULTURES

The earliest Native Americans hunted wild animals and gathered wild plants. About 1500 B.C., some groups began farming. The main crop was Indian corn, or maize, but beans and squash were also grown. In addition, they continued to gather nuts, berries, and wild grains. They rarely domesticated animals. Although some groups, or tribes, lived in a fixed place, many tribes moved as they followed the animals they hunted— the bison, or buffalo, of the great plains, for example. Along the northwest coast, cultures based on fishing developed.

DISEASE AND MASSACRE

In 1492, Christopher Columbus sailed to America from Europe. Over the next 400 years, the European settlers spread over most of the Americas. European diseases killed many Native Americans, who had no immunity. About 80 percent of the Mandan tribe in the northern plains was killed by smallpox. Many other

▲ This thriving smoked-fish business in Wisconsin shows how traditional skills have been adapted to modern times.

CULTURES

- Arctic
- Subarctic
- Northwest coast
- California
- Plains
- Eastern woodland
- Southwest

surviving tribes were driven from their lands or killed in warfare. The last battle of the Indian Wars was fought at Wounded Knee, South Dakota in 1890.

TRIBAL LANDS

In the late 1970s, some tribes started legal battles against the U.S. federal government to try to reclaim land that had been taken from them. Today, North America is home to about 2 million Native Americans. Many still live on reservations, keeping alive their traditional cultures. Some of these remain poor, others run thriving businesses.

SEE ALSO

Canada, North America

NAVIGATION

Navigation is the science of finding the way. It is used mainly to guide ships, aircraft, and spacecraft, but can also be used for vehicles on land.

The magnetic compass was invented in China around A.D. 1000.

The backstaff helped to find latitude by measuring the height of the sun and stars.

The astrolabe was used by navigators before the invention of the sextant.

The sextant, which also determines latitude, is still in use today.

For thousands of years, ever since people began to travel by sea, navigation has been necessary. Early navigators relied on skill and guesswork, but today they are helped by satellite technology and computers.

ANCIENT ARTS

Many early people traveled for trade or war, but the first to navigate seriously were the Phoenicians and Greeks, who sailed throughout the Mediterranean from about 750 B.C. By 300 B.C., some Greeks could find latitude by studying the stars, but after the fall of the Roman Empire, most navigational skills were lost.

HENRY THE NAVIGATOR

In 1418, Prince Henry of Portugal set up a school of navigation, which made many

MODERN NAVIGATIONAL SYSTEMS

The idea of bearings from beacons is used with satellite technology. The U.S. military Geostat system has satellites in orbit around the Earth positioned so that at least two are within radio range from any place on Earth. It is claimed a soldier with a computerized, handheld receiver can find his or her position to within 6.5 ft. (2m).

The lines of latitude and longitude marked on globes and atlases can be used to pinpoint specific places. Lines of latitude show how far north or south of the equator a place is. Lines of longitude run from the North to the South Pole.

Lines of longitude

Lines of latitude

advances in exploration and navigation. The tools developed depended on compass readings and sightings of the stars and sun. Although this early equipment underwent many changes, it remained the basis of navigation until well into the 1900s.

PINPOINTING A TARGET

World War II brought a major boost to navigation. Bomber aircraft needed to find their way to a target accurately. One way was to direct two radio beams into enemy territory so they crossed over the target. Aircraft followed one beam until they found the second. Another system was based on radio beacons. By taking a bearing on two beacons, the navigator could find his position to within a few hundred yards. The system was adapted to cover shipping lanes as well as air routes, and remains in use today as a major navigational aid for boats and ships.

Signals from satellites help aircraft pinpoint their position to within 300 ft. (100m)

Navigation satellites beam radio signals to Earth. The best known program is the U.S. owned GPS (Global Positioning System)

A receiver on board uses signals from land-based radio beacons to calculate the boat's position

Radar reflectors on floating buoys warn of hidden dangers

A computer on board uses satellite radio signals to guide the boat with great accuracy

An echo sounder measures the water depth by beaming high-pitched sound waves toward the seabed

SEE ALSO

Explorer, Magnetism

NETHERLANDS, BELGIUM, AND LUXEMBOURG

The Netherlands, Belgium, and Luxembourg make up a group of countries in northwest Europe called the Low Countries. The Netherlands is also known as Holland.

BELGIUM
Area: 11,787 sq. mi. (30,528km²)
Population: 11,491,000
Capital: Brussels
Languages: Dutch, French
Currency: Euro

LUXEMBOURG
Area: 998 sq. mi. (2,586km²)
Population: 605,000
Capital: Luxembourg
Languages: French, German, Letzeburgish
Currency: Euro

NETHERLANDS
Area: 16,040 sq. mi. (41,543km²)
Population: 17,085,000
Capitals: Amsterdam; The Hague (government seat)
Language: Dutch
Currency: Euro

The name Netherlands means "lowlands" —two fifths of the country lies below sea level and the countryside is crisscrossed with canals. Half the country's freight is carried on the inland waterways. The landscape is dotted with windmills, originally built for controlling the water level. Belgium is also low-lying and mostly flat, rising to hills called the Ardennes in the south, which extend across the border into the small country of Luxembourg.

TRADE AND NEW LAND
From the 1500s, the Dutch became seafarers, growing rich from fishing and trade, and built up an empire in Southeast Asia. Rotterdam remains the world's largest port. The Dutch became experts at flood control, draining the land and reclaiming it from the sea by building dikes and using pumps. This has created rich farmland—cheese and butter are major exports.

INDUSTRIES AND CITIES
Belgium's textile industry dates back to the Middle Ages. Today, the country is a heavily industrialized nation. Luxembourg is a leading steel producer, but Belgium's steel industry is in decline. The city of Luxembourg is a major center of banking, and Luxembourg is one of the wealthiest nations in Europe. The Netherlands is densely populated—in Europe,

only the tiny states of Monaco, Vatican City, and San Marino have moe people per square mile. Amsterdam, its largest city, is the national capital, although the government sits at The Hague.

HISTORY AND HERITAGE
The Netherlands fought for freedom from Spanish rule during the 1500s. Belgium and Luxembourg were part of the Netherlands until the 1800s. These three countrics remain closely linked as members of the European Union, which has its headquarters in Brussels.

◄ Cut flowers and bulbs are important crops in the Netherlands, as well as fruit and vegetables.

SEE ALSO

Europe

NEWSPAPER AND MAGAZINE

Newspapers and magazines are publications that print international or local news, alongside comments on important events and interviews with celebrities.

People all over the world find out about events by reading newspapers and magazines. National daily and weekly newspapers carry news from around the world. Some magazines specialize in one subject, such as football or medicine.

TABLOIDS AND BROADSHEETS

The first newspapers were printed in Europe in about 1650, after the introduction of the printing press. They may be printed every day or once a week, and may concentrate on local events or cover worldwide news. Most newspapers are either tabloid, with a page size of about 11.5x14 in. (30x40cm), or broadsheet, about twice as large. Although newspapers are all different, most have similar features. Sports news is usually printed toward the end of a paper and national, political, and international news stories are at the front.

GATHERING NEWS

News is gathered by reporters who may visit events, such as political conventions and baseball games, and interview people taking part. Personalities and commercial companies often write a press release and send it to reporters to let them know about events or new products.

MAGAZINES

Magazines may be published weekly or monthly. They often feature full-color, glossy pages with in-depth interviews and features. Some magazines cover a wide range of subjects, but some can be highly specialized. They may deal with fashion, sports, or celebrities. Those which concentrate on a particular business are called "trade press." Magazines often have a long lead time (written several weeks or months in advance).

ONLINE EDITIONS

The printed press makes money from advertising as well as sales. As advertisers have switched to the Internet, most newspapers have also had to produce online editions, and some have gone all-electronic. Online news may be offered free or by paid access.

©DC Thomson, Dundee
Children's comics appeared in the late 1800s. This one started in 1937.

©DC Comics
Superheroes, popularized by DC Comics, include Wonder Woman from 1941.

©Hachette Filipacchi Presse
Magazines may concentrate on particular subjects or age groups.

Tabloids are small-size newspapers that are easier to handle.

Broadsheets are larger, with more space for lengthy articles.

Game, set, and match to Murray

▲ Using computers, newspaper designers decide on the look of a page, choosing the style of type and the size and number of pictures.

► An editor and designer discuss the content of the lead, or front, page.

◄ A photographer shows the shots she took of an event to the art editor, using an onscreen digital light box. Later, the art editor will select the best images for publication with the article.

◄ Reporters write their stories straight onto the computer network. They are cut to length by a copy editor, who also checks facts and spellings.

CREATING A NEWSPAPER

Newspapers, magazines, and books are put together on computers (desktop publishing) before they are sent to be printed. A newspaper staff includes writers, photographers, designers, and copy editors working under a chief editor.

SEE ALSO
Cartoon and animation, Design, Language, Media, Printing

NEW ZEALAND

New Zealand lies in the South Pacific, 1,180 mi.
(1,900km) southeast of its nearest neighbor, Australia.
It has two main islands, both of which are long and narrow.

Area: 103,800 sq. mi.
(268,838km²)
Population: 4,510,000
Capital: Wellington
Language: English
Currency: New Zealand
dollar

◄ Most of New
Zealand's landscape
is hilly, but there
are fertile valleys
and plains, such
as South Island's
Canterbury Plains.

▲ In the greeting *hongi*,
Maoris rub noses. Other
traditions include carving,
weaving, and tattooing.

Eighty-six percent of New Zealanders
live in towns or cities. Three quarters
of the population lives on North Island,
where it is warmest, but South Island
is the largest of the two main islands.

LANDSCAPE AND WILDLIFE
The coasts are ideal for sailing,
surfing, and fishing, and the
mountains attract many skiers.
There are active volcanoes, geysers,
and pools of bubbling mud. Because
New Zealand has been isolated from
other land masses for millions of years,
it has developed distinct native wildlife
such as the kiwi, a flightless bird, and
many different kinds of fern.

EARNING A LIVING
Farming is in decline in New Zealand
and employs just one in 14 people.
Major exports include wood and wood
products, crude oil, dairy products, meat,
and manufactured goods. Industry is
concentrated around Auckland, the largest
city. Tourism is a fast-growing business.
More than two thirds of the country's
wealth comes from the service industries.

TWO TRADITIONS
New Zealand was first settled by Maoris
from Polynesia around the late 1200s A.D.
Today, less than a fifth of the population are
Maori or of mixed Maori-European herigage.
British settlement began in 1840. Settlers
transformed the country by founding cities
and introducing cereal crops, sheep, and
cattle. Independence came in 1907, but ties
between New Zealand and Britain remain
close through trade and sports.

◄ The All Blacks is New
Zealand's national rugby
football team. It is one
of the best in the world.

SEE ALSO

Custom, Pacific Islands

NIGERIA

Nigeria is a republic on the west coast of Africa. It has a greater population than any other African country and a rich blend of cultures.

Area: 356,669 sq. mi. (923,768km²)
Population: 203,453,000
Capital: Abuja
Language: English
Currency: Naira

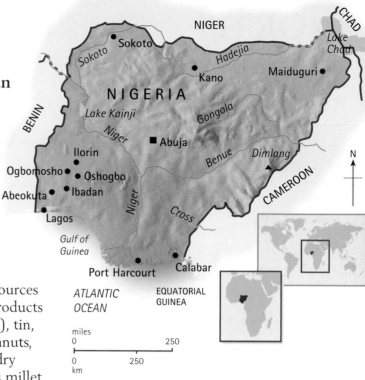

Nigeria's coastline consists of mangrove swamps. To the north of these lies a belt of dense tropical rain forest. Farther north, open woodland and savanna grassland merge into areas of semidesert.

RICH IN RESOURCES

Nigeria's most valuable natural resources are oil and gas. Other important products are palm oil (used for making soap), tin, cacao (used for making cocoa), peanuts, rubber, cotton, and timber. In the dry north, livestock and cereals such as millet and sorghum are important. In the wetter south, fish, rice, yams, and cassava are the main foods. The biggest city is the former capital Lagos, a major port and home to around 21 million people.

ARTS AND CRAFTS

Nigeria has a rich tradition in arts, music, and literature. The craftspeople of the kingdom of Benin were famous for casting fine sculptures in bronze 500 years ago. Wood carving and weaving are other traditional crafts. Nigerian authors writing in English, such as Chinua Achebe, have won fame, and in 1986, Wole Soyinka was the first African to be awarded the Nobel Prize for Literature.

NEW NATION OF OLD PEOPLES

Nigeria's boundaries were established by its British colonizers in the early 1900s. Nigeria became independent of British rule in 1960. The nation today brings together over 200 ancient tribes and kingdoms, as well as many different languages and religions. Half the people live in villages, and the rest live in towns. Half the people are Muslims who make up most of the population in the north. The other main religion is Christianity. There are more than 250 ethnic groups: the main ones are the Hausa and Fulani, living in the north, and the Yoruba and Igbo in the south.

▲ Markets are at the heart of Nigerian life. Nigeria is a democratic federation of states, with the largest population in Africa. It has become the wealthiest African nation, although many of its people remain poor.

◄ Zuma Rock dominates the landscape at Abuja. The city, which was built in 1979 to replace Lagos as the capital, is centrally located.

SEE ALSO

Africa

NORTH AMERICA

North America is the third largest of the world's seven continents and the fourth largest in population. It stretches from the Arctic Ocean to Central America.

▲ In the Canadian province of Quebec, average January temperatures range from 10°F (–12°C) to –20°F (–29°C).

KEY FACTS
- **Area:** 8,307,760 sq. mi. (21,517,000km²)
- **Population:** 567,762,000
- **Number of countries:** 23
- **Largest country:** Canada (3,851,810 sq. mi./9,976km²)
- **Smallest country:.** St. Kitts & Nevis (101 sq. mi./261km²)
- **Highest point:** Denali (20,308 ft./6,190m)
- **Largest lake:** Superior (31,796 sq. mi./82,350km²)
- **Longest river:** Mississippi-Missouri (3,740 mi./6,020kmkm²)

▼ The world's first skyscraper was built in Chicago in 1884. It no longer stands, but two other early skyscrapers, the Wrigley Building (left) and the Tribune Tower (right), are still Chicago landmarks.

The largest part of North America is made up of Canada and the United States. The rest consists of Mexico, the seven countries in Central America, and the islands in the Caribbean Sea, which include 13 independent countries and 18 overseas territories still linked to a colonial partner. The U.K. territory of Bermuda lies in the North Atlantic Ocean and is also part of North America.

LARGEST ISLAND
Greenland, in the north, is a self-governing territory linked to Denmark and is the world's largest island.

MOUNTAINS AND PLAINS
In the western half of the continent are the Rocky Mountains, the world's second-longest mountain chain. The continent's highest peak, Denali at 20,308 ft. (6,190m), is in Alaska. There are smaller mountain ranges in the east, including the Appalachians. The Canadian Shield is a huge area of ancient rock with poor soil, but it is rich in minerals. Across the center of the continent is the vast grassland region known as the prairies.

GREAT LAKES AND RIVERS
The five Great Lakes—Superior, Huron, Erie, Ontario, and Michigan—form the world's largest grouping of this kind. The thundering waters of Niagara Falls, on a strait between lakes Erie and Ontario, are an impressive spectacle. The Mississippi, Missouri, and Ohio rivers together form the continent's longest river system, at over 4,600 mi. (7,500km) long.

COLD AND HOT
North America has every kind of climate. The north has bitterly cold winters—in the Arctic regions of Canada and Alaska, it is too cold for trees to grow. In the south, huge forests of evergreen and deciduous trees cover the land. Still farther south, there are hot deserts and tropical forests.

GIANT TREES
Some of the world's tallest trees, the giant redwood and the sequoia, grow on the west coast of North America. In the eastern forests, the leaves of maple, hickory, and other deciduous trees provide a brilliant color show in the fall. Mesquite, prickly pear, and saguaro cactus grow in desert regions. ▶

NORTH AMERICA

ARCTIC OCEAN

GREENLAND
(Denmark)

KEY TO MAP
1 ST KITTS & NEVIS
2 ANTIGUA &
   BARBUDA
3 DOMINICA
4 BARBADOS
5 ST LUCIA
6 ST VINCENT &
   THE GRENADINES
7 GRENADA
8 TRINIDAD &
   TOBAGO

ALASKA
(USA)

Mt. McKinley

NORTH PACIFIC
OCEAN

YUKON
TERRITORY

Yukon

Mackenzie

ROCKY MOUNTAINS

CANADA

CANADIAN SHIELD

Hudson
Bay

GREAT PLAINS

Lake
Superior

Lake
Huron

Quebec

Ottawa

Lake Ontario

NORTH
ATLANTIC
OCEAN

Vancouver

UNITED STATES
OF AMERICA

Lake
Michigan

Lake Erie

New York

GREAT
BASIN

Chicago

CALIFORNIA

Washington D.C.

APPALACHIANS

Los Angeles

Missouri

Ohio

Mississippi

BERMUDA (UK)

Dallas

Rio Grande

MEXICO

Gulf of California

Gulf of
Mexico

BAHAMAS

DOMINICAN
REPUBLIC

PUERTO
RICO (U

CUBA

CARIBBEAN ISLANDS

PACIFIC
OCEAN

Mexico City

BELIZE

JAMAICA

HAITI

1 2
3
5
6
7

4

8

GUATEMALA

HONDURAS

CARIBBEAN
SEA

EL SALVADOR

CENTRAL AMERICA

VENEZUELA

NICARAGUA

COSTA RICA

COLOMBIA

PANAMA

miles
0 _____ 500

0 _____ 500
km

ANIMAL LIFE

Wildlife has been reduced by
hunting and settlement, so bison
(buffalo), wolves, and bears are no
longer as widespread as they once were.
There are caribou, moose, mountain
lions, wild goats, porcupines, beavers,
rattlesnakes, and alligators. Birds include
the turkey, macaw, roadrunner, and bald
eagle—the national symbol of the
United States.

FARMING

North America is rich in farmland,
and the continent is the world's biggest
grain exporter. The vast prairies have been
plowed for cereals or are used as grazing
land for cattle and sheep. Important
crops are corn, soya, cotton, wheat, and
flax. There are also plantations growing
bananas, coffee, cotton, and sugarcane, and
huge orchards of apples, oranges, cherries,
and other fruits.

▼ North American bison, also known as buffalo, graze
in Yellowstone National Park. These animals live mostly
in reserves. Their numbers have been greatly reduced by
overhunting, and strict laws now exist to protect them.

GOODS AND RESOURCES

Both Asia and Europe make more factory
goods than North America, but it is still
a major producer of vehicles, aircraft,
electronics, and chemicals. It is rich in
minerals, including silver, natural gas, oil,
copper, and coal. Some of the world's
leading companies are based here.

CITIES AND TRANSPORTATION

Most North Americans live in towns and
cities. The continent has some of the
world's largest cities, including Mexico
City, New York, and Los Angeles, where
skyscrapers form dramatic skylines and
where cars and trucks move along multilane

▲ At carnival time in Mexico, people dress in traditional costumes. Many Mexicans are of Spanish ancestry, but there are also descendants of the ancient Mayan people living in Mexico and Central America.

expressways. Many North Americans enjoy a high standard of living, but in the inner cities of the United States, and in Mexico and parts of the Caribbean, people are relatively poor.

VARIED ROOTS

North America has been a "melting pot" for people from many parts of the world. English is the main language, but French is used in parts of Canada, and Spanish is spoken in Mexico and by many people in Central America and the United States. Many North Americans have European or Asian roots. African Americans are the descendants of black people brought from Africa as slaves.

THE FIRST AMERICANS

People came to North America from Asia, before 20,000 B.C. and settled across the continent. They were hunters, some of whom, over the ages, became farmers and town-builders. Another group was the ancestors of the Inuit people, who settled in the far north. The Maya and Aztecs of Mexico created civilizations of which impressive ruins still remain.

EUROPEANS ARRIVE

Vikings came to North America more than 1,000 years ago but did not settle for long. In 1492, the explorer Christopher Columbus "discovered" the American continent, which soon became known as the New World. He was followed by explorers from Spain, who came seeking gold. From the 1600s, the British and French settled in Canada and along the east coast. Spain ruled Mexico, Florida, and Central America. Canada and Mexico became independent in the 1800s.

THE UNITED STATES

The United States was created in 1776, when the 13 colonies broke away from Britain. It rapidly grew into an industrial giant. Native Americans were driven from their lands as settlers moved west across the Great Plains and reached the Pacific coast. Immigrants from Africa, Europe, Asia, and Central America have helped shape the modern United States.

▲ Sequoias, growing on North America's west coast, are some of the world's tallest trees.

◀ Grenada is one of 13 independent island nations in the Caribbean. Its capital, St. George's, lies on the southwest coast among forested hills.

SEE ALSO

Aztec, Caribbean, Canada, Central America, Explorer, Maya, Mexico, Native American, Slavery, United States of America, Viking

NUCLEAR POWER

Nuclear power is the generation of electricity using heat released by changes in the nuclei of atoms. The process is known as a controlled nuclear reaction.

Lise Meitner (1878–1968) proved that heavy atoms can be split into lighter ones—a process she called "nuclear fission."

Otto Hahn (1879–1968) worked with Meitner to split the atom, for which he was awarded the 1944 Nobel Prize for Chemistry.

Enrico Fermi (1901–54) built the first nuclear reactor in a squash court in 1942 and later worked on the atomic bomb project.

The center of an atom is called the nucleus. Radioactive elements, such as uranium, have nuclei which sometimes split, releasing energy including heat. When these nuclei split, they throw out two or three tiny particles called neutrons. These can hit other nuclei, making them split, shooting out more neutrons.

AN IDEAL FUEL?

Compared to coal, oil, or gas, very small amounts of uranium can make a lot of electricity, and it does not pollute the air with chemicals or solids. Nuclear power generation is a low emitter of carbon waste, but the nuclear cycle as a whole is not.

▲ The mushroom cloud from a nuclear explosion is made up of particles of rock, soil, water, and other materials that eventually fall back to Earth as radioactive "fall-out."

THE NUCLEAR AGE

The world's first nuclear power station opened at Calder Hall, in the U.K., in 1956. This plant, and some of its successors, offered plutonium for the nuclear weapons programme, as well as a cheap source of power. Nuclear power still plays a major role globally, but today, some industrial nations such as Germany are turning away from nuclear power.

NEW DIRECTIONS

Scientists are researching nuclear fusion, which releases energy by joining atomic nuclei together rather than splitting them apart. Nuclear power costs are rising rapidly but renewable technology such as wind and solar power are becoming cheaper.

NUCLEAR HAZARDS

Terrible nuclear accidents have occurred, as at Chernobyl in the former Soviet Union in 1986 and at Fukushima, Japan, in 2011. Also, the problems of storing radioactive waste safely for thousands of years are huge.

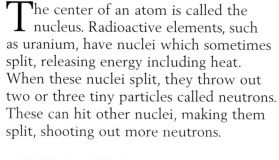

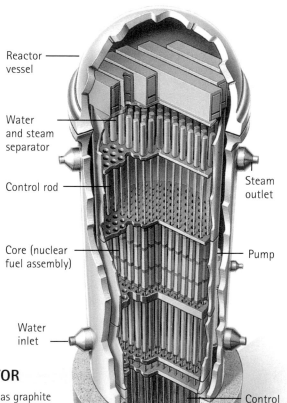

Reactor vessel

Water and steam separator

Control rod

Core (nuclear fuel assembly)

Water inlet

Steam outlet

Pump

Control rod drive

Concrete shield

THE NUCLEAR REACTOR

In a reactor, a moderator such as graphite or water is used to slow down the neutrons released from fuel rods containing uranium. Slowed neutrons are much better at splitting other uranium atoms, causing a sustained chain reaction that releases huge amounts of heat. Control rods stop the reaction going too fast by absorbing neutrons. The heat boils water into steam, which turns turbines to make electricity.

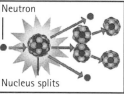

Neutron

Nucleus splits

▲ In nuclear fission, neutrons are used to split heavy atoms, such as those in uranium, which in turn release more free neutrons and energy.

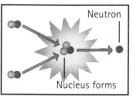

Neutron

Nucleus forms

▲ In nuclear fusion, two nuclei of a lightweight substance such as hydrogen combine to form heavier ones, releasing a further neutron and energy.

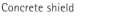

SEE ALSO

Atom and molecule, Electricity, Energy, Submarine, World War II

NUTRITION

Nutrition is the process by which we take in and use food. Chemical substances found in food, called nutrients, provide energy and help the body function.

▲ A Sudanese mother in a refugee camp shows all the food she has to feed her family. Lack of food can result in malnutrition and lowered resistance to disease.

Fruits and vegetables are rich in vitamins. We should eat five portions each day.

Carbohydrate foods contain natural sugars and starches for energy.

Fats can be animal (butter, milk, cheese) or vegetable— from plants and nuts.

Meat, fish, cheese, and pulses and nuts are sources of protein.

There are five important nutrients—carbohydrates, proteins, fats (in small quantities), vitamins, and minerals. In addition, we cannot live without water.

ENERGY AND GROWTH

Carbohydrates and fats provide the body with energy. Proteins are necessary for growth and repair of cells. Vitamins and minerals like calcium, potassium, and iron are essential for the health of nerves, skin, bones, muscles, and brain. Research has shown that eating food rich in vitamins A, C, E, and beta-carotene can help protect against the cell damage that causes cancer.

FIBER AND WATER

Fiber, the indigestible part of fruits and vegetables, is essential in the diet. It adds bulk to food and helps it move through the large intestine during digestion. Water

A BALANCED DIET

A healthy meal can take many forms. Most national diets are based on locally grown produce, animals or fish, and a traditional staple food that is usually starchy and relatively cheap, such as rice, bread, or pasta.

is vital. The human body is made up of about 65 percent water. Its cells need water to keep chemical reactions going. We need about 3.5 pt. (2 l) of water a day.

A BALANCED DIET

The energy value of food is measured in calories. The more work your body does, the more calories you need. A man needs, on average, 2,555 calories a day and a woman 1,925; a 16-year-old boy needs 2,755 calories a day and a girl 2,110.

FOOD SHORTAGES

Many people do not get enough to eat. Malnutrition (not getting sufficient nutrients) causes weakness and disease. Around 20 million people die each year from hunger-related causes, more than six million of whom are under five years old.

▼ Pasta is a good energy source; adding cheese increases protein. Tomato sauce provides vitamin C.

▼ The traditional Thanksgiving dinner in America is a well-balanced meal— unless you eat too much!

◀ Research shows the Japanese diet is especially beneficial to long-term health. Tofu (bean curd) contains protein, calcium, and other minerals. Raw fish is used to make sushi.

◀ A healthy meal in one bowl. In parts of West Africa, meat, beans, and nuts are mixed in a stew (gumbo), along with yam, a root vegetable.

▶ Many of our most popular foods originally come from South America.

▲ Fresh, raw vegetables are simply prepared in hot countries like Australia. Broiling meat reduces fat.

SEE ALSO

Farming, Food, Fruit, Vegetable

OCEAN AND SEA

Seventy-one percent of the Earth's surface is covered by water. Nearly all of this vast area is made up of saltwater oceans and seas.

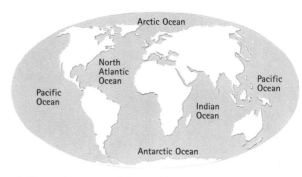

▲ The main oceans of the world cover more than two thirds of the Earth's surface.

The Earth's crust is of two types: dense oceanic crust and lighter continental crust. The continental crust forms the great land masses of the Earth, and these, being relatively light, stand high above the general level of the Earth's surface. The water-filled hollows that lie between the continents are called oceans.

OCEAN FOUNDATIONS

The ocean floor is made of denser crustal material, which is constantly being created and destroyed through the process of plate tectonics. Along each ocean lies a volcanic ridge, forming a vast underwater network that encircles the Earth. This is where new crustal material is generated. The old material is destroyed along the edges of some of the oceans as one crustal plate is drawn down and swallowed up beneath the edge of another.

OCEAN FEATURES

This movement creates the basic features of an ocean: the oceanic ridge, which can rise to about 3,000 ft. (1,000m) beneath the surface; the abyssal plains, the greatest area of ocean floor, on average

16,500–20,000 ft. (5,000–6,000m) deep; and the oceanic trenches, many over 30,000 ft. (9,000m) deep, with the deepest—the Marianas Trench—plunging to nearly 36,000 ft. (11,000m).

THE SOFT COVERING

The sediments of the ocean floor consist of tiny skeletons and shells, volcanic dust, and mud that has washed off the land. Sediments close to oceanic ridges are thin, but thicker farther away. This is because the new ocean crust close to the ridges has not had enough time to collect much debris.

SHALLOW SEAS

Seas differ from oceans in that they are much shallower. They are the areas of the continents that happen to be below sea level—the continents' flooded edges. Sea floors tend to be thickly covered in sediment, such as sand and mud, brought

High spring tides are caused by the combined gravitational pull of the Sun and Moon when they are in line with the Earth. This occurs at the full Moon and new Moon.

Weak neap tides occur during the Moon's first and third quarters, when the gravitational forces of the Sun and Moon are at right angles and their combined force is less.

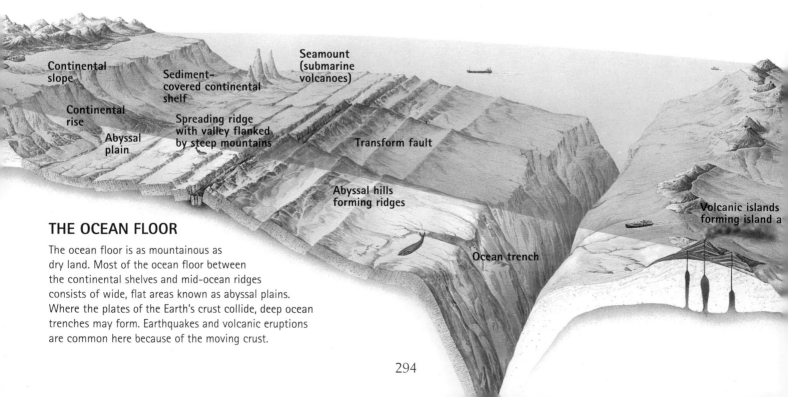

Continental slope

Continental rise

Abyssal plain

Sediment-covered continental shelf

Spreading ridge with valley flanked by steep mountains

Seamount (submarine volcanoes)

Transform fault

Abyssal hills forming ridges

Ocean trench

Volcanic islands forming island a

THE OCEAN FLOOR

The ocean floor is as mountainous as dry land. Most of the ocean floor between the continental shelves and mid-ocean ridges consists of wide, flat areas known as abyssal plains. Where the plates of the Earth's crust collide, deep ocean trenches may form. Earthquakes and volcanic eruptions are common here because of the moving crust.

down by the rivers. Some seas do not lie on the continental shelf but are inland. The Caspian Sea is completely landlocked, and the Black Sea is only narrowly connected to the Mediterranean Sea. The Red Sea is an oddity—although it is small and almost landlocked, its floor is true oceanic crust and it has a central ridge.

LIVING THINGS

Most ocean life is found within a layer of water about 300 ft. (100m) deep, where sunlight penetrates. Plankton is the mass of tiny plants and animals that drifts in the sea and is the basis of the entire ocean food chain. All sea creatures depend directly on plankton for food, or on animals that feed on plankton. Planktonic plants

MARINE LIFE

Life-forms in the ocean are more varied than those on land. New creatures are often discovered in the deep sea. **1** Herring **2** Sperm whale **3** Shrimp **4** Kat-tail **5** Anglerfish **6** Grenadier **7** Cod **8** Gulper eel **9** Sea spider, tube worms, clam, white ghost crab **10** Tripod fish **11** Viperfish **12** Swallower **13** Lanternfish **14** Swordfish **15** Yellowfin tuna **16** Giant squid **17** Hammerhead **18** Barracuda **19** Portuguese man-of-war **20** Plankton **21** Green turtle **22** Sea lion **23** Common dolphin

(*phytoplankton*) grow here and also planktonic animals (*zooplankton*), which include one-celled animals, baby crabs, and fish. Larger creatures feed upon these animals, and even larger predators feed upon them in turn. The final link in the food chain is humans—the sea provides a source of food for much of the world's population.

MYSTERIOUS DEPTHS

Although the oceans have been traveled by many generations, the sea retains its mystery. It has been the source of many legends, including the mermaid and the sea serpent, and has inspired artists throughout the centuries. Scuba divers and scientists in submersibles are still learning about the sea, studying its creatures and geological features, and discovering submerged cities and shipwrecks.

ATOLLS

An atoll begins as a coral reef surrounding a volcanic island. As the island sinks, the reef grows upward. Eventually, the island disappears completely, and all that remains is a ring-shaped reef, or atoll, surrounding a lagoon.

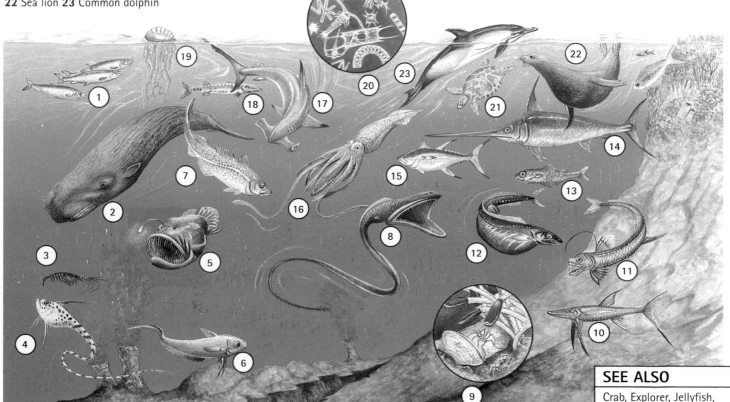

SEE ALSO

Crab, Explorer, Jellyfish, River, Seashore, Shark, Snail, Starfish, Swamp and marsh, Water

OIL

Oil, or petroleum, is a thick, black liquid, sometimes called crude oil. It is a valuable raw material for fuels such as gasoline, and in the chemical industry.

OTHER OIL SOURCES

Animal and vegetable sources provide us with different kinds of oil and oil products.

Animal fats, such as pig lard, are used for cooking.

Vitamin-rich cod liver oil is used in medicine.

Most of the world's olive crop is grown for its oil.

Oil from sunflower seeds is used to make margarine.

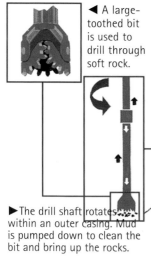

◄ A large-toothed bit is used to drill through soft rock.

► The drill shaft rotates within an outer casing. Mud is pumped down to clean the bit and bring up the rocks.

Oil is a complex mixture of chemical compounds consisting of the elements hydrogen and carbon. These hydrocarbons release heat when they burn. This is what makes them useful as fuels.

THE ORIGINS OF OIL

The story of oil began millions of years ago, with plants and animals that lived in the ancient seas. After they died, the bodies of these plants and animals decayed and gradually turned into oil. The oil has remained trapped in rocks ever since. Like coal and gas, oil is a fossil fuel.

FINDING OIL

The search for oil is called oil exploration. Crude oil is always found in certain patterns of rock, so geologists look for

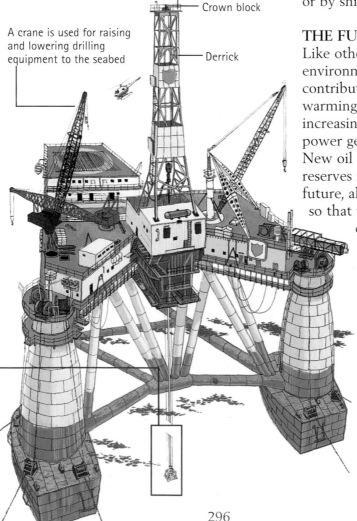

— Crown block

A crane is used for raising and lowering drilling equipment to the seabed

— Derrick

► In a refinery, parts, or fractions, of the crude oil are separated out in a process called fractional distillation. Fuels such as kerosene and gasoline are made by mixing these fractions. Other fractions are sent to chemical plants to be made into drugs, paints, plastics, and other products.

these patterns in areas where oil is likely to be found. They use magnetic and seismic surveys (which send sounds from explosions at ground level to bounce off rocks underground) to find rock formations that may contain oil.

DRILLING FOR OIL

To get the oil out, a hole is drilled down through the rocks. This is an oil well. The most expensive method is using oil rigs at sea (offshore), although onshore drilling is also common. The oil is sent by pipeline or by ship to an oil refinery for processing.

THE FUTURE OF OIL

Like other fossil fuels, oil pollutes the environment when it is burned. It also contributes to acid rain and to global warming. The modern world uses increasing amounts of oil for automobiles, power generation, heating, and industry. New oil finds are being made, but known reserves may have run out by 2060. In the future, alternative fuels will be needed so that the world's oil reserves do not completely run out.

OFFSHORE DRILLING

It is more dangerous to work on an offshore oil rig than a land rig because storms can damage the structure. It also costs about ten times more to build. The rig itself has to be floated out to sea in sections and then assembled; the equipment and crew are carried out to the site by helicopter. Because of the huge expense involved, several test drillings are done to make sure that there are enough oil reserves to justify the cost of setting up a permanent rig.

SEE ALSO

Coal, Gas, Medicine, Mining, Plastic, Pollution

OLYMPIC GAMES

The Olympic Games are a world athletic and sports competition that takes place every four years. About 208 nations enter competitors in about 28 different sports.

The first modern Olympic Games were opened by King George I of Greece in Athens on April 5, 1896. They were a huge success, but it took several attempts to get them established as a successful global event. The modern Olympics were inspired by the ancient Olympic Games, which were first held in Olympia, Greece in 776 B.C.

OLYMPIC SPIRIT

The aim of the Olympic Games is to promote peace, equality, and friendship and to inspire athletes around the world. Competition between individuals rather than countries is encouraged, and on the scoreboard at every Olympic Games is the message: "The most important thing in the Olympic Games is not to win but to take part…."

▲ The ancient Olympians, such as this discus thrower, competed naked.

FAST FACTS

• Since 1896, only five countries have been at all the Games: Australia, France, Greece, Great Britain, and Switzerland

• The marathon used to be 25 miles, but in the 1908 London Games it was extended to over 26 miles so that Princess Mary could see it start from the nursery window at Windsor Castle

• The Beijing Games' opening ceremony began at 8 P.M., on August 8, 2008. The number 8 means prosperity in Chinese culture.

• Newer Olympic sports include tae kwondo and the triathlon (introduced for Sydney 2000) and women's boxing (introduced for London 2012).

▲ The Olympic symbol of five linked rings represents the five continents of Africa, Asia, Australia, Europe, and North America. It was designed so that at least one of the six colors in the symbol (including the white background) would appear in all the flags of the competing nations.

OPENING CEREMONY

At every Olympic opening ceremony, a parade of nations is led by Greece, the founder nation, with the host country coming last and the nations in between appearing in alphabetical order. During the celebrations, the athletes and officials take the Olympic oath, the Olympic torch is lit, and the Olympic flag raised. As a sign of peace, doves are released into the stadium. ▶

THE 2016 RIO GAMES

The 2016 Summer Olympics were held in Rio de Janeiro and other cities in Brazil, the first South American nation to host the Games. Over 11,000 athletes competed, including a team representing refugees. Sports featured for the first time included golf and rugby sevens. Brazil is the land of carnival, and the games opened to the sound of the samba beat and a riot of color.

▲ U.S. athlete Jesse Owens became the star of the 1936 Games at Berlin, Germany, when he won four gold medals. In the face of Nazi propaganda for white superiority, Owens's victory was a huge embarrassment for Nazi officials.

▲ Almaz Ayana of Ethiopia was a star of the Rio de Janeiro Olympics in 2016, competing in the 5,000 and 10,000 metres, in which she won a gold medal and broke the world record.

THE OLYMPIC TORCH
Four weeks before the start of the Games, the Olympic flame is lit in Greece by magnifying the sun's rays with mirrors. It is then carried across the world in a torch by a series of runners. On the opening day of the Games, the last runner enters the stadium and the arena flame is lit. It stays burning until the close of the Games.

THE ANCIENT GAMES
The ancient Olympic Games were first organized as a religious, sporting, and cultural festival held in honor of Zeus, the ruler of the Greek gods. Every four years, Greek athletes traveled from all over the country to Olympia, a sanctuary in the region of Elis in southern Greece. Only Greek citizens could compete, although no women were allowed to take part in or even watch the Games on pain of death. The Games were taken so seriously that a truce between any warring states within Greece was called so that competitors could travel safely to Olympia.

BANNING OF THE GAMES
At the first ancient Olympic Games, in 776 B.C., there was only one event, a 200m stadium race. Gradually, more events were added, including chariot racing in 680 B.C. The Games were finally banned in A.D. 394 by the Roman emperor Theodosius. The Romans had conquered Greece, and Theodosius banned all pagan festivals, including the Olympic Games.

THE WINTER OLYMPICS
The modern Olympics fall into two parts: the Winter and the Summer Olympics. The first Winter Olympics were held in Chamonix, France, in 1924. Until 1994, they were always held in the same year as the Summer Olympics but they are now held two years earlier. Winter Olympic sports include ice hockey, luge (small sled), skating, skiing, and bobsled.

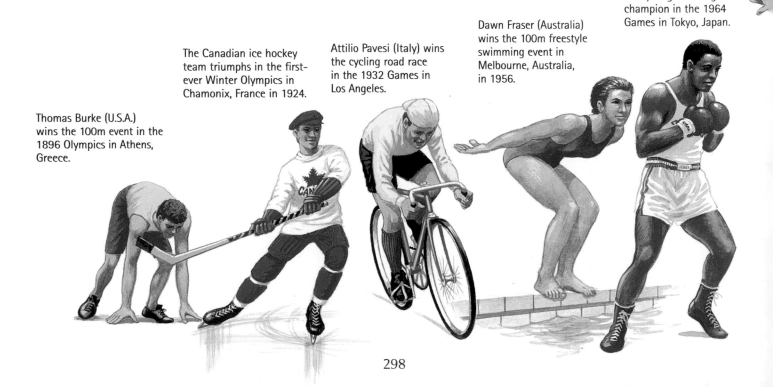

Thomas Burke (U.S.A.) wins the 100m event in the 1896 Olympics in Athens, Greece.

The Canadian ice hockey team triumphs in the first-ever Winter Olympics in Chamonix, France in 1924.

Attilio Pavesi (Italy) wins the cycling road race in the 1932 Games in Los Angeles.

Dawn Fraser (Australia) wins the 100m freestyle swimming event in Melbourne, Australia, in 1956.

Joe Frazier (U.S.A.) is heavyweight boxing champion in the 1964 Games in Tokyo, Japan.

THE SUMMER OLYMPICS

The Summer Olympics include hundreds of events across 28 sports (33 sports are planned for the 2020 Games). Combat sports include judo and boxing; ball games include volleyball and handball; court games include tennis and badminton; and water sports include rowing and swimming. Athletics is classified as one sport in the Olympics, but includes nearly 50 events, including 24 track events. As well as running events, athletics includes the high jump and long jump, the discus and javelin, and the decathlon (ten athletic events spread over two days).

POLITICAL PROBLEMS

Because the Olympic Games are the world's greatest sporting event, they have sometimes been used as a political tool. In 1972, Israeli competitors were attacked and killed by Arab terrorists at the Olympics in Munich, Germany. Eight years later, the Games in Moscow were boycotted by the United States and its allies because of the Soviet invasion of Afghanistan. In 1984, the Soviet Union and its allies refused to compete in the Olympics in Los Angeles because of fears over security arrangements.

TODAY'S GAMES

The Olympic Games are considered to be the ultimate sporting event and attract athletes from all over the world. The opening ceremony of the 2012 London Olympics was watched by 900 million television viewers worldwide. The 2020 Olympics are due to be held in Tokyo, Japan. The 2024 Games will be in Paris, France, while the 2028 Games will be in Los Angeles.

▲ The Paralympics is a competition for disabled competitors. It is separate from, and held after, the main Olympics, although it takes place in the Olympic stadium and is no less competitive. Here, the 4 x 400m wheelchair relay event at Atlanta was won by the German team.

Fourteen-year-old Nadia Comaneci (Romania) is gold medalist in the combined athletics event in the 1976 Games in Montreal, Canada.

Steffi Graf (Germany) wins the women's tennis singles event in the 1988 Games held in Seoul, South Korea.

Jan Zelezny (Czech Republic) wins the javelin event in the 1996 Games in Atlanta.

Sprinter Usain Bolt (Jamaica) competes in 2008 (Beijing), 2012 (London) and 2016 (Rio de Janeiro). He wins a total of eight gold medals.

SEE ALSO

Greece (ancient), Sports

PACIFIC ISLANDS

Before the 1960s, most of the islands in the Pacific Ocean were ruled by Britain, the United States, or France. There are now 13 independent countries.

 FIJI
Area: 7,055 sq. mi. (18,272km²)
Population: 921,000
Capital: Suva
Languages: English, Fijian
Currency: Fiji dollar

 KIRIBATI
Area: 313 sq. mi. (811km²)
Population: 109,000
Capital: Bairiki
Languages: English, Gilbertese
Currency: Australian dollar

 MARSHALL ISLANDS
Area: 70 sq. mi. (181km²)
Population: 75,000
Capital: Majuro
Languages: Marshallese, English
Currency: U.S. dollar

The Pacific Islands are part of a vast region called Oceania (which also includes Australia). Some of the islands are the mountainous tips of volcanoes, and others are coral islands that rest on the tops of sunken volcanoes.

ISLAND GROUPS

The Pacific Islands are divided into three areas. Melanesia, meaning "black islands" after the dark skin of the people, includes Fiji, Papua New Guinea, and the Solomon Islands. Micronesia, meaning "tiny islands," includes part of Kiribati, the Federated States of Micronesia, and several island groups associated with the United States. Polynesia, meaning "many islands," includes the islands in a triangle formed by New Zealand, Hawaii, and Easter Island.

 FEDERATED STATES OF MICRONESIA
Area: 271 sq. mi. (701km²)
Population: 104,000
Capital: Palikir
Language: English
Currency: U.S. dollar

 NAURU
Area: 8 sq. mi. (21km²)
Population: 9,600
Capital: Yaren
Language: Nauruan
Currency: Australian dollar

 NEW ZEALAND
Area: 103,800 sq. mi. (268,838km²)
Population: 4,510,000
Capital: Wellington
Language: English
Currency: N.Z. dollar

 PALAU
Area: 177 sq. mi. (458km²)
Population: 21,400
Capital: Koror
Languages: Palauan, English
Currency: U.S. dollar

 PAPUA NEW GUINEA
Area: 182,700 sq. mi. (462,840km²)
Population: 7,027,000
Capital: Port Moresby
Language: English
Currency: Kina

 SAMOA
Area: 1,093 sq. mi. (2,831km²)
Population: 201,000
Capital: Apia
Languages: Samoan, English
Currency: Tala

SOLOMON ISLANDS
Area: 11,157 sq. mi. (28,896km²)
Population: 660,000
Capital: Honiara
Language: English
Currency: Solomon Islands dollar

 TONGA
Area: 289 sq. mi. (748km²)
Population: 107,000
Capital: Nukualofa
Languages: English, Tongan
Currency: Pa'anga

TUVALU
Area: 9 sq. mi. (24km²)
Population: 11,000
Capital: Funafuti
Languages: Tuvaluan, English
Currency: Australian dollar

VANUATU
Area: 4,707 sq. mi. (12,190km²)
Population: 283,000
Capital: Port-Vila
Languages: Bislama, English, French
Currency: Vatu

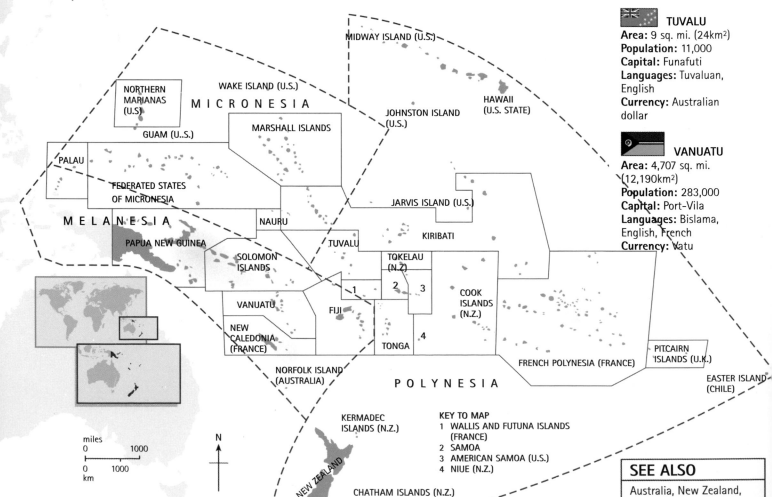

MIDWAY ISLAND (U.S.)

NORTHERN MARIANAS (U.S)
WAKE ISLAND (U.S.)
MICRONESIA
JOHNSTON ISLAND (U.S.)
HAWAII (U.S. STATE)
GUAM (U..S.)
MARSHALL ISLANDS
PALAU
FEDERATED STATES OF MICRONESIA
MELANESIA
NAURU
JARVIS ISLAND (U.S.)
PAPUA NEW GUINEA
KIRIBATI
SOLOMON ISLANDS
TUVALU
TOKELAU (N.Z.)
1
2
3
COOK ISLANDS (N.Z.)
VANUATU
FIJI
4
NEW CALEDONIA (FRANCE)
TONGA
PITCAIRN ISLANDS (U.K.)
FRENCH POLYNESIA (FRANCE)
NORFOLK ISLAND (AUSTRALIA)
POLYNESIA
EASTER ISLAND (CHILE)

miles
0   1000
0   1000
km

N

KERMADEC ISLANDS (N.Z.)

KEY TO MAP
1 WALLIS AND FUTUNA ISLANDS (FRANCE)
2 SAMOA
3 AMERICAN SAMOA (U.S.)
4 NIUE (N.Z.)

NEW ZEALAND

CHATHAM ISLANDS (N.Z.)

SEE ALSO
Australia, New Zealand, United States of America

PAINT AND DYE

Paint is a coloring which is used to cover a surface, usually to protect or decorate it. A dye is a substance that sinks into the material, coloring it inside and out.

Paints and dyes were traditionally produced in small batches from natural substances such as ocher, fruits, or flowers. Today, most are mass-produced in factories.

▶ Pigment gives paint its color. Today's pigments are usually made from chemicals, but artists often grind their own paints by hand.

▲ In textile dyeing, the cloth is immersed in the dyeing solution and the temperature is raised until enough dye has moved out of the solution and into the cloth fibers.

INSIDE PAINT
Paint is usually applied as a liquid. It dries by evaporation and forms a thin layer. It consists of a liquid—called a binder or medium—which may be water, an oil, or a resin and a solid—the pigment which gives paint its color. Chemicals are often added to improve the paint. They may prevent the paint from becoming solid in the can, or make the paint resistant to damage from exposure to the sun or frost once applied. Buildings or furniture may be treated with paints that, in the event of fire, break down chemically to slow up the spread of the flames.

◀ In 1856, English chemist William Perkin accidentally invented the world's first artificial chemical dye, a mauve derived from coal-tar waste.

USING DYES
Dyes are used to color plastics and paper as well as textiles. They usually need a fixative, or mordant, to help them penetrate fibers and stay in them. Most mordants are chemical solutions of metal salts. Until the 1850s, dyes were derived from natural substances such as leaves and berries. Indigo, a plant, was used to dye cloth blue, the cheapest color, usually worn by laborers in 18th-century France. By 1880, chemists had learned how to make an artificial indigo. Nowadays, almost all dyes are industrially produced. To make sure the color is even, the material being dyed must not resist the dye, and it must be moved continually during dyeing.

MAKING PAINT
In the first stage of making paint, oils, resins, and solvents (thinners) are blended together. Colored pigment is then added, and the mixture is ground in a ball mill until the paint is thoroughly mixed.

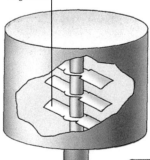

Oil and resin are blended together

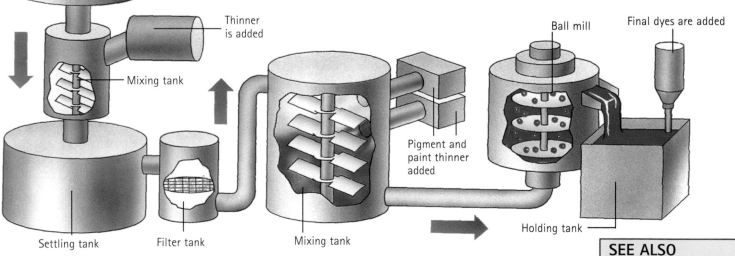

Thinner is added

Mixing tank

Settling tank

Filter tank

Mixing tank

Pigment and paint thinner added

Ball mill

Final dyes are added

Holding tank

SEE ALSO
Color, Textile

PAPER

Paper is a material made from plant fibers that are webbed together to form sheets. It is used for many different purposes, including writing and packaging.

Waxed paper can be used to make cartons for holding liquids.

Filter paper is used inside cars to stop grit from entering the engine.

Furnishings such as lampshades and wallpaper can be made from paper.

Paper is used for communication—it can be printed or written on.

Paper is used to mop up liquids, both in industry and in the home.

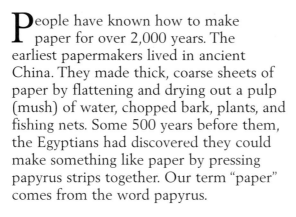

People have known how to make paper for over 2,000 years. The earliest papermakers lived in ancient China. They made thick, coarse sheets of paper by flattening and drying out a pulp (mush) of water, chopped bark, plants, and fishing nets. Some 500 years before them, the Egyptians had discovered they could make something like paper by pressing papyrus strips together. Our term "paper" comes from the word papyrus.

STRONG FIBERS

Like ancient Chinese paper, modern paper is made from a pulp, but most of it contains shredded, softened wood from coniferous trees such as pine, spruce, or fir. The fibers in wood, or any other plant, are made of a strong material called cellulose. This makes the paper very strong, so that it does not fall apart easily when pressed, folded, or stretched.

MAKING PAPER TODAY

In a papermaking machine, wood chips are boiled with sodium hydroxide or another chemical to soften them and strip them of everything but their long, stringy fibers. This pulp is spread over a conveyor belt, blasted with air, then squeezed between rollers to turn it into dry paper.

DIFFERENT SOURCES

Over the years, people have experimented with cellulose from sources other than wood. Paper currency and expensive writing paper often contain fibers from cotton rags, which are made from cotton plants. The fibers make the paper very smooth and tough.

WASTE PAPER

On average, every person in the United States uses about 750 lb. (510kg) of paper a year. Around 70 percent of the paper we use is recycled to make newspapers, toilet paper, and other low-quality papers. The rest is dumped in landfill sites.

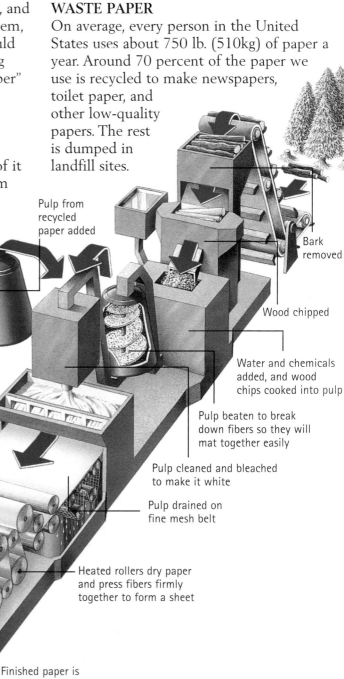

Pulp from recycled paper added

Bark removed

Wood chipped

Water and chemicals added, and wood chips cooked into pulp

Pulp beaten to break down fibers so they will mat together easily

Pulp cleaned and bleached to make it white

Pulp drained on fine mesh belt

Heated rollers dry paper and press fibers firmly together to form a sheet

Finished paper is wound onto reel

SEE ALSO

Conservation, Egypt (ancient)

PHILIPPINES

The Republic of the Philippines is a country in the southwest Pacific Ocean, off the coast of mainland Asia. It is made up of a total of 7,641 islands.

Area: 115,860 sq. mi. (300,076km²)
Population: 104,256,000
Capital: Manila
Languages: Filipino, English
Currency: Peso

The Philippines lie in one of the most violent geological zones, the "ring of fire," where there are many volcanoes. The dormant volcano Mount Apo (9,692 ft./ 2,954m) is the country's highest peak. The two largest islands are Luzon and Mindanao. Off the northeast coast of Mindanao is one of the deepest points in the Pacific, the Philippine Trench, reaching 34,580 ft. (10,540m) below the surface at Galathea Depth. The climate is tropical, with monsoon rains in July and August.

FORESTS AND FARMING
Forests cover a quarter of the land. The fiber from kapok trees is used for insulation, and bamboo provides a useful building material. With many trees being felled for timber, deforestation is a problem. In the fertile soil, farmers grow rice, corn, cassava, sweet potatoes, sugarcane, and abaca (Manila hemp). The seas provide fish, clams, and shrimp.

▲ Just over a third of the people live in rural areas, and many are farmers. The carabao, a type of water buffalo, is used to pull plows and haul loads.

▲ Gold is one of the Philippines' valuable resources. The country also has large reserves of copper, chromium, nickel, oil, and natural gas.

BOOMING CITY
Manila, founded in 1571, grew from a collection of shore villages into a teeming metropolis. It symbolizes the country's growth as an industrial nation. More than 21.3 million people live in metropolitan Manila. It is a busy port. Factories make clothing and electronic goods for export.

THE FILIPINOS
The people of the Philippines, Filipinos, are related to Malays. Chinese, Europeans, Indians, Japanese, and mountain people called Negritos also live there. Catholicism has been the main religion since the Spanish arrived on islands in 1565. The islands are named after Prince Philip II of Spain. They were ruled by the U.S. after 1898, invaded by Japan during World War II (1939–45), and became independent in 1946.

◄ Around 45 percent of the population is under 20 years old. Basketball is the country's national sport.

SEE ALSO
Asia, Volcano, World War II

PHOTOGRAPHY

Photography is the process of capturing images by focusing light onto a light-sensitive surface using a camera. Digital cameras use electronic light detectors.

Louis Daguerre produced the first successful photographs with his prototype camera.

The first popular camera by Kodak had an internal box to hold the film. The lens was part of the case.

A Polaroid camera takes a picture, develops the negative, and makes a print inside the camera.

The IXUS camera stores picture data on film, making it easy to improve the quality of prints.

▶ Julia Margaret Cameron's *The Parting of Sir Lancelot and Queen Guinevere* (1860s) is an example of early art photography. Cameron often posed her subjects as characters from stories.

Long ago in ancient China and ancient Greece, as well as in Arabia and medieval Europe, people described how an image could be made on the wall of a darkened room by letting light through a tiny hole in the opposite wall. This was called a *camera obscura*, meaning dark chamber. Apart from sketching it by hand, there was no way of recording the image until the 1700s, when the British scientists Sir Humphry Davy (1778–1829) and Thomas Wedgwood (1771–1805) caught outlines of leaves and faces on paper or leather coated with light-sensitive silver chloride.

THE FIRST PHOTOGRAPHS

The first photographs, called heliograms, were made in the 1820s by the French doctor Joseph Niépce (1765–1833) on bitumen-coated pewter plates using a camera obscura. In the 1830s, the French painter Louis Daguerre (1787–1851) made photographs on plates coated with light-sensitive silver iodide. The British inventor William Fox Talbot (1800–77) found a way to "fix" the silver iodide permanently so that it would not react to light and darken after a picture was taken. He also invented a process that made it possible to make many copies of one photograph.

PHOTOGRAPHY FOR EVERYONE

Photography was a complex procedure until 1889, when the American George Eastman (1854–1932) invented roll film and the small box camera. It soon became a hobby that any amateur could take up. More technical advances, such as the invention of flashbulbs and color film in the 1930s, led to the growing popularity of photography as it is enjoyed today.

▲ Lewis Hine captured the poverty-stricken conditions that many immigrant families in the United States endured during the early 1900s.

PHOTOJOURNALISM

Journalists quickly learned that a good photograph could often tell a story with more impact than written words. The first British war correspondent, Roger Fenton (1819–69), began taking battlefield photographs of the Crimean War in the 1850s. In the 1860s, the American Matthew Brady (1823–96) captured the grim reality of the U.S. Civil War.

SOCIAL REALISM

American sociologist Lewis Hine (1874–1940) was one of the first to use photography to show the terrible living conditions of poor people. His striking portraits of children at work in factories and mills helped to change child labor laws. Modern photojournalists often risk their lives to take pictures of war-torn countries or to reveal injustices in society.

ART PHOTOGRAPHY

Some early photographers used the principles of painting in their photographs. In the 1860s, the British photographer Julia Margaret Cameron (1815–79) created stunning portraits using blur and soft focus. The French photographer Nadar (1820–1910) captured many Paris intellectuals and artists, encouraging them to pose naturally. In the 1920s, the American photographer Man Ray (1890–1976) experimented with

artistic effects. His original style combined fantasy with reality, inspiring succeeding generations of budding photographers.

DIGITAL IMAGES

Since the 1990s, digital cameras have become smaller and easier to use. They are now built into smartphones, and images such as "selfies" can be forwarded instantly to social media. Images from a digital camera can be uploaded onto a computer for editing, printing, forwarding, or filing. Many applications allow images to be processed, recolored, manipulated, or resized.

▲ Fast shutter speeds freeze a moving image, but blur still occurs with a racing amusement park ride.

HOW A DIGITAL CAMERA WORKS

When you take a picture, the camera's shutter flicks open and closed to let light enter the camera and hit the charge-coupled device (CCD) for the correct length of time. The lens does the focusing, and the aperture controls how much light gets through. The CCD converts the light into binary digital code. The data is stored on the camera's memory chip and can then be displayed on the camera's screen or transferred to a printer or computer.

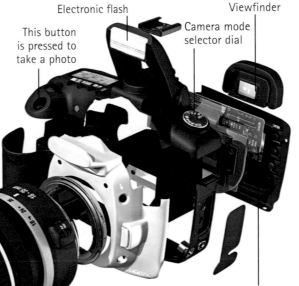

Electronic flash

This button is pressed to take a photo

Viewfinder

Camera mode selector dial

A large, precisely shaped lens captures plenty of light and brings the image to a sharp focus

A charge-coupled device (CCD) captures the image

▲ Digital images may be viewed immediately on a phone or camera, or uploaded onto computers or other electronic devices.

SEE ALSO
Art, Computer, Film, Internet, Lens, Newspaper and magazine, Printing

PILGRIM

Pilgrims are people who travel to take part in religious or spiritual events. Often they travel along a specific route or path known as a pilgrim way.

▲ Muslims who have completed the hajj pilgrimage decorate their homes with paintings of the journey.

Holy relics of Christian saints are often stored in jeweled boxes.

Buddhists climb Mount Fuji to view the dawn in the summer months.

Followers of Shinto in Japan return to their family shrine once a year.

Ancient Egyptians held festivals at Bubastis for the cat goddess Bastet.

PILGRIM WAYS

During the Middle Ages, a network of roads, called pilgrim ways, ran across Europe, linking major sites of pilgrimage. Pilgrims made donations and bought badges and relics, creating wealth for the churches and cities they visited. Monasteries were built along most routes to provide shelter for travelers.

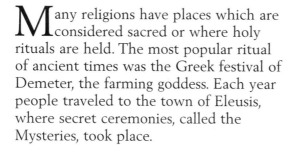

Many religions have places which are considered sacred or where holy rituals are held. The most popular ritual of ancient times was the Greek festival of Demeter, the farming goddess. Each year people traveled to the town of Eleusis, where secret ceremonies, called the Mysteries, took place.

CULT OF THE SAINTS

Many Christians believe that visiting the grave of a saint brings them closer to God. During the Middle Ages, Canterbury drew pilgrims from Britain and northern Europe to the tomb of St. Thomas à Becket, and Compostela in Spain held the tomb of St. James. But the greatest pilgrimage was to Jerusalem, where Christ was crucified. Today, Christians visit holy places such as Fatima in Portugal or Lourdes in France.

THE HAJJ

Muslims have a duty to visit Mecca at least once. This pilgrimage, the *hajj*, centers on a sacred black stone—which Muslims believe was given by God to Adam to absorb the sins of mankind—and on sacred pillars and hills.

PILGRIMS IN THE NEW WORLD

Sometimes people have to travel to a new place in search of religious freedom. In the early 1600s, a group of Puritans sailed from England on the *Mayflower* to set up a simplified, or "purified," church in America. They established Plymouth Colony in 1620, and became known as the Pilgrims.

SEE ALSO

Buddhism, Christianity, Crusades, Hinduism, Islam, Middle Ages, Religion

PLANET

Planets are the largest objects that circle around stars. They may be rocky, like the Earth, or made mostly of gas and liquid, like Jupiter.

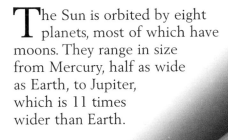

The Sun is orbited by eight planets, most of which have moons. They range in size from Mercury, half as wide as Earth, to Jupiter, which is 11 times wider than Earth.

Sir William Herschel (1738–1822) discovered Uranus in 1781.

In 1846, Urbain Le Verrier (1811–77) found the position of Neptune.

John Couch Adams (1819–92) predicted in 1845 that an eighth planet existed.

Percival Lowell (1855–1916) began the search for a ninth planet in 1905.

Clyde Tombaugh (b. 1906) found Pluto. It was classed as a planet from 1930–2006.

THE WANDERERS

The word planet is Greek for "wanderer." The name comes from the way planets appear to move against the stars over time. It is thought that the planets formed at about the same time as the Sun. As the original cloud of gas and dust collapsed to form the Sun, some matter was spun out into a flattened disc. Over several million years, the dust and gas gathered together to form the planets and moons. Denser rocks gathered near the Sun and lighter gases farther out.

MERCURY

Mercury is the planet closest to the Sun, at an average distance of 36 million

---

PLANETARY NAMES
Mercury The Roman god of merchants and travelers
Venus The Roman goddess of love
Mars The Roman god of war
Jupiter The king of the Roman gods
Saturn The Roman god of seeds and sowing
Uranus The Greek god of the sky
Neptune The Roman god of the sea

PLANET SYSTEMS

Planets in the solar system and around other stars share several features. The solid centre is often surrounded by layers of gas forming an atmosphere. Circling the planet may be smaller planet-like objects called moons. Around the equator may be bright rings consisting of tiny particles of rock and ice.

miles (58 million km). With a diameter of just 3,031 mi. (4,879km), Mercury is the smallest of the eight planets. During the day, its temperature soars to 806°F (430°C), hot enough to melt lead, but at night it cools down to –274°F (–170°C). Mercury's day, the time it takes to spin around once on its axis, is equal to 59 Earth days. Its year, the time it takes to go once around the Sun, is equal to 88 Earth days.

VENUS

With a diameter of 7,521 mi. (12,104km), Venus is nearly the same size as Earth. However, most of Venus's atmosphere consists of carbon dioxide, a gas that traps the Sun's heat. This "greenhouse effect" makes Venus hotter than Mercury, although it is about twice as far from the Sun. Most of its surface is covered in lava that flowed out of giant volcanoes millions of years ago. Venus is the only planet to spin the opposite way to the direction of its orbit. It spins so slowly that one of its days lasts for as long as 243 Earth days. ▶

MARS

The fourth planet from the Sun, Mars is only about half the size of Earth and is much cooler. Its strong red color is due to rust in the rocks on its surface. Its atmosphere consists mostly of carbon dioxide and is about 100 times thinner than Earth's. The largest volcano and the largest canyon ever discovered are to be found on the Martian surface. There are also features on Mars that look like dried-up riverbeds. This suggests that Mars was once warmer and wetter than it is now. Under these conditions, life may have developed and there is even a chance that primitive life may exist there today. Mars has two tiny moons: Phobos and Deimos. The larger of these, Phobos, is only about 15 mi. (24km) across.

JUPITER

The biggest of the planets, Jupiter, could swallow up over 1,000 Earths. It has a

MERCURY
The surface of Mercury is rocky, often covered in sand, and marked by large meteorite craters. There is no atmosphere and the planet is roasted by the nearness of the Sun.

VENUS
Venus has broken slabs of rock and some dust on its surface. Most sunlight is blocked by the clouds of sulfuric acid in the atmosphere of carbon dioxide and nitrogen.

EARTH
Only Earth is known to support life. The rocky surface is covered by water and soil. The atmosphere of nitrogen and oxygen contains clouds of water vapor.

MARS
The reddish surface of Mars is made up of rock and sand. The atmosphere is thin and consists mostly of carbon dioxide. Both poles are covered with caps of ice.

 The space probe *Voyager 2* was launched in 1977 and by 2017 had traveled 10.9 billion miles (16.9 billion km) from Earth, passing close to Jupiter, Saturn, Uranus, and Neptune.

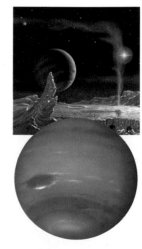

JUPITER
As a gas giant, Jupiter has no surface. Instead, dense layers of gas surround a core. Io, one of 67 known moons, has a rocky surface dyed red by sulfur from its many volcanoes.

SATURN
Like Jupiter, Saturn is a gas giant. The 91 percent hydrogen atmosphere has dense clouds of ammonia, water, and methane colored by phosphorus and other elements.

URANUS
Hydrogen and helium make up most of the gas giant Uranus. The planet is surrounded by rings of blackish particles "shepherded" by two small moons.

NEPTUNE
Gas giant Neptune's blue color is from methane gas. The surface of the moon Triton is frozen methane and nitrogen. Geysers of nitrogen gas erupt to 5 mi. (8km).

diameter of 88,732 mi. (142,800km), but most of this is made of gases and liquids rather than solid rock. Like the Sun, Jupiter contains a great deal of hydrogen. Jupiter spins so fast that its day lasts less than ten hours. But one year on Jupiter is nearly 12 times longer than one of ours. Jupiter has a single ring and 67 known satellites. One of these, Ganymede, is the largest moon in the solar system—bigger than Mercury.

SATURN
Measuring 74,974 mi. (120,660km) across, Saturn is second only to Jupiter in size. Like Jupiter, Uranus, and Neptune, it is a gas giant. It is famous for its bright rings, made up of billions of particles of rock and ice. The rings are more than 175,226 mi. (282,000km) across, but they are very thin. Saturn has at least 62 moons. The largest of these, Titan, is the only moon known to have an atmosphere.

URANUS
Orbiting the Sun 19 times farther out than Earth, Uranus receives very little heat. The temperature at the top of its clouds is –364°F (–220°C). With a diameter of 31,763 mi. (51,000km), Uranus is less than half the size of Saturn but still four times bigger than Earth. Uranus has a set of thin, dark rings and 27 known moons.

NEPTUNE
Similar in size and appearance to Uranus, the blue-green planet Neptune orbits the Sun at an average distance of 1.7 billion mi. (2.8 billion km). It is bitterly cold, and 85 percent of its atmosphere is hydrogen. Neptune has several thin rings and 14 known moons.

DWARF PLANETS
Smaller round objects, known as dwarf planets, also orbit the Sun. The best known is Pluto, which was classed as a planet from its discovery in 1930 until 2006. This cold, icy world is just 1,472 mi. (2,300km) across, and its orbit around the Sun takes 248 Earth years to complete. The other known dwarf planets are Ceres, discovered in 1801 and originally classed as an asteroid, Haumea, Makemake, and Eris.

PLANETS OF OTHER STARS
Planets that are orbiting stars other than our Sun are called extrasolar planets, or exoplanets. The first ones were discovered in the 1990s, and since then more than 2,337 have been confirmed as planets. Another 4,496 are waiting to be confirmed. The first planet found to be rocky like Earth was CoRot-7b. As more and more are found, the chances grow that billions of planets may exist, and that there may be life on some of them.

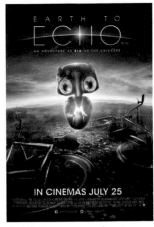

▲ Life from other planets has featured in the movies. The alien in the movie *Earth to Echo* was friendly.

▲ Saturn's rings are made up of dust, ice crystals, and rocks as large as mountains. The rings are 175,200 mi. (282,000km) wide, but only 0.6 mi. (1km) deep. As Saturn orbits the Sun, the rings are seen from Earth from different angles.

GREAT RED SPOT
The Great Red Spot on Jupiter has existed since at least 1665. It is a circular storm with winds blowing at about 260 ft. per second (80m per second). The red color may be due to sulfur in the clouds.

SEE ALSO

Astronomy, Moon, Solar system, Spacecraft, Space exploration, Sun

PLANT

Plants are living organisms that harness the energy of the Sun to feed themselves. Without plants for animals to feed on, there would be no animal life on Earth.

Ferns are among the oldest plants, appearing about 350 million years ago.

The dodder is a parasitic plant. It inserts suckers into other plants to get food.

The carnivorous Venus flytrap feeds on insects that it traps in its leaves.

We make textiles from the ripe fruit of the cotton plant.

Some plants are dangerous to eat—hemlock can be used to make poison.

Plants provide timber. Wood from the oak tree is heavy, hard, and strong.

Most plants are able to absorb sunlight by means of a green substance inside them called chlorophyll. They use the energy from the Sun's light to make food by a chemical process called photosynthesis. This results in the production of oxygen, which all plants and animals, including humans, need to live.

PLANTS OF ALL KINDS
There are about 400,000 different kinds of plant, ranging in size from tiny mosses only a few millimeters long to giant redwood trees, which grow to over 300 ft. (100m) tall. Each has adapted to absorb light, find water and minerals, and withstand the temperature range in its own habitat. Desert plants such as cacti have long, widely spreading roots to collect water, which they store in their expandable stems. Succulent plants store water in swollen, fleshy leaves. Plants in cold places grow in thick, low clumps that protect them from the cold and wind.

DESIGNED TO CATCH LIGHT
Plants need to catch as much light as possible. Each one has leaves which are shaped and arranged on the stem so they overshadow the leaves below as little as possible. Tall trees have strong, woody trunks to hold their leaves high above the ground and other plants. Plants like vines climb up through the trees with clinging tendrils. Plants called epiphytes grow entirely suspended in tree branches, never touching the ground.

OTHER SOURCES OF FOOD
Some parasitic plants, such as mistletoe, obtain extra nourishment by growing into the tissues of larger plants. Some plants, such as the dodder, cannot make any of their own food. The dodder attaches itself to another plant for nourishment. There are also carnivorous plants, such as the pitcher plant and the Venus flytrap, which can catch and digest insects.

PLANTS AND PEOPLE
People learned to grow plants as crops about 10,000 years ago. Today, over four fifths of the world's food comes from plants

GERMINATION

Inside the seed are all the parts needed to form a new plant. The stage when a seed starts to sprout is called germination. In order to begin the germination process, a seed must have warmth, moisture, and oxygen.

First leaves

Stem

Cotyledon

Plumule

Hypocotyl

Seed coat

Primary root

Stage 1

When a seed starts to germinate, it splits and the primary root is formed from the hypocotyl.

Stage 2

The stem pushes up through the soil and the cotyledon starts to break out of the seed coat.

Stage 3

The plumule breaks free of the cotyledon, the stem grows upward and the first leaves are formed.

NONVASCULAR

BRYOPHYTA

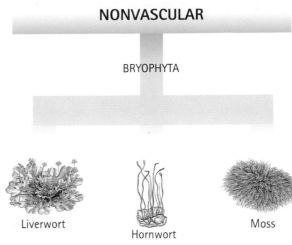

Liverwort
Hornwort
Moss

CLASSIFYING PLANTS

Plants are classified according to similarities that they share, or by a shared evolutionary history—or by both. The simple system shown here groups plants according to their similarities. For example, Bryophyta contains nonvascular plants, which do not have the tissues that carry food and water from one part of the plant to another. The other nine groups shown are all vascular. Anthophyta contains all flowering plants (also called angiosperms), which contain their reproductive cells in flowers. Angiosperms can be divided into two further groups: monocots and dicots. Monocots have one seed leaf (or cotyledon), and dicots have two. These groups are then further divided, so plants that share many key characteristics are put together. Some plants appear very similar but actually have different evolutionary histories. Modern classification systems based on the evolutionary history of plants are called cladistics.

VASCULAR

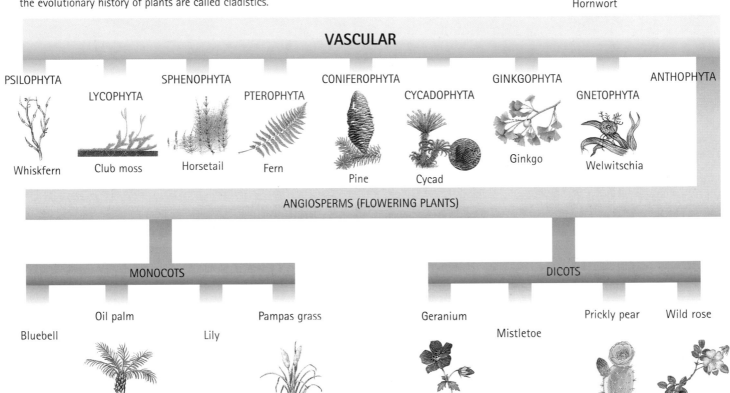

PSILOPHYTA — Whiskfern
LYCOPHYTA — Club moss
SPHENOPHYTA — Horsetail
PTEROPHYTA — Fern
CONIFEROPHYTA — Pine
CYCADOPHYTA — Cycad
GINKGOPHYTA — Ginkgo
GNETOPHYTA — Welwitschia
ANTHOPHYTA

ANGIOSPERMS (FLOWERING PLANTS)

MONOCOTS
Bluebell, Oil palm, Lily, Pampas grass

DICOTS
Geranium, Mistletoe, Prickly pear, Wild rose

such as wheat, rice, and potatoes. Humans eat a variety of fruits, nuts, and vegetables and make drinks from tea, coffee, and grains. Plants also provide products such as vegetable oils, cotton, rubber, and—perhaps the most useful of all—wood. Many of the drugs we use to treat disease come from plants. Even fuels such as coal are the fossilized remains of prehistoric plants.

PLANT BREEDING

Most plants we use today are quite different from their ancestors. Using methods such as genetic engineering, plant breeders have made improvements to cereals such as wheat to make them more productive or more resistant to pests.

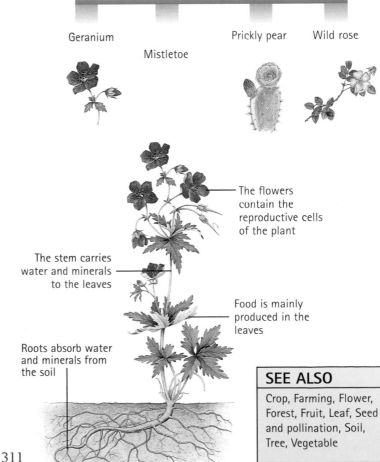

The flowers contain the reproductive cells of the plant

The stem carries water and minerals to the leaves

Food is mainly produced in the leaves

Roots absorb water and minerals from the soil

SEE ALSO

Crop, Farming, Flower, Forest, Fruit, Leaf, Seed and pollination, Soil, Tree, Vegetable

PLASTIC

Plastics are materials that can easily be stretched or molded into shape. Most are made from the chemicals obtained from petroleum oil.

Plastic replaces many metal items because it is light and durable.

Many items are wrapped and sealed in plastic rather than paper bags.

Strong and lightweight plastics can replace the metal bodywork in cars.

Polyester is a plastic widely used in clothing manufacturing.

Instead of wood, boats today are often made of strong, lightweight plastic.

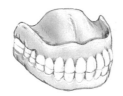

Plastic is used for replacement body parts, such as false teeth.

Plastics are man-made and consist of long chains of molecules called polymers. The way these chains are arranged gives plastics their different qualities. Hard plastics can be used to replace metals, such as car parts. Soft plastics can be used to create fabrics, leather, suedes, and even fur.

NATURAL INGREDIENTS
John W. Hyatt, a New York chemist, developed the first plastic in the late 1860s. The plastic, which was called celluloid, did not last well. It changed color and became brittle if left in strong light.

CHEMICALLY BASED PLASTIC
The first plastic to be chemically based was a material called Bakelite, which was invented in 1909. More modern plastics, however, such as polyvinyl chloride (PVC) and polyester, have become lighter and easier to color. They can also be flexible and are able to withstand moisture and strong sunlight.

HARD OR SOFT
Plastics do not all behave the same way when reheated. Some, called "thermoplastics," melt and can be reshaped after reheating. Polyethylene, a material used to make plastic bowls, is like this, which is why it often loses its shape if something hot is placed on it. Other plastics

PLASTIC MOLDING
Two common methods for molding plastic are that of injection molding, in which plastic pellets are heated and then injected into a mold, and hot extrusion, in which hot plastic is forced through openings to make rods or sheets.

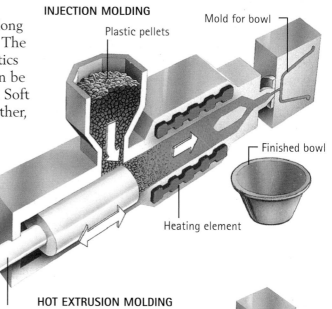

INJECTION MOLDING

Plastic pellets

Mold for bowl

Finished bowl

Heating element

Plunger

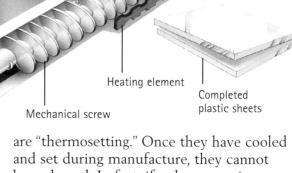

HOT EXTRUSION MOLDING

Plastic pellets

Extruded plastic sheet

Heating element

Completed plastic sheets

Mechanical screw

are "thermosetting." Once they have cooled and set during manufacture, they cannot be reshaped. In fact, if a thermosetting plastic is heated up, it gets harder.

PLASTIC POLLUTION
Although many plastics are recycled, huge amounts of plastic rubbish still choke rivers and harm wildlife. Tiny pellets of plastic collect in the oceans and enter the food chain of animals and humans.

◀ Plexiglas is an ideal plastic for a squash court, as it is transparent like glass but much stronger.

SEE ALSO
Clothing, Materials, Oil, Pollution

PLATYPUS

The platypus is an unusual mammal with a beak like a duck and a tail like a beaver. It lays eggs, but has fur, and it feeds its young with milk like other mammals.

▲ Platypuses are very good swimmers, pushing themselves through the water with their broad, paddlelike front feet and steering with their hind feet and tail.

The platypus is often called the duck-billed platypus because of the shape of its jaws, which resemble a duck's bill. It is one of only five mammals that lays eggs (monotremes). The others are four species of echidna, or spiny anteater. The platypus lives near rivers and lakes in Australia, including Tasmania. Each occupies its own stretch of water, where it digs a burrow in the bank with its strong claws. It sleeps in its burrow for most of the day and comes out to feed mainly at night, when it uses its flat bill to catch large numbers of insects and worms.

A FAKE?

The platypus is up to 30 in. (75cm) long, including its tail, and it weighs up to 5.5 lb. (2.5kg). When European scientists first saw the skin of a platypus, they thought it was a fake—as if someone had sewn a duck's beak and a beaver's tail onto the body of

▲ Echidnas are found in Australia and New Guinea. The female lays one egg a year, which hatches in a pouch on her belly. The young echidna stays in the pouch for several weeks, feeding on its mother's milk.

another animal. The platypus's bill is not hard like that of a duck. It is soft and leathery and very sensitive, and it has no teeth. The platypus stores energy-giving fat in its broad tail.

DEFENSE TACTICS

The male platypus has a poisonous spine on each back leg. The animals use their spines when they fight each other during the breeding season. Wounded platypuses are not seriously hurt by the poison, but there is enough in each spine to kill a dog.

HATCHING FROM EGGS

When the female is ready to lay her eggs, she makes a tunnel in the riverbank up to 100 ft. (30m) long. At the end of it she makes a nest of leaves for her eggs. Three or four months after hatching, the young leave the burrow, but they stay a few more weeks while they learn to swim and find food.

▶ The female platypus has no teats (nipples)—instead, the babies lap up the milk as it oozes from pores on her body.

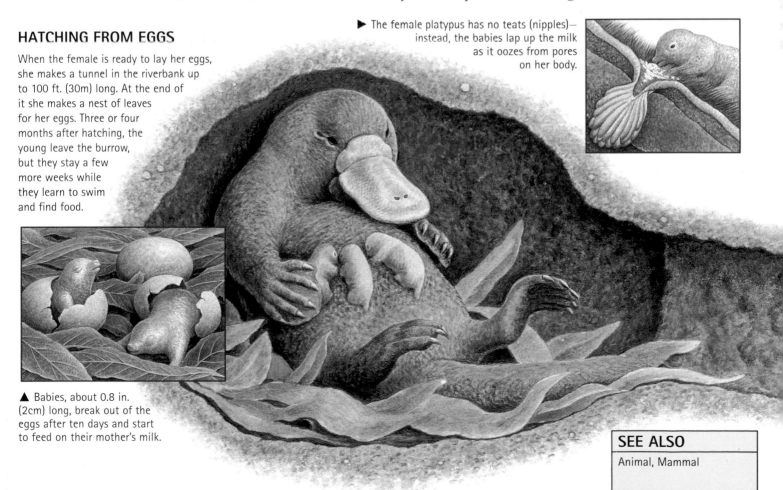

▲ Babies, about 0.8 in. (2cm) long, break out of the eggs after ten days and start to feed on their mother's milk.

SEE ALSO

Animal, Mammal

POLITICS

Politics means the actions and activities of people and organizations, such as political parties, councils, and trade unions, to gain power and influence the government of a country.

▲ Justin Trudeau, leader of Canada's Liberal Party, was elected Prime Minister of Canada in 2015. When he was born in 1971, his own father, Pierre Trudeau was serving as Canada's Prime Minister.

Politicians are people who seek power, use power to govern, or challenge power. They aim to bring about social, economic, or constitutional change. Politicians may be elected representatives, dictators, activists, or campaigners.

ELECTION POLITICS
During elections, parties put forward candidates and publish their ideas and programs. Politicians make speeches, appear on radio and television, and go out to meet the people. There are two main election systems: the "winner-takes-all" system (the candidate with the most

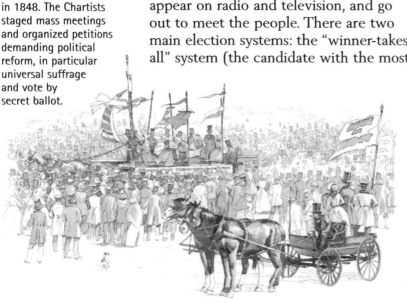

▼ A meeting of Chartists in London in 1848. The Chartists staged mass meetings and organized petitions demanding political reform, in particular universal suffrage and vote by secret ballot.

votes wins) and proportional representation (where voters may vote for more than one candidate, and for more than one party). Politics today has much to do with media management—the skillful use of Internet, TV, and advertising.

WHICH SIDE ARE YOU ON?
Politics is often divided into "left" and "right." These terms come from the French Revolution: those supporting the king sat on the right side of the assembly; those supporting a republic sat on the left. Today's right-wing politicians tend to support tough law and order and free-market economics. Left-wingers support public services and welfare. Alliances of political parties are called coalitions.

PILING ON THE PRESSURE
Pressure groups and lobbyists usually represent an organization, such as a union or manufacturer, or a single issue, such as stricter laws against drunk drivers. They mobilize opinion through the press or by organizing public demonstrations.

SEE ALSO

Communism, Democracy, Government, Revolution

POLLUTION

Pollution happens when a harmful substance is released into the environment in such large quantities that it causes damage to people, wildlife, or habitats.

The control of pollution is a major problem facing the world. Large areas may soon become uninhabitable, and many plants and animals may become extinct. Public opinion is now forcing governments and industry to combat pollution.

▲ Liquid waste dumped into rivers may poison wildlife and threaten supplies of drinking water for humans.

SMOKES AND SMELLS

Car exhausts and factories pump fumes into the air. Some of these gases mix with clouds to form acid rain, which kills plants. Carbon dioxide traps the sun's heat and may lead to global warming. Other gases, called CFCs, are thought to destroy ozone—the gas barrier that blocks harmful radiation from the sun. Noise can also be a form of pollution, with traffic or aircraft noise ruining the quality of life.

OIL SPILL

Oil tankers carry up to two million barrels of oil, so accidents may be devastating. The oil floats on the sea, forming a slick that blocks the sunlight required by seaweed and algae. Birds and fish may be trapped or poisoned by the oil. Thousands of creatures die, but most areas recover within a few years.

WASTE NOT . . .

Trash is created in large quantities, and the world is running out of places to put it all. Recycling glass, paper, and other waste reduces the need for dumping. Radioactive waste created by nuclear power plants remains dangerous for thousands of years.

DEAD RIVERS

Industrial waste dumped into rivers can kill all life. Fertilizers can produce growths of algae, which absorb the oxygen in the water, killing fish and plants. International agreements have been drawn up to stop countries dumping waste at sea and to reduce the pollution of lakes and rivers.

▲ Smoke and other pollutants can travel thousands of miles before falling as deposits or as acid rain.

> **SEE ALSO**
> Conservation, Ecology, Habitat

PREHISTORIC ANIMAL

Prehistoric animals are animals that lived before people began to record things in writing. Animal life began around one billion years ago in the oceans.

▼ *Diplocaulus*, an amphibian from the Permian period, was a pond dweller. His head shape would have made him hard to swallow.

We know that prehistoric animals existed because some of their remains have been preserved in rocks as fossils. The fossils tell us a lot about the shape and size of the animals. From this, scientists can work out how they lived and what they ate.

ARMORED CREATURES

The first living things appeared about 3.5 billion years ago. We don't know much about them because they were microscopic and did not leave many traces in the rocks. About 600 million years ago, animals began to develop shells or other hard coverings, and these hard parts were often preserved as fossils. Trilobites were among the earliest of the armored creatures. They looked like woodlice and lived mainly on the seabed. Corals and many kinds of shellfish lived with trilobites. Huge sea scorpions, or eurypterids, up to 6.5 ft. (2m) long, fed on smaller animals.

OUT OF THE WATER

The first animals with backbones were fish that appeared about 500 million years ago. Many of them had bony armor to protect them from sea scorpions. The earliest prehistoric animals all lived in the sea, but they gradually spread into fresh water and then onto the land. The amphibians were the first backboned animals to move onto

▶ *Meganeura* was like a giant dragonfly, with a wingspan reaching to about 30 in. (75cm). It probably grew large because of the warm Carboniferous forests.

the land. These early amphibians were like fish with stumpy legs that could only just about lift their bodies off the ground—some of them looked like big newts or salamanders. The early amphibians all lived in damp places and, just like today's frogs and toads, they had to go back to the water to breed. One group of amphibians started to change: their skins got thicker and they laid eggs with tough shells. These animals became the first reptiles. They could live in drier places and they spread all over the land.

TAKING TO THE SKIES

Some reptiles, called pterosaurs, learned to fly. Others went back to the sea, where they lived like today's dolphins. The best-known prehistoric reptiles were the dinosaurs, which ruled the Earth for over 100 million years during the Triassic, Jurassic, and Cretaceous periods. Many small, ratlike mammals wandered over the land at the same time as the dinosaurs. Some probably fed on dinosaur eggs, but only when the dinosaurs died out, about 65 million years ago, could mammals really have a chance of survival.

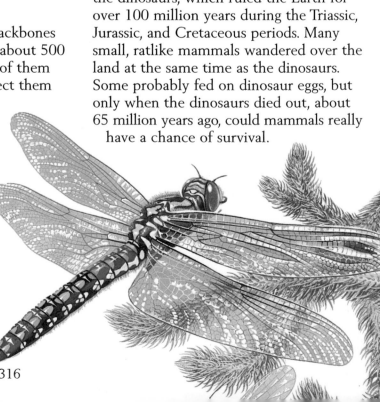
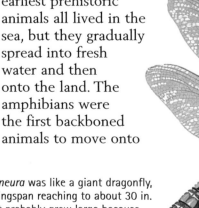

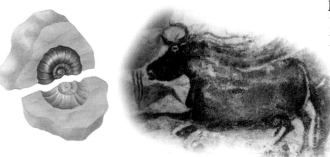

Dzungaripterus's pincerlike beak crushed shellfish.

Dimorphodon had strong jaws and sharp teeth.

Tropeognathus fed on fish caught by the mouthful.

FLYING GIANT

Quetzalcoatlus was the largest pterosaur. It lived in North America about 68 million years ago. Its wingspan was at least 40 ft. (12m)—almost five times bigger than our largest bird's—and its loose throat pouch could have held fish.

▲ Evidence of prehistoric animals comes from fossils and ancient cave paintings like those at Lascaux, France, showing deer, horses, elephants, and bison, which lived in Europe up to 50,000 years ago.

EXPERIMENTAL MAMMALS

As nature experimented with different shapes and sizes, many very strange prehistoric mammals appeared. Baluchitherium was a giant, giraffe-shaped rhinoceros that lived in Asia between 20 million and 30 million years ago. With its huge head carried about 25 ft. (8m) above the ground, it was probably the largest mammal ever to live on land. Most of these "experimental" mammals died out completely, but some of them survived and gradually evolved into the mammals that we see around us. Like the reptiles

before them, some invaded the sea and became whales and seals, and some, such as bats, developed wings and learned how to fly.

MAMMALS IN THE ICE AGES

During the last two million years, there have been several very cold periods called ice ages. Many northern parts of the world were covered with ice. Most animals moved south to avoid the cold, but some managed to survive close to the ice because they were able to grow thick coats, like the woolly rhinoceros and the woolly mammoth. These cold-climate mammals died out when the climate began to warm up about 10,000 years ago, and new species evolved to replace them.

▲ Scientists get clues to these pterosaurs' diets by studying their jaws. Strong jaws and sharp teeth were used for meat, and Tropeognathus's odd beak steadied it in the water.

▼ Smilodon was one of the saber-toothed cats of the Pleistocene period. It had massive fangs, about 6 in. (15cm) long, and huge neck muscles to power its jaws.

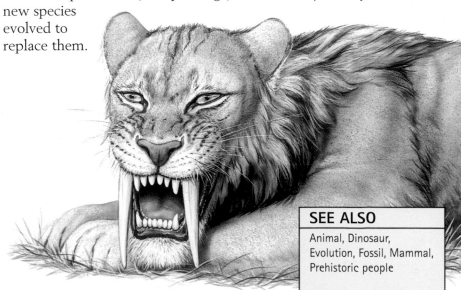

SEE ALSO
Animal, Dinosaur, Evolution, Fossil, Mammal, Prehistoric people

PREHISTORIC PEOPLE

Prehistoric people lived in "prehistory," that is, before about 3500 B.C. when people first began to write and so record their lives. They include our earliest ancestors.

▼ The various species of australopithecines, around 3.5 million years ago, were probably proficient hunters, using sticks and stones to kill prey and dig up edible roots.

Neanderthals shaped sophisticated hand tools.

Cro-Magnons made arrowheads from flint.

A bone needle used in the Palaeolithic era.

The first human beings lived in Africa more than two million years ago. But small, humanlike creatures who walked upright on their hind legs were living more than four million years ago. Today, scientists have named them australopithecines, and we know about them because their bones and footprints have been discovered. One of the most famous finds was the skeleton of a female, nicknamed "Lucy," who lived about 3.75 million years ago in Ethiopia.

APE MEN AND WOMEN

Australopithecus probably looked and lived very like the apes. This species was overtaken by a more advanced species, known as *Homo habilis* (skillful man),

ARRIVAL IN EUROPE

The Cro-Magnons (named after the site in France where their bones were first discovered) were the oldest known modern humans, (*Homo sapiens*) in Europe, appearing around 40,000 years ago. They were taller (5.6 ft./1.7m tall) and more slender than the Neanderthals and had bony chins and domed heads.

who was certainly a toolmaker, able to shape stones to make cutting and scraping tools. Animal bones have been found with scratches on them, suggesting that *Homo habilis* cut off the skins and meat from dead animals with stone tools.

STONE AGE PEOPLE

The early Stone Age, or Paleolithic period, began with *Homo habilis*. Some 1.8 million years ago, a new human species appeared. This was *Homo erectus* (upright man), who spread from Africa as far as Europe and Asia. *Homo erectus* had a bigger brain, made better tools, and

▲ An encampment of hunters in Eastern Europe, about 25,000 years ago. Hunting together they could kill large animals.

was probably the first human being to use fire. Some time after 230,000 years ago, yet another human species came on the scene. This was *Homo neanderthalensis.* One group, the Neanderthal people (named after a valley in Germany), lived in Europe and the Middle East until about 28,000 years ago, surviving the cold of the Pleistocene Ice Age by living in caves. The Neanderthals used simple tools and had probably developed a language to speak to one another.

PREHISTORIC CULTURES
Modern humans, *Homo sapiens*, appeared about 195,000 years ago and lived alongside the Neanderthals. The two species shared a common ancestor around 500,000 years ago and also interbred

around 45,000 years ago. When the Neanderthals died out, ours was the only human species left on Earth. Prehistoric peoples, such as the Cro-Magnons, lived all over Europe during the Stone Age period. They built simple wooden huts, fished, and hunted deer and wild cattle, moving on in search of food. They began to express themselves through art, drawing pictures on cave walls and carving stones into human shapes. There are famous examples of detailed cave paintings in Lascaux in France and Altamira in Spain.

SETTLING DOWN
In the Neolithic, or late Stone Age, people moved from a nomadic life based on food gathering and hunting to a more settled existence, growing crops and domesticating animals. This happened by about 11,000 years ago. People began to make metal tools about 5,500 years ago. The timing of events differs from area to area. The ancient Greeks were living in the Bronze Age at the height of their success 3,000 years ago, historical times for them, but in Britain, prehistory lasted until the Romans invaded 2,000 years ago in the Romans' Iron Age.

Mesolithic people learned to attach blades to handles.

Mesolithic antler spear thrower, still used by the Inuit.

FAST FACTS

- The Paleolithic period (early Stone Age) goes back two million years to the time of *Homo habilis*

- Mesolithic times (the Middle Stone Age) were when Europe was recovering from the Ice Age, around 18,000 B.C.

- The Neolithic period (late Stone Age) was marked by the beginning of agriculture

SEE ALSO
Evolution, Fossil, Prehistoric animal

◀ This mummy, found in 1991 in the Similaun glacier in Austria, is estimated to be 5,300 years old. Such finds tell us about our ancestors' lifestyles.

PRINTING

Printing is the mass production of identical images of writing or pictures on books, posters, packaging, and fabrics. It is used in education, business, art, and fashion.

The first attempts at printing were made in China during the A.D. 700s. Wooden blocks were carved with characters and pictures, which were then inked and pressed onto paper.

▲ With the Gutenberg press, books could be printed and circulated on a large scale. As printing became quicker and less expensive, books became cheaper, spreading information to a greater number of people. Printing inventions during the 1800s aided revolutions in science and mechanics.

EARLY PRESSES

The German Johann Gutenberg (c.1390–1468) invented the first printing press around 1455. Gutenberg used movable type, with raised pieces of metal for each letter so that words could be rearranged easily. The type was laid on a form and then covered with ink. A sheet of paper was placed over it, held down by screws to give a clear, even image. Later inventors added mechanisms for automating the printing press. By 1830, a steam press could produce 1,000 sheets per hour.

MODERN PRINTING

In 1904, the American printer Ira Rubel invented offset lithography printing. He discovered that the inked image from a printing plate could be offset, or stamped, onto a rubber roller, which could then be printed onto paper. In 1930, this system was combined with a method of making pictures up from small dots. When used with four basic ink colors, this made mass-production color printing possible. Today, many publications are printed from computer-generated pages. Laser printers work by spraying ink onto the page; dot matrix printers form images from tiny dots.

PICTURE PRINTS

Artists use intaglio to make engravings: they cut a design into the printing plate. Gravure printing uses a copperplate, which is engraved with a picture using a photographic process. Different tones and strengths of color are produced by engraving more deeply or shallowly.

OFFSET LITHOGRAPHY PRINTING

Rubber rollers are offset with a printing image, one for each of four basic colors: yellow, magenta, cyan (blue), and black. Paper is then printed with the colored inks alternating in turn until the complete picture is built up.

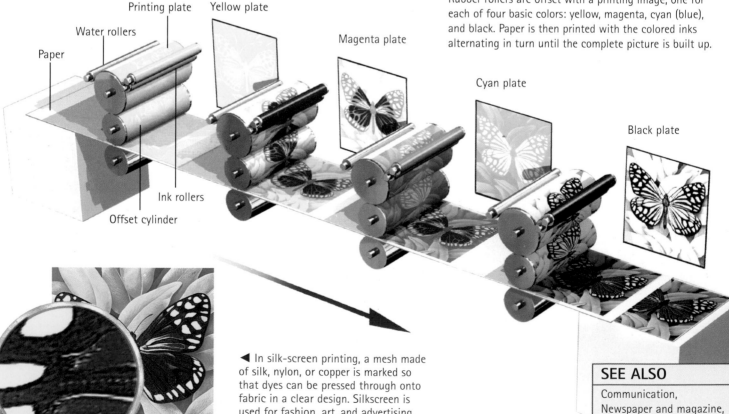

Paper · Water rollers · Printing plate · Yellow plate · Magenta plate · Cyan plate · Black plate · Ink rollers · Offset cylinder

◄ In silk-screen printing, a mesh made of silk, nylon, or copper is marked so that dyes can be pressed through onto fabric in a clear design. Silkscreen is used for fashion, art, and advertising.

SEE ALSO
Communication, Newspaper and magazine, Paint and dye, Paper, Textile

RADAR AND SONAR

Radar and sonar are systems that locate objects. They work by sending out waves, detecting echoes from objects, and measuring the distance in between.

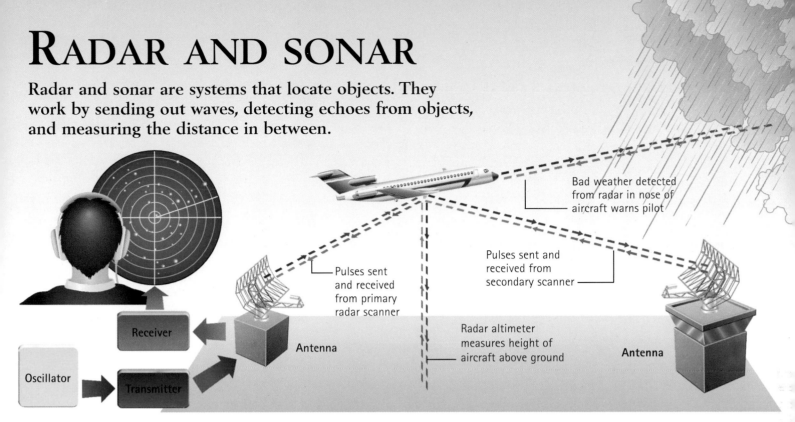

Pulses sent and received from primary radar scanner

Pulses sent and received from secondary scanner

Bad weather detected from radar in nose of aircraft warns pilot

Radar altimeter measures height of aircraft above ground

Receiver

Oscillator

Transmitter

Antenna

Antenna

Radar and sonar are used to find the location of objects that are difficult to see. They also help people to judge how fast objects are moving. Radar is used at airports to track aircraft in the surrounding airspace. Boats use sonar to measure the depth of the seabed or riverbed and to spot any obstacles under water.

HOW RADAR WORKS
Radar, which is short for Radio Detection And Ranging, works by sending out a narrow pulse of radio waves. Any car, aircraft, or other large metal object in the way of this pulse will reflect it, just like a mirror reflects light. A receiver on the radar system picks up the reflected

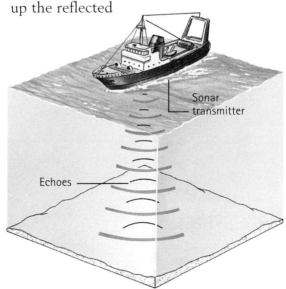

Sonar transmitter

Echoes

◀ Survey ships use sonar to chart the contours of the seabed. The time it takes sound waves to reflect back to the ship indicates the depth of the seabed.

AIRCRAFT RADAR
Air traffic controllers need to know the height and position of aircraft around busy airports to prevent collisions between planes. They have small display screens that relay information they have found. The displays show a realistic map of the area, marked with objects. Large aircraft have onboard radar to detect other planes and bad weather.

waves and measures how long the radio wave took to bounce back. This information can be used to calculate the object's distance. Radar is used by scientists to calculate the distance to other planets and by police to catch speeding drivers. It is also used to track storm fronts and forecast the weather.

HOW SONAR WORKS
Sonar, meaning Sound Navigation And Ranging, works in a similar way to radar. Instead of radio waves, it sends out a pulse of high-pitched sound. Known as ultrasound, the sound from a sonar system is so high that humans cannot hear it. The ultrasound bounces off any dense objects in its path, such as rocks, shipwrecks, and schools of fish, back toward the ship. Hydrophones (underwater microphones) pick up the reflected sound and use it to calculate the distance of the objects.

▲ Radar was first used to detect enemy aircraft during World War II. Information was sent to a central control room, where it was used to track enemy action and plot battle strategies on a map.

SEE ALSO
Aircraft, Medicine, Navigation, Radio, Ship, Sound, Submarine, Weather, World War II

RADIO

Radio is an invention we can use to send and receive information through air, and even deep into space, without connecting wires.

A radio wave is a form of energy that travels through the air. There are radio waves around all the time. But you are unaware of them until you turn on your radio (technically, your radio receiver) and tune in to one of them.

GUGLIELMO MARCONI
In 1895, this Italian inventor (1874–1937) was the first to send telegraph signals through the air without the use of wires.

DIFFERENT FREQUENCIES

All waves vibrate back and forth. The rate at which they do this is their "frequency." Radio waves vibrate at amazingly high frequencies—anything from a few thousand to a few billion times a second. Different radio stations broadcast on different frequencies so that their transmissions do not get mixed up.

1 A microphone turns sound waves from the DJ's voice into a vibrating electric current.

2 This current combines with another current that vibrates very rapidly.

MAKING A RADIO BROADCAST

When a disc jockey, or DJ, makes a radio broadcast, a microphone picks up his or her voice and turns it into an electric current. This current, which vibrates exactly as his or her voice does, is sent to a transmitter for broadcasting. In the transmitter, the vibrating current is mixed with another one that vibrates millions of times a second. This very rapid current is called a "carrier wave." Once they are mixed together, the two currents are turned into a radio wave which can be beamed out through the air.

SENDING OUT SOUNDS

There are two analogue ways of sending out radio waves: AM (amplitude modulation), and FM (frequency modulation). An AM broadcast sends out a radio program by varying the amplitude (extent of vibration) of a radio wave. An FM broadcast sends it out by varying the radio wave's frequency. An analogue radio picks up these changes and turns them back into sounds. In digital broadcasts, the analogue radio signal is turned into digital 1s and 0s and compressed to take up less bandwidth. A digital radio picks up the digital signal and turns it back into audio.

A VARIETY OF USES

Radio is regularly used by the police and by the crews onboard ships and airplanes to keep in touch with people back at base or ground control. Entertainers often use radio microphones on stage to relay their voices to amplifiers. Radio waves are also used to send signals to remote-controlled model cars, boats, and planes.

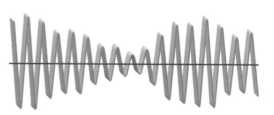

3 The combined currents are turned into radio waves, which are beamed through the air. A tuned-in radio picks up these waves.

4 The radio waves are amplified.

5 Circuits inside the radio pick out the current originally made by the DJ's microphone.

6 A loudspeaker turns this current into sound waves again.

SEE ALSO

Communication, Electronics, Sound, Telecommunication, Wavelength

RAIN FOREST

These dense, damp forests are mainly found near the equator. They contain more types of plants and animals than all other habitats put together.

The world's largest rain forests are the tropical rain forests of South America, Africa, and Southeast Asia, where the climate is always warm and wet. There is no winter at the equator, so there is nothing to stop the plants growing. The result is a huge variety of trees, ferns, vines, and epiphytes (plants that grow on other plants).

TROPICAL RAIN FORESTS

Although they cover only six percent of the Earth's surface, tropical rain forests contain about three fifths of all known plant and animal species. Wherever you look, there are always some plants in flower or producing fruit, so there is a constant supply of food for birds, bats, insects, snakes, tree frogs, monkeys, and a host of other animals. Most of the animals live in the trees.

◄ Tropical forest animals have adapted to life in the trees. The sloth uses its hooked claws to move from branch to branch.

RAIN-FOREST LIFE CYCLE

Tropical rain forests are made up of several layers. The main canopy (treetop layer) is usually 100–165 ft. (30–50m) above ground, where the slender trunks break out into a cluster of branches, but the tallest trees reach 200 ft. (60m). The understory, dark beneath the canopy, consists of tree trunks covered with lianas (woody vines) and laced together by creepers. The forest floor is surprisingly clear. Leaves, fruit, animal droppings, and bodies decompose quickly when they fall to the ground, and their chemical building blocks are immediately absorbed by plant roots and used to make new growth. It is nature's most efficient recycling system.

TEMPERATE RAIN FORESTS

Farther from the equator are temperate rain forests, formed in coastal regions where onshore winds bring constant rain. These lie chiefly in northwestern North America, southern Chile, Tasmania, southeastern Australia, and New Zealand. The dominant trees are redwoods and Sitka spruce in the Northern Hemisphere and eucalyptus and Antarctic beech in the Southern Hemisphere. Some temperate rain forest trees are even taller than those in the tropical forests, but the plant and animal life is not as rich.

THREATS TO THE FOREST

Large areas of the Amazon, Congo, and Malaysian rain forests have been destroyed by logging for timber. Vast areas have also been cut down to make way for plantations of rubber, coffee, bananas, and sugarcane, or to provide pastures for cattle. Rain forests play an important part in keeping the Earth's climate healthy, and they contain many medicinal plants. International organizations are trying to protect the remaining forests before it is too late.

Emergent tree

Canopy

Understory

Lianas wind around the tree trunks, and rafflesias grow on the forest floor

SEE ALSO

Brazil, Conservation, Forest, Habitat, Plant

RAT AND OTHER RODENTS

Rodents are mammals that have sharp, chisel-like front teeth. They use these for gnawing through food, as well as through anything that gets in their way.

Black (and brown) rats carry the germs of several diseases, including typhus.

The European red squirrel is one of several species of tree squirrel.

House mice live among people—"mouse" comes from a word meaning thief.

Most hamsters have large cheek pouches. They use these to carry food in.

Porcupines use their sharp, spiny quills to defend themselves.

Found in cold, northern regions, lemmings migrate to prevent overpopulation.

Rats belong to a large group of mammals called rodents. There are about 2,050 different rodents; they include rats, mice, voles, hamsters, squirrels, beavers, and porcupines. The smallest rodent is the swamp mouse from marshes and forests in Africa, which weighs just 0.2 oz. (5g). The biggest is the capybara from South America, which can weigh over 65 lb. (25kg). Rodents make up about almost half of the world's mammal species.

SHARP TEETH

All rodents share one important feature—a set of four sharp front teeth, called incisors, which work like chisels. They use these to gnaw their way through their food, to chop up nesting material, and to get through anything that blocks their path. Beavers use their incisors to gnaw through solid tree trunks, and rats and mice use them to gnaw through household lumber,

▲ In order to supply wood for its lodge (nest) and its winter food store, the beaver uses its sharp incisors to trim branches and even to fell small trees.

food packaging, and even electric wiring, which can set off fires.

FAST BREEDERS

Compared with many other mammals, rodents often breed very rapidly if they have enough food. A female brown rat can start to breed when only two months old, and can produce as many as five litters a year, with up to 12 in each litter. Poisons or traps are often used to keep rats under control, but their fast breeding rate makes this difficult.

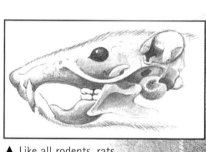

▲ Like all rodents, rats have four sharp front teeth. These are self-sharpening, and grow throughout the rodent's life.

WIRE CUTTERS

Both the black rat and the much more common brown rat (shown right) eat almost any kind of plant or animal. With their strong teeth, they are able to cut through materials as strong as wire to get to food. When eating, they often use their front feet to hold their food while their teeth gnaw at it.

SEE ALSO

Animal, Black Death, Mammal

REFORMATION

The Reformation was a period in Europe's history when the Christian Church in the West was split by disagreements and Protestantism became established.

LUTHER'S 95 THESES

In 1517, the German priest Martin Luther (1483–1546) was so upset at the scandal of the sale of indulgences (pardons for sins) by corrupt Church officials that he listed 95 theses, or arguments, against the practice and nailed them to the door of the church in Wittenberg.

John Calvin (1509–64) was influenced by Luther and set up a Protestant church in Geneva, Switzerland.

King Henry VIII of England (1491–1547) broke away from the Catholic Church in order to get a divorce.

John Knox (1514–72) established the Protestant faith in Scotland with help from Elizabeth I.

The Reformation grew out of the ideas of the Renaissance. People no longer shared the same beliefs about religion and wanted greater freedom of worship. Religious arguments became mixed with political struggles, leading to bitter wars. The Reformation led to great changes within the Roman Catholic Church.

BEGINNINGS

The pope in Rome was the head of the Catholic Church. However, by 1500, many people saw the Church as corrupt. Early protesters, such as Jan Huss (c.1370–1415) in Bohemia and John Wycliffe (c.1330–84) in England, spoke out against the Church. But the Reformation really began in 1517 when Martin Luther attacked Church corruption with his 95 theses. The pope expelled Luther from the Church. But Luther continued to lead the Protestant revolt until his death in 1546.

PROTESTANTISM SPREADS

Religious leaders, including Huldreich Zwingli and John Calvin in Switzerland, took up Luther's cause. In England, King Henry VIII broke with the pope over his divorce (which the Church refused), and made himself head of the Church of England. In the Netherlands, many Dutch people took up Protestantism in order to break free from Spanish (Catholic) rule.

MARTYRS AND WARS

Europe was split into two religious camps, often at war, with cruelties on both sides. Under Queen Mary I in England, Catholics persecuted Protestants. Under Mary's sister, Queen Elizabeth I, Protestants did the same to Catholics. France was torn by civil wars between Catholics and Protestants, and religious conflict reached its height during the Thirty Years' War (1618–48), which killed about one fifth of the people of Germany.

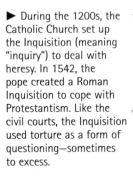

▶ During the 1200s, the Catholic Church set up the Inquisition (meaning "inquiry") to deal with heresy. In 1542, the pope created a Roman Inquisition to cope with Protestantism. Like the civil courts, the Inquisition used torture as a form of questioning—sometimes to excess.

SEE ALSO
Christianity, Crusades, Religion, Renaissance

REFUGEE

Refugees are people who are driven from their homes by war, revolution, natural disasters like floods, or because of political, racial, or religious persecution.

▲ Some refugees are forced to flee for religious reasons. The Huguenots in France suffered for 250 years. Many were murdered in the Massacre of St. Bartholemew's Day, 1572.

▲ Many refugees are forced from their homes by famine, drought, natural disasters, or disease.

When refugees flee from war or famine they can carry little with them. They travel in large, sudden movements, often bringing problems with them. Some refugees are welcomed in their new homelands, others are treated badly.

MASS MOVEMENTS
In the past, refugees were often met with hostility and forced to act brutally themselves. In A.D. 370, when the Huns invaded Europe from Asia, the Goths and other Germanic peoples were defeated and fled west into the Roman Empire. A lack of land and food led to fighting. Other refugees have been made more welcome. In the 1700s, the Protestants in Catholic France were persecuted and moved to nearby countries, like the Netherlands and Britain, bringing with them weaving and banking skills.

INTERNATIONAL HELP
In the 1920s, recognizing that refugees could disrupt stable nations, the League of Nations set up an agency for refugees. The United

Nations formed a new commission after World War II to help resettle the millions of displaced people. The aim was to provide food and shelter until the refugees could return home or find a new one.

HUMAN DISASTERS
Decades of invasion, civil war, terror, and persecution in Asia and Africa have been uprooting populations for many decades, but the refugee crisis today is worse than ever before. The United Nations High Commission for Refugees (UNHCR) reports that 65.6 million people worldwide have been forced from their homes, and 22.5 million are refugees. Ten million people are stateless, without a passport. Nearly 6 million people have fled Syria during the civil war that began in 2011. Daily life has become an impossible struggle for the inhabitants of areas controlled by fighters of IS, or Daesh, as well as in countries such as South Sudan and Yemen.

FAST FACTS

• About 5 million Hindus and Sikhs moved from West Pakistan into India in 1947, and Muslims left India for Pakistan

• After the Vietnam War ended in 1975, hundreds of thousands of Vietnamese fled by boat

• Almost 4 million Afghans left their homeland following Soviet invasion in 1979

• About one third of refugees worldwide are aged under 18

UNWANTED VICTIMS

Since 2011, millions of Syrian refugees have been cared for in camps in neighboring countries. Many others risked their lives trying to reach Europe on overcrowded boats, crossing from Turkey to Greece, or from Libya to Italy. Some were welcomed, but many were met with hostility. Many of these refugees, including children, were drowned at sea.

SEE ALSO
Israel, Gaza, and West Bank, Judaism, United Nations, Warfare

RELIGION

A religion usually involves a belief in a god or gods. It may have rituals, regard certain places as holy, and prescribe rules for living.

Zoroaster (c.600 B.C.) believed the Earth was fought over by good and evil gods.

There have been, and still are, many religions around the world. Most religions teach that people should lead good lives and behave in certain ways.

GODS

Gods are thought to be greatly superior to humans, endowed with wonderful powers. The ancient Greeks had hundreds of gods, each for a different thing—such as the sea, wind, or love. This group of gods is known as a pantheon. Many people, including the Vikings and ancient Egyptians, had such a pantheon. Other religions, including Judaism, Christianity, and Islam, have only one god.

Siddhartha Gautama (c.500 B.C.), the Enlightened One, founded Buddhism.

REVELATIONS

Some religions are based on a revelation— the passing on of sacred knowledge—from a god or gods to a human. Islam is based on the teachings of God as given to the prophet Muhammad in Arabia nearly 1,400 years ago. The Mormon Church of Latter-Day Saints is based on visions and a holy book revealed to Joseph Smith in Palmyra, New York in the 1820s.

Confucius (551–479 B.C.) established the way of life now called Confucianism.

▼ In New Guinea, dancers in colorful costumes take the roles of spirits during ceremonies.

TALKING TO THE GODS

The ancient Greeks believed that the Oracle at Delphi, dedicated to the sun god Apollo, could foretell the future. The chief priestess gave answers to questions in a trance. These answers were often ambiguous, but even the kings, lawmakers, and generals sometimes consulted the Oracle.

PRIESTS AND TEMPLES

Many religions have priests, who study holy teachings and make sure that rituals are carried out properly and that holy places are respected. Other religions, such as Islam, have no priests. The ancient Egyptians built vast temples that were considered to be the home of a god. In many societies, great wealth is lavished on the temple or church. However, Australian Aboriginals believe that certain places are sacred to the spirits and should not be built on.

HOLY COMMUNITIES

The followers of some religions may form a special community and treat nonbelievers as outsiders. In some religions, people form communities where they follow the teachings of the religion very strictly. Such dedicated communities include the monasteries and convents of Christianity and Buddhism.

Jesus Christ (c.4 B.C.–C.A.D. 30) preached and taught in Palestine.

Abu Bakr (c.573–634) led Islam after the death of the prophet Muhammad.

SEE ALSO
Buddhism, Christianity, Hinduism, Islam, Myth and legend, Pilgrim

RENAISSANCE

The Renaissance was a revival in arts and sciences that began in Italy around 1350. It spread across Europe, marking a shift from the Middle Ages to the modern world.

KEY DATES

1300s Florentine artist Giotto di Bondone is the first painter to show realistic (not symbolic) settings

1430s The Medici family dominates Florence's ruling class, paying architects to design impressive buildings

1518 Baldassare Castiglione writes *The Book of the Courtier*, describing proper conduct for noblemen

1519 Pope Leo X appoints the painter Raphael superintendent of Rome's antiquities

1526 The Bible is first translated into English

In the late 1300s, Italy was the richest and most populated area in Europe. However, Italy was not a unified country at this time—the region was divided up into about 250 states, and each state was based around a city and governed by the wealthiest families in that particular area.

Astronomers developed more accurate telescopes to observe the stars.

The invention of printing in Europe (1440) made the spread of learning possible.

THE REBIRTH

The word "renaissance" means rebirth. Italy had preserved much of the ancient Roman civilization, but this had been largely ignored until the 1300s. Then, around 1350, Italian scholars began to copy old manuscripts and circulate them. These manuscripts contained the history of the ancient (classical) world and passed on its knowledge of architecture, science, and art. There was also an influx of ancient Greek learning from the city of Constantinople after it fell to the Turks in 1453. Renaissance thinkers were increasingly influenced by the way ancient scholars studied subjects such as philosophy, literature, and science and wanted to recreate the spirit of the classical age. During the Middle Ages, which had immediately preceded the Renaissance, people had been much more concerned with theology (religion).

POWERFUL BACKERS

The rich noblemen who ruled the Italian cities paid for the classical manuscripts to be copied. In Florence, the powerful Medici family of bankers spent lavishly as patrons of the arts. Lorenzo Medici, who ruled Florence from 1469 to 1492, was called "the Magnificent" because he attracted the finest scientists and artists to the area. Francesco Sforza, a mercenary who became Duke of Milan in 1450, was another great Italian patron.

GREAT ARTISTS

Renaissance artists began painting and sculpting in a completely new style. Instead of stiff, formal poses, they drew people more naturally and put them in real landscapes and rooms. By 1424, Tomasso Masaccio was decorating churches in Florence with beautiful frescoes. At the same time, Filippo Brunelleschi was building startling new structures. His masterpiece is the dome on the cathedral in Florence, which he began in 1420. It blends excellent engineering with graceful design and was the largest dome in the world at the time.

◀ Hans Holbein's *The Ambassadors* (1533) typifies the spirit of the Renaissance: the richly robed ambassadors are surrounded by objects from science and the arts.

FUTURISTIC IDEAS OF FLYING MACHINES

The great minds of the Renaissance, like Leonardo Da Vinci, didn't take all their inspiration from the past. His sketch books show a fascination with flight and the possibility of flying machines long before the invention of the first successful aircraft.

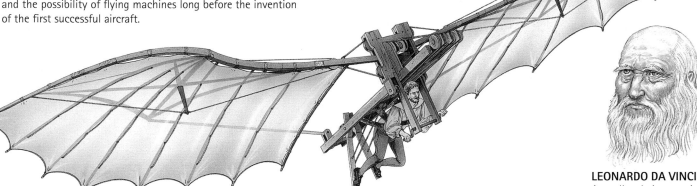

▲ A modern artist's impression of Leonardo's design for a flying machine

LEONARDO DA VINCI
As well as being a painter (masterpieces include the *Mona Lisa*) and inventor, da Vinci (1452–1519) studied biology, anatomy, and mechanics.

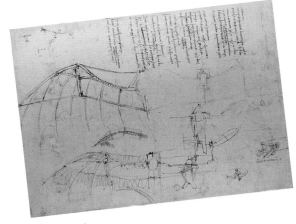

▲ Leonardo's original sketches

COMBINING SKILLS

The ability to mix very different skills was typical of the artists and scientists of the Renaissance. Michelangelo Buonarroti is best known for his marble sculptures, such as the famous *Pietá*, but he was also a painter and poet. He even worked as an architect on St. Peter's Basilica in Rome in 1547. Most versatile of all was Leonardo da Vinci, who created several great paintings, studied science, and designed irrigation systems for farms. Other famous figures of the era include the artists Giotto, Botticelli, and Raphael; sculptors Donatello and Ghiberti and the architect Bramante.

Scientists began to make their own detailed observations instead of simply accepting the teachings of the Church. The Polish astronomer Nicolaus Copernicus (1473–1543) realized that the Earth moved around the Sun. However, he was afraid to publish his findings until he was very close to death, because they opposed the Church view that the Earth was the center of the universe.

THE SPREAD OF LEARNING

As the new art and learning developed in Italy, other countries took note. The universities of Oxford, Cambridge, and Paris became centers of the Renaissance in England and France. Scholars such as Erasmus of Rotterdam in Holland and Thomas More of England developed and spread the ideas. In both Holland and Germany, artists such as the van Eycks, Dürer, and Holbein took Renaissance ideals and developed a distinct northern European style. In England, Shakespeare and Spenser began a revolution in poetry and drama. Then, in 1600, Marie de Medici married King Henri IV of France, taking Italian craftsmen, artists, and cooks with her, which further spread the ideas through Europe.

DESIDERIUS ERASMUS
(1466–1536) was a Dutch priest and leading Christian humanist whose writings attacked the morals of church leaders.

▲ Michelangelo's statue of Moses shows veins and muscles typical of the realistic style of Renaissance sculpture.

◄ Bramante's Tempietto in Rome reflects classical building styles.

SEE ALSO

Architecture, Art, Astronomy, Design, Explorer, Invention, Italy, Printing, Sculpture

REPRODUCTION

Reproduction is the process of producing new organisms so that life continues from one generation to the next. All living things make more of their own kind.

▲ Single-celled organisms, such as the amoeba, reproduce asexually by dividing in two—a process called "binary fission."

AVERAGE PREGNANCY TIME FOR MAMMALS	
Species	Days
Common shrew	15
House mouse	17
Horseshoe bat	45
Cat	63
Dog	63
Tiger	103
Goat	150
Moose	245
Gorilla	260
Human	266
Horse	333
Blue whale	350
Asian elephant	660

Reproduction is one of the most important functions of all living organisms—from the tiniest microbes to the largest trees, elephants, and whales. It means making more of your own kind, or species. There are two main types of reproduction: asexual and sexual.

ONE BECOMES TWO

The simplest form of asexual reproduction is that of organisms consisting of a single cell, such as amoebas or bacteria. These reproduce by simply dividing into two. Each offspring cell grows larger and then also divides, and so on. In suitable conditions, some bacteria can double their numbers like this every 15 to 20 minutes.

ONE-PARENT REPRODUCTION

Many plants reproduce asexually by vegetative propagation. A part of the plant grows roots into the soil and sprouts a stem, which then becomes a separate individual. Gardeners make use of this process by slicing off a part of a plant and growing it into a new individual. Some simple animals reproduce in a similar way, by budding. The parent sprouts a "bud" that grows into a new individual. Hydras, tiny anemonelike water creatures, multiply by budding.

FERTILIZATION

Reproduction is very similar in all mammals, including humans. The female or mother has reproductive organs called ovaries that make hundreds of tiny eggs. The male or father has reproductive organs called testes (testicles) that make millions of even tinier sperm. During mating, the male passes his sperm cells into the reproductive tubes, or tract, of the female. Here, one of the sperm joins with, or fertilizes, an egg. The genes in the egg and sperm come together to create a new individual.

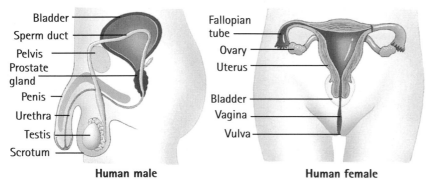

Human male

Bladder
Sperm duct
Pelvis
Prostate gland
Penis
Urethra
Testis
Scrotum

Human female

Fallopian tube
Ovary
Uterus
Bladder
Vagina
Vulva

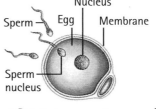

1 Day 1: a sperm cell penetrates and fertilizes an egg inside the Fallopian tube, forming a zygote.

Sperm — Egg — Membrane
Nucleus
Sperm nucleus

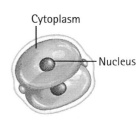

2 The zygote divides into two and continues to travel along the Fallopian tube toward the uterus.

Cytoplasm
Nucleus

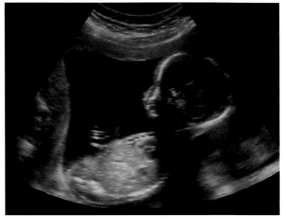

▲ Ultrasound scans, as of this 20-week-old fetus, are used to check on a baby's development in the uterus.

DIFFERENT GENES—VARIATION

Most plants and animals breed by sexual reproduction. This requires two parents—female and male. Each parent contributes a unique selection of genes, so the offspring vary in the genes they inherit and grow up to be slightly different from each other. This variation means that at least some offspring will be suited to the world's ever-changing conditions, and so will survive in the struggle for life.

HAVING BABIES

Some young mammals, such as mice, are born without fur, with eyes closed, and depend totally on their parents. A human baby is also helpless, although it does have certain reflexes, such as crying when it is hungry or cold. Other mammal babies, such as whales, giraffes, and antelope, are alert and able to move about within minutes of birth. The number of young born at one time varies. Mother seals, dolphins, bats, and humans usually have one baby. Mother dogs, cats, and rats have several babies. A mother opossum may give birth to more than 30 babies.

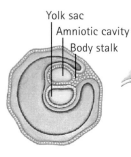

Yolk sac
Amniotic cavity
Body stalk

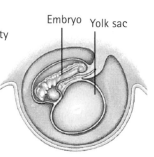

Embryo   Yolk sac

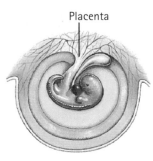

Placenta

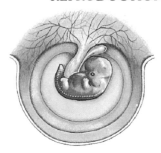

3 The cells continue to divide until, after 4 to 5 days, a tiny ball of 16 cells has formed.

4 Day 13: the ball settles into the lining of the uterus, which forms supportive structures.

5 Day 21: the embryo feeds off the yolk sac and its spine and brain begin to form.

6 Day 28: the stomach and arm and leg buds have all begun to form and the heart starts pumping blood.

7 Day 35: bones and muscles start to form, and the arms and legs continue to grow.

HOW THE HUMAN BABY DEVELOPS

During development, the cells multiply rapidly, move around, and change into specialized shapes, gradually forming the basic body organs. This rapid growth is called the embryo stage. As the tiny, tadpolelike body develops, it takes on a recognizable shape. It develops muscles, bones, skin, and other features. Eight weeks after fertilization, it is called a fetus. It is nourished by the mother through a specialized organ, the placenta. Finally, it leaves the uterus through the birth canal to begin life in the outside world.

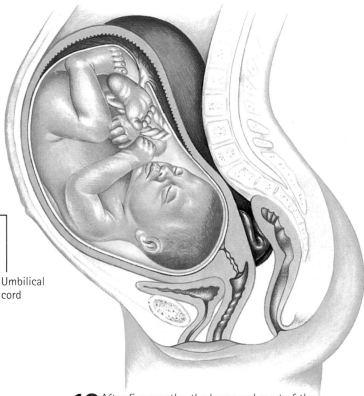

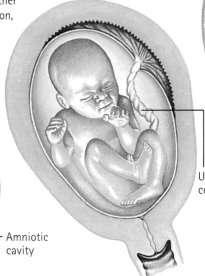

Umbilical cord

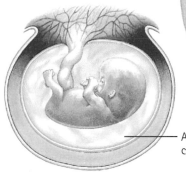

Amniotic cavity

8 Day 56: the 0.8-in. (2-cm) fetus has developed its main body parts, including fingers and toes; some muscles and nerves function.

9 After four months, the baby has doubled in size and has well-developed features such as fingers and toes.

10 After five months, the lungs and most of the other body organs are working properly. The fetus usually repositions itself, so that at the end of nine months (above) it is ready to be born head first.

LAYING EGGS

Mammals, some snakes and fish, and a few insects give birth to their young. But the vast majority of animal mothers reproduce by laying eggs, out of which the offspring hatch. On land, the eggs are usually encased in a tough shell for protection and to prevent drying out. Examples are bird and reptile eggs. These contain a yolk, which is the food store for nourishing the baby as it develops. Insects, spiders, and similar smaller creatures also lay tough-cased eggs, but without large food stores inside. The offspring must hatch out and feed immediately.

REPRODUCING IN WATER

Eggs laid in water do not need a waterproof casing. Amphibians' eggs are jellylike, and the eggs of most fish, crabs, and similar creatures have thin walls. On land, the male usually transfers his sperm into the female's body during mating, otherwise the sperm would dry out and die. In water, females can release their eggs, and males their sperm, without the risk of their drying out. Male and female cast their sperm and eggs into the water and fertilization is left to chance. In many fish and crabs, males and females come together and release their eggs and sperm into one place.

SEE ALSO

Amphibian, Animal, Butterfly and moth, Evolution, Fish, Flower, Human body, Insect, Mammal, Microorganism, Seed and pollination

REPTILE

Reptiles are air-breathing animals with backbones and a covering of tough scales. Most of them live on land, but some live in the sea or in fresh water.

▲ The Australian frilled lizard raises its collar in a display of aggression that frightens its attacker away.

Reptiles are usually described as cold-blooded creatures, and this means that their body temperature goes up and down as the air or water temperature changes. Most reptiles live in warm places, but they are found everywhere except in the far north or south. Those living in cooler places make themselves warm in the morning by sitting in the sun. Reptiles are vertebrates (they have backbones), and there are more than 10,000 different species divided into four main groups: turtles and tortoises; alligators and crocodiles; lizards and snakes; and the tuatara, a species in its own group.

The tuatara is described as a living fossil—it has hardly changed in 200 million years.

When frightened, the poisonous cobra rises and spreads its hood.

The crocodile is a large meat-eater that seizes its prey with powerful jaws.

TORTOISES—AN ANCIENT GROUP

Reptiles first appeared on the Earth over 300 million years ago, and many different kinds have come and gone since then. The oldest group of reptiles still living is the turtles and tortoises, which have not changed much in 200 million years. They are easily recognized by their shells, which are made of bone and usually have a horny covering. There are 300 different species. Those living in the sea are usually called turtles and those living on land tortoises. Freshwater species are called terrapins. In the United States, however, the name turtle is often used for all the shelled reptiles. Land-living tortoises feed mainly on plants, but the other species are mainly

OCEANGOING CREATURES

Most reptiles lay eggs. **1** The oceangoing marine turtle comes ashore to find a safe place in the sand for her young. **2** She lays her eggs in a sheltered spot. **3** Weeks later, the hatchlings break out of their shells. **4** They scramble out and race for the safety of the water. **5** Aquatic turtles all have limbs that act as paddles or flippers, making them excellent swimmers.

meat-eaters. Tortoises have no teeth, and they bite their food with sharp, horny beaks.

DINOSAUR RELATIVES

The huge dinosaurs that roamed Earth millions of year ago were reptiles. Their nearest living reptile relatives are the alligators and crocodiles. These dangerous meat-eaters live in and around tropical rivers. There are 23 species, and some reach lengths of about 30 ft. (9m).

LIZARDS AND SNAKES

These animals form the largest group of reptiles alive today. There are about 6,263 known species of lizard and 3,619 species of snake. Scientists believe that snakes descended from a group of burrowing lizards that gradually lost their legs about 100 million years ago. Some snakes are poisonous and bite with grooved fangs that inject venom from saclike glands. Lizards nearly all live on land and are mostly very active animals. They include both vegetarians and meat-eaters. The world's biggest lizard is the Komodo dragon, which lives in Indonesia. Up to 10 ft. (3m) long, it eats animals as large as pigs. It is one of the monitor lizards, which have long necks and powerful teeth. Some monitors steal crocodile eggs and even eat young crocodiles. Small lizards feed mainly on insects, slugs, and other species of invertebrate animals.

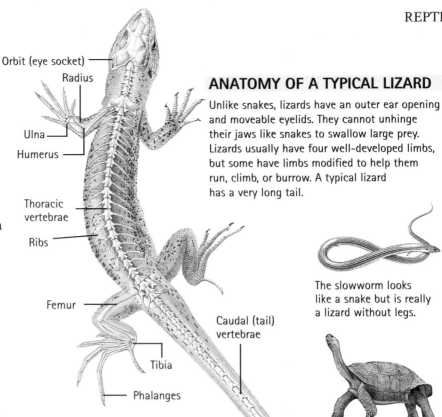

Orbit (eye socket)
Radius
Ulna
Humerus
Thoracic vertebrae
Ribs
Femur
Caudal (tail) vertebrae
Tibia
Phalanges

ANATOMY OF A TYPICAL LIZARD

Unlike snakes, lizards have an outer ear opening and moveable eyelids. They cannot unhinge their jaws like snakes to swallow large prey. Lizards usually have four well-developed limbs, but some have limbs modified to help them run, climb, or burrow. A typical lizard has a very long tail.

The slowworm looks like a snake but is really a lizard without legs.

The tortoise can pull its head, legs, and tail into its hard, protective shell.

The gecko can climb walls using suckerlike pads on its feet.

CHAMELEONS

These are slow-moving lizards, some of which are famous for their ability to change color. A chameleon surrounded by green leaves is usually some shade of green, but if it is then put among brown leaves or bare twigs it will gradually turn brown. Chameleons feed on insects, which they catch by firing out their long, sticky tongue at great speed. Their bulging eyes are also very unusual because each one can be moved separately: one eye can look forward while the other one looks behind. This is very useful for finding insects and also for spotting enemies.

A STRANGE SURVIVAL TRICK

Many birds and mammals like to eat lizards, but most lizards run away quickly when they are frightened. Their enemies often manage to grab no more than the tail—and then a surprising thing happens. The lizard snaps off its tail and races away, leaving the predator with just a wriggling tail. The lizard grows a new one.

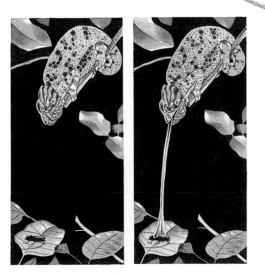

▲ A chameleon lashes out its tongue to catch a hapless insect. Its tongue is almost the same length as its body.

FAST FACTS

• The lifespan for a giant tortoise can be longer than 175 years.

• The Gila monster and the beaded lizard can kill people with their poisonous saliva

• The only oceangoing lizard is the marine iguana, which lives in the Galapagos Islands

SEE ALSO

Alligator and crocodile, Desert, Ocean and sea, Snake

REVOLUTION

A revolution is an overwhelming uprising by the people that aims to destroy the social or political system of a country and replace it with a new system.

▲ Medieval peasant revolts were generally aimed at abolishing harsh taxes. Rebels often burned the books in which taxes were recorded.

Revolutions are unpredictable. They may achieve all their aims or lose sight of the ideals that were fought for. Their leaders may go down in history as heroes or traitors.

Wat Tyler (d.1381) led the Peasants' Revolt of southern England in 1381.

MASS MOVEMENTS
Revolutions occur when most of the people in a country are suffering hardship, or when they want changes to be made. If they cannot gain what they want, anger and the demand for more radical change builds up. However, revolutions need an incident to start them. The uprising of Sicilians against French rulers in 1282 began when a Sicilian stabbed a Frenchman who had insulted his wife.

George Washington (1732–99) led colonial troops in the American Revolution.

REASONS FOR FAILURE
Most revolutions fail. The government has many advantages over ordinary people, including wealth, control of the army, and better organization. Revolutions are often disorganized, starting as separate protests

that can be put down by force. Even if rebel forces unite, they often argue later. The revolutions that succeed are those with a clear aim and strong leadership. But even these may fail. In 133 B.C., the Roman army officer Tiberius Gracchus led the poorer citizens in demands for reform of land and property laws. The revolution failed when noblemen killed Gracchus, his brother, and over 300 supporters.

MEDIEVAL PEASANTS
During the Middle Ages, the peasants of Europe had to pay taxes and work long hours for their masters. Some nobles treated their peasants harshly. In 1381, the

Simon Bolívar (1783–1830) led many revolts in South America.

FARMERS AGAINST SOLDIERS
During the American Revolution the British hired 30,000 German soldiers, mostly Hessians. The colonial militias, largely made up of farmers, won many skirmishes, but, compared with the soldiers, they were poorly trained. It was only after George Washington took charge of the Continental Army and began serious training that the rebelling forces won major battles and, eventually, the war.

Georges Danton (1759–94) led the republican faction in the French Revolution.

Giuseppe Garibaldi (1807–82) led revolutions in Italy to create a united nation.

peasants of England demanded an end to such conditions. The uprising collapsed, but reforms were slowly introduced. In 1524, German peasants launched a violent uprising. They murdered nobles and organized an army. The nobles hired foreign troops and defeated the peasants at Frankenhausen in 1525. Most of the rebels were killed.

THE AMERICAN REVOLUTION

The American Revolution began in 1775 when British colonists protested against being taxed by Britain with no representation in Parliament. At first, the uprising aimed at changing the status of the colonies, but in 1776 the colonies declared independence. After full-scale war with Britain, the new United States established a democratic republic.

THE FRENCH REVOLUTION

In the France of 1789, the king was seen as someone who spent vast sums of money on luxuries. Involvement in wars, including the American Revolution, had drained the treasury. At the same time, food prices had doubled after the harvest failed, and many were close to starvation. The middle

TO THE BARRICADES

The *sans-culottes*, the working class of Paris, formed the shock troops of the French Revolution. On July 14, 1789 they attacked the royal prison of the Bastille, marking the start of violence. July 14 is now the most important public holiday in France. During fighting, the *sans-culottes* built barricades across the narrow streets of Paris, from which to defy troops and police.

● Centers of revolution in 1848

Paris Frankfurt Berlin Warsaw
Vienna Prague Budapest
Milan Venice
Rome

◄ In 1848, people supporting democracy and social reforms rose against the monarchies of Europe. King Louis Philippe was overthrown in France, and major reforms were introduced in Belgium, Denmark, and the Netherlands. Elsewhere, the armies and peasants remained loyal to their monarchs. Revolts were crushed in Prussia and Italy, though some reforms were made. Only in Austria, Poland, and the smaller German states did the revolutions fail totally.

classes demanded an end to the injustices. In May 1789, Louis XVI called a meeting of the States General (parliament) for the first time in about 175 years. This body demanded tax reforms. Food riots broke out, and mob violence spread. The new government introduced radical measures to please the mob. The king tried to flee the country, was arrested, and beheaded. In the Reign of Terror that followed, almost 20,000 people were executed as enemies of the Revolution. Ten months later, moderates established a new government based on the ideals of the Revolution. ▶

▲ Demonstrations in Tunis and across Tunisia led to the overthrow of President Zine El Abidine Ben Ali's regime in 2011.

▲ Government symbols may be destroyed by revolutionaries, as was this portrait of Stalin by Hungarians in 1956.

▶ Civilians may take over military weapons in a revolution. The Hungarian uprising of 1956 failed when trained Soviet troops invaded.

REVOLUTION IN RUSSIA

In spring 1917, Russia's czar, or emperor, was overthrown by middle class democrats, but many social problems remained. Vladimir Lenin, leader of the Communist Party, began an uprising. It ended in 1921 with Communist victory.

REVOLUTION FROM ABOVE

In 1959, a force of Communist guerrillas overthrew the Cuban government. The guerrilla leader, Fidel Castro, then began a revolution from above by introducing communism to Cuba.

VELVET REVOLUTIONS

In 1956, the Hungarians tried but failed to peacefully overthrow their communist government. By 1989, however, Russia was too weak to interfere in Eastern Europe. Peaceful protests began in Poland, East Germany, Czechoslovakia, Bulgaria, and Hungary. These "velvet revolutions," replaced communism with democracy within a few months.

THE ARAB SPRING

In December 2010 a Tunisian market seller set himself on fire after his cart was confiscated by a police officer. He later died. The event triggered protests and, eventually, revolution in Tunisia. It also inspired other uprisings across the Arab world. During this wave of protest, known as the Arab Spring, the presidents of both Egypt and Libya were forced from office.

STORMING THE PALACE

Taking key buildings and communication centers is vital to any successful revolution. On October 25, 1917, Russian Communists and supporting troops seized government buildings, including the famous Winter Palace in St. Petersburg. Within days, the government of Russia was communist.

SEE ALSO

Civil war, Communism, Fascism, France, Russia, United States of America

RHINOCEROS

Rhinoceroses are large, thick-skinned mammals that are distantly related to the horse. They have one or two horns on the nose and three hoofed toes on each foot.

▲ Rhinos may fight each other with their horns, which can sometimes be torn from the nose in the struggle.

The two-horned black rhino has a hooked upper lip and lives on the African plains.

The one-horned African white rhino has square lips and lives on the scrubland.

The one-horned Indian rhino has large folds of skin and lives in marshy jungles.

The two-horned Sumatran rhino has hairy skin and lives in rain forests.

The one-horned Javan rhino lives in the rain forests, but is now nearly extinct.

There are five species of rhinoceros (or rhino). Two live in Africa and three in southern Asia. They are all plant-eaters. The African white rhino, which is actually gray like all the others, lives mainly on scrubland, where it feeds on grass. Nearly 6.5 ft. (2m) high, up to 13 ft. (4m) long, and over 2 tons, it is the largest of the five. The Sumatran rhino is the smallest, weighing only 1 ton; unlike the others it is very hairy.

HORN OR HAIR?

A rhino's horn is not made of bone or horn. It is actually made of very coarse hairs which are firmly stuck together. African black rhinos and white rhinos have two horns, and the one farthest foward can be nearly 5 ft. (1.5m) long. The Sumatran rhino also has two horns, but Indian and

A rhino's horns are used for self-defense and for digging up bushes and shrubs.

A black rhino uses its hooked upper lip for grasping leaves.

Javan rhinos have only one. A young rhino begins to grow horns when it is four or five weeks old.

ENDANGERED SPECIES

All rhinos are rare animals. There are probably only about 60 Javan rhinos left in the wild, and about 300 Sumatran rhinos. The animals have been hunted for their horns, which are often ground up and used to make traditional medicines in Asia. The white rhino lives in various national parks in Africa and is the most numerous, but the other rhinos are in serious danger of becoming extinct.

THE BLACK RHINOCEROS

Like all rhinos, the African black has excellent hearing and a good sense of smell. Its eyesight is not good, however, and the animal often charges almost blindly when it is disturbed by an unfamiliar smell or sound. A charging black rhino is terrifying, since it can run more than 28 mph (45kph), faster than a human.

A rhino's foot has three toes, each of which ends in a hoof. The middle toe takes most of the rhino's weight.

SEE ALSO

Africa, Animal, Indian subcontinent, Mammal

RIVER

When water falls as rain and snow over the land, it eventually flows back to the seas and oceans. Usually, it flows back in the form of a river.

A river that flows quickly down a steep slope, over hard rocks, cuts a deep gorge in the land.

When a river flows more slowly over softer rocks, the valley is worn back into an open V-shape.

▲ Waterfalls occur when a river tumbles over the edge of a steep cliff or ledge, as in the powerful Dettifoss Falls in Iceland.

A river goes through many stages in its development. First, water falls as rain on hills and mountainsides and seeps into the ground until the soil and rock are completely saturated with it—so full that they cannot hold any more. The top level of this saturated zone is called the water table. When the water table reaches the surface of the soil—on a steep slope, for example—water pours out, forming into a spring. Water from the spring runs downhill as a stream, and in time, many streams unite to form a river.

YOUNG RIVER
When a river is young, it runs swiftly down the hill or mountainside. High up, close to the springs, the falling water is full of energy and can carry rocks and boulders with it. This rocky debris scrapes and crashes along the bed of the river, carving out a deep V-shaped valley or gorge. This constant erosion is typical of

▼ Rivers are used all over the world to move goods and people. The floating market in Bangkok, Thailand is part of a river trade route, where people travel by boat to buy and sell goods.

a river in its early stage, and waterfalls and rapids (fast currents) are common.

MATURE RIVER
In the next stage of the river's development, some of the rocky debris begins to settle out in a process called deposition. However, erosion still takes place. The river valley becomes broad and flat, and the river winds, or meanders, around in it. When the course of the river swings toward the valley's edge, the sides are worn back, and the valley becomes wider. At the same time, rocks and sand are deposited on the valley floor, forming what is known as a floodplain. This whole area can be under water during flooding. As it flows, the river constantly changes direction and eats into the sediment (solid matter) that has already been dropped, lifting it and depositing it elsewhere.

LOOPING CURRENTS

When a river flows in a loop, its current is faster on the outside. The faster current can erode more quickly than the slower current on the inside, so the outside bank of the loop is worn back. At the same time, sand and pebbles are deposited by the slower current, and build up the inside bank. The loop gradually becomes more pronounced, and the course of the river changes.

OLD MAN RIVER

In its final stage of development, the river becomes so slow that there is no erosion anywhere, only deposition. The river is now a long way from its source high up in the mountains, and is meandering slowly across a flat plain. The river overflows its banks during times of flood, depositing fertile sediment on the plains as the water slows down away from the main current. The banks can get built up so that the river may actually flow at a higher level than the plain around it. Such a river alters its course continually during flooding, spreading valuable fertile soil on the plain, but making the water difficult to manage.

MEETING THE SEA

Eventually, the river reaches the sea at its mouth. If there are no currents at this point, the river's sediment is deposited as sandbanks. These sandbanks may form islands, and the river water splits up into individual streams between them, forming a delta. More often, the sediment is carried away, and the river has a broad tidal mouth called an estuary.

When the channel of a river flows in a snakelike pattern across its valley, it is said to meander.

1 Some meanders swell to broader loops than others.

2 The neck of the loop then becomes very narrow.

3 The old channel is cut off to form an oxbow lake.

Glacier
Meltwater
Waterfall
Rapids
Stream
Tributary stream
River
Oxbow lake
Estuary
Meander
Floodplain
River mouth

THE IMPORTANCE OF RIVERS

Although rivers make up only a tiny percentage of the Earth's surface water, they are very important. Rivers form the landscape and provide natural barriers. They also provide vital links from seas to inland areas, and are used for transporting goods. Most inland villages, towns, and cities began as settlements around rivers; when bridges were built, the settlements grew. Rivers supply food, and water for drinking, washing, and crop irrigation.

SEE ALSO

Lake, Mountain and valley, Transportation, Water

ROAD

People build and use roads for travel and for moving freight. Cars and trucks on the roads now carry most of the world's passengers and goods.

Natural soil

Compacted soil

Subbase

Base course

Pavement

Shoulder

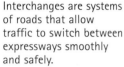

Interchanges are systems of roads that allow traffic to switch between expressways smoothly and safely.

Unpaved roads have stony or earthen surfaces and can be muddy after rain.

Track surfaces are often gravel. They are in remote areas with little traffic.

Main roads have all-weather surfaces and can support heavy trucks.

The earliest roads were rough tracks, made by people's feet as they traveled between villages. Sometimes, trackways of timber were laid over swampy ground. Few early roads were suitable for wheeled carts, especially in wet weather.

ROMAN ROADS

The Romans were among the first people to build good roads. Surveyors planned the route, following old tracks or setting out a new, straight line. The roads were suitable for wagons or an army on the march. Towns grew at points where roads crossed.

DECLINE AND REVIVAL

After the Romans, road building stopped in the Western world. Both the Inca of South America and the Chinese had advanced road systems, but in Europe, most roads were no better than rough tracks. Improvements were not made until

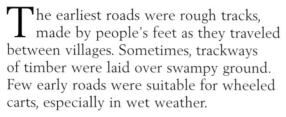

ROAD CONSTRUCTION

The lowest layer in modern highways is the subbase of stone which levels the ground. The base course is stones of about 1.5 in. (4cm). The top pavement may be made of concrete or of tar and small stones. Lane markings, lights, and signs make roads safer for driving.

the 1700s, when armies built better roads to move supplies. In 1816, British engineer John MacAdam (1756–1836) published new designs for roads. He used well-drained layers of stones and gravel bound together by sand. The design was used around the world for major routes.

AUTOMOBILES

In the 1890s, early drivers demanded better roads, because cars could not cope with cart tracks. By the 1930s, the first highway systems had been built in Italy and Germany. Today, many towns are dominated by roads and traffic, causing pollution and safety problems. Road building has opened up regions such as the Amazon, causing environmental damage. Roads are needed for business and pleasure, but urban planners need to solve the problems that roads create.

◀ Roman roads were built with flat stones laid over concrete. They were built and used by the army.

SEE ALSO

Car, Transportation, Truck and bus

ROBOT

A robot is a machine designed to imitate human actions. It can perform a range of tasks that are often too dangerous or monotonous for a human to do.

Robots are widely used in factories. Here, robotic hands solder parts onto electronic circuit boards.

The name "robot" comes from *robota*, the Czech word for the work peasants had to do for their landlords. Robots free humans from heavy and boring work; they perform routine tasks in industry, such as painting or welding. They can be used in dangerous conditions, for example where there are poisonous fumes or around volcanoes. Robots equipped with electronic "eyes" can also inspect or sort goods.

ROBOTS IN INDUSTRY

The first robot was introduced in 1961 by General Motors in New Jersey. Although they were invented in America, Japan soon became the world's leading maker and user of industrial robots. The first robot in Japan was bought from the U.S. in 1967. By 2019 over 1.4 million new industrial robots will be installed around the world. European factories are at the forefront of this revolution, and China, Japan and the USA are all huge markets for robotics.

Radio-controlled bomb disposal robots check out suspect packages and make controlled explosions.

ROBOTS VERSUS HUMANS

Robots have made themselves useful in all sorts of places, from sheep-shearing

▲ Early robots and movie robots (left) looked like humans. Later, useful robots were tiny and buglike or resembled industrial machines. By the 1990s, robotic research seemed to have gone full circle. Honda's (right) can walk, climb, and make simple decisions.

in Australia to the first humanoid robot in space, *Robonaut 2* (2011). However, robotics raises concerns with many people. Robots can take away jobs from humans. Robot vehicles and tiny airborne drones can spy on us. Robot soldiers can kill humans, with no sense of right or wrong. Realistic humanoid robots coupled with artificial intelligence might lead us into a world of science fiction made real.

Robots are popular in films. *Wall-E* (2008) tells the story of a single robot left on Earth to clear up the trash humans left behind.

▶ Tiny robots are used in microsurgery. Here a "bugbot" is sweeping away fatty cholesterol deposits clogging up human arteries.

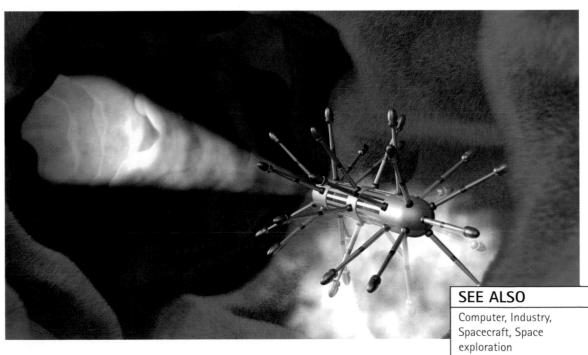

SEE ALSO

Computer, Industry, Spacecraft, Space exploration

ROCK

Rocks are the solid substances that make up the surface of the Earth. There are three types of rock, each of which forms in a different way.

▲ Basalt is an igneous rock formed from volcanic lava. It cools very fast, often producing columns such as the above.

Igneous rocks are those that have formed from heat. Sedimentary rocks are formed under water from layers of materials and organic remains. Metamorphic rocks are the result of changes made to existing rocks.

Granite is a coarse-grained igneous rock that has formed slowly underground.

Pumice is a light igneous rock that often forms in a volcanic eruption.

Marble is a medium-grained rock that forms in metamorphic terrains.

Slate is a dense, fine-grained metamorphic rock that splits into thin slabs.

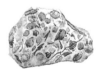

Limestone is a sedimentary rock that often contains tiny fossilized remains.

Sandstone is a sedimentary rock made of fine or coarse grains cemented into beds.

ROCKS FROM HEAT
Hot molten magma from inside the Earth can break out at the surface through a volcano as lava. It then cools and solidifies quickly, forming very fine rock such as basalt. Or, it may cool slowly underground, forming big, coarse mineral crystals. Granite is formed this way. In both cases, the rock is igneous—formed from fire.

ROCKS FROM WATER
Loose materials, such as sand or mud, can build up in layers at the bottom of the sea. These layers, or beds, may eventually be buried, compressed, and cemented into a solid mass. The resulting rock is called a sedimentary rock—built from layers. The layers may consist of small fragments such as sand, creating sandstone. Or they may be built from minerals dissolved in the seawater, like limestone, or built up from things that were once alive, like coal. We find fossils in sedimentary rocks.

NEW ROCKS FROM OLD
The third kind of rock forms when a rock that already exists is heated or squeezed. This may occur in the heart of a mountain chain when it is being pushed up, as the heat and pressure change the minerals that it contains. This produces a metamorphic rock—a rock of change. Great heat gives a rock with an even, crystalline structure, such as marble. Great pressure produces a rock in which the crystals are all twisted and deformed—schist, for example.

ROCK CYCLE
New rock is constantly being pushed up toward the Earth's surface, where it is broken down by the elements and deposited at the bottom of lakes, rivers, and seas. These sedimentary layers are compressed into new rock, which may later be uplifted or sink to depths where it melts to form igneous rocks. It can also become so roasted and compressed that it forms metamorphic rock.

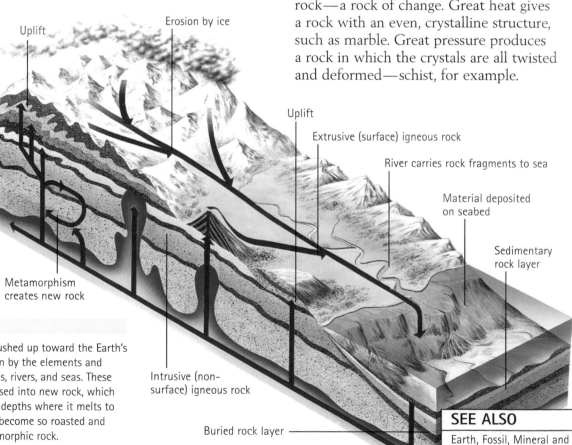

Uplift

Erosion by ice

Uplift

Extrusive (surface) igneous rock

River carries rock fragments to sea

Material deposited on seabed

Sedimentary rock layer

Metamorphism creates new rock

Intrusive (non-surface) igneous rock

Buried rock layer

SEE ALSO
Earth, Fossil, Mineral and gem, Mining, Oil, Soil

ROCKET

Rockets provide the thrust needed to lift spacecraft above Earth's atmosphere. They do this by burning fuel and shooting out the exhaust gases behind them.

Rockets make use of a law of physics: a force in one direction gives rise to an equal force in the opposite direction. The backward force of the escaping gases leads to an equal and opposite thrust that pushes the rocket forward. Because rockets have a supply of liquid oxygen, they can work in the emptiness of space.

MULTISTAGE ROCKETS
Most space rockets consist of three separate sections, or stages. After the powerful first stage has run out of fuel, it falls away and the second-stage engines ignite. After this fuel has been used up, the spacecraft completes its journey away from Earth, with the help of the third-stage engines.

SPACE SHUTTLE
The U.S. space shuttle had the first reusable rockets. It consisted of an orbiter; an external fuel tank that supplied the orbiter's main engines; and two solid-fuel rocket boosters. When the boosters ran out of fuel, they parachuted into the ocean, to be recovered. The empty fuel tank was jettisoned next, burning up on reentry into Earth's atmosphere. The orbiter continued into space to carry out its mission, returning to Earth to land on a runway like an airplane. During its 30 years of service, the five-strong shuttle fleet flew 135 missions.

FUTURE ROCKETS
A new generation of rockets is being developed, and should be seen on the launch pads from 2019. They are known as heavy-lift launch vehicles. The biggest and most powerful is the SLS (Space Launch System), being built by NASA to launch the Orion spacecraft. It can lift a huge load, but is extremely expensive to operate.

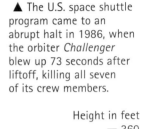

▲ The U.S. space shuttle program came to an abrupt halt in 1986, when the orbiter *Challenger* blew up 73 seconds after liftoff, killing all seven of its crew members.

MILESTONES IN ROCKETRY
c.1000 Chinese fireworks propelled by gunpowder
1805 Englishman William Congreve develops a rocket for use in battle
1903 Russian Konstantin Tsiolkovsky designs a spacecraft powered by liquid fuel
1926 First liquid-fueled rocket, Robert H. Goddard, U.S.
1944 Germany launches its destructive V2 rockets
1957 First rocket to lift a spacecraft into Earth's orbit
1981–2011 The space shuttle is the first reusable rocket system

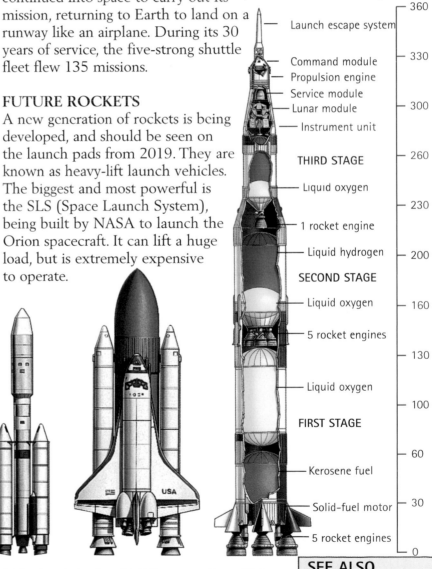

Height in feet

- Launch escape system — 360
- Command module — 330
- Propulsion engine
- Service module
- Lunar module — 300
- Instrument unit

THIRD STAGE — 260

- Liquid oxygen — 230
- 1 rocket engine
- Liquid hydrogen — 200

SECOND STAGE

- Liquid oxygen — 160
- 5 rocket engines — 130
- Liquid oxygen — 100

FIRST STAGE — 60

- Kerosene fuel
- Solid-fuel motor — 30
- 5 rocket engines — 0

German V2 first tested in 1942.

U.S. *Atlas* developed in 1960s.

Soviet *Soyuz II* launched in 1968.

European *Ariane IV* makes first flight in 1986.

U.S. *Titan* launched *Viking* spacecraft to Mars in 1974.

Reusable U.S. space shuttle makes first flight in 1981.

Saturn V takes U.S. *Apollo II* crew to Moon in 1969.

SEE ALSO
Engine, Spacecraft, Space exploration, Warfare

ROMAN EMPIRE

The Romans ruled the Mediterranean and much of Europe for hundreds of years. Many modern legal and government systems are based on those of Rome.

Julius Caesar (c.100–44 B.C.) was a dictator, taking power from the Senate.

Caligula (A.D. 12–41) ordered many executions and may have been insane.

Hadrian (76–138) ordered the building of defenses along the empire's borders.

Septimus Severus (146–211) reformed the empire into a military state.

The cruelty of Commodus (161–192) plunged the empire into civil war.

Constantine the Great (c.280–337) was the first Christian emperor.

Over hundreds of years, the Romans defeated the other peoples of Italy and then built up a vast empire. This reached its largest extent in A.D. 117. Social organization and military discipline kept the Romans in power. The common language of their empire was Latin.

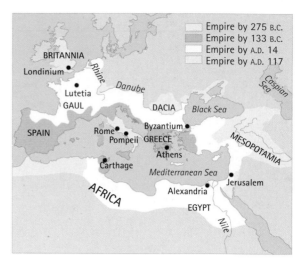

▲ The territory of the Roman Empire expanded rapidly during wars with Egypt, Carthage, and Greece. After A.D. 117, remote areas, such as Mesopotamia, were abandoned.

THE REPUBLIC

According to legend, Rome was founded in 753 B.C., and in 509 B.C. became a republic. Rome's main rival was Carthage, a city in North Africa, and in 218 B.C. the two went to war. The Carthaginian leader, Hannibal, wiped out the main Roman army at Cannae in 216 B.C., but he could not capture Rome. Carthage was finally defeated in 146 B.C. By 44 B.C., Rome had conquered Greece and large areas of the Near East, North Africa, Spain, and France.

AGE OF AUGUSTUS

As the Roman Empire grew, patricians, or noblemen, gained vast wealth and the ordinary citizens, or plebeians, lost political power. The army was more loyal to successful commanders than to the

government. These tensions led to a series of civil wars from 49 B.C. to 30 B.C. The wars were won by Octavian, nephew of the dictator Julius Caesar. He took the title Augustus, meaning "the sacred one," and established a new type of government, giving power to the emperor.

CITIZENS OF ROME

Male citizens of Rome could vote, stand in elections or work in government. Female citizens and slaves were not allowed to vote. At first, only people from Rome were citizens, but gradually men from other cities or who had served in the army for 30 years became citizens. Finally, in A.D. 212,

THE ROMAN ARMY

The Roman army was organized into legions of about 4,000–6,000 armored infantry, with a few archers and cavalry. In battle, the legion was trained to fight in tight formations, such as the *testudo*, or tortoise (below). The army was skilled at building forts to guard the frontiers. Each legionary had to carry all his equipment, including weapons, cooking pot, blanket, and tools (right).

ROMAN HOUSING

Most Romans lived in the countryside or in apartment blocks (*insulae*), but wealthy families would have a town house, or *domus*. The front rooms were rented out to shopkeepers. The family lived in rooms around the atrium courtyard or the peristyle garden. The *triclinium* (dining room) was close to the kitchen.

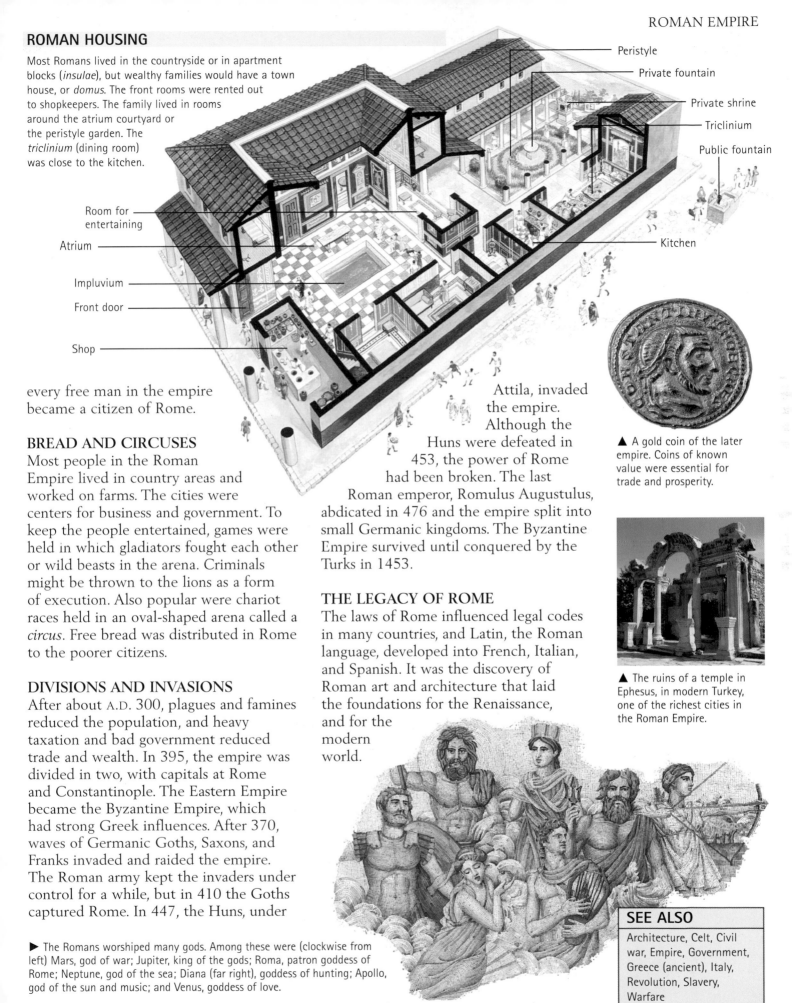

Peristyle
Private fountain
Private shrine
Triclinium
Public fountain
Room for entertaining
Atrium
Impluvium
Front door
Shop
Kitchen

▲ A gold coin of the later empire. Coins of known value were essential for trade and prosperity.

▲ The ruins of a temple in Ephesus, in modern Turkey, one of the richest cities in the Roman Empire.

every free man in the empire became a citizen of Rome.

BREAD AND CIRCUSES

Most people in the Roman Empire lived in country areas and worked on farms. The cities were centers for business and government. To keep the people entertained, games were held in which gladiators fought each other or wild beasts in the arena. Criminals might be thrown to the lions as a form of execution. Also popular were chariot races held in an oval-shaped arena called a *circus*. Free bread was distributed in Rome to the poorer citizens.

DIVISIONS AND INVASIONS

After about A.D. 300, plagues and famines reduced the population, and heavy taxation and bad government reduced trade and wealth. In 395, the empire was divided in two, with capitals at Rome and Constantinople. The Eastern Empire became the Byzantine Empire, which had strong Greek influences. After 370, waves of Germanic Goths, Saxons, and Franks invaded and raided the empire. The Roman army kept the invaders under control for a while, but in 410 the Goths captured Rome. In 447, the Huns, under Attila, invaded the empire. Although the Huns were defeated in 453, the power of Rome had been broken. The last Roman emperor, Romulus Augustulus, abdicated in 476 and the empire split into small Germanic kingdoms. The Byzantine Empire survived until conquered by the Turks in 1453.

THE LEGACY OF ROME

The laws of Rome influenced legal codes in many countries, and Latin, the Roman language, developed into French, Italian, and Spanish. It was the discovery of Roman art and architecture that laid the foundations for the Renaissance, and for the modern world.

▶ The Romans worshiped many gods. Among these were (clockwise from left) Mars, god of war; Jupiter, king of the gods; Roma, patron goddess of Rome; Neptune, god of the sea; Diana (far right), goddess of hunting; Apollo, god of the sun and music; and Venus, goddess of love.

SEE ALSO

Architecture, Celt, Civil war, Empire, Government, Greece (ancient), Italy, Revolution, Slavery, Warfare

RUSSIA

The Russian Federation is the largest country in the world. It takes in northeastern Europe and, beyond the Ural mountains, northern Asia.

RUSSIA
Area: 6,592,850 sq. mi.
(17,075,400km²)
Population: 142,905,000
Capital: Moscow
Language: Russian
Currency: Rouble

▲ Russian ballet became internationally famous in the 1800s. The Moscow State Academy of Choreography is one of the training centers for children.

Western Russia is part of a great plain stretching through eastern Europe to the Urals. The vast eastern region, Siberia, includes tablelands and great rivers. Mountains ring the northeast, southeast, and southwest. Russia borders both the Arctic and Pacific oceans. Much of the north is tundra, treeless land where the soil is permanently frozen beneath the surface. To the south are vast forests of conifer and birch, known as taiga, giving way to grassy steppes.

WINTER AND SUMMER
Most of Russia has long, cold winters. Half the country is covered by snow for six months of the year. Many northern ports are closed by ice in winter, although the Arctic climate has been warming in recent years. Summers are mild or warm. Rivers such as the Volga, Don and Dnieper, along with a network of canals, are part of the transport system.

RICH IN RESOURCES
Russia has a great wealth of natural resources, including gas, oil, coal, iron, copper, gold, and platinum. Many of these reserves, however, are in remote areas,

▲ A Russian *matryoshka* is a set of wooden dolls painted in traditional dress, placed one inside another.

and access to them is hampered by the harsh climate and high transport costs. The railway system radiates out from Moscow and St. Petersburg, around which industry is concentrated. About three-quarters of the population now live in towns and cities, and many rural villages have been abandoned. Cattle and, in the Arctic, reindeer are herded and agricultural produce includes cotton, wheat, barley, maize, sunflowers, and wine.

PEOPLE AND RELIGION
Ethnic Russians account for about 78 percent of the population. Minority peoples include Tatars, Ukrainians, Bashkir, Chechens, and Chuvash. The former Soviet Union (1922–91) was officially an atheist country, but since its fall the

▶ Lake Baikal in Siberia is the world's deepest lake—5,712 ft. (1,731m).

miles
0   500
0   500
km

N

ARCTIC OCEAN

Franz Josef Land

Severnaya Zemlya

New Siberian Islands

BERING SEA

Novaya Zemlya

Kolyma

Indigirka

Lena

SEA OF OKHOTSK

Kuril Islands

CENTRAL SIBERIAN PLATEAU

R U S S I A

Sakhalin

NORWAY

ESTONIA
LATVIA
LITHUANIA
RUSSIA
POLAND
BELARUS

FINLAND

Murmansk

Tallinn

Arkhangel'sk

Riga
Vilnius
St. Petersburg

W. Dvina
Dnieper

Moscow

Nizhniy Novgorod

Ural Mts.

Ob

Yenisey

UKRAINE

Don

Kazan

Perm

Volga

Samara

Yekaterinburg

Chelyabinsk

Rostov-na-Donu

Omsk

Novosibirsk

Lake Baikal

Amur

CHINA

JAPAN

Vladivostok

KAZAKHSTAN

CASPIAN SEA

GEORGIA

AZERBAIJAN

CHINA

MONGOLIA

Russian Orthodox branch of the Christian faith has regained some popularity, and is followed by up to 20 percent of Russians. About 10–15 percent of the population is Muslim.

RUSSIA'S EXPANSION

The Russian state emerged from the Rus civilization in the 9th century. Its rulers took the title of tsar. Peter the Great, tsar from 1682 to 1725, introduced Western European culture and technology and founded a new capital, St Petersburg. By conquering Estonia and Latvia, he began a program of expansion, which his successors extended to Lithuania, Belarus, Ukraine, and the Crimea. Russian settlement of Siberia began in the 18th century and in the 19th century Finland, the Caucasus and Central Asia were added to the Russian Empire.

EARLY 20TH-CENTURY RUSSIA

Russia was a large and powerful country, with a rich culture that saw the development of modern ballet, the music

of Tchaikovsky and the writings of Tolstoy and Chekhov. However, under the tsars (rulers) Russia failed to modernize and bring in democratic reforms. By 1905 the country was in a state of revolution. ▶

▼ St Basil's Cathedral, in Moscow's Red Square, dates back to 1561.

347

▲ Siberian tigers survive in the snowy forests of the Russian Far East.

WARS AND LOSSES

During World War II, the U.S.S.R. fought with the Allies from 1940 to 1945, and suffered massive human losses. After the war, the victorious U.S.S.R. was directly or indirectly in control of much of Eastern and Central Europe. A period of political tension and confrontation with the U.S.-led Western democracies (the "Cold War") lasted until 1991.

RUSSIAN REVOLUTION

In 1917, Tsar Nicholas II was overthrown. A moderate government led by Alexander Kerensky came to power, but in turn was overthrown by radical communists known as Bolsheheviks, led by Vladimir Ilyich Ulyanov (better known as Lenin). After a bitter civil war, Lenin founded the Union of Soviet Socialist Republics (U.S.S.R., or Soviet Union) in 1922.

PUTIN'S RUSSIA

When the Soviet Union broke up, many of its border territories became independent nations. In the new Russian Federation there was democratic reform, but also economic chaos. Vladimir Putin came to power in 2008. He brought more stability, but tensions soon grew again with the West and with Russia's neighbors.

▲ Vladimir Putin has served as Prime Minister and as President. His supporters say he is a strong leader, standing up for Russia. His critics claim he has too much personal power.

THE SOVIET UNION

After Lenin's death in 1924, Joseph Stalin ruled as a brutal dictator. He developed heavy industry but his agricultural reforms led to mass starvation, and many of his opponents were killed by the feared secret police, or imprisoned in labor camps.

▼ The Kremlin, in Moscow's Red Square, was originally a fortress. Under communist rule, it became the government headquarters.

▲ Long, harsh winters are an accepted part of life in Siberia. Local people use sleds to carry shopping.

SEE ALSO

Asia, Astronaut, Cold War, Communism, Eastern Europe, Europe, Revolution

SATELLITE

Satellites are objects that move in orbit around other objects of greater mass. A satellite may be natural, like the Moon, or artificial, like an orbiting spacecraft.

Spacecraft orbiting high above Earth can be used to relay messages over very long distances. Some satellites are used to send television signals around the world or to track the movement of hurricanes and large weather fronts. Communication satellites are used to pass on telephone conversations and computer data. These satellites receive signals from a transmitting station on Earth, amplify them, and beam the signals down to another Earth station, which may be thousands of miles away.

GEOSYNCHRONOUS ORBIT
Most communication satellites move in a special orbit known as a geosynchronous orbit, which is about 22,310 mi. (35,900km) above the equator. This orbit allows the satellite to remain over the same point on Earth's surface at all times.

ASTRONOMICAL SATELLITES
By carrying telescopes and other instruments above Earth's atmosphere, astronomical satellites can see distant objects, such as stars, nebulae, and galaxies, much more clearly than we can from the ground. They can also pick up types of waves, such as infrared, ultraviolet, X rays, and gamma rays, which are partly or totally blocked by the atmosphere. For example, X-ray satellites have helped scientists to study black holes and dense, remote binary (double) stars.

SURVEYING THE EARTH
Remote-sensing satellites, equipped with powerful cameras and other equipment, provide valuable information about our planet's natural resources. They can reveal changes to the polar ice caps or the rate at which human beings are destroying the rain forests. Weather satellites can track the movement of hurricanes and supply data that allows accurate weather forecasts several days in advance.

▲ *Sputnik 1*, the world's first artificial satellite, was launched by Russia on October 4, 1957. It was used to broadcast scientific data and orbited the Earth for six months.

▼ Satellites can sometimes give us a clearer picture of activity on Earth's surface than we can get from the ground. Earth is surrounded by craft designed specifically for different purposes.

Landsat 5 can spot areas where the Brazilian rain forest has been cleared

The European Remote Sensing satellite (ERS) carried instruments to monitor Earth's land, oceans, and atmosphere. It was replaced by Envisat in 2011.

Spy satellites use powerful telescopes to detect potential trouble spots

Aqua (EOS PM-1) is a research satellite that studies the Earth's water cycle

The Meteosat Second Generation (MSG) satellite stays in geostationary orbit above the Atlantic to track weather fronts such as hurricanes and cyclones

SEE ALSO

Communication, Telecommunication, Telephone, Television, Weather

SCANDINAVIA

Scandinavia consists of the neighboring northern European countries of Denmark, Norway, Sweden, Finland, Iceland, and the Faeroe Islands.

DENMARK
Area: 16,639 sq. mi. (43,094km²)
Population: 5,809,000
Capital: Copenhagen
Language: Danish
Currency: Krone

FINLAND
Area: 130,558 sq. mi. (338,145km²)
Population: 5,518,000
Capital: Helsinki
Languages: Finnish, Swedish
Currency: Euro

ICELAND
Area: 39,699 sq. mi. (102,819km²)
Population: 340,000
Capital: Reykjavik
Language: Icelandic
Currency: Krona

NORWAY
Area: 125,021 sq. mi. (323,802km²)
Population: 5,320,000
Capital: Oslo
Language: Norwegian
Currency: Kroner

SWEDEN
Area: 173,860 sq. mi. (450,295km²)
Population: 10,040,000
Capital: Stockholm
Language: Swedish
Currency: Krona

▶ Stockholm, the capital of Sweden, is built on 14 small islands connected by about 50 bridges.

▲ Norway's coast is famous for its many fjords—long, narrow inlets of the sea that make fine natural harbors.

The name Scandinavia refers to the large peninsula made up of Sweden and Norway. Often included in this term are the neighboring countries of Denmark and Finland, as well as Iceland and the Faeroe Islands, which have cultural and language links with the region. Danish, Swedish, Norwegian, and Icelandic all come from a common ancestor language, but Finnish is distinctly different.

THE FAEROE ISLANDS

These 18 islands in the North Atlantic Ocean have a population of about 48,600. They were ruled by Norway until 1380, and many of the inhabitants are of Norse origin. For the last 600 years, they have been under Danish control. In 1948, they became self-governing. The representatives of their *Lagting* (assembly or parliament) sit in the Danish assembly in Copenhagen.

LONG SUMMER DAYS

Due to their northerly location, the countries of Scandinavia have long, cold, snowy winters. In Iceland and the northernmost parts of Finland, Norway, and Sweden around the Arctic Circle, it is light for 24 hours a day around midsummer and dark for most of the day toward the end of December.

RICH IN RESOURCES

Flat Denmark is famous for its agriculture, Finland for its lakes, Sweden for its forests, Norway for its spectacular coastal fjords (inlets), and Iceland for its dramatic geysers (hot springs) and volcanoes. The region is rich in natural resources, including oil, gas, iron, and timber. From the 1960s, Norway became expert at oil production and platform construction, but North Sea oil reserves are now in decline. Sweden is the most industrial of the Scandinavian nations and is one of the wealthiest countries in Europe. Fishing and shipbuilding have been important industries for the whole region. Modern

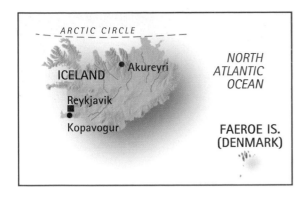

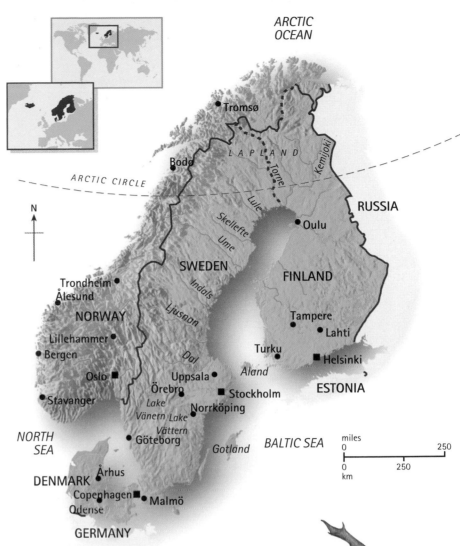

Scandinavian styles of architecture and design, especially of furniture, metalwork, and glassware, are influential worldwide.

NORTHERN PEOPLE

Most Scandinavians are descendants of Germanic people who moved into the area around 2,000 years ago, while most Finns migrated around the same time from western Russia. North of the Arctic Circle are the Sami—descendants of the earliest inhabitants of Sweden and Finland. Some Sami live a traditional way of life herding reindeer, which they keep for their meat, milk, and hides. But most earn a living from farming, fishing, or mining. In Norway, Finland, and Sweden, the Sami have their own parliaments, or Sametings.

SCANDINAVIAN POLICIES

Norway, Denmark, and Sweden are all

▼ In Denmark, surrounded as it is by sea, both fishing and shipbuilding are important. Danish fishing fleets bring in mackerel, herring, cod, shrimp, and flatfish.

constitutional monarchies, but Finland and Iceland are republics. The Scandinavian countries have traditionally been strong supporters of international organizations, human rights, health and welfare programs, and conservation. In recent years, the welfare state model has been under strain, mainly as a result of a drop in oil revenues and political swings to the right.

NORSE MYTHOLOGY

In pre-Christian times, early Scandinavian and Germanic people shared a common mythology, known as Norse mythology. The myths, originally passed on by word of mouth, were first written down in the 1200s. Four of the early Norse gods—Tiw, Odin, Thor, and Freya—are remembered in the days of the week: Tuesday, Wednesday, Thursday, and Friday. Today, Lutheran Protestant Christianity is the main religion in all Scandinavian countries.

▲ Found in arctic regions, reindeer migrate several hundred miles a year in search of food.

SEE ALSO

Arctic, Europe, Myth and legend, Viking

351

SCULPTURE

Sculpture is a piece of three-dimensional art that gives you different views as you walk around it. It can be carved, molded, or shaped out of a range of materials.

▲ *Cloud Gate* (2006) by Sir Anish Kapoor is a public sculpture in Chicago, Illinois, USA. Made of 168 stainless steel plates welded together, it has no visible seams.

The two traditional ways of making a sculpture are carving and molding. Carving means cutting into wood or stone; molding involves making a model in clay and using it to cast a replica in concrete or a metal. Sculpture can also be carved in relief, by cutting a raised picture into flat stone or wood. Modern sculptures have been made from plastic, glass, and everyday objects—one British artist, David Mach, uses papers and magazines.

▲ Michelangelo's bold and lifelike marble statue of *David* (1504) followed the classical Greek style.

GODS AND IDOLS
Since people began using tools, they have made figures of people and animals or religious idols to please their gods and scare away evil spirits. Tiny figures made by shamans (magician-priests) about 30,000 years ago are among the earliest known sculptures. The ancient Egyptians cut huge figures out of solid rock, and there are other massive ancient sculptures in the Americas and Asia. Tribal totem poles are a form of sculpture. The ancient Greeks created impressive lifelike figures.

CHANGING IMAGES
In the Middle Ages, European sculpture was mostly religious—the architectural decoration in and on church buildings. During the Renaissance, artists returned to the realism of the classical Greeks. Their works were for religious and private patrons who paid for marble and bronze sculptures.

BREAK WITH TRADITION
In the 1900s, sculptors began to explore new styles, using solid shapes to represent abstract ideas and feelings. This included using ordinary objects in unusual ways, like assembling moving pieces or mobiles—known as installation art. American artist Christo wrapped buildings in plastic, which linked art and architecture in a new way.

▲ British sculptor Andy Goldsworthy's *Sentinel* (2009), a form of land art, shows that art isn't confined to museums.

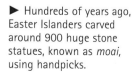

▶ Hundreds of years ago, Easter Islanders carved around 900 huge stone statues, known as *moai*, using handpicks.

SEE ALSO
Art, Renaissance

SEASHORE

There are many types of seashore, from rocky cliffs to sandy beaches. Each habitat has its own creatures and plant life, specially adapted to live there.

Tidal pools contain plants and small marine animals.

Rocky cliffs are a favorite nesting place for kittiwakes.

Many salt-resistant grasses thrive on sand dunes.

The seashore, the narrow zone where land and sea meet, is one of the most varied and fascinating habitats on Earth. It contains creatures that have evolved to live half their lives on land and half at sea.

BEACHES
The most common type of shore is the sandy beach, made of tiny particles of rock (sand) worn down by being constantly rolled together by waves. Plants can't grow in the loose sand between high- and low-water marks, but just below the surface, sandworms and burrowing shellfish feed on tiny food particles washed in with the tide. Sandy and muddy shores are favorite feeding places for shorebirds.

CLIFFS
Where waves hammer against hard rocks, a steep cliff may form. Here, the tiny ledges and cracks are home to specialized plants that can survive the salt spray and cold winter winds. Cliff ledges also provide nesting places for many seabirds such as gulls, guillemots, and gannets, and puffins live in burrows in the soil on the cliff top.

ROCKY SHORES
Rocky coasts are home to a huge variety of red, brown, and green seaweeds, some like long leather belts, some like mosses. The seaweed fronds provide a cool, damp hiding place for sand hoppers (beach fleas), crabs, barnacles, winkles, and limpets. Rock pools provide another place in which sea creatures can survive while the tide is out. Some mollusks, such as mussels and limpets, attach themselves to rocks.

SANDY SEASHORES
A vast array of birds, plants, mollusks, and crustaceans live around the world's seashores. Crashing waves constantly change the shape of sandy beaches, so all forms of life must be adaptable—most shore plants and animals are able to live in and out of water. Shorebirds feed on worms, fish, and other small creatures.

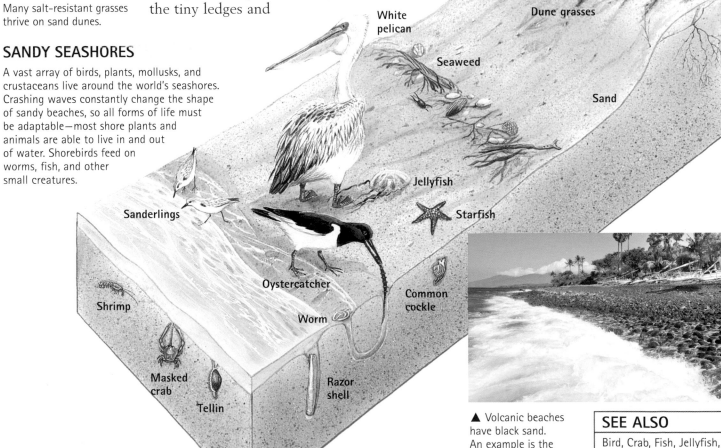

White pelican

Seaweed

Dune grasses

Sand

Jellyfish

Starfish

Sanderlings

Oystercatcher

Common cockle

Worm

Shrimp

Masked crab

Tellin

Razor shell

▲ Volcanic beaches have black sand. An example is the Tulamben in Bali, Indonesia

SEE ALSO
Bird, Crab, Fish, Jellyfish, Ocean and sea, Snail, Starfish, Volcano, Worm

353

SEASON

As Earth orbits the Sun, the tilt of its axis causes changes in the length of day and the temperature. This creates what we call the seasons.

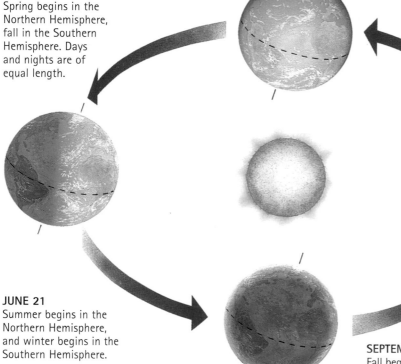

MARCH 21
Spring begins in the Northern Hemisphere, fall in the Southern Hemisphere. Days and nights are of equal length.

DECEMBER 21
Winter begins in the Northern Hemisphere, and summer begins in the Southern Hemisphere.

JUNE 21
Summer begins in the Northern Hemisphere, and winter begins in the Southern Hemisphere.

SEPTEMBER 23
Fall begins in the Northern Hemisphere, and spring begins in the Southern Hemisphere. Days and nights are of equal length again.

▲ December in Alberta, Canada, brings the typically snowy and cold weather of a Northern Hemisphere winter.

The seasons affect everything we do. They determine when we plant our crops and harvest them, what kind of clothes we wear, what we eat, how much energy we use for heating and lighting, and even how we feel. The seasons are caused by the tilt of Earth's axis during its yearly journey around the Sun.

EARTH'S TILT
Earth is always spinning, tilted at an angle of 23.5°, so that the North Pole tilts toward the Sun for part of the year. In the Northern Hemisphere, the Sun is high in the sky and the days are long and warm, resulting in summer. At the same time, the South Pole is tilted away from the Sun, and the Southern Hemisphere has its winter.

THE SOLSTICES
As Earth orbits the Sun, its axis points toward the same spot in space, so that six

months later, the North Pole tilts away from the Sun. It is now winter in the Northern Hemisphere and summer in the Southern Hemisphere. In the Northern Hemisphere, the longest day (the summer solstice) is June 21 and the shortest day (the winter solstice) is December 21. For the Southern Hemisphere, the longest day of the year is December 21 and the shortest day is June 21.

THE EQUINOXES
Halfway between the solstices are the fall, or autumn, and spring equinoxes. On March 21 and September 23, tilted Earth is sideways-on to the Sun, and day and night are of equal length. Spring in the Northern Hemisphere begins on March 21, when the Southern Hemisphere has fall. On September 23, the Northern Hemisphere's fall begins, and it is spring south of the equator.

▲ Southern Hemisphere areas like Green Island Beach, Australia, enjoy the beginning of their summer season in December.

SEE ALSO
Climate, Earth, Hibernation, Sun, Weather, Wind

354

SEED AND POLLINATION

Seeds are the means by which flowering plants reproduce to make other plants of the same species. But pollination must take place before a seed is formed.

Stone fruits (drupes) such as the peach have a large stone that contains a seed.

The coconut is a very large seed, with edible flesh and milk inside its tough husk.

The acorn is the fruit of the oak tree. Its woody cup holds a hard, smooth nut.

Maple seeds have papery wings that help them scatter on the wind.

An apple has several seeds in its core, to increase its chances of reproduction.

A seed consists of a tiny new plant, called an embryo, and a store of food, all contained within a tough protective coat. Some seeds can remain dormant (in a resting state) for over 100 years before they grow into new plants. To make a seed, pollen (male cells) from one plant must fertilize, or pollinate, the eggs (female cells) of another plant.

POLLINATION

Some plants, like grasses and trees, rely on the wind to blow their pollen from one plant to the next. Other plants have large flowers, with bright colors, scents, and nectar, to attract insects, bats, birds, or small animals. These visitors feed on the nectar, and as they do so, the pollen sticks to them and is carried to the next flower they visit. When a pollen grain sticks to another flower's stigma, it sends out a pollen tube that grows down inside the stalk leading to the ovary, so male cells can reach the egg and fertilize it. Once the egg has been fertilized, it develops into a seed.

GERMINATION

A seed must have moisture, warmth, and oxygen to grow into a new plant. This process, called germination, begins with the seed absorbing water. The embryo begins to grow, and its root pushes its way through the seed coat. The seed leaves, or cotyledons, and the shoot soon follow.

SEEDS AS FOOD

When a seed falls to the ground, its starchy food store feeds the young plant, and it is this starch that people use as food. The seeds of wheat, barley, corn, rice, and other members of the grass family are cooked to make basic foods, or ground into flour to make bread and pasta.

SEED DISPERSAL

Plants scatter, or disperse, seeds using many methods. Mice and other small animals eat grass seeds (grain) and berries, and spiky burrs from plants such as thistles stick to their fur. Later, mouse droppings move seeds to a different area, and burrs drop off along the way. Dandelion seeds have soft, feathery tufts, and poppies have tiny, light seeds, which make it easy for them to become windborne.

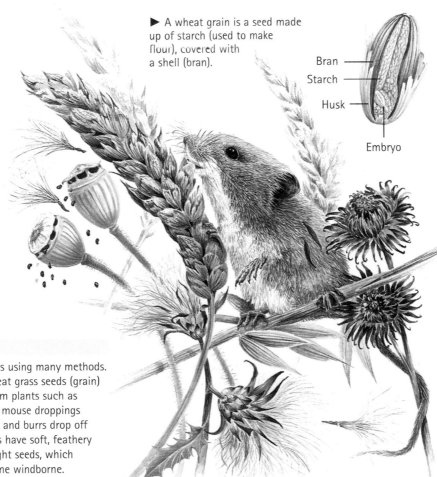

▶ A wheat grain is a seed made up of starch (used to make flour), covered with a shell (bran).

Bran
Starch
Husk
Embryo

▲ When a windborne seed falls to the ground, its food store gives it the nutrients it needs to take root.

▲ The soil provides additional nutrients so that the plant can push above ground level and grow to full size.

SEE ALSO
Crop, Flower, Fruit, Plant, Tree, Vegetable

SEVEN WONDERS OF THE WORLD

The Seven Wonders of the World were the most impressive and famous buildings and monuments known to the ancient Greeks.

In about 146 B.C., the Greek architect Philo of Byzantium produced a list of the finest engineering feats of the known world. Of these, only the Pyramids of Giza remain, although archaeologists have found foundations and fragments of the Temple of Artemis and stone blocks from the Pharos.

IN MEMORY

The greatest Egyptian pyramids were built at Giza as tombs for the pharaohs Cheops (Khufu), Chephren (Khafre), and Mycerinus (Menkure) between 2600 B.C. and 2500 B.C.

The Mausoleum was built as the tomb of King Mausolus of Caria in 353 B.C. by his widow, Artemisia, in the city of Halicarnassus (modern Bodrum in Turkey). Even today, elaborate tombs are called mausoleums. The legendary Hanging Gardens of Babylon were built in about 580 B.C. by King Nebuchadrezzar II of Babylon to remind his wife, a princess from the mountain kingdom of Media, of home.

BUILT FOR THE GODS

The second Temple of Artemis was built in 350 B.C. (the first was destroyed in 356 B.C.) It had over 100 columns, each 65 ft. (20m) tall and decorated with sculptures. It was dedicated to Artemis, goddess of nature. The statue of Zeus at Olympia, home of the Olympic Games, was made in 433 B.C. by Phidias of Athens. The wooden statue, covered in ivory and gold, stood 43 ft. (13m) tall. The Colossus of Rhodes was a 130-ft. (40-m)-tall bronze statue of the sun god Helios, erected by the city of Rhodes after invaders were defeated in 305 B.C. It fell in an earthquake in 224 B.C. and was sold for scrap in A.D. 653.

THE FIRST LIGHTHOUSE

The approach to the harbor of Alexandria in Egypt was extremely dangerous. To help ships arrive safely, the great Pharos was built in about 280 B.C. The tower stood over 460 ft. (140m) tall and was topped by a statue of a god, thought to be Zeus Soter. The tower could be seen from far out to sea and led ships into harbor. At night, it is said, a fire was lit to guide ships. The tower gradually crumbled into ruins after 1,500 years.

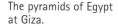

The pyramids of Egypt at Giza.

The Colossus on the island of Rhodes.

The Mausoleum of Halicarnassus.

The statue of Zeus at Olympia.

The Hanging Gardens of Babylon.

The Temple of Artemis at Ephesus.

SEE ALSO

Babylon, Egypt (ancient), Greece (ancient)

SHARK

Sharks are fish whose skeletons are made of gristly cartilage instead of bone. Almost all of them live in the sea and they feed mainly on other fish.

The aggressive tiger shark can grow to over 23 ft. (7m) long and has been known to attack human beings.

The hammerhead shark can grow up to 20 ft. (6m) long and has a flattened head like the head of a hammer.

The basking shark can grow to 50 ft. (15m) long and swims close to the surface to feed on plankton.

The fast and powerful mako shark grows up to 11.5 ft. (3.5m) long and is a popular catch for sea fishermen.

The thresher shark grows to about 20 ft. (6m) long and uses its long tail to stun the fish it feeds on.

The harmless whale shark grows up to 50 ft. (15m) long but feeds only on plankton and small fish.

There are over 450 species of shark, from the little dogfish, less than 19 in. (0.5m) long, to the huge whale shark, which is 50 ft. (15m) long and weighs 15 tons. Most sharks are fast swimmers, with streamlined bodies. Their fins are thick and leathery and cannot be folded like those of other fish.

GILL SLITS FOR BREATHING
A shark has five to seven gill slits just behind the head on each side. Water taken in through the mouth flows out through these slits after passing over the gills, where life-giving oxygen is taken from it. Most sharks must keep swimming to keep this oxygen flow going.

SKIN LIKE SANDPAPER
The skin of a shark is covered with denticles—toothlike scales that make it very rough. In fact, sailors once used shark skins as sandpaper to scrub the decks of their wooden ships. A shark's teeth have

THE GREAT WHITE
Up to 26 ft. (8m) long, the great white is the most dangerous of all sharks. It preys on large animals such as dolphins, sea lions, and other sharks. It will also attack human beings and even fishing boats.

serrated, razor-sharp edges and can easily slice through flesh. Its digestive juices are strong enough to corrode steel.

THE LARGEST FISH
Although most sharks are ferocious hunters, the largest ones are actually harmless. The whale shark is the largest fish in the world. It has a huge mouth, but it feeds by straining tiny animals and plants from the water, just as many whales do.

SKATES AND RAYS
Skates and rays are closely related to sharks, but their bodies are very flat. Their head and body and massive front fins are all fused together to form a circular or diamond-shaped disk. They live mainly on the seabed and feed on shellfish and other bottom-dwelling animals, which they crush with rows of flat teeth. Some of them are armed with poisonous spines.

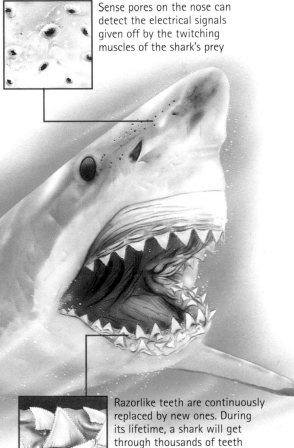

Sense pores on the nose can detect the electrical signals given off by the twitching muscles of the shark's prey

The skin consists of tiny, toothlike scales and is used to make rough shark leather

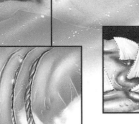

Gill slits open and close to take in oxygen from the water

Razorlike teeth are continuously replaced by new ones. During its lifetime, a shark will get through thousands of teeth

SEE ALSO
Fish, Ocean and sea, Whale and dolphin

SHIP

Ships are large sea-going craft that are used to carry passengers and freight or to catch fish. They may also be used in warfare.

▲ Tankers transport liquids, usually oil, in bulk. The liquid is stored in tanks, and empty chambers give added buoyancy. The engines and crew quarters are usually placed at the rear.

Viking longships of A.D. 900 had open decks and were powered by sails and oars.

Galleons during the 1500s had high sides on which to mount guns.

Clippers of the 1800s had streamlined hulls for extra speed.

Large wooden ships were first made in the countries around the Mediterranean Sea and in the Far East from about 2,500 B.C. These ships were powered by sails or oars and were up to 165 ft. (50m) in length. Later wooden ships, with tall masts and several sails, reached 380 ft. (115m).

IRON AND STEAM

Modern ships were made possible by two important developments. The first was the use of iron or steel construction, which is strong enough for very large ships. The second was the steam engine, which made ships independent of the direction in which the wind was blowing. The only practical limit to the size of a steel ship is the depth of coastal waters and the size of docks. The largest ships now afloat are the supertankers. These sail between oil fields and refineries in Europe, America, and Japan. Supertankers are far bigger than any liner or warship, weighing up to one million tons when fully loaded and measuring over 1,300 ft. (400m) long.

The *Great Eastern* of 1855 combined steam and sail power and was the first liner.

CARGO CARRIERS

Modern cargo ships include bulk carriers and container ships. The bulk carrier transports large, solid cargoes such as coal or iron ore, using special equipment to load and unload. The container ship carries standard-sized containers, each small enough to be loaded onto a truck. A very large ship may carry several thousand containers. These big merchant ships have an "island" at the back (the stern) containing the bridge, the crew quarters, and the engine room. They also have a long center deck above the cargo holds, and a further small island close to the front (the bow).

PASSENGER SHIPS

Luxurious passenger ships called liners were used to carry passengers between continents, but today, large passenger-carrying ships are used for cruising. They take people on vacation, allowing them to visit different ports while enjoying a luxurious life on board. Another passenger ship is the ferry, used for carrying people and vehicles on short sea crossings. Ferries are designed to load and unload their passengers quickly, usually through huge doors at the bow and stern. A modern cruise liner may weigh 80,000 tons, and some ferries weigh over 20,000 tons.

WARSHIPS

As trade by sea became more important and nations competed for dominance, they began to develop navies of fighting ships. Warships now include destroyers, cruisers, and submarines, armed with guns, missiles, and torpedoes. The largest warships are aircraft carriers, which can weigh 80,000 tons or more. They act as offshore air bases from which air strikes on enemy targets can be made.

ENGINES AND STEERING

Most modern ships are driven by one or two propellers, powered by large diesel engines or by gas turbines, although some warships use nuclear power. The diesel engine is cheaper and more reliable, and the gas turbine is small and light. A rudder is used for steering, but small propellers, or thrusters, are used to control the ship when it is maneuvering.

SKIMMING THE SURFACE

A ship uses most of its energy pushing the water aside, so some modern craft skim above the water. Hydrofoils are supported by "wings" under the water, and hovercraft float on a cushion of air. Both are fast, but cannot be built too large.

▲ A multipurpose cargo ship carrying containers. Lifting equipment along the center of the ship is used to load and unload the cargo.

Air strikes against enemy fleets are launched from aircraft carriers.

Cruise ships are luxurious floating hotels that carry thousands of passengers.

Missiles and torpedoes are launched from submarines beneath the sea surface.

FACTORY FISHING

Factory ships catch large numbers of fish. The net is hauled in, spilling the catch into the fish bin where it is sorted before passing to the cleaning room where heads and guts are removed. The waste is processed into fish meal, while the clean fillets are packed and frozen. The frozen fish is stored in the refrigerated hold until the ship reaches port. Sonar and other electronic aids help the skipper to find giant shoals of fish. In some places, factory ships have put local fishing boats out of business, or reduced fish stocks by overfishing.

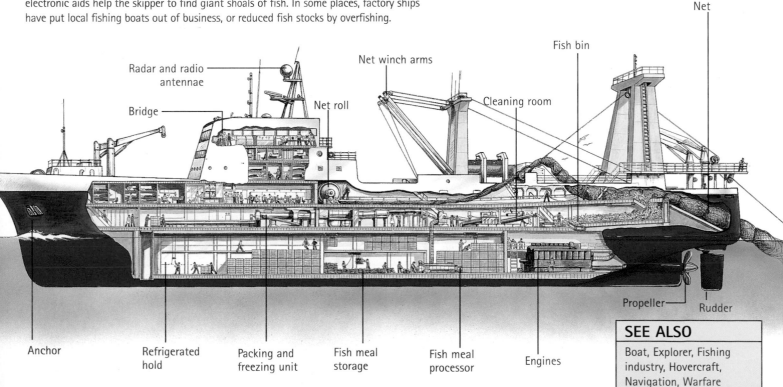

Net

Fish bin

Net winch arms

Cleaning room

Radar and radio antennae

Bridge

Net roll

Anchor

Refrigerated hold

Packing and freezing unit

Fish meal storage

Fish meal processor

Engines

Propeller

Rudder

SEE ALSO

Boat, Explorer, Fishing industry, Hovercraft, Navigation, Warfare

SIGHT

Sight is the ability to detect light and form it into an accurate view of the shapes, colors, and distances of surrounding objects.

Insect compound eyes have a mosaic of cells that build up an image.

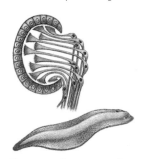

Flatworms have cupped organs able to detect the direction of a light source.

Sight is the most important sense for most animals, providing over half of all the information that enters the brain. Animals use their eyes to look for food and mates and to watch for danger. Most invertebrates (creatures without backbones) have simple eyes, able to give only a rough picture of their surroundings.

ADVANCED VISION

Animals with backbones (vertebrates) have eyes that are able to see clearly. At the front of the eye is a transparent area, known as the cornea, through which light enters. Behind the cornea is a colored ring of muscle, the iris, with a central hole, the pupil. The iris changes shape to make the pupil wider in dim light, so that more light enters the eye, for clearer vision. Behind the pupil is the lens, which focuses light rays. A ring of ciliary muscles changes the shape of the lens to adjust the focus.

THE HUMAN EYE

The human eyeball, about 1 in. (25mm) across, is set into a bowl-shaped socket in the skull. Six small muscles move the eye up, down, and sideways. The eye's whitish outer layer, the sclera, is strong and tough. Inside is the choroid layer, soft and blood-rich, which nourishes the inner parts of the eye. The main bulk of the eyeball is filled with clear jelly, or vitreous humor, which keeps it firm.

▲ A cat's eyes stand out in poor light (left). They have an extra layer, the guanine, which reflects light back past the retina. The guanine allows cats to see clearly in poor light (right), although they cannot distinguish colors very well.

LIGHT TO NERVE SIGNALS

Light rays focused by the lens shine onto the retina. This contains millions of light-sensitive cells, known as rods and cones. They send nerve signals to the brain, which forms them into a picture. The rods are sensitive in dim light, and detect movement and the contrast between black and white. The cones, which are clustered in one small area, see color. Only humans and a few other types of animal can see in full color.

TWO EYES

Most animals have two eyes, which help judge distance in two ways. Each eye sees an object from a slightly different point. The brain compares these two views, and the more different they are, the nearer the object. Also, when looking at closer objects, the eyes swivel inward, and the brain can measure the distance of the object from the amount of swivel.

Image focused on retina

Iris

Cornea

Lens

Sclera

Choroid

Retina

Optic nerve

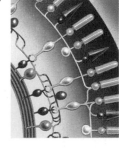

▲ Nerve cells on the retina react to light. They send signals along the optic nerve to the brain.

SEE ALSO

Brain, Cat, Eagle, Human body, Insect, Lens, Light, Wavelength

SILVER

Silver is a white-colored precious metal. It is best known for its use in jewelry, coins, and silverware, but it is also used in electronics and photography.

Silver on calcite

Silver ore

Silver wiry form

In addition to its beauty, silver has important properties that make it unique. One of the most important is its conductivity: it allows heat and electric current to pass through (conduct) it more easily than any other metal.

MINING SILVER

The amount of silver found on Earth is tiny, but it occurs in many types of rock. Some rocks contain pure silver metal. Others combine silver with other chemical elements in silver ores. Silver is separated from these ores (smelted) using heat and electricity. Like gold, silver is a by-product of copper and lead mines. Mexico leads in the world's production, followed by Peru and China.

SILVER JEWELRY AND COINS

Silver jewelry has been made for at least 6,000 years, even before the smelting of metals began. Most modern silver jewelry is made of an alloy (mixture) of 80 percent silver and 20 percent copper.

◄ Silver is often used with turquoise in Native American jewelry such as necklaces.

This ewer from the ▼ 1600s is an example of Italian silver tableware.

▼ Pegasus features on this ancient silver coin from Corinth, c.350 B.C.

Like gold, silver is used as a form of money. Coins have been made out of silver for at least 2,800 years. For much of that time, large quantities of silver have been held in reserve by governments as a sign of their wealth. Today, however, silver has other more important uses.

OTHER USES OF SILVER

At one time, nearly two fifths of all silver went into making photographic film. The rise of digital cameras means that now less than ten percent of silver is put to that use. Silver is used in modern electronic circuit boards and in some surgical equipment. Most mirrors are made by coating glass with a thin layer of silver.

SILVER ELECTROPLATING

In electroplating, a metal object is coated with a plate (thin layer) of another metal, such as silver or gold, using an electric current. The pitcher is immersed in a water and silver solution. One wire is connected to a strip of silver, and another is connected to the pitcher. The wires are both connected to a power source. When the current is turned on, electrolysis occurs: silver moves from the solution to coat the pitcher with a smooth layer.

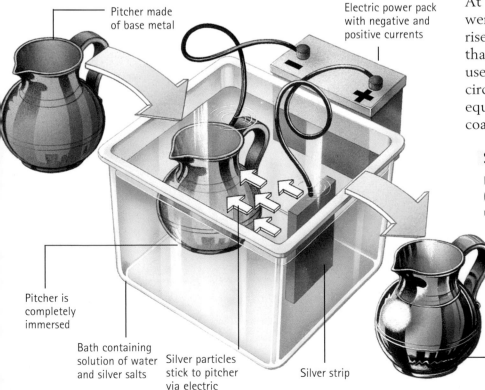

Pitcher made of base metal

Electric power pack with negative and positive currents

Pitcher is completely immersed

Bath containing solution of water and silver salts

Silver particles stick to pitcher via electric current

Silver strip

Finished silver-plated pitcher

SEE ALSO

Electronics, Metal, Mineral and gem, Mining, Money

SINGAPORE

Singapore is a small island nation in Southeast Asia. It lies at the southern tip of the Malay Peninsula, to which it is connected by a causeway.

SINGAPORE
Area: 269 sq. mi.
(697km²)
Population: 5,889,000
Capital: Singapore City
Languages: English,
Malay, Chinese, Tamil
Currency: Singapore dollar

▲ Traditional life mixes with modern—Chinese rickshaws ferry passengers along Singapore's main highways.

The Republic of Singapore is made up of over 60 small islands, and a large one linked to Malaysia by road across the Johor Strait. It is a flat country with a warm, wet, tropical climate. Nearly one quarter of Singapore is made up of rainforest and nature reserves.

PROSPERITY

Singaporeans enjoy one of the highest living standards in Asia. Lacking raw materials of its own, Singapore has prospered from the skills of its well-educated, hardworking people. Although 74 percent of the population is Chinese, 13 percent Malay, 9 percent Indian, English is the main language of government, business, and education. Singapore is one of Asia's leading international financial centers. Other main industries include electronics, building and repairing ships, refining oil, fishing, and tourism.

NEW COUNTRY, NEW NATION

Singapore supported small farmers and fishermen until Sir Stamford Raffles, a British trader, saw the advantages of its natural harbor and location on major trade routes and made it a British possession in 1819. Under British rule, the population grew, gaining many Chinese and Indians, who came as traders and laborers. The port handled products like rubber, tin, and timber from Malaya. British rule ended in 1959, and Singapore became part of the Federation of Malaysia (1963–65). Since then, it has been an independent republic.

▼ The city of Singapore developed around its harbor. It is the second biggest container port in the world, after Shanghai in China.

SEE ALSO

Asia, Southeast Asia

SKELETON

The strong framework of more than 200 bones called the skeleton gives the body shape, support, and protection, and allows it to move.

A bird's skeleton is very light in weight, making flight easier.

Large mammals such as cows need strong bones to carry their body weight.

Fish have spiny bones to support fins and flexible backbones for swimming.

The body's firmness, shape, and strength are due to its skeleton. The skeleton has two main parts. The skull, backbone, and ribs form the central, or axial, skeleton and the arms and legs make up the appendicular skeleton. This system of 206 tough, rigid parts, called bones, forms the body's internal framework and protects delicate organs such as the brain, heart, and lungs. Bones are linked to each other at joints and are anchored to muscles, which pull on them to move the body.

BONE STRENGTH

Each bone's size, shape, and strength depend on how it supports its part of the body and its muscle attachments. Bones are stiff because they contain crystals of minerals such as calcium and phosphate. But they are also slightly flexible, because they contain fibers of the body protein collagen, so that they bend slightly under stress, rather than crack.

INSIDE A BONE

Bones are pale yellow and have their own blood vessels and nerves. Bones are a combination of living cells and minerals. Bone cells, called osteocytes, produce tiny rodlike structures of bone minerals, called osteons (Haversian systems). Most bones have a strong outer layer of compact bone, with the osteons packed together. Inside this is a layer of spongy, or cancellous, bone.

BONE MARROW

In the middle of some bones is jellylike marrow. This makes new cells for the blood, producing millions every second. All of a baby's bones contain marrow, but by adulthood, marrow is found mainly in the sternum, backbone, ribs, and skull.

THE HUMAN SKELETON

The skull consists of 8 bones joined together; the face has 14 bones. Inside each ear are 3 of the body's tiniest bones called ossicles. The backbone has 26 bones called vertebrae; 12 pairs of ribs join the sternum at the front of the chest. Each shoulder and arm has 32 bones, including 8 carpals in the wrist. Each hip and leg has 31 bones, including 7 tarsal bones in the ankle.

◄ About one third of bone is living tissue. The rest consists of minerals like calcium and phosphate, which produce a hard, yet slightly elastic, material.

Head
Spongy bone
Shaft
Compact bone
Haversian canals (ringed by bone cells)
Marrow
▲ Human thighbone

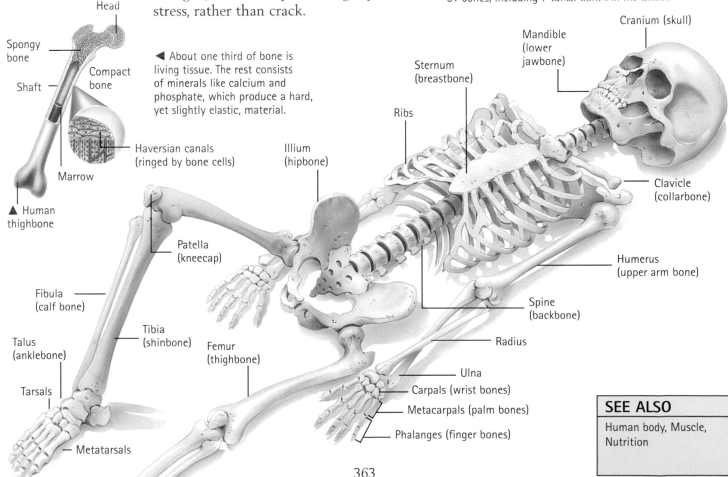

Mandible (lower jawbone)
Cranium (skull)
Sternum (breastbone)
Ribs
Illium (hipbone)
Clavicle (collarbone)
Patella (kneecap)
Humerus (upper arm bone)
Fibula (calf bone)
Spine (backbone)
Tibia (shinbone)
Talus (anklebone)
Femur (thighbone)
Radius
Tarsals
Ulna
Carpals (wrist bones)
Metacarpals (palm bones)
Phalanges (finger bones)
Metatarsals

SEE ALSO
Human body, Muscle, Nutrition

SKIN AND HAIR

Skin protects our delicate insides from wear, damage, dirt, germs, and rain. It also helps cool or warm the body and gives us our sense of touch.

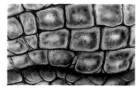

Reptiles such as lizards have dry, scaly skin.

Pigskin: only mammals' skin is covered with hair.

Slug skin: glands secrete slime on the skin.

Skin is a hard-wearing, living tissue, covering about 22 sq. ft. (2m²). It weighs almost 9 lb. (4kg). The eyelids are 0.02 in. (0.5mm) thick, the soles of the feet 0.2 in. (5mm); average thickness is 0.08–0.1 in. (1–2mm). Skin continuously grows and renews; with pressure and wear, it becomes thicker and tougher.

THE OUTER LAYER

The skin's surface, the epidermis, is dead, but just underneath it is one of the body's busiest parts, the dermis. Microscopic cells at the base of the epidermis continually multiply, which pushes old cells upward. Over about four weeks, these cells fill with the tough body protein, keratin (which also makes up hair and nails), flatten, and die. The dead cells then reach the surface and rub and flake off with daily wear and tear.

GETTING UNDER YOUR SKIN

There is an outer and inner layer of skin. The outer layer is the epidermis, underneath is the thicker dermis. This contains fibers of stiff collagen and stretchy elastin, making it strong yet flexible. In the dermis are sweat glands, hair roots, tiny blood vessels, and microscopic nerve endings for our sense of touch. Each hair is anchored in a follicle. It has a sebaceous gland that makes a natural wax or oil called sebum.

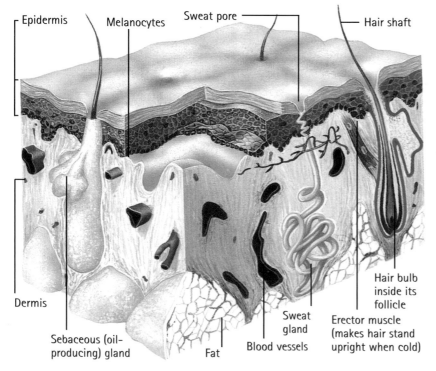

Epidermis — Melanocytes — Sweat pore — Hair shaft

Dermis

Sebaceous (oil-producing) gland — Fat — Blood vessels — Sweat gland — Erector muscle (makes hair stand upright when cold) — Hair bulb inside its follicle

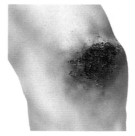

When skin is damaged, a scab forms to protect the body from germs while new skin develops under it.

1 Broken blood vessels become narrow to stop blood loss. White blood cells destroy bacteria.

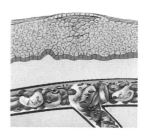

2 Substances in the blood called platelets cause it to clot. This clot hardens into a scab.

3 In the dermis, cells called fibroblasts produce new tissue. When healed, the scab falls off.

SKIN COLOR

Our melanocyte cells produce tiny flecks of dark brown melanin (pigment). More active melanocytes make more melanin and thus produce darker skin. We inherit our normal level of melanocyte activity, and therefore our skin color, from our parents. However, strong sunlight makes melanocytes more active to protect the body from the sun's ultraviolet rays—and this produces a suntan.

COOLING SWEAT

Skin helps control our temperature. If the body is too hot, tiny blood vessels in the dermis widen, allowing more blood to lose heat to the air. The microscopic sweat glands also ooze sweat through the pores (tiny holes) onto the skin. As this dries, it draws more warmth from the body.

HAIR AND GOOSE BUMPS

If the body is too cold, the blood vessels narrow, to reduce heat loss. The erector muscle, attached to a hair, pulls it upright. This traps air near the skin's surface, which keeps warmth in, and causes goose bumps. Hairs are long rods of dead, keratin-filled cells. The only living part is the hair bulb.

SEE ALSO

Amphibian, Blood, Cell, Gland, Human body, Snail, Touch

SKYSCRAPER

Skyscrapers are very tall buildings found in cities where land is expensive. Usually built from concrete on a metal frame, they contain offices and apartments.

▲ Working on high-rise buildings is a risky operation. These window cleaners are abseiling down the Shard, London.

When U.S. mechanic Elisha Graves Otis created an elevator with a safety device in 1852, he made skyscrapers possible—tall buildings could now be used comfortably. In 1884, William Le Baron Jenney built the world's first skyscraper in Chicago (now demolished). Its ten stories would not qualify as a skyscraper today, but its metal frame structure set a new trend.

HIGH-RISE LIVING

From 1895, the lead in skyscraper-building passed to New York. Famous examples include the Woolworth Building (1914), the Chrysler Building (1930), and the Empire State Building (1931), which was the world's tallest building until the 1960s.

SWAYING WEIGHT

A skyscraper must support a heavy weight (the Empire State Building weighs around 400,000 tons) and resist strong winds. Its strong, stable frame is vital. It can be made of prestressed or reinforced concrete, although steel girders form the skeleton of most skyscrapers. The Willis Tower (1974) used nine huge steel tubes welded together to form one structure.

UNDERGROUND SUPPORT

The right foundation is crucial in order to stop a skyscraper from falling over or collapsing. Piles (columns of concrete and metal) are driven deep into the ground. The world's tallest skyscraper, Burj Khalifa, rests on a thick raft supported by 164-foot-long (50m) piles.

GOING UP

Some skyscrapers (like the John Hancock Center) have their steel skeleton on the outside; others show a wall of glass. During construction, manufactured sections of glass, concrete, and steel are brought onto the site and put into place by cranes. The wiring and service ducts go between the floors.

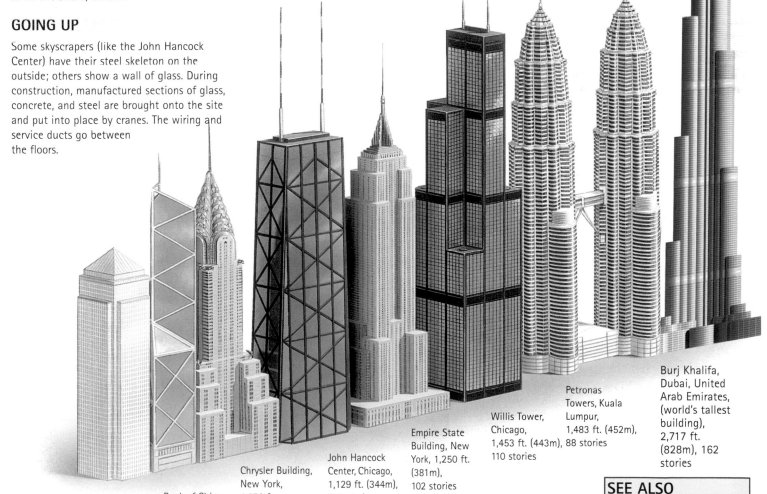

Canary Wharf, London, 800 ft. (244m), 50 stories

Bank of China, Hong Kong, 1,033 ft. (315m), 72 stories

Chrysler Building, New York, 1,076 ft. (319m), 77 stories

John Hancock Center, Chicago, 1,129 ft. (344m), 100 stories

Empire State Building, New York, 1,250 ft. (381m), 102 stories

Willis Tower, Chicago, 1,453 ft. (443m), 110 stories

Petronas Towers, Kuala Lumpur, 1,483 ft. (452m), 88 stories

Burj Khalifa, Dubai, United Arab Emirates, (world's tallest building), 2,717 ft. (828m), 162 stories

SEE ALSO
Architecture, City, Construction, North America

SLAVERY

Slavery is when one person becomes the property, or slave, of another. The slave must do as the owner wishes and has few, if any, rights under the law.

William Wilberforce (1759–1833) led Britain to abolish slavery in 1833.

Ex-slave Harriet Tubman (c.1820–1913) helped 300 slaves escape in the U.S.A.

Nat Turner (1800–31) led a failed uprising of slaves in America in 1831.

Today, the idea of slavery is horrifying, but it was once an accepted part of society.

BONDAGE OF WAR
In early times, prisoners captured in battle belonged to the victors. In some areas of the Roman Empire, over half the people were slaves. From 1250 until the 1800s, Egypt was ruled by slaves called Mamelukes. Children captured on raids were made slaves and trained to be the next generation of Mameluke rulers.

THE SLAVE TRADE
By the 18th century, the slave trade was a major industry. Thousands of slaves were transported from Africa to the Americas to work on plantations. Some were treated well, but many suffered from harsh conditions. In the U.S., the North campaigned to abolish slavery. In 1861, several southern states left the Union, partly because they wanted to keep slavery, and this began the U.S. Civil War (1861–65). Slavery was abolished in 1865 after the victory of the northern states.

SLAVERY CONDEMNED
After about 1780, public opinion in many

▲ An Arabian slave market in the 1200s. The Arabs traded slaves from Africa, Europe, and Asia through the great markets of Zanzibar, Samarkand, and Mombasa.

countries began to turn against slavery. Slavery was abolished in the British Empire from 1833, and by the 1890s most other countries had followed. In 1948, the United Nations declared that freedom from slavery was a universal human right.

SLAVERY TODAY
Slavery is illegal in all countries, but it still goes on. Some slaves are working to pay off a family debt. Others (including children) are being forced to work against their will in sweatshops and labor camps, for example. According to some estimates, nearly 46 million men, women and children are being kept as slaves worldwide.

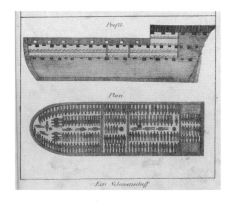

THE TRIANGULAR TRADE
The largest slave trade was between West Africa and the Americas—the Triangular Trade. Ships left Bristol or Liverpool in England with weapons and tools to be traded in Africa for slaves. The slaves were so tightly packed onto ships (above) that many died during the voyage to the Americas, where they were sold for sugar or tobacco destined for England. Between 1680 and 1800, about seven million slaves were traded.

SEE ALSO
Civil rights, Civil War (American)

SLEEP

Sleep is a state of decreased consciousness, during which the body rests from its normal activities. It is essential for a healthy body and mind.

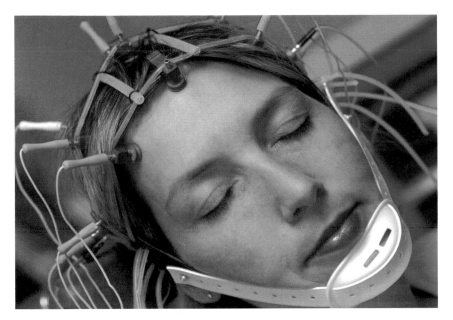

SLEEP CYCLES

Laboratory studies show the electrical patterns the brain produces during sleep. Electrodes from an EEG, or electroencephalograph, are attached to the sleeper's head—these record changes in brain activity, shown as a wavy line on the graph. In an 8-hour sleep period, sleepers go through REM and NREM cycles every 90 minutes, starting with NREM in Stage 1. Sleep gets deeper until Stage 4, the deepest sleep. After 60 to 90 minutes, dreaming (REM) occurs during Stage 2, when the brain becomes more active again. Longer REM periods occur as sleep continues.

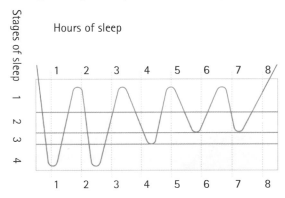

When we sleep, the electrical activity of the brain slows down in stages, along with heart rate, temperature, and breathing. However, when we dream, the brain's activity increases again, and the eyes move rapidly under the eyelids in REM (rapid eye movement) sleep. We go through several cycles of non-dreaming (NREM, or non-rapid eye movement) and dreaming sleep every night.

SLEEP AND GROWTH

Although we spend a third of our lives asleep, no one really knows why it is so important. Sleep rests the body, but we use almost as much energy asleep as when we are awake. Sleep is important for growth, which is why children need more than adults. It may also help with learning and memory. As people age, they need less sleep. A baby sleeps most of the time, and a four-year-old needs 10 to 14 hours of sleep a night. A young adult may sleep for 8 hours, but people over 60 sleep only about 5 to 6 hours, and wake often during the night.

SLEEP DISTURBANCES

Sleep is essential. When a person has insomnia (the inability to sleep) for even one night, he or she feels irritable and clumsy. If insomnia continues, lack of concentration and hallucinations (seeing things that are not real) can occur. Some people have nightmares; others get out of bed and walk around while they are asleep (sleepwalking). Jet lag is the disruption of sleep caused by air travel across time zones.

DREAMS

Many people believe that dreams are the working through of thoughts and feelings that happen during the day. Some people remember dreams and some do not. Dreams are often fantastic and colorful, and provide people with inspiration for art, music, stories, and movies.

◀ Many artists are inspired by their dreams. This picture captures the strange, surreal qualities of a dream.

SLEEP FACTS

• Human beings are mostly diurnal—they are awake during the day and they sleep at night

• Some animals, such as badgers, are nocturnal—they sleep by day and are active at night

• Reptiles, fish, and insects have periods of inactivity that resemble a sleeping state

• Donkeys need 3 hours of sleep per day

• Bats need 20 hours of sleep per day

SEE ALSO

Animal, Hibernation, Human body, Season, Time

SOIL

Soil is the loose material that lies on the Earth's surface and in which plants grow. It consists mainly of small particles of broken-down rock and plant material.

Deciduous forests form deep, humus-rich soils.

Dry, lime-rich soils form on grasslands.

Mountains have only a thin covering of poor soil.

Desert soils are rich in salts, but lack humus.

Tropical rain forests form fertile, but thin, soils.

Swamps have wet and often acidic soils.

▶ Farmers add manure and other organic matter to soil to boost the fertility of their land.

Soil covers the rocks of the Earth and is sometimes very deep. It consists of small pieces of rock, along with plant material, fungi, bacteria, and a host of tiny animals.

HOW SOILS FORM

Rocks are broken down by rain and wind to produce a layer of grit. Leaves and stems falling on the grit rot away to provide food for fungi, worms, and microscopic organisms. Some plant fibers remain in the soil as humus, which holds the grit together and helps it hold water. The rest of the plants, and the remains of animals, are broken down by fungi and bacteria into simple chemicals that provide nutrients for new plants.

A MATTER OF LAYERS

Soil is made up of layers. The dark topsoil is rich in humus and nutrients. Below that is the subsoil, a layer of fine material containing a lot of clay. The thickness of the layers and their chemical composition vary according to the climate, the type of rock the soil is made from, and the kind of vegetation growing in it.

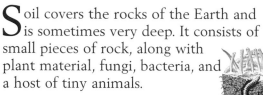

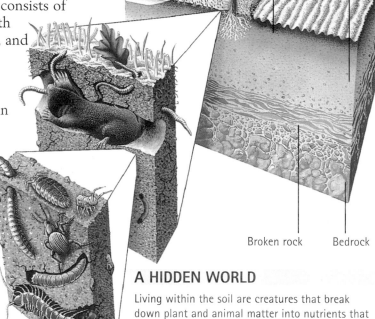

Water table | Topsoil | Subsoil

Broken rock | Bedrock

A HIDDEN WORLD

Living within the soil are creatures that break down plant and animal matter into nutrients that can be absorbed by plant roots. Earthworms pull plant waste into the soil and are eaten by moles whose tunnels help to circulate air. Microscopic beetles, centipedes, and other creatures feed on rotting plant and animal matter, and on each other.

VALUABLE RESOURCE

The plants that take root in soil form the basis of the food chain for all land animals. People plant food crops in the soil as well as fodder crops to feed farm animals. Most farmers care for their soil, but in some areas, cutting down trees or intensive farming leads to soil erosion and crop failure.

SEE ALSO

Climate, Conservation, Crop, Farming, Habitat, Seed and pollination

SOLAR POWER

Solar power harnesses the energy in the sun's rays. It is a nonpolluting source of energy that will not run out until the sun dies, billions of years from now.

The sun is our chief source of energy. Coal, oil, and gas come from the fossilized remains of ancient plants that used sunlight to grow. The sun's energy is stored in oceans and rivers, and in the winds. All living things need the sun. Yet we use only a fraction of the energy reaching us from the sun.

SOLAR POWER PLANTS

By using mirrors, the sun's rays can be used to heat a water-filled boiler. Steam from the boiler turns a turbine which makes electricity. A power plant called Solar 1 in California uses 1,818 computer-controlled mirrors to concentrate the sunlight onto a boiler tower 300 ft. (91m) high. Solar power plants need to be in sunny places, and much of the electricity they make is lost during distribution.

▼ Solar cells mounted in winglike panels are used to power satellites because they require almost no maintenance.

SOLAR HEATING

Sunlight can provide heat for the home, saving other energy resources. Modern buildings with large windows and heat-absorbing collectors on the roof can take in enough energy from sunlight to provide room and water heating, even on cloudy days. Just a simple, insulated glass panel with a black-coated bottom will collect enough solar energy to warm the water inside, since black absorbs the most sunlight.

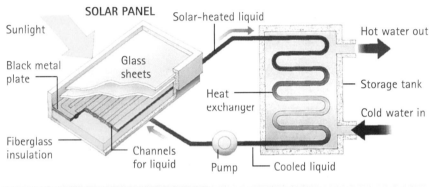

▲ A solar furnace uses a huge curved mirror to focus the sun's rays. It uses the sun's energy to provide a clean, nonpolluting source of heat.

▼ Energy from the sun can be used directly to heat water for a home's hot-water system through the use of solar panels.

SOLAR PANEL

Sunlight · Solar-heated liquid · Hot water out · Black metal plate · Glass sheets · Heat exchanger · Storage tank · Cold water in · Fiberglass insulation · Channels for liquid · Pump · Cooled liquid

ELECTRICITY FROM SUNLIGHT

Solar photovoltaics (PV) use semiconductors such as silicon to generate electricity from sunlight. Solar panels have long been used to power spacecraft such as the Hubble Space Telescope (HST) shown below. In the past 20 years solar PV panels have been mass-produced as a clean source of energy on Earth. By 2016 solar PV was meeting 2 percent of the world's energy needs. Solar PV is set to become a leading source of electricity by 2050.

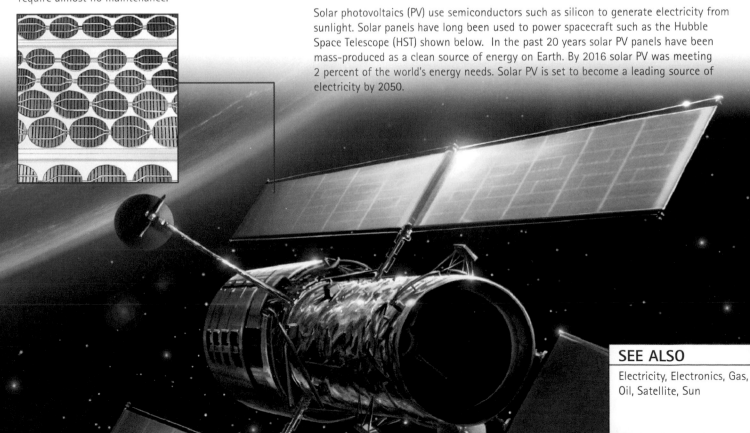

SEE ALSO
Electricity, Electronics, Gas, Oil, Satellite, Sun

SOLAR SYSTEM

Our solar system is made up of the Sun and the objects that orbit it. These include the nine planets and their moons, as well as asteroids, comets, and meteors.

THE PLANETS	
Distance from Sun (million mi.)	Average time to orbit Sun
Mercury	
58	88 days
Venus	
108	225 days
Earth	
150	1 year
Mars	
228	1.9 years
Jupiter	
778	11.9 years
Saturn	
1,427	29.5 years
Uranus	
2,870	84 years
Neptune	
4,498	164.8 years

The Sun is at the center of the solar system. Its mass, which makes up 99.86 percent of all of the mass in the solar system, holds the planets and other objects in their orbit through gravity.

ROCKY WORLDS AND GAS GIANTS

Most of the matter from which the planets formed consisted of hydrogen and helium. The planets nearest the Sun—Mercury, Venus, Earth, and Mars—were too warm to hold on to these plentiful light gases, and instead became small worlds of rock and metal. Farther from the Sun, where temperatures were very low, the planets attracted huge amounts of hydrogen and helium. They became the gas giants— Jupiter, Saturn, Uranus, and Neptune.

ASTEROIDS AND COMETS

Between the orbits of Mars and Jupiter is a band of space where asteroids are common. This is the asteroid belt. Occasionally asteroids collide. When this happens, bits break off that may arrive on Earth as meteorites. A vast cloud of frozen comets is thought to lie much farther from the Sun than Pluto. This cloud, which may be 100 times farther from the Sun than the Earth is, marks the outer edge of the solar system.

HOW THE SOLAR SYSTEM FORMED

The Sun was born about five billion years ago out of a great cloud of gas and dust in space. Scientists believe that the planets, as well as the asteroids and comets, gradually formed out of this spinning cloud.

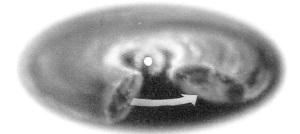

1 Material that was left over from the cloud of dust and gas formed a disk that circled the Sun.

2 As particles within the disk collided, they began to stick together, forming larger objects.

3 The objects grew into planets, moons, asteroids, and comets, which often collided.

4 Eventually, the remaining objects circled the Sun in orbits that rarely crossed.

◄ The planets of our solar system drawn to scale:
1 Mercury; 2 Venus;
3 Earth; 4 Mars; 5 Jupiter;
6 Saturn; 7 Uranus;
8 Neptune.

SEE ALSO
Astronomy, Big Bang theory, Comet, meteor, and asteroid, Constellation, Galaxy, Planet, Star, Sun, Universe

SOLID, LIQUID, AND GAS

Solid, liquid, and gas are the three states in which substances, or matter, can exist. Each state depends on how strongly the molecules are bound together.

BOILING POINTS (at sea level)		
Substance	°C	°F
Iron	2,800	5,072
Mercury	357	675
Water	100	212
Ethanol	78	172
Oxygen	−183	−297
Nitrogen	−195	−319

MELTING POINTS (at sea level)		
Substance	°C	°F
Iron	1,535	2,795
Mercury	−39	−38.2
Water	0	32
Ethanol	−117	−179
Oxygen	−218	−360
Nitrogen	−210	−346

As you read this book, you may be sitting at a table or desk. It is probably made of wood, plastic, or steel. At room temperature, these materials are all solids. They are made of molecules that are strongly bound together. That is why the table keeps its shape. Scientists call a solid a state of matter.

LIQUIDS

If you have a filled glass, you can see another state of matter: liquid. Water, milk, and ethanol (ordinary alcohol) are all liquid at room temperature. Like all other liquids, they are made of molecules that are only loosely bound together. When you pour a liquid into a glass, its molecules are able to flow around the bottom of it. That is why the liquid fills the container evenly, forming a level surface.

GASES

All around you is air. Air is in another state, called a gas. Gases are made of molecules that are hardly bound to each other at all. When you release a gas into any space, its molecules are free to move around the space randomly, spreading around and filling the whole space evenly. That is why a beach ball forms a spherical shape even though you only blow air into one end of it.

CHANGING STATE

If we change a substance's temperature enough, its state will usually change. When iron is over 2,802°F (1,539°C), for instance, it melts into a liquid. Similarly, if water is below 32°F (0°C), it freezes to form ice, a solid. Oxygen, one of the gases that makes up air, will condense to form a liquid if we cool it to a chilly 297°F (−183°C).

HOW TEMPERATURE CHANGES MATTER

At room temperature, water is in a liquid state. However, water can be turned into a gas by heating it until it boils and turns into water vapor. Alternatively, if the water's temperature is lowered to below freezing point, it will turn into ice, which is its solid state. These changes take place because temperature affects the way in which the individual atoms and molecules of a substance are bound together.

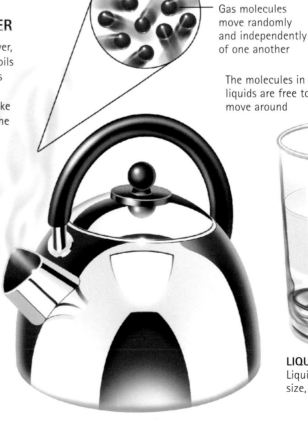

Gas molecules move randomly and independently of one another

The molecules in liquids are free to move around

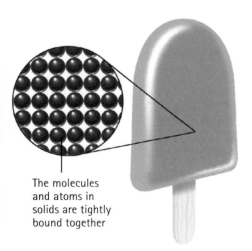

The molecules and atoms in solids are tightly bound together

SOLID
Solids, such as ice, have a fixed shape and size.

GAS
Gases, such as water vapor from boiling water, have no fixed shape or size.

LIQUID
Liquids, such as water, have a fixed size, or volume, but no fixed shape.

SEE ALSO

Atom and molecule, Heat, Iron and steel

SOUND

Sound is a form of energy that can be heard. It is caused by vibrations and travels in waves through solids, liquids, and gases.

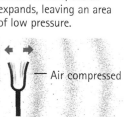

▼ When you tap a tuning fork against a hard surface, it starts to vibrate rapidly, giving out a constant pitch. When the prongs vibrate outward, they compress the air near them, creating high pressure. When they vibrate inward, the air expands, leaving an area of low pressure.

— Air compressed

— Air expanded

We usually think of sound traveling only through air, but it can also move through other substances. When you are swimming under water in a pool, you can still hear the sounds going on around the pool. That is because sound can travel through water—or any other liquid. Noisy neighbors are a problem because the sounds they make can travel through walls and floors—solid materials.

MAKING SOUND

You can make a sound in the air if you hit two objects together, a pair of pot lids, for example. The objects create sound because you give them some energy, making them vibrate (shake). As the objects vibrate, they compress, then release the air each side of them, over and over again. This makes the air pressure around them rise and fall repeatedly.

THE HUMAN VOICE

The human voice produces sound when air from the lungs is forced past the vocal cords. How high or low the voice is depends on how quickly or slowly these cords vibrate. The diaphragm controls the flow of air in and out of the lungs. The muscles around the mouth turn the noise produced by the vocal cords into recognizable sounds. The cavities in the nose, throat, and chest help the sounds to resonate.

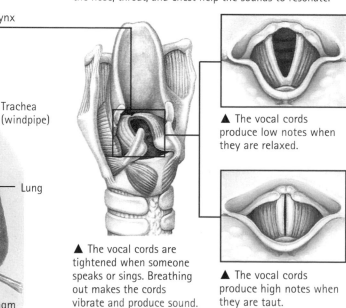

— Nasal cavity

— Mouth

— Epiglottis

— Larynx

— Trachea (windpipe)

— Lung

Diaphragm

▲ The vocal cords are tightened when someone speaks or sings. Breathing out makes the cords vibrate and produce sound.

▲ The vocal cords produce low notes when they are relaxed.

▲ The vocal cords produce high notes when they are taut.

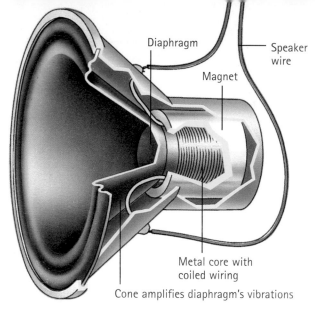

Diaphragm

Speaker wire

Magnet

Metal core with coiled wiring

Cone amplifies diaphragm's vibrations

▲ Loudspeakers turn electrical signals back into sounds. The signals cause a diaphragm inside the speaker to vibrate, and this motion reproduces the original sound.

AIR VIBRATIONS

Sound is caused by only tiny changes of air pressure. When someone nearby talks to you, they make the air pressure rise and fall by about 1/10,000 of normal air pressure. That is roughly the pressure change you feel when you put a single sheet of paper in your palm. As air vibrates, it shakes a thin membrane in the ear—the eardrum. That is why we hear the vibrations as sound. Our ears cannot pick up all kinds of vibration. They have to be loud enough for us to hear. They also have to happen at a rate that our ears can detect—in other words, they have to be the right frequency.

SPREAD OF SOUND

When an object vibrates, sound waves spread out from it. The farther you are from the object, the more the energy from it has spread, so the quieter it is. Sound waves bounce off hard objects such as brick walls or windows. When you listen to someone speaking in a room, for example, you hear both the sound that has come directly from their voice and the sound that has bounced off the walls, ceiling, and floor. This effect is reverberation.

LOUDNESS

The harder you hit something, the louder the sound you make with it. That is because it vibrates more, creating a greater pressure change in the air around it. Our

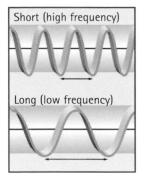

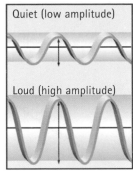

▲ The pitch of a sound—whether it is high or low—depends on its frequency or wavelength. Long waves have a lower frequency and pitch than short waves.

▲ A sound's loudness depends on the height of its waves, called its amplitude. Quiet sounds have a smaller amplitude than loud sounds.

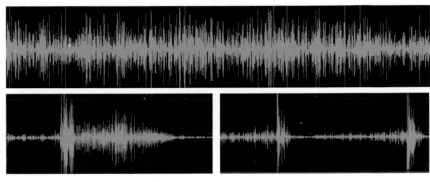

▲ A visual display of three different sounds: a complete symphony orchestra (top); the spoken word "hello" (above left); and two hand claps (above right). Rich, complex sounds involve thousands of waveforms, of differing amplitudes and frequencies, all intermingling at the same time to make up the waveform shapes above.

ears can pick up a wide range of pressure changes. At best, they can detect sounds made by pressure changes that are a mere 5 billionths of normal air pressure. A pin dropping is this quiet. At the other extreme, our ears can detect pressure changes about one fifth of normal air pressure. A pneumatic drill is this loud.

FREQUENCY AND PITCH

Whistles and women's voices make sounds that are much higher in pitch than bass guitars and men's voices. That is because they make sounds that have a higher frequency, or shorter wavelength. Frequency

BREAKING THE SOUND BARRIER

When a vehicle, such as the British jet car Thrust SSC (below), travels at the speed of sound, pressure waves build up in front of the vehicle and form a shock wave. As the car accelerates through the sound barrier and travels faster than sound, the shock wave breaks away and can be heard, after the car has passed, as a sonic boom. You cannot hear a vehicle approaching at supersonic speeds.

is measured in hertz (Hz). Our ears can only pick up sounds that are between 20 Hz and 20,000 Hz.
A car horn makes a sound with a frequency of about 200 Hz, women can sing notes as high as 1,200 Hz, and men can sing notes as low as 60 Hz.

SPEED OF SOUND

On a warm day, sound travels through air at about 1,082 ft./sec. (330m/sec). On colder days, it travels more slowly. Sound travels at different speeds through other materials. It travels four times faster through water than air. Sound travels through solid concrete (such as the concrete partition between two offices) over ten times faster than it travels through air.

LOUDNESS SCALE

Loudness is measured in decibels (dB). Since the sound energy increases ten times, the decibels go up by the number ten. The following table shows the loudness of some sounds.

• Rocket liftoff	150–190 dB
• Jet takeoff	120–140 dB
• Thunder	95–115 dB
• Motorcycle	70–90 dB
• Vacuum cleaner	60–80 dB
• Orchestra	50–70 dB
• Talking	30–60 dB
• Whispering	20–30 dB
• Falling leaves	20 dB

Shock wave

Sound waves

SEE ALSO

Hearing, Musical instrument, Radar and sonar, Radio, Wavelength

SOUTH AFRICA

Occupying the southernmost tip of the African continent, the country of South Africa consists mostly of a vast plateau, 3,940 ft. (1,200m) above sea level.

Area: 470,693 sq. mi. (1,219,090km²)
Population: 55,380,000
Capitals: Cape Town (legislative), Pretoria (administrative)
Languages: Afrikaans, English
Currency: Rand

South Africa's high, flat-topped hills are surrounded by fertile, low-lying coastal strips, measuring from 34–150 mi. (55–240km) across. The spectacular Drakensberg Mountains rise to 11,424 ft. (3,482m), and the Limpopo River marks much of the country's northern boundary. The separate, mountainous kingdom of Lesotho is entirely surrounded by South African territory. South Africa's climate is mostly dry and sunny, with an average temperature of 63°F (17°C).

DESERT, GRASSLAND, AND SCRUB
In the north, the Kalahari Desert stretches into neighboring Botswana. Most of the vast central plateau is occupied by an area of coarse grassland called the Highveld. The Middleveld, in the northwest, is more suited to livestock than crops because of its poor soil, owing to erosion and little rain. The northeast of the plateau is the Transvaal Basin, where farmers grow citrus fruit, corn, and tobacco. Elephants, lions, leopards, and great herds of antelope and zebras live on Transvaal's thorny scrub and are protected in the Kruger National Park.

▲ Apartheid forced many blacks to live in sprawling slums, called townships. One is Soweto—South Africa's largest black residential area.

PRECIOUS RESOURCES
South Africa has a vast wealth of natural resources—in particular, minerals. It exports more diamonds than any other country, and also produces gold, platinum, chrome and manganese. It has large reserves of gas, coal, copper, iron, asbestos, silver, nickel, and uranium. It is Africa's most industrial country and could be one of the world's richest nations. It can provide enough of its own grain and meat to feed its population, and nearly one third of its wealth comes from industries such as chemicals, textiles, and machinery.

▲ The Drakensberg Mountains form a long line of sharp cliffs where South Africa's high central plateau drops down toward coastal lowlands.

► For many visitors, the first sight of South Africa is Cape Town, set against the dramatic backdrop of Table Mountain, at the southern tip of the country.

POLICY OF APARTHEID

The wealth of South Africa's natural resources has benefited only a minority of the population. This is because a policy of apartheid (separateness) was introduced in 1950 by the white government; this separated blacks from whites and refused blacks equal rights. With black people making up almost three fourths of the population, millions of people were left in abject poverty. Many other countries protested against the cruelty of apartheid, and imposed sanctions which limited South Africa's overseas trade.

THE AFTERMATH OF APARTHEID

The process of apartheid began to collapse in 1990, under the presidency of F. W. de Klerk. In 1994, the first multiracial elections were held in South Africa, bringing to power a majority black government. Nelson Mandela served as president from 1994 to 1999, and died in 2013. Although a black government was a positive force for equality, the young democracy still faced enormous problems: supplying education, social services, electricity, and clean water, for example, as well as tackling unemployment, crime, and diseases such as HIV-AIDS. After 2009, the ruling African National Congress party, under President Jacob Zuma, entered a period of turbulent politics.

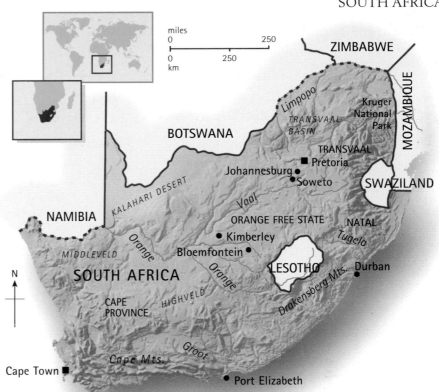

▲ The elections of 1994 brought to power the African National Congress (ANC), headed by Nelson Mandela. Between 1964 and 1990, Mandela had been imprisoned for his opposition to the apartheid regime.

FIGHTING FOR TERRITORY

The first South Africans were the San and the Khoi peoples. From about A.D. 300, Bantu-speaking peoples such as the Zulus, Xhosa, and Sesotho moved into the region. From 1652, Dutch settlers came by sea, soon followed by other Europeans. In 1806, the British took over the coastal areas, where the Dutch farmers (called Boers or Afrikaners) had settled. In order to keep their independence and claim new land for themselves, the Afrikaners made the Great Trek inland in 1834–38; during this time they founded Transvaal and the Orange Free State. The discovery of gold and diamonds on Afrikaner territory led to two wars between the Boers and the British. Final Afrikaner defeat in 1902 led to a united South Africa in 1910.

PLANS FOR THE FUTURE

South Africa's population is 80 percent black, 8 percent white, 9 percent mixed race, and 2 percent Asian. Mandela hoped to build a "rainbow society," where all people could live in harmony. Public holidays celebrate Human Rights, the Family, Freedom, Workers, Youth, Women, Heritage, Reconciliation, and Goodwill.

▲ One of the main peoples of South Africa is the Zulus. More than 11 million of them live here, mainly in the province of Natal.

SEE ALSO

Africa, Civil rights

SOUTH AMERICA

Covering 12 percent of the planet's land area, South America is the fourth largest continent. Its people make up around 6 percent of the world's population.

▲ Ecuador's Cotopaxi (19,347 ft./5,897m), seen from the volcano Illinizais, is the continent's highest active volcano.

South America's varied landscape includes the rocky islands of Tierra del Fuego (belonging to Argentina and Chile) and the immense grasslands of Argentina and Venezuela. There are also snowcapped mountains and active volcanoes. The Andes, running along the Pacific coast for 5,000 mi. (8,000km), form the longest mountain range in the world. Aconcagua in Argentina is the highest peak.

WET AND DRY

The Amazon River basin holds one fifth of the world's fresh water. It occupies two fifths of the continent and is the world's largest tropical rain forest. The Amazon is second to the Nile in length. Quibdo in Colombia is South America's rainiest place, receiving over 350 in. (8,890mm) of rain a year. The Atacama Desert in Chile is one of the world's driest places— the port of Arica in northern Chile averages less than 0.04 in. (1mm) of rain a year—but the hottest temperatures are recorded in the Gran Chaco region of northern Argentina.

CLIMATIC DIFFERENCES

The great range of climates is because there is a wide variation in the distance of the different countries from the equator and in the height of different areas above sea level. Lake Titicaca, between Bolivia and Peru, is the highest lake in the world, 12,503 ft. (3,811m) above sea level.

COASTAL CITIES

High mountains, dense forests, and vast distances make overland transportation difficult and costly. Most major cities lie along the coast or on large rivers, where they can be served by shipping. Away from the cities, most roads are unpaved,

▲ Venezuela's Angel Falls has a longer drop (3,212 ft./ 979m) than any other waterfall in the world.

▶ In Bolivia, llamas graze high up in the Andes and are kept for their wool and meat. They are also able to carry heavy loads.

GALAPAGOS IS.
(Ecuador)

▲ The giant tortoise is one of the many unusual forms of wildlife on the Galapagos Islands, which lie 600 mi. (960km) off the coast of Ecuador.

Map labels:

CARIBBEAN SEA
PANAMA
Quibdó
San Agustín
Bogotá
Quito
Cotopaxi ▲
ECUADOR
COLOMBIA
Lake Maracaibo
Caracas
VENEZUELA
Georgetown
GUYANA
Paramaribo
Kourou
Cayenne
SURINAME
FRENCH GUIANA
(France)
Angel Falls
Amazon
BRAZIL
PERU
Andes
Lima
Lake Titicaca
BOLIVIA
La Paz (seat of government)
Arica
Sucre (legal)
GRAN CHACO
Brasilia
São Paulo
Rio de Janeiro
PARAGUAY
Asunción
PACIFIC OCEAN
ATACAMA DESERT
Aconcagua ▲
Valparaíso
Santiago
CHILE
ARGENTINA
Andes
Buenos Aires
URUGUAY
Montevideo
N
ATLANTIC OCEAN
FALKLAND IS. (UK)
Stanley
Tierra del Fuego
SOUTH GEORGIA (UK)
SOUTH SANDWICH IS. (UK)

miles
0   500
0   500
km

and in rural areas, donkeys and carts drawn by oxen or horses are used to carry goods. Aviation has developed rapidly since about 1950, especially in Brazil, which has more than 725 airports and 3,300 landing strips.

UNIQUE WILDLIFE

South America's isolation from the rest of the world has led to the evolution of many unique forms of wildlife. These include the rhea (a large, flightless bird), the capybara (the world's largest rodent), and the llama. Other South American creatures include the tapir, armadillo, jaguar, condor, iguana, giant anteater, tree sloth, vicuña, piranha fish, manatee, and many varieties of parrot and monkey.

PLANTS AND PRODUCTS

The Amazon region contains more kinds of plants than anywhere else in the world, including at least 16,000 species of tree and hundreds of species of orchid. South American plants yield products such as rubber, quinine, sisal, and chocolate and woods such as mahogany and balsa.

▼ The Pan-American highway, which runs through the Atacama Desert, links most South American countries to each other and to North America.

VARIED DESCENT

The native people of South America came from Asia by way of North America. From 1500 onward, Europeans came to settle, mostly from Spain and Portugal. Many intermarried with local people, producing children of mixed race known as *mestizos*. In Andean countries such as Bolivia and Peru, native people still make up a large proportion of the population. Argentina's population is largely white, with many people of Italian, German, or British descent, while Brazil's population includes many descendants of African slaves brought to work on sugar plantations. Since 1940, South America's population has more than tripled. ▶

▲ Sugarcane is Guyana's most important crop. It is grown near the coast.

▲ Brazil produces a third of the world's coffee. The beans must be washed in order to remove the outer skin.

TODAY'S PEOPLE

One person in three in South America is under 15. About three fourths of the population lives in cities, the three largest cities being Brazil's São Paolo and Rio de Janeiro, and Argentina's Buenos Aires. Ninety percent of adults can read and write. Most of the people are Roman Catholics. In most South American countries, there is a small governing class of officials, businessmen, landowners, and military leaders; a growing professional middle class; and a poor majority, many of whom are unemployed and living in overcrowded conditions. Living standards are lower in rural areas, many of which still lack electricity, telephones, schools, and medical care. Official development programs are trying to improve rural conditions to reverse the movement of people to the cities.

▲ Indians make up much of the population in Bolivia. Many wear traditional clothes, especially for festivals.

SPORT AND LEISURE

Soccer has passionate fans throughout the continent—Brazil's Pelé (born 1940) has been called the world's greatest soccer player. Bullfighting is still popular in Colombia, Venezuela, and Peru. South America has produced many popular forms of music and dance, such as the tango and samba. Colorful *fiestas* (festivals) are held on national and religious holidays. South American writers who have won the Nobel Prize for Literature include Chilean poets Gabriela Mistral and Pablo Neruda, and Colombian novelist Gabriel Garcia Marquez.

MINERAL RESOURCES

Since European settlement began, South America has developed as a supplier of raw materials. At first this meant gold and silver, then timber, sugar, coffee, and rubber, and, after the coming of railroads and steamships, beef, wheat, and wool. Venezuela is rich in oil, Brazil in iron,

▼ Bolivia is rich in tin. Local people sift through the mountains of slag looking for tin ore.

manganese, and bauxite. Colombia has nickel and emeralds, and Chile has copper as well as guano (bird droppings) and nitrates, used as fertilizer and to make explosives. Mineral exports pay for imports of manufactured goods, but modern mining creates few jobs.

INDUSTRIALIZATION

Brazil is the most industrialized South American country, producing cars and trucks, light planes, televisions, and machinery for the rest of the continent. Shortages of money and skills hold back industry in other countries, but most now produce basic items such as clothes, shoes, furniture, and drinks for local use, reducing the need for imports.

NEW VERSUS OLD

Brazil and Argentina both have vast plantations and ranches. Large-scale forest clearance has created environmental problems, as well as disturbing the traditional way of life of tribal people, who live by hunting and gathering. Offshore fishing is a major industry for both Chile and Peru.

EUROPEAN SETTLEMENT

During the 1400s, the Inca built up a great empire in the Andes. In the early 1500s, European settlers from Spain and Portugal—greedy for gold and silver— enslaved or killed many native people, and brought with them diseases unknown to the continent, which wiped out millions of others. Missionaries introduced Christianity to replace

▲ Paraguay's capital city Asunción was built by the Spanish, who arrived in the 1500s and ruled the country for 300 years.

traditional beliefs. The Napoleonic Wars in the early 1800s, however, weakened the hold of Spain and Portugal on their South American colonies.

TO INDEPENDENCE

Revolutions in the early 1800s brought independence. The leading revolutionary figures were Simón Bolívar and José de San Martín. The former Spanish colonies became republics, but Brazil was ruled by emperors until 1889. South American trade remained tied to Europe and, from the late 1800s onward, increasingly to the United States. Centuries of European influence are clearly shown in the Spanish-style architecture of many older cities.

MILITARY RULE

Many South American countries have been ruled by dictators, usually backed by the military, and revolutions were once common. Since the 1980s, civilian rule has been restored across South America and all its 12 nations enjoy democratic rule.

STONE STATUES

Some 300 stone statues have been found in the hills near San Agustín in Colombia. They are at least 1,000 years old and appear to mark burial sites. Colombia was originally home to many groups of indigenous people, some living in rainforest settlements, others wandering the open plains.

▲ *Ariane IV* is one of a number of rockets launched from the Kourou Space Center in French Guiana.

SEE ALSO

Argentina, Brazil, Continent

SOUTHEAST ASIA

The region of Southeast Asia consists of seven mainland countries and four island nations that lie east of India and south of China.

BRUNEI
Area: 2,226 sq. mi.
(5,765km²)
Population: 450,000
Capital: Bandar Seri
Begawan
Language: Malay
Currency: Brunei dollar

Southeast Asia covers an area over 1,550,000 sq. mi. (4 million km²). Its population of nearly 650 million is growing rapidly. The landscape is mainly mountainous uplands and tropical forests, with swampy coastland. Countries north of the equator, like Thailand, get heavy rain from May to October; Indonesia, south of the equator, has its rainy season from November to April. Temperatures are usually above 77°F (25°C) all year round.

VOLCANIC LAND
A chain of volcanoes runs through the Indonesian islands of Sumatra, Java,

and the Lesser Sunda Islands. Seventy six have erupted in the last 200 years. The eruption on the island of Krakatoa, which took place in 1883, was the loudest explosion in modern history.

OLD CULTURES
Early centers of civilization emerged in the valleys of rivers such as the Irrawaddy, Chao Praya, and Mekong, where annual flooding fertilized the soil. Rich harvests of rice supported ruling classes of warriors and priests. The harvests also fed the

BURMA (MYANMAR)
Area: 261,228 sq. mi.
(676,577km²)
Population: 55,124,000
Capital: Rangoon
(Yangon)
Language: Burmese
Currency: Kyat

CAMBODIA
Area: 69,898 sq. mi.
(181,035km²)
Population: 16,205,000
Capital: Phnom Penh
Language: Khmer
Currency: Riel

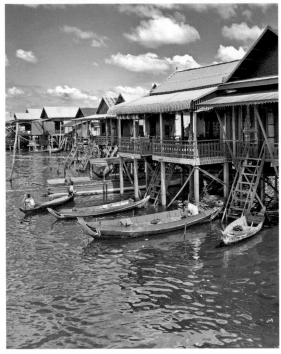

▲ Most Cambodians live in farming villages and work in paddy fields. On Cambodia's Lake Tonle Sap, there are colorful houses built on stilts.

craftsworkers and laborers who made their luxuries and built their palaces, forts, and temples. Thailand and Burma (Myanmar) are famed for their historic pagodas. In Cambodia are the ruins of the temple-city of Angkor Wat, the capital of the great Khmer Empire (802 C.E. to 1431).

MATERIALS FOR TRADE

Southeast Asia is rich in raw materials such as oil, tin, and timber. Burma and Thailand are the two leading ruby producers. Burma also has sapphires (only Madagascar produces more). Five hundred years ago, European merchants came trading for spices such as cloves, nutmeg, and cinnamon. Apart from Thailand, the whole region gradually came under European rule and plantation crops such as rubber and coffee were introduced.

Many Chinese and Indians moved there as traders and laborers.

MODERN TIMES

Since regaining their independence after 1945, Southeast Asian countries have dramatically raised their standards of living, health, and education, despite the damage caused by the Vietnam War (1955 to 1973). Malaysia, Singapore, and Thailand have developed modern industries, making cars and electronic goods. Farming is the main occupation in East Timor, Laos, and Burma, the cief crops being rice, corn, palm oil, sugar, tea, and coffee.

FUTURE CONCERNS

The rapid use of the region's resources is raising concern about pollution problems, the destruction of forests, and threats to wildlife. All the region's nations (except East Timor) belong to the Association of South East Asian Nations (ASEAN), which was founded in 1967 to help cooperation in trade, education, and development.

▲ The Komodo dragon, the largest living lizard, is named after the Indonesian island on which it is found.

PHILIPPINES
Area: 115,860 sq. mi. (300,076km²)
Population: 104,256,000
Capital: Manila
Languages: Filipino, English
Currency: Peso

SINGAPORE
Area: 269 sq. mi. (697km²)
Population: 5,889,000
Capital: Singapore City
Languages: English, Malay, Mandarin Chinese, Tamil
Currency: Singapore dollar

THAILAND
Area: 198,114 sq. mi. (513,115km²)
Population: 68,414,000
Capital: Bangkok
Language: Thai
Currency: Baht

VIETNAM
Area: 124,020 sq. mi. (321,120km²)
Population: 96,160,000
Capital: Hanoi
Language: Vietnamese
Currency: Dong

EAST TIMOR
Area: 5,743 sq. mi. (14,874km²)
Population: 1,291,000
Capital: Dili
Language: Tetum, Portuguese
Currency: U.S. dollar

INDONESIA
Area: 735,358 sq. mi. (1,904,569km²)
Population: 260,581,000
Capital: Jakarta
Languages: Bahasa, Indonesia, Javanese
Currency: Rupiah

LAOS
Area: 91,430 sq. mi. (236,800km²)
Population: 7,127,000
Capital: Vientiane
Language: Lao
Currency: Kip

MALAYSIA
Area: 127,355 sq. mi. (329,847km²)
Population: 31,382,000
Capitals: Kuala Lumpur and Putrujaya
Language: Malay
Currency: Ringgit

SEE ALSO
Asia, Indonesia, Malaysia, Philippines, Singapore

SPACECRAFT

There are three main types of spacecraft: artificial satellites, unmanned probes, and manned spacecraft. All require powerful rockets to lift them into space.

Satellites are spacecraft that orbit Earth without a crew. They are used for surveying our planet, communication, forecasting the weather, or, as in the case of the Hubble Space Telescope, investigating the universe. They carry equipment, including radio receivers and transmitters, measuring instruments, cameras, and computers. The energy needed to run the onboard equipment comes from solar panels that convert sunlight into electricity.

GETTING THERE

The space shuttle took off like a rocket, landed like a plane, and could reach speeds of 17,400 mph (28,000kph). The launch in 1981 of the first space shuttle, *Columbia*, by NASA meant that a reusable vehicle could launch craft into space instead of a new rocket needing to be built for each mission.

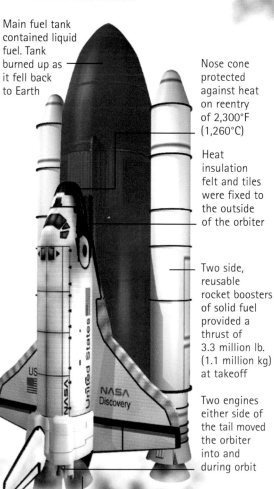

Main fuel tank contained liquid fuel. Tank burned up as it fell back to Earth

Nose cone protected against heat on reentry of 2,300°F (1,260°C)

Heat insulation felt and tiles were fixed to the outside of the orbiter

Two side, reusable rocket boosters of solid fuel provided a thrust of 3.3 million lb. (1.1 million kg) at takeoff

Two engines either side of the tail moved the orbiter into and during orbit

The shuttle had three main rocket engines

▼ Two minutes after launch, the booster rockets fell away; six minutes later, the main liquid-fueled tank dropped away. The boosters splashed down in the Atlantic Ocean and were retrieved by ships.

▲ The shuttle launched its cargo into orbit—here, a satellite. The shuttle's speed at the time of launch was crucial: if it was too fast, the satellite would fly off into space; too slow and it would drop to Earth.

Sputnik (U.S.S.R.), the first satellite, launched in 1957, orbited for six months.

Mir space station (U.S.S.R., 1986) was almost continuously occupied.

Luna 9 was the first craft to land on the Moon and send back pictures, in 1966.

ROBOTS IN SPACE
Robotic spacecraft called probes have been sent to fly past, orbit, or land on other planets. They carry cameras and instruments to gather data that is sent back to Earth as a stream of radio signals. Space probes have small rocket engines that are fired to alter course or slow down before they enter orbit. Some probes send a lander to a planet's surface, where it soft-lands.

MANNED SPACEFLIGHT
Early manned spacecraft include the U.S.S.R.'s 1961 *Vostok I*, which carried the first human into space, and the U.S.'s 1969 *Apollo* craft, which carried the first astronauts to the Moon. Later came orbital space stations and the space shuttle. Manned spacecraft must carry enough air, food, and water to keep astronauts alive and working for what may be months in space. Fresh supplies can be brought from Earth in unmanned vehicles that dock with the manned spacecraft. In this way permanent space stations can be maintained in orbit.

ROCKETS
To gather enough speed to go into orbit around Earth or to escape from Earth's gravity spacecraft need rocket-launch vehicles. These usually come in three parts, or stages. As one stage runs out of fuel it falls away, and the next stage fires.

The European Space Agency's *Ariane* rocket was first launched in 1981.

SEE ALSO
Astronaut, Planet, Rocket, Satellite, Solar system, Space exploration

SPACE EXPLORATION

Space exploration began in 1957, with the launch of the first artificial satellite. By 1961, people were orbiting Earth. All the major planets have now been investigated.

▲ A dog named Laika was the first "astronaut," sent into orbit in *Sputnik 2* in 1957. It stayed up for two weeks.

The *Luna 2* (U.S.S.R.) was the first spacecraft to reach the Moon, in 1959.

Five *Surveyor* spacecraft (U.S.A.) landed on the Moon in the 1960s.

Radio-controlled *Lunokhods* (U.S.S.R.) traveled on the Moon's surface in 1970 and 1973.

The Moon was the first target for space probes. In 1959, Russia's *Luna 1* flew past the Moon at a distance of 3,700 mi. (5,955km). Later that year, *Luna 2* crash-landed on the Moon, and *Luna 3* went around it, to send back the first pictures of the far side. In the 1960s, several U.S. and Russian probes landed on the Moon and sent back pictures. Manned landings began with Apollo 11 in 1969. Altogether, the six successful Apollo missions brought back 840 lbs. (381kg) of lunar rock and dust. Many probes have since visited the Moon, and in 2013 a Chinese spacecraft landed there to deliver *Yutu*, a robotic rover.

HOT VENUS
Venus is the planet closest to Earth (about 26 million mi./41 million km away), but its surface is hidden by thick clouds, so it's hard to get a clear picture of it by telescope or spacecraft. In 1967, the Russian probe *Venera 4* parachuted down through the gaseous clouds and sent back information about their makeup.

SEARCHING PROBES
During the 1970s, several Russian probes landed on Venus and took measurements of their surroundings. But in scorching temperatures of over 840°F (450°C), none of the spacecraft survived for more than about an hour. In 1990 the *Magellan* orbiter began to map the planet, completing its mission in 1994. From 2006 until 2014 the European orbiter *Venus Express* studied the planet's atmosphere, and in 2016 Japan's *Akatsuki* arrived to continue these studies. ▶

APOLLO **COMMAND MODULE**

UNITED STATES

APOLLO **LUNAR MODULE**

A GIANT LEAP FOR MANKIND

In 1969, U.S. astronaut Neil Armstrong made history when he stepped from *Apollo 11*'s lunar module onto the Moon. Later missions, like this fourth U.S. landing in 1971, used lunar rovers to explore and collect soil samples. The lunar module took them back to the orbiting command module.

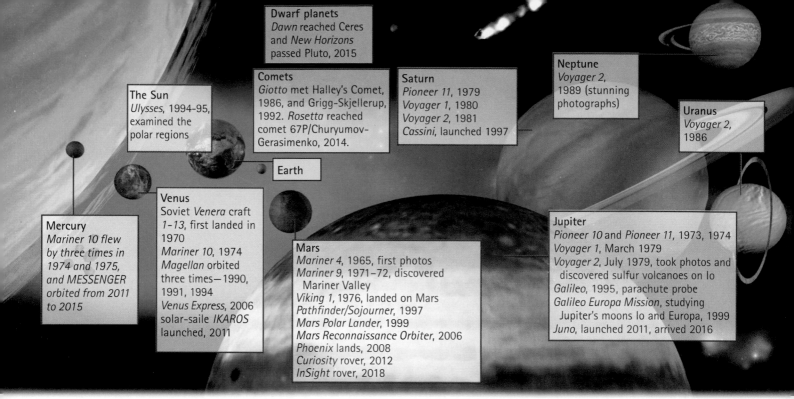

Dwarf planets
Dawn reached Ceres and *New Horizons* passed Pluto, 2015

The Sun
Ulysses, 1994-95, examined the polar regions

Comets
Giotto met Halley's Comet, 1986, and Grigg-Skjellerup, 1992. *Rosetta* reached comet 67P/Churyumov-Gerasimenko, 2014.

Saturn
Pioneer 11, 1979
Voyager 1, 1980
Voyager 2, 1981
Cassini, launched 1997

Neptune
Voyager 2, 1989 (stunning photographs)

Uranus
Voyager 2, 1986

Earth

Venus
Soviet *Venera* craft *1-13*, first landed in 1970
Mariner 10, 1974
Magellan orbited three times—1990, 1991, 1994
Venus Express, 2006
solar-saile *IKAROS* launched, 2011

Mercury
Mariner 10 flew by three times in 1974 and 1975, and MESSENGER orbited from 2011 to 2015

Mars
Mariner 4, 1965, first photos
Mariner 9, 1971–72, discovered Mariner Valley
Viking 1, 1976, landed on Mars
Pathfinder/Sojourner, 1997
Mars Polar Lander, 1999
Mars Reconnaissance Orbiter, 2006
Phoenix lands, 2008
Curiosity rover, 2012
InSight rover, 2018

Jupiter
Pioneer 10 and *Pioneer 11*, 1973, 1974
Voyager 1, March 1979
Voyager 2, July 1979, took photos and discovered sulfur volcanoes on Io
Galileo, 1995, parachute probe
Galileo Europa Mission, studying Jupiter's moons Io and Europa, 1999
Juno, launched 2011, arrived 2016

Mars 96 Penetrator (U.S.S.R.) has a 20-ft. (6-m) spike full of instruments to monitor composition of the ground.

Artist's impression of the *Magellan* radar-mapping spacecraft orbiting Venus in 1994.

Earth-controlled exploring robot designed to roam Mars or the Moon and send back images.

▲ Unmanned probes have now visited all of the major planets—and *New Horizons*, launched in 2006, flew past faraway dwarf planet Pluto in 2015. Other ventures include further deep-space missions and the 2011 launch of *Juno*, which arrived at Jupiter in 2016.

MISSIONS TO MERCURY

The *Mariner 10* probe flew by Mercury in 1974 and 1975, sending back the first clear photos of this small world's heavily cratered surface. In 2011, NASA's *MESSENGER* (MErcury Surface, Space ENvironment, GEochemistry, and Ranging) probe went into orbit around Mercury, remaining there until 2015 when it crashed into the planet. *MESSENGER* found water on Mercury, both deep below the surface and in the form of ice in craters near the planet's north pole.

LIFE ON MARS?

In 1971 NASA's *Mariner 9* probe discovered dried-up riverbeds on Mars, and in 1976 the American landers *Viking 1* and *Viking 2* tested the soil in a search for life. Many other craft have orbited around or landed on Mars since, including four robotic rovers, which have crawled over and dug into the surface of Mars, named the Red Planet after the color of its soil. A great deal of ice, and small amounts of liquid water, have been found on Mars and we know that long ago there was plentiful running water on its surface. So far, however, no trace of life has been found there.

Solar panels generating power from the Sun

Telescopes and solar observation unit

Apollo command module

Docking unit

Living quarters and orbital workshop

◄ *Skylab*, launched in 1973, was built by NASA as a laboratory in space. It lasted until 1979, when it broke up and fell back to Earth. Astronauts now live and work in orbit in the *International Space Station*.

IS ANYONE OUT THERE?

World	Evidence
Mars	In the past, Mars had a thick atmosphere and plenty of liquid water, so life could have evolved there—and may still survive, deep underground
Enceladus	One of Saturn's moons, Enceladus, has underground oceans of water that spray out through surface cracks. Life exists in similar conditions deep in Earth's oceans
Titan	Saturn's largest moon, and the only other world we know with lakes (of a tar-like liquid) on its surface. Many of the chemical ingredients for life are to be found there
Europa	A moon of Jupiter, Europa has an underground ocean larger than all of Earth's oceans together

◀ The *Mars Global Surveyor*, launched in 1996, orbited Mars (the Red Planet) taking photographs, assessing the planet's geology, and finding a landing site for the next mission due to land there.

GIANT PLANETS

In 1973, the first probe to Jupiter, *Pioneer 10*, flew past the planet. Many more probes have since flown by Jupiter, but it was not until 1995 that the first orbiter arrived – *Galileo*, which released a probe that dropped by parachute through Jupiter's clouds and sent back details of the weather conditions and make-up of the atmosphere before burning up. In 2016, NASA's *Juno* probe became the second Jupiter orbiter. Two of the other giant planets, Uranus and Neptune, have been visited only by the *Voyager 2* flyby probe, in 1986 and 1989.

SMALL WORLDS

In 2014 the *Rosetta* spacecraft reached comet 67P/Churyumov–Gerasimenko after visiting two asteroids. It released a probe called *Philae*, which landed on the comet. In 2015, the *Dawn* orbiter reached Ceres, a dwarf planet, which is the largest member of the asteroid belt. In the same year the *New Horizons* probe flew by dwarf planet Pluto as part of a mission to explore the Kuiper Belt, a region of the outer solar system containing many tiny worlds and smaller objects about which we know very little.

MANNED EXPLORATION

More than 520 astronauts have flown in space, and 12 have set foot on the Moon. The next target for manned exploration is Mars. A craft to make this journey could be built in space by astronauts on board the *International Space Station* orbiting Earth.

▼ *Huygens* took two and a half hours to parachute to Titan's surface, sending information back to *Cassini* about the moon's atmosphere, which relayed it back to Earth.

TO SATURN AND BEYOND

Launched in 1997, NASA's *Cassini* spacecraft took seven years to reach Saturn. In 2004, it reached the planet and released a robot probe, *Huygens*, which successfully landed on the surface of Titan, Saturn's largest moon. The probe sent back images of the surface of Titan showing ice blocks strewn around and sampled the chemical composition of the atmosphere. *Cassini* continued to orbit Saturn, studying the planet and its rings and moons, until 2017, when it ran out of fuel and was allowed to burn up in the planet's atmosphere.

SEE ALSO

Astronaut, Planet, Satellite, Solar system, Spacecraft, Star, Sun

SPAIN AND PORTUGAL

Spain and Portugal lie in the most southwesterly part of Europe, in an area known as the Iberian Peninsula. The countries have a linked history.

SPAIN
Area: 195,124 sq. mi. (505,370km²)
Population: 48,958,000
Capital: Madrid
Languages: Spanish, Catalan, Galician, Basque
Currency: Euro

PORTUGAL
Area: 35,556 sq. mi. (92,090km²)
Population: 10,840,000
Capital: Lisbon
Language: Portuguese
Currency: Euro

Much of the Spanish mainland is a huge plateau called the Meseta. The country's high mountains include the Sierra Nevada and the Cantabrian ranges. The Pyrenees separate Spain from France. The Mediterranean coastline consists of fertile plains, and, together with Spain's Balearic Islands, it attracts many tourists. The Canary Islands in the Atlantic are also popular; Spain's highest peak, Pico de Teide at 12,198 ft. (3,718m), lies on the island of Tenerife. Central Spain has hot summers, reaching 108°F (42°C) and cold winters; the coasts have a more moderate climate. Portugal is also mountainous, with high cliffs along its sandy Atlantic coastline. It has a milder climate than Spain. Its territory includes the islands of the Azores and Madeira in the Atlantic.

KEY CITIES
Spain's capital city, Madrid, is in the center of the country. Other major cities include the industrial ports of Barcelona, Valencia, Malaga, and Bilbao, as well as the historic fortress-cities of Granada, Cordoba, Seville, and Murcia. Portugal's capital city, Lisbon, stands on the Tagus River, which divides the country. Lisbon was rebuilt after being

▲ Traditional costumes, like those of these women and children from Seville, are still worn by many Spanish people for festivals and other celebrations.

destroyed by an earthquake in 1755. Portugal's other major city, Porto, is the center of the port wine trade. Over one third of the Portuguese people live in rural villages.

TOURISM AND TRADE
In Spain, tourism and industry have grown rapidly since the 1950s, alongside traditional crafts, winemaking, fishing, and growing fruit and vegetables. Portugal's main products are textiles and clothing, wine, fish, cork, and marble. Portugal also depends heavily on tourism. Many Portuguese work abroad, sending money back home. Nearly seven percent of the country's adults cannot read or write.

THE SPANISH LANGUAGE
Southern Spain was ruled by Moors—Muslims from North Africa—from A.D. 711 to 1492. Moorish civilization left its mark on language, architecture, food, and

▲ Forests of cork oak trees in Portugal provide natural cork for export, but this traditional industry is threatened by the use of plastic stoppers in wine bottles.

► Spain has about 1,400 castles and palaces. The fortified Alhambra Palace in Granada was built in the 1200s and 1300s.

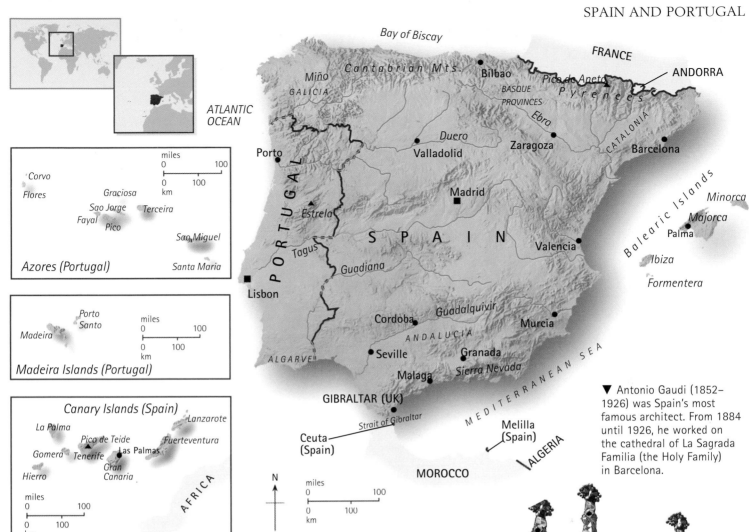

Bay of Biscay

Cantabrian Mts.

FRANCE

ANDORRA

Bilbao

Pico de Aneto

Pyrenees

Miño

GALICIA

BASQUE
PROVINCES

Ebro

CATALONIA

Porto

Duero

Valladolid

Zaragoza

Barcelona

PORTUGAL

Madrid

Estrela

S P A I N

Balearic Islands

Minorca

Majorca

Palma

Tagus

Valencia

Ibiza

Guadiana

Formentera

Lisbon

Guadalquivir

Cordoba

Murcia

ANDALUCIA

Seville

Granada

MEDITERRANEAN SEA

ALGARVE

Malaga

Sierra Nevada

GIBRALTAR (UK)

Strait of Gibraltar

Melilla
(Spain)

Ceuta
(Spain)

ALGERIA

MOROCCO

N

ATLANTIC
OCEAN

miles
0   100
0   100
km

Corvo

Flores

Graciosa

Sao Jorge

Terceira

Fayal

Pico

Sao Miguel

Azores (Portugal)

Santa Maria

*Porto
Santo*

Madeira

Madeira Islands (Portugal)

miles
0   100
0   100
km

Canary Islands (Spain)

Lanzarote

La Palma

Pico de Teide

Fuerteventura

Gomera

Tenerife

Las Palmas

Hierro

*Gran
Canaria*

AFRICA

miles
0   100
0   100
km

miles
0   100
0   100
km

▼ Antonio Gaudi (1852–
1926) was Spain's most
famous architect. From 1884
until 1926, he worked on
the cathedral of La Sagrada
Familia (the Holy Family)
in Barcelona.

music. By 1516, Spain's several kingdoms were united under one ruler and the Roman Catholic Church. Wealth from a newly conquered empire in South America made Spain the greatest military power in Europe, and colonization, especially in the Americas, made Spanish a world language.

SETBACKS TO PROGRESS

From 1800, Spain was weakened by wars, revolutions, and poverty. After the Spanish Civil War of 1936–39, General Francisco Franco ruled as a dictator until his death in 1975. The monarchy was then restored with King Juan Carlos I, and a democratic form of government was established.

PORTUGAL'S HISTORY

Although overshadowed by Spain, Portugal has managed to keep its language, identity, and independence. Like Spain, Portugal has a Moorish heritage, is strongly Roman Catholic, and has suffered from wars, dictatorship, and poverty. From 1400,

Portuguese sailors such as Vasco da Gama took the lead in Europe's expansion overseas and helped create a Portuguese-speaking empire stretching from Brazil to Macao in China. Portugal's power began to weaken in the late 1500s. Portugal has been a democracy only since 1976. In 1986, Spain and Portugal joined the European Union.

SEE ALSO

Civil war, Empire, Europe, Explorer

SPIDER AND SCORPION

Spiders and scorpions are invertebrates (animals with no backbone) belonging to a group called arachnids. They have four pairs of legs—insects have only three.

The wind scorpion (or sun spider) uses the wind to run and has huge jaws.

Mites, like this giant desert mite, are members of the arachnid family.

Unlike spiders, harvestmen have just one body section and eight slender legs.

A scorpion has large claws at the front to crush prey, and a sting in its tail.

All spiders and scorpions are predatory animals, feeding mainly on insects. Some of the big tropical spiders eat lizards and mice and even take baby birds from their nests.

WEB OF DEATH

Spiders are famous for the silk webs they spin to trap their prey. There are lots of different web designs, the best known being the circular orb webs. These have sticky spiral threads fixed to a set of radial threads that look like the spokes of a bicycle wheel. They are designed to catch flying insects. Other webs are designed to trap insects that scuttle over the ground.

HUNTING OR TRAPPING

The Australian dinopis spider spins a net, and holding this in its front legs, waits for an insect to pass by. Then it throws the net over the insect. But not all spiders make webs. Wolf spiders run after their prey, and crab spiders usually sit on plants, seizing insects that come within range.

POISONOUS FANGS

A spider kills its prey with poison, which is injected with a pair of needlelike fangs close to its mouth. The poison also starts to digest the prey, making it liquid, so the spider can suck the juices into its tiny mouth. It

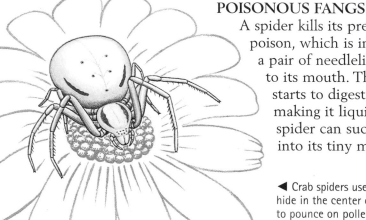

◀ Crab spiders use their colors to hide in the center of flowers, ready to pounce on pollen-hunting bugs.

Spiders have two body parts—an abdomen (back end) and a cephalothorax (head and chest). The legs are joined to the cephalothorax

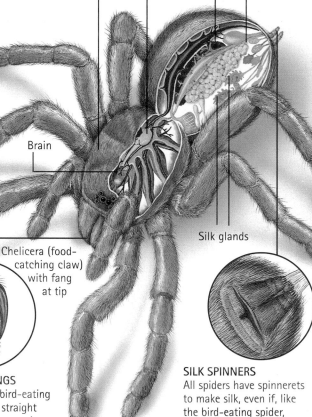

Sucking stomach

Heart

Ovaries

Brain

Hairs

Silk glands

Claws

Chelicera (food-catching claw) with fang at tip

DEADLY FANGS
The fangs of bird-eating spiders point straight down. In other species, they point sideways.

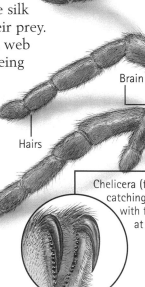

SILK SPINNERS
All spiders have spinnerets to make silk, even if, like the bird-eating spider, they don't make webs.

BIG, HAIRY BIRD EATER

Bird-eating spiders are among the largest spiders, with a leg span of up to 10 in. (25cm) and 2.5 in. (6cm)-wide bodies. Despite their eight eyes, they have poor eyesight and use their sense of touch and body hairs to detect vibrations. They leave trails of silk to help would-be mates find them, to help them climb, and to wrap their eggs.

cannot eat solid food. Some spider poisons are powerful enough to kill people, but only about 30 of the 40,000 or so species of spider are really dangerous. They include the black widow and the funnel-web spiders. The most venomous spider known to humans is the wandering spider from Brazil, and there is still no antidote for the bite of the recluse spider, also found in South America. The fangs of most spiders are too small or weak to pierce human skin.

▲ Scorpions are fluorescent. Their outer shell glows bright green when an ultraviolet light is shined at it. This helps scientists to spot them at night when they are most active.

SENSITIVE HAIRS

Each leg of a spider has seven segments. Most species have three claws at the tip of the leg and a pad of hairs that helps them stick to surfaces. The legs are covered with three kinds of sensory hairs. On most spiders, the hairs are irritants that can be rubbed off onto attackers. They are also used to taste (by detecting chemicals in the surroundings), to feel, and to "hear," picking up vibrations either on the ground or in the web. A male spider often drums on a female's web as a mating signal.

A DANGEROUS COURTSHIP

Mating can be dangerous for many arachnids. The male spiders are mostly smaller than the females and often risk being mistaken for prey and eaten when they approach a would-be mate. In fact, the female often eats the male after, or even during, mating. The male nursery web spider gives his partner a gift of an insect wrapped in silk. As she eats the insect, he can mate safely.

EGGS IN SILK BAGS

A female spider wraps her eggs in silk bags, or sacs. Wolf spiders carry these around with them, and even carry their babies on their backs for a while. Some spiders, such as the pink-haired bird-eating spider, lay 3,000 eggs in one batch—the hatched spiderlings are larger than many fully grown species.

▶ A scorpion's sting is at the end of a long flexible tail, which it can quickly flick over to inject venom into its prey. The poison comes from two glands at the base.

STICKY TRAPS

Spiders have a variety of ways to trap prey. The orb-web spider (like many common garden spiders) creates a circular web in which unsuspecting flies get stuck. Bolas spiders fish for prey using a sticky line of silk which they throw at nearby insects. Trap-door spiders lurk in tunnels with little trapdoors. They dart out to catch passing insects and drag them below.

SCORPIONS

There are almost 2,000 species of scorpion, and all live in hot countries. Many of them live in deserts, where they can survive the high temperatures without ever needing a drink. Scorpions range from 0.8–8 in. (2–20cm) in length, the largest being the imperial scorpion of West Africa. All scorpions and spiders molt or shed their skin around 5 to 10 times as they grow.

A STING IN THE TAIL

Scorpions have large pincers—pedipalps— at the front and use them to catch lizards, insects, and other small animals. A scorpion also has a sting at the end of its slender tail. The sting is used mainly for defense, and some species are dangerous to people. The fat-tailed scorpion (found in parts of north Africa and the Middle East) is one of the most venomous scorpions. Its sting can kill a human in 6 to 7 hours.

Common garden spiders spin sticky, circular orb webs between branches.

Water spiders make a tent of silk under water, using air bubbles to breathe.

Trap-door spiders make a silk-lined tunnel in the ground with a lid on top.

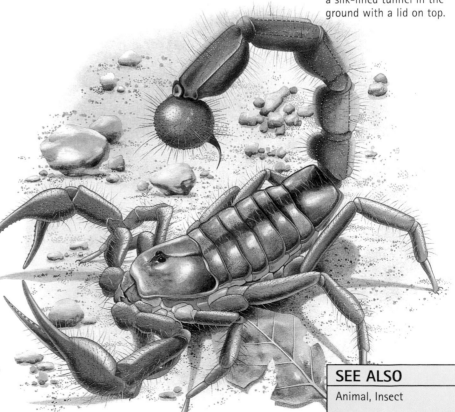

SEE ALSO
Animal, Insect

SPORTS

A sport is a game or activity involving physical skills, often in competition. It is enjoyable as a form of exercise and also provides big-business entertainment.

Sports can be played either in teams or individually, on a professional or an amateur basis. Most sports are competitive and winning may be decided in a number of ways: by timing speeds (running or swimming events), measuring distances (jumping or throwing events), scoring points (most ball games), or judging performances (diving, boxing, and gymnastics).

Ice hockey players reach 30 mph (48kph) and drive a hard, disk-shaped puck at 100 mph (160kph).

In motorcross, strong, light bikes with chunky tires race across rough and hilly cross-country terrain.

A discus thrower spins around one and a half times before releasing the discus from his hand.

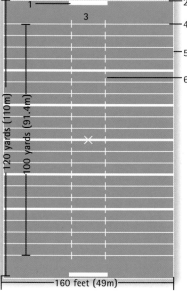

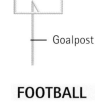

— Goalpost

KEY

1 Goalpost
2 End line
3 End zone
4 Goal line
5 Sideline
6 Inbounds lines

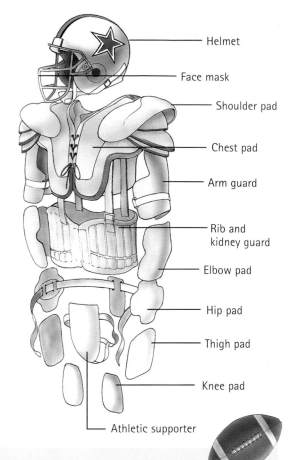

Helmet
Face mask
Shoulder pad
Chest pad
Arm guard
Rib and kidney guard
Elbow pad
Hip pad
Thigh pad
Knee pad
Athletic supporter

FOOTBALL

Football evolved from English soccer and rugby. Professional teams have squads of up to 45 players divided into three areas: one for offense, another for defense, and the third for kicking. The team in possession (offense) has four plays, or "downs," to advance the ball 10 yards (9.1m) by running with it or passing it. If successful, the team has another series of plays. If it fails, the opposition takes possession of the ball. All plays start on or between the inbounds lines. Six points are awarded for a touchdown, plus an extra point for converting the ball over the crossbar. Placekicking the ball over the crossbar from anywhere in the field gains three points. The defense can also score two points from a "safety" either by tackling the ball carrier in his own end zone or if the carrier steps out of the back or side of his zone.

TENNIS

The modern game of lawn tennis was developed in Britain in the 1860s. The object of the game is to score points by hitting the ball with a racket over the net into the opponent's court so that it cannot be returned. The ball may be struck either before it has hit the ground or after one bounce. Tennis is played in sets, usually the best of three or five. A set is won when one side wins six games, with a lead of at least two games. A game's scoring goes from "love" (0) to 15, 30, 40, and "game." If the score reaches 40–40 ("deuce"), it continues until one side leads by two clear points.

◄ Success in men's tennis depends greatly on having a powerful serve, as Pete Sampras demonstrates.

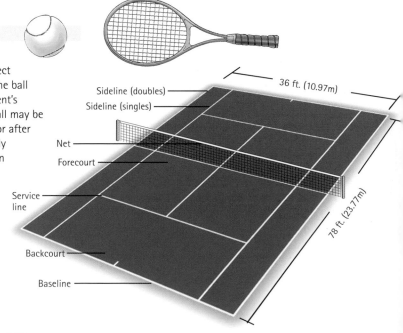

Sideline (doubles)
Sideline (singles)
36 ft. (10.97m)
Net
Forecourt
Service line
Backcourt
Baseline
78 ft. (23.77m)

SOCCER

Professional soccer is played 11 to a team, with three substitutes allowed, and consists of two 45-minute halves. The object of the game is to kick or head the ball into the opponents' net to score a goal. The team with the most goals at the end of play wins. Players can move the ball with their feet, head, or body, but not their hands or arms. Only the goalkeeper may handle the ball, and then only inside the penalty area. A free-kick is given if a player commits a foul or is offside. A player is offside when fewer than two defending players are positioned between him and the goal line as the ball is being passed forward to him.

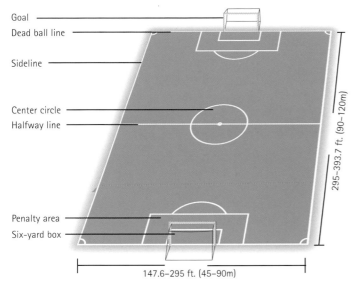

Goal
Dead ball line
Sideline
Center circle
Halfway line
Penalty area
Six-yard box

295–393.7 ft. (90–120m)

147.6–295 ft. (45–90m)

▲ It's a foul! Israel's Etay Schechte tackles Marco Verratti of Italy in 2017, during a qualifier for the 2018 FIFA World Cup.

TRACK AND FIELD EVENTS

Outdoor running events, except for the marathon, take place on the 400m track. They include the 100m, 200m, and 400m sprint. The longest middle-distance track race is 10,000m (25 laps), and other running events include the steeplechase and relay. Field events include: high, long, and triple jump; hammer, discus, and javelin throwing; pole vaulting; and shot putting. Combined track and field events include the ten-event decathlon and seven-event heptathlon.

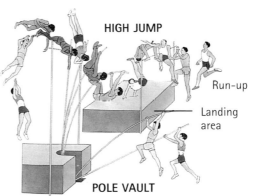

HIGH JUMP

Run-up

Landing area

POLE VAULT

◀ Leading high jumpers use a technique called the "Fosbury flop." This involves clearing the bar head first, followed by the back, and, last of all, the legs. In pole vaulting, the pole may be of any length or width.

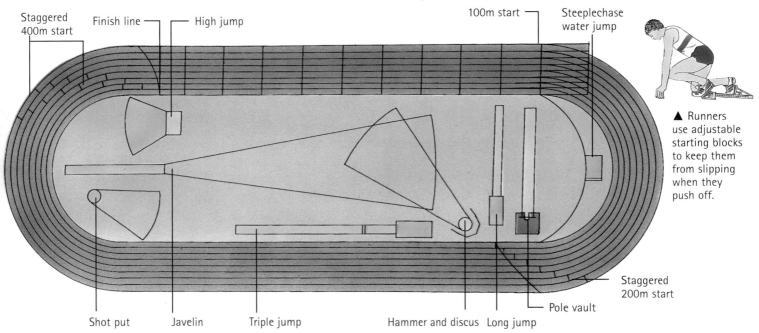

Staggered 400m start
Finish line
High jump
100m start
Steeplechase water jump

Shot put   Javelin   Triple jump   Hammer and discus Long jump

Pole vault

Staggered 200m start

▲ Runners use adjustable starting blocks to keep them from slipping when they push off.

393

An old Scottish game, golf is now one of the most popular sports worldwide.

Horse racing can either be flat racing or racing over jumps and is a major betting sport.

Skiing is a snow sport that includes downhill, slalom (obstacle course), ski-jumping, and cross-country.

BASKETBALL

Basketball was invented in Massachusetts in 1891 and is now one of the most popular sports worldwide. It is played by two teams of ten, although only five players may be on court at any one time. The object of the game is to score points by throwing the ball into the opposition's basket. Players move the ball around with their hands by passing, dribbling, and shooting. Running with the ball is not allowed. Baskets may be scored from any part of the court and are worth three points from outside the three-point arc, two from inside it, and one from a free throw.

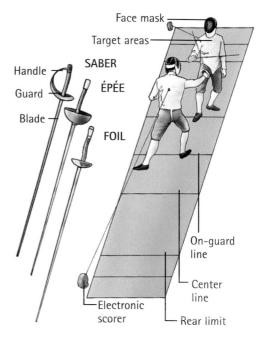

Backboard

Basket

Free-throw line

▲ Michael Jordan slam dunks for the Chicago Bulls.

Sideline

End line

Center circle

FENCING

As a combat practice, fencing dates from the Middle Ages. Three weapons are now used—the épée, saber, and foil. The object of fencing is to touch your opponent on the target area with your sword to score a hit. The fencers are wired up so that any hit can be registered electronically. Only the point of the weapon may be used in épée and foil, but with the saber the edge of the blade also counts.

Face mask

Target areas

Handle — SABER

Guard — ÉPÉE

Blade —

FOIL

On-guard line

Center line

Electronic scorer

Rear limit

CRICKET

Organized cricket began in England in the late 1600s, but its origins probably go as far back as 1300. The modern game is played 11 on each team. At each end of the pitch is a wicket, which is defended by a batsman. The object of the game is to get the opponents' side out with the least number of runs. A side's innings ends when ten batsmen have been dismissed, caught, or run out. Any member of the fielding side may bowl an "over" consisting of six balls. After each over, another bowler starts from the other end of the pitch. A run is scored when a batsman hits the ball with the bat and both batsmen run to the opposite end of the pitch without being dismissed. A hit over the boundary scores four runs, or six runs if it does not touch the ground first.

Batting glove

Bails

▲ The possible fielding positions for a right-handed batsman (only 11 fielders allowed): 1 Bowler; 2 Wicket keeper; 3 First slip; 4 Second slip; 5 Gully; 6 Point; 7 Cover point; 8 Extra cover; 9 Silly point; 10 Silly mid-off; 11 Mid-off; 12 Deep mid-off; 13 Long-off; 14 Long-on; 15 Deep mid-on; 16 Mid-on; 17 Mid-wicket; 18 Silly mid-on; 19 Deep square-leg; 20 Square-leg; 21 Forward short-leg; 22 Backward short-leg; 23 Leg slip; 24 Short extra cover; 25 Backward point; 26 Short third man; 27 Third man; 28 Deep mid-wicket; 29 Deep extra cover.

Leg pad

Stumps

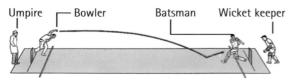

Umpire — Bowler — Batsman — Wicket keeper

BASEBALL

Baseball probably developed from games such as cricket and rounders. It was first played in 1846 in New Jersey, USA. It is played nine to a team on a square field, the diamond, within a larger outfield. At one point of the diamond is home plate, where the batter stands, and at the other points are first, second, and third bases, each of which is defended by a baseman. The pitcher throws the ball from a mound in the center of the diamond. To score a run, the batter moves around the bases to reach home plate. He may do this with one hit or on hits of succeeding batters. Each team has nine turns at bat. The fielding team must get three batters out to close an inning and take its next turn at bat.

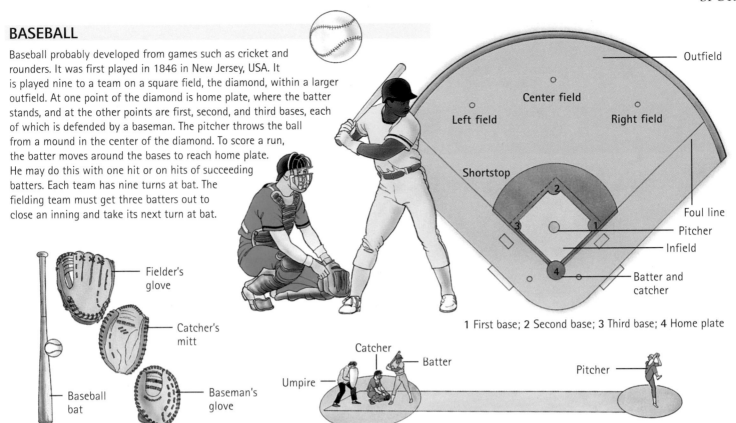

Outfield

Center field

Left field   Right field

Shortstop

Foul line

Pitcher

Infield

Batter and catcher

1 First base; 2 Second base; 3 Third base; 4 Home plate

Fielder's glove

Catcher's mitt

Baseman's glove

Baseball bat

Umpire   Catcher   Batter   Pitcher

GYMNASTICS

Born in ancient Greece, the idea of gymnastics was revived in the late 1700s and was an event at the first modern Olympic Games in 1896. In competition, gymnasts are marked out of ten by a panel of judges. The classic events involve floor exercises, high bar, parallel bars, pommel horse, rings, and vault. Rhythmic gymnastics is performed to music and involves ballet steps and hand apparatus. Its individual exercises include twirling, throwing, catching, rolling, bouncing, or swinging the apparatus. Sports acrobatics, for individuals or teams, includes somersaults and springs.

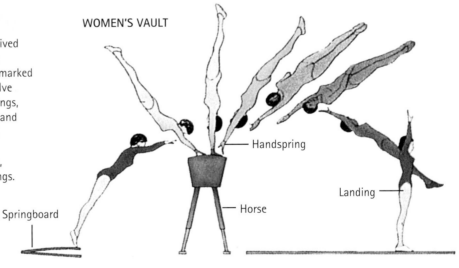

WOMEN'S VAULT

Handspring

Landing

Springboard

Horse

SWIMMING AND DIVING

The earliest swimming races took place 2,000 years ago in Japan. Today, they involve four main strokes—front crawl, backstroke, breaststroke, and butterfly—as well as freestyle. There are also separate diving events, either from a highboard or springboard, which involve specific somersaults, twists, and turns while in the air.

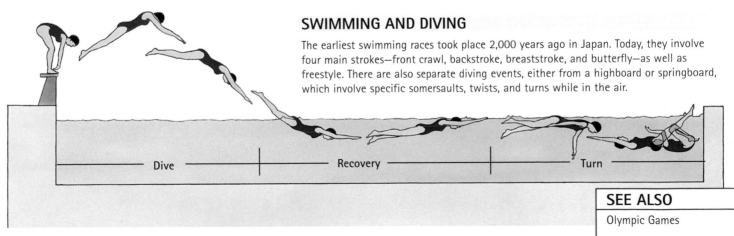

Dive   Recovery   Turn

SEE ALSO
Olympic Games

STAR

Stars are large balls of hot gas that produce light and heat through nuclear reactions. Our Sun is an average yellow star, but seems bright because it is so close.

THE BIRTH OF A STAR

A star begins its life by condensing out of material from a cloud of dust and gas. When the star's temperature is hot enough, nuclear reactions begin, and hydrogen converts to helium, creating a steady glow. Yellow stars, such as the Sun, may shine steadily for billions of years before expanding and cooling into red giants. Finally, they collapse into small, dense white dwarfs, and then die.

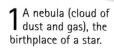

1 A nebula (cloud of dust and gas), the birthplace of a star.

2 The gas and dust condense, and the star begins to form.

3 Nuclear reaction takes place: hydrogen is converted to helium.

4 The new star generates light and heat.

5 The yellow star remains stable for billions of years.

▲ The constellation of Orion is a place where new stars are being born, in areas such as the Orion Nebula (M42).

Stars form from large clouds of gas and dust in space, called nebulae. These clouds shrink due to the inward pull of their own gravity. At the center of a shrinking cloud, the gas becomes hotter and denser. Eventually, nuclear reactions start, in which hydrogen is turned into helium by a process known ias nuclear fusion, and a new star is born.

STAR TEMPERATURES

At the center of a star, where nuclear fusion occurs, it is over 50 million°F (10 million°C). Stars may be classified according to their temperature. The temperature at the surface varies from star to star. A red dwarf may be 5,432°F (3,000°C), and a blue supergiant may be over 37,832°F (20,000°C). Stars also have different luminosities, or brightnesses, so a bright, distant star may look closer than a nearby star that is very dim.

STARS IN OLD AGE

When all the hydrogen at the center of a star is used up, the star begins to change. Its outer layers swell until the star is many times larger than before, and it becomes a red giant. After this, the fate of the star is decided by its mass. Stars such as the Sun end up as small, hot stars called white dwarfs. More massive stars, however,

are shorter-lived and blow up in huge explosions called supernovae. One of two final stages may follow: in the first, the remaining part of the star collapses until it becomes a neutron star, the densest type of star. A handful of its material weighs billions of tons. The second possibility is that a star of very great mass may collapse and become a black hole, a funnel-like shape that sucks all nearby material into it—even light cannot escape.

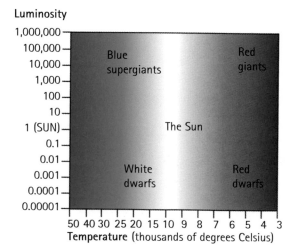

▲ The diagram plots the temperature and luminosity of stars. The more material a star has, the hotter it is. Blue supergiants are the hottest, and red dwarfs the coolest.

BRIGHTEST STARS

Name	Constellation
Sun	–
Sirius	Canis Major
Canopus	Carina
Rigil Kent	Centaurus
Arcturus	Bootes
Vega	Lyra
Capella	Auriga
Rigel	Orion
Procyon	Canis Minor
Achernar	Eridanus

SEE ALSO

Astronomy, Black hole, Color, Constellation, Galaxy, Sun, Universe

396

STARFISH AND OTHER ECHINODERMS

Starfish are star-shaped, marine invertebrates with between 5 and 40 arms. Other echinoderms include brittle stars, sea urchins, and sea cucumbers.

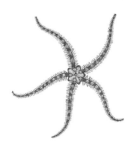

A sea cucumber can grow up to 20 in. (50cm). It has suckered feet for climbing.

A brittle star has no suckers. It uses its long arms to pull itself along.

A rock urchin grows up to 2.5 in. (6cm) and has sharp spines. It eats algae.

A violet heart urchin has furry spines on top. It burrows in sand and mud.

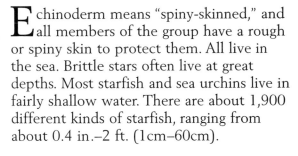

Echinoderm means "spiny-skinned," and all members of the group have a rough or spiny skin to protect them. All live in the sea. Brittle stars often live at great depths. Most starfish and sea urchins live in fairly shallow water. There are about 1,900 different kinds of starfish, ranging from about 0.4 in.–2 ft. (1cm–60cm).

POWERFUL SUCKERS
Using its suckers, a starfish can move in any direction it chooses. It feeds on other small animals, including fish and worms, and can even open the shells of cockles and other bivalves with its powerful suckers. The starfish wraps its arms around a shell and grips with its suckers, which gradually pull the two halves of the shell apart. The starfish then pushes its stomach through the crack and digests the soft body inside.

DRIFTING YOUNGSTERS
Starfish do not mate. The males and females release clouds of sperm and eggs into the water, and fertilization takes place there. The young starfish (or larvae) are

▲ A starfish digests a bird egg. It turns its stomach inside out and pushes it into the shell to eat the soft body.

bloblike with no arms and, instead of living on the seabed, they float near the surface of the sea so they spread to new areas. They alter shape as they grow, and metamorphose (change) into adults.

SLENDER RELATIVES
Brittle stars look like starfish, but their arms are more slender and are clearly separated from the central disk. Some brittle stars catch small animals with their arms, but most species shovel mud into their mouth and digest any tiny creatures living there. Sea cucumbers have feeding tentacles around their mouth to filter food from water. Some sea urchins also feed like this.

SOFT SUCKERS
Rows of circular tube-feet with suckers at the ends are spaced along the arms.

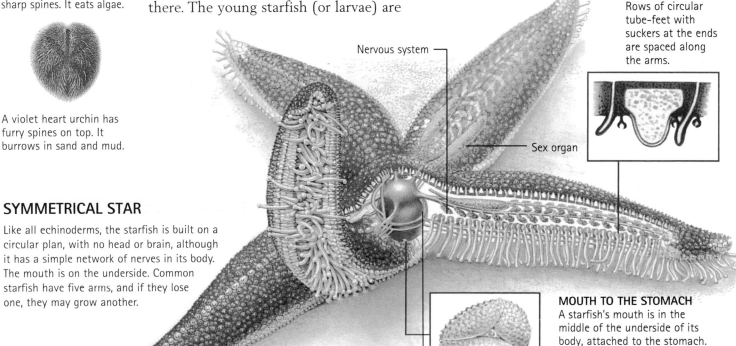

Nervous system

Sex organ

Stomach

SYMMETRICAL STAR
Like all echinoderms, the starfish is built on a circular plan, with no head or brain, although it has a simple network of nerves in its body. The mouth is on the underside. Common starfish have five arms, and if they lose one, they may grow another.

MOUTH TO THE STOMACH
A starfish's mouth is in the middle of the underside of its body, attached to the stomach.

SEE ALSO
Animal, Ocean and sea, Seashore

STOMACH AND DIGESTIVE SYSTEM

The food we eat is broken down into nutrients by the stomach and intestines, and then taken into the body for energy, growth, maintenance, and repair.

The stomach is the widest part of the digestive system, a long passageway or tube within the body. This begins at the mouth and continues through the throat, gullet, stomach, small intestine, and large intestine, ending at the anus. The whole tube is about 30 ft. (9m) long.

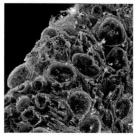

▲ A magnified view of human taste buds, which detect sweet, sour, bitter, salt, and umami flavors.

CHEWED TO A PULP
Chewing mashes food into a pulp so that digestive juices can reach it more easily.

DIGESTIVE JOURNEY

Food takes 24 to 36 hours to pass through the human digestive system. It is digested, or broken down, by squeezing and mashing, and by strong chemical juices called digestive enzymes.

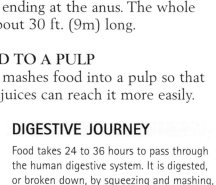

1 In the mouth, food is chewed into a pulp and mixed with watery saliva. This makes food slippery and easy to swallow. (Each mass of swallowed food is called a bolus.)

2 As food passes down the throat and the esophagus (gullet), it is squeezed and massaged along by wavelike contractions of the muscles in the wall.

3 Strong muscles in the stomach wall churn and squash the food. After 3 to 6 hours, the soupy, semidigested food, called chyme, trickles into the small intestine.

4 In the small intestine, the chyme is broken down into chemicals. The nutrients are taken into the bloodstream.

5 Undigested food and wastes pass into the large intestine. Water and body salts are absorbed by the bloodstream before the feces are expelled through the anus.

▲ Sugar and fat contain important nutrients. Too much, however, can damage health.

Three pairs of glands pour saliva into the mouth. The saliva contains enzymes to break down starches and sugars.

DIGESTING AND ABSORBING
In the stomach, the food is mixed with powerful acid and digestive enzymes. From there food passes to the small intestine, 1.6 in. (4cm) wide and 20 ft. (6m) long. Its lining is covered with thousands of villi (tiny projections), each about 0.04 in. (1mm) long. This provides a huge area for absorbing nutrients. The small intestine lining and nearby pancreas gland make more strong enzymes to digest chyme (semidigested food). Another digestive fluid, bile, is made in the liver and stored in the gallbladder. Bile is especially good at digesting fatty substances in food.

LARGE INTESTINE
Undigested food passes into the large intestine, about 2.4 in. (6cm) wide and 5 ft. (1.5m) long. The semisolid feces are stored near the end of the tract, in the rectum, until it is convenient to expel them through the anus.

LIVER
Blood from the intestines flows to the liver, which stores some nutrients from digestion, and converts sugars into starch for storage. It also breaks down possibly harmful substances, such as alcohol.

SEE ALSO
Food, Gland, Human body, Nutrition, Taste and smell

SUBMARINE

A submarine is a craft that can travel under the sea. It can be a deadly naval weapon, but can also explore the seabed and carry out repairs on underwater pipelines.

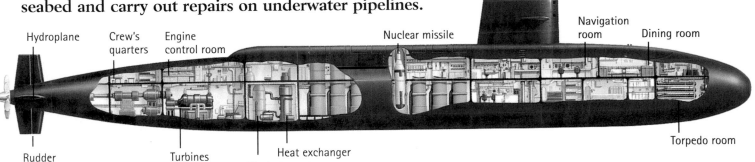

Periscope, radio, and radar antennae

Navigation room

Nuclear missile

Dining room

Hydroplane

Crew's quarters

Engine control room

Rudder

Turbines

Heat exchanger

Nuclear reactor

Torpedo room

▲ David Bushnell's *Turtle* was the first submarine to be used in warfare, in the American Revolution, 1776. The craft was driven by hand- and foot-propellers and steered by a rudder.

KEY DATES

c.1620 First submarine is built by Dutchman Cornelius Drebbel

1864 USS *Hunley* becomes first submarine to sink an enemy ship, in American Civil War

1954 USS *Nautilus* is the first nuclear submarine

1960 *Trieste* submersible dives to a record 6.8 mi. (10.9km) in the Pacific

The earliest submarines were barrel-like vessels powered by hand-cranked propellers or oars during the 1600s and 1700s. American engineer Robert Fulton (1765–1815) tried in vain to interest the French navy in his submarine in 1800. Submarine warfare was tried during the American Civil War (1861–65), and it was the U.S. Navy that accepted the first practical submarine, built in 1898 by Irish-born inventor John P. Holland (1840–1914).

SUBMARINES IN WAR

Submarines armed with torpedoes sank ships in both world wars. They had electric motors for use underwater, but moved faster on the surface, using diesel engines to recharge the electric motors' batteries. The United States launched the first nuclear-powered submarine in 1955. Modern naval submarines have nuclear reactors driving turbine engines and can travel around the world underwater without refueling. They can fire guided missiles and, with the aid of computerized navigation systems, can go almost anywhere in the world's seas.

▲ Much of the space in a nuclear submarine is taken up by the turbines that drive it and the reactor. The crew's quarters and operating area take up a very small space.

HOW A SUBMARINE WORKS

A submarine's depth in the sea is controlled by ballast tanks. When the tanks are filled with water, the submarine sinks. When water in the tanks is forced out by compressed air, the submarine rises. Underwater, the submarine is steered by rudders, while its depth is controlled by winglike hydroplanes at the front and rear. The submarine's whalelike shape helps it slip through the water with the least resistance. The largest nuclear submarines are huge, weighing more than 22,000 tons, and have room for about 150 crew members and 16 nuclear missiles.

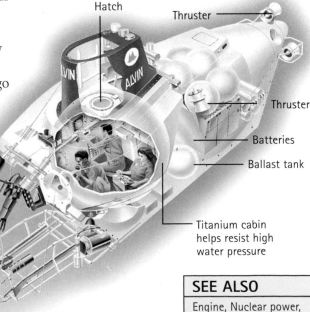

Hatch

Thruster

Thruster

Batteries

Ballast tank

Titanium cabin helps resist high water pressure

SUBMERSIBLES

Submarines used for scientific and industrial work are called submersibles. Some have no crew and are guided by remote control as they explore the oceans. Others, such as the U.S.'s *Alvin* (right), can seat up to three crew members. The *Alvin* can dive to 13,100 ft. (4,000m) and has been used to locate ocean mineral deposits and marine life. A remotely operated vehicle, *Jason Junior* (near right), can be operated from within the submersible to explore places too small or dangerous for the *Alvin*.

Video camera

Thruster

Strobe light

Cable for remote control

SEE ALSO

Engine, Nuclear power, Ship, World War I, World War II

SUDAN AND SOUTH SUDAN

Sudan was formerly a single country, the largest in Africa. In 2011, South Sudan broke away to become a separate independent nation. Sudan is now second largest after Algeria.

Area: 718,723 sq. mi. (1,861,484km²)
Population: 43,120,000
Capital: Khartoum
Language: Arabic
Currency: Sudanese pound

Area: 248,777 sq. mi. (644,329km²)
Population: 13,026,000
Capital: Juba (new capital will be built at Ramciel)
Languages: English, Dinka, Nuer
Currency: South Sudan pound

▲ Khartoum is divided into three areas: Khartoum itself, Omdurman (above) and Khartoum North. Omdurman has the largest population.

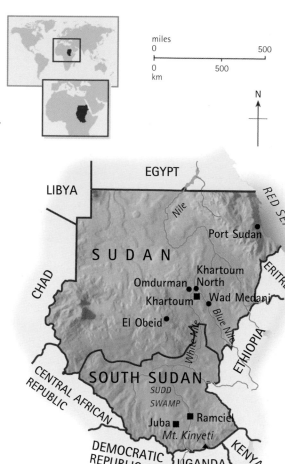

Most of the people of Sudan and South Sudan live along the banks of the White Nile and the Blue Nile. These rivers join at Sudan's capital, Khartoum, flowing north into Egypt. Much of Sudan is desert, which gives way to grassy plains. In South Sudan, where there is more rainfall, there are forests and a swamp called the Sudd which is the size of Alabama. South Sudan is rich in wildlife, including giraffes, lions, leopards, and elephants, with hippos and crocodiles along the Nile. The climate is hot, reaching 115°F (46°C) in the north in the summer.

A DIVIDED LAND

For centuries, the north of this region has been home to Arabs, who were Muslims. The south was home to dozens of different black African peoples. From the late 1800s, some of these peoples became Christians, but most remained followers of traditional African religions. Today, more than 100 different African languages are spoken in South Sudan.

FARMING AND INDUSTRY

Cotton is Sudan's major export, while wheat and millet are the main food crops. Mining produces chromium, gypsum, and gold. Sudan is also the world's largest supplier of gum arabic, used in ink and medicines. South Sudan is much poorer.

More than 75 percent of its people are farmers. However, it has oil reserves that it exports through Sudan to Port Sudan.

ANCIENT LAND

People first settled in the Sudan region around 9,000 years ago and farming began 6,000 years ago. Missionaries brought Christianity from A.D.500 but Muslims later conquered the area. Britain and Egypt controlled Sudan from 1899, until Sudan became an independent country in 1956. Civil war between the north (now Sudan) and south (now South Sudan) broke out in the 1950s and 1960s and fighting recurred from 1983. War and drought created a major refugee problem and stopped the development of oil fields in the south. A peace agreement signed in 2005 led to a vote in the south in favour of independence. In 2011 South Sudan became a separate republic and Africa's newest country, but it remains divided by fighting between ethnic groups.

◄ The Dinka people make up South Sudan's largest black African group. They live by herding and farming.

SEE ALSO

Africa

SUN

The Sun is the nearest star to Earth. It is a globe of hot gas, mostly hydrogen, and lies at the center of our solar system. It contains no solid material.

The Sun is so large that more than a million Earths would fit inside it. It looks different from other stars because it is so much nearer to Earth. At the Sun's core, high temperatures and pressures cause nuclear reactions to take place in which hydrogen is turned into helium. This process releases huge amounts of energy, which eventually finds its way to the Sun's surface, called the photosphere. From there, it escapes into space as light, heat, and other radiations.

EVER-CHANGING

Cooler areas of the Sun form dark patches on the Sun's surface known as sunspots. From these, releases of energy, called solar flares, send bursts of radiation into space. Other eruptions, known as prominences, reach into the Sun's inner atmosphere,

the chromosphere, and into its outer atmosphere, the corona. From the corona, there is a constant stream of particles into space, called the solar wind.

GOOD AND BAD RAYS

Without the warmth and light of the Sun, life on Earth would be impossible. But the Sun also gives off other kinds of radiation, including ultraviolet rays and X rays, which can be harmful. We are shielded from most of this damaging radiation by the ozone layer of Earth's atmosphere, but enough ultraviolet radiation penetrates to the surface to be able to cause sunburn.

LIFE STORY OF THE SUN

The Sun was formed about five billion years ago from a cloud of gas and dust. In another four or five billion years, its supply of hydrogen will run out and the core will collapse. The outer layers will swell as it becomes a red giant, then it will end its life as a slowly cooling white dwarf star.

THE SUN'S ENERGY

The Sun's energy is produced in the core. It flows out as radiation, through the radiative zone to the convective zone. The energy reaches the visible surface of the Sun (the photosphere) by a churning motion called convection. Hot gas rises to the surface, gives off its energy and cools, then sinks back. The surface gives off the energy as light and heat.

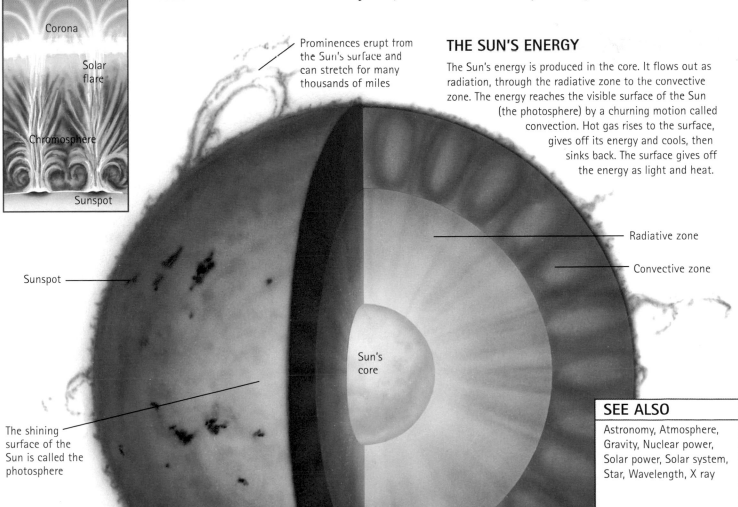

▼ Solar flares occur over sunspots. They can disturb Earth's magnetic field and interfere with radio transmissions on Earth.

Corona

Solar flare

Chromosphere

Sunspot

Prominences erupt from the Sun's surface and can stretch for many thousands of miles

Sunspot

The shining surface of the Sun is called the photosphere

Sun's core

Radiative zone

Convective zone

SEE ALSO

Astronomy, Atmosphere, Gravity, Nuclear power, Solar power, Solar system, Star, Wavelength, X ray

SURGERY

Surgery is a branch of medicine that involves cutting into the body to remove or repair a body part that is damaged or diseased.

A surgical procedure is called an operation and is usually done in the hospital. Operations are performed in an operating room—a room designed to protect the patient from infection.

Artificial limbs were made over 2,000 years ago. In the 1500s, they were made of metal or wood.

Military surgeons in the 1700s carried their surgical instruments with them in a wooden case.

The surgeon Joseph Lister (1827–1912) used carbolic acid to disinfect the air during operations.

An early surgical knife is the forerunner of the modern-day scalpel, used to cut into the body.

Anesthetics can be given as gases inhaled through a mask, but they are now more likely to be injected.

THE SURGICAL TEAM

Operations are carried out by a specially qualified doctor called a surgeon. He or she works with an assistant, a surgical (or OR) nurse, and an anesthesiologist (a doctor who administers an anesthetic). The surgical team all wear sterile gowns, gloves, and masks to make sure that they neither receive nor transmit germs.

SURGICAL INSTRUMENTS

The surgeon uses various instruments during an operation. A scalpel is a knife that cuts into the body. Retractors hold the incision (cut) open. Forceps are used to handle tissue, which may be cut with surgical scissors. After the operation, the surgeon stitches the incision closed or seals it with special tape.

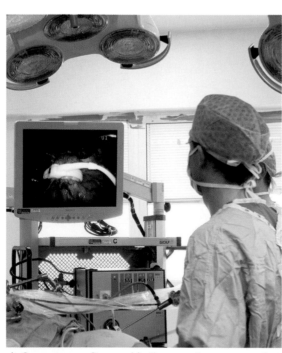

▲ Cameras are often used in the operating room, so that the surgical team can see the area they are operating on in greater detail on a video screen.

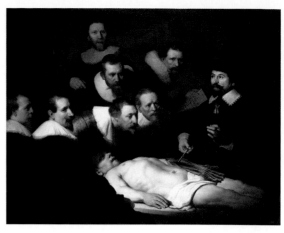

▲ Until the 1600s, the Church did not allow people to cut open human bodies for scientific purposes. The study of anatomy, shown here in Rembrandt's 1632 painting, enabled surgeons to perform more complex operations.

TYPES OF SURGERY

There are several types of surgery. In transplant operations, diseased organs such as the liver or heart are removed and replaced by healthy organs from human donors. Plastic surgery involves repairing skin that has been damaged by burns or injury. It is also done to improve a person's appearance. Today, many operations are done using keyhole surgery, which helps the patient recover more quickly. Here, the surgeon makes a tiny incision and uses miniature instruments to do the surgery.

DULLING THE PAIN

Without anesthetics, most of the surgery done today would be impossible. An American dentist, William Clarke, was the first to use anesthesia in 1847. He used ether to make a patient unconscious while he pulled out a tooth. Nitrous oxide, which is still used today, was another early anesthetic.

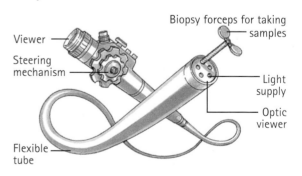

Viewer

Steering mechanism

Biopsy forceps for taking samples

Light supply

Optic viewer

Flexible tube

▲ The endoscope is a long, flexible tube with its own fiber-optic light source. This allows doctors to see inside the body before making an incision.

SEE ALSO
Drug, Medicine

SWAMP AND MARSH

Swamps, marshes, bogs, and fens are all varieties of wetlands, in which the soil is permanently waterlogged or even completely covered with water.

A swamp is a wetland area dominated by trees and shrubs—a kind of permanently flooded forest. Waterlogged areas without trees are called marshes.

UNDERWATER ROOTS
The species found growing in swamps are those that can withstand having their roots permanently under water. Some of the world's largest swamps are found in southern Asia. Here, mangrove swamps form a tangle of tall, stiltlike roots along thousands of miles of coast. Strange fish called mudskippers scurry around on exposed areas of mud, and archerfish spit water to knock insects off overhanging branches. Other creatures include crab-eating frogs and monkeys, and some of the world's most poisonous water snakes.

MARSHLAND
Marsh vegetation consists mainly of grasses and sedges. Dense patches of reeds and rushes surround patches of open water, which may contain water lilies, rooted to the bottom but with their leaves floating on the surface, or true floaters, such as the water hyacinth and duckweed. Many of Europe's large rivers have marshlands alongside them, providing homes for a huge variety of birdlife—from herons, egrets, and avocets to tiny reed warblers and bearded tits. Salt marshes are common around the coasts in temperate regions. They contain a variety of grasses, depending on how saline (salty) they are and whether they are permanently flooded. Like freshwater marshes, they contain huge numbers of insects, snails, and frogs and are vital breeding and feeding areas for waterbirds.

BOGS AND FENS
The term "bog" is usually used for a waterlogged area consisting of thick layers of peat. There is often no water on the surface, but the ground is soggy, and the surface is usually covered with spongy sphagnum moss. The peat is so acidic and contains so little oxygen that 2,000-year-old bodies have been found in it, perfectly preserved. Less acidic wetland areas are often called fens.

THE EVERGLADES
The Florida Everglades are the best-known Northern Hemisphere swamps, extending over 9,500 sq. yds. The region is essentially a river filled with coarse grasses and rushes, and scattered with dense stands of cypress, red maple, and gum trees, draped with Spanish moss.

Rough green snake

Pileated woodpecker

Zebra butterfly

Raccoon

Roseate spoonbill

Green tree frog

Mississippi alligator

Terrapin

Oxeye tarpon

Mangrove roots

SEE ALSO
Alligator and crocodile, Bird, Fish, Habitat, Insect, Snake, United States of America

SWITZERLAND AND AUSTRIA

Switzerland and Austria lie north of Italy, in Europe, with Liechtenstein sandwiched between them. The Alps cover a large area of the two countries.

AUSTRIA
Area: 32,383 sq. mi. (83,871km²)
Population: 8,754,000
Capital: Vienna
Language: German
Currency: Euro

SWITZERLAND
Area: 15,937 sq. mi. (41,277km²)
Population: 8,236,000
Capital: Bern
Languages: German, French, Italian, Romansh
Currency: Swiss franc

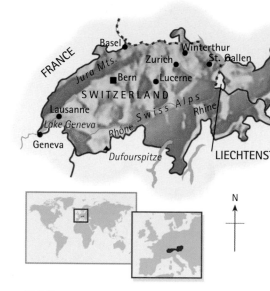

▲ Switzerland is famous for its beautiful lakes, including Lake Geneva.

▲ Swiss banks are probably the most secure in the world. Gold bars are stored in their vaults.

Two great rivers, the Rhine and the Rhône, start in the Swiss Alps within 15 mi. (25km) of each other, and the mighty Danube flows through Austria. The mountainous landscape of both countries attracts many tourists.

ALPINE INDUSTRY

Switzerland is one of the richest countries in Europe, despite its lack of natural resources and flat farmland. Its wealth has come from banking, tourism, and industry —it produces cheese, chocolate, medicines, machinery, and watches. Almost half of Austria is wooded, supplying timber and paper. Austria's mountain waters feed hydroelectric plants that provide more than two thirds of the nation's power.

SWISS GOVERNMENT

Switzerland is divided into 26 self-governing regions called cantons, although the central government controls the army, railroads, and mail, and links with foreign countries. Twenty-five major international organizations have their headquarters in Switzerland, including the Red Cross, founded there in 1864. Through all the wars of modern history, Switzerland has remained neutral, but all Swiss men must train as soldiers. About one fifth of the population was born outside Switzerland.

AUSTRIA'S PEOPLE

Until 1918, Austria ruled Europe's sprawling Austro-Hungarian Empire from Vienna. Vienna is Austria's capital city today, and almost one fourth of the population lives there. The majority of Austrians are Roman Catholics and keep up old customs and festivals. Many country people wear traditional dress, like lederhosen.

POPULAR PASTIMES

Austria has a rich musical history as the home of the waltz and of the composers Mozart, Schubert, and Strauss. Favorite Swiss and Austrian pastimes include folk dancing, yodeling, shooting, and cycling.

▲ Skiing is a popular pastime in both countries and attracts many tourists. In Austria alone, there are around 60 resorts.

SEE ALSO

Europe

TASTE AND SMELL

Taste and smell are two of our five main senses. They warn us of harmful fumes or rotten food—and also allow us to enjoy a delicious meal.

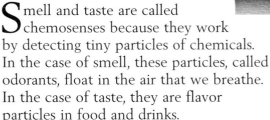

FAST FACTS

- We can identify 10,000 or more smells

- There are only five kinds of flavors—other "flavors" are really the same five, combined in different proportions

- When we have a cold, food seems bland because we cannot smell it

- The middle of the tongue has hardly any taste buds

Smell and taste are called chemosenses because they work by detecting tiny particles of chemicals. In the case of smell, these particles, called odorants, float in the air that we breathe. In the case of taste, they are flavor particles in food and drinks.

DETECTING SMELLS

When odorant particles land on the sticky liquid, or mucus, at the top of the nose, they touch the hairs of the smell cells. Different smells have differently shaped particles and the hairs have differently shaped pits or holes, called receptors. If an odorant particle fits exactly into a receptor, this triggers the smell cell to generate a nerve signal. This passes along the olfactory nerve to the brain, where it is analyzed and identified.

Unlike other senses, smell has direct nerve connections with the parts of the brain that deal with memory and emotion. This is why certain aromas can arouse strong memories and feelings.

▲ A snake uses its tongue to pick up scents in the air, so it can tell whether a mate, a meal, or an enemy is near.

▲ There are five tastes: sweet, salty, sour, bitter, and umami (savory). The first four are detected by a certain part of the tongue but umami tastes are senses throughout.

DOWN IN THE MOUTH

The tongue's upper surface has pimple-like protrusions called papillae, which help to grip and move food during chewing. It also has 10,000 microscopic taste buds, scattered mainly between and on the sides of the papillae. A taste bud is a tiny pit containing a ball-shaped cluster of 20 to 30 gustatory (taste) cells, which are arranged like segments of an orange. Flavor particles dissolve in saliva, and, as in the nose, probably fit into receptors on the hairs of the gustatory cells. This triggers nerve signals that travel along two main nerves to the taste center of the brain for analysis and identification.

TASTING SMELLS

When we eat, the mouth mainly tastes the food, but we also smell it. This is because some odorant particles in the mouth float around the back of the roof of the mouth up into the nasal cavity. There, they are smelled in the same way as odorant particles breathed in through the nose.

NOSE AND MOUTH CELLS

Inside the nose is a two-part chamber called the nasal cavity. The roof of each part has a thumbnail-size patch of lining which contains about 12 million microscopic olfactory (smell) cells. The tip of each of these cells is covered with 10 to 20 tiny hairs, called cilia. These stick in the thin, sticky mucus that coats the nasal cavity lining. The gustatory (taste) cells of the tongue's taste buds also have tiny hairs, projecting into the saliva that coats the tongue.

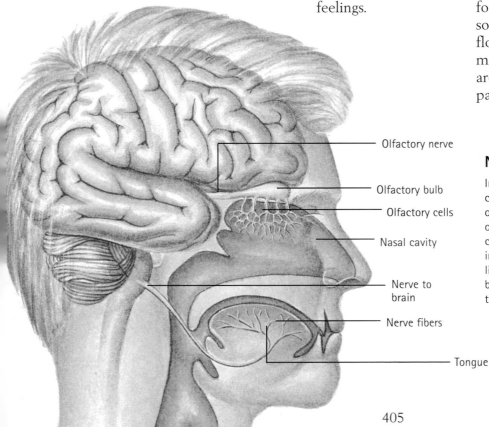

Olfactory nerve

Olfactory bulb

Olfactory cells

Nasal cavity

Nerve to brain

Nerve fibers

Tongue

SEE ALSO

Brain and nervous system, Cell, Food, Human body

TECHNOLOGY

Technology is the practical use of knowledge to construct things, to make work easier, and to make our lives more comfortable. It is also used to cure diseases.

The invention of the wheel meant easier travel—now chariots and carts could carry goods and people.

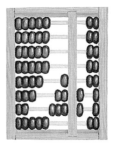

The abacus—a type of early calculator—has been used in China from around 5000 B.C.

No one knows when technology began. The earliest examples—hand-ax flints—are at least 1.6 million years old. Technology is now advancing very quickly, dramatically changing the way we live.

MATERIALS
Before 6000 B.C., wood, bone, hide, stone, and shell were used to make things. By controlling fire, ancient peoples learned to heat ores, such as iron and bronze, to make tools, weapons, and jewelry. In India and Egypt, people became skilled at making pottery and glass. Eventually, processed natural materials such as leather, rubber, and bricks were developed. Synthetic materials, such as plastics, have been made only since the mid-1800s.

POWER AND PRODUCTION
The invention of the wheel (c.3500 B.C.) eventually led to the watermill and the windmill, which provided power for manufacturing. The steam engine paved the way for the Industrial Revolution of the 1700s. The internal combustion engine of 1876 led to the use of road vehicles. Machines using wheels, gears, cranks, and cams were built to carry out repetitive processes like weaving.

▶ The Romans developed expert engineering skills to construct viaducts and aquaducts across valleys.

MODERN TECHNOLOGY
Nanotechnology, using tiny, computerized robots, is allowing us to make ever-smaller and more complex machines. Medical technology, used to help people live longer and healthier lives, includes biotechnology (manipulating cells) and genetic engineering (manipulating genes). Today's technologists must find ways to enrich our lives in ways that respect the Earth's environment, and do not cause pollution.

VIRTUAL REALITY

Sophisticated computer graphics make it possible for people to experience things in virtual reality (VR) that would not normally be possible. A VR headset (and sometimes gloves) are worn. These are connected to a computer, which sends sensory impulses to eyes and ears (and sometimes hands), enabling people to see a new version of reality. Doctors use VR to practice surgery.

SEE ALSO
Architecture, Construction, Engine, Genetics, Industrial Revolution, Machine, Materials, Medicine, Telecommunication

TEETH

Teeth are hard, bonelike, enamel-coated structures embedded in the jawbones of animals, including humans. They are used mainly for biting and chewing.

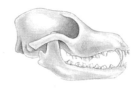

Meat-eaters such as the hyena have sharp teeth for tearing and crushing.

The male African savannah elephant's tusk is the largest incisor tooth of any animal.

Snakes have teeth that curve backward to help pull prey into the throat.

A spider's fangs are hollow and filled with poison for paralyzing its victims.

A shark's teeth are serrated and are regularly replaced as they fall out.

Teeth are extremely strong and hard-wearing and are covered with the body's hardest substance—enamel. But to prevent toothache, tooth decay, and gum disease, they need regular cleaning.

TYPES OF TEETH
Our four main kinds of teeth do different jobs. Incisors at the front are thin and square-tipped, like a chisel or spade, to slice and bite off food. Next are canines, or eye teeth, which are longer and more pointed in order to tear and rip. Premolars and molars, or cheek teeth, at the back of the mouth, are broad and wide-topped for powerful grinding and chewing.

FIRST SET OF TEETH
Humans grow two sets of teeth. The first set—baby, milk, or deciduous teeth— numbers 20. It begins to appear about six months after birth and is complete by the age of three. Baby teeth consist of two incisors, one canine, and two premolars in both the left and right halves of the upper jaw, and the same in the lower jaw.

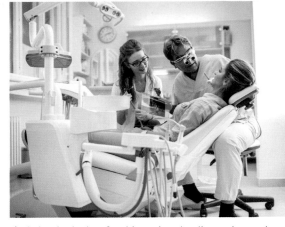

▲ A dentist looks after his patient by diagnosing and treating diseases of the teeth and gums. Regular visits to the dentist help detect problems early.

SECOND SET OF TEETH
From the age of about seven, a child's first teeth loosen and fall out naturally, to be replaced by 32 permanent, or adult, teeth. In each half of each jaw there are two incisors, one canine, two premolars, and three molars. The rear molars, or wisdom teeth, are usually the last to erupt, or grow, above the gum, which happens at around the age of 20. In some people they never erupt, staying small and hidden in the jawbone.

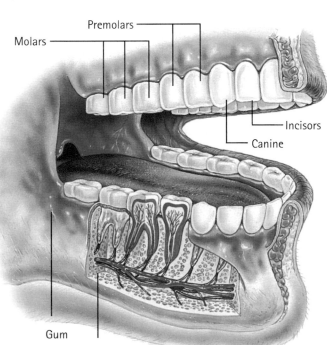

Molars
Premolars
Incisors
Canine
Gum
Lower jawbone

Crown — Enamel
— Pulp cavity
— Gum
Root canal — Dentine
Oxygenated blood in
Jawbone
Nerves
Deoxygenated blood out

INSIDE THE TOOTH
All teeth have the same basic structure. The upper part, or crown, of the tooth shows above the gum, and the root is in the jawbone. At the base of the crown, soft gum tissue (gingiva) joins to the neck of the tooth. In between the crown and root is the pulp cavity. This contains tiny blood vessels to nourish the tooth and nerves to detect pressure, temperature, and pain. The vessels and nerves pass into the jawbone through a tiny hole, the root canal, at the root's base.

SEE ALSO
Elephant, Horse, Human body, Shark, Spider and scorpion

TELECOMMUNICATION

Telecommunication is the transmission of words, sounds, images, or other data over long distances as electronic or electromagnetic signals.

Simple communication systems were already in use in the early 1800s. A code, known as semaphore, that used two movable arms for each letter, or a mirror called a heliograph to flash sunlight, allowed people within sight of each other to send messages.

▲ Semaphore telegraphy became the fastest way to send messages across long distances in the early 1800s.

ELECTRIC PULSES

The electric telegraph allowed coded messages to be sent much farther, as pulses of electric current along copper wires. It was invented in Britain in 1837 by William Cooke and Charles Wheatstone and was soon used by railroad companies. Developed at the same time, Samuel Morse's American telegraph system used coded pulses to transmit messages from place to place. The dots and dashes of the Morse code were internationally authorized right up until 1999.

▲ The first submarine cables were laid between Dover in southern England and Cap Gris-Nez in northern France in 1850.

MESSAGES WITHOUT WIRES

In 1876, Alexander Graham Bell discovered how to send the human voice along wires. In doing so, he invented the telephone. Then, using the discoveries about electromagnetic waves made by German physicist Heinrich Hertz in 1894, the Italian inventor Guglielmo Marconi made a "wireless" telegraph. Sending messages as radio waves, Marconi linked telegraph operators on opposite sides of the Atlantic Ocean in 1901. As the use of radio developed, speech, and later pictures, could be transmitted. High-frequency microwave radio signals can now carry tens of thousands of telephone conversations, text messages, emails, Internet chats and tweets all at the same time, together with television and data signals.

▲ ATMs, use telephone lines for fast communication with a cardholder's bank. Once the bank has sent its approval of the cash withdrawal, the ATM dispenses the money.

AROUND THE WORLD IN SECONDS

Microwave radio signals travel in straight lines, so they need to be passed along by relay stations in order for them to carry smoothly around the curve of the Earth's surface. The British science fiction

▲ The invention of radio in 1901 helped police and armed forces keep in contact with those working outside.

writer Arthur C. Clarke came up with an ingenious solution to the problem in 1945. He suggested putting the relay equipment on satellites which could orbit the Earth every 24 hours, staying fixed in one point in the sky 22,370 mi. (36,000km) above the ground. His dream become a reality in 1964, when the first geostationary satellite *Syncom 3* was successfully launched and put into orbit. Complete networks of satellites and ground stations can now link any two places on the Earth almost instantly.

TOO MUCH INFORMATION?

The kinds and amount of information being carried by telecommunication systems is increasing all the time. Converting voice, sound, and pictures into digital code allows increasingly more

▲ Smart phones have not only revolutionized telecommunications, they have changed the way we live. The range of their applications is amazing. However some people fear that they are addictive, getting in the way of personal interaction and social skills.

THROUGH THE CABLES
Multimode fibers have glass cores which can carry several light messages at once over short distances.

Outer sheath
Filter
Fiber
Cushion

Satellite

▲ Improvements in technology mean that email can now zip between continents in a matter of seconds.

CHATTING ELECTRONICALLY

The rapid growth of the Internet has revolutionized the telecommunication industry. An electronic mail (E-mail) message sent from one country to another can travel by a variety of routes. Here, it travels from the computer by fiber-optic cable, then by microwaves relayed by a satellite. It finishes its journey by cable.

Ground station transmits and receives signals

information to be carried across continents and seas, and this information travels almost instantaneously. Today, fiber-optic cables made of bundles of fine glass fibers are used to transmit telephone calls. A caller's voice is changed into digital signals that are carried as rapidly flashing pulses of laser light. Fiber-optic cables channel light around corners and can carry far more digital information than the copper wires that carry analog signals.

USING BROADBAND

It is now possible to squeeze more information through existing networks by compression. The capacity, or bandwidth, of the networks is increased, and this helps to ease the flow of data while new networks are designed and built. A purely digital system called ISDN (Integrated-Services Digital Network) began operating in Japan in 1988 and has since been adopted by many countries.

FAST FACTS

• Worldwide there are about 972 million fixed landlines and more than 4.8 billion mobile phone subscriptions

• Cable carries 90% of all Internet traffic

• There are nearly 3.9 billion Internet users across the world

• About 2.4 billion emails are sent every second

▲ By checking her electronic mailbox, this user can receive mail and reply immediately. She doesn't have to rush out to mail a letter.

SEE ALSO

Communication, Computer, Internet, Laser, Satellite, Telephone

TELEPHONE

Telephones are instruments for communicating over long distances. They send speech to another location as electric currents, laser light, or radio waves.

Alexander Graham Bell's prototype telephone (1876) had an exposed coil, electromagnet, and wires.

The telephone was invented in 1876 by the Scottish engineer Alexander Graham Bell (1847–1922). He had been working in the United States on improvements to the telegraph, which could only send Morse code dots and dashes. By 1880, the first public telephone systems were in use, although at first they had very few customers.

GETTING CONNECTED

Early telephones were connected by wires to a telephone exchange, where operators connected one line to another by hand. The invention of automatic switches in the 1890s allowed exchanges to connect calls without going through an operator. Modern telephone systems change the varying electrical signal of older telephones into a digital signal made up of pulses that are handled by computerized exchanges, removing the need for mechanical switches.

The telephone of 1919 had a body with a mouthpiece, a rotary number dial, and a separate earpiece.

HOW DOES A TELEPHONE WORK?

A telephone handset has a mouthpiece and an earpiece. When a caller speaks, sound waves made by their voice hit a diaphragm (thin metal disk) in the mouthpiece, making it vibrate. This pushes against carbon grains, making their resistance to an electric current flowing through them vary in a pattern that copies the sound wave pattern. At the receiver's end, this current causes an electromagnet to make the diaphragm in their earpiece vibrate. This makes sound waves that reproduce the sound of the caller talking.

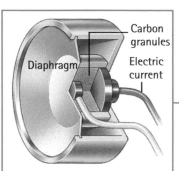

Cell phones can deliver a wide range of applications as well as calls and text messages.

▲ Until the late 1800s, telephone operators connected phone calls manually through a switchboard. A caller gave the operator the number; the operator then connected the caller's line to the line of the person being called.

SENDING THE SIGNAL

Calls can be sent around the world as radio signals relayed by satellites, or digital signals can be sent as pulses of laser light along fiber-optic cables under the oceans. The fiber-optic cables can carry thousands of calls at once. Cellular phones use microwave radio frequencies to connect to nearby transceivers, which transmit and receive calls in a network.

NEW TECHNOLOGY

Phones are becoming even more useful as the technologies of telephones and computers mix. Internet access, E-mail, and video telephones, which display images of the caller, are all possible from a small, mobile handset using digital technology.

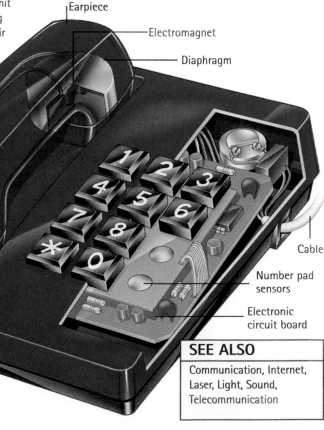

Earpiece

Electromagnet

Diaphragm

Mouthpiece

Cable

Number pad sensors

Electronic circuit board

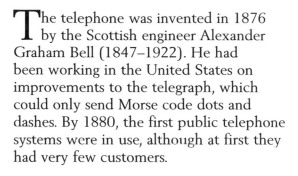

Carbon granules

Electric current

Diaphragm

◄ Sound waves vibrate the diaphragm, compressing carbon granules to alter the flow of electricity and send the caller's voice.

SEE ALSO

Communication, Internet, Laser, Light, Sound, Telecommunication

TELESCOPE

Telescopes are instruments for studying objects that are far away. Astronomers use various kinds of telescopes to find out more about stars and planets.

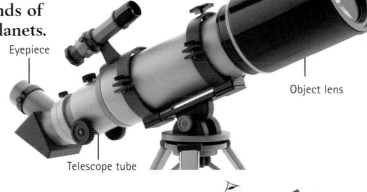

Viewfinder

Eyepiece

Object lens

Telescope tube

OPTICAL TELESCOPES

The two main types of optical telescope are refractors and reflectors. Refractors, such as the Simmons 100X magnification telescope, use a lens to form an upside-down image. Reflectors have a large, curved mirror instead of a lens. The mirror gathers light, which is reflected off a second mirror into the eyepiece. The image seen is right-side up.

Sir Isaac Newton (1642–1727) invented a reflecting telescope that used curved mirrors to reflect light.

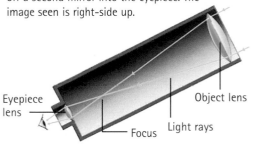

Eyepiece lens

Object lens

Focus

Light rays

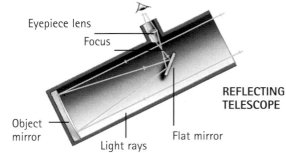

Eyepiece lens

Focus

REFLECTING TELESCOPE

Object mirror

Flat mirror

Light rays

Galileo (1564–1642) used this telescope to view the phases of Venus and the moons of Jupiter.

The first telescope was built by a Dutch scientist called Hans Lippershey (c.1570–1619) in 1608. It was an optical telescope, with glass lenses that made distant objects appear larger.

REFRACTING TELESCOPES

Refractors have two lenses. A large lens at the front of the telescope, called the objective, collects light. A small eyepiece lens focuses the light into the observer's eye. Galileo used this kind of telescope in 1609 to look at the Moon, which he could see 30 times more clearly than before.

William Herschel (1738–1822) built a reflector with a 47-in. (120-cm) aperture to study faint objects.

REFLECTING TELESCOPES

Modern astronomers mainly use reflectors with a big, curved mirror to collect light, and a small, flat mirror to shine the light through an eyepiece lens. The first reflector, built by Isaac Newton in 1668, used a primary mirror only 3 in. (7.5cm) wide. Modern reflectors use larger ones. The Keck telescope in Hawaii has 36 six-sided mirrors joined to make a mirror 33 ft. (10m) across. Images are viewed on a computer screen or camera film.

Edwin Hubble (1889–1953) used this 8-ft. (2.4-m) reflector to discover the expansion of the universe.

The Hubble Space Telescope orbits Earth and sends back pictures from the farthest parts of the universe.

SEEING THE UNSEEN

Light reaching us from distant parts of the universe is very faint, and the Earth's atmosphere blurs what we can see through optical telescopes. To record faint images, astronomers use electronic detectors called charged-coupled devices (CCDs) instead of their eyes. The Hubble Space Telescope (HST) orbits high above the Earth's atmosphere, so the light it collects is not distorted. Radio, X-ray, infrared, gamma-ray, and microwave telescopes collect other kinds of energy radiating from stars and galaxies that we cannot see with our eyes.

◄ The Hanbury Brown radio telescope in New South Wales, Australia, picks up long-wavelength radio waves from space.

SEE ALSO
Astronomy, Lens, Radio, Satellite, Wavelength, X ray

TELEVISION

Television (TV) is the transmission of pictures and sound from one place to another. It is one of the most important means of mass communication in the world.

John Logie Baird's 1926 television system used lenses set in revolving discs to scan an object.

The first regular high-quality television broadcasts began in 1936, from Alexandra Palace in London. Several scientists had worked on developing television, including Scotsman John Logie Baird and Americans Vladimir Zworykin and Philo Farnsworth.

Some large-screen televisions use a back projection system with mirrors to enlarge the image.

IN THE PICTURE
Television pictures are made up of electronic signals produced by a camera and recreated by a television set. A TV camera has lenses which focus the picture onto a surface that converts light to electronic signals. These can be recorded for later transmission. The signals can be turned into radio waves, to be broadcast from radio transmitters, beamed via a satellite or sent along cable networks directly to the TV sets in homes.

▲ Television allows us to observe world events as they happen. This news crew's camera is on hand as Crimean troops and soldiers under Russian command clash in Crimea in 2014.

MAKING A TV PROGRAM
Producing a TV show is a team effort. Camera operators take the pictures, while mike boom operators keep microphones in position. The director in a control room cuts from one camera to another. There are also script writers, make-up artists, costume designers, caterers, lighting crews, post-production teams, and technical staff.

TV TODAY
Most of today's televisions use either liquid crystal displays (LCDs) or plasma screens. These screens can be very large, but are also light and thin enough to mount on a wall. They give very sharp images—especially when showing programs on High Definition TV (HDTV) channels.

HOW TELEVISION WORKS

Light detectors in a TV camera convert light into electronic signals, which are processed before being transmitted as radio waves to a television receiver. The TV camera will also convey sound information to the receiver. The television set displays the transmitted information, displaying moving pictures on its screen and producing sound from its speakers. An LCD television contains tiny crystals with light behind them. The crystals twist when electricity is applied and this allows light to shine through them onto the screen.

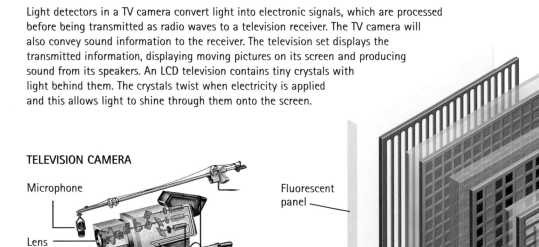

TELEVISION CAMERA

- Microphone
- Lens
- Light detectors
- Trolley
- Viewfinder
- Cable carries signal from camera

- Rear glass plate
- Subpixel electrodes
- Front glass plate
- Fluorescent panel
- Vertical polarizing filter
- Layer of liquid crystal
- Color filter
- Horizontal polarizing filter
- Front screen of LCD television

SEE ALSO
Electricity, Invention, Media, Radio, Telecommunication, Video

TEXTILE

The word textile means "woven fabric" and the first textiles were woven by hand. Now they can be created from natural fibers using chemical processes.

Originally, textiles were fabrics made by spinning natural fibers into threads and then weaving them together on a loom. Textiles are also produced by other methods such as knitting (using a single yarn or set of loops) or felting (matting fibers together by heat and pressure), and include such materials as lace, braid and net.

▲ A Chinese woman weaves silk on a hand loom. Woven fabrics use two sets of yarns: one lengthwise (the warp) and one crosswise (the weft).

GROWING MATERIALS

The five most important natural fibers are wool, cotton, silk, linen, and jute. Wool comes from sheep, goats, or llamas; cotton has been grown in Egypt and India since ancient times; and silk was first made in Ancient China. Linen, made from the flax plant, is used for shirts, sheets, and table napkins, and jute, which grows best in India and Bangladesh, is used to make sacks, matting, ropes and twine.

WEARING CHEMICALS

The chemical industry produces synthetic (artificial) fibers such as nylon and acrylic, which can be made stronger, cheaper, more elastic, and easier to wash than natural fibers. These include neoprene, a synthetic rubber used in wet suits, Gore-Tex, a waterproof fabric used in climbing and outdoor clothing, and stretchy nylon Lycra, used in everyday casual wear.

▲ Cotton machines in a Ugandan factory. The raw cotton has been arranged into long fibers and coiled. The fibers are twisted into yarn and woven.

▶ Tapestries are textiles woven in different colored threads to create a picture. This beautiful unicorn was woven from wool, silk, and silver thread, in the South Netherlands in 1495-1505.

FROM HOME TO FACTORY

Textile-making has often made great use of women's labor. Weaving was traditionally practiced at home and still is in many parts of the world. Textile-making was the first industry to be completely mechanized, starting with cotton in Britain in the 18th century. Modern textile machinery is often computer-controlled to produce intricate designs.

A WAY OF LIFE

Many areas of the world have depended on textiles for employment. Special types of cloth, such as denim, duffel, muslin, and chantilly, take their names from the towns which specialized in making them. Making rugs and carpets is still a major industry in countries such as Turkey, Iran, Afghanistan, and Pakistan. Indonesia is famous for a resist-dyeing process called batik.

TEXTILE USE

The largest demand for textiles comes from the clothing industry, but they are also used for upholstery, sports, and car accessories.

▶ A young child makes a traditional Jaipur carpet in India.

◀ Some textiles are still hand-printed by batik or screen printing (left). In a factory, textile patterns are printed using rollers on a rotary printer—each prints a single color.

SEE ALSO
Clothing, Design, Paint and dye, Printing, Technology

THEATER

Theater is the production of a drama, comedy, music, or other artistic performance in front of an audience. It usually takes place in a specially designed building.

Sophocles (c. 496–406 B.C.) wrote 123 tragedies in Ancient Greece.

William Shakespeare (1564–1616) was England's finest playwright.

Okuni (c.1620) established the Japanese style of theater called Kabuki.

Molière (1622–73) created a new kind of comedy in the French theater.

Irishman Samuel Beckett (1906–89) wrote abstract, philosophical plays.

Tennessee Williams (1911–83) wrote tense plays set in the southern U.S.A.

THE GLOBE THEATER

The Globe Theater was built in London in 1614 after a fire destroyed an earlier theater. The audience sat in galleries or stood around the stage. Most of Shakespeare's plays first appeared here.

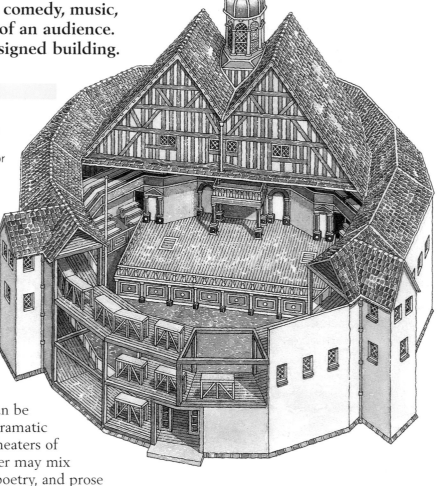

Modern theater can be traced back to dramatic performances in the theaters of ancient Greece. Theater may mix design, music, dance, poetry, and prose to create drama in front of an audience.

ANCIENT PLAYS

The ancient Greeks established both tragedy and comedy. In Greek theater, the chorus (a group of singers) chanted the story, while the actors mimed their roles. At first, the audience sat on hillsides, and the action took place on a level space—known as the orchestra. By 450 B.C., theaters with banks of stone benches for the audience, like the one at Epidaurus, had been constructed. The Romans added an elaborate "scene house," which provided backdrop scenery for the action. In front of this, there was a raised stage above the orchestra, as in modern theaters.

REVIVAL IN EUROPE

During the Middle Ages, theater in Europe took different forms, such as mystery and religious plays. In the 1500s, William Shakespeare and others led a revival. All the roles were played by men and boys,

not women. Actresses first appeared in Europe with the Italian traveling players performing *commedia dell'arte*—plays with themes of love and intrigue. In Japan, actors developed the formal *Noh* form of theater and popular, stylized Kabuki dramas.

ARCHES AND STAGES

In the 1590s, English theaters were circular wooden buildings with an open stage. In the 1600s, the proscenium arch—a frame around the front of the stage—was introduced. This masked the areas where actors or sceneshifters waited. An important figure of 18th-century European theater was David Garrick (1717–79), an actor-manager who put on new plays, as well as works by Shakespeare.

MUSIC HALL AND DRAMA

Increasingly popular during the 1800s was music hall, known as vaudeville in North America. These shows had actors, singers, and comedians performing to enthusiastic and noisy audiences. Opera (drama in which the actors sing) and ballet (dance drama) also flourished in the 1800s. At the same time, electric lighting, larger sets, revolving stages, and exciting special effects with water, smoke, and illusions developed. Productions became so elaborate that, by 1910, some directors preferred a simple approach with little scenery. New ideas included the open-thrust stage, which projected forward, theater-in-the-round (with the audience all around the stage), and open-air theater.

THEATER TODAY

Modern theater productions involve a team of backstage people—designers, set-builders, technicians, and wardrobe and make-up artists, as well as the actors and director. Professional theaters offer the latest electronic gadgetry, lighting, and sound systems, although plays are still performed very successfully by amateurs in small halls and schools. The ancient Greek theater of Epidaurus continues to stage classic Greek dramas. In London, the reconstructed Globe Theater offers modern audiences the opportunity to experience Shakespeare's plays as they were originally performed.

"THE MET"

There has been a Metropolitan Opera House, known as "the Met," in New York City since 1833. The new house at Lincoln Center opened in 1966, and both opera and ballet are presented there. Each time a performance is put on, the theater employs a team of about 1,000 people.

▲ These Indian puppets are 10 ft. (3m) high. They are used in dramatic performances to tell tales of love and bravery.

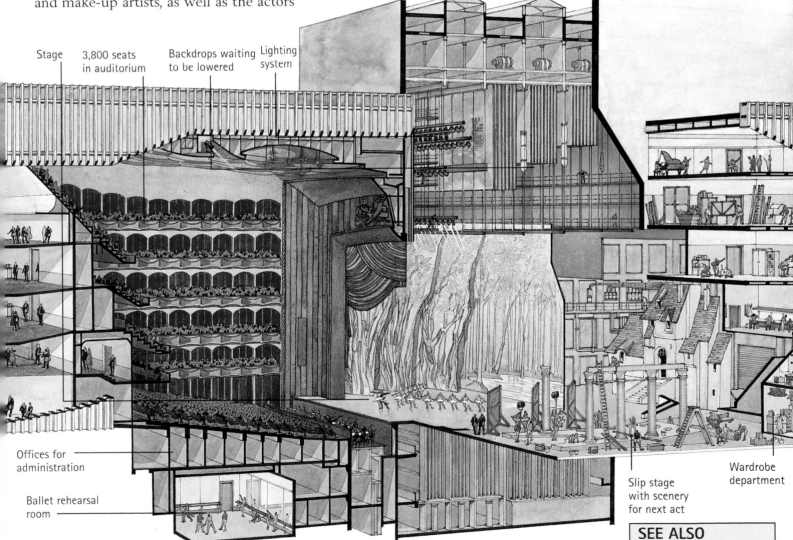

Stage — 3,800 seats in auditorium — Backdrops waiting to be lowered — Lighting system

Offices for administration

Ballet rehearsal room

Slip stage with scenery for next act

Wardrobe department

SEE ALSO

Dance, Greece (ancient), Literature

TIGER AND OTHER BIG CATS

Tigers, lions, and leopards belong to a group of the cat family known as "big cats." The cat family also includes many smaller wildcats, as well as the domesticated cat.

▲ Although not classed as a big cat, the puma is as big as a leopard. Also known as the cougar, mountain lion, or panther, it ranges through the Americas and eats a varied menu, from deer to birds.

The cheetah is the only cat to outrun its prey rather than stalk it.

The black panther is a natural, black-furred variation of a leopard or jaguar.

The lynx is a wildcat that lives in the forests of Asia, Europe, and North America.

Tigers belong to the cat family (*Felidae*). So do four other species of big cat— lions, jaguars, leopards, and snow leopards. The cat family also includes about 35 species of smaller wildcat, from the cheetah, puma, bobcat, and lynx down to the smaller margay, kodkod, and sandcat. The black-footed cat of southern Africa is even smaller than a domesticated cat.

CAT FEATURES
All cats are meat-eaters, members of the carnivore group. They live by hunting, although a few scavenge dead meat. They have sharp senses, with excellent sight even at nighttime, and amazing balance for climbing. Long whiskers feel the way in darkness. The cat's body is lithe and agile, with stealthy movements. The fur is striped, spotted, or patterned for camouflage, so the cat can creep silently and unseen. Long claws grip, scratch, and slash and can be pulled or retracted into the toe tips, keeping them sharp. Long, sharp teeth bite and tear apart prey.

NIGHT HUNTER
Like other cats, the tiger hunts mainly at twilight or night. It prefers dense, swampy forest and ambushes deer, wild pigs, wild cattle, and the occasional baby elephant or rhino. Very rarely, a tiger preys on people. The record-holding man eater killed over 400 people.

BIGGEST OF THE BIG CATS
Tigers live across India, on some islands of Indonesia, and in parts of China. Siberian tigers of Manchuria are huge and powerful predators, up to 13 ft. (4m) from nose to tail and over 660 lb. (300kg). Like most cats, tigers live alone. They are only together when mating, or when a mother is with her cubs.

▲ Lions are the only cats that live and hunt in groups (or prides). The lionesses do the hunting, usually at night. One lioness stalks the prey, driving it toward the other lionesses who lie in wait. The adult male does not join in, but claims a share of the kill. Lions sleep during the day.

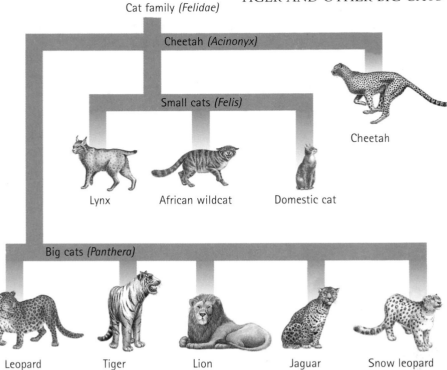

Cat family (Felidae)

Cheetah (Acinonyx)

Small cats (Felis)

Cheetah

Lynx

African wildcat

Domestic cat

Big cats (Panthera)

Leopard

Tiger

Lion

Jaguar

Snow leopard

THE LEOPARD

The leopard is the most widespread big cat, ranging across Africa and Southern Asia, into China and Indonesia. It is adaptable, too, living in high hills, deserts, scrub, rain forests, and even near towns and villages. Leopards eat a wide variety of prey and will drag a carcass into a tree to store it away from scavengers. The rare snow leopard, or ounce, lives in the Himalayas and nearby mountains. It has long, thick, pale fur for warmth and camouflage.

THE CHEETAH

This lean, long-legged cat is the fastest land animal. It sprints at almost 60 mph (100kph) after swift prey such as antelope, hares, and even young ostriches. It has spotted fur and a long tail to help it balance and turn at high speed. The cheetah is the only cat that cannot retract its claws. For this reason, it is classed on its own in the cat family.

THE LION

Prides of lions were once common in Europe, Africa, and Asia, but now can be found only in protected areas south of the Sahara Desert in Africa and in the Gir Forest, a wildlife sanctuary in India. They live in open, grassy plains, where water is available and are territorial, fiercely protecting their hunting ground, where they stalk zebras, wildebeest, and antelope.

THE CAT FAMILY

The cat family is divided into three groups. The *Panthera* group is made up of the five big cats: the leopard, tiger, lion, jaguar, and snow leopard. The *Felis* group includes the domestic cat, as well as around another 34 types of small cats. The cheetah forms a group of its own.

THE JAGUAR

The only American big cat, the muscular jaguar is found in the southern U.S.A. and in Central and South America. With its spotted coat, it resembles a leopard, but is larger and more powerful, weighing about 220 lb. (100kg). Jaguars like thick forests with swamps, lakes, and rivers. They are excellent swimmers.

▼ The leopard has a full body length of about 60 in. (150cm). As with most cats, the males are larger than the females, at 130–155 lb. (60–70kg). The leopard's larger spots are not single black patches, but circular groups, or rosettes.

SEE ALSO
Animal, Cat, Mammal

TIME

We use time to track the passing of days, in hours, minutes, and seconds. In addition to natural units of time, people have invented other ways to measure it.

One day

One day is exactly the time it takes for Earth to revolve on its axis once.

One year

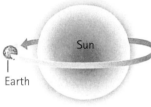

One year is approximately the time it takes for Earth to orbit the Sun.

One lunar month

A month is based roughly on the time it takes Moon to orbit the Earth.

When you need to know the time, you look at a watch or clock. This tells you how many hours and minutes it is since noon (midday) or midnight. For example, if your watch says the time is exactly 3:30 ("three-thirty") in the afternoon, you know that three hours and thirty minutes have passed since noon. If your watch is very precise, it may also tell you how many seconds have passed.

DAYS

The measurement of time is based on the position of the Sun in the sky. Every day, the Sun seems to rise at dawn, move across the sky, then set at dusk. This happens because Earth is continually spinning around. Each place on Earth can only see the Sun for part of the day; when the Sun is out of view, it is nighttime in that part of the world. The Sun appears to rise as it comes into view and set as it disappears again. At one moment in the day, each place faces the Sun directly. When this happens, the Sun is highest in the sky and the daylight is brightest (on a sunny day).

THE AZTEC CALENDAR

▲ The Greenwich Observatory in England is the place where astronomers first devised the Greenwich Meridian in 1866. This is the line at zero longitude that divides east from west; time zones are still calculated from it.

HOURS

As early as 2400 B.C., the Babylonians divided the day into 24 equal parts, called hours. The modern day starts at midnight, a time when the sky is dark in most areas. A few hours later, the Sun rises. Twelve hours after midnight it is noon, the time when the Sun is highest. In another 12 hours, it is midnight again.

CALENDARS

Every civilization has used some kind of calendar to keep track of years, months, weeks, and days. Calendars are used to plan planting and harvesting, and also to mark special holidays and festivals. The Julian calendar was instituted by Julius Caesar in 46 B.C. Pope Gregory XIII (1502–85) adjusted it in 1582, and his Gregorian calendar is still used in Western countries today. The Chinese calendar is lunar, with a 60-year cycle, but the Chinese use the Western calendar, too. The Jewish calendar combines solar and lunar cycles, and has 12 or 13 months.

CALENDARS OF THE AMERICAS

The Aztecs of Central America made a calendar in the ground from a huge stone shaped liked the Sun. The face of the Sun god, Tezcatlipoca, was carved in the middle, and signs for the days were carved around the edges. The Maya—also of Central America—used a calendar with two interlocking cog wheels to represent circular time. Native American tribes kept track of time by watching the seasons and phases of the Moon.

TIME ZONES

Because the Earth is spinning, different places on Earth face the Sun at different times of day. When it is midday in London, it is dawn in New York, and in Adelaide, Australia, it is still night. If people read the time directly from the Sun's position, watches worldwide would be set to thousands of different times. Chaos would result; for example, it would be impossible to write accurate train timetables.

GREENWICH MEAN TIME

To get around this timing problem, governments approximate time by dividing the world into 24 time zones. These zones follow the Earth's longitude lines, and are based on Greenwich Mean Time (GMT), the time at Greenwich, England. Tokyo, Japan, is nine hours ahead of GMT, so when it is 2:00 A.M. in Greenwich, it is 11:00 A.M. in Tokyo.

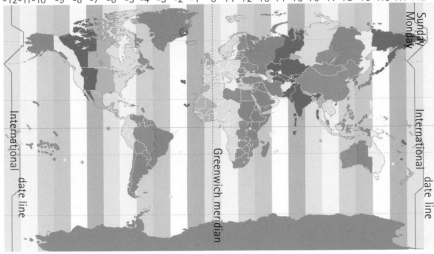

Hours -12 -11 -10 -9 -8 -7 -6 -5 -4 -3 -2 -1 0 +1 +2 +3 +4 +5 +6 +7 +8 +9 +10 +11 +12

International date line · Greenwich meridian · International date line · Sunday · Monday

▲ The world is divided into 24 time zones, centered on the prime meridian at Greenwich. Each zone west of the meridian is an hour earlier than the last. Each zone to the east is one hour ahead.

THE FOURTH DIMENSION

All objects have three dimensions: width, height, and depth (the dimensions of space). Scientists believe that objects also have a fourth dimension: time. Every day, we move through the four dimensions (called space-time). We can move in all directions through space (up and down, or from side to side); however, it is believed that we can only move forward through time. Many science-fiction writers have played with the idea that time travel into the future (or into the past) is possible.

▲ H. G. Wells's (1866–1946) remarkable science-fiction novel, *The Time Machine* (1895), tells the story of a man who builds a machine that carries him into the future. In the 1960 film, above, the machine vanishes forward in time.

▲ The giant Sun clock in New Delhi, India, tells the time as the Sun casts shadows on graduated markings.

▼ Stonehenge in England (begun c. 2700 B.C.) is a stone circle thought to have been used as an astronomical observatory and calendar. Its axis was aligned with midsummer sunrise (June 21), which suggests it was used to track the movements of the Sun, Moon, and planets.

SEE ALSO

Astronomy, Clock, Earth, Moon, Navigation, Season, Star, Sun

TOUCH

Touch is one of the body's five main senses. It allows us to detect not only physical contact, but also temperature, pressure, heat, cold, and pain.

▲ Touch sensors are packed closer together in places such as the lips and fingertips, with hundreds in a pinhead-size area. These body parts are most sensitive to touch.

Touch can distinguish between light and heavy pressure, and between things that are soft and hard, cold and hot, dry and wet, rough and smooth, still and moving. From this variety of information, we build up an impression of what our skin comes into contact with—from a cold, slippery ice cube to a warm, furry kitten.

TOUCH SENSORS

There are millions of microscopic sensors in the skin. Each is the specialized ending of a nerve fiber. When stimulated, the sensor sends bursts of nerve signals along its fiber to the brain. Touch sensors are all over the body in the skin. Hairs are mostly dead, so they cannot feel. But touch sensors are

▲ Braille is a special raised-dot type system that enables blind people to read with their fingertips. The system was invented by Louis Braille (1809–52).

wrapped around each hair root. When the hair is rocked or tilted, the sensors send out nerve signals. Similarly, nails are dead but have touch sensors in the skin underneath.

TYPES OF SENSOR

There are different types of touch sensor. Merkel sensors are tiny disks in the base of the skin's upper layer, or epidermis. Meissner sensors are slightly larger and egg-shaped, in the upper part of the skin's lower layer, or dermis. Krause sensors, also egg-shaped, and Ruffini sensors, larger and sausagelike, are in the middle of the dermis. Pacini sensors are multilayered, like onions. At up to 0.04 in. (1mm) long, they are the largest sensors and are just visible to the naked eye. The most numerous sensors are free nerve endings, each one resembling a tiny, many-branched tree.

WHAT DO THEY DETECT?

Some types of sensor respond better to certain kinds of touch. Meissner and Merkel sensors detect light touch, and Pacini sensors respond better to heavier pressure. Ruffini sensors pick up vibrations well. But in daily life, most types of sensor respond to most kinds of touch. Free nerve endings, which are the most widespread, respond to almost any kind of touch, including heat and cold, as well as the great pressure and damage that cause pain.

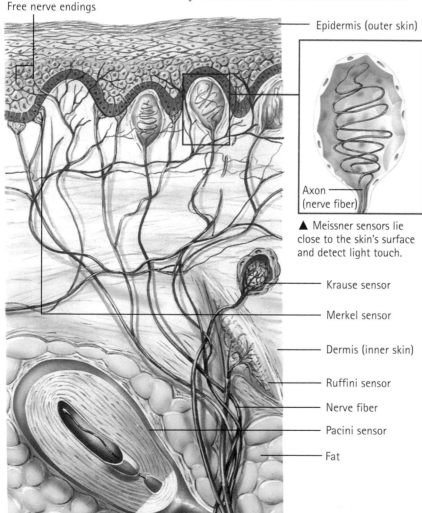

Free nerve endings

Epidermis (outer skin)

Axon (nerve fiber)

▲ Meissner sensors lie close to the skin's surface and detect light touch.

Krause sensor

Merkel sensor

Dermis (inner skin)

Ruffini sensor

Nerve fiber

Pacini sensor

Fat

SEE ALSO
Brain and nervous system, Skin and hair

TRADE

Trade is the buying and selling of goods. It takes place between individuals or companies, but the largest exchanges take place between different countries.

▲ During the Renaissance (1400–1600), trade in Europe increased greatly until it overtook farming as a source of wealth.

▲ A customs officer uses a dog to sniff out smuggled goods. People sometimes try to smuggle goods that are illegal or will be heavily taxed.

International trade allows countries to exchange what they have for what they need. A country with plenty of farmland but no coal mines can export (sell abroad) food and import (buy in) coal. Some countries specialize in one product, others produce a variety of goods and services.

VISIBLES AND INVISIBLES

International trade is divided into visible and invisible trade. Most goods, such as food, computers, and washing machines, which are moved from one country to another are visibles. Invisibles include banking charges, insurance policies, and people spending money on vacation. Some countries, such as Switzerland and Britain, rely heavily on invisible trade.

PROTECTION

Some countries limit import trade to try to protect jobs and industries at home. A special tax, called a tariff, may be placed on imported goods, or a limit set on imports. This is known as protection.

LAISSEZ FAIRE

Free trade, also known as laissez faire, means that people are free to import or export without restrictions or tariffs. A laissez-faire policy encourages trade and is believed to increase employment and wealth. International trading organizations, such as the European Union (EU) and the North American Free Trade Agreement (NAFTA), establish free trade between members. The World Trade Organization, works to reduce trade barriers with all countries.

BALANCE OF PAYMENTS

The difference between the money coming into and going out of a country (both for visible and invisible items) is called the balance of payments. Large amounts of money or goods continually flowing in one direction may damage the economy of the country. If the value of the nation's currency is allowed to fall or rise, it affects the price of imports and exports and helps to bring the balance of payments back to zero.

▼ Most visible trade is carried out by sea. Ships transport goods relatively cheaply, using large, packed containers. Goods that need to be moved quickly are carried by aircraft.

SEE ALSO
Explorer, Great Depression, Industry, Money, Slavery, Transportation

TRAIN

Trains are simply lines of passenger or freight cars pulled along a steel track by an engine. They provide fast transportation either above or below ground.

The fastest steam train was the *Mallard* at 125 mph (201kph).

The first diesel train was built in Germany in 1912.

Diesel locomotives haul heavy goods trains.

Rapid transit trains, often underground, carry people around cities.

Rack and pinion trains climb steep slopes up hills.

Trains were developed during the Industrial Revolution in the 1700s. At first, horses were used to pull trucks carrying heavy loads along simple metal tracks at mines and factories. Later, steam engines mounted on wheels were developed, which were used to link cities with one another and achieved much higher speeds.

GETTING GOING

In 1802, the British engineer Richard Trevithick patented a high-pressure steam engine mounted on wheels. In 1825, British engineer George Stephenson overcame problems with engine power and track laying to build the Stockton and Darlington Railway. He went on to build the Liverpool–Manchester line in 1829.

STEAM TRAINS

After the success of George Stephenson's Liverpool–Manchester Railway, trains quickly became extremely successful and popular for moving both freight and passengers. At the time, there were few good roads and no powered vehicles to run on them. By 1900, most of the developed countries of the world had built extensive networks of railroad lines that were able to carry millions of passengers and a great deal of freight.

STEEL ON STEEL

Most modern trains have steel wheels that run on twin steel rails. This arrangement means that resistance to motion is small,

▲ On February 21, 1804, Cornish engineer Richard Trevithick won a bet when he built the first steam locomotive able to haul 10 tons of freight over 10 miles (16km).

so that a heavy train can be propelled using relatively little power. It also means that there is no need to worry about steering, since the train will always follow the rails. A railroad line therefore needs to be only slightly wider than the widest train intended to pass along it.

UNDERGROUND RAILWAYS

Many cities have railways running in tunnels under their streets. These ease congestion and move people quickly. The first underground railroad was the Metropolitan, in London, England, which opened in 1863. The smoke from the steam engines caused problems, so later lines used electric trains. Other cities began building underground railroads— Boston in 1895, Budapest in 1896, Paris in 1898, and New York in 1904.

▼ In 1981, the French national railroads introduced the TGV, or *Train à Grande Vitesse*—a high-speed service between major cities. Today, it is one of the fastest train services in the world, reaching 199 mph (320 kph) on its eastern line. On test lines it has traveled even faster—its record was more than 357 mph (574kph).

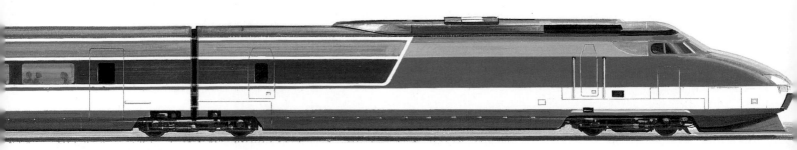

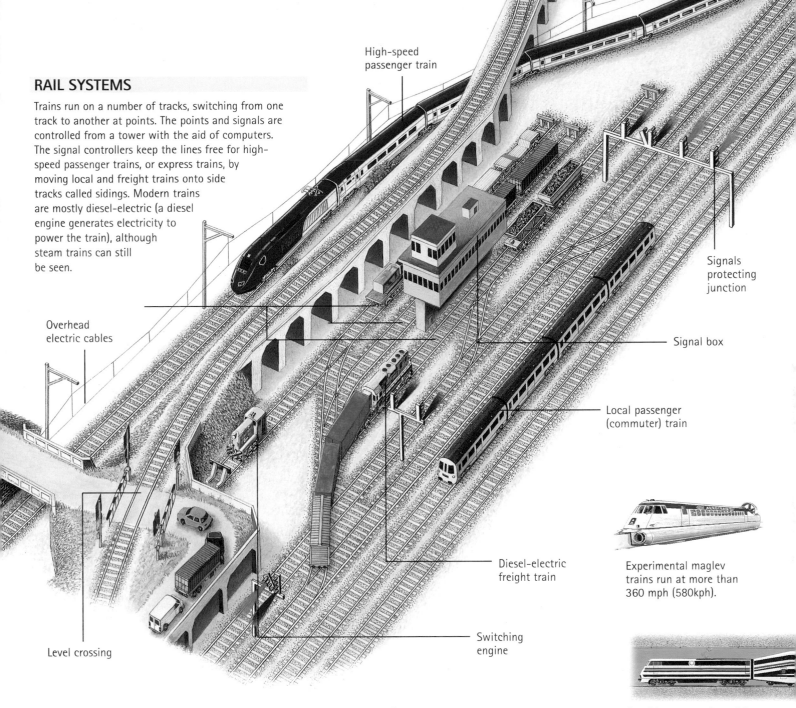

RAIL SYSTEMS

Trains run on a number of tracks, switching from one track to another at points. The points and signals are controlled from a tower with the aid of computers. The signal controllers keep the lines free for high-speed passenger trains, or express trains, by moving local and freight trains onto side tracks called sidings. Modern trains are mostly diesel-electric (a diesel engine generates electricity to power the train), although steam trains can still be seen.

High-speed passenger train

Overhead electric cables

Signals protecting junction

Signal box

Local passenger (commuter) train

Diesel-electric freight train

Level crossing

Switching engine

Experimental maglev trains run at more than 360 mph (580kph).

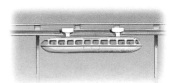

Car drivers can relax while they travel on car trains.

Monorails have been built above crowded streets.

RAILROADS DECLINE

In the second half of the 1900s, railroads began to lose both passenger and freight traffic to the roads and to the airlines. Railroads were not "flexible"—they could not deliver to everyone's front door as the roads could—and they were very expensive to maintain to the high standard that safety demanded. Trains need long distances for acceleration and braking. This meant that they had to be a long way apart, limiting the number that could use a line. Railroads began to lose money. During the 1970s, several U.S. railroad companies declared bankruptcy.

FUTURISTIC DESIGNS

Railroad engineers worked hard to attract passengers and freight back to trains. After many years when train speeds remained almost the same, most systems now operate some kind of high-speed train running at 125 mph (200kph) or more, for example the French TGV. More adventurous designers have eliminated the steel rails altogether. They have used magnets, for example, to lift the train above a track. This "maglev" system, which has been pioneered in Germany, China, and Japan, allows even higher speeds while at the same time reducing noise.

SEE ALSO

City, Engine, Industrial Revolution, Transportation

TRANSPORTATION

Transportation is a means of carrying people, animals, or goods from one place to another. This can be by land, water, or air, or through space.

Britain's *Flying Scotsman* made the world's longest nonstop run in 1928, from London to Edinburgh.

The Japanese intercity bullet train can travel up to 186 mph (300kph) and provides smooth and noiseless transportation for thousands of commuters daily.

Humans have always needed to move from place to place and to carry their goods. This is why the earliest civilizations were built along rivers. Eventually, people began to ride on horseback to cover long distances more quickly. They also used pack animals and carts to carry goods.

TRADE BY WATER

As civilizations developed, the need for transportation grew. Any trading center close to water built a harbor and began to send heavy goods to other centers by boat. At the same time, vehicles with wheels also became important. But few roads were strong enough to support heavily laden carts.

So, up until the 1800s, water transportation, in the form of ships and barges, developed more quickly than land transportation, and most of the world's trade went by sea.

STEAM ENGINES

At the end of the 1700s, the first practical steam engine was invented. This gave birth to the steamship and, in 1804, a locomotive to carry passengers. Railways became so successful that they soon put inland canals out of business. At the same

ON THE ROAD

The first travelers had to carry or drag their belongings. Then they trained animals to carry loads and drag sleds. Around 3200 B.C., the Sumerians began to use wheeled carts. From that time and for hundreds of years, people travelled in various types of carriages pulled by animals. However, for many years there were no roads. Since the invention of the automobile, a vast network of roads and expressways has run across countries.

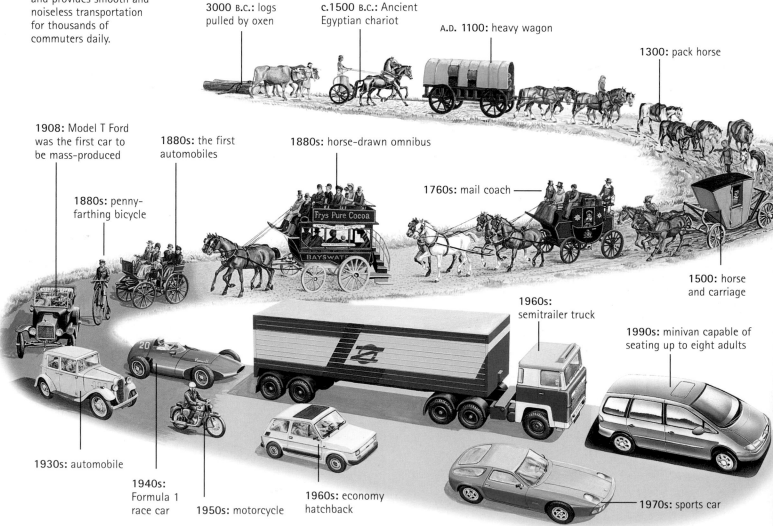

3000 B.C.: logs pulled by oxen

c.1500 B.C.: Ancient Egyptian chariot

A.D. 1100: heavy wagon

1300: pack horse

1908: Model T Ford was the first car to be mass-produced

1880s: the first automobiles

1880s: horse-drawn omnibus

1760s: mail coach

1880s: penny-farthing bicycle

1500: horse and carriage

1960s: semitrailer truck

1990s: minivan capable of seating up to eight adults

1930s: automobile

1940s: Formula 1 race car

1950s: motorcycle

1960s: economy hatchback

1970s: sports car

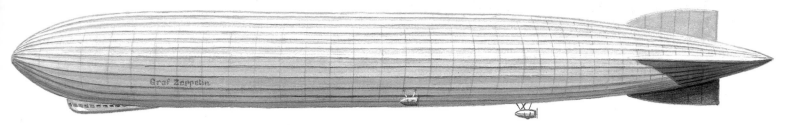

▲ The German Zeppelin was a successful form of transportation in the early 1900s until 1937. These airships could be up to 790 ft. (240m) long with a speed of 80 mph (130kph),

time, larger, faster steamships were carrying more and more passengers and goods across the oceans.

TRADE BOOM

This progress had the effect of further boosting trade. By the end of the 1800s, the world's major ports were huge places employing thousands of people and the railroads in most countries had been fully extended. Also, networks of blacktopped roads were being built. This meant that goods could be delivered from the ports and railroad yards directly to the front doors of stores and houses and people could travel to work. The development of the roads was aided by two inventions: the pneumatic (air-filled) tire and the internal combustion engine, which, between them, led to modern automobiles and trucks.

▲ The largest jet airliners, known as jumbo jets, can carry as many as 850 pasengers.

THE AGE OF THE CAR

Roads quickly became the most useful form of transportation. Anyone with a car could travel almost anywhere, for business or pleasure. At first, few people could afford a car of their own. During the 1920s, however, cheap motor cars began to be mass-produced and heavy trucks became much more efficient. By about 1950, road transportation had taken a lot of business away from the railroads. In addition, by this time, air transportation, with the development of larger planes and jet engines, was attracting passengers away from oceangoing liners, which had become too expensive to run.

Great ocean liners have six or more decks with luxuries for passengers such as elevators, suites, ballrooms, and swimming pools.

MERCHANT SHIPPING

Today, most short-distance transportation —of people or goods—is by road, while almost all long-distance transportation is by air and sea. Heavy cargo is transported mostly by merchant shipping, which consists of specially built cargo carriers, such as oil tankers, bulk carriers, and container ships.

DEATH OF THE RAILROADS

Despite the increase in air traffic, rail travel has come back into favor, with high-speed intercity and international services, new metro and light rail lines, and suburban commuter networks. This has helped reduce congestion and pollution, particularly in those inner cities where road traffic is restricted.

▲ In modern cities such as Los Angeles, California (shown here), the vehicle emissions from road vehicles are a constant cause of air pollution. Widespread use of electric cars may help to solve this problem.

The bicycle remains an efficient means of short-distance transportation and causes no pollution.

SEE ALSO

Aircraft, Bicycle and motorcycle, Boat, Car, Horse, Hovercraft, Road, Ship, Train, Truck and bus

TREE

A tree is a large, upright plant with a single, woody main stem. The biggest trees are among the largest, heaviest, and longest-living organisms on Earth.

Trees come in all shapes, with most over 20 ft. (6m). Some, like oaks, have a short trunk dividing into huge, spreading branches. Others, like redwoods, are tall and conical; trunks are 330 ft. (100m) tall, 30 ft. (9m) thick at the base.

CLASSIFYING TREES

The two main tree families are the conifers, or softwood trees, and the deciduous trees, or hardwoods. Scientists refer to conifers as gymnosperms (meaning "naked seeds"), because their seeds form on the woody scales that make up their cones. Deciduous trees are called angiosperms ("enclosed seeds"), because their seeds are enclosed inside fruit. Pines, firs, spruces, larches, and hemlocks are all conifers—also called evergreens because most keep their thin, needle-shaped leaves throughout the year. Deciduous trees, such as the oak, ash, maple, beech, elm, and horse chestnut, shed their leaves in the fall, or autumn.

TREE PARTS

The three main parts of a tree are its roots, trunk, and leaves. The roots take in water and nutrients from the soil. The trunk supports the tree and carries water and nutrients to the leaves through tubes, and food from the leaves back down to the rest of the tree.

The silver birch has pure white bark, often pocked with black marks. It has a tall and elegant shape.

Like the sugar maple, the silver maple is tapped for its syrup. Its five-lobed leaves are deeply toothed.

▶ Acorns are the fruit of the oak tree. On the English oak, they are attached to stalks.

Oak leaf

Acorn

The bark of the oak tree is fissured (ridged) and brownish-gray in color.

▲ Many species of oak grow in the Americas and Europe. Most are deciduous, such as the English oak, which can survive for 1,000 years. Its trunk is stout and burred.

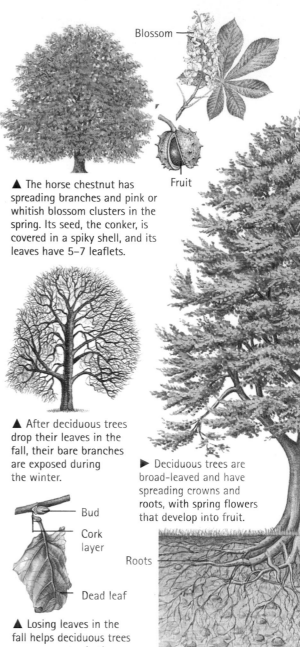

Blossom

Fruit

▲ The horse chestnut has spreading branches and pink or whitish blossom clusters in the spring. Its seed, the conker, is covered in a spiky shell, and its leaves have 5–7 leaflets.

▲ After deciduous trees drop their leaves in the fall, their bare branches are exposed during the winter.

Bud

Cork layer

Dead leaf

▲ Losing leaves in the fall helps deciduous trees conserve water in the winter. The leaf is sealed off from the stem's food supply near the bud; it dies and falls.

▶ Deciduous trees are broad-leaved and have spreading crowns and roots, with spring flowers that develop into fruit.

Roots

▲ The banyan tree, native to India, has branches that hang down to the ground and root themselves. On one banyan in Sri Lanka, over 3,300 trunks have been counted.

Monkey puzzle
female pine
cone

Monkey
puzzle
bark

Chinese windmill
palm leaf

Stem

▲ The monkey puzzle is an unusual conifer with sharp, leathery leaves. Male and female cones grow on separate trees; the bark is ringed.

▲ The spiky, fanned fronds of the Chinese windmill palm leaf can spread to a width of 3 ft. (1m).

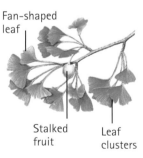

▲ Deciduous trees produce vivid and beautiful fall colors in North American woodlands. Leaves may change from green to shades of red, orange, purple, and gold.

PHOTOSYNTHESIS

The leaves are the tree's chemical factory. Through a process called photosynthesis, sunlight acts with the chemical chlorophyll (which also gives the leaves their green color) to break down molecules of water and carbon dioxide, rearranging their atoms to make the starch and sugars the tree needs to grow. Oxygen is the waste product of this process, and whatever is not needed for respiration passes back into the air.

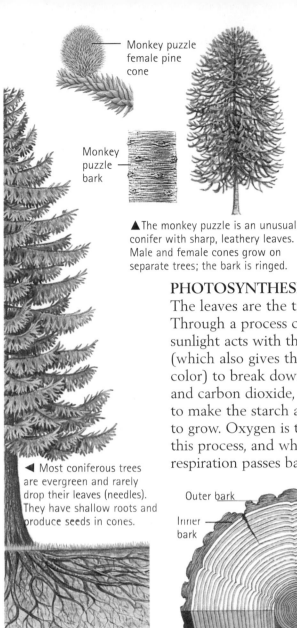

◄ Most coniferous trees are evergreen and rarely drop their leaves (needles). They have shallow roots and produce seeds in cones.

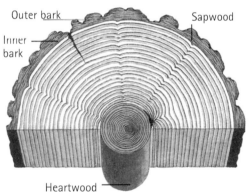

Outer bark

Inner
bark

Sapwood

Heartwood

▲ The heartwood of a tree trunk section is surrounded by lighter sapwood. A fresh growth ring is added every year; the number of rings shows the tree's age.

USES OF TREES

Trees were among the first natural resources used by people. They provided fuel for fires; wood for shelters, tools, and weapons; and fruit and nuts for food. Today, three billion people in developing countries still rely on wood for fuel. The industrial world also uses huge amounts of lumber, plywood, and hardboard. Wood pulp is used to make paper and fibers.

TREES AND THE ENVIRONMENT

Trees help keep the atmosphere healthy, because they remove carbon dioxide from the air and give off oxygen not used during photosynthesis. Trees also protect the land from erosion. Their giant canopies of leaves and branches absorb heavy rainfall; their roots bind the soil and prevent it from being washed away. This is why it is important to preserve rain forests in Brazil and Indonesia. In parts of Africa, where natural forests have been cut down, fast-growing trees are being planted to help prevent the desert from taking over.

◄ Bristlecone pines of North America are the world's oldest trees. Some are over 6,000 years old.

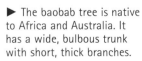

► The baobab tree is native to Africa and Australia. It has a wide, bulbous trunk with short, thick branches.

▲ Bonsai is the art of growing miniature trees. Almost any tree seedling can be grown as a bonsai by pruning its roots and branches, but evergreens are the most popular.

Fan-shaped
leaf

Stalked
fruit

Leaf
clusters

▲ The *ginkgo biloba*, or maidenhair tree, has remained unchanged for 160 million years. The tree was cultivated for centuries in Chinese temple gardens.

SEE ALSO

Conservation, Ecology, Forest, Fruit, Habitat, Leaf, Plant, Rain forest, Seed and pollination

TRUCK AND BUS

Trucks and buses are commercial road vehicles. Trucks are used to carry goods and products, while buses provide public transport for people.

A Foden C-type steam lorry of 1922. Steam trucks were popular until the 1930s.

A 1914 Hallford 3-ton truck used by the British army in World War I.

A London double-decker bus. The second deck boosts passenger capacity.

Modern trucks carry pre-packed containers of goods for easy loading.

Commercial trucks and buses have many features in common and are often built by the same companies.

RANGE OF SIZES
Unlike cars, most trucks and buses have a separate chassis, or wheeled frame, on which is mounted a body designed for a particular purpose. A truck may be a light local delivery vehicle, a middle-range goods transporter or a heavy-load carrier weighing up to 44 tons. The largest public service buses—articulated buses—carry as many as 200 passengers.

ROAD TRAINS
There are two main types of truck: rigid and articulated. Rigid trucks are built as a single unit, with all the wheels attached to one chassis. The articulated truck consists of a "tractor" unit, which contains the engine and cab, and a trailer which carries the goods. It is easier to handle and more flexible in operation. Truck chassis may be adapted for special purposes, for example, tankers (which carry liquids such as milk, fuel, or chemicals), cement mixers, and fire engines. In some countries, such as Australia, heavy trucks may tow many trailers as a "road train".

▲ Long-distance bus routes were established in the United States in 1925 by the Greyhound Corporation, and are now found in most countries with a good road system.

CARRYING PASSENGERS
Buses may be single-decked or double-decked. A double-decker can carry more passengers in the same road space. Very long single-deck buses are hinged near the center so they can turn tightly. Most buses operate in cities, but others run long-distance routes, usually offering much lower fares than the railroad. The tram, a streetcar on rails, follows a fixed route through a city. Many cities use streetcar lines to solve traffic jams.

▲ Road trains (articulated trucks pulling several trailers) are used for long-haul transportation in remote areas.

ARTICULATED TRUCKS
An articulated truck is made up of a tractor and a semitrailer. The tractor contains the engine, cab, fuel tanks, brakes, and other equipment. The semitrailer carries the main load. It has wheels at the rear, and rests on the tractor at the front by means of a device called the fifth wheel.

SEE ALSO
Car, Engine, Road, Transportation

TUNNEL

Tunnels are natural or artificial passageways built underground. They can be built through hills or mountains, or under land or water.

Tunnels are constructed to carry roads, railroads, water, sewage, or cables. They are also built to reach mineral deposits, or to create underground shelters or storage areas. Tunnels that carry traffic or people need ventilation systems to remove fumes and circulate fresh air.

ANCIENT TUNNELS

Tunneling began in prehistoric times when cave dwellers began to extend natural caves and dig for useful flints to make into tools. Ancient empires had tunnels built to house royal tombs and temples and to carry water to irrigate fields. The Romans built tunnels to connect the aqueducts that carried their water supply.

EXPLOSIVES AND SHIELDS

The first major traffic-carrying tunnel was built in the 1670s, when a 518-ft. (158-m) tunnel was blasted through a rocky hill near Béziers in France. Tunnel builders today still use explosives to blast through solid rock. Building tunnels through less dense materials

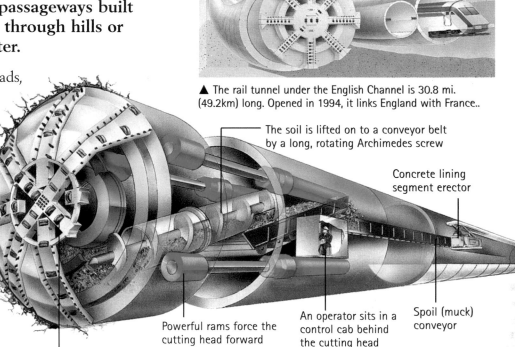

▲ The rail tunnel under the English Channel is 30.8 mi. (49.2km) long. Opened in 1994, it links England with France..

The soil is lifted on to a conveyor belt by a long, rotating Archimedes screw

Concrete lining segment erector

Powerful rams force the cutting head forward

An operator sits in a control cab behind the cutting head

Spoil (muck) conveyor

The cutter head has tough cutting rollers and teeth

TUNNEL–BORING MACHINE (TBM)

Modern tunneling machines use very tough, tungsten carbide cutting teeth. These can bore through soft rock, like chalk, at a rate of up to 3,280 ft. (1,000m) a month. A segment erector follows the cutting machine and places the lining sections in position.

requires a tunneling shield. Invented in Britain in 1825 by the French-born engineer Marc Isambard Brunel (1769–1849), the shield protects laborers as they dig. As the shield is gradually moved forward in sections, the walls of the tunnel are shored up with brickwork or concrete to stabilize them. Brunel used this method to build the first tunnel under the River Thames, London, completed in 1843.

UNDERWATER TUNNELS

A cheaper method of building tunnels under water is to dig a trench, drop in preformed sections of metal or concrete, and then, after divers have fitted them together, pump out the water and fill in the trench. The Hong Kong Cross Harbor Tunnel was built this way.

◀ The Thames Tunnel, built by Marc Brunel in the early 1840s, was the first underwater tunnel. It is still in use today as part of London's Underground train system.

FAST FACTS

• The world's widest tunnel, which is 207 ft. (63m) wide, is the eight-lane Fort McHenry Tunnel, Baltimore

• The world's longest road tunnel is the Laerdal Tunnel in Norway. It was completed in 2000 and is 15.2mi. (24.5km) long

• The world's longest and deepest railroad tunnel is the Gotthard Base Tunnel in Switzerland, which opened in 2016. Its route length is over 38 mi. (57km)

▲ A mole can dig five times faster than a TBM using just its two front paws, although its tunnels are, of course, smaller.

SEE ALSO

Hibernation, Mining, Oil

UNITED KINGDOM

England, Scotland, and Wales lie on the island of Great Britain in northwest Europe. Together with Northern Ireland, they form the United Kingdom (U.K.).

UNITED KINGDOM
Area: 94,058 sq. mi. (243,610km²)
Population: 65,105,000
Capital: London
Languages: English, Welsh, and Gaelic
Currency: Pound sterling

▲ Many commuters traveling in and out of London have to cope with crowded train stations.

Much of England is lowland, with the flattest areas in the east. Upland regions include the Lake District and the Pennines. Scotland, Wales, and Northern Ireland are more mountainous than England. Scotland's Ben Nevis (4,413 ft./ 1,345m) is the United Kingdom's highest peak. Loch Neagh, in Northern Ireland, is its largest lake. The Severn (210 mi./ 338km), which runs through Wales and England, is the longest river. In most parts, summers are generally cool and winters mild, with rainfall all year round.

TOWN AND COUNTRY
The U.K. is a crowded nation. Four out of every five British people live in cities and towns. England—especially the southeast around London—is the most densely populated part of the U.K. London is one of the world's great cultural centers. The U.K. has an extensive road system with many expressways, and London's Heathrow is one of the world's busiest airports. Since 1994, the Channel Tunnel, under the English Channel, has linked Great Britain with France.

INDUSTRY AND FARMING
Resources include oil deposits in the North Sea, although these are now in decline. The nation's many rivers provide drinking water, as well as water for crops. Much of the countryside is farmed, and the crops include wheat, sugar beet, potatoes, and oilseed rape. Dairy cattle and sheep are raised as well as pigs and poultry. Manufacturing industries include aerospace, chemicals, telecommunication, and electronics. Scotland also produces fine woolens and Northern Ireland is famous for its pure white linen. Industries such as banking, publishing, and tourism are also important.

▲ Northern Ireland has been the scene of violent conflict between Catholics and Protestants. Here, the Protestant Orange Order celebrates the anniversary of the victory of William of Orange over Catholic King James II in the Battle of the Boyne in 1690.

▶ Wales is a scenic land of green valleys, grassy plains, rugged seaside, hill farms, and mountains.

430

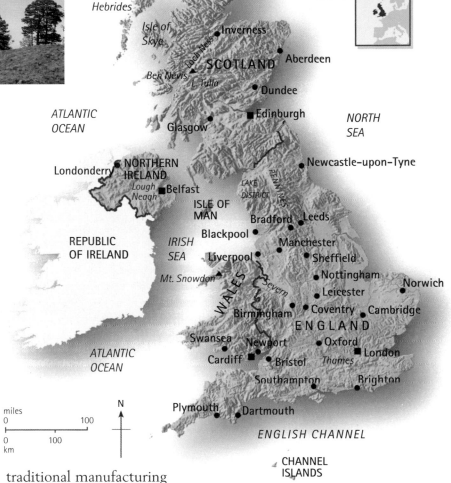

◀ Loch Tulla is a small lake in Scotland's Grampian Hills, between the Lowlands and the Highlands.

Shetland Is.
Orkney Is.
Outer Hebrides
Isle of Skye
Inverness
SCOTLAND
Aberdeen
Ben Nevis ▲
L. Tulla
Dundee
ATLANTIC OCEAN
Glasgow
■ **Edinburgh**
NORTH SEA
Londonderry
NORTHERN IRELAND
Lough Neagh ■ **Belfast**
Newcastle-upon-Tyne
PENNINES
LAKE DISTRICT
ISLE OF MAN
REPUBLIC OF IRELAND
Bradford **Leeds**
IRISH SEA
Blackpool ●
Manchester
Liverpool **Sheffield**
Mt. Snowdon ▲
WALES
Severn
Nottingham
Leicester
Norwich
Birmingham
Coventry **Cambridge**
ENGLAND
Swansea
Newport
Oxford
London ■
Cardiff ■
Bristol
Thames
ATLANTIC OCEAN
Southampton
Brighton
Plymouth
Dartmouth
ENGLISH CHANNEL
CHANNEL ISLANDS

miles
0 — 100
0 — 100
km

N

FROM CONQUEST TO KINGDOM

The Romans conquered lowland Britain from A.D. 43. After the Romans came Anglo-Saxons, Vikings, and Normans. The United Kingdom of Great Britain and Ireland was formed in 1801. It became the United Kingdom of Great Britain and Northern Ireland in 1922, after the southern part of the island of Ireland became independent.

WORLD POWER

During the 1700s, Britain colonized large parts of North America, Africa, and Asia. Wealth from the colonies supplied money for the Industrial Revolution to begin at home, and factories and machinery were built. By 1900, the British Empire had become the world's largest empire, defended by the greatest navy.

DECLINE OF THE EMPIRE

In the first half of the 1900s, two world wars caused loss of life and economic strain. From the 1950s, the U.K.'s wealth and power declined as many of the colonies became independent and Britain's traditional manufacturing industries such as coal, iron, steel, and shipbuilding declined.

THE U.K. TODAY

The U.K. remains a major player in finance and the service industries. The U.K. is a member of the United Nations and the Commonwealth. It is currently negotiating a British withdrawal from the European Union. The U.K. is a constitutional monarchy, which means the king or queen is head of state but political power is controlled by Parliament. In 1997, a degree of power was devolved to a regional parliament in Scotland and an assembly in Wales. Northern Ireland has had its assembly since 2007. The Isle of Man and the Channel Islands (Jersey and Guernsey) are largely self-governing.

▲ England's south coast, such as the town of Dartmouth in Devon, is popular with tourists for its scenery and climate.

▲ London's Tower Bridge, opened in 1894, is a symbol of the city and a magnet for tourists.

SEE ALSO

Civil war, Empire, Europe, Government, Industrial Revolution, Ireland (Republic of), United Nations, Viking, World War I, World War II

UNITED NATIONS

The United Nations is an international organization based in New York. Governments send representatives there to discuss problems and to try and find solutions.

The United Nations flag features the world surrounded by the olive branch, a symbol of peace.

Founded in 1945 by the Allied countries who won World War II, the United Nations (UN) has grown to include 193 of the nearly 200 independent states on Earth. The UN sponsors negotiations between countries that have disputes, and has many agencies that carry out humanitarian work.

GENERAL ASSEMBLY
Each UN member country has one vote in the General Assembly, which meets in New York City. The General Assembly approves UN work, debates important issues, and decides how to spend money. The 15-member Security Council is responsible for peace and security. It can send a peacekeeping force to any country, and may condemn aggressive action. Five countries are permanent members: China, France, Russian, the U.K., and the U.S.

HUMANITARIAN WORK
The UN works to promote trade, health education, and cultural understanding. This work is carried out by the bodies of the Economic and Social Council

(ESC), which pays for aid projects in poor countries, encourages healthcare, and promotes the rights of minorities. UNICEF (UN Children's Fund) promotes the welfare of children in poor countries. In 1991, the UN held an Earth Summit in Rio de Janeiro so that world leaders could agree on solutions to environmental problems.

PROBLEMS IN THE UN
The UN cannot always find solutions that suit all its member states. Some believe that the Security Council has too much power. Some ignore UN resolutions. There has sometimes been criticism of UN peace-keeping troops in the field. However, the work of the UN in areas such as health and the care of refugees is essential for peace and progress.

▲ Maize and cooking oil are distributed in Somalia as another famine threatens the Horn of Africa in 2017. UN agencies play an important part in preventing or dealing with starvation and malnutrition.

UN AGENCIES

- World Health Organization (WHO)
- Food and Agriculture Organization (FAO)
- International Monetary Fund (IMF)
- UN Educational, Scientific, and Cultural Organization (UNESCO)
- International Civil Aviation Organization (ICAO)
- World Bank
- UN Children's Fund (UNICEF)

◄ The United Nations General Assembly meets for three months every autumn to decide on important issues. It can hold a special session during an emergency, such as the Soviet invasion of Hungary in 1956.

SEE ALSO

Civil war, Education, Government, Politics, World War II

UNITED STATES OF AMERICA

The United States is the third largest country in the world in terms of population and area. It is rich in natural resources and highly advanced in technology.

Area: 3,796,742 sq. mi. (9,833,517km²)
Population: 329,256,000
Capital: Washington, D.C. (District of Columbia)
Language: English
Currency: U.S. dollar

▼ The Statue of Liberty stands at the entrance to New York Harbor. It was a gift from France in 1884 and represents freedom for the people of the United States.

The United States (U.S.) consists of 50 states, 48 contiguous (touching) and two apart from the rest. Alaska lies west of Canada and includes Mount Denali (Mt. McKinley) (20,308 ft./6,190m), North America's highest peak. Hawaii is a group of islands in the Pacific Ocean, 2,425 mi. (3,900km) from the U.S. mainland.

THE 48 STATES
Climate and geography divide the 48 states below Canada into groups from east to west and north to south. Those on the Atlantic coast consist of the New England, Middle Atlantic, and Southern states. The Midwest and Southwest form the center of the country. To the west are the Rocky Mountain states, and west of these are the Pacific Coast states, running south to Mexico.

VIGOR AND VARIETY
The United States is a country of vast plains and bustling cities, everglades and deserts, spectacular seacoasts, and majestic mountains. Southern plantations grow cotton and tobacco. Midwestern prairies run gold with grain crops. The West Coast has rugged mountains and endless Pacific beaches. Business

▲ New York is the largest city in the U.S. One of its key symbols is the yellow cab, a common sight on the streets of Manhattan and the other four boroughs.

booms from coast to coast: New York and Chicago are major financial centers; Detroit and Cleveland are industrial bases; Atlanta, Dallas, and Houston have become hubs of commerce; Los Angeles and San Francisco dominate the West Coast. The country's historical roots still live in Boston and Philadelphia. Images of Washington, D.C. symbolize the country around the world. New Orleans, Miami, Seattle, St. Louis—all make their unique contribution to the mosaic that is the modern United States. ▶

▲ The Grand Canyon lies in northwestern Arizona. It is one of the most spectacular river gorges in the world, carved from the desert rock by the Colorado River over six million years.

▲ The 800 mi. (1,300km) Trans-Alaska pipeline carries oil from the frozen north of the state to the Gulf of Alaska in the south.

the Revolutionary War (1775–83), and on July 4, 1776, a group of colonial leaders signed the Declaration of Independence. The war ended in victory for the colonists, led by General George Washington.

THE PEOPLE

Since 1940, the population of the United States has more than doubled. Native Americans, who lived in North America for thousands of years before Europeans began arriving, now make up just one percent of the population. About half of all U.S. citizens are Protestants; nearly a quarter are Roman Catholics. About two percent of the population are Jewish and less than one percent is Muslim.

NEW LAWS

In 1787, the Constitution was drawn up and sent to the states for approval. In it, power was divided between the federal government and the individual states. In 1789, a number of amendments that guaranteed specific rights were proposed. Ten were approved by the states and are known as the Bill of Rights. There are now 27 amendments.

SETTLEMENT AND REVOLUTION

Permanent European settlement of what was to become the U.S. began with a British colony founded in 1607 at Jamestown, Virginia. British colonists spread along America's eastern coast. In the South, they grew tobacco, cotton, and indigo on plantations worked by slaves shipped from Africa. In the North, timber and furs were key products, and fishing was a major industry. French and Spanish explorers and colonists began to settle other territories to the west. Disputes between Britain and its 13 colonies over trade, taxes, and defense led to

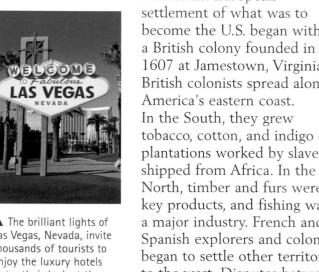

▲ The brilliant lights of Las Vegas, Nevada, invite thousands of tourists to enjoy the luxury hotels or try their luck at the world-famous casinos.

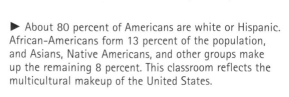

▶ About 80 percent of Americans are white or Hispanic. African-Americans form 13 percent of the population, and Asians, Native Americans, and other groups make up the remaining 8 percent. This classroom reflects the multicultural makeup of the United States.

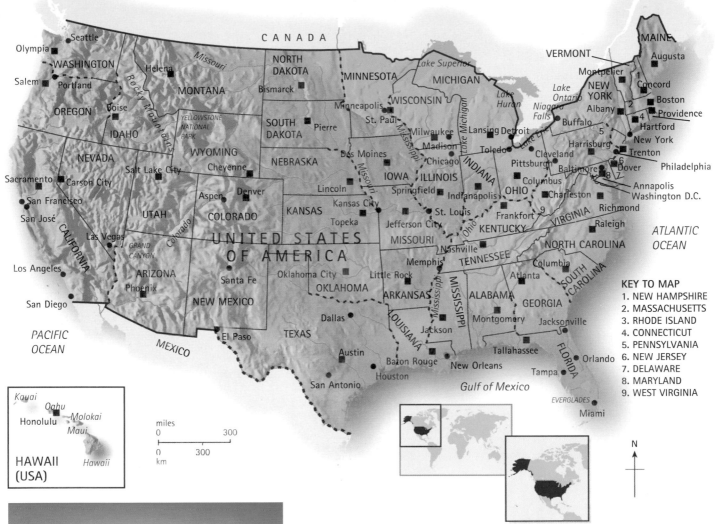

HAWAII
(USA)

KEY TO MAP
1. NEW HAMPSHIRE
2. MASSACHUSETTS
3. RHODE ISLAND
4. CONNECTICUT
5. PENNSYLVANIA
6. NEW JERSEY
7. DELAWARE
8. MARYLAND
9. WEST VIRGINIA

▲ The Midwestern states of North Dakota and Kansas are the country's largest producers of wheat.

GROWTH OF A NATION

George Washington was the first president, and a new national capital was founded and named in his honor. In 1802, the third president, Thomas Jefferson, bought vast western territories claimed by France, doubling the size of the new nation. In 1804, Jefferson sent an expedition to explore the continent from east to west. War against Mexico (1846–48) led to the conquest of the southwest and

Pacific coast. Lured by the discovery of gold in California in 1849 and by the prospect of free land on the prairies, Americans headed west. Meanwhile, Washington Irving and other writers helped create a new national identity, and Noah Webster compiled the first dictionary of American English.

WAR AND PEACE

From 1861 to 1865, America was torn by a civil war which made the South poor, but boosted industry in the North. Peace brought a boom in railroad building. By 1869, railroads joined the East and West coasts. San Francisco, Chicago, and St. Louis grew from frontier posts into great cities. ▶

▼ Surfing and other water sports are popular in the Hawaiian islands, including Oahu, where 76 percent of Hawaii's population lives.

▲ Football, a popular professional and college sport, developed in the 1800s.

▲ The White House had to be rebuilt after it was damaged by fire in the War of 1812.

INDUSTRY AND IMMIGRATION

Millions of Europeans moved to the U.S., and Native Americans were driven from their traditional lands. America grew rich from its farms and factories. By 1900, the average American was better off than the average European. Half of all Americans still lived on farms, but cities were booming. American inventions, such as the lightbulb, elevator, skyscraper, and airplane, were to change the world.

A WORLD POWER

In 1867, the United States bought Alaska from Russia. In 1898, it took over the Pacific islands of Hawaii and also went to war with Spain. This led to independence for Cuba and American rule over the Philippines. The U.S. developed a great navy. In 1917, the country joined in World War I to help Britain and France defeat Germany and its allies.

BOOM, BUST, AND WAR

In the 1920s, the United States was the first country in which millions of people drove cars, listened to the radio, and enjoyed the movies. But the "roaring twenties" ended in a business collapse in 1929, with millions out of work. President Franklin D. Roosevelt used government money from taxes to create new jobs. Following Japan's attack on the naval base at Pearl Harbor (Hawaii) in 1940, Roosevelt led the country during World War II, but died just before the German surrender.

SUPERPOWER

War boosted industry in the United States and left the country as a superpower, armed with atomic bombs and with a new role as leader of the democratic world. U.S. wealth helped Europe recover from war damage. Today, the United States is the world's most powerful nation, and its culture has spread across the world.

▲ In 1620, a group of English Puritans who called themselves Pilgrims founded a colony at Plymouth, Massachusetts. A recreation of their settlement now stands on the site of the original colony.

◄ In the early 1900s, jazz emerged in New Orleans and developed as a new and distinctly American style of music. Today, the New Orleans jazz festival is world famous.

SEE ALSO

Civil rights, Civil War (American), Cold War, Habitat, Native American, North America, Slavery, World War I, World War II

UNIVERSE

The universe is made up of stars, planets, and other matter scattered throughout space. It may contain as many as 2 trillion galaxies with 100 billion stars in each.

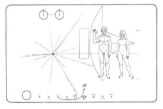
Most scientists believe that the universe began with an enormous explosion called the Big Bang, which happened about 13.7 billion years ago. During this event, all the matter and energy that would ever exist was created in a fraction of a second, in an area smaller than the size of a grape. Ever since the Big Bang, the universe has been expanding outward into space.

SEEING INTO THE PAST

A galaxy that is five billion light-years away is seen by astronomers as it was five billion years ago. Therefore, looking at very remote objects gives us a way of seeing the universe when it was much younger than it is today. The most distant objects ever seen are newborn galaxies or galaxies that are still being formed. At even greater distances and earlier times, astronomers can detect only faint radio waves, which come from all parts of space. These are the cooled down remains of the fireball that erupted out of the Big Bang.

HISTORY OF THE UNIVERSE	
Time after Big Bang	Event
0 minutes	Time, space, and energy created
3 minutes	Universe made of 90 percent hydrogen and 10 percent helium
300,000 years	Atoms were formed
1 billion years	First galaxies appeared
13.7 billion years	The present day

MYSTERIES OF THE UNIVERSE

Scientists ask: will the universe go on expanding forever, or will it eventually begin to shrink and end in a Big Crunch? At present, the answer is unknown, but it seems that the universe may be delicately balanced between the two options. Another question is: does life exist elsewhere in the universe? Again, the answer is not yet known, but the evidence suggests that life may be common throughout space. Space probes sent to other planets search for water, the main ingredient that supports life as we know it. Over 90 percent of the universe consists of dark matter, which cannot be seen. The composition of this remains another great mystery.

SEE ALSO

Astronomy, Big Bang theory, Galaxy, Planet, Solar system, Star, Time

VEGETABLE

Vegetables are plants grown to provide food. Most are grown from seeds, bulbs, or tubers, then harvested within a year. A few grow on long-lived plants.

EDIBLE VEGETABLE PARTS

Eight different parts of vegetable plants are eaten: the bulbs of onion and garlic; the flowers of broccoli and cauliflower; the leaves of lettuce and kale; the roots of carrots and turnips; the seeds and pods of peas and beans; the stems of celery and rhubarb; and the tubers of potatoes and yams. Tomatoes, peppers, eggplants, and squashes such as pumpkins are really fruits, since they contain seeds, but are grown as vegetables.

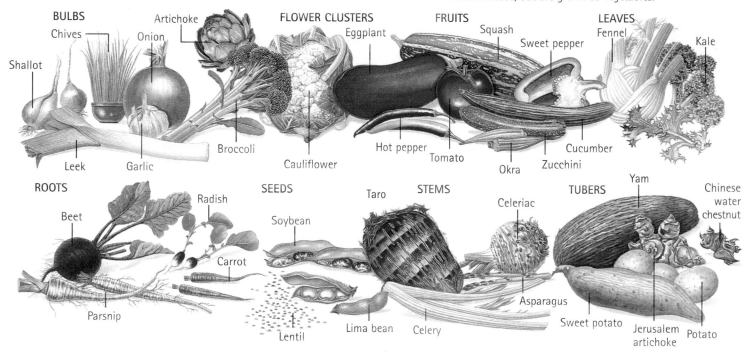

BULBS — Chives, Shallot, Onion, Artichoke, Leek, Garlic

FLOWER CLUSTERS — Eggplant, Broccoli, Cauliflower

FRUITS — Squash, Sweet pepper, Hot pepper, Tomato, Okra, Zucchini, Cucumber

LEAVES — Fennel, Kale

ROOTS — Beet, Radish, Carrot, Parsnip

SEEDS — Soybean, Lentil, Lima bean

STEMS — Taro, Celeriac, Celery, Asparagus

TUBERS — Yam, Chinese water chestnut, Sweet potato, Jerusalem artichoke, Potato

VEGETABLE FACTS

• Potatoes, tomatoes, peppers, and corn are native to the Americas and were unknown in Europe before A.D. 1500

• Some types of beans are poisonous if they are eaten raw

• Organic vegetables are grown without pesticides

Vegetables are very important to a healthy diet: they are low in fat, and different types provide protein, carbohydrates in the form of starches and sugars, vitamins, minerals, and fiber. Some vegetables, such as potatoes, must be cooked before being eaten; others are best eaten raw, and many vegetables may be eaten either way. Cooking vegetables for too long destroys some of their vitamins.

SEASONAL VEGETABLES

Vegetables are harvested at different times of the year. Some, like lettuce, are usually eaten fresh, but others, such as peas and beans, can be dried or frozen and cooked later. Root vegetables last for a long time when stored in cool, dry conditions—they can even be left in the soil. Freezing and canning make it possible to eat from a wide selection throughout the year, although fresh vegetables have the highest nutritional value.

CROPS AND BREEDING

All vegetables contain nutrients. Cultivated crops have more nutrients than their wild ancestors. Many people, particularly in developing countries, have to rely on their own crops for food. If crops fail, they face starvation, so over thousands of years, farmers have selected and bred edible plants that give the best yield for the climate in their area. Through plant-breeding techniques, scientists have developed new varieties of vegetables that are resistant to attack by pests and diseases.

◀ Giant vegetables, such as pumpkins, are grown for contests, but they are too tough to eat.

SEE ALSO

Crop, Farming, Nutrition, Plant, Seed and pollination

VIDEO

Video technology turns moving pictures and sounds into electronic form, stores them on a magnetic tape or disc, and then plays them back on a screen.

▲ Computer-controlled video-editing setups are used to assemble images and add special effects.

The first videocassette recorder (VCR) was made by Sony in 1969. Signals from TV aerials, cables, satellite dishes, or video cameras can be recorded in many ways: on optical discs (including DVDs and Blu-rays), computer hard disc drives, an electronic system called "flash memory" or online.

▲ Camcorders store images in digital form. These give high-quality recordings, which can be edited on a computer and uploaded to video-sharing sites such as YouTube.

GET THE PICTURE
A century ago, silent home movies were made using reels of photographic film. These had to be sent off for developing before they could be played back with a projector. In the 1950s, a method of recording moving images and sound on magnetic tape was invented, and in the 1980s portable video cameras called camcorders were introduced. Now, most mobile phones and laptops include camcorders.

▲ Closed-circuit television (CCTV), with small video cameras, is used for security surveillance in buildings and public places.

VIDEO CAMERAS
In a camcorder, a lens bends the incoming light to form a sharp image on a flat light sensor called a charge-coupled device (CCD). This turns the image into an electronic signal, which is recorded together with a sound track. Software reduces wobble and can also be used to track moving objects automatically or to start recording when movement is detected. 3D camcorders are also now available.

VIDEO-CONFERENCING
The use of video has become increasingly widespread. For instance, video-equipped police cars and traffic cameras help to monitor roads and enforce speed limits. Thanks to the Internet and to web-cams (small cameras mounted on computer monitors) people can see and talk to each other even when they are on different continents. By combining special headsets with video cameras that can record in all directions at once, users can experience distant (or made-up) sights and sounds as if they are really there.

DIGITAL FILES
Films and programs can be recorded from TV broadcasts or purchased online and downloaded over the Internet. They can then be stored on hard disc drives (HDDs) as digital files, either on a computer or on a separate unit that can be plugged into a TV. These units can usually also save the files on optical discs (DVDs or Blu-ray discs).

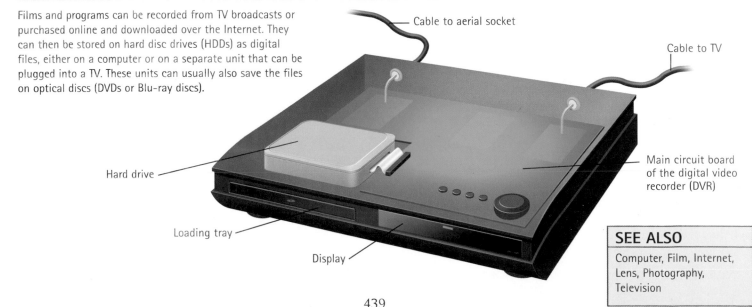

Cable to aerial socket

Cable to TV

Hard drive

Main circuit board of the digital video recorder (DVR)

Loading tray

Display

SEE ALSO
Computer, Film, Internet, Lens, Photography, Television

439

VIKING

The Vikings were peoples from Norway, Sweden, and Denmark. They were traders, raiders and explorers, who settled many lands during the ninth and tenth centuries.

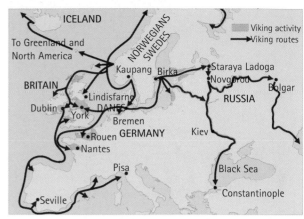

Why did Viking warriors sail for new lands? They may have been looking for better farmland, for riches or slaves, or simply for adventure. They had perfected the longship, a fast vessel that could ride the ocean waves.

Thor was the Viking god of thunder and war. Thursday is named after him.

In battle, Vikings often used a spear made of ash wood with an iron head.

A Viking silver amulet in the shape of Thor's hammer and decorated with a face.

EARLY RAIDS
The first Viking raids were small; one or two longships would raid a few coastal villages and escape with the loot. Around 800, they began to attack in force. They destroyed the monastery on Holy Island (Lindisfarne) and created fear with a series of ferocious attacks from northern France to the coast of Ireland.

FIERCE RELIGION
The Vikings believed in many different gods, spirits, and monsters. They told stories about gods and heroes in long poems called sagas. They believed the world would end in a war between the gods and giants at Ragnarok ("twilight of the gods"). Odin was their chief god. Men who died bravely in battle were thought to be taken by the Valkyries, 12 handmaidens from Odin's court, to Valhalla, a great hall, to spend eternity feasting and fighting.

▲ Viking trade and expansion routes in the 800s and 900s ran east through Russia, as far south as Seville and Pisa, and, by A.D. 1000, west to North America.

INVASION OF ENGLAND
In 851, Vikings arrived in England with a great army and 350 ships. They invaded Kent, destroying Canterbury. In 866, an even larger Viking army, led by Halfdane and Basecg, invaded Kent. Within five years nearly all of England had been defeated and conquered. The victory of King Alfred the Great (849–99) over Guthrum's Viking army at Edington in 878 saved southern and western England.

VIKING SETTLEMENTS
Large numbers of Vikings sailed to England and settled in the conquered lands as farmers and traders. York, Lincoln, and Derby became Viking towns. In Ireland, the Vikings founded Dublin and Waterford as trading cities. A large section of northern France—later known as Normandy (from Norsemen)—was captured by Earl Rollo and settled by Vikings. Some Vikings sailed east to travel up the rivers of eastern Europe. At Kiev, they founded a kingdom called the Russ, or Russia.

◀ The Vikings believed not only that there was life after death, but also that people would need some of their possessions in the afterlife. The greatest possession a Viking warrior could take with him was his longship—and many Vikings were either buried or burned in their longships, along with some everyday possessions.

FEARLESS RAIDERS FROM THE SEA

From the late 700s to about 1100, fearless Viking warriors from the Scandinavian countries of Norway, Sweden, and Denmark made several raids on the coasts of Christian countries, inflicting terror on the local inhabitants. They plundered monasteries and churches, killing, burning houses, and driving away the cattle.

OCEAN VOYAGES

The Vikings were skilled navigators. By studying the stars and the Sun they could travel accurately across vast distances of open sea. In about 825, they reached and settled the Faeroe Islands. Fifty years later, they reached Iceland. There, they founded an assembly—it still meets to discuss and decide communal matters. The Althing is the world's oldest governing assembly. In 982, the first Viking settlements on Greenland were founded. About the year 1000, a Viking named Leif Ericsson traveled to Newfoundland in search of

timber, which was scarce in Greenland. They continued to visit North America over many years, but the Vikings never settled there long.

VIKING TWILIGHT

By 900, the great Viking raids were over. Wars between Viking settlements and surrounding kingdoms remained common, but most Vikings settled down to a more peaceful existence. The Viking kingdoms in England and Ireland were taken over by the native kingdoms by 970.

CHRISTIAN CONVERTS

The Vikings and English lived side by side and, for a time, England became part of the Scandinavian Empire, under Canute (1016–35). A last attempt at conquest was made by the Norwegian Viking Harald Hardrada when he invaded England in 1066, but he was defeated and killed. From then on, most of the Vikings adopted Christianity and turned to farming and trading, abandoning raiding and conquest.

▲ Swords were highly valued by the Vikings and were often richly decorated with gold and silver.

▲ A Viking man and woman dressed in everyday clothes.

SEE ALSO

Myth and legend, Religion, Ship, Warfare

VOLCANO

When lava bursts through an opening in the Earth's crust, a volcano forms. The word "volcano" comes from Vulcan, the Roman god of fire and metalworking.

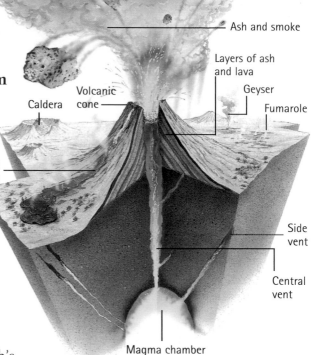

The Earth's surface is continuously moving through the action of plate tectonics, as sections of the Earth's crust are moved by currents in the molten rock below. There are two types of volcano: basaltic volcanoes found where new plate material is being created, and andesitic volcanoes in areas where plates are being destroyed.

BASALTIC VOLCANOES

Where new crust forms along oceanic ridges, the molten material from the Earth's mantle wells up and spreads out, pushing the plates apart. This usually happens at the bottom of the sea, but in Iceland it has risen above the sea and produced a whole island. The molten material, or lava, that erupts from these basaltic volcanoes is very runny and flows a long distance before becoming solid. Basaltic volcanoes are also found a long way from the edges of the plates. The Hawaiian islands were formed as basaltic material pushed its way up through the plate from the Earth's mantle. These "hot-spot" volcanoes have produced many other islands of the Pacific, including the Galapagos Islands and Fiji.

▲ Volcanic activity has formed the whole landscape of Iceland. The terrain is littered with jets of boiling water, called geysers.

FAMOUS ERUPTIONS

• In A.D. 79, Vesuvius erupted, destroying the Roman city of Pompeii

• About 90 eruptions have been recorded at Mount Etna, in Sicily, since 1800 B.C.

• Krakatoa, a volcanic island in Indonesia, erupted in A.D. 1883 and killed 36,000 people

• In 1980, the eruption of Mount St. Helens was predicted—the area was evacuated and only a few people died

INSIDE A VOLCANO

A typical volcano has a crater and a cone of solidified lava and ash. Eruptions take place through a chimney-like vent. Far below the surface is a chamber of magma (molten rock), containing bubbling gases that make some volcanic rock frothy. A caldera forms when a violent eruption empties the magma chamber that feeds it. The roof then collapses, leaving a hole. Fumaroles are openings that let out only gas and steam, and geysers sometimes shoot fountains of boiling water high into the air.

Ash and smoke
Layers of ash and lava
Geyser
Fumarole
Volcanic cone
Caldera
Lava flow
Side vent
Central vent
Magma chamber

VIOLENT ERUPTIONS

Andesitic volcanoes are found where plates are being drawn beneath one another and destroyed. Molten plate material rises through the overriding plate and bursts through at the surface. These andesitic volcanoes occur in the great mountain chains, and in island arcs around the edges of oceans, close to deep ocean trenches. The lava of an andesitic volcano is stiff and sticky, and when it erupts, it does so explosively. Mount St. Helens, in Washington, and the island of Montserrat are recent examples of such violent and destructive eruptions. Because of accurate forecasting, few were killed, but the hot ash from Mount St. Helens destroyed trees up to 19 mi. (30km) away.

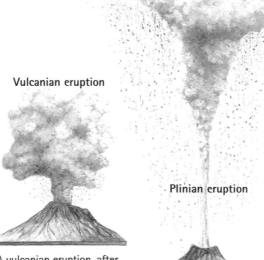

Vulcanian eruption

Plinian eruption

Hawaiian eruption

Volcano cones created by Hawaiian eruptions slope gently, because the lava flow is quite runny

A vulcanian eruption, after Vulcano, in Italy, throws almost solid magma during an explosion

Plinian eruptions, such as the one that destroyed Pompeii in A.D. 79, explode with great clouds of ash and pumice

SEE ALSO

Earth, Earthquake, Mountain and valley, Ocean and sea, Rock

WARFARE

Warfare is armed conflict between the military forces of two nations or states, or between organized groups within a state.

Much of recorded history is a recounting of war and conflict. This is often because one group seeks to impose its will on another for some form of gain, such as territory, food, or natural resources.

TURNING TO ARMS

Wars start for different reasons. The Crusades and the Thirty Years' War, in the 1600s, started for religious reasons. In 1701, the Ashanti fought for freedom from another African people and created a great trading nation. The Indian Wars of the late 1800s saw Native Americans defending their way of life against those who wanted their land. Involvement in Korea and Vietnam stemmed from opposition to communism in the Cold War.

OUTBREAK OF WAR

Countries going to war want to appear to be in the right. This encourages citizens to support the war and deters other countries from helping the enemy. Often a relatively minor incident will trigger a war.

▲ Samurai warriors used their discipline and skill with weapons to control Japan from 1200 to 1871.

In 1914, the Hapsburg Empire declared war on Serbia after a Serb killed the Austrian archduke. But the Hapsburgs really wanted to stop Serbia from encouraging unrest within the empire.

INTELLIGENCE

Once at war, commanders need to know about the strengths and plans of the enemy. The lack of such knowledge left France vulnerable to the German attack of 1940. Information may be gathered by watching the enemy from satellites and aircraft, by capturing or decoding messages, or by using spies. Information would then be given to commanders to help make battlefield decisions. ▶

Ancient Egyptians used stone for maceheads, knives, and arrowheads and spearheads.

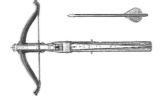

Medieval crossbows shot bolts accurately, but were slow to load and use.

OARS AND RAMS

The Battle of Salamis in 480 B.C. was fought between the oared galleys of Greece and the Persian Empire. The Greeks defeated the larger Persian fleet because their triremes (ships with three banks of oars) were faster and easier to handle than the Persian ships.

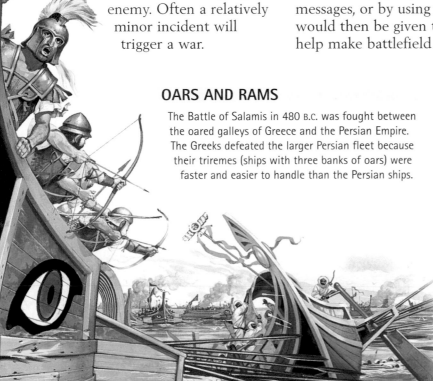

▲ Hand weapons of the Middle Ages included:
1 Daggers for stabbing; 2 Maces to crack metal armor; 3 War hammers, used as maces; 4 Spiked staffs; 5 Pikes with handles up to 6.5 ft. (2m) long to keep horsemen at a distance.

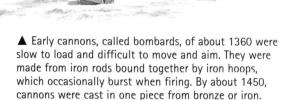

TOTAL WAR

In a total war, an entire country is organized for fighting. In the Zulu Empire, during the 1800s, every young man had to serve in the army and boys, older men, and women provided supplies. Both world wars of the 1900s were total wars. Men were conscripted into the armed forces, and many industries switched to producing weapons. It was considered fair to bomb cities in which factories were located, even though this might mean killing civilians.

▲ Early cannons, called bombards, of about 1360 were slow to load and difficult to move and aim. They were made from iron rods bound together by iron hoops, which occasionally burst when firing. By about 1450, cannons were cast in one piece from bronze or iron.

THE FATE OF PRISONERS

Prisoners are taken in all wars, but their treatment has differed. The Romans sold prisoners as slaves. The Aztecs sacrificed prisoners to their gods. During the 1800s, in wars with the British, the Afghans tortured all prisoners to death—the British often shot their men if they could not rescue them. World War II prisoner of war camps in Japan were notorious for bad conditions. The Geneva Convention of 1864, and its later revisions in 1906, 1929, 1949, and 1977, lays down strict rules about prisoners of war. They cannot be tortured. They must be given the same food and shelter as their captors, and they cannot be forced to do work to help the war effort. Prisoners are usually released at the end of a war.

▲ In Europe in the 1400s, armor covered the body with carefully shaped metal plates, each curved and ribbed to deflect blows.

▲ Helmets fringed with chain mail gave protection while allowing movement.

KEY DATES

c.5000 B.C. Cities in Mesopotamia form first armies

c.90 B.C. Marius reforms the Roman armies into professional and full-time forces

c.800 Feudal armies made up of semiprofessional knights form in Europe

c.1350 Gunpowder is invented

1916 Tanks are used for the first time

1945 Nuclear weapons are used for the first time

1991 The first major use of cruise missiles in the Gulf War by the United States

LIMITED BLOODSHED

War by its nature is violent. Soldiers may kill civilians, steal goods, and burn houses, so attempts have been made to reduce the violence. During the 1100s, the idea of chivalry encouraged knights to avoid hurting women or children. Nobles were taken prisoner (for their ransom); lesser captives were often slaughtered. In 1631, the German city of Magdeburg was captured by an army of Croats and Walloons. The soldiers looted the city and slaughtered thousands. European monarchs were appalled and developed

THE BATTLE OF WATERLOO

The Battle of Waterloo was fought in 1815 between the French, led by Napoleon Bonaparte, and a joint British, Dutch, and German army. The muskets and cannons of the time had only a limited range. The colorful uniforms helped soldiers tell friend from foe in the smoke of the battlefield.

the idea of limited war, which meant that civilians were to be unharmed and armies could surrender peacefully.

OBEYING THE RULES

Many wars have been fought according to a set of rules. In ancient Greece, most cities depended on olive oil for food, so olive trees were usually not destroyed when an enemy city was captured. The people of each city knew that they might be defeated at some time and wanted to have enough food to survive. During the Middle Ages, prisoners were given a chance to buy their freedom immediately by paying a ransom.

WAR CRIMES

Before 1945, any enemy soldier or leader who broke the rules of war was hanged or put in prison. At the end of World War II, the Allies set up special courts to

▲ In 1906, HMS *Dreadnought* was a new type of battleship, armed with 12-in. (30-cm) guns and able to steam at over 20 knots (30 mph/50kph). Battleships remained the most powerful ships afloat until aircraft carriers in the 1940s.

try people as war criminals for breaking the Geneva Convention and for the mass murder of Jews and others in the Holocaust. In the 1990s, new war crimes courts were set up to try people who had killed civilians during the Bosnian civil war.

GUERRILLAS

Some wars are fought by irregular troops called guerrillas. Such wars are usually fought when the enemy is too strong to be faced in battle. Using any weapons at hand and operating in small groups, ▶

▲ The British Mark IV tank of World War I was designed to crush barbed wire and cross trenches while protecting its crew from machine-gun fire.

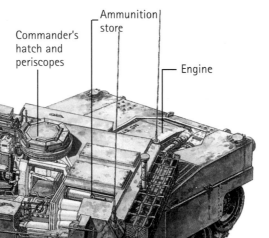

Commander's hatch and periscopes
Ammunition store
Engine
Machine gun
105-mm cannon
Sloped armor
Driver's seat
Tracks

A handgun of 1400

A 1500s' wheel lock

A 1600s' flintlock

The Colt revolver of 1851

A matchlock musket

A breechloading rifle of the 1800s

The German Mauser pistol of 1896

The Gatling gun of 1862 was an early machine gun

A German 50-ton siege cannon of 1867

THE MAIN BATTLE TANK

The Abrams M1 is the main battle tank (MBT) of the United States. MBTs are any army's most important weapon. They have guns up to 120mm caliber that are able to destroy strongholds and enemy tanks; armor protects the crew from all but the heaviest guns; mobility allows them to move through enemy territory to reach targets.

Modern warships have guns, missiles, and complex electronics.

The Mustang was the fastest American fighter of World War II.

The German V1 could fly 150 mi. (240km) with a 2,000 lb. (900kg) warhead.

The American Honest John missile could reach a range of 12.4 mi. (20km).

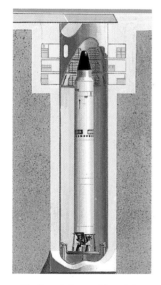

Modern Intercontinental Ballistic Missiles (ICBMs) carry nuclear warheads.

FIGHTING TOMCAT

The Grumman F14-A Tomcat is a twin-engined, 2-seater fighter. It served as part of the US Navy fleet from 1974 until 2006 and is still in use by the Iranian Air Force.

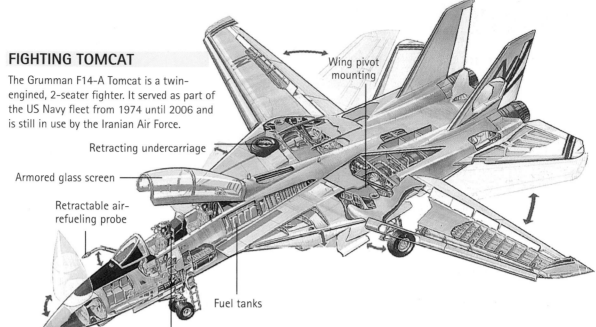

Wing pivot mounting

Retracting undercarriage

Armored glass screen

Retractable air-refueling probe

Fuel tanks

Ejector seat

guerrillas cut enemy supply lines and ambush patrols. The aim is to wear down the enemy forces, so that they give in.

PSYCHOLOGICAL WEAPONS

Many commanders try to persuade the enemy to surrender or to retreat by tricking them. In the 1740s, Frederick the Great of Prussia had a special regiment of men over 7 ft. (2.2m) tall. Because he only used his "giants" when he thought he would win, enemies seeing them advancing would think they were beaten. In World War II, British aircraft dropped leaflets on Germany urging troops to surrender. They failed because the leaflets contained obvious lies.

RADIO TRICKS

During World War II, a British radio station aimed at German troops claimed to be broadcast by a German army officer. Because the "officer" used army slang, many Germans believed the stories of German defeats. Tokyo Rose, a Japanese radio show, mixed stories of American defeats with popular music during World War II.

▶ Soldiers of the U.S. 82nd Airborne Division wear gas masks during the Gulf War of 1991. Chemical and biological weapons can cause massive casualties.

PEACEFUL SOLUTIONS

At the end of every war is a period of peace. This is often agreed between the two sides in a document called a treaty. Treaties set out conditions, such as the handing over of territory and the return of prisoners, which are signed by all parties. The Treaty of Amiens ended a war between Britain and France in 1802, but it left so many issues unresolved that the two were at war again just one year later. Other treaties have been more successful. The Treaty of Vienna in 1815 was signed by every nation in Europe and meant that peace lasted for decades. After World War II, the United Nations was set up to solve international disputes with the aim of preventing war from breaking out.

SEE ALSO

Castle, Celt, Civil war, Crusades, Greece (Ancient), Mongol Empire, Napoleonic Wars, Rocket, Roman Empire, United Nations, World War I, World War II

WATER

Water is the most common substance on Earth. It is the main ingredient in all living organisms–without water, life on the planet could not exist.

WATER FACTS

- A person drinks over 11,600 gal. (44,000 l) of water in a lifetime

- Human beings will die if they lose more than 20 percent of the body's normal water content

- Each flush of the toilet uses 12-36 pts. (6-17 l) of water; it takes 37 gal. (140l) to fill a bathtub; nearly 11 gal. (4l) to wash the dishes; and up to 32 gal. (120l) to run a washing machine

- The wettest place on Earth is Mawsynram in India, where about 1,020 in. (26,000mm) fell in 1985

▲ Climate change is reducing the amount of fresh water frozen in glaciers and polar ice caps.

Water vapor condenses and forms clouds

Rain and snow

Transpiration from plants

Water vapor in atmosphere

River flows back to oceans

Evaporation from seas and lakes

Water vapor cools and forms rain

Groundwater runs off

THE WATER CYCLE

Water is constantly being recycled. When the Sun heats Earth's surface, water evaporates into the atmosphere. Over 80 percent of this comes from seas, but some comes from plants giving off water vapor (transpiration). As water in the atmosphere cools, it condenses to form clouds. Some of this water falls again as rain.

Water vapor   0.05 percent
Moisture in soil   0.2 percent
Rivers and lakes   0.35 percent
Saltwater lakes
and inland seas   0.4 percent

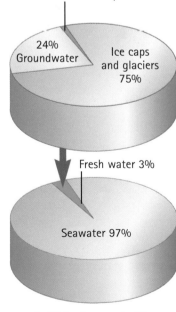

24% Groundwater

Ice caps and glaciers 75%

Fresh water 3%

Seawater 97%

▲ Of the 3 percent of the world's water that is not in the seas, 75 percent is locked in ice and glaciers.

Water exists naturally in three different forms: solid (frozen as ice), liquid (water), and gas (water vapor in the air). It can dissolve more substances than any other liquid. The force of natural water power has shaped the world's mountains, valleys, coastlines, and plains.

UNIVERSAL SUBSTANCE

Water covers 70 percent of Earth's surface—over 5.6 billion cu. mi. (1.4 billion cu km)—but only a tiny fraction is of use to humans. Almost 97 percent of all water is seawater, with up to about 77 lb. (35kg) of dissolved salts in every ton—eight times too salty to drink or to use for crops. Only about three percent of all water is fresh—and three fourths of that is in polar ice caps and mountain glaciers. Every living thing depends on the small amount of fresh water (under one percent of the total) that falls as rain and fills rivers and lakes.

WATER FOR LIVING

Life began in the sea 3.5 billion years ago, and water is still essential for all life-forms. The human body consists of about two-thirds water. People need 5 pt. (2.5l) of water a day to stay alive, but many of us use far more—the average American uses 150 gal. (570 l), the average Norwegian uses 80 gal. (300 l), and the average Briton 40 gal. (150 l). We also use vast amounts of water in industry and agriculture. It takes 264 gal. (1,000 l) of water to grow 2.2 lbs. (1kg) of wheat and 63.5 gal. (240 l) of water to produce 2.2 lbs (1kg) of steel.

SHAPING THE LAND

Water is the most important force in shaping the land. Rivers and glaciers carve valleys, wear down mountain ranges, and carry gravel, sand, silt, and clay onto lowland plains and eventually out into the sea. Even spectacular desert scenery is carved mainly by water from flash floods.

SEE ALSO

Lake, Mountain and valley, Ocean and sea, River, Waterpower, Weather

WATERPOWER

Waterpower uses the movement of water to turn machinery or to generate electricity. It is a renewable, nonpolluting source of energy.

▲ A huge wave crashing against the shore shows the awesome force of natural waterpower. The sea can be harnessed to generate electricity in tidal power plants and wave-power generators.

Waterwheels have been used to grind grain into flour since the time of ancient Greece. In Britain in the 1800s, they provided the power for big textile mills during the Industrial Revolution. Electric generators that could convert the turning motion of a waterwheel into electricity led to the rapid development of hydroelectric power in the early 1900s.

HYDROELECTRIC POWER

Water is first stored in a reservoir, often made by damming a river and flooding its valley. The water flows down pipes through turbines, propeller-like blades that are spun around by the flow of the water. In turn, these spin the electric generators. Pumped storage plants can push the water back up into the reservoir using off-peak electricity, then generate electricity again when demand is high, like charging up a giant battery. Just over six percent of the world's electricity comes from hydroelectric power, but it is available mainly in mountainous areas, far away from large cities, where most of the power is needed.

▲ In the Middle Ages, waterwheels were used to power hammers for ironworking. They saved time and labor.

TIDAL POWER

Dams built across river estuaries trap the rise and fall of ocean tides. The trapped water turns turbines as it flows through holes in the dam. These use the "head" of water made by the rise and fall of ocean tides to spin turbines. The largest tidal power plant, on the Rance River in Brittany, France, has been generating 240 megawatts of electricity since 1966.

WAVE POWER

The up-and-down movement of sea waves can be used to make electricity, but this is more difficult than using flowing water to turn a turbine. Since the 1980s, more than a dozen different types of device have been developed to harness wave power. There are wave farms off the coasts of Scotland, Australia, and Portugal.

TURBOGENERATOR

Water flows past turbogenerators inside the dam wall of a hydroelectric power plant. A turbogenerator converts the energy of flowing water into electrical energy. The shaft is turned by the pressure of water against its curved blades, and this moves the generator rotor, which generates (produces) an electric current.

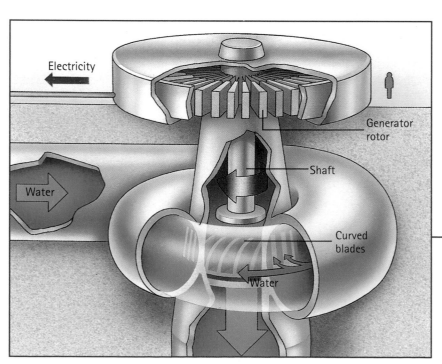

Electricity

Water

Generator rotor

Shaft

Curved blades

Water

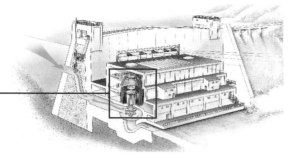

SEE ALSO
Dam, Electricity, Energy, Engine, Water

WAVELENGTH

Wavelength is the distance between two identical points on a wave. This is usually measured from one peak of the wave to the next.

Most of us have seen waves on the sea. Before they reach the coast, these waves make the seawater ripple. The highest points of these ripples are called peaks; the lowest points are called troughs. The distance between one peak and the next is called the wavelength of the waves.

SOUND WAVES
All forms of moving energy, including sound, light, and heat, travel in waves. All of them have a wavelength just like waves on the sea. When sound waves travel through air, for example, they create tiny changes in the air pressure. The peaks of a sound wave are where the air pressure is greatest. Our ears pick up the changes in air pressure and send signals to the brain.

DIFFERENT WAVELENGTHS
Just like frequency (the rate at which a wave moves up and down), wavelength affects a wave's properties because wavelength and frequency are closely related. For instance, low-frequency sound waves have a longer wavelength than high-frequency ones. Similarly, red light waves have a longer wavelength than blue ones. Light is one of a range of energy waves, including radio waves, micro-waves, infrared rays, ultraviolet rays, X rays, and gamma

rays, all of which travel at 186,400 mi./sec. (300,000km/sec). Together, these form the electromagnetic spectrum.

▲ Police often use radar to catch speeding motorists. Radar waves from a gun bounce off a moving vehicle. The frequency at which they return gives its speed.

WAVELENGTH AND FREQUENCY
If you divide the speed of a wave (measured in meters per second) by its frequency (measured in Hertz), you can work out its wavelength (in meters). For example, a sound wave that travels at 344m/sec and has a frequency of 688 Hz has a wavelength of 0.5m (because 344 ÷ 688 = 0.5).

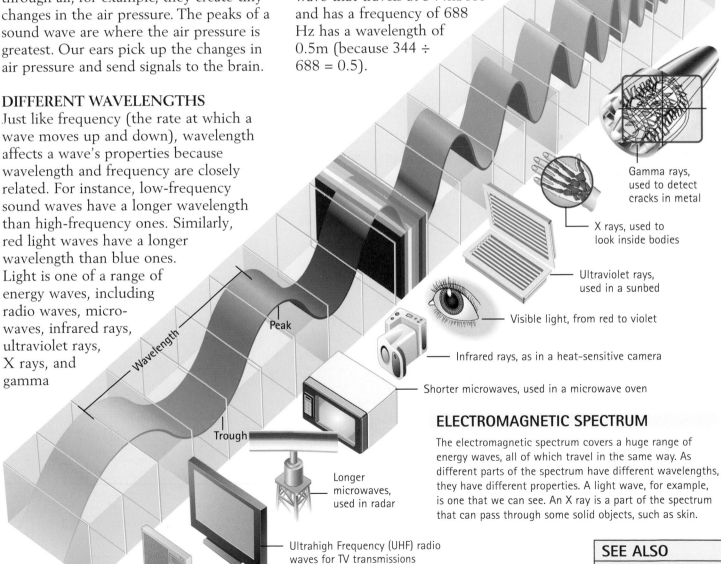

Wavelength

Peak

Trough

Gamma rays, used to detect cracks in metal

X rays, used to look inside bodies

Ultraviolet rays, used in a sunbed

Visible light, from red to violet

Infrared rays, as in a heat-sensitive camera

Shorter microwaves, used in a microwave oven

Longer microwaves, used in radar

Ultrahigh Frequency (UHF) radio waves for TV transmissions

Radio waves used in radio broadcasts

ELECTROMAGNETIC SPECTRUM
The electromagnetic spectrum covers a huge range of energy waves, all of which travel in the same way. As different parts of the spectrum have different wavelengths, they have different properties. A light wave, for example, is one that we can see. An X ray is a part of the spectrum that can pass through some solid objects, such as skin.

SEE ALSO
Energy, Light, Musical instrument, Radar and sonar, Radio, Sound, X ray

WEATHER

Atmospheric conditions, such as rain, wind, and sunshine, make up the weather at a particular place and time. Weather may change slowly or rapidly.

An anemometer is used to measure the speed of the wind. Its sensitive shells move in the wind's path.

A barograph records changes in air pressure on a rotating drum, using an inked pen to draw a graph.

The psychrometer uses a dry bulb and a wet bulb to measure the humidity in the air.

Thermometers measure air temperature. Many meteorological instruments are now digital.

The weather depends on the way air masses move around the globe. The climate of a place is the average of these weather conditions over a long period of time. Though weather may change within hours, climates change over years. Meteorologists study the weather and its causes, and work on weather forecasts.

CAUSES OF WEATHER
The way that air masses are driven depends on factors such as distance from the equator and the presence of mountains or seas. When an air mass moves from the sea over high ground, it cools, and the water it contains falls as rain. If an air mass moves from the center of a continent, it contains no water and brings dry weather. If a mass of air rests over tropical waters for a long time, it becomes extremely moist and warm, leading to severe storms.

REGULAR CYCLES
The weather follows regular cycles. In many areas, the summer means warmer weather than the winter because more solar (sun) energy is received during long, hot days. In Southeast Asia, the monsoon period is dominated by warm, wet winds from the Indian Ocean, causing heavy rains. Every ten years or so, a phenomenon called El Niño occurs: the temperature of the southeast Pacific Ocean rises slightly, which alters the movements of air masses. This can lead to drought, severe rainstorms, and economic disaster.

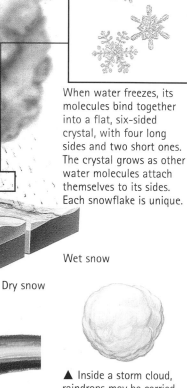

Stratus cloud

When water freezes, its molecules bind together into a flat, six-sided crystal, with four long sides and two short ones. The crystal grows as other water molecules attach themselves to its sides. Each snowflake is unique.

Wet snow

Dry snow

Sleet

Rain

Drizzle

Temperature

▲ When rain clears quickly after a shower, a colorful rainbow may stretch across the sky. Sunlight shines on water droplets, and light is bent, or refracted, until it is split into spectrum colors.

▲ Inside a storm cloud, raindrops may be carried up by air currents and frozen in the clouds. Layers of ice build up as water vapor freezes onto these icy crystals. The growing hailstones fall to warmer levels, then rise again until they are heavy enough to fall from the clouds.

RAIN AND SNOW

Two main types of rain occur. In the tropics, rain forms when tiny droplets come into contact in a cloud, join together, and fall. Rain outside the tropics can be caused by melting snowflakes. If the base of a stratus cloud is low enough, rain falls as drizzle. Dry snow falls when the ground temperature is cold, but if snow falls into air that is above freezing, sleet (a mixture of rain and snow) occurs.

1 The Sun heats one area of ground, such as bare soil, more than others. On warm days, bubbles of hot air form over these areas, and rise up through the cooler air around them.

2 Warm air rises into low-pressure air, then expands and cools. The air cools so much that water vapor condenses into droplets, and a small cumulus cloud is formed.

3 As it is fed by a series of air bubbles, the cloud grows, and the wind detaches it. Fair-weather cumulus clouds look like cotton balls. They do not carry enough water to cause rain.

▲ Radiosondes are balloons that carry instruments to measure temperature, air pressure, and humidity in the upper atmosphere.

HIGH AND LOW PRESSURE

In most parts of the world, weather is determined by areas of low air pressure (cyclones) or areas of high pressure (anticyclones). Some last for months; the Bermuda High is an anticyclone that appears in the North Atlantic during the summer. Others last only a few days or weeks. In tropical areas, belts of low pressure can be massive and move slowly westward. As they suck in warm air, heavy rain and storms are created.

FRONTS

When a mass of cold air meets a mass of warm air, a front develops. If cold air cuts sharply under warm air, a cold front forms. The warm air rises rapidly, cools, and produces heavy rains. If warm air rises slowly, it produces a warm front marked by long periods of gentle rain and drizzle.

DESTRUCTIVE WEATHER

Although most thunderstorms are harmless, a large storm can produce strong winds, heavy rain, lightning, and hail. In 1986, a storm in Gopalganj, India, created a downpour of hailstones weighing 2.2 lb (1kg) each, killing 100 people in a few seconds. Lightning kills around 200 people a year and starts over 20,000 fires. Tornadoes form when thunderstorms create strong updrafts. The spinning air can reach 310 mph (500kph) and wreak destruction along a path 0.6 mi. (1km) wide and 62 mi. (100km) long.

FORECASTING

Traditionally, people have forecast weather either by watching the sky or noticing the behavior of animals, which is affected by basic weather changes. Modern weather forecasting is based on the global movement of areas of low and high pressure and fronts, which is tracked using satellite photographs.

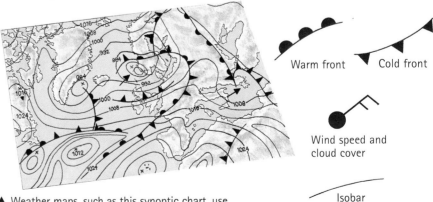

▲ Weather maps, such as this synoptic chart, use standard symbols. Isobars are lines that connect places where air pressure is the same. Winds flow parallel to isobars; the closer together they are, the stronger the wind. Air pressure (in millibars) is shown at centers of low and high pressure. Wind speed, and warm and cold front symbols, are also shown.

◀ ▲ As water droplets collide in a large cloud, water becomes electrically charged. Positive charges collect at the cloud's top, and negative charges at the bottom. As a negative charge meets a positive charge on the ground, forked lightning flashes; sheet lightning flashes between clouds. Thunder is the sound of hot air expanding.

Warm front   Cold front

Wind speed and cloud cover

Isobar

SEE ALSO

Climate, Ecology, Electricity, Light, Satellite, Season, Water

WEIGHTS AND MEASURES

Weights and measures are the standard units that we use to work out how much we have of things. Each form of measurement needs its own kind of "ruler."

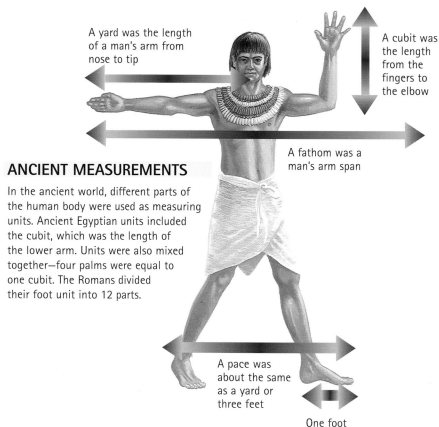

A yard was the length of a man's arm from nose to tip

A cubit was the length from the fingers to the elbow

A fathom was a man's arm span

A pace was about the same as a yard or three feet

One foot

ANCIENT MEASUREMENTS

In the ancient world, different parts of the human body were used as measuring units. Ancient Egyptian units included the cubit, which was the length of the lower arm. Units were also mixed together—four palms were equal to one cubit. The Romans divided their foot unit into 12 parts.

▲ Units based on the hand included the digit, which was the width of a finger. This later became the inch. A span was the length from thumb to little finger, and there was also the palm unit.

E ver since people started making things, trading goods, or carrying out experiments, they have needed to measure amounts. Ancient civilizations based their measurements on parts of the body. These were standard (the same) only within each civilization. An Egyptian cubit, for example, was different from a Greek or Roman cubit. This caused many problems, especially when people needed to trade with one another. That's why, over time, standard measurement systems have come into use.

TRADITIONAL MEASUREMENTS

Most people in the U.S. use the imperial system of measurement. This measures length in inches, feet, yards, and miles; and weight in ounces, pounds, and tons. The use of the foot as a unit of measurement dates back to Anglo-Saxon times. The inch (3 grains of barley, lengthwise) dates to the 1300s, when it was established as one

twelfth of a foot. The mile has its origins in measuring thousands of paces. Ounces and pounds are units of the *avoirdupois* ("goods sold by weight") system, in use since at least the 1400s. The imperial system isn't always easy to use, however, and people who took complex measurements realized they needed a simpler system. In the 1790s, the metric system was created in France.

METRIC SYSTEM

Most countries now use the metric system, or SI (Système International). The basic units are the meter (length) and the kilogram (weight). There are many other units with their own special names such as the joule, the newton, and the volt. However, scientists can relate most of them to the basic set: one newton (1N), for example, the unit of force, can also be written as one kilogram meter per second per second (1kg m/sec^2).

SETTING STANDARDS

A laboratory near Paris holds examples of the SI units—the Standard Meter is the length of a certain number of wavelengths of a specially made laser beam. The Standard Kilogram is the weight of a special ingot of platinum-iridium metal, stored at a controlled temperature.

▲ Scales have been used to weigh objects for sale for thousands of years. Here, they are used to weigh dried flower and plant remedies for sale at an herbalist dispensary.

WEIGHT

Metric

1,000 milligrams (mg)	=	1 gram (g)
1,000 grams	=	1 kilogram (kg)
100kg	=	1 quintal (q)
1,000kg	=	1 metric ton or tonne (t)

Standard

16 ounces (oz.)	=	1 pound (lb.)
112 lb.	=	1 hundredweight (cwt.)
20 cwt.	=	1 (long) ton (= 2,240lb.)
2,000 lb.	=	1 short ton

Conversions

1 gram	=	0.035oz.
1kg	=	2.205 lb.
1 metric ton or tonne (t)	=	2,200 lb.
1t	=	0.984 (long) tons
1 oz.	=	28.35g
1 lb.	=	454g
1 (long) ton	=	1.02t

AREA

Metric

100 square mm (mm^2)	=	1 square cm (cm^2)
10,000cm^2	=	1 square metre (m^2)
100m^2	=	1 are (a)
100a	=	1 hectare (ha)
100ha	=	1 square kilometre (km^2)

Standard

144 square inches (in.^{2})	=	1 square foot (ft.^{2})
9 ft.^{2}	=	1 square yard (yd.^{2})
4,840 yd.^{2}	=	1 acre
640 acres	=	1 square mile (mi.^{2})

Conversions

1cm^2	=	0.155 in.^{2}
1m^2	=	10.76 ft.^{2}
1 hectare	=	2.47 acres
1km^2	=	0.386 square miles
1 in.^{2}	=	6.45cm^2
1 ft.^{2}	=	0.093m^2
1 acre	=	0.405 hectares
1 sq. mi.	=	2.59km^2

LENGTH

Metric

10 millimeters (mm)	=	1 centimeter (cm)
100cm	=	1 meter (m)
1,000m	=	1 kilometer (km)

Standard

12 inches (in.)	=	1 foot (ft.)
3 ft.	=	1 yard (yd.)
1,760 yd.	=	1 mile (mi.)

Conversions

1mm	=	0.0394 in.
1cm	=	0.394 in.
1m	=	1.094 yd.
1km	=	0.621 mi.
1 in.	=	2.54cm
1 ft.	=	30.48cm
1 yd.	=	0.914m
1 mi.	=	1.609km

VOLUME

Metric

1,000mm^3	=	1 cubic centimeter (cm^3)
1,000cm^3	=	1 cubic decimeter (dm^3)
1,000dm^3	=	1 cubic meter (m^3)

Standard

1,728 cubic inches (in.^{3})	=	1 cubic foot (ft.^{3})
27 ft.^{3}	=	1 cubic yard (yd.^{3})

Conversions

1cm^3 = 0.06 1 in.^{3}	1m^3 = 35.3 ft.^{3}
1 in.^{3} = 16.4cm^3	1 ft.^{3} = 0.028m^3

CAPACITY

Metric

1,000 milliliters (ml)	=	1 liter (l)
100 liters	=	1 hectoliter (hl)

Standard

4 gills	=	1 pint (= 16 fluid ounces)
2 pints	=	1 quart
4 quarts	=	1 gallon

Conversions

1 liter = 0.908 quart	1 pint = 0.473 liters
1 deciliter = 0.21 pint	

The Egyptians used delicate balancing scales to weigh gold and precious stones. Later, the Babylonians (who lived in what is now Iraq) made standard weights from metal to use at markets.

The builders of the pyramids in Egypt had to measure length so that they knew how many stones they needed, as well as how to drive shafts accurately through the huge structures.

The measuring cup is used to measure liquids in fluid ounces (imperial units) and milliliters (metric units). Wine bottles usually hold 700 or 750 milliliters (ml) of wine when they are full.

SEE ALSO

Babylon, Clock, Gravity, Time

WHALE AND DOLPHIN

Whales, dolphins, and porpoises are collectively known as cetaceans, which means "large sea animal." They are divided into two groups: toothed and baleen whales.

A white-sided dolphin eats fish and has 92–128 teeth. It is found in large schools of up to 1,000 dolphins.

A rough-toothed dolphin is a small (up to 8 ft./ 2.5m), tropical species known to follow ships.

Porpoises are the smallest cetaceans (up to 6.5 ft./ 2m). The most common species is the harbour porpoise.

The adult beluga, or white whale, is pure white, but the young are gray. Belugas have no dorsal fin.

True's beaked whale has a single pair of teeth, in the lower jaw. It is found in the North Atlantic.

A male bottle-nosed dolphin grows up to 13 ft. (4m). It eats squid, cuttlefish, and herring.

There are 14 species of baleen whale and about 74 toothed whale species, including 38 species of marine dolphin, four river dolphin species, and six species of porpoise. Cetaceans may look like fish, but whales and dolphins are warm-blooded, air-breathing mammals.

FROM EARTH TO SEA

Whales first appeared on Earth over 50 million years ago. Their ancestors once lived on land, but then moved into the water and gradually lost their back legs; their front legs became flippers. The flippers are used for steering and balance, but the power comes from the big tail with its horizontal fins or flukes. The tail is waved up and down to drive the whale forward. (Fish have vertical tail fins, waved from side to side.)

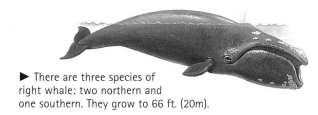

▶ There are three species of right whale: two northern and one southern. They grow to 66 ft. (20m).

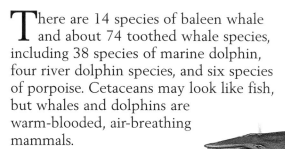

◀ Fin whales belong to the rorqual and humpback family that have grooved throats. They grow to 65 ft. (20m).

▶ Bowhead whales grow up to 60 ft. (18m), and their baleen plates can be 9 ft. (3m) long. They belong to the right whale family.

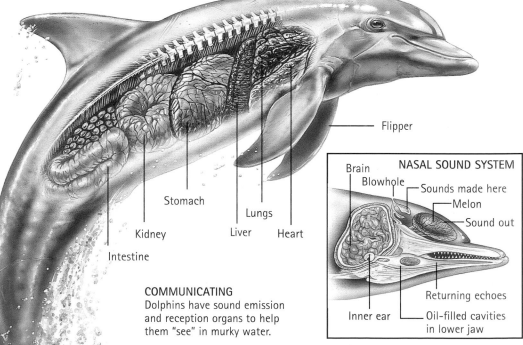

Flipper

Stomach

Kidney

Lungs

Liver   Heart

Intestine

COMMUNICATING
Dolphins have sound emission and reception organs to help them "see" in murky water.

NASAL SOUND SYSTEM

Brain
Blowhole
— Sounds made here
— Melon
— Sound out

Returning echoes

Inner ear   Oil-filled cavities in lower jaw

SEEING WITH SOUND

Dolphins communicate, find food, and navigate using a kind of radar sound system under water. They make high-frequency clicking noises by blowing air through their nasal passages. Then the melon (a waxy cavity in the dolphin's head) focuses the sound into a beam. Sound vibrations travel through the water and bounce off objects. A dolphin receives the sound echoes through an area in its jaw, where the bones are thinner. The echoes then travel to the inner ear.

STRAIN OR BITE

There are two types of whale: baleen whales and toothed whales. Baleen whales are filter feeders that strain tiny creatures from the water through fringed curtains of a horny material called baleen or whalebone.

◀ Blue whale

▲ The number and size of teeth varies with species. Dolphins (above) have conical, interlocking teeth, porpoises have spade-shaped teeth, and most beaked whales only have two visible pairs.

THERE SHE BLOWS

Whales come to the surface to breathe. As they breathe out, warm moist air rushes out through nostrils on the top of the head—the blowhole. This "blow" may reach 33 ft. (10m) into the air. They then take a few breaths through the blowhole and dive down for several minutes. Toothed whales have just one blowhole; baleen whales have two.

FRIENDLY GIANT

The blue whale is the largest animal that has ever lived on Earth. It can reach a length of 100 ft. (30m) and a weight of 165 tons—as heavy as 20 full-grown elephants. Like most of the other large whales, the blue whale has no teeth. It is a baleen whale that feeds on tiny plankton and krill living near the surface of the sea. Other whales and dolphins have many teeth and feed on fish, squid, seals, and penguins.

SMILING DOLPHINS

Dolphins are small whales with a pointed snout and appear to have a permanent smile. They are playful and intelligent animals. They live in groups called schools and communicate with clicks and whistles. They use sound location to navigate and find fish to eat. An injured dolphin will usually be helped by other members of the school. There are even reports of dolphins helping drowning people. Like all whales, dolphins never come ashore. They mate and give birth to their young in the sea. A mother dolphin feeds her baby on her milk for a year and they often stay together for several years.

▲ Narwhals grow up to 18 ft. (5.5m) with no dorsal fin and two teeth. In males, one tooth develops into a spiral tusk up to 9 ft. (2.7m) long.

▲ Sperm whales are a family of three species. They are the largest toothed whales (growing to 66 ft./20m) and the deepest divers. They eat mostly squid.

◀ Orcas, or killer whales, are dolphins with a tall (6.5 ft./2m), sharklike fin. They have long, sharp teeth and eat young whales, seals, squid, or fish.

SEE ALSO

Animal, Conservation, Mammal, Migration

WIND

Wind is the movement of air over Earth's surface. It can range from a gentle summer breeze to the destructive power of a hurricane or tornado.

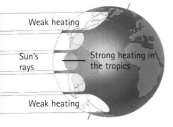

▲ The Sun is strongest in the tropics, where it is almost overhead. Closer to the poles, the Sun's rays are more spread out and therefore weaker.

North Pole (high pressure)

Sun's rays

South Pole (high pressure)

▲ Wind is the flow of air from high- (H) to low-pressure areas (L). This creates six main bands of air across the globe.

Wind is the movement of air from an area of high pressure to an area of low pressure. A wind is named after the direction from which it is blowing. So a north wind is one blowing from the north.

BLOWING HOT AND COLD

Big global wind systems such as the trade winds and easterlies are caused by the heating effect of the Sun. Near the equator, the Sun is almost overhead, and so the land, sea, and air receive the maximum amount of heat. Warm air tends to rise (just as a hot-air balloon rises), and because it is rising, it does not press down so much on Earth's surface. This creates a low-pressure area. Colder, heavier air sinks down toward Earth's surface in cooler regions, farther from the equator, and this creates high-pressure areas. The cooler, heavier air flows over Earth's surface from high-pressure areas to low-pressure areas, creating winds.

▲ Hurricanes form in the late summer and fall over warm areas in the Atlantic, Pacific, and Indian oceans. They then move westward, along the coasts.

LOCAL WINDS

Local winds arise from a combination of weather patterns and the shape of the land. Land heats up and cools down quicker than water, and this produces the gentle breezes you often feel at the coast. During the day, the land heats up, the air above it warms up and rises, and moist air flows in from the sea to replace it, creating a cool sea breeze. At night, the land cools quickly, the air above it descends and spreads out, and this produces a light offshore breeze. Other local winds form around mountains, especially where there are glaciers. At night, cold, heavy air pours down the hillsides and valleys, and out over the surrounding lowlands.

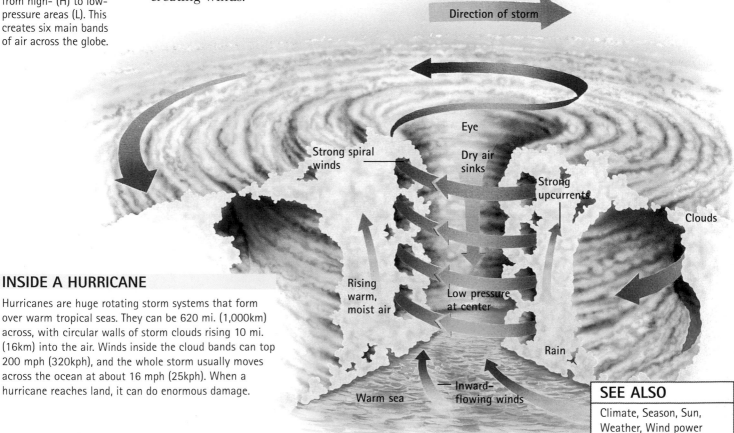

Direction of storm

Eye

Dry air sinks

Strong spiral winds

Strong upcurrents

Clouds

Rising warm, moist air

Low pressure at center

Rain

Inward-flowing winds

Warm sea

INSIDE A HURRICANE

Hurricanes are huge rotating storm systems that form over warm tropical seas. They can be 620 mi. (1,000km) across, with circular walls of storm clouds rising 10 mi. (16km) into the air. Winds inside the cloud bands can top 200 mph (320kph), and the whole storm usually moves across the ocean at about 16 mph (25kph). When a hurricane reaches land, it can do enormous damage.

SEE ALSO
Climate, Season, Sun, Weather, Wind power

WIND POWER

Wind power uses the power of the wind to turn machinery or generate electricity. It is a renewable, nonpolluting source of energy.

Fantail

Windmills have been used to grind corn or pump water from the ground for hundreds of years. Simple windmills may have been used in ancient Persia (now Iran) in the A.D. 600s. Modern windmills, called wind turbines, use the turning motion of the blades to spin a turbine, which generates electricity.

▲ The addition of a fantail, invented in 1745, automatically turned the top of the mill so that the sails caught the wind.

SPINNING SAILS
In a windmill, four to eight wind sails, each 10–30 ft. (3–9m) long, catch the wind. As they spin, a shaft turns. Gears transfer the power to turn a heavy grinding stone at the bottom of the building. Spring sails made of wooden shutters, invented in 1772, could be adjusted to turn steadily in varying winds.

WIND TURBINES
Windmills were largely replaced in the 1900s by engine power. But wind turbines are a growing energy source. Pioneered in Denmark in the 1890s, they use airfoils like airplane propellers to turn a turbine and

▲ Although often only 1,640 ft. (500m) across, tornadoes unleash a devastating force. They form over land, like dark funnels of cloud and can contain winds of over 250 mph (400kph)—strong enough to demolish buildings and throw around cars like toys.

make electricity. Used to supply electricity in remote areas, wind farms may have hundreds of wind turbines, with blades 50–100 ft. (15–30m) in diameter. The largest wind farms can generate more than 750 megawatts, nearly as much electricity as a nuclear power plant produces. Although non-polluting, wind farms use great areas of land.

WIND FARMS
Wind turbines need to be made so that they turn, even in gentle wind, and also cope with gales. They also need to be built where there is plenty of wind, such as along the coast or on flat plains. These places are usually a long way from where the electricity is needed, and much energy is lost sending it along power lines.

FAST FACTS
• The sailboat is one of the most common users of wind power

• China is the country with the biggest installed wind power capacity (34 per cent of global wind capacity).

• By 2050, between 25 and 30 percent of the world's electricity may be generated using wind power

SEE ALSO
Boat, Electricity, Wind

WOLF AND OTHER WILD DOGS

Wolves, coyotes, jackals, and foxes are all kinds of wild dog. They are strong, quick, alert carnivores, many of which hunt in packs.

A skillful hunter, the red fox lives in Asia, Europe, and North America.

In winter, the long fur of the Arctic fox turns from brown or gray to white.

Known for its eerie howl, the coyote is found in Canada, the U.S., and Mexico.

Wolves belong to the group known as *Canidae*, or the dog family. This group also includes the gray, red, and maned wolf, coyote, and dingo, African and Asian (dhole) wild dogs, raccoon and bush dogs, 4 kinds of jackal, about 20 kinds of fox—as well as the hundreds of breeds and varieties of domestic dog. These were probably tamed and bred from wolf ancestors at least 10,000 years ago.

FEATURES OF THE HUNTER

All members of the dog family are meat- eaters, or carnivores. They live by hunting or scavenging. But they eat almost anything if they are hungry, even fruits and berries. They have acute senses, including sharp eyesight and hearing, and an excellent sense of smell. Their long, strong legs, which they use for fast running and relentless pursuit, have clawed toes for good grip and scratching. Their long, sharp teeth bite and tear flesh.

WHERE WOLVES LIVE

The gray, or timber, wolf, usually just known as the wolf, is widespread across North America, parts of Europe, the Middle East, and northern Asia. It prefers forests but can live in mountains, grasslands, and even deserts. The red wolf is extremely rare,

◄ When gathering to begin a hunt, wolves greet each other with loud howls. This warns wolves from other packs to stay out of their territory.

▲ In each pack, some wolves are more dominant than others. Here, a dominant wolf stands with its tail and ears held up, while a subordinate wolf approaches it in a crouched position, tail between legs and ears flattened.

limited to a small area of southeast North America. The maned wolf, which is really more like a long-legged fox, dwells in grassy scrubland in central South America.

WILD DOGS AROUND THE WORLD

The coyote, with its mournful howl, is a wolflike wild dog that has extended its territory from the southwestern United States and Mexico. In Australia, the dingo is probably descended from the part-tamed dogs of Aboriginal people, brought to the continent more than 7,000 years ago. Jackals live across Africa, the Middle East, and southern Asia. Different kinds of bushy-tailed fox dwell in almost every habitat, from the Arctic fox of the snowy far north, to the Cape fox of southern Africa's deserts, and the well-known, widespread, and adaptable red fox, which scavenges trash in towns and cities.

KEY FACTS

• Various members of the dog family can breed with each other. For example, a domestic dog and a coyote produce coydog puppies. This interbreeding makes it difficult to know exactly how many true species are in the dog family

• The main difference between wolves and dogs that look like them is that wolves carry their tail hanging down while dogs carry it curled up

• The crab-eating fox of South America really does eat crabs, and tortoises, too, but it prefers easier meat, such as mice, birds, lizards, insects, and eggs

HUNTING IN PACKS

Many wild dogs, especially wolves and African and Asian wild dogs, hunt with others of their kind. The group is called a pack. It can catch much larger prey than one dog hunting alone. A pack of wolves can bring down a full-grown moose over 6.5 ft. (2m) high. Each pack has dominant males, or leaders, who get the best food and mate with females at breeding time.

A VARIETY OF PREY

Other wild dogs, especially foxes, live and hunt alone, or with a mate. Jackals have a reputation as scavengers. In fact, they usually hunt live prey—from frogs, lizards, and mice to small gazelles and young zebras. Smaller wild dogs usually eat smaller meals. Most foxes have a diet of mice, voles, fish, frogs, birds, eggs, and insects. The smallest kind, the fennec fox, with huge ears, survives in the Sahara and Middle Eastern deserts by consuming small beetles, spiders, locusts, and worms.

▲ The dingo, which can be bred with the domestic dog, howls, but rarely barks. Dingoes come together to run down and kill large prey, such as kangaroos.

A DOG'S LIFE

Wolves have long been feared in legend and have therefore been persecuted. In fact, wolves attack people only when threatened or if they are extremely hungry. Many other wild dogs are also hunted, and some are endangered. People shoot, poison, or trap them in case they raid farm animals. Also some kinds, especially foxes, are still killed for their handsome fur pelts.

The jackal is up to 30 in. (75cm) in length. It has a strong body smell.

The raccoon dog lives throughout eastern Asia and is mainly nocturnal.

The African wild dog lives in large parts of Africa, and hunts its prey in packs.

PACK HUNTERS

Wolves hunt in packs, feeding on almost any animal that they can catch. In order to kill prey such as reindeer and elk, which are faster and stronger than they are, wolves must be quick and skillful. Wolves hunt by day and by night, roaming through territory until they find prey. They stalk it by moving toward it against the wind to prevent it from picking up their scent. Once close enough, the wolves break into a run and the chase begins. If they succeed in catching their victim, they weaken it through injury, then grab it by the throat.

SEE ALSO

Animal, Desert, Dog, Mammal

WOMEN'S RIGHTS

Women's rights are those civil rights that have traditionally been denied to women in many societies. Women have had to struggle to gain these rights.

MARY WOLLSTONECRAFT (1759–97), Irish–English writer of one of the first feminist books, *Vindication of the Rights of Women* (1792). A later pamphlet, *Thoughts on the Education of Daughters* (1797), criticized girls' schooling.

ELIZABETH CADY STANTON (1815–1902), organized the first women's rights assembly in the U.S.A. in 1848. She fought for fair property and divorce laws for married women, coeducation, and the right to vote (suffrage).

EMMELINE PANKHURST (1858–1928), a women's rights leader in the U.K., founded the Women's Social and Political Union (1902), campaigning for the right to vote. She and her daughter, Christabel, were imprisoned many times.

I n different societies the status of men and women has varied greatly. Today it is generally thought that men and women should have equal rights, and some countries have laws to make forms of discrimination (unfair treatment) illegal.

ANCIENT RIGHTS
The role of women within society has varied greatly. In ancient Greece, women had few rights. They were expected to stay at home and to take no part in social life. Some Greek teachers believed it was wrong to teach women to read in case they learned too much and disagreed with the men. In ancient Egypt, however, women played a full part in society. They could take jobs, own property, and divorce their husbands. Some became rulers, but usually after the death of a husband.

DIVISION OF LABOR
In traditional farming communities, the work of a family was divided. Men mainly carried out heavy physical work. Women took on

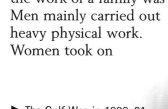

▶ The Gulf War, in 1990–91, was the first conflict that saw female soldiers of the U.S. Army fighting alongside men.

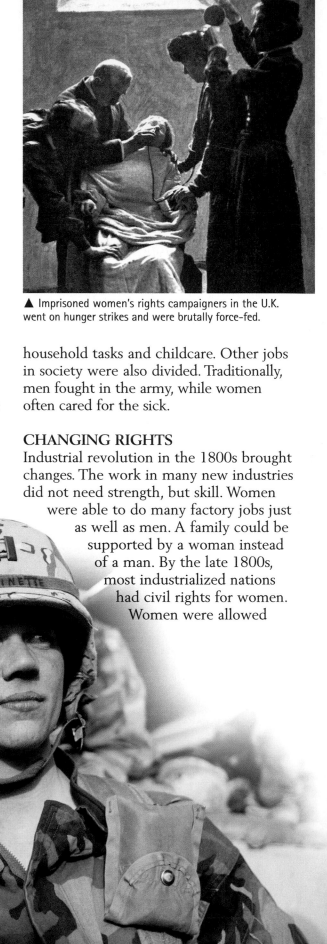

▲ Imprisoned women's rights campaigners in the U.K. went on hunger strikes and were brutally force-fed.

household tasks and childcare. Other jobs in society were also divided. Traditionally, men fought in the army, while women often cared for the sick.

CHANGING RIGHTS
Industrial revolution in the 1800s brought changes. The work in many new industries did not need strength, but skill. Women were able to do many factory jobs just as well as men. A family could be supported by a woman instead of a man. By the late 1800s, most industrialized nations had civil rights for women. Women were allowed

to keep their own property when they married, instead of giving control to their husbands. They could enter into contracts and sign legal papers, teach, and become nurses and doctors, although education for girls was still less formal than for males and ended at an earlier age.

THE VOTE

For a long time only those who owned property could vote. During the 1800s, this was challenged. The right to vote (suffrage) was extended to poor men, but not to women. In 1869, Elizabeth Cady Stanton and Susan B. Anthony founded the National Woman Suffrage Association;

▲ During the two world wars, many Western women took jobs making weapons in factories. It was their war efforts that led to greater recognition of women's value.

in the same year Lucy Stone set up the rival National American Woman Suffrage Association. Activists were called suffragists. In the U.K., Emmeline Pankhurst organized the Women's Social and Political Union; U.K. activists were called suffragettes.

SLOW PROGRESS

Women in New Zealand were the first to get the vote, in 1893—but Maori women had to wait until 1967. By the 1920s, most democracies had given women the vote, although Swiss women won it only in the 1970s. Many Arab countries only gave women the right to vote in the early 2000s.

SHIFTING HORIZONS

During the 1960s, a movement called Women's Liberation sought to make women equal to men in social and economic terms. Gradually women's choices have widened. Today there are female doctors, lawyers, and judges. The number of women running companies is slowly rising. It is not unusual to see women as bus drivers, firefighters, or construction workers. Women have taken frontline roles in some Western armies. Even so, balancing a career and motherhood is still a dilemma for many women.

▲ Israel's Golda Meir was deputy foreign minister in 1948 and later foreign minister. She became the Israeli prime minister in 1969.

◄ In 1996, the Taliban (fundamentalist Muslims) took over the government in Afghanistan. They banned girls from schools, women from working, and made women cover themselves. In 2001, the Taliban government was overthrown.

SEE ALSO

Civil rights, Democracy, Education, Industrial Revolution, Israel, Textile, World War II

WORLD WAR I

World War I was a terrible war fought between 1914 and 1918 in which millions of people died. It began in Europe, but spread to many parts of the globe.

Kaiser Wilhelm II (1859–1941) of Germany led an aggressive foreign policy against other nations.

Lloyd George (1863–1945), British prime minister from 1916, reorganized the war effort for victory.

Russia's Tsar Nicholas II (1868–1918) backed Serbia against Austria, bringing Russia into the war.

People living at the time called World War I "the Great War" because no other war had been so widespread nor so destructive. Millions of soldiers were killed and the world economy changed forever.

OUTBREAK OF WAR

In 1914, Europe was divided into two major alliances. The Hapsburg Empire was allied to Germany to block Russian moves in the Balkans, while France sided with Russia against the growing might of Germany. On June 28, 1914, the Hapsburg archduke Franz Ferdinand was shot dead by a Serb terrorist, prompting the Hapsburgs to declare war on Serbia. Serbia, in turn, asked for help from the Russians, who then declared war on the Hapsburgs. This brought Germany and France into the war. Britain joined the war when Germany invaded Belgium.

EARLY BATTLES

In the east, Russian armies were smashed by the Germans at Tannenberg, while Hapsburg armies were defeated by the Russians in several encounters during the month of September. In the west, the Germans intended to capture Paris and defeat France, but were stopped on the Marne River on September 8, 1914, while the British army blocked outflanking moves to the north. By October, the armies had settled into trenches for the winter.

NEW WEAPONS

Barbed wire barriers, machine guns, and artillery made defense so strong that attacks were almost useless. Troops experimented with poison gas to help attackers, but it rarely had much effect. Tanks, first used by the British in 1916,

▲ World War I began after Serb terrorist Gavrilo Princip killed the Hapsburg archduke Franz Ferdinand. Princip was sentenced to 20 years in prison, but got sick and died in 1918.

could defeat barbed wire or machine guns, but they often broke down. Aircraft were more successful and were used to spy on enemy troops, target artillery shells, and drop bombs. The German pilot Manfred von Richthofen, nicknamed the "Red Baron," successfully shot 80 enemy aircraft down in flames.

WORLD WAR

In Africa, British and French troops attacked German colonies. In 1915, Australian and New Zealand troops attacked Turkey at Gallipoli, but were badly defeated and sustained heavy losses. At sea, German ships and submarines sank Allied ships, and in 1917 began attacking any ships heading for Allied ports. The United States first protested about these attacks on its ships, and then joined the Allies, declaring war on Germany.

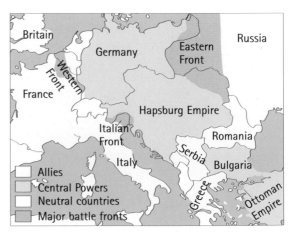

▲ Trench warfare led to small battlefronts. Only on the Eastern Front were sweeping movements made.

◄ Russian Cossacks and other cavalry were used for scouting, but were useless in the trenches.

Aircraft were a new weapon, used for scouting and fighting.

The small Serb army was driven out of Serbia into Greece in December 1915.

FINAL MOVES

In 1917, the Communists took over Russia and made peace. The German troops, freed from Russia, launched a massive attack in March 1918 in France. American troops helped stop the attack. But Bulgaria, Turkey, and the Hapsburgs were close to collapse and Germany asked for peace. A ceasefire was finally agreed on November 11, 1918.

TRENCH WARFARE

The war in the West was fought from trenches guarded by barbed wire and machine guns. Conditions were appalling, with knee-deep mud, constant shelling, sniping, and raids. The battles of the Somme and Verdun in France in 1916 cost over two million casualties, although neither side managed to advance more than a few hundred yards.

THE WAR ENDS

The cost of World War I was immense. Germany lost 1.9 million men, Russia 1.7 million, France 1.5 million, and Britain and the Hapsburgs 1 million each, as well as vast amounts of money. The Hapsburg Empire was split into Austria, Hungary, Czechoslovakia, and Yugoslavia. Poland, Estonia, Latvia, and Lithuania became independent. European countries lost economic power as others built up their industries. The world was changed forever.

Britain had the smallest army in 1914, but it was made up of professionals.

In 1914, the German army was the largest and best trained in the world.

Machine gun post in the French trenches

German troops

SEE ALSO
Communism, Empire, Warfare, World War II

WORLD WAR II

World War II was fought between 1939 and 1945. It involved more countries, cost more lives, and caused more destruction than any other war.

The American B17 Flying Fortress

Erwin Rommel (1891–1944) was a daring leader of German armored units.

Yamamoto Isoroku (1884–1943) planned Japan's attack on Pearl Harbor.

Bernard Montgomery (1887–1976) led the British in North Africa and Europe.

Georgy Zhukov (1896–1974) commanded the Soviet Red Army.

Dwight D. Eisenhower (1890–1969) led the D-Day invasion of 1944.

Adolf Hitler in Germany, Benito Mussolini in Italy, and General Tojo Hideki in Japan wanted to extend the power and territories of their countries. They formed a pact, called the Axis, to gain what they wanted.

BLITZKRIEG

In September 1939, Germany invaded Poland to regain land it had lost in World War I. Britain and France supported Poland. The Germans used a tactic called *blitzkrieg*—lightning war. Bomber aircraft began the attack, then tanks, or panzers, plunged deep behind enemy lines, followed by infantry and artillery. Poland was defeated in just five weeks. In April 1940, Hitler invaded Denmark, Belgium, Holland, Norway, and France. By July, only Britain had not surrendered. In the Battle of Britain, the determined Royal Air Force beat off German air attacks.

INTO RUSSIA

Hitler wanted to expand Germany and create *lebensraum* ("living space") for the German nation. In June 1941, 3.5 million German, Italian, Romanian, and Hungarian troops stormed into Russia, capturing vast territories. In December, a reinforced Red Army finally stopped the invaders just outside Moscow.

The Japanese Mitsubishi Ki-67, codenamed "Peggy"

The German Dornier Do217

The British Avro Lancaster

▲ Small bombers, such as the Dornier and Mitsubishi, were used to destroy battlefield targets, such as tanks and artillery. The Lancaster, Flying Fortress, and other heavy bombers pounded cities and factories.

PEARL HARBOR

Japan wanted to capture large areas of Southeast Asia to secure industrial raw materials. The Japanese hoped that a quick defeat would persuade the United States to allow Japanese expansion, so they launched a surprise attack on Pearl Harbor. The U.S. did not give way, but declared war. The same day, Japan invaded Southeast Asia. By May 1942, Japan had conquered Burma (Myanmar), Malaya, the Philippines, and the East Indies.

THE TIDE TURNS

After three years of war, the Allies had built up their armed forces. In North Africa, German and Italian troops were defeated at El Alamein in October 1942, and in December 1942, the German 6th Army was

◄ On December 7, 1941, 360 Japanese aircraft attacked Pearl Harbor, Hawaii, the base of the U.S. Pacific Fleet. The attack opened the way for Japanese conquests and brought the U.S. into the war.

▶ Germany, Japan, and their allies made large conquests in 1939–42. But the greater resources of the Allies were brought into action after 1942.

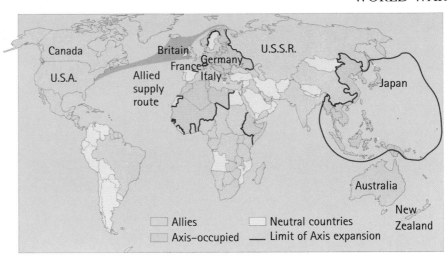

wiped out at Stalingrad. The Japanese were halted in February 1943. The Allies then organized strike forces to retake Burma, and to use island-hopping tactics in the Pacific.

GERMANY COLLAPSES

In June 1944, Germany was caught between the landings in Normandy, France and the Russian advance. On April 30, 1945, Hitler killed himself; a week later Germany surrendered. The Allies found that the Nazis had murdered millions, six million of them Jews, in the worst case of mass human extinction in history. It has come to be called the Holocaust. Jewish people refer to it as the Shoah, meaning "chaos" or "annihilation."

THE ATOMIC BOMB

With the war over in Europe, President Truman wanted to bring U.S. troops home from the Pacific—Japanese forces were determined to fight on. To end the war and cut casualties, the U.S. decided to use the atomic bomb. It obliterated the cities of Hiroshima and Nagasaki; 200,000 people died. Japan surrendered on September 2, 1945.

PEACE AND COLD WAR

The war had cost the lives of some 15 million troops and 35 million civilians. After the war, the world divided into two powerful blocs: the communist countries, led by the Soviet Union and China, and the democratic world, led by the United States. The Cold War had begun.

▲ The Allied leaders, Winston Churchill (left), Franklin D. Roosevelt (center), and Joseph Stalin, met at Yalta in 1945 to decide the postwar arrangements for Europe.

D-DAY

At dawn on June 6, 1944, the largest invasion fleet in history landed Allied forces on the coast of Normandy. In all, 1,200 warships and 4,100 landing craft put 132,500 soldiers ashore, while 10,000 aircraft attacked German positions inland. The success of the D-Day invasion allowed American, British, and French troops to drive the Germans out of France.

SEE ALSO

Cold War, Fascism, Great Depression, Warfare, World War I

WORM

Worms are legless invertebrates (animals with no backbone). There are four major groups: ribbon worms, flatworms, roundworms, and segmented worms.

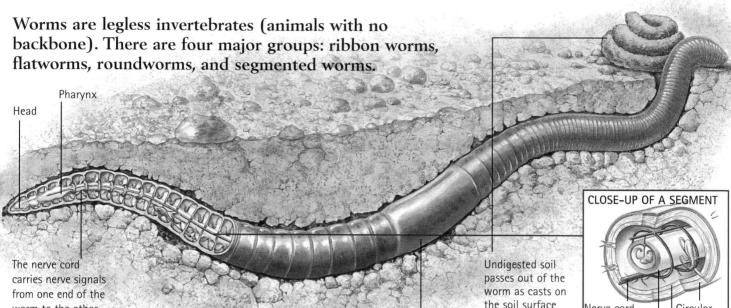

Head

Pharynx

The nerve cord carries nerve signals from one end of the worm to the other

Clitellum—produces cases for worm eggs

Undigested soil passes out of the worm as casts on the soil surface

CLOSE-UP OF A SEGMENT

Nerve cord

Intestine

Longitudinal muscle

Circular muscle

A lugworm (segmented) has feathery gills.

A horse leech (segmented) can grow to 1 ft. (30cm).

Flatworms can cause serious illnesses in humans.

Roundworms make up the largest group of worms.

Ribbon worms live in the sea and can be 6.5 ft. (2m).

A ragworm (segmented) has strong jaws to eat prey.

There are thousands of kinds of worm. The simplest, such as flatworms, are found mostly in the sea or are parasites that live inside animals and humans. Ribbon worms are like long flatworms— the bootlace worm grows to 85 ft. (25m).

EARTHWORMS
The earthworms that tunnel in gardens belong to a group called annelids, or segmented worms. Their bodies are made of many ringlike sections. There are hundreds of species of earthworm and all feed by swallowing soil and digesting any decaying matter in it. They also pull dead leaves into their tunnels and eat them. Earthworms are important for farmers and gardeners because their tunnels drain and bring air into the soil and allow plant roots to grow. There are no separate male and female worms: each one has both male and female parts. After mating, which usually takes place above ground at night, each worm lays its own eggs.

BLOOD-SUCKING LEECHES
Leeches are related to earthworms, but instead of having bristles for moving they have a large sucker at each end. Most of them live in water or damp soil and feed on other animals. Some of the bigger ones are bloodsuckers and may attack people.

SLITHERING SEGMENTS
Each segment of an earthworm's body has several little bristles on the underside and these enable the worms to move through their tunnels. The bristles of one group of segments dig into the walls like anchors while powerful muscles push or pull the others forward. There are no lungs; respiration takes place through the body surface.

PARASITIC WORMS
Many flatworms and roundworms (also called nematodes) live inside other animals as parasites. Hooks or suckers on their head cling to the lining of the host's intestines and the worms soak up digested food. Tapeworms, which can reach 98 ft. (30m), produce many eggs, which pass out with the host's droppings. Some eggs find their way into new host animals.

▲ Peacock worms live in the sea. They catch food with bristles and live in a tube made from secretions.

SEE ALSO

Animal, Blood, Earth, Sight, Zoology

X RAY

X rays are a form of energy that can pass straight through many solid materials. We use X rays to look inside bodies and machines and to kill some cancers.

▲ X ray radiation was discovered by the German physicist Wilhelm Roentgen (1845–1923), who was awarded the first Nobel Prize for Physics in 1901.

▼ High doses of X rays can damage body cells. The harmful effects of X rays are often used to help cure cancers. Powerful beams of X rays are directed at cells in a tumor, killing them off.

If you break a bone, you will probably go to the hospital for an X ray. An X ray image lets the doctor see where your bone is fractured or damaged. A special machine directs a narrow beam of X rays at the part of your body that needs examining. Unlike light waves, these X rays can pass right through the soft parts of your body, the skin and muscles.

X RAY IMAGE

When X rays come through your body, they hit a photographic plate, where they form an image. Because your bones and teeth are heavy and dense, they block the path of the X rays. This is why they leave blank areas on the X ray image. Trained people can look at these blank areas and work out the exact shape of your skeleton.

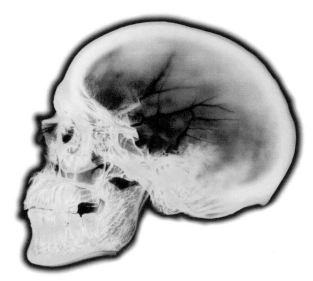

▲ This X ray image of a human skull found at a Roman burial site reveals a missing top molar tooth.

SOFT TISSUE

Sometimes, doctors use X rays to look at softer, lighter parts of your body, such as the liver or bladder. To do this, they inject you with a special chemical called barium sulfate. This makes these tissues block the path of X rays. The body gets rid of this chemical naturally after a few hours.

MACHINES AND CRYSTALS

X rays are not only used to look inside people. They are also used to examine the insides of certain machines. Aircraft makers, for example, take X ray images of various machine parts to make sure they have no inner cracks. Chemists take X ray images of crystals. They use these to study how the X rays bounce off a crystal's inner structure. This can help them work out how the atoms in the crystal are arranged.

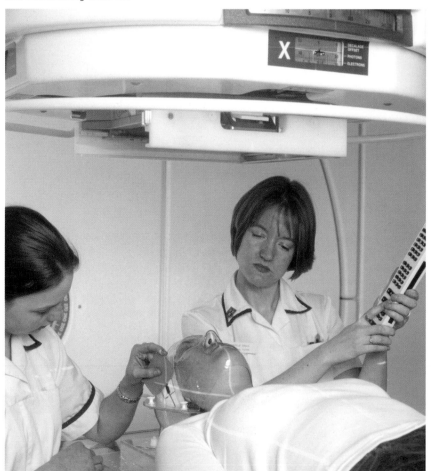

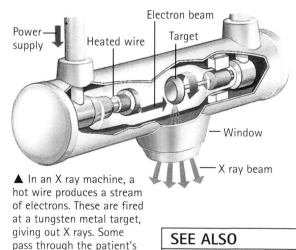

▲ In an X ray machine, a hot wire produces a stream of electrons. These are fired at a tungsten metal target, giving out X rays. Some pass through the patient's body, making an image on film or a fluorescent screen.

Power supply — Heated wire — Electron beam — Target — Window — X ray beam

SEE ALSO

Astronomy, Atom and molecule, Light, Medicine, Wavelength

ZOOLOGY

Zoology is the scientific study of all animals–their body structure, how they live, feed, breed, move, and behave–in nature or captivity.

Nearctic Realm

Palearctic Realm

◀ The roe deer is one of the few animals that is naturally confined to the Palearctic Realm. It has relatives in other areas.

Oriental Realm

▲ The giant panda weighs up to 350 lb. (160kg), lives in China, and eats mainly bamboo. Most attempts to breed it have failed.

▲ The bald eagle is a species of eagle found in the Nearctic Realm. It is the U.S.A.'s national bird.

Neotropical Realm

Ethiopian Realm

Australasian Realm

◀ A pygmy hippopotamus can be up to 6 ft. (1.8m). It faces extinction through being hunted in Africa.

▲ Australia has many marsupials, such as the kangaroo rat, found only in the Australasian area.

▶ Sloths are a family of South American animals that move slowly and hang upside down through trees.

GROUPING ANIMALS

Zoologists divide the Earth into six distinct regions, or realms, following the work, in the 1800s, of British wildlife expert, Alfred Russel Wallace. He first noticed that whole orders or families of animals, birds, and freshwater fish may be confined to one region. This map shows the six realms and an example of the animals found only in each area.

The animal kingdom is vast, varied, and complicated. Zoology has many specialist branches. These often overlap. Some branches deal with particular groups of animals. For example, entomology is the detailed study of insects. Ichthyology specializes in fish. Herpetology is the study of amphibians and reptiles.

LEARNING ABOUT ANIMALS

Other branches of zoology deal with the features that animals share. Anatomists study the structure of an animal's body and the parts inside, such as the heart, nerves, intestines, and kidneys. Physiologists look at how these parts work, for example how worms take food from soil or how fish take in oxygen through gills. Embryologists deal with development of animals before birth.

THE LIVING AND THE DEAD

Some areas of zoology are very wide-ranging. Ethologists watch animal behavior—their actions and instincts. Ecologists study how a creature fits into its surroundings or habitat. They observe its needs, such as food and shelter, and its predators. Paleontologists study fossil remains that tell us about prehistoric life, such as dinosaurs. They deal with dead remains, but still need a good knowledge of living animals to reconstruct finds and compare them with other creatures.

WHAT ZOOLOGISTS DO

Some zoologists are desk-based, writing reports or books. Others work in laboratories, carrying out tests and experiments. Some are based in museums, zoos, or wildlife parks, and others are in the field—watching, taking notes on, and photographing animals in the wild. Many deal with the media: for example, campaigning to save endangered creatures or giving pet advice.

▼ A keeper at Chester Zoo (U.K.) bottle-feeds a baby giraffe. Breeding threatened species is one invaluable role of a zoo. Many breed animals in captivity to help boost their dwindling numbers in the wild.

SEE ALSO

Animal, Conservation, Evolution, Mammal, Prehistoric animal

Propelled by rocket engines, the supersonic X-15 holds the world air-speed record at 4,510 mph (7,274kph) set in 1967.

The funeral mask of the pharaoh Tutankhamen was found in his tomb, discovered in 1922.

The first washing machine (invented by Hamilton Smith, U.S.A., 1858) still relied on muscle power.

On April 12, 1961, Yuri Gagarin of the U.S.S.R. became the first person in space onboard *Vostok 1*.

The steam gun carriage of 1769, invented by French engineer Cugnot, was the first motorized vehicle.

FACTFINDER

Whether for school projects, or just for fun, this section provides facts, figures, and other essential information– from a world map to presidents and states, and on to biographies of famous figures, finishing with the highlights of the past 10 years. Timelines present key international (top) and U.S. (bottom) developments.

The *chanoyu*, a Japanese tea ceremony which can last four hours, actually originated in China.

In 1834, Charles Babbage (1792-1871) designed the first mechanical computer, but he never saw it built.

The Venus flytrap is a carnivorous plant that feeds on the insects it traps in its leaves.

U.S. astronauts use a Manned Maneuvering Unit (MMU) to guide themselves when floating free in space. This contains several small rocket thrusters pointing in different directions. When one is fired, the astronaut moves in the opposite direction.

The Arctic tern is a long-distance flyer, making an annual round trip of up to 25,000 mi. (40,000km).

Camptosaurus was an ornithopod ("bird-footed") dinosaur that lived about 150 million years ago.

Edgar Allan Poe (1809-49) was one of America's greatest poets and an early writer of horror stories.

COUNTRIES OF THE WORLD

A R C T I C

Greenland
(Denmark)

Jan Mayen
(Norway)

Arctic Circle

UNITED STATES
OF AMERICA
(ALASKA)

ICELAND

Faeroe Islands
(Denmark)

C A N A D A

UNITED
KINGDOM   DENMARK

A T L A N T I C   REPUBLIC OF   NETHERLANDS
IRELAND   BELGIUM

O C E A N   Channel Islands   LI
(UK)   SW
FRANCE
MONACO

St Pierre &   ANDORRA
Miquelon
(France)   PORTUGAL   SPAIN

UNITED STATES
OF AMERICA   Azores   Gibraltar
(Portugal)   (UK)

Bermuda   Madeira
(UK)   (Portugal)   MOROCCO

Tropic of Cancer   Canary Islands (Spain)   ALGERIA

BAHAMAS   WESTERN
SAHARA
Hawaiian Islands   Turks Is (UK)   British   (occupied by Morocco)   MAURITANIA   MALI
(US)   MEXICO   CUBA   Navassa   Virgin Is (UK)
Island   DOMINICAN   Virgin Is
Johnston Atoll   Cayman Is   Puerto Rico   St Martin (France and Neth)   CAPE VERDE
(US)   (UK)   HAITI   REPUBLIC   (US)   Anguilla (UK)
JAMAICA   St Barthélemy (France)
BELIZE   ANTIGUA & BARBUDA   SENEGAL
GUATEMALA   Montserrat (UK)   GAMBIA
HONDURAS   Guadeloupe (France)   GUINEA-BISSAU   GUINEA
Kingman Reef (US)   EL SALVADOR   DOMINICA   SIERRA LEONE
Palmyra Atoll (US)   NICARAGUA   Martinique (France)   LIBERIA   IVORY
Clipperton Island   Aruba (Neth)   ST LUCIA   COAST
(France)   COSTA   Bonaire (Neth)   BARBADOS   EQUATORIAL GUINE
Jarvis Island   RICA PANAMA   Curaçao (Neth)   ST VINCENT & THE GRENADINES
Equator   (US)   GRENADA
KIRIBATI   VENEZUELA   TRINIDAD & TOBAGO   SÃO TOM
& PRINCI
Galapagos Islands   French
(Ecuador)   ECUADOR   COLOMBIA   GUYANA   Guiana
(France)

P A C I F I C   SURINAME

American   Cook   O C E A N   PERU   B R A Z I L   Ascension
Samoa   Islands   Island
(US)   (NZ)   (St Helena)

Niue   BOLIVIA
(NZ)   St Helena
French Polynesia   (UK)
(France)   PARAGUAY
Tropic of Capricorn   Pitcairn Islands
(UK)   A T L A N T I C

Easter Island
(Chile)   URUGUAY   O C E A N
Juan   A R G E N T I N A
Fernández Islands
(Chile)   Tristan da Cunha
(St Helena)

Gough Island
(Tristan da Cunha)

Falkland Islands
(UK)

South Georgia   Bouvet Island
(UK)   (Norway)

South Sandwich Islands
(UK)

S O U T H

Antarctic Circle

A N T A R C T I C A

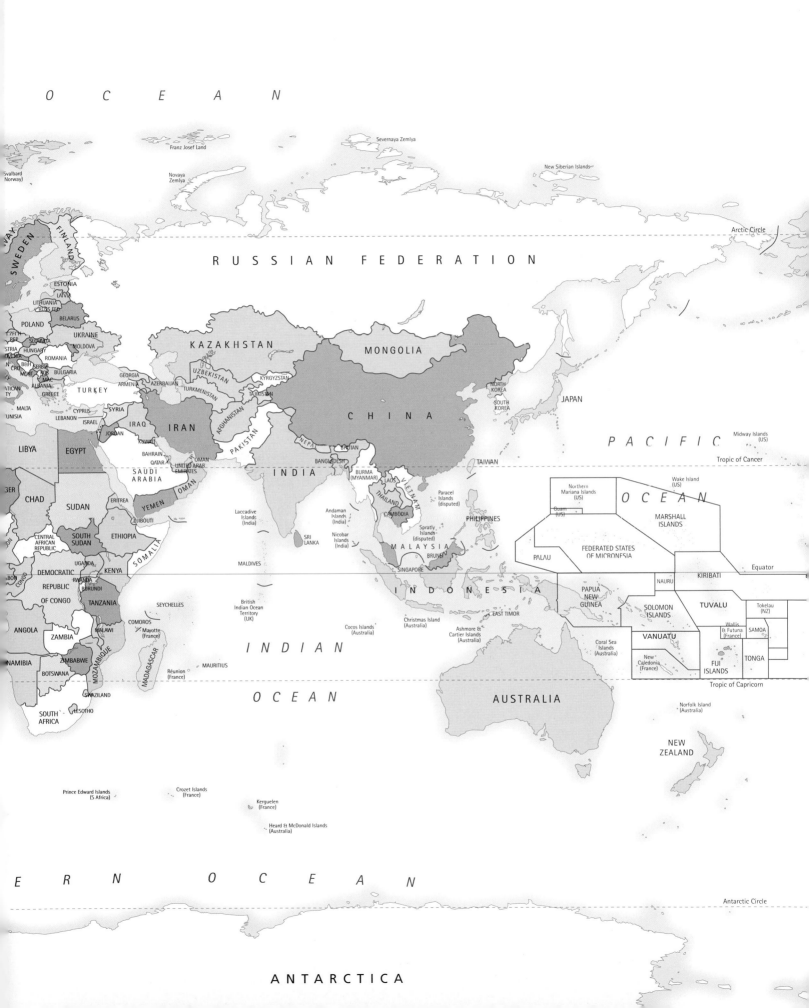

STATES OF THE UNITED STATES

STATE	CAPITAL	POPULATION (2017 ESTIMATE)	(RANK)	AREA (IN SQ. MI.)	(RANK)	ENTRY INTO UNION	(ORDER)
Alabama	Montgomery	4,872,725	(24)	52,419	(30)	December 14, 1819	(22)
Alaska	Juneau	746,079	(48)	663,267	(1)	January 3, 1959	(49)
Arizona	Phoenix	7,044,577	(14)	113,998	(6)	February 14, 1912	(48)
Arkansas	Little Rock	2,998,643	(32)	53,179	(29)	June 15, 1836	(25)
California	Sacramento	39,506,094	(1)	163,696	(3)	September 9, 1850	(31)
Colorado	Denver	5,632,271	(21)	104,094	(8)	August 1, 1876	(38)
Connecticut	Hartford	3,568,174	(29)	5,543	(48)	January 9, 1788	(5)
Delaware	Dover	960,054	(45)	2,489	(49)	December 7, 1787	(1)
Florida	Tallahassee	20,979,964	(3)	65,755	(22)	March 3, 1845	(27)
Georgia	Atlanta	10,421,344	(8)	59,425	(24)	January 2, 1788	(4)
Hawaii	Honolulu	1,431,957	(40)	10,931	(43)	August 21, 1959	(50)
Idaho	Boise	1,713,452	(39)	83,570	(14)	July 3, 1890	(43)
Illinois	Springfield	12,764,031	(6)	57,914	(25)	December 3, 1818	(21)
Indiana	Indianapolis	6,653,338	(17)	36,418	(38)	December 11, 1816	(19)
Iowa	Des Moines	3,147,389	(30)	56,272	(26)	December 28, 1846	(29)
Kansas	Topeka	2,907,857	(35)	82,277	(15)	January 29, 1861	(34)
Kentucky	Frankfort	4,449,337	(26)	40,409	(37)	June 1, 1792	(15)
Louisiana	Baton Rouge	4,694,372	(25)	51,840	(31)	April 30, 1812	(18)
Maine	Augusta	1,333,505	(42)	35,385	(39)	March 15, 1820	(23)
Maryland	Annapolis	6,037,911	(19)	12,407	(42)	April 28, 1788	(7)
Massachusetts	Boston	6,839,318	(15)	10,555	(44)	February 6, 1788	(6)
Michigan	Lansing	9,938,885	(10)	96,716	(11)	January 26, 1837	(26)
Minnesota	St. Paul	5,557,469	(22)	86,939	(12)	May 11, 1858	(32)
Mississippi	Jackson	2,988,062	(34)	48,430	(32)	December 10, 1817	(20)
Missouri	Jefferson City	6,109,796	(18)	69,704	(21)	August 10, 1821	(24)
Montana	Helena	1,052,967	(44)	147,042	(4)	November 8, 1889	(41)
Nebraska	Lincoln	1,920,467	(37)	77,354	(16)	March 1, 1867	(37)
Nevada	Carson City	2,996,358	(33)	110,561	(7)	October 31, 1864	(36)
New Hampshire	Concord	1,339,479	(41)	9,350	(46)	June 21, 1788	(9)
New Jersey	Trenton	8,953,517	(11)	8,721	(47)	December 18, 1787	(3)
New Mexico	Santa Fe	2,081,702	(36)	121,589	(5)	January 6, 1912	(47)
New York	Albany	19,743,395	(4)	54,556	(27)	July 26, 1788	(11)
North Carolina	Raleigh	10,258,390	(9)	53,819	(28)	November 21, 1789	(12)
North Dakota	Bismarck	759,069	(47)	70,700	(19)	November 2, 1889	(39)
Ohio	Columbus	11,623,656	(7)	44,825	(34)	March 1, 1803	(17)
Oklahoma	Oklahoma City	3,939,708	(28)	69,898	(20)	November 16, 1907	(46)
Oregon	Salem	4,162,296	(27)	98,381	(9)	February 14, 1859	(33)
Pennsylvania	Harrisburg	12,776,550	(5)	46,055	(33)	December 12, 1787	(2)
Rhode Island	Providence	1,057,245	(43)	1,545	(50)	May 29, 1790	(13)
South Carolina	Columbia	5,027,404	(23)	32,020	(40)	May 23, 1788	(8)
South Dakota	Pierre	872,989	(46)	77,116	(17)	November 2, 1889	(40)
Tennessee	Nashville	6,707,332	(16)	42,143	(36)	June 1, 1796	(16)
Texas	Austin	28,295,553	(2)	268,581	(2)	December 29, 1845	(28)
Utah	Salt Lake City	3,111,802	(31)	84,899	(13)	January 4, 1896	(45)
Vermont	Montpelier	623,100	(49)	9,614	(45)	March 4, 1791	(14)
Virginia	Richmond	8,456,029	(12)	42,774	(35)	June 25, 1788	(10)
Washington	Olympia	7,415,710	(13)	71,300	(18)	November 11, 1889	(42)
West Virginia	Charleston	1,821,151	(38)	24,230	(41)	June 20, 1863	(35)
Wisconsin	Madison	5,789,525	(20)	65,498	(23)	May 29, 1848	(30)
Wyoming	Cheyenne	584,447	(50)	97,814	(10)	July 10, 1890	(44)

American Indian ancestors arrive from Asia — 38000 B.C.–8000 B.C.

Folsom culture in the Great Plains — 9000 B.C.–8000 B.C.

Olmec civilization in Mexico and Central America — 1200 B.C.–100 B.C.

Maya civilization in Central America — A.D. 300–900

Mound Builders in Mississippi Valley — 700

Vikings explore NE coast of North America — 1000

PRESIDENTS OF THE UNITED STATES

	NAME (PARTY)*	BIRTH-DEATH DATES	TERM IN OFFICE	VICE PRESIDENT(S)
1.	George Washington (F)	1732 – 1799	Apr. 30, 1789 – Mar. 4, 1797	John Adams
2.	John Adams (F)	1735 – 1826	Mar. 4, 1797 – Mar. 4, 1801	Thomas Jefferson
3.	Thomas Jefferson (D–R)	1743 – 1826	Mar. 4, 1801 – Mar. 4, 1809	Aaron Burr George Clinton
4.	James Madison (D–R)	1751 – 1836	Mar. 4, 1809 – Mar. 4, 1817	George Clinton Elbridge Gerry
5.	James Monroe (D–R)	1758 – 1831	Mar. 4, 1817 – Mar. 4, 1825	Daniel D. Tompkins
6.	John Quincy Adams (D–R)	1767 – 1848	Mar. 4, 1825 – Mar. 4, 1829	John C. Calhoun
7.	Andrew Jackson (D)	1767 – 1845	Mar. 4, 1829 – Mar. 4, 1837	John C. Calhoun, Martin Van Buren
8.	Martin Van Buren (D)	1782 – 1862	Mar. 4, 1837 – Mar. 4, 1841	Richard M. Johnson
9.	William Henry Harrison (W)	1773 – 1841	Mar. 4, 1841 – Apr. 4, 1841	John Tyler
10.	John Tyler (W)	1790 – 1862	Apr. 4, 1841 – Mar. 4, 1845	—
11.	James K. Polk (D)	1795 – 1849	Mar. 4, 1845 – Mar. 4, 1849	George M. Dallas
12.	Zachary Taylor (W)	1784 – 1850	Mar. 4, 1849 – July 9, 1850	Millard Fillmore
13	Millard Fillmore (W)	1800 – 1874	July 9, 1850 – Mar. 4, 1853	—
14.	Franklin Pierce (D)	1804 – 1869	Mar. 4, 1853 – Mar. 4, 1857	William R. King
15.	James Buchanan (D)	1791 – 1868	Mar. 4, 1857 – Mar. 4, 1861	John C. Breckinridge
16.	Abraham Lincoln (R)	1809 – 1865	Mar. 4, 1861 – Apr. 15, 1865	Hannibal Hamlin, Andrew Johnson
17.	Andrew Johnson (R)	1808 – 1875	Apr. 15, 1865 – Mar. 4, 1869	
18.	Ulysses S. Grant (R)	1822 – 1885	Mar. 4, 1869 – Mar. 4, 1877	Schuyler Colfax Henry Wilson
19.	Rutherford B. Hayes (R)	1822 – 1893	Mar. 4, 1877 – Mar. 4, 1881	William A. Wheeler
20.	James A. Garfield (R)	1831 – 1881	Mar. 4, 1881 – Sept.19, 1881	Chester A. Arthur
21.	Chester A. Arthur (R)	1829 – 1886	Sept.19, 1881 – Mar. 4, 1885	—
22.	Grover Cleveland (D)	1837 – 1908	Mar. 4, 1885 – Mar. 4, 1889	Thomas A. Hendricks
23.	Benjamin Harrison (R)	1833 – 1901	Mar. 4, 1889 – Mar. 4, 1893	Levi P. Morton
24.	Grover Cleveland (D)	1837 – 1908	Mar. 4, 1893 – Mar. 4, 1897	Adlai E. Stevenson
25.	William McKinley (R)	1843 – 1901	Mar. 4, 1897 – Sept.14, 1901	Garret A. Hobart Theodore Roosevelt
26.	Theodore Roosevelt (R)	1858 – 1919	Sept.14, 1901 – Mar. 4, 1909	Charles W. Fairbanks
27.	William H. Taft (R)	1857 – 1930	Mar. 4, 1909 – Mar. 4, 1913	James S. Sherman
28.	Woodrow Wilson (D)	1856 – 1924	Mar. 4, 1913 – Mar. 4, 1921	Thomas R. Marshall
29.	Warren G. Harding (R)	1865 – 1923	Mar. 4, 1921 – Aug. 2, 1923	Calvin Coolidge
30.	Calvin Coolidge (R)	1872 – 1933	Aug. 3, 1923 – Mar. 4, 1929	Charles G. Dawes
31.	Herbert Hoover (R)	1874 – 1964	Mar. 4, 1929 – Mar. 4, 1933	Charles Curtis
32.	Franklin D. Roosevelt (D)	1882 – 1945	Mar. 4, 1933 – Apr. 12, 1945	John N. Garner Henry A. Wallace Harry S. Truman
33.	Harry S. Truman (D)	1884 – 1972	Apr. 12, 1945 – Jan. 20, 1953	Alben W. Barkley
34.	Dwight D. Eisenhower (R)	1890 – 1969	Jan. 20, 1953 – Jan. 20, 1961	Richard M. Nixon
35.	John F. Kennedy (D)	1917 – 1963	Jan. 20, 1961 – Nov. 22, 1963	Lyndon B. Johnson
36.	Lyndon B. Johnson (D)	1908 – 1973	Nov. 22, 1963 – Jan. 20, 1969	Hubert H. Humphrey
37.	Richard M. Nixon (R)	1913 – 1994	Jan. 20, 1969 – Aug. 9, 1974	Spiro T. Agnew Gerald R. Ford
38.	Gerald R. Ford (R)	1913 – 2006	Aug. 9, 1974 – Jan. 20, 1977	Nelson A. Rockefeller
39.	Jimmy Carter (D)	1924 –	Jan. 20, 1977 – Jan. 20, 1981	Walter F. Mondale
40.	Ronald Reagan (R)	1911 – 2004	Jan. 20, 1981 – Jan. 20, 1989	George Bush
41.	George Bush (R)	1924 –	Jan. 20, 1989 – Jan. 20, 1993	Dan Quayle
42.	Bill Clinton (D)	1946 –	Jan. 20, 1993 – Jan. 20, 2001	Al Gore
43.	George W. Bush (R)	1946 –	Jan. 20, 2001 – Jan. 20, 2009	Richard Cheney
44.	Barack Obama (D)	1961 –	Jan. 20, 2009 – Jan. 20, 2017	Joe Biden
45.	Donald J. Trump (R)	1946 –	Jan. 20, 2017 –	Mike Pence

*Federalist (F), Whig (W), Democratic–Republican (D–R), Republican (R), Democrat (D)

George Washington refused a third term as the first U.S. President.

Abraham Lincoln was the first president assassinated in office.

Franklin D. Roosevelt led the U.S. during the Depression and WWII.

John F. Kennedy symbolized the young spirit of the 1960s.

The Statue of Liberty welcomes all who enter New York Harbor.

Sir John A. MacDonald led the first government of Canada as a Dominion.

POPULATION OF LARGEST AMERICAN CITIES (2017 estimate)

RANK	CITY	POPULATION	RANK	CITY	POPULATION	RANK	CITY	POPULATION
1.	New York City, NY	8,516,502	26.	Portland, OR	630,621	51.	Pittsburgh, PA	303,864
2.	Los Angeles, CA	3,949,149	27.	Oklahoma City, OK	630,618	52.	Cincinnati, OH	298,654
3.	Chicago, IL	2,713,596	28.	Las Vegas, NV	622,448	53.	Anchorage, AK	298,312
4.	Houston, TX	2,284,816	29.	Baltimore, MD	621,402	54.	Lincoln, NE	276,611
5.	Phoenix, AZ	1,582,904	30.	Louisville, KY	614,748	55.	Orlando, FL	270,483
6.	Philadelphia, PA	1,564,964	31.	Milwaukee, WI	599,413	56.	Buffalo, NY	258,351
7.	San Antonio, TX	1,468,037	32.	Albuquerque, NM	557,448	57.	Madison, WI	248,613
8.	San Diego, CA	1,390,915	33.	Tucson, AZ	528,441	58.	Reno, NV	240,667
9.	Dallas, TX	1,297,327	34.	Fresno, CA	518,503	59.	Baton Rouge, LA	228,320
10.	San Jose, CA	1,022,627	35.	Sacramento, CA	489,202	60.	Boise, ID	220,281
11.	Austin, TX	930,152	36.	Kansas City, MO	474,862	61.	Des Moines, IA	214,814
12.	Jacksonville, FL	867,164	37.	Atlanta, GA	462,970	62.	Spokane, WA	213,080
13.	San Francisco, CA	862,004	38.	Colorado Springs, CO	455,535	63.	Rochester, NY	209,734
14.	Indianapolis, IN	852,295	39.	Raleigh, NC	449,947	64.	Little Rock, AR	198,195
15.	Columbus, OH	850,044	40.	Omaha, NE	445,273	65.	Grand Rapids, MI	195,094
16.	Fort Worth, TX	834,171	41.	Miami, FL	440,864	66.	Salt Lake City, UT	191,438
17.	Charlotte, NC	826,395	42.	Oakland, CA	417,870	67.	Tallahassee, FL	189,802
18.	Seattle, WA	683,505	43.	Minneapolis, MN	410,116	68.	Knoxville, TN	185,196
19.	Denver, CO	680,032	44.	Tulsa, OK	403,105	69.	Chattanooga, TN	176,220
20.	El Paso, TX	678,570	45.	New Orleans, LA	389,738	70.	Sioux Falls, IA	171,622
21.	Detroit, MI	676,336	46.	Cleveland, OH	387,812	71.	Fort Collins, CO	161,854
22.	Washington, DC	670,377	47.	Tampa, FL	368,494	72.	Syracuse, NY	144,053
23.	Boston, MA	665,984	48.	Honolulu, HI	352,048	73.	Charleston, SC	132,454
24.	Memphis, TN	654,454	49.	Corpus Christi, TX	324,508	74.	Ann Arbor, MI	118,765
25.	Nashville, TN	654,078	50.	St. Louis, MO	314,875	75.	Fargo, ND	118,542

THE PROVINCES AND TERRITORIES OF CANADA

PROVINCES	CAPITAL	POPULATION (2016 CENSUS)	(RANK)	AREA IN SQ. MI.	(RANK)	DATE BECAME PROVINCE
Alberta	Edmonton	4,067,175	(4)	255,287	(4)	1905
British Columbia	Victoria	4,648,055	(3)	365,948	(3)	1871
Manitoba	Winnipeg	1,278,365	(5)	250,947	(6)	1870
New Brunswick	Fredericton	747,101	(8)	28,355	(8)	1867
Newfoundland	St. John's	519,716	(9)	156,649	(7)	1949
Nova Scotia	Halifax	923,598	(7)	21,425	(9)	1867
Ontario	Toronto	13,448,494	(1)	412,581	(2)	1867
Prince Edward Island	Charlottetown	142,907	(10)	2,185	(10)	1873
Quebec	Quebec City	8,164,361	(2)	594,860	(1)	1867
Saskatchewan	Regina	1,098,352	(6)	251,866	(5)	1905

TERRITORIES	CAPITAL	POPULATION (2016 CENSUS)	AREA IN SQ. MI.
Northwest Territories	Yellowknife	41,786	503,951
Nunavut	Iqaluit	35,944	818,959
Yukon Territory	Whitehorse	35,874	186,661

PRIME MINISTERS OF CANADA

NAME	SERVED	POLITCAL PARTY
Sir John A. Macdonald	1867–1873	Conservative
Alexander Mackenzie	1873–1878	Liberal
Sir John A. Macdonald	1878–1891	Convervative
Sir John Abbott	1891–1892	Conservative
Sir John Thompson	1892–1894	Conservative
Sir Mackenzie Bowell	1894–1896	Conservative
Sir Charles Tupper	1896	Conservative
Sir Wilfrid Laurier	1896–1911	Liberal
Sir Robert Borden	1911–1917	Conservative
Sir Robert Borden	1917–1920	Unionist
Arthur Meighen	1920–1921	Unionist
W.L. Mackenzie King	1921–1926	Liberal
Arthur Meighen	1926	Conservative
W.L. Mackenzie King	1926–1930	Liberal
Richard Bennett	1930–1935	Conservative
W.L. Mackenzie King	1935–1948	Liberal
Louis St. Laurent	1948–1957	Liberal
John Diefenbaker	1957–1963	Progressive Conservative
Lester B. Pearson	1963–1968	Liberal
Pierre E. Trudeau	1968–1979	Liberal
Charles Joseph Clark	1979–1980	Progressive Conservative
Pierre E. Trudeau	1980–1984	Liberal
John Turner	1984	Liberal
Brian Mulroney	1984–1993	Progressive Conservative
Kim Campbell	1993	Progressive Conservative
Jean Chrétien	1993–2003	Liberal
Paul Martin	2003–2006	Liberal
Stephen Harper	2006–2015	Conservative
Justin Trudeau	2015	Liberal

INTERNATIONAL ORGANIZATIONS

United Nations (UN)

was founded in 1945. Its goals are to maintain international peace and security, and solve cultural, social, and humanitarian problems. By 2011, it had 193 member nations. Its headquarters are in New York City. The UN's main organs include: the General Assembly, with representatives of all members; the Security Council, with 15 members, 5 of whom (China, France, Russia, U.K., and U.S.) have permanent seats and 10 of whom are elected for 2 years; and the International Court of Justice, or World Court, which sits in The Hague, Netherlands.

Following are eight of the UN's specialized and related agencies:

Food and Agriculture Organization (FAO)

helps improve production and distribution of food and world dietary standards. Headquarters: Rome, Italy.

International Bank for Reconstruction and Development (IBRD),

or World Bank, provides loans and technical help for economic projects in developing countries. Headquarters: Washington, D.C.

International Monetary Fund (IMF)

promotes monetary cooperation and the expansion of world trade. Headquarters: Washington, D.C.

United Nations Children's Fund (UNICEF)

helps children in developing nations. Headquarters: New York City.

United Nations Educational, Scientific, and Cultural Organization (UNESCO)

promotes exchange of information, ideas, and culture. Headquarters: Paris, France.

United Nations High Commissioner for Refugees (UNHCR)

provides assistance to refugees worldwide. It is based in Geneva, Switzerland.

World Health Organization (WHO)

fights disease and helps improve health standards. Headquarters: Geneva, Switzerland.

World Trade Organization (WTO)

administers trade agreements and attempts to settle disputes. Headquarters: Geneva, Switzerland.

Other international organizations include:

AU

African Union, formerly the Organization of African Unity, which was founded in 1963 to promote African unity and co-operation. It has 55 member states.

Caribbean Community and Common Market (CARICOM)

was founded in 1973. Its full members are Antigua and Barbuda, Bahamas, Barbados, Belize, Dominica, Grenada, Guyana, Haiti, Jamaica, Montserrat, St. Kitts & Nevis, St. Lucia, St. Vincent and the Grenadines, Suriname, and Trinidad and Tobago. Headquarters: Georgetown, Guyana.

The Commonwealth,

founded in 1949, is a loose association of Great Britain and more than 52 other nations that were once part of the British Empire. Mozambique, the most recent member, had not been part of the British Empire. Headquarters: London, England.

European Union (EU),

founded in 1952 with 6 members, was originally a free-trade and customs union. It is now a closer political and economic union with 28 members, although the U.K. is currently negotiating withdrawal.

Group of Seven (G7),

is an informal group of seven leading industrialized nations that meet to discuss economic issues. Members are Canada, France, Germany, Japan, Italy, the U.K., and the U.S.

Group of Twenty (G20)

is a group of 19 countries, plus the EU, founded in 1999 to promote international financial stability. Its members contribute more than 80 percent of the world's trade. Members are Argentina, Australia, Brazil, Canada, China, the EU, France, Germany, India, Indonesia, Italy, Japan, Mexico, Russia, Saudi Arabia, South Africa, South Korea, Turkey, the U.K. and the U.S.

International Criminal Police Organization (Interpol),

founded in 1956, promotes cooperation between police authorities in 190 countries. Headquarters: Lyon, France.

League of Arab States,

also known as the Arab League; promotes economic, social, political, and military cooperation among members. Founded in 1945, it has 22 members, including Palestine, which it considers an independent nation. Headquarters: Cairo, Egypt.

North Atlantic Treaty Organization (NATO)

is a military alliance of 29 Western nations. It was founded in 1949 to defend Western Europe, the U.S., and Canada from military aggression. Members are Albania, Belgium, Bulgaria, Canada, Croatia, Czech Republic, Denmark, Estonia, France, Germany, Greece, Hungary, Iceland, Italy, Latvia, Lithuania, Luxembourg, Montenegro, the Netherlands, Norway, Poland, Portugal, Romania, Slovakia, Slovenia, Spain, Turkey, the U.K., and the U.S. Headquarters: Brussels, Belgium.

Organization for Economic Cooperation and Development (OECD)

was founded in 1961. Its goals are to promote economic growth, financial stability, and social welfare in its 35 member nations and to assist developing nations. Headquarters: Paris, France.

Organization of American States (OAS)

was founded in 1948. Its major goal is the peaceful settlement of disputes between nations. It has 35 members. Cuba was suspended from OAS activities from 1962 to 2009. Headquarters: Washington, D.C.

Organization of Petroleum Exporting Countries (OPEC)

was founded in 1960 to coordinate oil production and prices. Members are Algeria, Angola, Ecuador, Equatorial Guinea, Gabon, Iran, Iraq, Kuwait, Libya, Nigeria, Qatar, Saudi Arabia, United Arab Emirates, and Venezuela. Headquarters: Vienna, Austria.

Logo for the League of Arab States, which mediates disputes among its member nations.

Logo for the European Union. This was known as the European Community (EC) until 1994.

The AU flag features an outline of Africa and a circle of stars that stand for its member states.

Since the end of the Cold War in the 1990s, NATO has had to reassess its military role.

BIOGRAPHIES

Leonardo was not only an artist, but also an inventor, mathematician, engineer, and anatomist.

Picasso was the most famous artist of the 20th century. His work changed the course of modern art.

Chaucer's *Canterbury Tales* is a collection of stories told by pilgrims on their journey to Canterbury.

Brought up in poverty himself, Dickens wrote knowledgeably about the lives of the poor.

ARTISTS

Audubon, John James (1785–1851), a U.S. artist and naturalist, was noted for his paintings of birds.

Botticelli, Sandro (c.1445–1510) was an Italian painter. Works such as *Primavera* (Spring) and the *Birth of Venus* reflect the humanist and classical interests of his time.

Copley, John Singleton (1738–1815) is considered the greatest painter of colonial America. He painted portraits of people such as Paul Revere in natural poses.

Cézanne, Paul (1839–1906), a French painter, started out as an impressionist. His paintings showed the effects of light on objects rather than the objects themselves. He later painted colorful, more solid forms.

Degas, Edgar (1834–1917), a French painter and sculptor, was influenced by impressionism and Japanese woodcuts. He was interested in the human form, and many of his subjects were ballet dancers. His paintings include *The Rehearsal* and *Dance Class.*

Giotto (c.1266–1337), an Italian painter, revived the art of painting in the early Renaissance period. He was especially known for his religious frescoes, including *Life of Christ* and the *Last Judgment.*

Goya y Lucientes, Francisco José de (1746–1828), a Spaniard, painted realistic portraits and scenes from everyday life, including *The Disasters of War.*

Hopper, Edward (1882–1967) painted ordinary American scenes. The people in many of his paintings are often shown as lonely or sad.

Homer, Winslow (1836–1910) is considered one of the greatest U.S. artists. His paintings, including *Breezing Up* and *Gulf Stream,* captured the power and beauty of the sea.

Leonardo da Vinci (1452–1519), an Italian painter and scientist, was a genius. His greatest works include the *Last Supper* and the *Mona Lisa.*

Michelangelo (1475–1564), an Italian painter, sculptor, and architect, created the frescoes on the ceiling of the Sistine Chapel and sculptures of the *Pietà* and *David.*

Monet, Claude (1840–1926), a French painter, was one of the creators of the impressionist movement. Among his most famous works are *Impression: Sunrise*, the Rouen Cathedral series, and the Water Lily series.

Picasso, Pablo (1881–1973), a Spaniard, is thought by many to be the greatest artist of the 20th century. With Georges Braque, he developed cubism, a style in which forms are broken down into geometric shapes.

Pollock, Jackson (1912–56), an American, one of the most influential artists of the 20th century, was an abstract expressionist who made the colors and shapes of his paintings reflect his feelings. Among his works are *Autumn Rhythm.*

Rembrandt (Harmenszoon van Rijn) (1606–69) was the greatest of the Dutch old master painters. He did many group portraits and self-portraits. Among his works are *The Night Watch* and *Syndics of the Cloth Guild.*

Rubens, Peter Paul (1577–1640), a Flemish painter, master of the baroque style. He painted portraits, landscapes, and religious and historical subjects.

Turner, Joseph M. W. (1775–1851) was a British landscape painter. He painted in both watercolors and oils. His atmospheric paintings include *The Fighting Téméraire* and *Old Chain Pier at Brighton.*

Van Gogh, Vincent (1853–90), a Dutch painter, was famous for his use of color. His paintings include *Sunflowers* and *Starry Night.*

Warhol, Andy (1926–87) was a U.S. pioneer in "pop art." He painted pop culture objects, such as Campbell's soup cans, and comic-strip characters.

Wren, Sir Christopher (1632–1723) is considered the greatest English architect. His best-known creation was St. Paul's Cathedral in London.

Wright, Frank Lloyd (1869–1959), the greatest U.S. architect of the 20th century, designed such masterpieces as the Falling Water House and the Guggenheim Museum.

WRITERS

Alcott, Louisa May (1832–88), a U.S. author, is best known for the novel *Little Women*, a story about the four March sisters and their family during the Civil War.

Andersen, Hans Christian (1805–75), a Danish writer, was one of the world's greatest storytellers. He is best known for his fairy tales, such as "The Emperor's New Clothes," "The Snow Queen," "The Little Mermaid," and "The Ugly Duckling."

Austen, Jane (1775–1817), an English novelist, wrote about the middle class of English country life in such novels as *Emma*, *Pride and Prejudice*, and *Sense and Sensibility.*

Cervantes, Miguel (1547–1616) was a Spanish novelist and dramatist. His greatest work, *Don Quixote*, details the life of a poor gentleman who wants to be a knight and do knightly deeds.

Chaucer, Geoffrey (c.1345–1400) was an English poet whose most famous work was a group of stories called the *Canterbury Tales.*

Cooper, James Fenimore (1789–1851) wrote novels about the American frontier in the 1700s. His most famous book was *The Last of the Mohicans.*

Dante Alighieri (1265–1321) was Italy's greatest poet. His most famous work was the *Divine Comedy.*

Dickens, Charles (1812–70) was one of England's greatest novelists. Some of his novels, including *Oliver Twist* and *David Copperfield*, drew attention to the plight of the poor and underprivileged.

| 1854 | | 1859 | 1869 | | 1870 | 1870–1914 | 1894–95 |

1854 — Japan opens its doors to trade with the West

1859 — Darwin writes *Origin of Species*

1869 — Suez Canal opens

1870 — France defeated in Franco-Prussian War

1870–1914 — European colonization of Africa and Asia

1894–95 — China defeated in Sino-Japanese War

Dickinson, Emily (1830–86)
was one of the most important U.S. poets of the 1800s. She wrote 1,775 poems, but only a few were published when she was alive.

Frost, Robert (1874–1963)
was one of the most important U.S. poets of the 20th century. He wrote about the people and the land of New England. Among his books of poetry are *New Hampshire* and *In the Clearing*.

Goethe, Johann Wolfgang von (1749–1832)
was a poet, novelist, and playwright of unequaled importance in German literature. His greatest work was *Faust*.

Hawthorne, Nathaniel (1804–64),
born in Massachusetts, was one of the most important American writers of the 1800s. His greatest novel was *The Scarlet Letter*.

Henry, O. (1862–1910)
was one of America's foremost short-story writers. His real name was William Sydney Porter. He wrote more than 300 stories, many with surprise endings. One of his most popular stories is "The Gift of the Magi."

Keats, John (1795–1821),
an English poet, wrote beautiful odes, including "To a Nightingale," "On a Grecian Urn," and "To Autumn."

Longfellow, Henry Wadsworth (1807–82)
was a modern language professor and popular poet who wrote poems about American history including such long poems as *The Song of Hiawatha*.

Melville, Herman (1819–91)
was one of the great U.S. writers. He used his experiences as a sailor when writing his most popular books, *Moby Dick* and *Typee*.

Poe, Edgar Allan (1809–49),
a U.S. author, has been called the father of modern mystery and horror stories. His short stories include "The Fall of the House of Usher" and "The Pit and the Pendulum." Poems include "The Raven" and "The Bells."

Sandburg, Carl (1878–1967)
was one of the most beloved U.S. poets, as well as a biographer. His biography of Abraham Lincoln won the 1940 Pulitzer Prize for history.

Shakespeare, William (1564–1616),
an English dramatist and poet, is considered by many to be the world's greatest writer. His plays include *A Midsummer Night's Dream*, *Hamlet*, and *Macbeth*.

Stevenson, Robert Louis (1850–94)
was a versatile Scottish author. He wrote *A Child's Garden of Verses*, and such adventure stories as *Treasure Island* and *Kidnapped*.

Stowe, Harriet Beecher (1811–96),
a U.S. author, was famous for her novel *Uncle Tom's Cabin*. It made a powerful case against slavery.

Swift, Jonathan (1667–1745)
was an English writer whose books poked fun at the silly, cruel behavior of people and governments. His most famous book is *Gulliver's Travels*.

Tolstoy, Count Leo (1828–1910)
was a Russian novelist. Two of his greatest books were *War and Peace* and *Anna Karenina*.

Twain, Mark (1835–1910)
was a popular U.S. novelist and journalist. His real name was Samuel Clemens. Among his bestselling books were *The Adventures of Tom Sawyer* and *The Adventures of Huckleberry Finn*.

Wordsworth, William (1770–1850)
was one of England's greatest poets. His poetry explores the lives of ordinary people in contact with nature. Together with his friend Samuel Taylor Coleridge, he wrote the *Lyrical Ballads*, which included his poem "Tintern Abbey."

COMPOSERS AND MUSICIANS

Bach, Johann Sebastian (1685–1750),
a German, was one of the world's greatest composers. He wrote concertos and sacred cantatas. His masterpieces include the six *Brandenburg Concertos*, *St. Matthew Passion*, and *B Minor Mass*.

Beethoven, Ludwig van (1770–1827),
a German, wrote sonatas, symphonies, choral and chamber music, and concertos. Major works include his Ninth Symphony, the Piano Concerto no. 5, and the opera *Fidelio*.

Berlin, Irving (1888–1989)
was one of the greatest U.S. writers of popular music. He wrote nearly 1,000 songs, including "*Alexander's Ragtime Band*," "*This Is the Army*," and "*God Bless America*."

Bizet, Georges (1838–75),
a French composer, is most famous for his opera *Carmen*.

Brahms, Johannes (1833–97),
a German Romantic composer and gifted pianist, wrote piano sonatas, symphonies, and choral works.

Britten, Benjamin (1913–76),
a British composer, wrote such operas as *Billy Budd* and *Death in Venice*. He also wrote large-scale instrumental works, including *The Young Person's Guide to the Orchestra*.

Copland, Aaron (1900–90),
U.S. composer best known for using jazz and American folk tunes in his classical compositions. His works include the music for such ballets as *Billy the Kid*, *Rodeo*, and *Appalachian Spring*.

Ellington, Duke (1899–1974)
was the greatest U.S. jazz composer. He wrote more than 2,000 jazz compositions, plus concert works, religious music, and scores for theater, ballet, and film.

Gershwin, George (1898–1937)
was one of the most important U.S. songwriters of the 20th century. He produced many concert works and Broadway musicals. Gershwin's best-known works include *Porgy and Bess*, an opera, and *Rhapsody in Blue*, an orchestral work.

Handel, Georg Frideric (1685–1759),
a German-born British composer, was famous for the oratorio *Messiah*. His orchestral works include *Water Music* and *Music for the Royal Fireworks*.

Haydn, Franz Joseph (1732–1809),
an Austrian composer, was the most famous composer of his day, and he is known as the "father of the symphony." His output included 104 symphonies, about 50 concertos, and 84 string quartets, among other works.

Ives, Charles (1874–1954)
was one of the most important US composers of the 20th century. His works

Tolstoy introduced a new form of Christianity into Russia, writing religious works as well as novels.

Tom Sawyer's adventures on the Mississippi River were based on Twain's own boyhood experiences.

Beethoven's music is among the greatest in the world and still influences composers today.

Duke Ellington was one of America's best-known jazz band leaders of the 1930s. He wrote over 50 hits.

U.S. buys Alaska from Russia — 1867

Spanish-American War; U.S. annexes Hawaii — 1898

U.S. fights in World War I — 1917–18

19th Amendment gives women the vote — 1920

Great Depression — 1930s

U.S. fights in World War II — 1941–45

Mozart began writing music at the age of five. Two years later, he was playing concerts.

Marie and Pierre Curie devoted their lives to research, spending their own money on equipment.

Edison's first phonograph, a recording machine, led to the development of the record player.

Aristotle studied under Plato for 20 years before becoming tutor to Alexander the Great.

included symphonies, sonatas, and orchestral, choral, and chamber music. He also wrote some 150 songs. Many of his compositions used themes from American folk music.

Monteverdi, Claudio (1567–1643), an Italian composer, wrote *Orfeo*, which is considered to be the first opera.

Mozart, Wolfgang Amadeus (1756–91), an Austrian, was one of the world's greatest composers. He began composing at the age of five and eventually wrote more than 600 pieces of music, including symphonies, piano concertos, and operas such as *Don Giovanni* and *The Marriage of Figaro*.

Rodgers, Richard (1902–79) was one of the most successful U.S. composers in the history of entertainment. He wrote the music for such Broadway musicals as *Oklahoma!*, *Pal Joey*, *The King and I*, *South Pacific*, and *The Sound of Music*.

Sousa, John Philip (1854–1932) wrote so many U.S. marches he was known as the "March King." His most famous works include "The Stars and Stripes Forever," "The Washington Post March," and "Semper Fidelis."

Stravinsky, Igor (1882–1971), a Russian-born U.S. composer, wrote symphonies and operas, as well as the music for such ballets as *The Firebird* and *The Rite of Spring*.

Tchaikovsky, Peter Ilyich (1840–93) was a Russian composer. He wrote ballet music, symphonies, piano concertos, and operas. Among his best-known works are the ballet *Swan Lake* and his First Piano Concerto.

Verdi, Giuseppe (1813–1901) was the leading Italian operatic composer of his day. *Rigoletto*, *La Traviata*, and *Aida* are among his best-known works.

Vivaldi, Antonio (c.1675–1741) was a Venetian violinist and composer. He wrote operas, sacred music, and concertos such as *The Four Seasons*.

Wagner, Richard (1813–83), a German composer, is best known for his opera cycle *The Ring of the Nibelung*, which consists of four works based on old Germanic mystical legends.

SCIENTISTS AND INVENTORS

Bell, Alexander Graham (1847–1922), a Scottish-born American, invented the telephone.

Benz, Karl (1844–1929), a German engineer, built the first practical gasoline-powered automobile.

Copernicus, Nicolaus (1473–1543), a Polish astronomer, proved that the Earth moves in orbit around the Sun.

Curie, Marie (1867–1934), a Polish physicist, discovered radium, a radioactive substance. She worked with her husband Pierre.

Daguerre, Louis (1789–1851), a French painter, invented the first practical photographic process.

Darwin, Charles (1809–82), a British naturalist, formulated the theory of evolution by natural selection.

Edison, Thomas Alva (1847–1931), a U.S. inventor, patented more than a thousand inventions, including the telegraph and electric lightbulb.

Einstein, Albert (1879–1955), a German-born American physicist, changed our view of the universe with his General Theory of Relativity (1915).

Faraday, Michael (1791–1867), a British physicist and chemist, was a pioneer in the field of electricity. His work made the generator (dynamo) and the electric motor possible.

Fermi, Enrico (1901–54), an Italian nuclear physicist, built the first nuclear reactor.

Fleming, Alexander (1881–1955), a British bacteriologist, discovered penicillin, the first antibiotic.

Franklin, Benjamin (1706–90), a U.S. scientist, publisher, and statesman, proved that lightning is a form of electricity.

Galilei, Galileo (1564–1642), an Italian astronomer and physicist, was the first to use the telescope. He also showed that light objects fall as fast as heavy ones when they are pulled toward Earth by gravity.

Gutenberg, Johann (c.1400–68), a German printer, was the first to develop a way to print books with speed and accuracy.

Harvey, William (1578–1657), a British physician, discovered that the heart acted as a pump to circulate blood through the body.

Kepler, Johannes (1571–1630), a German astronomer, showed that the planets went around the Sun in elliptical paths.

Marconi, Guglielmo (1874–1937), an Italian-born British engineer, was the first person to transmit long-distance radio signals.

Mendel, Gregor (1822–84), an Austrian priest, biologist, and botanist, researched the laws of heredity using pea plants.

Morse, Samuel F.B. (1791–1872), a U.S. inventor, invented the first successful electric telegraph (1837).

Newton, Isaac (1642–1727), an English mathematician, devised laws of motion, theorized about gravity, and showed the nature of light and color.

Pasteur, Louis (1822–95), a French scientist, proved that disease is spread by bacteria, or germs.

Rutherford, Sir Ernest (1871–1937), a New Zealand-born British physicist, was a pioneer in the study of the atom's structure. His work led to the development of nuclear energy.

Watt, James (1736–1819), a British engineer who improved the steam engine to make it a suitable power plant for all kinds of machinery.

Wright, Orville (1871–1948) and Wilbur (1867–1912), two U.S. aeronautical engineers who built and flew (1903) the first successful heavier-than-air aircraft.

PHILOSOPHERS AND REFORMERS

Aristotle (384–322 B.C.), a Greek philosopher, studied under Plato. He opened a school of philosophy in Athens. His work gave rise to the science of logical reasoning.

Calvin, John (1509–64)
was a French religious reformer and leader of the Protestant Reformation. He believed that all people, not just bishops and kings, should share in religious and political policy making.

Confucius (c. 551–c. 480 B.C.)
was a Chinese philosopher whose teachings on moral responsibility have been a strong influence on Chinese thinking for over 2,000 years.

Gandhi, Mohandas Karamchand (1869–1948),
Indian spiritual and political leader, helped free India from British control through nonviolent resistance. He was known as Mahatma, or "Great Soul."

Gautama, Siddhartha (Buddha) (c. 563–483 B.C.),
Indian religious teacher, founder of Buddhism, one of the world's great religions. He gave up his life as a prince to become a wandering monk in search of enlightenment.

Jesus Christ (c. 4 B.C.–c. A.D. 33)
was the great religious leader on whose teachings the Christian religion was founded.

Joan of Arc, Saint (c. 1412–1431),
French national leader and heroine, believed God had chosen her to free France from English rule and led French armies to many victories.

King, Martin Luther (1929–68)
was a black American minister and leader of the U.S. civil rights movement. King won the 1964 Nobel Peace Prize, but was assassinated four years later.

Luther, Martin (1483–1546)
was a German religious reformer and leader of the Reformation—the religious movement that led to the birth of Protestantism.

Marx, Karl (1818–83)
was a German political philosopher and main founder of the socialist and communist movements. Wrote *The Communist Manifesto*, with Friedrich Engels, and *Das Kapital*.

Montessori, Maria (1870–1952),
Italian educator and doctor, she designed an educational system to help children develop their intelligence and independence. This system is used throughout the world.

Mother Teresa of Calcutta (1910–1997)
was a Roman Catholic nun born in Yugoslavia. She founded a religious order in Calcutta in 1950 called Missionaries of Charity, which now works in more than 130 countries.

Muhammad (A.D. 570–632)
was an Arabian prophet and founder of the Islamic religion. He felt himself called as God's prophet and preached that there is only one God (Allah).

Nightingale, Florence (1820–1910),
English nursing pioneer, reformed the nursing profession.

Pankhurst, Emmeline (1858–1928)
was an English political reformer. She led the fight for women's right to vote in England.

Plato (c.427–c.347BC),
a Greek philosopher, founded what is probably the first-ever university, known as the Academy. He wrote *The Republic*, in which he outlined the ideal state or society.

Sanger, Margaret (1883–1966)
was the American leader of the birth control movement.

Socrates (c.469–399 B.C.),
a Greek philosopher and teacher, devoted himself to seeking truth and goodness.

Stanton, Elizabeth Cady (1815–1902)
was a leader of the U.S. women's rights movement. She also worked toward the abolition of slavery.

Wesley, John (1703–91),
English clergyman, founder of Methodism. He traveled over 5,000 mi. (8,000km) a year, preaching.

Wilberforce, William (1759–1833)
was an English politician and reformer. He led the fight to abolish slavery in the British Empire.

Wollstonecraft, Mary (1759–97)
was an English author who argued that women should have equal rights to men in her book, *A Vindication of the Rights of Women*.

EXPLORERS

Amundsen, Roald (1872–1928),
a Norwegian, discovered the Northwest Passage and was the first man to reach the South Pole (1911).

Balboa, Vasco Núñez de (1475–1519),
a Spaniard, was the first European to sight the east coast of the Pacific Ocean (1513).

Bird, Richard E. (1888–1957),
a U.S. polar explorer, was the first to fly over the North Pole (1926) and the South Pole (1929).

Cabot, John (c.1461–98),
an Italian-born English explorer, claimed North American territory for England.

Champlain, Samuel de (1567–1635),
a French explorer, explored the Atlantic coast of Canada and founded Quebec (1608).

Columbus, Christopher (1451–1506),
an Italian explorer, discovered the New World while seeking a route to Asia.

Cook, James (1728–79),
an English sea captain, was the first to sight Antarctica and explore the Pacific Ocean.

Cortés, Hernán (1485–1547),
a Spanish explorer, conquered the Aztec Empire of Mexico (1521).

Da Gama, Vasco (c.1469–1524),
Portuguese navigator and explorer, sailed around Africa to India and back to Europe.

Ericsson, Leif (fl. 900–1000),
a Viking sailor, was the first European to land in North America (c.1000).

Livingstone, David (1813–73),
a Scottish explorer, traveled through much of Africa's interior.

Magellan, Ferdinand (c.1480–1521),
a Portuguese explorer, led the first expedition to sail around the world (1519–22). He was killed by natives in the Philippines before the journey was completed.

Peary, Robert E. (1856–1920),
a U.S. explorer, claimed to be the first person to reach the North Pole (1909).

Pizarro, Francisco (c.1475–1541),
a Spanish explorer, conquered the Inca Empire of Peru (1533).

Polo, Marco (c.1254–1324),
a Venetian (Italian) explorer, traveled through Asia and met Kublai Khan, the Mongol emperor.

Elizabeth Cady Stanton began the U.S. women's suffrage movement in 1848.

Gandhi is often called the "father of modern India" for his work in freeing India from British rule.

Vasco da Gama reached India in 1498 by sailing around the Cape of Good Hope in southern Africa.

Henry Morton Stanley, a reporter, found Livingstone (feared dead in Africa) at Lake Tanganyika in 1871.

History highlights since 1900

In Germany, Adolf Hitler's aggressive policies led to the outbreak of World War II.

DNA determines which traits children inherit from their parents.

Personal computers became commonly available in the early 1980s.

U.S. spacecraft *Viking 1* and *2* landed probes on Mars by parachute.

Over a million industrial robots work in factories around the world.

In 1953, Hillary and Tenzing were the first to scale Mt. Everest.

SPACE EXPLORATION

1957: The Soviet Union launches *Sputnik 1*, the first artificial satellite to orbit Earth.

1961: Soviet cosmonaut Yuri Gagarin, aboard the *Vostok 1* spacecraft, becomes the first man to orbit Earth.

1962: Astronaut John H. Glenn, Jr., aboard the *Mercury 6* spacecraft, becomes the first American to orbit Earth.

1963: Soviet cosmonaut Valentina Tereshkova orbits Earth becoming the first woman in space.

1965: Soviet cosmonaut Aleksei Leonov takes the first space walk.

1968: *Apollo 8* becomes the first spacecraft to orbit the Moon.

1969: *Apollo 11* astronauts Neil Armstrong and Edwin Aldrin become the first men to land on the Moon.

1970: *Venera 7*, a Soviet spacecraft, lands on Venus and transmits data back to Earth.

1975: The Soviet Union's *Venera 7* takes the first photographs of the surface of Venus.

1976: *Viking 1* and *Viking 2*, U.S. spacecraft, land on Mars and send photos and data back to Earth.

1977: The U.S. launches *Voyager 2*, which will later photograph Jupiter (1979), Saturn (1981), Uranus (1986), and Neptune (1989).

1981: The U.S. launches the space shuttle *Columbia*, the first reusable manned spacecraft.

1986: The U.S. space shuttle *Challenger* blows up shortly after launch, killing all seven astronauts.

1990: The U.S. space probe *Magellan* orbits Venus and sends radar images of the planet back to Earth. The Hubble Space Telescope is launched.

1997: The U.S. Mars *Pathfinder* spacecraft lands on Mars and deploys *Sojourner*, a roving vehicle to analyze Martian rocks and soil.

1998: Water is discovered frozen in rocks on the Moon.

2003: Space shuttle *Columbia* explodes on re-entry.

2005: Space shuttle *Discovery* docks to the ISS.

2006: Spacecraft *Venus Express* orbits Venus, taking detailed images.

2011 (July): Final shuttle mission.

POLITICAL EVENTS

1914: World War I starts when Archduke Francis Ferdinand of Austria is assassinated. The war ends in 1918.

1917: The Communists seize power in Russia during the Russian Revolution.

1929: The Wall Street Crash sets off the Great Depression.

1933: Adolf Hitler becomes the dictator of Germany.

1939: The German invasion of Poland starts World War II.

1941: The U.S. enters World War II after Japan attacks Pearl Harbor.

1945: World War II ends after the U.S. drops two atomic bombs on Japan. Tens of millions of people were killed during the war. The United Nations is founded.

1948: The state of Israel is founded.

1949: The Communists take control of China.

1950: Communist North Korea invades South Korea, starting the Korean War. The fighting ended three years later.

1952: European Community (now European Union) is founded.

1965: U.S. combat troops enter the Vietnam War. The war ends with the defeat of the U.S. in 1975.

1989: Communism begins to collapse in Eastern Europe, with democratic governments replacing communist dictatorships.

1990: Apartheid ends and black rule begins in South Africa.

1991: Gulf War. Break up of Soviet Union.

2001: Terrorist attacks on U.S.

2003: U.S.-led coalition invades Iraq.

2009: Barack Obama is the U.S.A.'s first African American president.

2010–2011: Arab Spring revolutions and protests.

SCIENCE AND MEDICINE

1905: German-born U.S. physicist Albert Einstein publishes his special theory of relativity.

1913: Hungarian-born pediatrician Bela Schick discovers an immunity test for diphtheria.

1915: Physicist Albert Einstein publishes his general theory of relativity.

1921: Canadian physicians Frederick Banting and Charles Best discover the hormone insulin, a treatment for diabetes.

1928: Scottish bacteriologist Alexander Fleming discovers penicillin.

1942: U.S. physicist Enrico Fermi directs the first controlled nuclear reaction.

1945: The first atomic bomb is detonated in New Mexico.

1953: Work by Francis Crick, Rosalind Franklin (U.K.), and James Watson (U.S.) leads to the discovery of the double-helix structure of DNA.

1954: Harvard University physicians perform the first successful organ (kidney) transplant.

1955: U.S. microbiologist Jonas Salk develops the first vaccine against polio, a crippling disease.

1967: South African surgeon Christiaan Barnard performs the first heart transplant.

1982: U.S. surgeons working at the Utah Medical Center implant the first artificial heart.

1990–2003: Human Genome Project sequences the human genome.

2010: A da Vinci robot surgeon and McSleepy robot anesthetist carry out the first all-robot surgery.

TELECOMMUNICATIONS

1901: Italian-born inventor Guglielmo Marconi, using Morse code-like dot-and-dash signals, sends the first radio message across the Atlantic Ocean.

1906: U.S. engineer Reginald A. Fessendon broadcasts the first radio program of voice and music.

1915: First transcontinental telephone call between inventor Alexander Graham Bell in New York and his assistant Thomas Watson in San Francisco, over 3,000 mi. (5,000km) away.

1929: Russian-born American electronic engineer Vladimir Zworykin demonstrates the first electronic television system.

1936: The British Broadcasting Corp. makes the first TV broadcasts

1946: U.S. engineers J. Presper Eckert, Jr., and John W. Mauchly build ENIAC, the first electronic digital computer.

1951: Eckert and Mauchly build UNIVAC I, the first commercially available computer.

1953: Color television broadcast begins in the U.S.

1960s: Internet begins as a military security network.

1965: Early Bird, the first commercial communications satellite, is launched.

1977: The Apple Computer Company introduces the first personal computer.

1983: Cellular phone service begins.

1993: Mosaic web browser helps to popularize public use of the Internet.

2001: Broadband technology enters mainstream usage.

2006: Social networking site Facebook is launched for everyone.

INDEX

Page numbers in **bold** indicate where the main reference to a subject can be found. Page numbers in *italic* refer to captions and illustrations.

ACKNOWLEDGMENTS

The publishers wish to thank the following for supplying photographs for this book:

ABBREVIATIONS (*t* = top; *b* = bottom; *c* = center; *l* = left; *r* = right)

Cover all images by Shutterstock; Pages iiit IStock/luminis; iiib IStock/DaddyBit; iv IStock/mtruchon; viii Penny Tweedie/Getty; 1tl World History Archive/Alamy; 1br John Shaw/NHPA/Photoshot; 1tr ChameleonsEye/Shutterstock; 1bl The Image Bank/Getty; 2tr hadynyah/IStock; 2b Franz Aberham/Getty; 3b Edeantoine/Shutterstock; 4tr Paul Fearn/Alamy; 4tl Eco Images/Getty; 4bl Delbars/Shutterstock; 5tl Anton Ivanov/Shutterstock; 5cr Action Plus Sports Images/Alamy; 5bl Ulrich Mueller/Shutterstock; 8tr Angelo Giampiccolo/Shutterstock; 9tr IStock; 10tr John Cancalosi/Alamy; 12tl IStock/Nnehring; 12tr IStock/Ecopic; 16tl Classic Image/Alamy; 16cr Roger Clark ARPS/Shutterstock; 16bl Adfoto/IStock; 17bl BennettEgyptArch/Alamy; 17br Science History Images/Alamy; 18tr pxl.store/Shutterstock; p20cr Georg Kristiansen/Alamy; 20bc kovalchuk/IStock; p21cl Bildagentur Zoonar GmbH/Shutterstock; 21cr FrankvandenBergh/IStock; 21bl Hemis/Alamy; 22clt PhotoBliss/Alamy; 22tl Granger Historical Picture Archive/Alamy; 22cl James Jenkins - Visual Arts/Alamy; 22cr Alexander Makarov/Alamy; 22bl Peter Barritt/Alamy; 22br Wikicommons; p23bl Dan Kitwood/Getty; 23tl The Image Zone/Alamy; 23cr Kumar Sriskandan/Alamy; 23br Ian Dagnall/Alamy; 24tr Shi Yali/Shutterstock; 24bl Warren Metcalf/Shutterstock; 24b Ky Cho/Shutterstock; 25b SUC/Shutterstock; 26tl hadynyah/IStock; 26b Claudioviri/Shutterstock; 26tr Jimmy Tran/Shutterstock; 27cr Hemis/Alamy; 27tl rmnunes/IStock; 27cl World History Archive/Alamy; 28tl Heritage Images/Getty; 28tr MSFC/NASA; 28br JSC/NASA; 28clb NASA/MFSC; 28clt ESA/INT; 28bc JSC/NASA; 30trt den-belitsky/IStock; 30trb NASA/JPL; 32tl IStock; 32tr NASA/JPL; 34tr AustralianCamera/Shutterstock; 34bc Stanislav Fosenbauer/Shutterstock; 35bc apsimo/IStock; 35br mary416/Shutterstock; 36tl Haireena/Shutterstock; 36bc Siwawut/IStock; 37tl ChameleonsEye/Shutterstock; 37tr Bill Bachman/Alamy; 37c Benny Marty/Shutterstock; 37b Chronicle/Alamy; 43tr Parilov/Shutterstock; 44tr NASA; 46br Shutterstock; 49br NASA; 50tl Chronicle/Alamy; 50tr Steve Gschmeissner/SPL; 51br Gregory Dubus/IStock; 54tr James Davis Photograph /Alamy; 54b Catarina Belova/Shutterstock; 54cl Andrea Delbo/shutterstock; 55cl Rich Carey/Shutterstock; 55br Shutterstock; 55br IStock; 57br IStock; 57tr southtownboy/iStock; 57cl Wanchanta/IStock; 58c Avalon/Photoshot/Alamy; 58bc Shutterstock; 60tr mtnmichelle/IStock; 60b uzbuzzer/IStock; 60cr VisualCommunications/IStock; 60cl Fertnig/IStock; 61cl JHVEPhoto/IStock; 61br Shaun Cunningham/Alamy; 62b Natursports/Shutterstock; 63t fStop Images GmbH/Alamy; 64tr guenterguni/IStock; 64b piccaya/IStock; 65br cdwheatley/IStock; 65cl Diego Grandi/Shutterstock; 66tl Anton Ivanov/Shutterstock; 70clt James Benet/IStock; 70tl Dr Linda Stannard/SPL; 70cl BlackJack3D/IStock; 70clb Francois Paquet-Durand/SPL; 70bl Dr Microbe/IStock; 71tl The Ardagh Chalice, Reerasta, County Limerick, early 8th century (silver with silver gilding, enamel, brass and bronze) (Celtic, (8th century)/National Museum of Ireland, Dublin, Ireland/Photo © Boltin Picture Library/Bridgeman Images; 72tr Mlenny/IStock; 72b loca4motion/shutterstock; 73tr evenfh/Shutterstock; 73b meunierd/Shutterstock; 73cl GARDEL Bertrand/hemis.fr/Alamy; 75tr LeeYiuTung/IStock; 75cl Alex Potemkin/IStock; 75b aphotostory/Shutterstock; 76b Mlenny/IStock; 77tc PurpleImages/IStock; 77tr Vanzyst/IStock; 77bl IStock; 77br OSTILL/IStock; 78tr Huw Jones/Getty; 78bl Samson Opus/Alamy; 78br neneo/Shutterstock; 79c Ilyas Kalimullin/Shutterstock; 79bcl Digitalsignal/Shutterstock; 79bl Kiev.Victor/Shutterstock; 79bcr olli0815/IStock; 79br ChameleonsEye/Shutterstock; 80tl Amnesty International; 80tr Sandro Tucci /Getty; 80b Rolls Press/Popperfoto /Getty; 81tl Cloete Breytenbach /Getty; 81bl Pierre Verdy/Getty; 81br ITAR-TASS Photo Agency/Alamy; 82tl Granger Historical Picture Archive/Alamy; 82t World History Archive/Alamy; 86tr sandyman/Shutterstock; 86cl Pictorial Press Ltd/Alamy; 87tc ostislavv/IStock; 87tr Paul Hastie/Alamy; 87c Eugene Onischenko/Shutterstock; 87br Sally and Richard Greenhill/Alamy; 88cr Cultura Creative (RF)/Alamy; 89t Getty; 89b Tony Vaccaro/Getty; 90tr Hulton Fine Art Collection/Getty; 91tl Heartwood Films/Shutterstock; 91clt NASA/JPL/USGS; 91clb StephanHoerold/IStock; 91bl solarseven/Shutterstock; 92tr Photographee.eu/Shutterstock; 93bl jorisvo/Shutterstock; 93clb emkaplin/Shutterstock; 93br Pictorial Press Ltd/Alamy; 94bc Jstone/Shutterstock; 95tr Shutterstock; 96tl Gavran333/Shutterstock; 96tr dpa picture alliance archive/Alamy; 98tr georgeclerk/IStock georgeclerk, 104br Hemis/Alamy; 106bl Paolo Bona/Shutterstock; 106br Robbie Jack/Getty; 107tr PeopleImages/IStock; 107tl Robert Fried/Alamy; 107cr Mila Atkovska/Shutterstock; 107br Yaacov Dagan/Alamy; 108b Hindustan Times /Getty; 109tl Aleksey Stemmer/Shutterstock; 110tr Slaven/Shutterstock; 110clt Chris Willson/Alamy; 110cbl Elizabeth Whiting & Associates/Alamy; 110bl Cultura Creative (RF)/Alamy; 110bl Italyan/Shutterstock; 112cl The Natural History Museum/Alamy; 114tl Olivier Asselin/Alamy; 114bl Eye of Science/SPL; 115br clearviewstock/Shutterstock; 120b yankane/Shutterstock; 121tr smereka/Shutterstock; 121b Scanrail1/Shutterstock; 122b Lucian Motatu/Shutterstock; 123tl Kenan Kaya/Shutterstock; 123tr T photography/Shutterstock; 124b Sovfoto /Getty; 124br Christopher Scott/Alamy; 125tl monkeybusinessimages/IStock; 125cl Graham Oliver/Alamy; 125cr Hulton Archive/Getty; 125b Monkey Business Images/Shutterstock; 126tl Colin13362/IStock; 126bl holgs/IStock; 126br Richmatts/IStock; 127tr fmajor/IStock; 133cr 06photo/iStock; 134bc Blend Images/Shutterstock; 136tl Aviation History Collection/Alamy; 136cl RGB Ventures/SuperStock/Alamy; 136tr Artur Janichev/Shutterstock; 138t Adellyne/Shutterstock; 138b Getty; 139br Stefonlinton/IStock; 140tl prmustafa/IStock; 140tr Cameris/IStock; 140bl Marco Iacobucci EPP/Shutterstock; 141tr Pictorial Press Ltd/Alamy; 141cl Tramino/IStock; 141b Alexandra Lande/Shutterstock; 145 Monika Gruszewicz/Shutterstock; 146cl Protasov AN/shutterstock; 147tl Keystone Pictures USA/Alamy; 147bl Keystone Pictures USA/Alamy; 147clb Keystone Pictures USA/Alamy; 147b David Cole/Alamy; 147br Everett Collection Inc/Alamy; 149tr Moviestore collection Ltd/Alamy; 149cr Pictorial Press Ltd/Alamy; 149br Moviestore collection Ltd/Alamy; 149bl Moviestore collection Ltd/Alamy; 150tr aDam Wildlife/Shutterstock; 152cr Elzbieta Sekowska/Shutterstock; 156bc CreativeNature_nl/IStock; 158c VTG/IStock; 159cl Marco Ossino/Shutterstock; 159c Freisian cow/Shutterstock; 160tr dwphotos/Shutterstock; 161tl Zoka74/Shutterstock; 161cl TEK Image/SPL; 162tl michieldb/IStock; 164tr Rolf E. Staerk/Shutterstock; 164br Reidl/IStock; 164cl gorillaimages/Shutterstock; 165tl FashionStock.com/Shutterstock; 165bl dpa picture alliance/Alamy; 165br WDG Photo/Shutterstock; 168tr ratmaner/IStock; 169tl NASA; 169clt NASA; 169clb NASA; 170bl Tigergallery/Shutterstock; 170bcl IStock; 170br IStock; 170bcr Shutterstock/ plprod; 171tr jeremy sutton-hibbert/Alamy; 172tr Victor FlowerFly/Shutterstock; 172cl imageBROKER/Alamy; 172b lexan/Shutterstock; 173cl SeanPavonePhoto/IStock; 173b footageclips/Shutterstock; 176cl a454/Shutterstock; 177tr studiocasper/IStock; 177bc BanksPhotos/IStock; 177cl World History Archive/Alamy; 178cr robertharding/Alamy; 179tl Yugan/Shutterstock; 180tl Hulton Archive /Getty; 180 b 2happy/Shutterstock; 181 tr MPI/Getty; 181 cr General Photographic agency/Getty; 182tr imageBROKER/Alamy; 182b Rich Lynch/Shutterstock; 183cl wronaphoto.com/Alamy; 183br Alamy; 185tr Landscape Nature Photo/Shutterstock; 186tr vblinov/Shutterstock; 186tl Brian E Kushner/Shutterstock; 186bl Birute Vijeikiene/Shutterstock; 186cr COffe72/IStock; 186r Rich Carey/Shutterstock; 186bc reisegraf.ch/Shutterstock; 189tr robas/IStock; 192tr SoumenNath/IStock; 192b Russell Kord/Alamy; 193tr Tatiana Grozetskaya/Shutterstock; 194tr Diane Garcia/Shutterstock; 194br Catwalk Photos/Shutterstock; 196tr Grassetto/IStock; 197tr rkl_foto/Shutterstock; 197bl mRGB/Shutterstock; 197br guppyimages/IStock; 198tr BreatheFitness/IStock; 199tr Shutterstock; 199br 4x6/IStock; 199bl adynyah/IStock; 199 clt visionchina/IStock; 199clb Imgorthand/IStock; 199cl valeriebarry/IStock; 199tl Mr_Khan/IStock; 201tc Ermolaev Alexander/Shutterstock; 204tr Alexander Mazurkevich/Shutterstock; 204b Nicholas DeVore/Getty; 205cr age fotostock/Alamy; 205bl Vold77/IStock; 206tl hadynyah/IStock; 206tr somchaisom/IStock; 206b hadynyah/IStock; 207tl eezsnow/IStock; 207bl Andrey Bayda/Shutterstock; 207r Pictorial Press Ltd/Alamy; 208r Em Faies/Shutterstock; 208 bl Kertu/Shutterstock; 210t Heritage Image Partnership Ltd/Alamy; 212tr Likoper/Shutterstock; 212cr Joerg Boethling/Alamy; 213cr Cas Photography/IStock; 213br Mark Brandon/Shutterstock; 214tl Simon002/IStock; 214clt blickwinkel/Alamy; 214clb Ronnakron Kaewseenuan/Shutterstock; 214bl Claude Nuridsany & Marie Perennou/SPL; 214br TommyIX/IStock; 216 tr kali9/IStock; 217tr age fotostock/Alamy; 218cl Paul Springett D/Alamy; 218bl Leonid Andronov/Shutterstock; 218 br acceptphoto/Shutterstock; 219tr Panksvatouny/Shutterstock; 220cl leolintang/Shutterstock; 220b ESB Professional/Shutterstock; 221 tr vvvita/Shutterstock; 221 tr Drazen Lovric/IStock; 221 bl Eddie Gerald/Alamy; 222tr Claudio Giovanni Colombo/Shutterstock; 222b Pfeiffer/Shutterstock; 222cl francesco de marco/Shutterstock; 223cr Trinity Mirror/Mirrorpix/Alamy; 223bl Arndale/Shutterstock; 223tl Viacheslav Lopatin/Shutterstock; 224 tr Bloomberg/Getty; 224b vichie81/IStock; 224cl NetaDegany/IStock; 225cr J. Henning Buchholz/Shutterstock; 225b kirati apivattakakul/Shutterstock; 226tr MattiaATH/Shutterstock; 227tr ChameleonsEye/Shutterstock; 227cl nicolay_bastos/IStock; 227bl Africa Studio/Shutterstock; 227bc Assaf Frank/Alamy; 229cl wollwerth/IStock; 229bl Andrzej Kubik/Shutterstock; 229br LOOK Die Bildagentur der Fotografen GmbH/Alamy; 230tl Phanie/Alamy; 232tl Ivaylo Sarayski/Alamy; 232b Ian Dagnall/Alamy; 233tl tobiasjo/IStock; 233tr BSIP SA/Alamy; 233 cl Francis DEMANGE/Getty; 233bl Fertnig/IStock; 234 Maximilian Weinzierl/Alamy; 237tr Shutterstock; 237tl Ian Dagnall/Alamy; 237cl Andrew Koturanov/Shutterstock; 237c gyn9037/Shutterstock; 237bl Dom Greves/Alamy; 237bc Solvin Zankl/Alamy; 238tl Africa Studios/Shutterstock; 244tr Peter An/Shutterstock; 245cl Attila JANDI/Shutterstock; 245bl evarak/IStock; 245br BartCo/IStock; 249tr saac74/IStock; 250tr Iago Fernandez/IStock; 251tr Clive Brunskill/Getty; 251bl MishAi/Shutterstock; 251bl James Boardman/Alamy; 251tr Chris Jobs/Alamy; 252bc Jim West/Alamy; 253tr Alina555/IStock; 255cr DEA/M. CARRIERI /Getty; 256tl honix_a/IStock; 257tr dpa picture alliance/Alamy; 257cl Ken Welsh/Alamy; 257bl Richard Ellis/Alamy; 257 tl A. Dowsett, Health Protection Agency/SPL; 257clt Crown copyright/Health & Safety Laboratory/SPL; 257bl Gerd Guenther/SPL; 259tr Monty Rakusen/Getty; 259bc BSIP SA/Alamy; 259tl DR. Fred Hossler/Visuals Unlimited Inc. /SPL; 259clt Biomedical Imaging Unit, Southampton General Hospital/SPL; 259clb Dennis Kunkel Microscopy/SPL; 259bl Steve Gschmeissner/SPL; 261tr suc/iStock; 261b Bloomberg/Getty; 262c oneinchpunch/IStock; 263tl Louai Beshara /Getty; 263tr Peter Jordan/Alamy; 263b Orhan Cam/IStock; 264bl perfectStills/IStock; 265tr BookyBuggy/IStock; 267tl Neil Cooper/Alamy ; 271cr Angus McComiskey /Alamy; 276tl Anton Ivanov/Shutterstock; 276cl Pictorial Press Ltd/Alamy; 276bl Granamour Weems Collection/Alamy; 276b Alen Ferina/alamy; 277br Dean Mitchell/Getty; 278cr Pavel L Photo and Video/Shutterstock; 278b Tom Lynn/Getty; 283tr Marc Deville/Getty; 287tc kovgabor79/IStock; 287cl age fotostock/Alamy; 287bl Dianne Wilson/Getty; 288 cl agafapaperiapunta/IStock; 288b Irene Abdou /Alamy; 289tr Shutterstock; 289bl ziggymaj/IStock; 290bl JohnnyGreig/IStock; 291tl valentinrussanov/IStock; 291tr Stephen Moehle/Shutterstock; 292bl Studio Barcelona/Shutterstock; 292tr Shutterstock; 293tr Images & Stories/Alamy; 296tr IStock; 297cr age fotostock/Alamy; 297b Newscom/Alamy; 298tl Roger Sedres/Alamy; 299tr AFP/Getty; 301tl wsfurlan/IStock; 301tr Cakelo/IStock; 303cl Art Phaneuf/Alamy; 303bl Universal Images Group/Getty; 303bc imageBROKER/Alamy; 304clb Wisnu Haryo Yudhanto/Alamy; 304bl Qrt/Alamy; 304b The Artchives/Alamy; 305tr Pictorial Press Ltd/Alamy; 305cr ArliftAtoz2205/Shutterstock; 305br wavebreakmedia/IStock; 306tr Eddie Gerald/Alamy; 308 NASA; 309tr AF archive/Alamy; 312b John Fryer/Alamy; 313tl Dave Watts/Alamy; 313tr Paul Looyen/Shutterstock; 314t NBC/Getty; 315b Sintez/IStock; 317c Ruth Hofshi/Alamy; 319bl Leopold Nekula /Getty; 321b RBM Vintage Images/Alamy; 322 zhudifeng/IStock; 323cl Damsea/Shutterstock; 324tr SERGEI BRIK/Shutterstock; 326tl Bettman/Getty; 326tr Granger Historical Picture Archive/Alamy; 326b Sophie Elbaz/Getty; 327b Michal Knitl/Shutterstock; 328bl World History Archive/Alamy; 329cl Painting/Alamy; 330cr GagliardiImages/Shutterstock; 336tl AFP/Getty; 336tr Keystone Pictures USA/Alamy; 336cl Jack Esten/Getty; 337tr Johan Swanepoel/Shutterstock; 338bl Innvar/Shutterstock; 338b nimon/Shutterstock; 340tl Ingus Kruklitis/Shutterstock; 340bc MaxyM/Shutterstock; 340ct Sumikophoto/Shutterstock; 340bl Michelle Mealing/Shutterstock; 340br Stephen Seibel/Shutterstock; 341tl Asharkyu/Shutterstock; 341tcr niscene/IStock; 341tr wikicommons/Morio; 341 United Archives GmbH/Alamy; 341cl Radharc images/Alamy; 341br Animated Healthcare Ltd/SPL; 342tr Shutterstock; 343tr NASA; 345crt Shutterstock; 345crb Pixachi/Shutterstock; 346b Chamille White/Shutterstock; 346 vlcm/IStock; 347br Shutterstock; 347 yulenochekk/IStock; 348tl Unniversal Images Group/Getty; 348cl discus63/IStock; 348bl Dmitry Feoktistov /Getty; 348 rpbirdman/IStock; 348br alexeyart/Shutterstock; 350tr Sergey_Bogomyako/Shutterstock; 350b Scanrail1/Shutterstock; 351bl Niels Quist/Alamy; 351br Sylvie Bouchard/Shutterstock; 352tl ceba/Shutterstock; 352tr AndreyKav/IStock; 352cl South West Images Scotland/Alamy; 352br Olga Danylenko/Shutterstock; 353tl Shutterstock; 353clt cuxy58/Shutterstock; 353bl Shutterstock/Nowak Lukasz; 353br Vladimir Zaplakhov/Shutterstock; 354cr BGSmith/Shutterstock; 354br jordieasy/IStock; 359tc Dan Prat/IStock; 361t igitalfarmer/IStock; 361cr DEA/A. DAGLI ORTI/Getty; 361cl PjrStudio/Alamy; 362tr Asia Images Group/Shutterstock; 362b Prasit Rodphan/Shutterstock; 365tl Philip Pound/Alamy; 366br Chronicle/Alamy; 366tr Granger Historical Picture Archive/Alamy; 367tl Phanie/Alamy; 367br jamesteohart/Shutterstock; 368tr blickwinkel/Alamy; 369tr Mark Kostich/IStock; 370b Peter Gudella/Shutterstock; 371tr Arterra Picture Library/Alamy; 375b Jamal Nasrallah/Getty; 376cl JeremyRichards/IStock; 376tr cglade/IStock; 376b Comaniciu Dan/Shutterstock; 377bl Per-Anders Pettersson /Getty; 377cr Stock Connection Blue/Alamy; 378tr Ecuadorpostales/Shutterstock; 378cl Janne Hamalainen/Shutterstock; 378b MP cz/Shutterstock; 379tl Constantin Iosif/Shutterstock; 379bl Art Konovalov/Shutterstock; 379br Jeff Greenberg /Getty; 380 tl Ruslana Iurchenko/Shutterstock; 380b Ian Nellist/Alamy; 380tr Alf Ribeiro/Shutterstock; 381tr Donyanedomam/IStock; 381cr ESA–Stephane Corvaja, 2016; 381bl IStock; 381br TheOldhiro/Shutterstock; 383tl Aleksandar Todorovic/Shutterstock; 383c Anna Kucherova/Shutterstock; 385tr Sovfoto/Getty; 385bl NASA; 386cl David Ducros CNES/SPL; 386clb Julian Baum/SPL; 386bl Henning Dalhoff/SPL; 388tr Cynthia Liang/Shutterstock; 388cl Nessa Gnatoush/Shutterstock; 388b WillSelarep/Shutterstock; 389b Veniamin Kraskov/Shutterstock; 391tl Erwin Niemand/Shutterstock; 392bl PCN Photography/Alamy; 393tr Valerio Pennicino /getty; 394tc zuma press/Alamy; 396cl Sololos/IStock; 397tr WaterFrame/Alamy; 398tl Prof. P. Motta/Dept. of Anatomy /University "La Sapienza", Rome/SPL; 398tr ertnig/IStock; 400cl Christophe Cerisier/IStock; 400bl Joerg Boethling/Alamy; 402tr classicpaintings/Alamy; 402b Life in View/SPL; 404cl Alxpin/IStock; 404bl farakos/IStock; 404br mbbirdy/IStock; 406b Jacob Ammentorp Lund/IStock; 407tr Solis Images/Shutterstock; 408tl INTERFOTO/Alamy; 408cl World History Archive/Alamy; 408bl Andrey Arkusha/shutterstock; 408tr Chicago History Museum/Getty; 408br franckreporter/IStock; 409tl Ricardo Mayer/Shutterstock; 410clb Leszek Kobusinski/Shutterstock; 411tc adventtr/IStock; 411br Joe Gough/IStock; 412tr Etienne De Malglaive /Getty; 413tr Gift of John Davison Rockefeller, Jr. (January 29, 1874 – May 11, 1960), 1937/Wikicommons; 413bl mauritius images GmbH/Alamy; 413br Art Directors & TRIP/Alamy; 418tr Maksim Budnikov/Shutterstock; 419cl saiko3p/Shutterstock; 419cr Moviestore collection Ltd/Alamy; 419b Mr Nai/Shutterstock; 420tr Billy Hustace/Getty; 421b Nattanan726/Shutterstock; 421cl Bill Helsel/Alamy; 424cl icosha/Shutterstock; 425bl trekandshoot/Shutterstock; 427tr Thorsten Schier/Shutterstock; 428tr YankeePhotography/Alamy; 429bl Pictorial Press Ltd/Alamy; 430cl andrew chittock/Alamy; 430tr urbancown/IStock; 430b leighcol/ iStock; 431tl Shutterstock; 431bl Oscar Johns/Shutterstock; 431br anyaivanova /Shutterstock; 432cr Giles Clarke/Getty; 432b Drop the light/Shutterstock; 433tr Songquan Deng /Shutterstock; 433bl Matej Hudovernik /shutterstock; 433br Anton Ivanov /Shutterstock; 434tl Sam Chadwick /Shutterstock; 434cl wsfurlan/IStock; 434br Jamie Grill/Getty; 435cl ArtistGNDphotography/IStock; 435br Richinpit/IStock; 436tl Alexey Stiop/ Shutterstock; 436cl Andrea Izzott/Shutterstock; 436cr Hemis/Alamy; 436b Siouxsnapp/Shutterstock; 437tl Courtesy Pioneer Project, ARC, and NASA; 438b Lyd39/Shutterstock; 439tl Keela/Shutterstock; 439tr Chainfoto24 /Shutterstock; 439cl Eldar Nurkovic /Shutterstock; 442tl Kavram/Shutterstock; 446br DOD/Getty; 447tc Volodymyr Goinyk/Shutterstock; 448tl Zacarias Pereira da Mata/Shutterstock; 449tr Alan Fraser/Alamy; 451c Vasin Lee /Shutterstock; 452br African Studios/Shutterstock; 457tr Solar Seven/Shutterstock; 457b garytog/IStock; 459tc Arco Images GmbH/Alamy; 460b David Turnley/Getty; 460t Heritage Image Partnership Ltd/Alamy; 461t Leonard McCombe /Getty; 461cr Granger Historical Picture Archive/Alamy; 461bl Stefan Smith/Getty; 462tl Alamy; 462cl Keystone Pictures USA/Alamy; 462bl David Cole/Alamy; 465b Prisma by Dukas Presseagentur GmbH/Alamy; 466br Natural Visions/Alamy; 467tr David Roberts/SPL; 467bl Simon Fraser/NCCT, Freeman Trust, Newcastle-Upon-Tyne/SPL; 468br Christopher Furlong/Getty.

The publishers would also like to thank the following for their help in supplying information used as visual reference: **6–7:** Boeing Aircraft Corporation (Boeing 747); **11:** Zoological Society of London (fire salamander cutaway); **17:** Geoscan Research (scanner); **19:** Ove Arup & Partners (Sydney Opera House); **30–31:** W.M. Keck Observatory (Keck observatory); **62–63:** John Willoughby, The Mustang Owners Club of Great Britain, Selby (Mustang); **146:** Fullwood Ltd (milking shed); **190:** Bell Helicopter Textron (helicopter cutaway); **196:** Dyson Appliances Ltd (Dyson vacuum cleaner cutaway); **198:** The Hovercraft Museum Trust; **242–243:** Otis plc, Ove Arup & Partners (lift), **252–253:** Picker International Ltd, Siemens Medical Engineering (CAT scanner); **292:** Nuclear Electric (nuclear reactor); **296:** British Petroleum (platform); **297–299:** Olympic Museum; **361:** Balco Ltd (electroplating system); **410:** British Telecom (telephone); **425:** Ford Motor Company (people carrier).